The Soho Manufactory, Mint and Foundry, West Midlands

George Demidowicz

The Soho Manufactory, Mint and Foundry, West Midlands

Where Boulton, Watt and Murdoch Made History

George Demidowicz

Historic England

Published by Liverpool University Press on behalf of Historic England, The Engine House,
Fire Fly Avenue, Swindon SN2 2EH
www.HistoricEngland.org.uk

Historic England is a Government service championing England's heritage and giving expert, constructive advice.

The views contained in this book are those of the author alone and not Historic England, English Heritage or Liverpool University Press.

First published 2022

ISBN: 978-1-80034-928-5 cased

British Library Cataloguing in Publication data
A CIP catalogue record for this book is available from the British Library.

Typeset in Georgia Pro Light 9.5 on 11.75pt
Edited by Sarah Enticknap
Page layout by Carnegie Book Production

Printed in Poland by Akcent

Front cover: Watercolour of the Soho Manufactory from the north. © The British Library Board (shelfmark Ktop XLII, item number 82-n, Topographical Drawing)
Back cover: Axonometric projection of the Soho Manufactory showing the mill waterworks. (© George Demidowicz)

Contents

List of figures and credits

Abbreviations

BL	The British Library Board
BMT	Birmingham Museum Trust
GD	George Demidowicz
HE	Crown Copyright Historic England Archive
LoB	Library of Birmingham Archives and Local Studies Collections
Sandwell CHAS	Sandwell Community History and Archives Service
SMG	Science Museum Group Collection

Frontispiece

Chapter 1

Chapter 2

Chapter 3

Chapter 4

Chapter 5

Chapter 6

Chapter 7

Tables

Appendix 1

Appendix 2

Acknowledgements

This book owes a major debt to Stephen Price, without whose initiative Soho House might not have been acquired in 1989 by the City of Birmingham as a museum. He had previously commissioned me to research the watermills of the River Cole in order to improve the interpretation of Sarehole Mill, already established as a branch museum. I was intrigued to find that a watermill at the Soho Manufactory operated as late as the 1840s, a site better known for its production of steam engines. Stephen asked me to investigate this curious survival, the evidence for which lay in the massive Soho collection lodged in the archives of the former Birmingham Reference Library. I was immediately hooked and could not resist extending the research further.

I am grateful to all the archive staff for dealing patiently over many years with my searches, often speculative, through this astonishing and unrivalled collection, which when I began had not the advantage of the comprehensive calendar it now possesses. The monumental task of re-cataloguing was undertaken by Fiona Tait, Tim Proctor and Adam Green, who would obligingly alert me to relevant material coming to light during their work. A large part of the book was originally written using the old references; more recently, Fiona, having retired from archives, helped me over what seemed to me the insurmountable obstacle of converting about 800 of these from old to new. This was financed by Mike Gibbs, whose deep interest and support of local history in the West Midlands continues. There still remained a stubborn rump of references that could not be found, and Peter Dore, who now curates the Soho collection, doggedly tracked down the elusive items.

The Covid pandemic delayed the publication of the book. On the eve of lockdown about fifty images from the Soho and other collections in the Library of Birmingham still needed to be photographed. It was not until May 2021 that the archives could accommodate a photographic session. Many thanks go to Nicola Crews for painstakingly tracking down the items which were expertly photographed by Luke Unsworth. There are many other collections all over the country, too many to mention here, that have supplied images and permitted their publication.

I must thank John Townley, my collaborator on other research projects, for sharing with me his knowledge of steam engines and Birmingham history in general. He also helped find elusive references and images.

Rita McLean and Val Loggie, the first members of staff appointed to the Soho House museum, provided valuable comments on early versions of the text. They also generously shared their research on Matthew Boulton and his house and garden. Nick Molyneux, formerly field officer in the Local History Department of Birmingham Museum, continues his interests in Soho matters and was able provide useful comments on my texts, allowing me to use his initial findings on the Mint.

The more complete text was meticulously proofread by my cousin, Zenon Demidowicz, which helped considerably in providing a more acceptable manuscript for publishers. His notes were vital to Fiona's task of converting old references to new. Malcolm Dick also read my early chapters and suggested editorial improvements.

Tim Taylor, the producer of the Channel 4 *Time Team* programme must be thanked for taking the risk of filming for the first time industrial archaeology in the difficult conditions of suburban back gardens. Of the many members of the team, Mick Worthington deserves special mention in helping to set up the initial evaluation. All this needed a local contact with knowledge of the area, and I could not have had a better representative than Dylan Close to negotiate access to gardens facing considerable upheaval. Born and bred in the area, he persuaded, among others, his parents to have their patio dug up, where to my relief an important fragment of the Latchet (Crescent) Building was found inches below the surface. Without the agreement of the residents of South Road, the programme could not have been made.

At about this time Soho Foundry came under threat of demolition, and I am grateful to Rita Mclean once again for inviting me to join a Lunar Society visit to the site, where it was obvious to me that large amounts of original Boulton & Watt fabric were still standing. A campaign to save the buildings was initiated, much helped by members of Smethwick Local History Society and in particular Mary Bodfish and Steve Cemm. The Royal Commission, now Historic England, surveys were also invaluable in achieving statutory listing for the site. I am thankful to the Sandwell Borough archaeologists for giving me the opportunity to help develop an understanding of the Soho Foundry, Ruth Waller initially commissioning my study of the unlisted Soho Foundry Mint to establish its significance, verified a short while later by the excavations carried out by the University of Leicester Archaeological Unit. She was followed by Shane Gould, who commissioned my report on the Soho Foundry itself, without which material no book on the Soho industrial sites could be regarded as complete. During this research, the buildings were in relatively good condition, and Tony Adcock of Avery Berkel allowed access to the site and to the company deeds. The Avery weighing museum at the Foundry, managed by Howard Green at the time, was an important source of addition information.

Unfortunately, the buildings continued to deteriorate, and I am very grateful to three parties for jointly funding the considerable sum needed for the protective cover over the main foundry building: Sandwell Borough Council, Avery Weigh-Tronix and Historic England.

The book has achieved publication owing to the support of Ellen McAdam, until recently Director of Birmingham Museums Trust. She initiated the application to Historic England for funding the publication, and employed Jenni Butterworth to prepare the bid and estimates of costs. Jenni has taken much of the administrative strain of nursing the application through its various stages, which culminated in a successful bid and an approved manuscript. I am very grateful, therefore, to Historic England for its agreement to finance and Liverpool University Press, its preferred publishers, for undertaking the major task of a profusely illustrated book. Bringing the manuscript and images to a press-ready state was a major task and I must thank the following: Alison Welsby, Editorial Director and Senior Commissioning Editor, and Patrick Brereton, Head of Production at Liverpool University Press; assisted by the staff at Carnegie Book Production: Sarah Warren, Senior Production Editor, Lucy Frontani, design layout and typesetting, Claire McGann, Editorial Assistant, Sarah Enticknap, Copy Editor, and Alan Rutter, Indexer.

This is the first time that I have drawn my figures entirely on the computer, but I am grateful to Tara Moore for setting me off on this course by producing Fig 1.2 and for helping me to master a simple software package (Paint.Net).

Last, but not least, my enduring debt is to my wife, Toni, who has been a reader of various versions of the manuscript over the years and also suffered long periods of Soho widowhood while I was writing, drawing, excavating on site and researching in the archives. Relief at publication at long last is jointly shared.

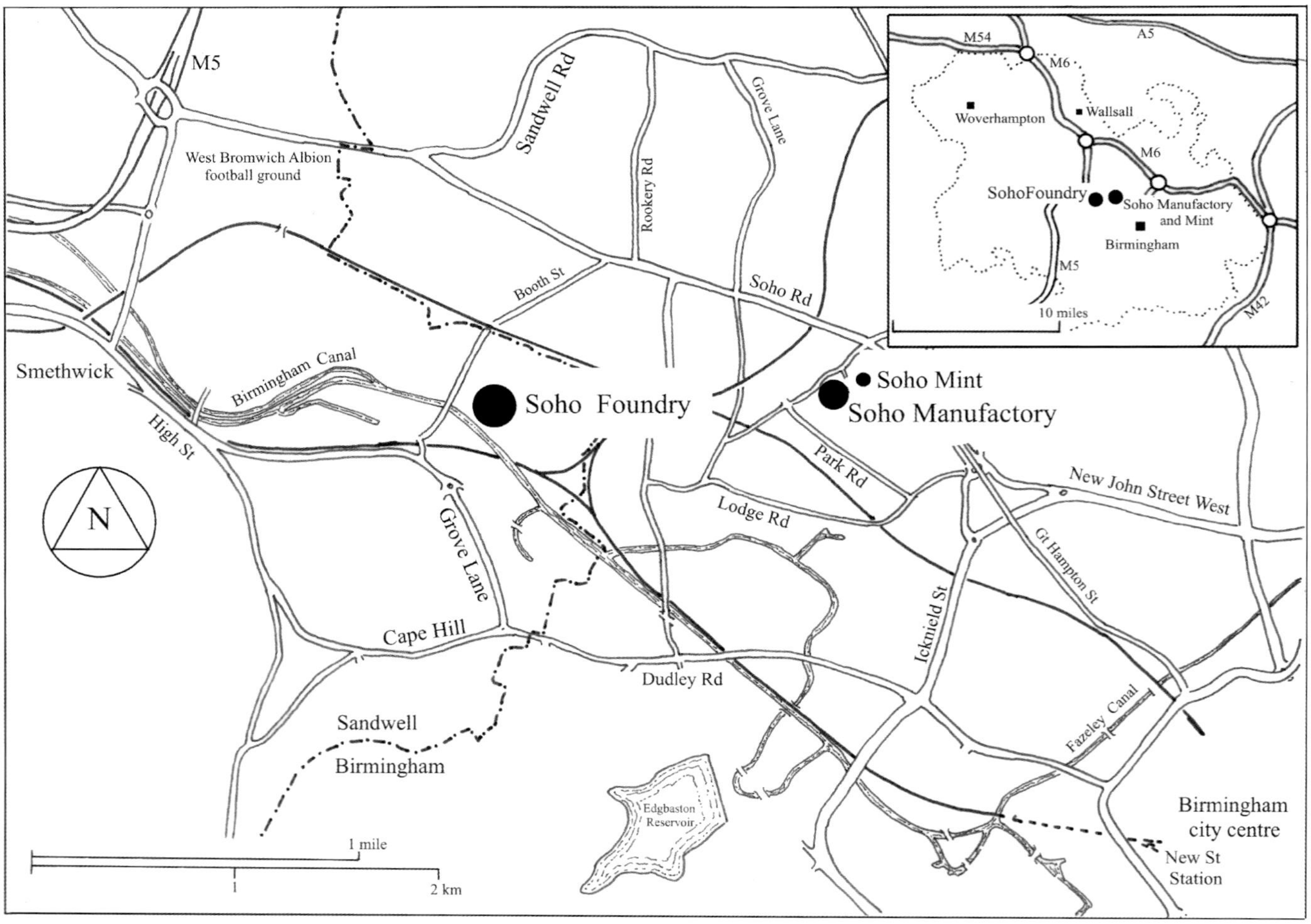

Fig 1.1
Location plan; the dotted line on the inset map indicates the built-up area.

1

Introduction and background

This book is intended to provide another dimension to the study of Matthew Boulton, James Watt and the Soho enterprises, a subject of national and international significance in the history of the Industrial Revolution. It is the study of Soho as a place, rather than more traditionally of its people and products, although the three areas of study are deeply connected.

The name Soho is a useful shorthand for the people and the products, but it was also a physical place, or more accurately three: the Soho Manufactory, the Soho Mint and the Soho Foundry. There is a vast written output on the Soho personalities and, in particular, the triumvirate of Matthew Boulton, James Watt and William Murdoch. Likewise, the attention of scholars of wide interests and expertise has been attracted to the staggering and uniquely wide range of products that originated from the three Soho sites: steam engines, gas plants, coins and commemorative medals, silverware, plated ware and ormolu for townhouse and mansion, buttons, buckles and myriad other personal adornments, and wear such as sword hilts, watch chains, chatelaines, cane heads and snuff boxes (Figs 1.5 to 1.8). On the other hand, the buildings themselves, in which the people worked to devise, invent and manufacture the products, have been surprisingly neglected. The three Soho sites are well known by name but not well studied. As a consequence, there was little published material available to help guide the author.[1] There are cases where the buildings have been cursorily treated, limited to the reproduction of well-known images, but often misinterpreted and misidentified.[2] This book, it is hoped, will help rectify this matter. It is primarily concerned, therefore, with the origins, development and decline of the three Soho industrial sites, the principal historical narrative supported with information on the form and function of specific buildings, their internal layout and their power systems, where appropriate. It is intended to fill a gap in the Soho literature more traditionally focused on its heroes and its extensive product range. This approach chimes with the growing interest in and status of industrial archaeology, the study of the material remains of past industrialisation, particularly in the late 18th and early 19th century, when an important and transformative phase in economic development took place.

The Soho Manufactory (1761–1863) and Soho Mint (1788–early 1850s) were situated in the historic parish of Handsworth, Staffordshire, now an inner-city suburb within the boundary of the city of Birmingham (Fig 1.1). Today there is nothing to be seen of these two industrial sites, the last building having disappeared in 1863 (Fig 1.2). Soho House, Matthew Boulton's home, has fortunately survived, and since 1996 has functioned as a branch of Birmingham Museums Trust. It stands well above the industrial sites, its view now impeded by housing, where more than 200 years earlier Boulton could survey all that he had built directly below. The physical remains of the Soho Manufactory and Mint all now lie below the ground and can only be observed through archaeological excavation (Figs 1.3a and 1.3b). This book includes an account of the excavations that took place in 1996 filmed by the Channel 4 *Time Team* programme. The excavations fixed the exact locations of the Manufactory and Mint accurately for the first time and proved conclusively that there are substantial below-ground remains in the later domestic back gardens and factory forecourts.

The interest of the author in the Soho Manufactory was first aroused by the intriguing fact that this world-famous site, associated with Boulton and Watt and the steam engine, still retained its waterwheel as late as the 1840s. This led to the discovery that the first working James Watt steam engine in the world had been installed at the Manufactory to return water to the waterwheel turning in the rolling and polishing mill. When attention was transferred to the Soho Mint, it was quickly realised, given the importance of the national coinage produced by Boulton, that little has been written on how the

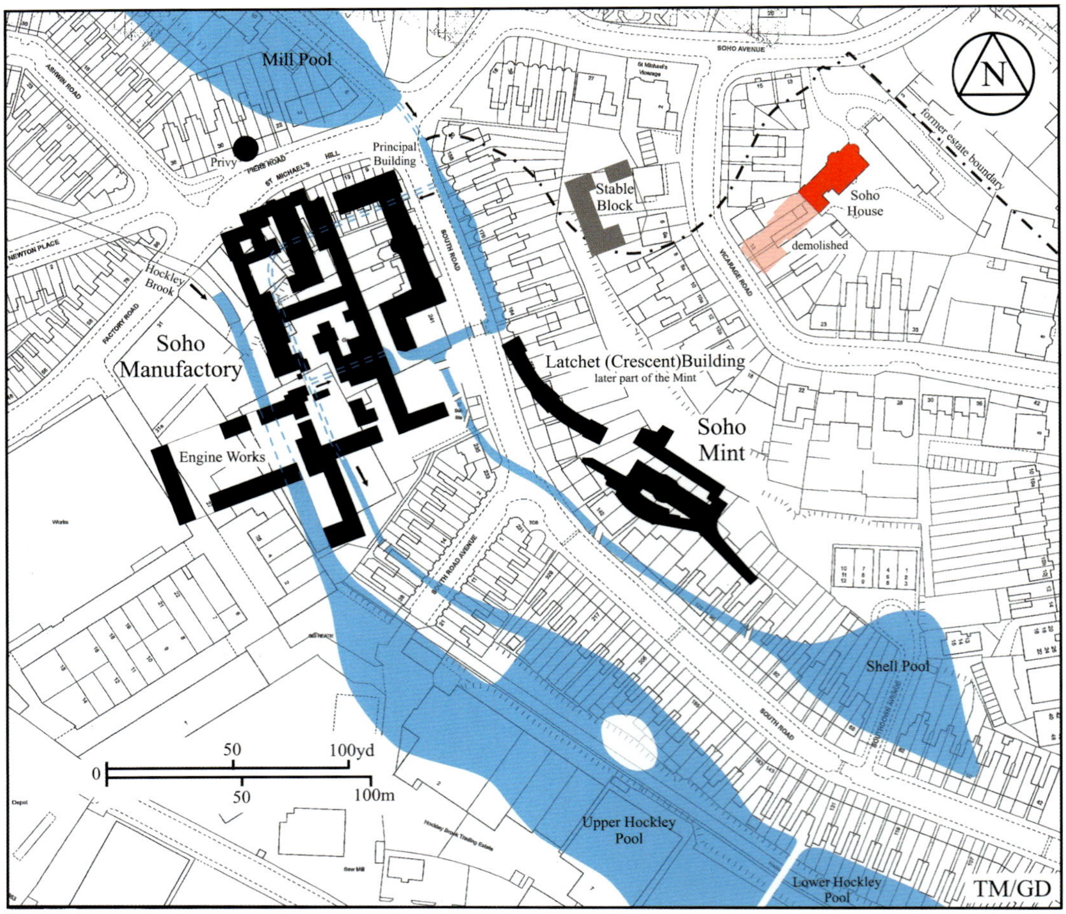

Fig 1.2
The Soho buildings overlaid on a current OS map. None of the buildings have survived above ground except for Soho House (red). Most of the water has disappeared except for the part-culverted and much straightened Hockley Brook.

conversion from copper cake to impressed coin had been physically arranged in the first steam-powered mint in the world.[3] Here the discovery was of three radically different layouts, all less than ideal, idiosyncratic even, and so arranged because of a need for secrecy and a desire to reuse redundant buildings.

The Soho Foundry (1795–1895) is to be found in the township of Smethwick, the northern part of the ancient parish of Harborne, Staffordshire, now a part of Sandwell Metropolitan Borough (Figs 1.4a and 1.4b). In comparison to the Manufactory and Mint, the Foundry has fared better, an obsolete steam engine works saved from demolition through a takeover by Avery's, the weighing machine manufacturers, in 1895. Many of the Foundry buildings were demolished subsequently, but there is sufficient surviving from the very earliest and latest phases of the first purpose-built steam engine manufactory in the world for them to be statutorily listed grade II*. It is hugely significant that these buildings still stand, enabling their fabric to be studied directly to gain understanding of their development without depending entirely on archaeological excavation or archival research. Avery's had gradually abandoned the site in the post-war period, the foundry itself last used in 1956, so that by the time the author began to make his site visits to the redundant buildings from the mid-1990s, they were visibly deteriorating. The main foundry building is fortunately now protected from the wind and weather by a temporary roof supported by scaffolding. The whole complex remains forlorn and empty, a new use desperately needed, and is out of bounds for reasons of health and safety. In 2021 there is at last some prospect that the buildings will be restored and a new use found.

The great bonus in the study of Soho, in all its aspects, is the vast archive housed in the Library of Birmingham: the Matthew Boulton, the Boulton and Watt, and James Watt collections. Its depth and extent is breathtaking, even intimidating, to researchers arriving to use it for the first time, but it hardly needs stating that without this material this book could not have been written. In view of its wealth, particularly in the Boulton & Watt engine portfolios, it is ironic, with so many plans of industrial sites elsewhere in the country, that the Soho Manufactory has so few such plans to illustrate its early development from a modest watermill. This deficiency does not apply to the Boulton & Watt engine works at the Manufactory, to the Soho Mint or to the Soho Foundry. In the case of the Manufactory there is some compensation, however, in the vast collection of letters that passed between Matthew Boulton, James Watt, their chief engineers, managers and clerks, in the images of the Manufactory, and in a bewildering variety of other documents. This material permitted a 3-D reconstruction to be attempted with some confidence (*see* Fig 2.26). The Soho collections were also a vital aid in the positioning of trenches during the filming of the *Time Team* programme, for their normal 'hopping about in a field' was not an option in a dense sequence of back gardens where well-tended plots had to be avoided.

Although this is a study of material history, it must be emphasised that it is not confined to 'bricks and mortar', machinery, steam engines and drive shafts. Traditionally there has been much emphasis on the two of the so-called 'heroes' of the Industrial Revolution, Matthew Boulton (1728–1809) and James Watt (1736–1819); less so, unjustifiably, on William Murdoch (1754–1839), the 'Third Man'.[4] These protagonists cannot be ignored, and new insights can be gained into their personality and achievements. There are many differences in temperament and expertise between Matthew Boulton and James Watt, but one in particular is revealed in the study of the Soho buildings. Boulton was the builder 'par excellence', developing the Manufactory into one of the largest hardware industrial complexes in the country and establishing the first mint powered by a steam engine. Watt, on the other hand, saw himself first and foremost as an innovator; how the products of his inventive mind were to be housed or manufactured was usually a matter of concern for others, and Boulton ably fulfilled this task. This is not to downplay Boulton's own inventiveness; in his wider perspective and ambition to produce the national coinage, for example, he conceived not only mechanised coining but also resolved how existing non-industrial buildings could be adapted and secretly extended to accommodate such innovatory processes. It is telling that James Watt had little to do with the establishment of the Soho Foundry in 1795, except in funding the purchase of the land. Its construction, layout and fitting were left to his son, James Watt Jr Boulton, on the other hand, had by this time established in underused mint buildings and in the first phase of a new 'Crescent' building the manufacture of a type of buckle, known as a 'latchet'. This venture was soon to fail, due to changes in fashion, but its buildings eventually found a use in the reconstruction of the Soho Mint in 1824–6 by Boulton's son, Matthew Robinson Boulton.

There are several others, however, who will make an appearance in the book. The contributions of the second generation, James Watt Jr and Matthew Robinson Boulton, for example, have been somewhat overshadowed by their fathers' achievements. This book is intended to rebalance their reputations, for in reading the massive correspondence and documentation relating to the establishment of the Soho Foundry (1795–6), the engine works at the Manufactory (1802–4) and the reorganisation of the Soho Mint (1824–6), one cannot fail to be impressed by the initiative, technical knowledge, diligence and managerial competence of the two sons. James Watt Jr took responsibility for the Foundry, but he knew, when matters were failing, whom he could rely on to solve the more intractable technical problems. This was William Murdoch, whose role at the Foundry in its formative years is recounted and assessed in some detail and, it is hoped, his reputation much enhanced as a result. The extent to which Matthew Robinson Boulton masterminded both the construction of an extended engine works at the Manufactory and the radical reorganisation of the Soho Mint long after his father's death has certainly not been appreciated. John Southern, engineer and head of the drawing office, has been given the attention he deserves. The role of the main protagonists will, therefore, in this book be elaborated through their contribution to the development of Soho buildings, plant and machinery. Many of the engineers who worked for Boulton & Watt will receive scant attention, however, unless the record demonstrates that they made a mark on the development of buildings and their power systems.

Such is the complexity and long history of the three Soho sites that a single study cannot possibly deal adequately with all that went on within their walls. The many workers that plodded every day to and from the three Soho sites (all being relatively isolated) have received scant attention traditionally, a matter that could not be

Fig 1.3a
The classic view of the Soho Manufactory, focused on the principal building. To the left lies the Latchet (Crescent) Building and to the right, the steeply descending frontage to more extensive buildings can be glimpsed.

Fig 1.3b
The same view today from the junction of St Michael's Road, St Michael's Hill and South Road. The beginning of South Road corresponds roughly with the forecourt to the principal building.

rectified in this book.[5] A proper study of the workforce can only be dealt with separately, and I highlight this as an excellent opportunity for others to further enhance our knowledge of the three Sohos.

The next chapter in the book (Chapter 2) provides a summary history of the whole Manufactory and Mint complex, with an emphasis on the physical development of the site. There will be more detail here, however, for buildings not covered by the more specialist chapters that follow (Chapter 3 – the Mill; Chapter 4 – the Engine Works; Chapter 5 – the Mint). In Chapter 2 information will be found not only on the button and plated-ware buildings and, in particular, the 'principal building', but also on the latchet (buckle) works. There are few details available unfortunately on the layout of the Boulton & Watt copying-machine works. The structure adopted will involve some repetition as, for example, the Mint is discussed in Chapter 2 and in Chapter 5. In the former will be found a short overview; in the latter a detailed analysis. On balance, it is thought that there is a benefit in providing in Chapter 2 a relatively succinct and more easily assimilated history of the Soho

Fig 1.4a
Soho Foundry, 1895. The large building in the background is the main foundry building with the boring mill and turning shop closer to the photographer.

Fig 1.4b
Soho Foundry, 2006. The interior of the main foundry building looking east. The main central arch in the east wall, constructed in 1795–6, can be seen in Fig 1.4a; the two flanking arches also date from this earliest phase.

Manufactory and Mint. For readers interested in water-power, steam-engine or coin production, for example, Chapters 3, 4 and 5, respectively, can be immediately consulted.

Chapter 6 takes the story of the Manufactory and Mint sites from their demolition in the 1850s and early 1860s to the present day. Although the Manufactory and Mint were located in mainly rural Handsworth at the time of their demolition, it was inevitable that their sites would be swallowed up by their near neighbour, Birmingham, expanding rapidly from the east. Not far away to the west, Smethwick, in which the Soho Foundry was situated, was also urbanising and industrialising at a rapid pace. Handsworth was incorporated into the city of Birmingham in 1911. As a result, the Manufactory and Mint are regarded as being

Birmingham industrial sites, although, strictly speaking, they were demolished when still in Handsworth. This statement needs qualification, however, as part of the Soho Manufactory engine works was built in 1802–4 on the Birmingham side of the Hockley Brook boundary.

The last events chronicled at the Handsworth site in this book are the excavations that took place between 1994 and 1996, principally with the help of the Channel 4 *Time Team* programme in 1996. The results are summarised here for the non-specialist reader, successful for the fact that remains of both the Soho Manufactory and Mint were located in relatively difficult circumstances. The more detailed archaeological report is in Appendix 1.

Chapter 7 is entirely devoted to a history of the Soho Foundry where, unlike the Soho Manufactory and Mint, a substantial area of buildings survive above ground as well as in a basement 'subterranean' level (two sequences of pattern stores). A large number of Boulton & Watt buildings were, however, demolished by Avery's, the weighing machine manufacturers, during their occupation and expansion on the site after 1895, including the important boring mill and engine house. Owing to the deep and robust nature of industrial archaeological remains, however, they are likely to survive well over the whole site, both in open areas and beneath later buildings. The Foundry differs from the Soho Manufactory in having detailed building and machinery accounts, many more plans, and relevant correspondence from its earliest years. This made it significantly easier to chronicle its foundation in 1795–6 and to reconstruct with some confidence its physical expansion and the layout of its various power systems over the following hundred years. The function of most of the buildings at each phase could also be identified. A series of over 80 photographs taken in 1895 were invaluable in providing evidence of the interior and exterior appearance of various buildings at the end of the Foundry's life as an engine works. By contrast there are only five photographs of the Soho Manufactory, and none of the Mint. With the survival of so much Boulton & Watt aboveground fabric, it is surprising that this fact was not recognised until the mid-1990s. Today the Soho Foundry is instantly identifiable on a train journey from Birmingham to Wolverhampton by its massive temporary roof and scaffolding.

The concluding chapter (8) presents a synthesis of the evidence by summarising key facts and features at all three sites. Their significance is identified, a process that inexorably leads to the conclusion that the Soho industrial enterprises constitute one of the earliest and most important sites of the industrialising world, regionally, nationally and internationally. This is exemplified in a series of world 'firsts': the first steam-engine-powered mint, the first purpose-built steam engine manufactory, the first factory in the world to be lit by gas. Their significance is enhanced by the association with 'heroes' of the Industrial Revolution, who have appeared recently on British banknotes and are commemorated in Westminster Abbey. On a special issue

Fig 1.5
The Titus Clock Case, 1776–78, one of number made by Boulton and Fothergill, ormolu and marble.

Fig 1.6
This penny token commemorates the abolition of the slave trade in 1807 and was produced in 1814 for Macauley and Babington, the largest European mercantile traders in Freetown, Sierra Leone; struck at the Soho Mint.

of stamps, Matthew Boulton stands in front of his beloved Manufactory, while James Watt stares proudly at a model of his improved steam engine.

The wholesale demolition of the Soho Manufactory and Mint during the 1850s and early 1860s left no building or structure standing above the ground. The area had been developed with housing and factories in the early 20th century. Historically important industrial buildings had stood here for nearly 200 years; was anything left of them? By the early 1990s sufficient research had been completed by the author to fix the approximate position of the Soho buildings, but nothing was known about their state of preservation below the ground. There was potential for much new information to be revealed and, in particular, to fix their location accurately for the first time. Appendix 1 provides a detailed record of the initial exploratory trenches dug in 1994 and 1995, followed by the *Time Team* excavations that took place over three days during Easter 1996. This was one of the first *Time Team* programmes where careful plotting before the cameras arrived was essential. Instead of open fields there were private rear gardens and factory forecourts with little flexibility if the wrong spot had been chosen. A limited number of owners were willing to have their gardens transformed into archaeological excavations. There were certainly risks involved, but the Soho archive yet again revealed its worth. The successful results proved that documentary research combined with archaeological excavation is a most efficacious, but regretfully still a rare, method of studying the material past.

Appendix 2 provides a short summary of the main Soho businesses to help alleviate the confusion that is apparent in the literature, mainly caused by the interrelated nature of the concerns with the Boulton and Watt families as their nexus. This was not always the case, however, as the later years of the plated-ware company and the steam engine works at the Manufactory and Foundry demonstrate. A time-line diagram is offered to help disentangle the commercial relationships. The book is not intended, however, to provide a business history of the Soho enterprises, which is a monumental task for even one of the sites. For the Manufactory, its multitude of products makes the undertaking even more daunting.

Appendix 2, and the book more generally, has another related aim: to distinguish without any ambiguity the difference between the Soho Manufactory and the Soho Foundry, the sharing of the name Soho being the cause of much confusion by researchers of all levels of expertise, from professional scholars to the simply curious. The existence of an engine works at the Manufactory as well as at the Foundry has further contributed to misunderstandings. The internet has only made matters worse, its history content being notorious for error, inaccuracy, the propagation of myth, and the repetition of unsubstantiated 'facts'. Fortunately, however, the Soho Mint in Handsworth is rarely confused with the much later Soho Foundry Mint built in 1860 by James Watt and Company at the Soho Foundry, for the simple reason that the latter is hardly known.

In writing this book it was evident from the beginning that only a small proportion of the information that had been amassed over two decades on the three Soho buildings could find a place in the text. The author hopes that others will be inspired to follow and enhance further our knowledge of the historically significant places that were the Manufactory, Mint and Foundry.

Fig 1.7
This medal commemorates the various British victories of the Napoleonic wars in the year 1798, the design by the master engraver, Conrad Heinrich Küchler, superbly expressive of the nation's triumph; struck at the Soho Mint.

Fig 1.8
This token manufactured by Peter Kempson in 1797, describing himself on the reverse side as a 'maker of buttons and medals &c Birmingham', is rare in depicting the principal building of the Manufactory, but its poor rendition contrasts with the quality of design and manufacture at the Soho Mint at this time.

Fig 1.9a An unusual view of the principal building of the Soho Manufactory from the south-east. The mill pool can be seen immediately to the right. The only other known version of this image is in the William Salt Library, Stafford.

Fig 1.9b The classic view of the Soho Manufactory dominated by the principal building, part of Handsworth Heath having been taken into Boulton's park and planted along the approach road. To the right, the mill pool fed water to the canal in front of the principal building and to the watermill behind. To the left lies the Latchet (Crescent) Building, the wing closest to the viewpoint probably not completed until 1824–6. Farther to the left, and partially hidden by the trees, is the Soho Mint of which there are no known complete images.

2

A short history of the Soho Manufactory and Mint

Introduction

In 1761, Matthew Boulton came to Soho Mill on Handsworth Heath in search of water power, and within a few years he claimed he had erected 'the largest Hardware Manufactory in the World'.[1] As a result, he quickly outgrew the capabilities of his mill, or – more strictly speaking – the water supply to it. Many would have just grumbled and cursed the droughts, floods and frosts that would periodically bring the waterwheel to a stop. Matthew Boulton, with his engineering and business talents, realised that James Watt's condenser could produce a more efficient steam engine for pumping water back to the mill pool and wheel, thereby extending the working time of his mill. Making another imaginative leap, Boulton foresaw that, with a patent, Soho could become the centre for the development and production of the Watt steam engine. In 1774, the diffident Scot was persuaded to leave his native country and one of the greatest partnerships of the Industrial Revolution was born. Despite the fact that the firm of Boulton & Watt became world famous, and therefore the Soho concerns synonymous with steam-engine production, it is ironic that a waterwheel produced power until the last years of Soho. Matthew Boulton had indeed solved the problem of water supply with the help of a steam-pumping engine, but it took more than a new-fangled condenser to oust water power.

The association between Soho and steam engines should not be overemphasised, as the Manufactory was also renowned in its time for many other products such as coins, plated ware, ormolu and 'toys' in general.[2] Peter Jones reminds us that it 'started off life as a "toy" emporium – a place of manufacture of "buttons, buckles, etwees [boxes], belt hooks, watch chains and trinkets, snuff-boxes, [buckle] chapes etc," to quote from a regional directory printed in 1780'.[3] Another diverting Boulton interest was coin and medal production, which led to the establishment of a separate group of buildings known as the 'Soho Mint'. Previous studies of Matthew Boulton and Soho have tended to concentrate – with some justification – on the intellectual gifts and enterprise of the man and the quality, design and ingenuity of the Soho range of products. Little work has been done on the physical layout, organisation and development of the Manufactory as a group of buildings housing myriad industrial processes. Owing to the richness of the Matthew Boulton, Boulton & Watt, and James Watt collections in the Library of Birmingham, it has been possible to establish for the first time a detailed chronology of the origins, development and decline of the Manufactory, together with its offshoot, the Mint. For certain periods, reasonably reliable plans of the whole site can be reconstructed, together with more detailed plans of particular buildings or sections of the works. It has been less easy to understand from the surviving documents how production was organised, both from a managerial and a technical point of view, especially as these operations were being continually altered. Information on the Mint is, however, more revealing and it can be supplemented by examining the material on the foreign mints.

In just over 40 years, from 1761 to 1804, Soho expanded from a single watermill to an industrial complex covering over 86,000 sq ft (7,989.4 sq m). The diversification of Boulton's businesses over his lifetime was reflected in the buildings that were erected and in the technology that was installed within them. After Boulton's death in 1809, there was relatively little change to the buildings (except in the Mint), reflecting a stability in business interests that has often been interpreted as the loss of the dynamism of innovation on the part of the succeeding generation.

It is clear, moreover, that a definitive history of the Soho button and plated-ware business has yet to be written. In fact, from the point of view of the development of its buildings, the story was more or less complete in the six years to 1767, a period from which only chance references to building operations – but no plans – have survived in correspondence. The birth and explosive growth of Boulton's toy and plated-ware manufactory is poorly chronicled in relation to later developments.

A general chronology

Ruston and Eaves, 1757–61

The Manufactory was established on open heathland just less than two miles (3km) north-west of the centre of Birmingham in the parish of Handsworth, close to the main road from Birmingham (turnpiked in 1727) to West Bromwich and Wednesbury. The heath stretched from Handsworth southwards into Birmingham parish, with the Hockley Brook forming the boundary between the two (Fig 2.1). In 1757, Edward Ruston and John Eaves (both toymakers) obtained a 99-year lease, at an annual rent of £14 14s 0d (£14.70), of a 'Cottage or Tenement called ... Soho', with other buildings, a garden, three pieces of enclosed land, Soho Warren, Crabtree Brake Warren, and about 4 acres (1.62ha) of heath to be enclosed.[4]

Edward Ruston and John Eaves pulled down the cottage and erected a house and a mill.[5] Four years later, in 1761, Matthew Boulton, describing himself as a toymaker of Birmingham, bought out the lease for £1,000. This assignment of the lease was a momentous event, but few, if any, appreciated it at the time. The grandiose scheme for the Manufactory may not have yet germinated in Boulton's mind. In the poorly documented years before Soho, Boulton occupied Sarehole Mill, situated about 6 miles (9.66km) away by road on the other side of Birmingham in Yardley parish. In the early 1960s, R A Pelham discovered that Matthew Boulton held Sarehole Mill as a subtenant from at least 1756 to 1760 and that until his death in 1759, Boulton's father, Matthew Boulton Sr, lived at Sarehole farm.[6] A connection between Sarehole and Soho had been established through John Eaves, who held a financial interest in Sarehole Mill, and it may have been this same link that provided the opportunity for Boulton to move from Sarehole (*see* p 41). It must be emphasised that Boulton retained his father's premises in Snow Hill on the north-eastern edge of Birmingham on the same turnpike road that passed Soho. The advantages of relocation must have been obvious.

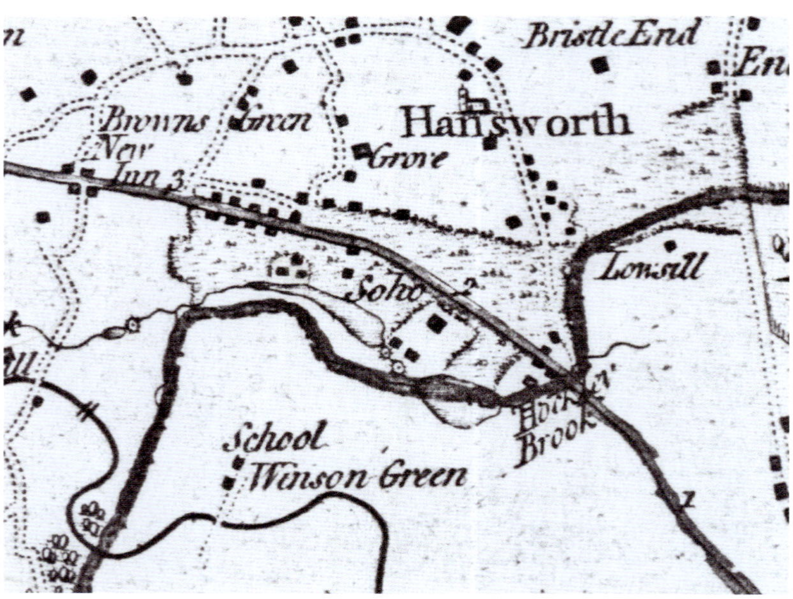

Fig 2.1
Detail from William Yates's Map of Staffordshire, 1777, showing the Soho encroachment and the curving mill pool on Handsworth Heath, the Manufactory buildings represented symbolically.

Boulton's first years at Soho, 1761–4

It is not known why Ruston and Eaves were willing to sell their lease on after only four years. According to the memorandum already quoted, Boulton applied to Edward Ruston for the lease after conceiving a plan in January 1761 to manufacture hardware and toys 'in w'ch a water Mill was essentially necessary'.[7] The new lease was dated 21 April 1761,[8] and by July Boulton had gathered together sufficient 'workmen Timber Brick &c' to build some workers' dwellings, a warehouse and several workshops. He also demolished and rebuilt the mill – though it was only four years old – because it did not suit his new plan. The work was not finished that season and had to be extended into 1762, starting up again in the spring, and in August the water-wheel was set in motion for the first time.[9] In these circumstances, it is not surprising that Boulton wished to retain the sublease of Sarehole Mill for a short time.

There are no contemporary maps or plans, and the buildings erected at this time can only be identified by eliminating those that came later. It is likely that the first Boulton manufactory buildings at Soho were grouped around an area that, within a few years, found itself below and immediately behind the principal building.[10] The east

Fig 2.2
The principal building, designed to look like a Georgian country mansion and housing the plated-ware works, warehouses, showroom and staff accommodation, hides the more utilitarian Manufactory buildings lying on the lower level. [Monthly Magazine, *1797*]

side was formed by a major break-of-slope about 16–20ft high (4.9–6.1m), the *raison d'être* for the watermill. Henceforth, for convenience, this feature will be referred to as the 'Great Bank' (although it was not called this at the time) and it was later to divide the Manufactory into two main levels.[11] The watermill provided a fixed point around which the first grouping of buildings developed. As this position was well away from the mill-pool edge, it is possible that the mill was not only rebuilt but also relocated to provide sufficient room for the first yard to develop around it. Of the other known buildings at this time, the warehouse may have been located on the north side in what was to be called Rolling Mill Row. Workers' houses faced the Hockley Brook on the west, forming the terrace known as Brook Row. Workshops probably completed the south side of the yard. These first buildings already constituted industrial premises on more than the average local scale, and throughout the history of Soho continued to be used for toy manufacture and, in particular, buttons.

Before the second season of building started in spring 1762, Boulton had entered into a partnership with John Fothergill, which he hoped would open up a much wider market for his Soho products, already entering the Continent. It is interesting that, early in the following year, Fothergill describes the new buildings as a 'Chape Manufactory', even though a much wider variety of goods, e.g. buttons and watch chains, was being made.[12] On 26 July 1763, Matthew Boulton mortgaged his Soho lease, borrowing £1,300 from Henry Carver and Girton Peake, both of Birmingham.[13] This may have been to finance the recent and imminent investment in buildings, but about this time Fothergill had temporarily deserted their partnership, precipitating an immediate crisis.[14] Nevertheless, overinvestment in buildings in relation to business turnover was to bedevil the Soho venture for many years to come. In September 1763, William Wyatt (of Burton) referred to building works in progress that may relate to the Manufactory. His brother, possibly Samuel, drew 'the Plan' and this fraternal partnership may represent the first association of the Wyatt family of architects with Soho.[15] At this stage, the most architectural element of the Manufactory was the north side, Rolling Mill Row, a three-storey gabled block containing a central entrance, which was later to be filled in. Within the gable was a Diocletian window. Two-storey wings on either side terminated in taller bays with pyramidal or near-pyramidal roofs, certain of the pitches having a hipped dormer window. The eastern bay was, in fact, the highest (perhaps equivalent to four storeys) as it had to straddle the Great Bank. In the approach to the

Manufactory from the main road, this north elevation was one of the two most prominent, though it suffered in being partially hidden by the break-of-slope of the Great Bank. The other elevation, facing east and containing the end of the mill, was soon to be transformed by the construction of the principal building (*see* pp 12–18). In the summer of 1764, additional workshops were constructed for button making (as demand was outstripping production) and a new stamping shop was erected.[16] These facilities may have been constructed on the Great Bank.

At about this time, another important development took place that has not been appreciated hitherto. Despite the fact that Boulton had rebuilt Soho Mill in 1761–2, he soon took out a sublease on Holford Mill, this move following the abandonment of Sarehole Mill (*see* pp 48–9). With a new mill at Soho, why would Boulton have needed Holford? The latter, situated about 2.1 miles (3.5km) to the north-east on the River Tame in the same parish of Handsworth, rolled metal, and it is apparent that there was insufficient capacity for this kind of work at Soho, which had probably been rebuilt primarily as a lapping and polishing mill. Buttons, buckles and chains used relatively little rolled metal, but the demand for this material rose considerably when Boulton established his plated-ware business around the year 1765. A stylish and impressive building was erected to accommodate plated-ware manufacture, but without the requisite rolling mill capacity. Holford Mill was to serve as Soho's principal rolling mill until at least 1782.

The principal building, 1765–7

The best-known image of the Soho Manufactory is that of the principal building, which was erected in 1765–7. From the very beginning, the building 'engaged the attention of all ranks of people' and became the most frequently illustrated part of the Manufactory (Fig 2.2).[17] The choice is understandable given the building's imposing façade and size. It created – deliberately, it must be stressed – the impression of a Georgian country mansion. The numerous illustrations, however, are not matched by a plentiful documentary record of its construction and only fragments of letters and a single memorandum record the long and expensive building works. As mentioned above, Matthew Boulton first came to Soho for water power, and originally he did not intend that the whole of his operations should be located on one site. In Boulton's own words, 'one thing required another to be there until one half of the business became settled there and great inconveniences were formed by its being divided'.[18] Boulton had retained his premises at Snow Hill but losses were being incurred by trying to manage both the Soho and Snow Hill sites, and Fothergill and all of the 'Clarks and assistants ... cryed out for a Building equal to the Whole Manufactory'.[19] Boulton later stressed that the decision to build was made jointly and that he was not solely to blame for 'Building the great building at Soho'.[20] William Wyatt was commissioned to provide a design, which he estimated would cost £2,000 to build. The actual figure proved to be more like £10,000, 'which was a sore grievance to an infant undertaking'. Much of the dispute that ensued is seen from the Boulton camp, but there is one letter from William Wyatt apologising for 'bad estimates' and 'Money missapplied'.[21] Wyatt also preferred to talk the matter over rather than write upon it, and certainly the Wyatt–Boulton correspondence barely mentions these 'disagreeable circumstances'.[22] Perhaps there was too little contemporary documentation and supervision and therefore too few clear instructions from William Wyatt for such a large building operation.

Work on the principal building probably began in the spring or early summer of 1765. On 26 April 1765, Boulton asked Samuel Wyatt (William's brother) for the price of Westmorland slate.[23] In view of this consultation, it is possible that the brothers collaborated on the design and execution of the Soho buildings. In June, 'another new Mill also New Warehouses work shops and Workmens Houses' were under way.[24] It is unlikely that a new mill building or site was involved here, perhaps more a refit of equipment such as laps (buffing or polishing discs), and the introduction of a little rolling capacity for the plated-ware trade.[25] Most of the accommodation listed was located in the principal building. '[We] are now actuly Building one Building that will hold 400 Workmen'.[26] On 2 July, all was 'in great forwardness' and Boulton was anxious to obtain his slate before winter; 10 tons was to arrive by early November via Bewdley.[27] It was not until 12 November that 'Soho's Walls' were 'within a Days Labour of their destind hight except the Tower and Gavel ends', but by this time building operations had 'already consumed almost as much as the whole was to have cost'.[28] More bricks were needed and these were to be made on site to 'complete the whole of the mansion and out buildings'.[29] Fortunately, the weather was fine enough in December for work to be done on the roof, including the winding up of its timbers.[30]

By 8 March in the following year (1766), the new building had not yet been occupied.[31] Although the rest of the year was mainly devoted to fitting-out, as late as Christmas there were still 'several obligations on the Build'g branch' to be cleared.[32] In fact, in 1767 a further £1,500 was spent on 'finishing of our Building & in new erections'.[33] Some of the finance for this work may again have been obtained by mortgaging the Soho property: on 13 December 1766, Matthew Boulton borrowed another £400 on top of the £1,300 he still owed Henry Carver and Girton Peake.[34] The ratio of capital investment to business turnover had grown even more out of proportion with the construction of the principal building.[35] The grandiose design and the scale of the new Manufactory building quickly began to attract wealthy tourists and customers from both home and abroad. Soho established itself as a new 'wonder of the world', a marvel of industry to be visited *de rigueur* on any Grand Tour: 'during this summer [1767] scarcely a Day hath passd without haveing one two or 3 Companys of foreigners or Strangers to wait upon, as well as many of our Nobility who are all much delighted w'th the extension & regularity of our Manufactory'.[36] Although William Wyatt was both an architect and a builder, it appears that he took on the former role for the principal building, as a Mr Newbold was employed as the builder.[37] The principal building, in being designed by an architect, was innovative for industrial premises in this period. Except for royal establishments such as the Royal Brass Foundry at Woolwich, polite architecture for industrial buildings had been confined to minor embellishment, such as a lunette or Venetian window. Arkwright's Masson Mill in the Derwent valley, Derbyshire, for example, displays both as surface decoration on an awkwardly positioned central bay.[38] None could match the sophistication of the principal building. It was a courageous exercise in the full Palladian style; a confident assertion that the manufactory as well as the mansion could now share the topmost rank in the architectural 'hierarchy of decorum'. The chosen style not only symbolised social aspirations but also principles of order and reason that underpinned the fast-accelerating Industrial Revolution. It was no wonder that the building was likened to an aristocrat's house and that the old social order came from far and wide to gaze at the brazen ambition of the new manufacturing class and its awe-inspiring innovations.

The frontage of the principal building,

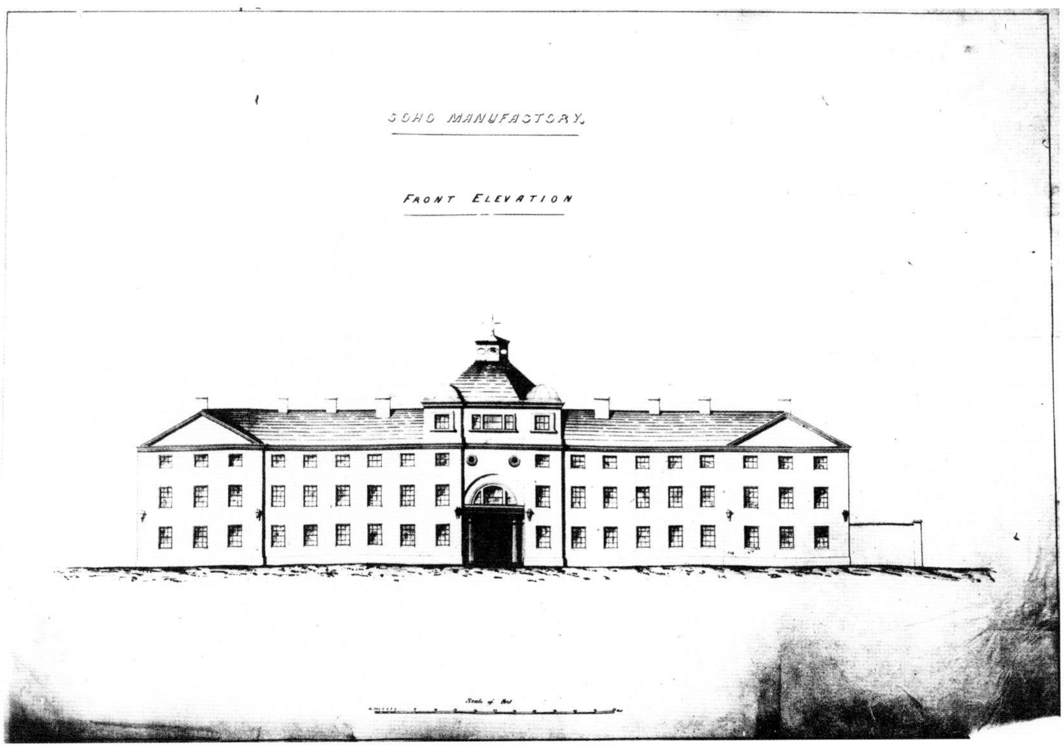

Fig 2.3
The front elevation of the principal building, drawn in 1858 by Robert McLeish Jr, five years before it was demolished. One of four drawings all now lost.

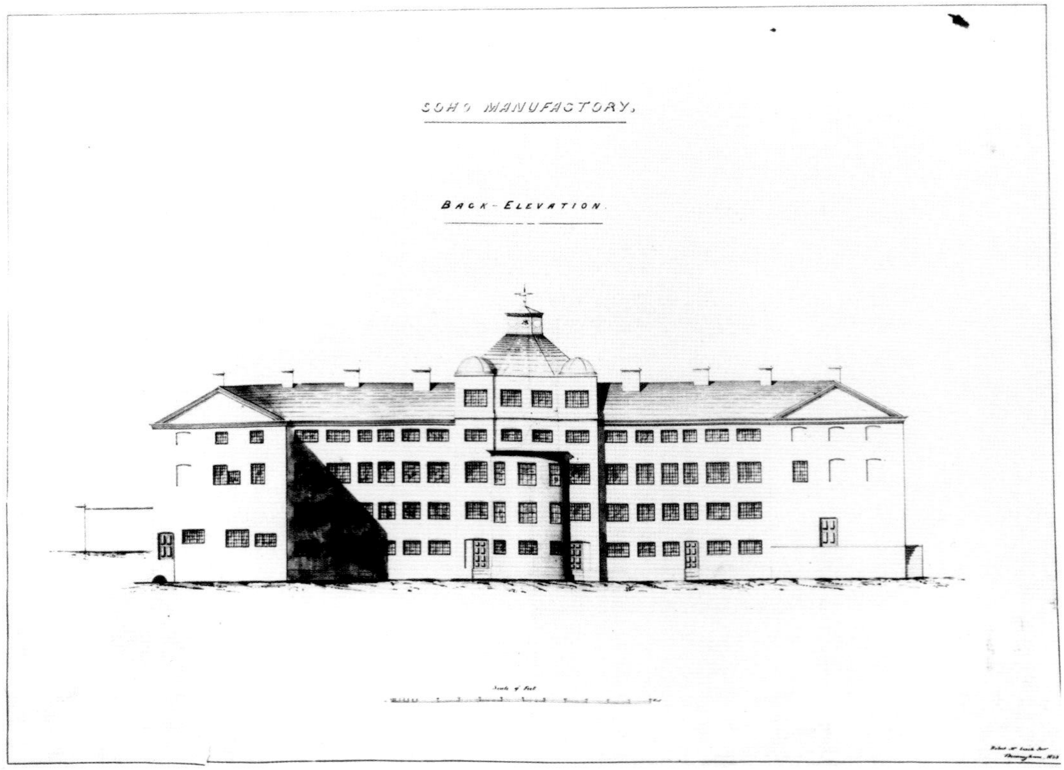

Fig 2.4
The rear elevation of the principal building by Robert McLeish Jr, 1858, showing the more utilitarian workshop widows on this less visible façade.

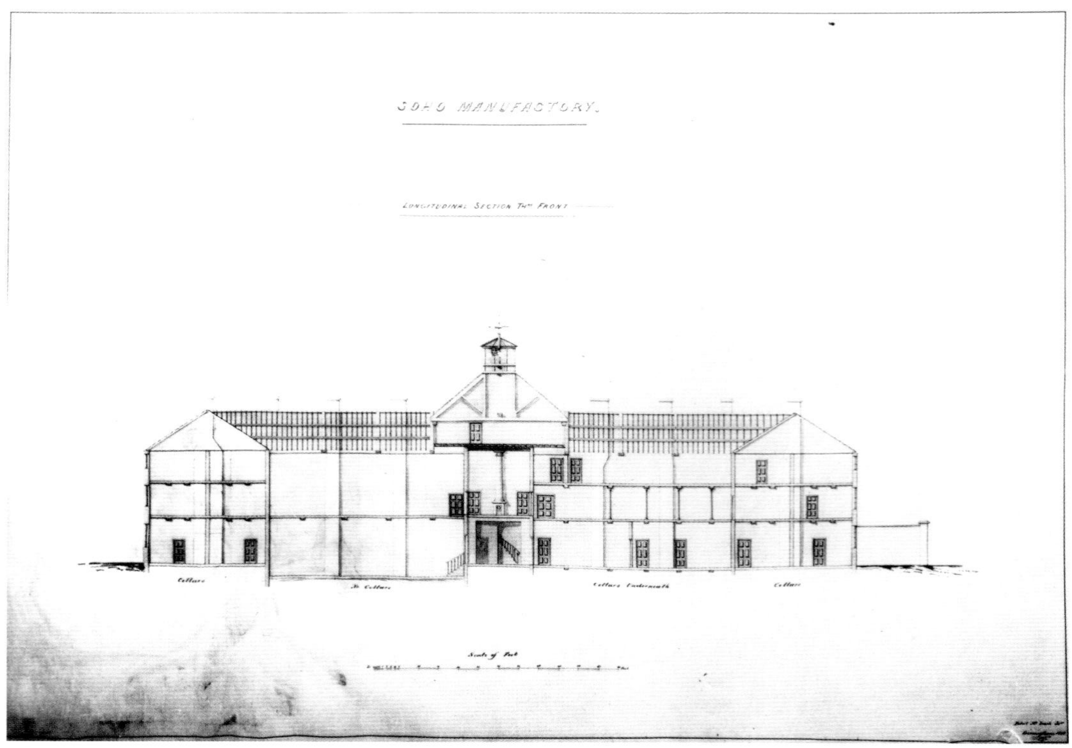

Fig 2.5
Cross section of the front half of principal building by Robert McLeish Jr, 1858, revealing that the left-hand side of the building had only two storeys, although the frontage gives the impression of three storeys.

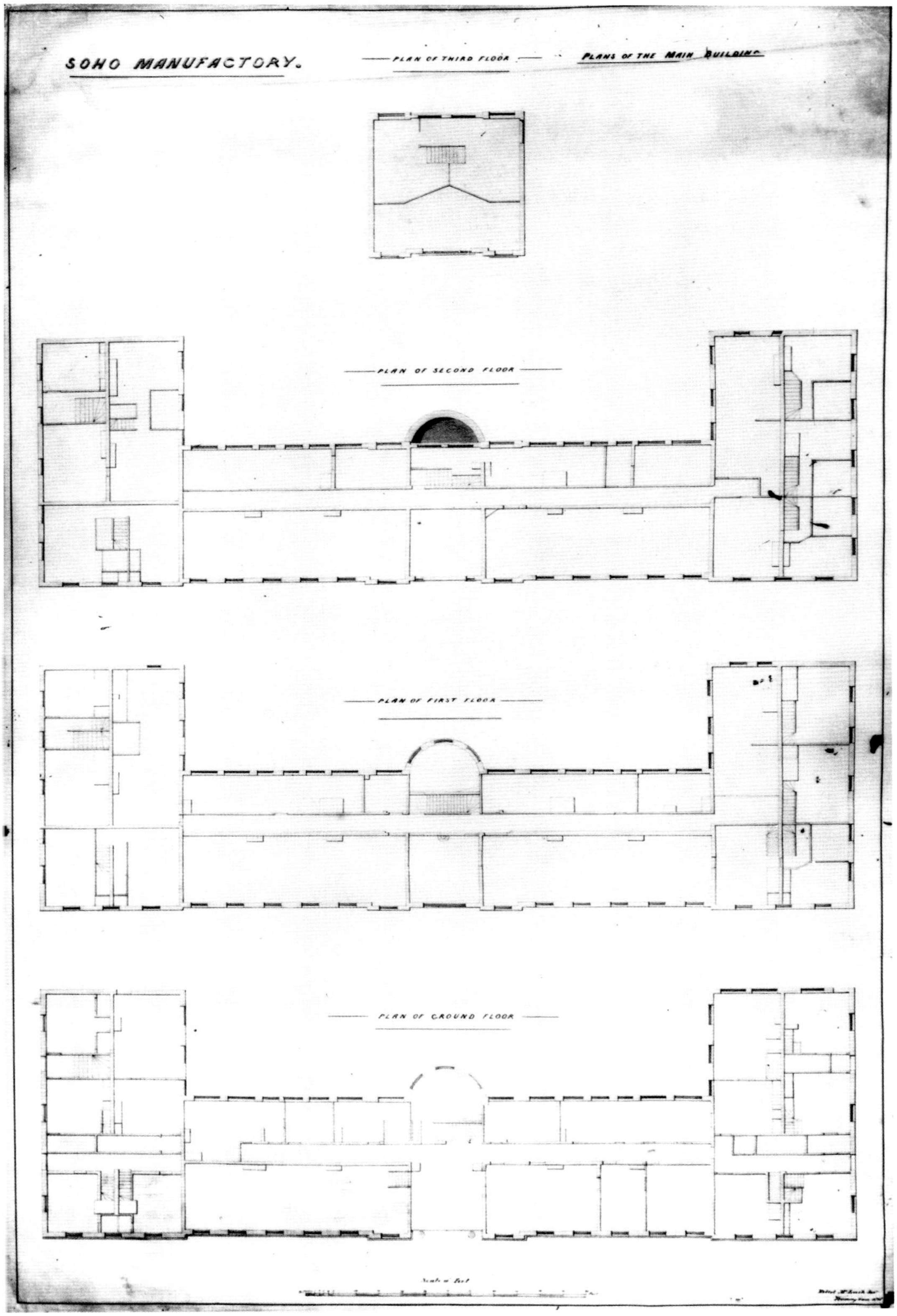

Fig 2.6
Floor plans of the principal building by Robert McLeish Jr, 1858. The staff accommodation can be seen in both end wings, each approached from a passage leading from the entrance hall and staircase.

presumably rendered, was of three storeys with 3+5+4+5+3 bays, the outermost sections breaking forward with simple triangular pediments (Fig 2.3). The centre, also projecting forward (but only on the outer two bays), was further emphasised by a fourth floor below a pyramidal octagonal roof and lantern. In the space left on the roof between the octagon and the four corners of the central section were placed circular domes, two visible on the front and two on the rear elevation. The main centre piece was recessed throughout its four storeys back to the line of the main five-bay wings. Below a Diocletian window at first-floor level, and supported by a simple entablature, was a doorway flanked by two Doric columns that allowed a deeper recess in which hung a two-leaf, six-panel door. Above the Diocletian window, lighting the second floor, were two oculi, and on the top floor a tripartite window with a central ten-pane light flanked by two four-pane lights. As well as the main eaves and pediments, moulded cornices defined the eaves of the central four-storey section.

Why did Boulton conceive the principal building? Ostensibly, it was to diversify the business by setting up a plated-ware manufactory and to consolidate on the Soho site. But it is clear that business decisions provided the opportunity for display and ostentation. The building was a hybrid industrial establishment with no powered machinery. Rooms were set aside for the production of plated ware, but these were concentrated in the rear half, overlooking the rest of the Manufactory and were well lit by large workshop windows (Figs 2.3–2.6). The front and side façades contained sash windows giving light to rooms which, in the wings, provided housing for the more senior Soho employees (*see* Fig 2.14); curtains can be seen in many of these windows in a view of *c* 1780 (Fig 2.7). The centre was given over to a counting house and office, and part of the main front, at least, to warehousing and showrooms where Boulton could show off his goods, having already impressed his customers with the scale and architecture of the building. As well as the functional division between front and back, and between the main block and the wings, there was a more subtle difference in the layout of rooms on either side of the main entrance in the main block itself. To the left, despite the impression of three storeys to preserve symmetry, there were (in fact) only two levels of equal height. The lower level was sunk slightly into the ground and lit by one range of windows, while the upper was served by two rows of windows ostensibly of the first and second storeys. These tall and capacious rooms were probably used for warehousing. To the right of the main entrance there was a more conventional arrangement where windows corresponded with floors on three storeys, but the function of these rooms is unknown. Beneath this side were cellars that had to make

Fig 2.7
A closer and dramatic view of the principal building, c *1780, its frontage busy with visitors' carriages.*

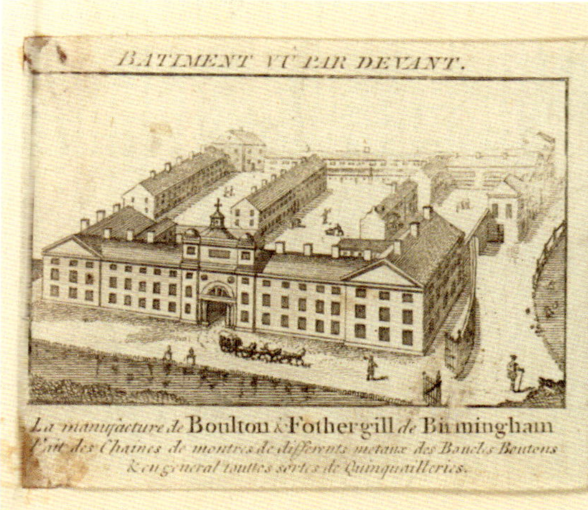

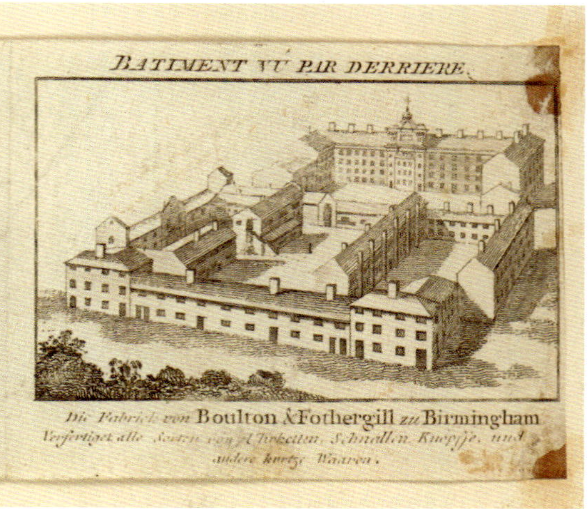

Fig 2.8
Bird's-eye view of the front of the Manufactory, probably drawn by Edward Rooker, c 1768. This is the earliest image of all the buildings at the rear of the principal building, but is inaccurate in showing them at the same level.

Fig 2.9
Bird's-eye view of the rear of the Manufactory, probably drawn by Edward Rooker, c 1768. The terrace of workers' housing enclosed the lower yard, but here drawn at the same level as the principal building.

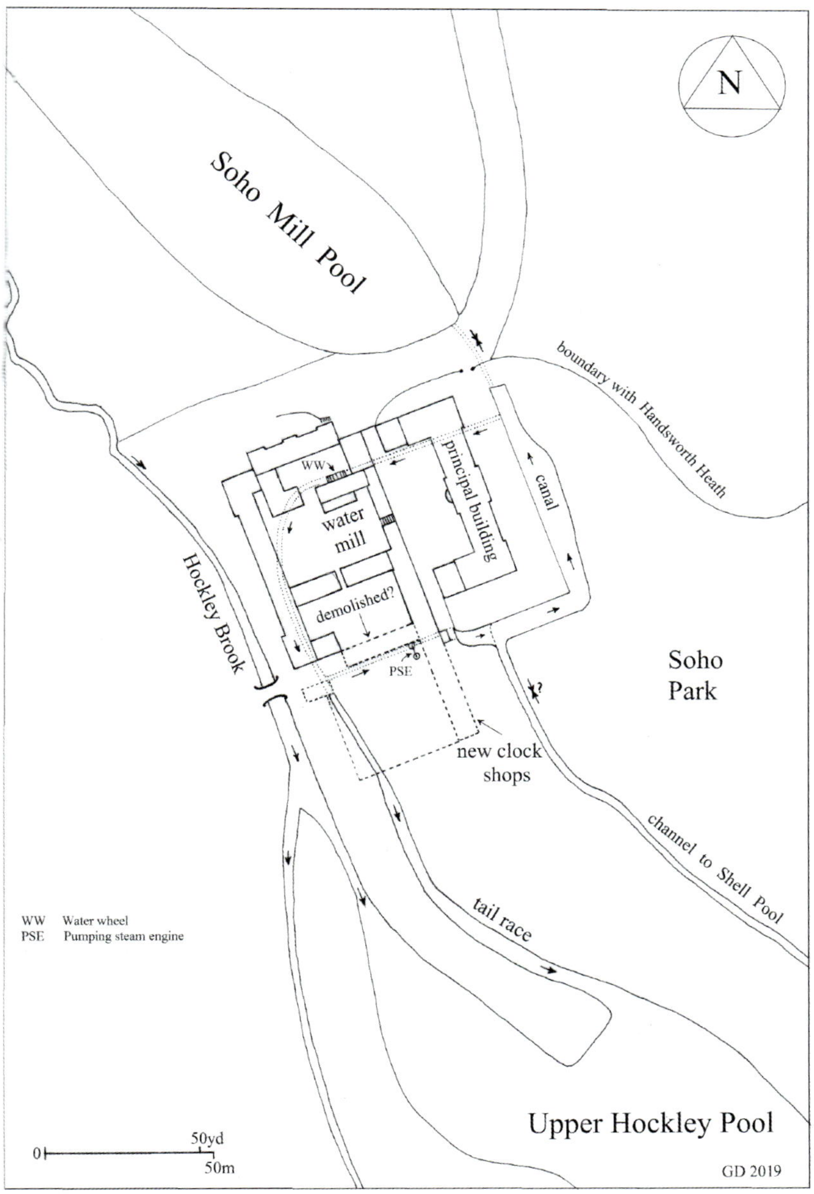

Fig 2.10
Plan of the waterworks at the Soho Manufactory, c 1775, showing how water was recirculated to the mill with the aid of James Watt's pumping engine.

space for the culvert leading from the pool to the mill. Taking advantage of the slope from the front of the building to the back, the shopping at the rear was built on four storeys.

There are in existence two small perspectives of the whole Manufactory, which probably date from soon after the principal building was constructed (Figs 2.8 and 2.9).[39] The bird's- eye view of the front has a French title, and that of the rear bears the equivalent in German; they were probably used by Fothergill on his marketing journeys in Europe. In 1768, William Jupp was commissioned to draw the 'Fair Front for Mr Rooker to Engrave', which, together with the back, was to be executed in perspective.[40] Mr Rooker was probably Edward Rooker, father of the better-known Michael Angelo Rooker, and an accomplished engraver of architectural subjects.[41] The Jupp and Rooker views cannot be earlier than 1765–6 (the date of the construction of the principal building) or later than 1775 (the year of the construction of the first Watt engine house, which is not shown). Four enclosed courts are visible all lying to the rear of the principal building, and the terrace of workmen's houses (Brook Row) dominates the rear perspective. Providing the only source of power at this time, the small watermill is hardly distinguishable. Eventually, the Manufactory was to extend to nearly twice this area.

On 18 April 1769, Boulton repaid with interest the £1,700 he had borrowed from Henry Carver and Girton Peake.[42] This repayment did not reflect a healthy business state, but was the result of restructuring borrowings. Later in 1769, not only the Soho lease but also the buildings, machinery, tools and implements were mortgaged for £8,000 through a Dutch banking house.[43]

The first steam pumping engines and clock manufacture, 1774–8

Boulton had come to Soho for water power but he quickly discovered that it was insufficient for his purposes; in dry summers horses had to be attached via a gin to the mill to move the lapping machinery.[44] He resolved to intercept the water that had left his mill and pump it back into the top pool using a steam engine. The atmospheric engine was being secretly improved in Scotland by James Watt who, on the way back in 1768 from patenting his condenser in London, called at Soho and met the already illustrious Matthew Boulton for the first time. The story of this historic meeting and its consequences has been told many times and there is no need to repeat it here.[45] On the other hand, the alterations made to the Manufactory to accommodate the first Watt pumping engine, and those that followed it, have received scant attention.

In 1773, Watt's engine was shipped down from Kinneil in Scotland to Soho via Hull but was not assembled until the following year when, on 31 May 1774, Watt himself arrived to settle permanently.[46] Although the engine was experimental, Boulton needed it to be put to work as soon as possible. It is probable, therefore, that the engine was at once sited where it could most conveniently return used water to the mill pool. This was on the Great Bank, which separated the principal building from the main complex of toy workshops and workers' housing below (Fig 2.10). The engine came too late to be shown on the perspectives mentioned above, but it would have been on the left and right edge of the front (*see* Fig 2.8) and back (*see* Fig 2.9) views respectively, just outside the existing yards. It is difficult to be certain, but a row of buildings may have been demolished to make way for it. This row does not appear on the first large-scale plan of the Manufactory made in 1788 (*see* Fig 2.14). The engine house was completed in the summer and autumn of 1774, accompanied by significant expenditure on new waterworks.[47]

In about August or September 1775, the

Fig 2.11
James Watt's Soho 33in pumping engine ('Old Bess') on display in the Science Museum, London.

fledgling firm of Boulton & Watt constructed a new forging shop, their first premises.[48] Following on quickly from the partnership agreed on 1 June 1775, they were probably built to fashion smaller engine parts.[49] Shortly before this, Boulton ventured into the invention and manufacture of clock movements, though he had been making decorative clock cases since about 1771 (Fig 1.5).[50] Based on James Keir's memoir, Dickinson speculated that Dr Small was intended to play an important development role here, but the latter died in 1775.[51] Boulton was obviously preoccupied with establishing the ultimately successful engine business. It appears that the clock-making enterprise was one project too many in the circumstances and was, therefore, stillborn.

At the end of 1776, the engine house was eventually added to the building inventory of Boulton & Fothergill, together with a new three-storey clock shop, a regulating shop, a little forging shop and a burnishing shop, all built during the preceding year. Their total cost was £550.[52] These shops were built on the Great Bank close to the pumping engine, and the new Boulton & Watt forging shop was aligned at right angles (but not connected to them) forming a new yard. Thus, the mid 1770s represent the next phase in the development of the Manufactory in extending south of the existing toy and hardware workshops. The new yard was soon to enclose the steam engine completely, though the south end of Brook Row already formed part of the west side.

The earliest complete inventory of the Manufactory survives from this period and lists 128 rooms occupying a total area of 32,039.75 sq ft (2,976.42 sq m) and valued at about £11,000.[53] Unfortunately, the location of most of the rooms cannot be identified precisely, although their dimensions are given.

In the summer of 1777, the original 18in (457mm) cylinder was exchanged for a 33in (838mm) cylinder working on the expansive action of steam; the engine soon became known as 'Beelzebub'.[54] Following a fire (the first known conflagration at the Manufactory) that broke out in July 1778 in the engine house, improvements were made both to the engine and to the building (*see* pp 46–8). As a result, 'Beelzebub' became known affectionately as 'Old Bess' and her remains now grace the Science Museum in London (Fig 2.11).

The copying-press company and extensions to the engine works, 1780–3

In 1780, a copying-press company was established to produce the letter- and plan-copying machines invented by James Watt. These were the first practical document copiers using special inks that were transferred from the original by rollers onto unsized damp tissue paper, the impression as a result being readable on the reverse side. Plans were printed in reverse onto normal thicker opaque paper and were marked accordingly. The firm was originally organised under the partnership of Boulton, Watt and James Keir, but was later transferred to James Watt & Co.[55] The company originally occupied modestly sized premises, using three existing workshops, including a clock shop and a clock room, part of the redundant three-storey building constructed on the Great Bank.[56] These workshops, in occupying the Great Bank, were consequently one storey high on the upslope elevation (east) and three storeys high facing the new yard (west) (*see* Fig 2.35).

In autumn 1781, a new workshop was constructed for Boulton & Watt in order 'to fit up little Engines' and in which a double-expansive 15in (381mm) engine was tested (*see* Fig 4.2).[57] The workshop was placed at right angles to the existing 'Smiths Shop', or forging shop of 1775, on the west side of the yard, almost completing the enclosure. An open tail-race channel still ran within the yard parallel to the new shop. Important developments in steam-engine technology, such as the double-acting (reciprocating) engine and its application to rotative motion, were imminent. Both these advances were tested at Soho and the engine-yard buildings modified and extended as a result (*see* pp 65–70).

In October and November 1782, some months after the invention of the 'sun-and-planet' crank, work began on an engine house for a new 18in (457mm) rotative engine that, in the following year, was connected to corn-grinding machinery to create the first steam-engine-powered corn mill in the world (*see* Fig 4.5). The experiments on the Soho corn mill led quickly to the establishment of the first commercial enterprise using this machinery, the Albion Mill on the Thames at Blackfriars Bridge in London. By 1788, the new yard had been divided east–west in line with the steam pumping engine. Two courts to the north belonged to

Matthew Boulton's hardware businesses and the larger one to the south to the Boulton & Watt steam engine company and the letter-copying works.[58]

Buttons and plated ware, 1782–9

Although there had been relatively little building at the rest of the Manufactory after 1776, major changes in the organisation of the businesses had taken place. The Boulton and Fothergill partnership was dissolved on 31 December 1781 following an acrimonious dispute. Immediately after Fothergill's death in June 1782, an extremely detailed inventory of all the tools, utensils and goods contained in about 70 rooms was taken.[59] Unfortunately, comparable inventories of the buildings, machinery and fixtures have not survived. By 1783, Boulton – free of Fothergill – had divided his firm into two: the button business managed by John Scale (Boulton & Scale), and the plated-ware business managed by John Hodges (Matthew Boulton & Plate Co, after a short spell as William Bingley & Co). At the end of December 1783, an inventory of the Manufactory was made that was not 'room by room', but a listing of whole buildings, the dwellings, the boundary/retaining walls, culverts and watercourses.[60] This was intended as a survey of the physical fabric of the Manufactory, which was the personal possession of Matthew Boulton. For this reason, the watermill machinery and the steam pumping engine appear on the list but no other machinery, which was normally assessed as part of the Soho businesses. Other items of interest include the 'School for Children or Gateway converted into a Dwelling House', brewhouses, barbers shop and an 'Engine to Quench fire'. Although Boulton had a financial interest in all the Soho businesses, he was to charge each of them rent payable to his personal estate. He, in turn, was responsible for the maintenance of the steam engines and buildings. The 50 items of the physical fabric of the Manufactory were valued at £6,973 8s 0d, just over half of the 1776 assessment based on floor area (*see* p 19).

An inventory made in about 1789 lists all the rooms belonging to the button company and the plated-ware company.[61] The former had the larger floor area (just over 14,000 sq ft/1,300.6 sq m in about 55 rooms), while the latter measured nearly 10,500 sq ft/975.45 sq m in 31 rooms. The discrepancy of about 7,500 sq ft/696.75 sq m between the 1777 total of just over 32,000 sq ft/2,972.8 sq m and the 1789 total of 24,500 sq ft/2,276.05 sq m is made up of 5,400 sq ft/501.66 sq m assigned to Boulton & Watt (the letter-copying and engine company) and much of the balance by the steam pumping-engine house and the rolling and lapping mill rebuilt in the 1780s.

The new watermill, 1785 (*see* pp 48–53)

Although Boulton had come to Soho because he needed a mill for rolling and polishing, the mill was never adequate and hence Holford Mill was leased. When Soho Mill was eventually rebuilt in 1785 and 1788, this work was undertaken not only to remedy a long-term deficiency but also to prepare for an entirely different line of business: coining. The 1780s represent an important conjuncture in the development of Soho, and early in the decade Matthew Boulton was forced to become independent of outside rolling-mill capacity, a necessary condition in the establishment of a coining business.

In April 1780, the lease of Holford Mill was offered to Boulton, but he was advised not to take it by his own managers who wished to have the installation at Soho rebuilt and made more powerful.[62] Holford Mill was given up in 1781 and the Soho Mill used for a few years despite its deficiencies.[63] At this time, Boulton's mind was without doubt wrapped up in the development of rotary power and steam engines. It was not until 1784, however, that the rebuilding of the mill was seriously considered, prompted by the immediate need to repair the waterwheel.[64] In the summer and early autumn of 1785 the old building was demolished and a much larger and more powerful rolling and lapping mill constructed at right angles to the former site. The old waterwheel position was more or less retained, but a new wider and larger-diameter wheel was installed and placed under cover.[65] John Rennie helped to design and install the new machinery in the mill and his work here (and at the Albion Mill, London) established his reputation.[66]

It is not known whether Boulton was convinced of the necessity of rebuilding by the requirements of his old businesses or by the germ of a new idea regarding coining. In 1786, however, Boulton secured his first coining contract – for the East India Company – though only blanks were made at Soho (*see* pp 87–9).

The new mint, 1788

In typical fashion, the lure of novelty and necessity propelled Matthew Boulton into the construction at Soho of the first steam-powered mint in the world, a venture that was, however, to maintain his interest to his dying day. For Boulton – ever receptive to a new idea – coining (at a rapid rate with fixed diameters, width and metal content) was an attractive and timely proposition. The coinage of the realm was in a pitiful state, with acute shortages of small change, and counterfeiting rampant.[67] Much of the forgery took place two miles away in Birmingham under Matthew Boulton's own nose. He found this situation intolerable and looked for a solution in a combination of new technologies: the rotative steam engine, vacuum power, and a new collar for holding the coin blank in the press. The forgers' task was to be made even more difficult by applying the well-established mark of Soho – high art and craftsmanship – translated (in this case) into exquisite design by some of the best die sinkers in the country.[68]

Matthew Boulton had set his mind on producing a new national copper coinage and he lobbied the Committee of the Privy Council appointed to deal with the problems of the national coinage.[69] When the Committee began its deliberations in 1787, Boulton could only offer the results of experiments. However, in January 1788, in anticipation of orders, he began building a mint on a site separate from the main Manufactory complex.[70] It was situated in his private garden about 120yd (109.73m) south-east of the principal building, behind the menagerie, tea room, fossil room and laboratory (Fig 2.12; for wider orientation *see* Fig 5.21). The decision to locate there seems as much influenced by the need to hide his new technology from prying eyes as it was to keep the minted coins secure from thieving hands. This adaptation and extension of existing garden buildings created a less-than-ideal layout and a peculiarly distinctive group of buildings. For the first time, production was established away from the main Manufactory complex, a decision that was to be repeated only once more, in the establishment of the Latchet (Crescent) Building six years later (*see* pp 26–8).

At first, the new building contained only a single-storey coining room and an attached two-storey engine house; the other ancillary functions, most notably the cutting-out of blanks, were performed some distance away in and around the rolling mill. An initial layout of eight coining presses, in two parallel lines of four, was soon abandoned in late 1788 for presses arranged in a circle (*see* pp 89–97). The circular arrangement appears in the patent specification drawing of 1790, which was 'made from the real machine'.[71] Strictly speaking, the presses were not directly steam powered. The steam engine drove a horizontal wheel that produced, via levers and cams, a vacuum in air pumps linked to each press. The release of the vacuum spun the fly arm of the screw press and the screw and its die underside descended in the usual manner to impress the coin blanks (*see* Fig 5.13).

The expected orders for the national coinage did not, however, materialise, and it was not until 1797 that Boulton's investment in buildings and new machinery was fully realised on his terms.

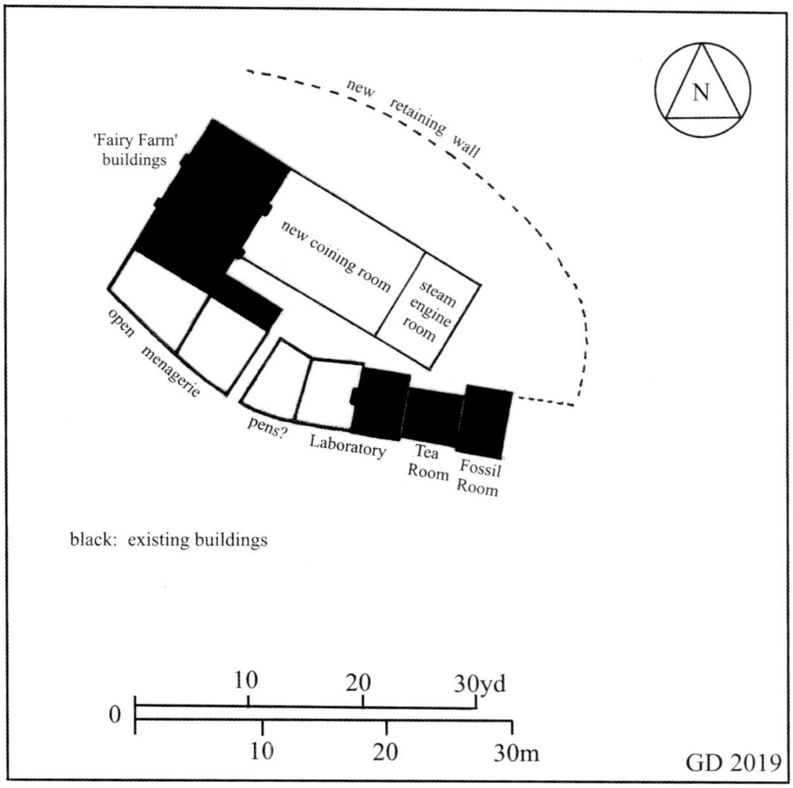

Fig 2.12
Sketch plan of the Soho Mint, 1788, showing how it was deliberately hidden behind existing garden buildings.

The lap engine, 1788

The automated coinage presses of the new mint required a considerable amount of rolled copper, which could not be supplied in sufficient quantities by Boulton's existing watermill, though newly built in 1785. To one side, the waterwheel powered

Fig 2.13
The Soho lap (and cutting-out) engine on display in the Science Museum, London.

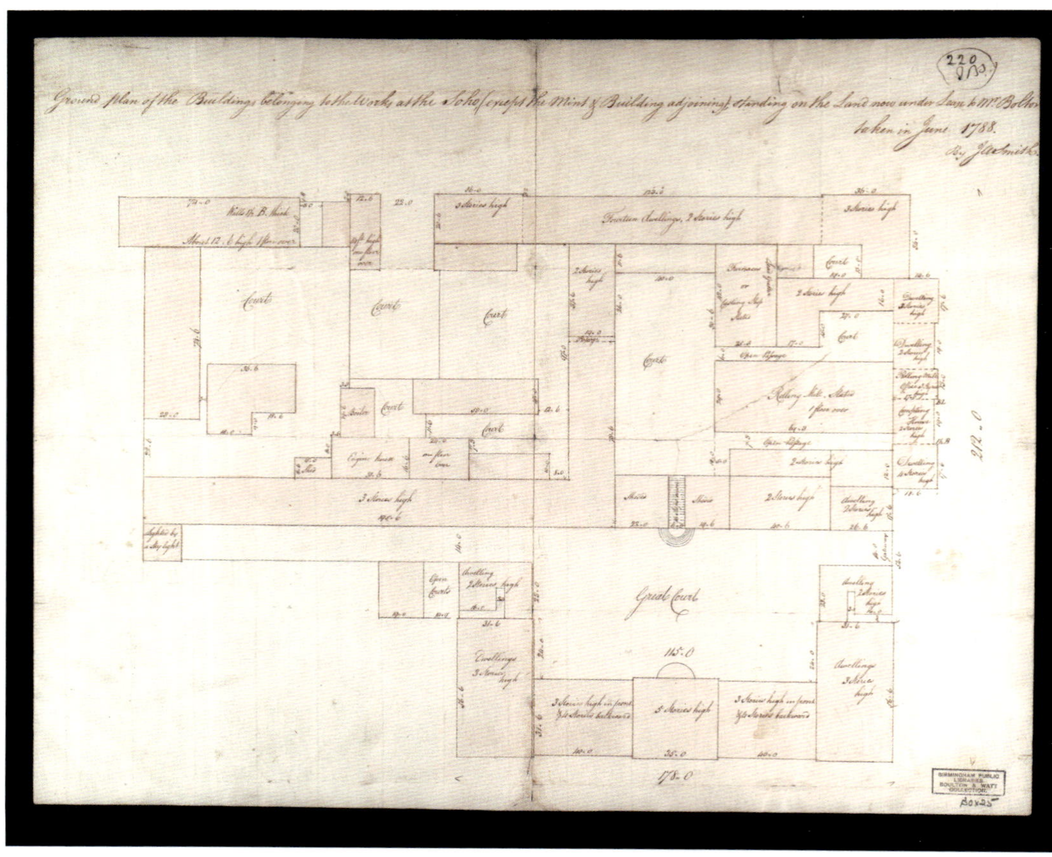

Fig 2.14
Large-scale plan of the Soho Manufactory by James Smith, June 1788, the earliest known.

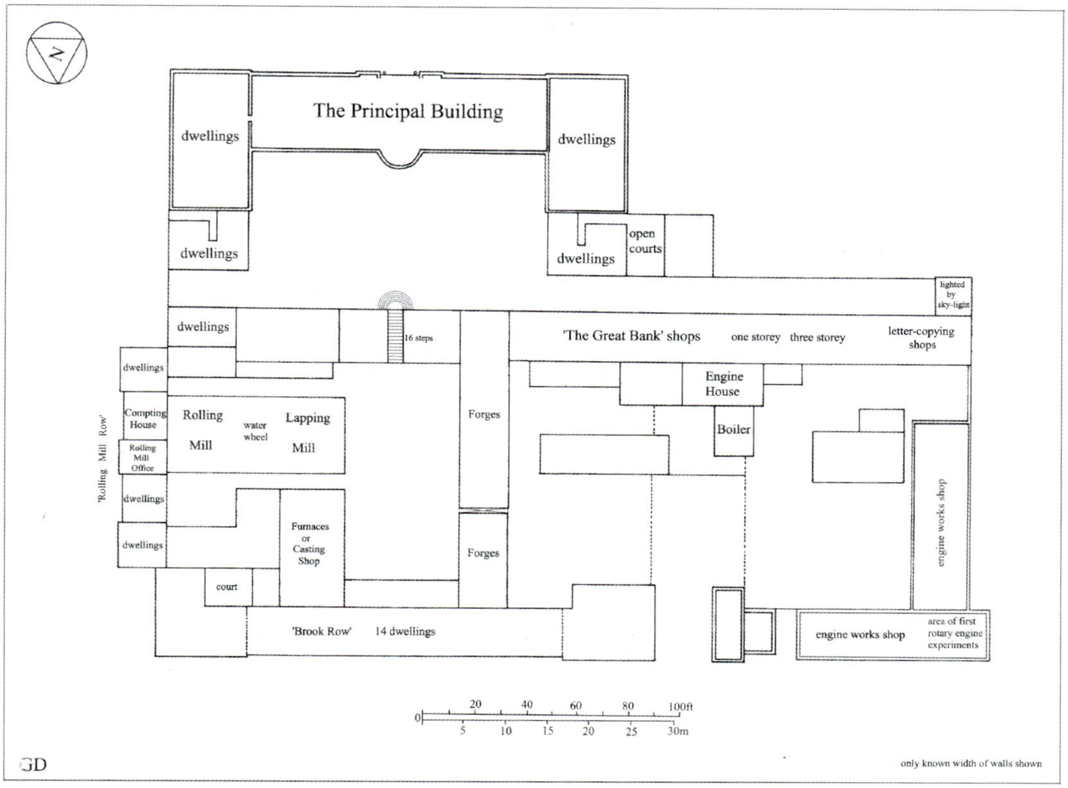

Fig 2.15
Plan of the Soho Manufactory, 1788, including the Boulton & Watt engine works buildings.

several sets of rolls, and to the other a large number of laps. Boulton, after considering a number of ideas, decided to attach a rotative steam engine to the lapping end of the mill where there was space for an engine house.[72] Consequently, the water-wheel was freed to move the rolls alone, which were then to be engaged mainly in making sheet and strip copper for coinage. The engine hence became known as the lap engine and is now on display (Fig 2.13) in the Science Museum, London, having been fortunately saved when the mill was demolished in the early 1860s.

The new engine was also connected to a cutting-out machine, which produced the copper blanks ('dubs') for the coining presses in the mint.[73] These presses were arranged in a circle and worked by the same principle as those for coining in the mint. Work began on the new lap-engine house in the summer of 1788, but many alterations and additions to the rolling machinery and lap gearing were also carried out, and equipment was still being installed early in 1789.[74] It was in this rebuilding that another young Scottish engineer, Peter Ewart, cut his teeth and went on to enjoy a distinguished career.[75] In fact, he was employed at Soho to implement the plans jointly agreed by the absent John Rennie and Matthew Boulton.

A number of sources (the most important being a plan, dated June 1788; Fig 2.14),[76] have been used to produce a plan of the Manufactory as it was just after the construction of the lap-engine house (Fig 2.15). Unfortunately, the scale of the original plan is too small for most of the workshops listed in the *c* 1789 inventory to be distinguished.[77] Furthermore, many of the workshops were two or three storeys high and there are no separate floor plans. Though useful, only the number of storeys in each building is given, but rarely their function. The laying out of the buildings on a rectilinear pattern created a series of interconnected yards or 'courts'.

Extensions to the engine works and lap-engine house, 1790–2

In about 1790, the lap engine was moved out of the engine house and attached to the external wall, leaving the chimney in the same position (*see* pp 53–8). In the meantime, the increasing demand for steam engines required further additions to the engine works. Between 1790 and 1792, several new workshops and rooms appear in the annual inventories of the Boulton & Watt premises.[78] Apart from adding extra floors to buildings around the main engine yard,

Fig 2.16
Watercolour by John Phillp, 1796, showing the extreme southern end of the Manufactory at the Boulton & Watt engine works overlooking the Upper Hockley Pool. The Soho Manufactory and Park were unashamedly adjacent to one another.

Fig 2.17
Pen-and-ink drawing by John Phillp, 1796, showing the southern end of the Manufactory at the Boulton & Watt engine works from a slightly different perspective. The water to the right would enter the Upper Hockley Pool from the watermill tail race.

Fig 2.18
Pen-and-ink drawing by John Phillp, 1796, of the Soho Manufactory and Soho Park taken from Birmingham Heath. The two levels of the Manufactory can clearly to be seen on the left, but farther to the right and partially hidden amidst the trees lie the incomplete Latchet (Crescent) Building and the Soho Mint with its smoking chimney.

a single-storey wing, running south into an area that was formerly Matthew Boulton's kitchen garden, was attached to the main engine house and served as a new forging shop. It broadened into a two-storey hipped-roof building with large workshop windows and prominent chimneys overlooking the garden (Figs 2.16 and 2.17).[79]

A view of the Manufactory from the rear, dating from a few years after this phase of building was completed (1796), is shown in Fig 2.18. Although the new buildings are only just visible above the trees, the drawing gives a good impression of how the Manufactory had spread into the landscaped grounds of Soho House and clearly shows the principal building at the upper level overlooking the remainder of the Manufactory complex.[80]

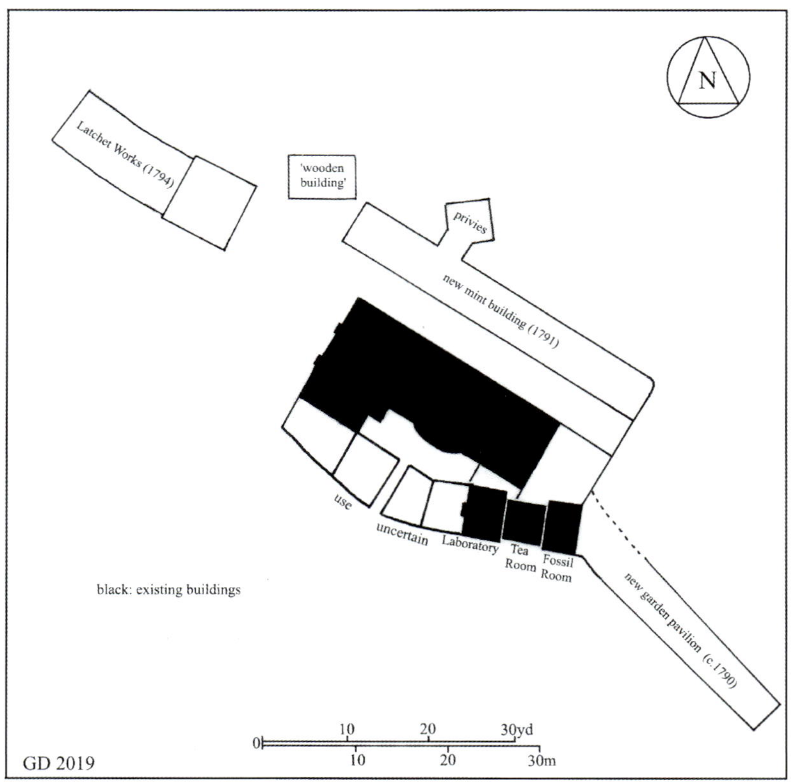

Fig 2.19
Sketch plan of the Soho Mint, 1791, together with the first phase of the Latchet (Crescent) Building constructed in 1794 and garden pavilion, c 1790.

A new mint building, 1791

The division of mint activities between the new coining presses tucked away in the garden and the manufactory mill was certainly not ideal. In 1791, Boulton decided to transfer some of the cutting out, shaking and pickling – which was overcrowding the mill – to a more convenient location close by the coining presses. Steam-powered cutting out, however, remained in the lapping mill.

In the summer and early autumn of 1791, a two-storey range of shopping, 14ft (4.27m) wide, was erected to the north-east of, and parallel to, the mint and engine house, leaving an open yard in between of about the same width (Fig 2.19; for wider orientation *see* Fig 5.21). It contained, on the ground floor, an office, a warehouse, a room for four presses (presumably for cutting out by hand), a shaking and drying shop, and an unnamed room. It is not clear how all the upper rooms of the new range were intended to be used (*see* Fig 5.12).[81] The warehouse room in this building was discovered and excavated in 1995 and re-excavated in April 1996 (*see* Appendix 1).

The construction of the Soho Foundry, 1795–6 (*see* Chapter 7)

The Foundry was primarily established to cast and bore engine cylinders so that the company of Boulton & Watt would no longer be dependent on the outside foundries to which such work had previously been contracted. Their main suppliers had been the brothers John and William Wilkinson, but they fell out with each other, and their Bersham works in Shropshire, where the cylinders were made, were threatened with closure.[82] The collapse of the Wilkinson firm was a primary cause in the establishment of the Soho Foundry, the first purpose-built steam-engine manufactory in the world, but it is by no means certain that this event on its own was sufficient to influence this course of action. The expiry of Watt's patent in 1800 must also have provided a strong motive for Boulton & Watt to set up their own production of cylinders and eventually all engine parts. A site was chosen about a mile away in Smethwick alongside the Birmingham Canal for easier transport of raw materials and finished engines. The Manufactory concentrated, as before, on smaller engines and more precisely made components, although considerable expansion of its premises was to take place within a few years (*see* pp 29–31). Finished engine parts were probably exchanged between the two establishments so that both could assemble and despatch completed engines, but the actual working relationship between the two establishments is not yet fully understood and merits further detailed study.

The Latchet Works (Crescent Building), 1794–9

After the 1791 phase of construction of the Mint, the contracts for coining that Boulton expected did not materialise and he was left with spare workshops, machinery and underemployed workmen.[83] In about 1792, two Birmingham button makers, James and Benjamin Smith, offered to make their patent shoe buckle, known as a 'latchet', in partnership with Boulton at Soho. The latchet was a flexible sheet-metal buckle with hooks attached, which engaged with the lace-holes on a shoe, holding them under tension. Thus, the same shoe could be worn with a number of different buckles or vice versa (Fig 2.20). The Smith offer was attractive as Boulton 'conceived the Buckle Manufacture might be Established at Soho for 1/10 part of the Expence & 1/10 part of the time which wd have cost to have gone into new Shops'.[84] By early 1794, the new company had taken over all of the 1791 building. The 'Buckle Shops' that caught fire in early February 1794 lay within its centre. The fire was limited to the 'lower shop where the Great presses are fixt (next to the shaking shop)' and 'the chamber over it'.[85]

However, for reasons which are perplexing, a completely new building – sumptuous in scale and appearance – was planned between the Manufactory and the Mint (Fig 2.21). It was to be crescent-shaped, with a slightly projecting three-storey section in the centre, originally intended to carry a dome. Boulton thought this too pretentious and had the design altered to a

Fig 2.20
A Boulton & Smith latchet; the springy metal with two pairs of hooks fixed to the underside allowed the buckle to be used on more than one shoe.

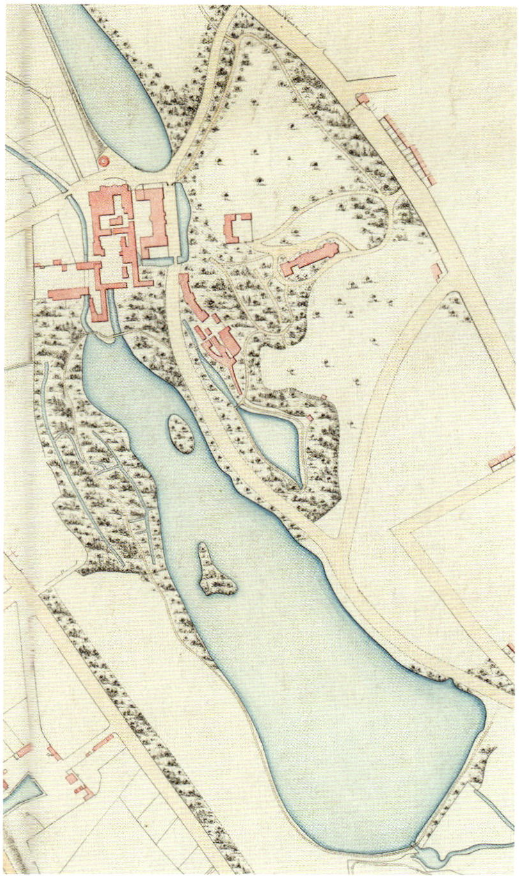

more modest pediment instead.[86] Francis Egínton's engraving (Fig 2.22) shows this later version, although the dome is to be seen on another view (Fig 2.23). On either side of the central bay, forward curving wings (two storeys in height) were to end with bays slightly breaking forward, as at the centre (Fig 2.24).

The two drawings by Eginton and Phillp, respectively, are, however, part fiction, as the Latchet building was not completed as intended until 1824–6. It is a useful reminder that views of buildings commissioned by their proud owners are not always reliable, particularly if proposed constructions are shown. The south bay and wing (1,614 sq ft/150 sq m) were constructed in 1794–5 and the central bay (699 sq ft/65 sq m) in 1798–9.[87] The north wing and its end bay were subsequently constructed as a single storey but it is not certain when this phase was carried out.

Drawings for the 'Latchetary', as it was also called, were produced in the Boulton & Watt drawing office in July and August 1794 and the plan staked out on the ground on 6 August. Unfortunately, none of this material has survived.[88] It appears that construction work began soon after as accounts show entries (beginning in April) for the delivery of several consignments of bricks appearing in the accounts, the largest, numbering 60,550, arriving on 16 August. James Webster was appointed as builder, with Charles Glover supplying the timber components, the stone detailing and the metalware for

Fig 2.21
Detail from the Board of Health map, c 1850–5, showing the completed Latchet (Crescent) Building lying between the principal building and the Mint.

Fig 2.22
Detail from Francis Eginton's engraving of the Soho Manufactory showing the Latchet (Crescent) Building with pediments, this end probably not completed to its full height until 1824–6.

Fig 2.23
Detail from John Phillp's pen-and-ink drawing, c 1796, of the Latchet (Crescent) Building with its original design for a dome on the central bay and hipped roofs on the end bays.

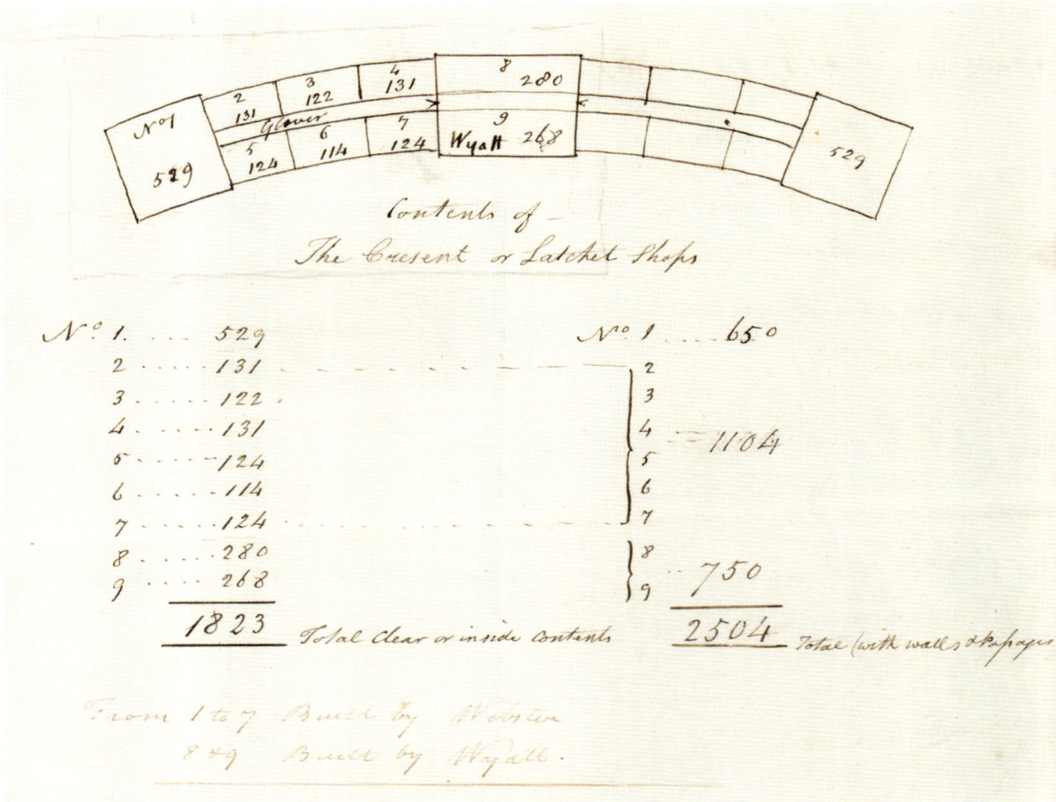

Fig 2.24
Sketch plan by Matthew Boulton, c 1800, of the Latchet (Crescent) Building.

doors and windows. Charles Glover submitted accounts, dated 1794, for the Crescent totalling £382 8s 6d.[89] The full cost of this phase of the work was given as £877.[90] In this same period, Glover also erected or reconstructed buildings about the Mint for the Latchet Company. This included 'new narrow shopping near the Crescent ... Buckle Shops near the Tea Room', the latter with a gallery above. In 1798, Benjamin Wyatt (of Sutton Coldfield) (1755–1813) was called on to build the central three-storey bay, for which he charged £435.[91]

The Latchet Company came to occupy many of the underused Mint buildings as well as the Crescent shops. In fact, around 1800, the firm rented 11,955 sq ft (1,110 sq m) compared to the 5,946 sq ft (552 sq m) of the Mint.[92] Production of latchets seems to have ceased in about 1806 when the patent ran out and rent for part of the mill at Soho ceased to be paid by Boulton and Smith.[93] An inventory was made in November 1807.[94] Thenceforth, the building was progressively taken over by the Mint, most dramatically in 1824–6 when the north end was heightened according to the original plan and power introduced for the first time for ancillary minting operations such as cutting out (*see* pp 34–5 and Chapter 5).[95] The whole building was probably demolished, along with the rest of the Mint, in the early 1850s.

Mint reconstruction, 1798–9

It was not until 1797 that Matthew Boulton finally achieved his ambition of coining for the government when he signed a contract with the Treasury to supply a total of 500 tons (508 tonnes) of coin consisting of 20 tons (20.3 tonnes) of 2d pieces and 480 tons (487.7 tonnes) of 1d pieces.[96] The national coinage contract precipitated plans to construct a new type of mint machinery, which Boulton and John Southern (the head of the drawing office and one of his principal engineers) had been working on for some time (*see* pp 100–9).[97] This was to involve an entirely different method of applying power to the coining presses: the steam engine was applied directly to the production of a vacuum in a tube that ran parallel to the presses arranged in a line. Shafts and a horizontal cam wheel were eliminated, but the mechanism was no less complicated for that. In fact, the circular arrangement, dependent on an overhead cam wheel, continued to be used for cutting out coin blanks.

A new minting room was established, taking over the area of redundant walled enclosures (Fig 2.25). John Southern's plan is dated 14 May 1798 and the room can be located to the north-west of the tea room and to the south-west of the earlier coining room[98] (*see* Fig 5.21). It was a slightly curving two-storey building cut into the slope of the hill, with its first floor at the level of the remainder of the Mint complex. In November and December 1798, a new 8hp 16in-cylinder steam engine was installed in a former workshop, bringing its power through vacuum pumps onto the north-east side of the minting room.[99] It was not until 1 May 1799 that the intended eight presses worked together for the first time, making the nation's pennies, halfpence and farthings.[100] The middle bay of the Crescent Building was completed about this time and the ground floor appropriated for a workshop housing vices and a lathe.[101]

The machinery of the Soho Mint installed in this period was (with minor modifications) the technology that was to be exported across the globe in the next few decades. Indeed, within a few years, a Boulton mint had been established at St Petersburg in Russia.[102]

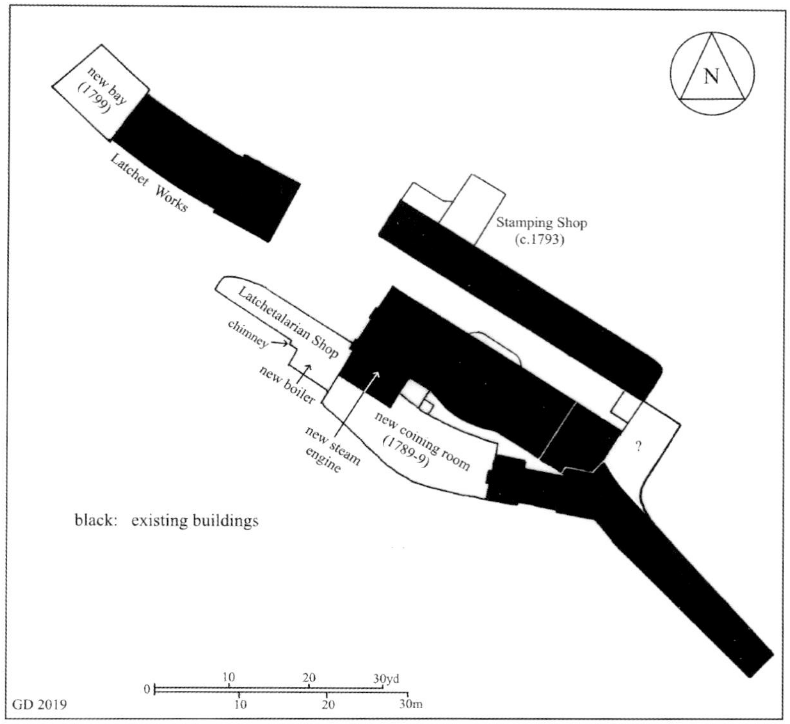

Fig 2.25
Sketch plan of the 1798–9 Soho Mint including the central bay of the Latchet (Crescent) Building.

The engine works – major extensions and alterations, 1801–4

The construction of the Soho Foundry in 1795–6 enabled the newly constituted firm of Boulton Watt & Sons to produce larger cast-metal parts, such as cylinders and condensers, for the first time. Demand for steam engines, particularly of the rotary type, rose steadily throughout the late 1780s and the 1790s. The Foundry solved a production bottleneck on one front, but it was found that the engine works at the Manufactory could not produce sufficient of the smaller parts, e.g. nozzles (valve boxes), parallel motions and communicating gearing, to keep pace. It was therefore decided to undertake a major rebuilding and expansion of the engine yard at the Manufactory.

Detailed planning for the extensions started in 1800 and seems to have been entirely the province of Boulton's son, Matthew Robinson Boulton (1770–1842) (*see* pp 73–9).[103] There was little flat land available immediately south of the existing engine yard and perhaps further encroachment into the Soho House garden was not permitted by Boulton Sr. It was decided for the first time to extend at right angles to the main axis of the Manufactory across the Hockley Brook into Birmingham parish, which was in Warwickshire. From this time, the Manufactory could no longer be strictly referred to as being situated at Soho, Handsworth, Staffordshire. The new yard was attached to the existing engine works, creating the last enclosed court of the Manufactory, and measured approximately 62yd (56.69m) × 35yd (32m). A section of the Hockley Brook was enclosed within the yard and culverted.

Documents in Matthew Robinson Boulton's hand reveal the meticulous planning that went into the reorganisation and extension of the engine works. A 15in (421mm) engine, which had some time before replaced the old 18in (457mm) corn-mill engine, was encumbered with lathes and a drill in a complicated arrangement of gearing.[104] It, in turn, made way for three separate small engines (of 6hp, 3hp and 1hp respectively), powering the same drills and lathes but entailing a considerable rebuilding of the engine house. The oldest forging shop became the nozzle and drilling shop, and the forge built ten years previously was altered to the 'lower fitting shop'. The existing 'fitting up shop', where once the first rotary engines were tested, was converted into a parallel motion shop. A new forge was constructed at the very end of the new engine yard. Around the rest of the perimeter (and facing inwards on the south

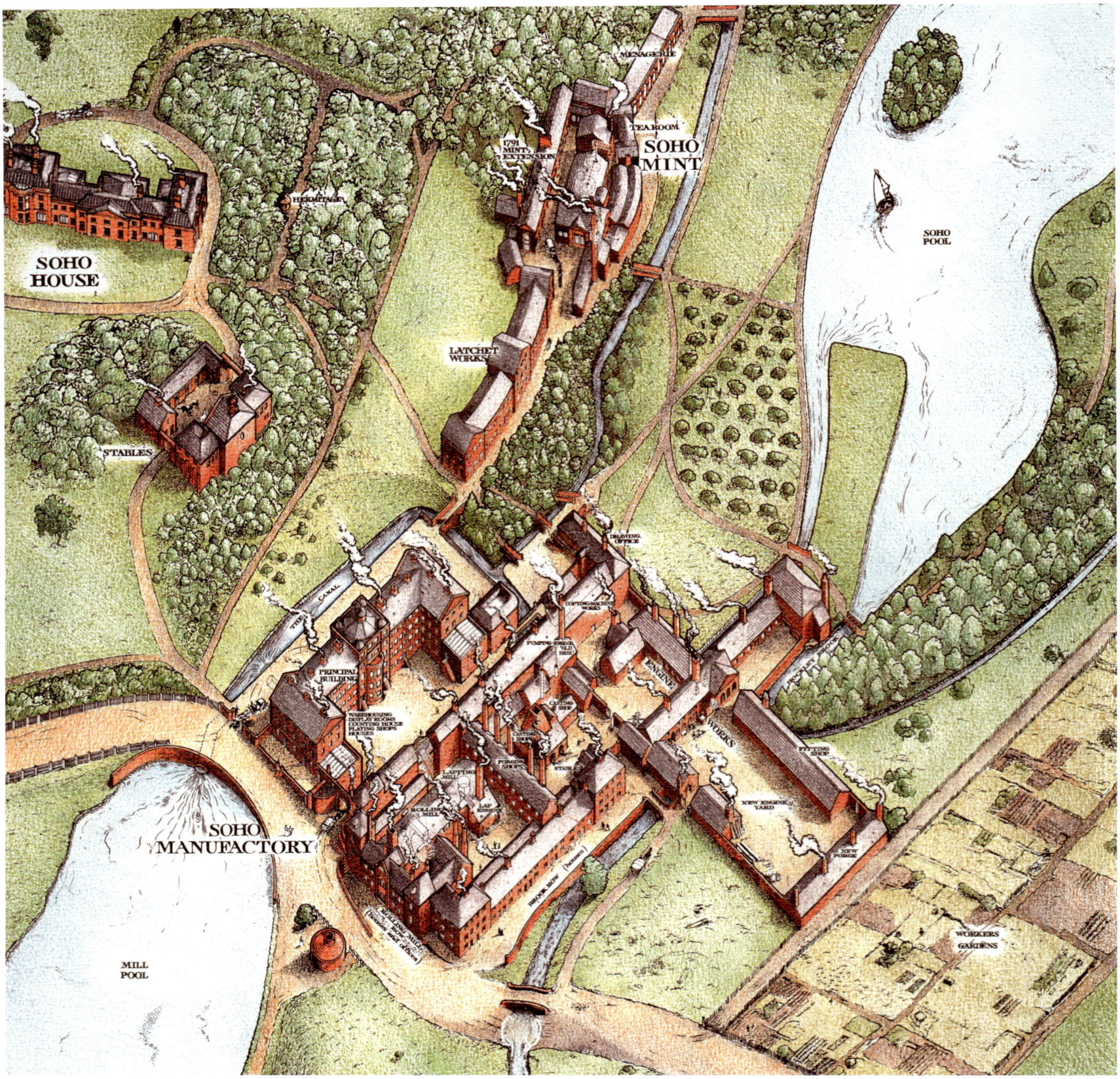

Fig 2.26
Axonometric view of the Soho Manufactory and Mint, c 1805, at nearly their maximum extent. Original drawing by George Demidowicz, subsequently coloured, with Soho House, stable block and workers' gardens added by Bremner and Orr. The northern bay of the Latchet (Crescent) Building was not completed by this time.

side) was built the new 'upper fitting shop' and on the north side, divided by a main gate onto the heath, a magazine and a workshop. Casting was removed from the end of the old 'fitting up shop' and a 'counting house' installed next to the new magazine. The old magazine or store, known as 'Solomon's Temple', was converted into the new casting shed. Boulton and Watt's room, and another alongside it, were expensively refurbished.

These alterations were to be the last substantial capital investment at the Manufactory, which in *c* 1805 covered an area of about 90,000 sq ft (8,361 sq m) (*see* Fig 2.38). The actual ground-floor area of the buildings (measured from plans) was approximately 409,950 sq ft, (4,640 sq m), a figure that could easily be doubled as many stood to a height of two and three storeys. Domestic accommodation not exceeding 8,550 sq ft (793 sq m) has been included in the latter total. The total area of just over 33,000 sq ft (3065.7 sq m) given in the 1776 inventory is not easily compared with these *c* 1805 estimates since the inventory includes only the internal dimensions

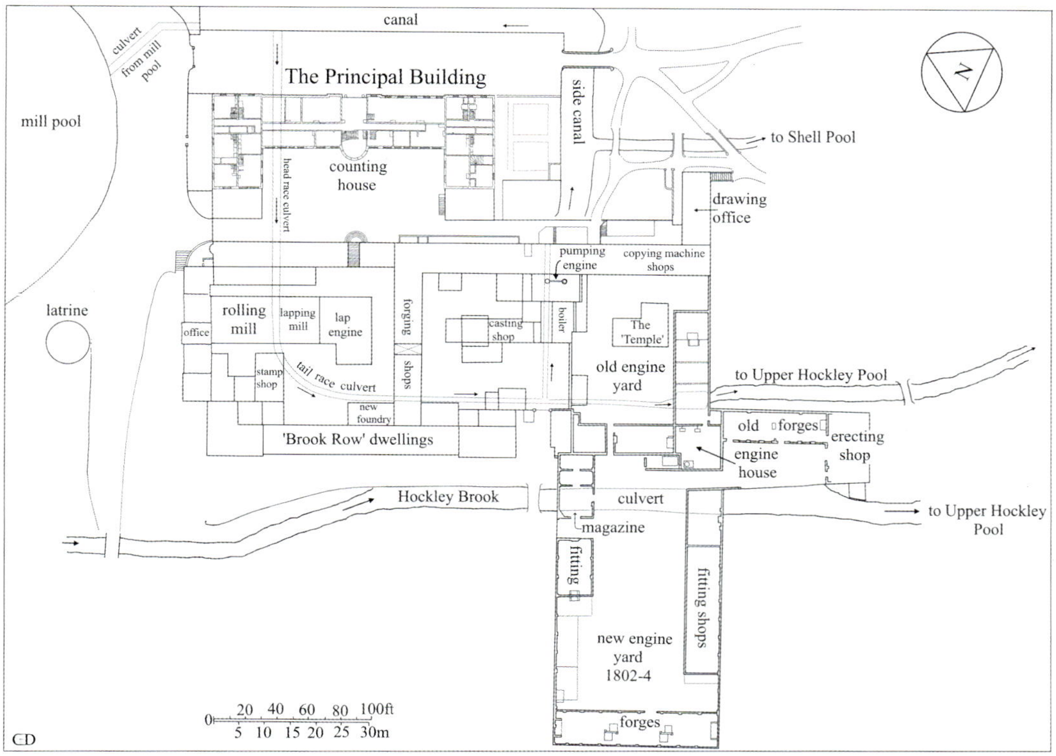

Fig 2.27
Plan of the Soho Manufactory with its engine works, c 1805.

of the workshops and few, if any, corridors, staircases or landings. There are no extant 19th-century inventories for the whole Manufactory.

Over the next 60 years, additions to the main Manufactory buildings were to be relatively minor. The Mint was to have one more significant phase of rebuilding in 1824–6, but this did not add substantially to the floor area. In the first years of the 19th century, its buildings covered a ground area of about 10,224 sq ft (950 sq m). The whole Crescent Building, albeit constructed in three phases, occupied an area of about 3,928 sq ft (365 sq m).

Based on the available plans and illustrations (and supplemented by evidence from correspondence), a three-dimensional drawing of the Manufactory and Mint (as they looked in about 1805) has been attempted (Fig 2.26). Using the axonometric projection, the buildings have been raised directly off a plan compiled from the same map sources (Fig 2.27). After these drawings were made, a watercolour of the rear of the Manufactory came to light (Fig 2.28). It was painted in 1801 as part of Matthew Boulton's evidence submitted in the trial of burglars who had broken into the principal building.[105] It had a similar viewpoint to the Phillp pen-and-ink sketch of 1796 (*see* Fig 2.18) and it added useful information on building materials.

The button and plated-ware works, 1790–1834

The Mint and the engine works had seen the greatest expansion of buildings at Soho in the period from 1788 to 1805. The button and plated-ware companies were left in the shadow of these two expanding businesses, the making of plated ware less buffeted by the vagaries of

Fig 2.28
Watercolour of the rear of the Manufactory, 1801, produced as evidence for a robbery case. Apart from demonstrating clearly the distinct difference in levels at the site, it reveals that clay-tiled roofs predominated on the buildings below the Great Bank, but that the principal building was topped with slate, as was also the rolling and lapping mill below.

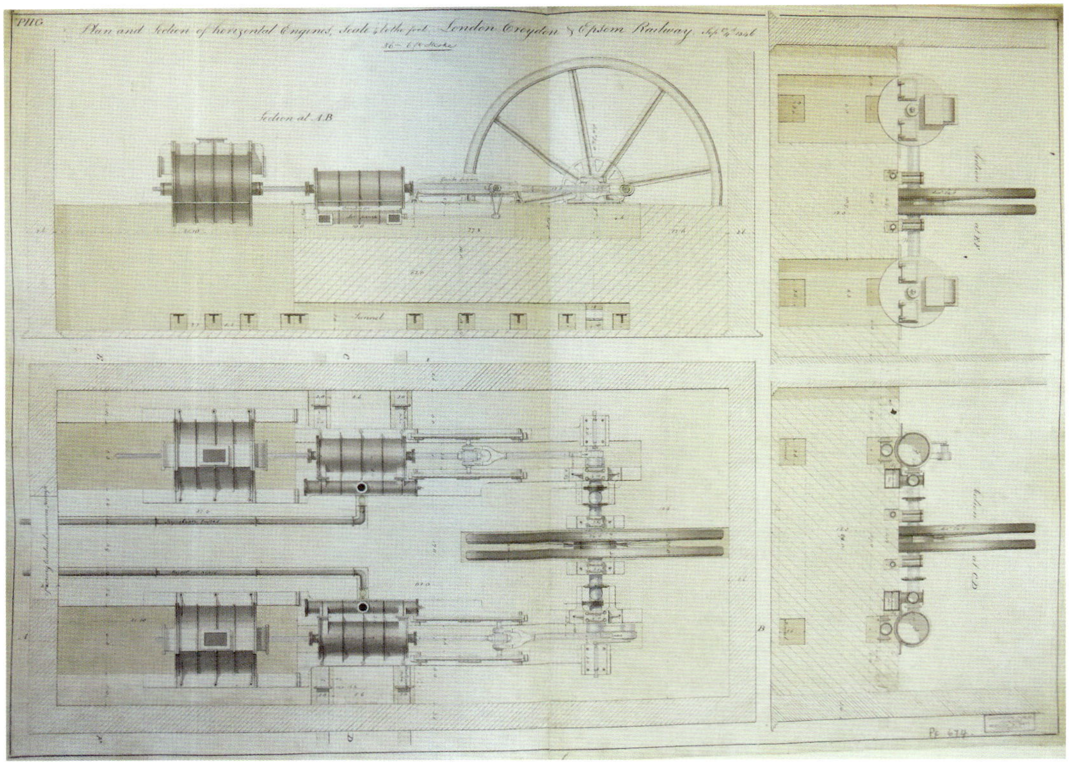

Fig 2.33
The James Toy and Son horizontal steam engine placed in the rear yard of the principal building, originally intended for the London, Croydon and Epsom Railway, drawn 4 September 1846.

inevitable reorganisation that took place within the workshops themselves over the decades (changing their function, internal layout and machinery) have not survived.

The casting shop that used to stand between the rolling mill and Brook Row was demolished after 1800 and rebuilt ('New Foundry') on a reduced plan in the same yard in the corner against Brook Row and the forging shops (*see* Fig 2.32). The original building can be seen in two of the rear views of the Manufactory (*see* Figs 2.18 and 2.28) as a gabled roof with two tall furnace chimneys immediately behind the Brook Row houses. However, before 1800, another furnace had been established in the yard serving the pumping engine, and its chimney can be seen in the same two views and in a photograph of *c* 1860 (*see* Fig 2.35). Attached to the south was a casting shop.[130] On the 1850s map, there was also a casting shop on the north side and the furnace was being additionally used for hardening. Throughout the 19th century, it appears that coal for the furnace was stored against the west side. The workshops on the Great Bank between the rolling mill and the principal building seem to have narrowed their footprint between the two plans but, on closer examination, this is the result of the inaccuracy of the 1788 plan. By the 1850s, the old carriageway under the former rolling-mill offices, constructed in the earliest days of Soho, had been opened as a passage again.

In 1850, the Soho Plate Company ceased production and its premises were apparently left empty for about two years when, in 1852, they were reoccupied by James Toy and Son, who were brass founders and makers of tubes, chandeliers, gas joints and metal bedsteads (*see* Appendix 2).[131] They overcame the lack of a power unit in the old plated-ware company premises by installing a steam engine and boiler house in the yard immediately at the back of the principal building. The last of the steam engines installed at Soho was one of a number of horizontal engines originally ordered from James Watt & Co by the London, Croydon and Epsom Railway (Fig 2.33).[132] It was sold to James Toy and Son in 1852 and installed in the latter half of that year.[133] The only known view of the rear of the Manufactory in this period shows that the engine was housed in a great lean-to structure attached to the back of the principal building and occupying all of the yard (Fig 2.34). The 1850s map (*see* Fig 2.32) seems to indicate that James Toy and Son occupied a far more extensive area than the traditional plated-ware company premises, for they had also taken on part of the old engine works and copying-machine

Fig 2.34
A view of the rear of the Manufactory, c 1853 described as 'Messrs Toy and Sons Soho Works'. The lean-to at the rear of the principal building contained the horizontal steam engine installed in 1852.

manufactory on the Great Bank. The reason for this is not clear, for it was only a short time later, in 1853, however, that all the engine and copying-machine workshops were demolished. Alfred Toy also leased Soho House in 1852.

The same 1850s map shows how William Toney's steel-button and fire-iron business had remained in the traditional position of button-making at Soho, scattered in workshops surrounding the rolling mill, but having taken over the plated-ware company's stamping shop, new in 1801 (*see* pp 31–2). Toney also maintained a grinding shop in the lapping mill. Frederick Jenks, a *papier mâché* maker who took over the greater part of the rolling and lapping mill in 1853, agreed to supply power to this workshop from the lap engine (*see* p 63).

The demolition of the Mint, early 1850s

Matthew Piers Watt Boulton, son of Matthew Robinson Boulton, appears not to have shared the motivation of his father and grandfather to make the mint business succeed. Eight years after he had inherited the Manufactory, he decided to close the Mint and on 29 April 1850 (and over the next few days) the machinery and plant of the Soho Mint were auctioned. The sale also included the contents of the rolling mill and of the ancillary buildings that had been directly linked with the coining business since the late 1780s.[134] The Mint and Crescent Building were demolished gradually in the early 1850s (*see* pp 121–5). The rolling-mill buildings survived until 1862 at least, as they lay within the main Manufactory complex for which temporary tenants (e.g. Frederick Jenks) were found.

Causes for decline and the final years

The successors to the original Boulton & Watt partnership could not maintain the innovative genius that made such a major contribution to the Industrial Revolution of the late 18th century. Nevertheless, Matthew Robinson Boulton and James Watt Jr continued to be heavily involved throughout their lives in the activities of the Soho enterprises and were more than competent engineers, production designers and businessmen in their own right. But there was relatively little investment in new ideas and plant to maintain the cutting edge, so the Soho buildings and machinery gradually became obsolete. Only three new steam engines were erected at the Manufactory after 1805, and all of these in the engine works. James Toy's engine of 1852, mentioned above, was an unsold Boulton

Fig 2.35
The Soho Manufactory, c 1860, photographed by W B Osbourne, showing the site of the demolished engine works in the foreground and the buildings straddling the Great Bank in section.

& Watt engine constructed for an entirely different purpose. After the first decade of the 19th century, there was no major investment in new buildings except at the Mint in 1824–6. Even though the machinery was new, it was based on technology already 25 years old. The mint technology that John Southern had devised at the end of the 18th century continued to be used with minor refinements into the late 1840s. Boulton & Watt steam engines persisted in using low pressure, particularly in their application to boats and ships to avoid the danger of boiler explosions at sea. In the 19th century, the development of the most successful and efficient steam engines took the other course towards high-pressure steam.

The clearance of the Mint in the early 1850s coincided with the demolition of the engine works in 1853, though the two sites were no longer in common ownership. There was, however, a more immediate reason for the Manufactory's demise, whose origins can be traced to a century earlier. In 1766, Matthew Boulton decided to live at Soho House, which he enlarged and embellished. The old warren was landscaped and beautified, and for many decades the tree plantations, lawns and shrubberies provided a backdrop and a balance to the smoky din and vibrancy of the industrial buildings below.[135] In the 19th century the town of Birmingham had slowly advanced towards Soho and the landscaped gardens (long known as 'Soho Park') were an obvious site for 'superior and aristocratic' villas. In the late 1840s, the Boultons accordingly began to develop the Park with such success that the new residents, annoyed and disturbed by the clamour and smell emitted from the old Manufactory below, threatened legal action. This was avoided by the promise to quit all operations and to demolish all except the principal building, which was to be gutted and converted into four dwellings.[136] It is a great tragedy that this scheme was not executed and that, as a result, this most impressive and symbolic of the Manufactory buildings did not survive into a period when it would have been appreciated as such.

Happily, at least three photographs of the Manufactory were taken before the remainder of it was demolished (Figs 2.35–2.37).[137] Fig 2.35 clearly shows that demolition work had proceeded from the engine works, exposing, when the photograph was taken, the south end of Brook Row, the casting shop and furnace, with the old pumping-engine house lying demolished before it. Also visible is the internal gable of the shops that were built into the Great Bank and used for many decades by the copying-machine company, and in the background the old forging shops that connected Brook Row to the Great Bank, thereby separating one court from another.

The final demolition, 1862–3

Matthew Piers Watt Boulton (1820–94), grandson of Matthew Boulton, gave in to the pressure exerted by the new Soho residents and transferred the tenants of the Manufactory, together with some machinery, to new premises named

Fig 2.36
The Soho Manufactory, c 1860, photographed by W B Osbourne. A road (the future South Road) has been laid along the front terrace of the principal building. In the distance Birmingham is advancing towards the site.

Fig 2.37
The last known classic view of the principal building, c 1860, photographed by W B Osbourne about three years before it was demolished. It appears to be abandoned, with its open windows and broken glazing, but its original Palladian splendour has not been significantly diminished. A great loss to industrial history.

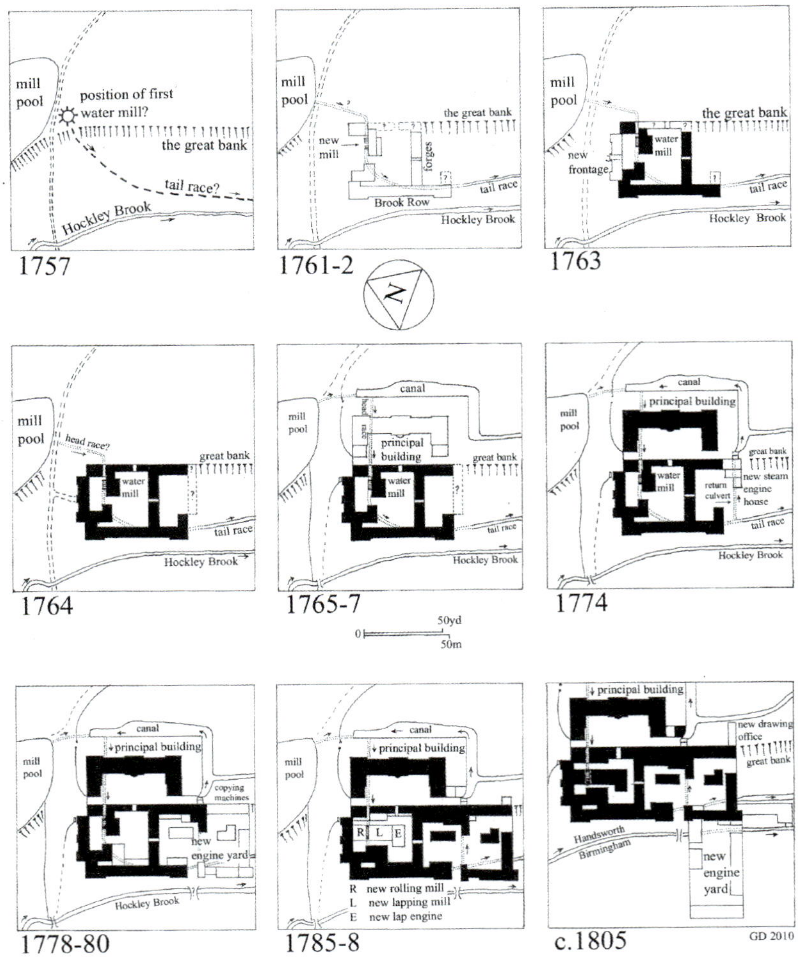

Fig 2.38
Phase plans of the development of the Soho Manufactory.

'Soho Works' at Spring Hill (Eyre Street, Birmingham), thus adding to the confusion between the various Soho factories.[138] His father, Matthew Robinson Boulton had, two years before his death in 1842, allowed himself to be bought out of the steam-engine business by James Watt Jr, though the firm continued to be called Boulton, Watt & Co.[139] The Boultons, therefore, played no part in the demolition of the Soho engine works but, nevertheless, brought on the unavoidable destruction of the remainder of the Manufactory. In March 1862, F Cotterill was paid £41 1s 9d 'for pulling down old buildings' and on 29 May, Aaron Smith agreed to pay £100 for material he could salvage after he demolished (at his own expense) Brook Row, the rolling mill, Rolling Mill Row and the Steel Company premises, but not the principal building.[140] The conversion of the latter into residences was apparently still being considered but, unfortunately, it seems that no 'developer' was ever found.

By the turn of the new year, only the principal building was left standing in forlorn isolation, but it was reported that its 'hour of disappearance draws nigh'.[141] The article mentioned an advertisement, which had just previously appeared in the press, announcing that 'the materials of which the old building is composed' were for sale. On 8 January a letter to the *Birmingham Daily Post* implored photographers to visit the site before it was too late as 'demolition was progressing rapidly every day.[142] The exact date of demolition is not known but it could not have been very long after. An estate road had been built across the principal building's frontage in about 1850 and this was later to become South Road.[143]

The Manufactory site remained clear of buildings for 50 years. A few terraced houses appeared between 1904 and 1914, and in the interwar period, on the west side of South Road, factories were built over a mass of material that had been deposited over the area to form an extended terrace at the level of the former principal building.[144] As a consequence, the archaeological remains of the Manufactory west of the Great Bank lie sealed below about 10m of fill. The Mint site falls in the back gardens of private houses on the east side of South Road. Sand extraction before the First World War removed the coining room and engine house but left the 1791 building and the Crescent Building undisturbed (*see* Fig A1.1). A very small part of the principal building and a larger area of the 1791 mint were excavated in November 1994 and September 1995, respectively. Subsequently, *Time Team* (the Channel 4 television archaeology series) was persuaded to produce a programme on Soho and in the Easter of 1996 five areas were excavated, including the principal building, the Crescent Building and the mint. The excavations established for the first time the position of these buildings accurately and their state of preservation. A detailed account of all the excavations can be found in Appendix 1.

3

The Soho Mill

Water power gave birth to the Soho Manufactory, and its role, later supplemented but not entirely ousted by steam power, is crucial to understanding how the various businesses and industrial processes interlinked and developed. For a Birmingham 'toy maker' such as Matthew Boulton, a watermill provided the power to roll metal into sheets (an essential material) and, at the other end of the process, to polish finished articles. Much of the work in between was not mechanised or, at most, aided by hand- or foot-operated machines such as stamps, presses and lathes.

Sarehole Mill[1]

As mentioned in Chapter 2, Matthew Boulton was a tenant of Sarehole Mill, Yardley, from at least 1756 to late 1762, retaining it while he rebuilt the rolling mill at Soho. Sarehole still stands today and is in the care of Birmingham Museum Trust. During much of the 18th century, however, various members of the Eaves family held a complicated financial interest in Sarehole Mill and it may have been the Eaves family, rather than the Boultons, who was the first to establish the Sarehole–Soho connection. Richard Eaves Sr disappeared in 1745 (leaving his wife, Sarah, and her children) only to return from parts unknown in 1762. In the meantime, in about 1750, John Baskerville, the famous printer, took Sarah and her children into his own house at Easy Hill, Birmingham, and married her in 1764, shortly after Richard Eaves Sr died. Baskerville trained John Eaves, Sarah's eldest son, to become a printer in order to succeed to the Easy Hill press.[2] It is tempting to suggest that the first Soho Mill was financed by John Baskerville, perhaps to make paper or to gloss paper by rolling.[3] This idea was first proposed by William Bennett but never repeated.[4] In fact, the 1757 Soho lease coincides with Baskerville's first successful publication, *Virgil*, but John Eaves and Edward Ruston, Eaves' brother-in-law, are described in the same lease as toymakers. The statement by Stebbing Shaw that the mill was erected 'for the purpose of rolling metal' makes sense if it were to be used in toymaking.[5] John Eaves, in fact, may not have been the principal partner as he was preoccupied with the printing trade, and Boulton refers only to Edward Ruston in his negotiations to transfer the lease.[6]

John Eaves died in 1762 aged 30, a year after giving up the lease and two years before his father, Richard Eaves Sr, died. In 1756, the latter had begun proceedings in Chancery for the recovery of the Sarehole estate from the Dolphin family, to whom it had been mortgaged. The process dragged on until 1765, so his son, Richard Eaves Jr, younger brother of John, was beneficiary of the judgement against the Dolphins.[7] During this time, Boulton was tenant of Sarehole Mill, but he was anxious to expand his business and, more importantly, to move closer to Black Country raw materials and to his Snow Hill base in Birmingham. It was either through his acquaintance with John Baskerville or with John Eaves that he became aware that the Soho lease was up for sale. Further research has revealed that Matthew Boulton did not give up Sarehole Mill in 1761, but maintained his lease until at least the latter part of 1762.[8] This decision makes sense in view of Boulton's building operations at Soho in 1761–2, which disrupted the working of the mill there.

Ruston and Eaves' mill, 1757–61

Little is known about the Soho lease that Boulton acquired in 1761; the mill had only recently been built by Edward Ruston and John Eaves who, it was claimed, had spent £1,000 on the premises.[9] This figure, though it included the cost of a new house, is much higher than the

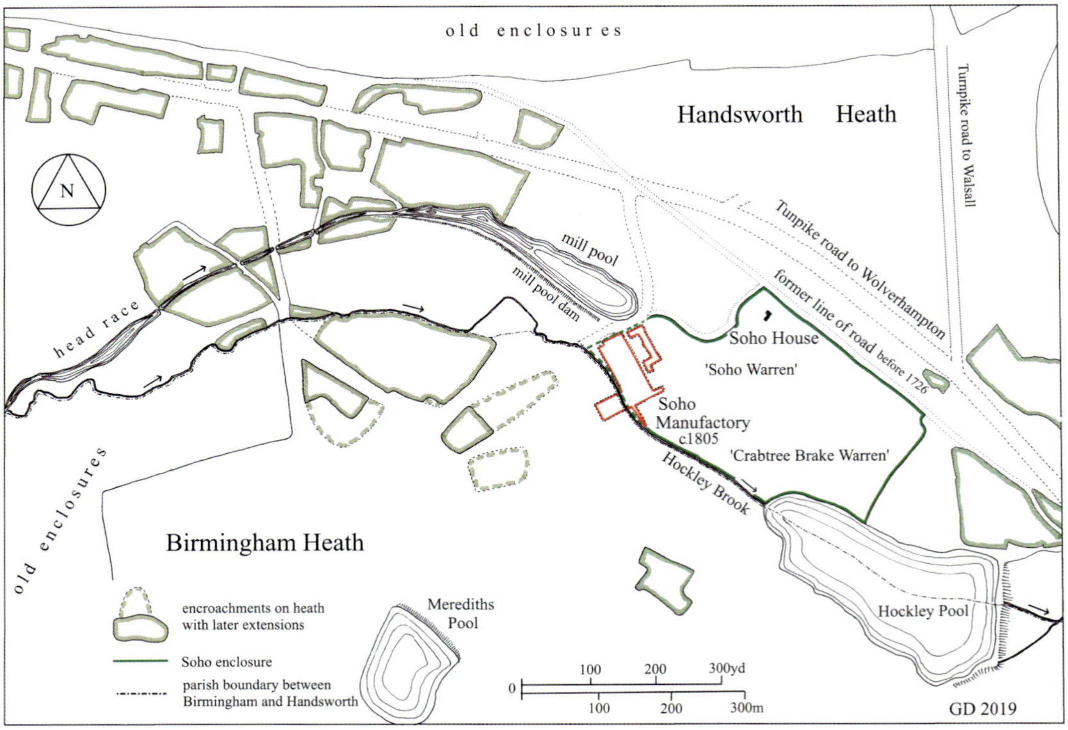

Fig 3.1
Plan of the environs of Soho Mill, c 1760, showing its waterworks and the position of the future manufactory, c 1805, overlaid in the north-west corner of the Soho encroachment. The Upper Hockley Pool is yet to be constructed (c 1774).

minimum (£150) they were required to spend under the lease.[10] There were expensive waterworks involved; in particular, the head race, reputed to have been half a mile (804.6m) long and not to be 'made more than five feet [1.52m] wide', led to a mill pool from the furthest possible point on the Hockley Brook at the boundary of Handsworth parish. The head race actually measured about 650yd (594.36m). The mill pool was no more than a swelling at the extremity of the new cut, gradually widening to about 55yd (50.29m) at its maximum, measuring 400yd (365.76m) in length and retained by a dam along the whole of the south-west side (Fig. 3.1). The exact position of the Ruston mill is unknown.

The rebuilding of the mill and the reorganisation of the waterworks, 1761–6

In February 1761 Boulton wrote: 'I have lately purchased the most convenient Water-Mill in England for my Business which I shall not work before Lady day by the conveniency of which & other alterations I shall make about that time I hope then to send you some patterns'.[11] Contradicting what he had written to Hollis in the summer of 1761, Matthew Boulton pulled down the short-lived rolling mill, which he 'ill favoured'.[12] He seemed less interested in rolling metal than in applying a rapid and superior polish to his products. It may be that the water supply, despite Ruston and Eaves' major investment, could only supply power for one or the other function, and Boulton was therefore forced to select his greater priority. The rolling that he required had mostly to be done in Holford Mill, which he was to sublet for almost 20 years (*see* pp 48–9). In developing a polishing or lapping mill, he displayed an early innovative skill, as it was not usual at the time to use water power for this process in the Birmingham area. James Watt claimed that 'Mr Boulton was the first Inventor of the inlaid button, & the first to have applied a mill to turn Laps'.[13] If this were so, then it was no wonder that Boulton rebuilt the rolling mill to his own designs. There is evidence, however, that Boulton was helped in the millwrighting by John Wyatt, the inventor, whose genius in innovation was not matched by financial acumen and a worldly practicality.[14] In a fortuitous survival of a copy letter, John Wyatt gives the date upon which the new waterwheel was turned for the first time (29 Aug [1762]): 'The Water was yesterday for the first time let upon Mr Boulton's Mill Wheel'.[15] Of particular interest is John Wyatt's application of his 'frictionless rollers', an early form of roller bearings, in what he called 'our Gimcrack Mill', probably one of the first watermills to use them. Further fitting-out work may have followed, but by January 1763 John Fothergill was able to write 'of having compleated our Mills to carry on our Chape Manufactory to greatest perfection'.[16]

It is possible that, in 1761, Boulton not only rebuilt, but relocated the mill he acquired from Ruston and Eaves. It is not until about the year 1768, however, that there is evidence to locate the mill precisely, about 45yd (41.15m) from the mill-pool edge (*see* Figs 2.8 and 2.9). In this position, there had to be a leat to connect the mill and its pool. This arrangement is unlikely to have existed in the Ruston and Eaves years, since it was unusual in the Birmingham area to place a mill away from its pool dam owing to gentle river gradients and topography. Only the artificial dam itself could provide the difference in level locally for the head of water so eagerly sought for the waterwheel. A possible reason to abandon the old site in 1761 was the fact that there was insufficient space for the substantial number of early Manufactory buildings to develop around it. In the very early years, these did not include the principal building, though its construction was later to affect the pool-to-mill waterworks. It must be stressed that when Boulton first came to Soho he nurtured no grand plan to unite all his operations or to build a grand fronting 'mansion'.[17] But once it was decided to have such a building, a high-level site at the top of the Great Bank was, to a large extent, predetermined. Here, prominence of the architectural composition was assured and, at the same time, a grand screen to more utilitarian buildings could be created. The spot chosen coincided with the pool-to-mill leat, which had to be culverted and perhaps also realigned so it could pass under the new building. A new foreboy, also described as a 'trough to the water wheel', was constructed in November 1765 and the mill pool was 'rendered quite beautilly to its original form'.[18] Thenceforth, mill water made its way from the pool along a complicated route via the first part of the 'canal', which fronted the principal building. It then turned through 90 degrees into a culvert that passed under the principal building to emerge as an open channel in the yard at the rear. The water entered through or under a building straddling the Great Bank and emerged onto a timber foreboy (the head-race trough) to complete its journey at the top of the wheel at the mill itself (*see* Figs 2.10 and 3.8). It is not known exactly when the even-longer channel linking the mill pool with Shell Pool in Boulton's garden was constructed. Its first section was probably completed in 1765–7 as the 'canal' running along the front and side of the principal building. A virtue was then made of the necessity to bring mill water along the front of the principal building by transforming the leat into a picturesque body of water at the boundary between the garden of Soho House and the Manufactory. Later still, its practical value, but not necessarily its water quality, was enhanced by receiving spent mill water from Watt's first pumping engine. It comes as no surprise, therefore, that the phase of works associated with the erection of the principal building, including the new waterworks, eventually cost about £10,000.

The records provide evidence of an unreliable water supply. In June 1763, oats were supplied for horses harnessed to a gin connected to the mill machinery. Further payments for oats and hay were made in July and November 1763 and in January and July 1764.[19] On 18 August 1764, the first breakdown at the mill was reported; there were many more to come: 'our principle Wheel is ... broke ... wch hath put an intire Stop to the pollishing of all our work particularly st[ee]l chains'.[20]

In the summer of 1765, Boulton blamed 'the dryness of the season, no water no pollishing' for delays in the supply of goods to customers.[21] It may be no coincidence that the foundations of the principal building were being laid at this time, interrupting the water supply to the mill. Certainly through August, September and October horses were being used to move the mill machinery.[22] The horse gin was apparently connected directly to the waterwheel, which was external at this time. Six to ten horses were required, costing '5 to 6 guineas a week besides Injuring the Mill'.[23] In October, the carelessness of workmen caused an accident 'which broke our Mill into above 100 pieces'.[24] A considerable amount of work was done to the pool dam in August and September of 1766.[25] The tail race, or 'Flem', had been cleaned and widened in January.[26]

The water crisis deepens, 1767–74

When James Watt visited Soho for the first time in 1767, he observed that 'A Mill with a water wheel was employed in Laminating metal for buttons, plated goods &c and to turn Laps for

Fig 3.2
Water-coloured elevation of the complete 33in Soho pumping engine, c 1777. Few drawings of this engine survive owing to the engine house fire in 1778.

grinding & polishing steel work'.[27] There was another invention of Boulton's 'put in motion by the mill' – a shaking box for scouring button blanks and other small pieces of metal, applied more widely later on to shake newly minted coins dry after immersing them in a cleaning solution. In 1768, Erasmus Darwin described 'a large water-wheel in one of the courts', which communicated 'motion to a prodigious number of different tools'.[28] If the attribution to Edward Rooker is correct, the first illustrations of the mill must date from these years (*see* Figs 2.8 and 2.9). They show, in two perspectives, a rectangular two-storey structure. A shaped gable graces the side facing the rear of the principal building. An external waterwheel is attached to the main north wall and on the opposite side there is a single-storey lean-to. The other gable has a first-floor door approached by an external staircase. No other known drawing shows the mill so completely, such is the rarity of views showing the rear of the Manufactory (*see* Fig 3.8).

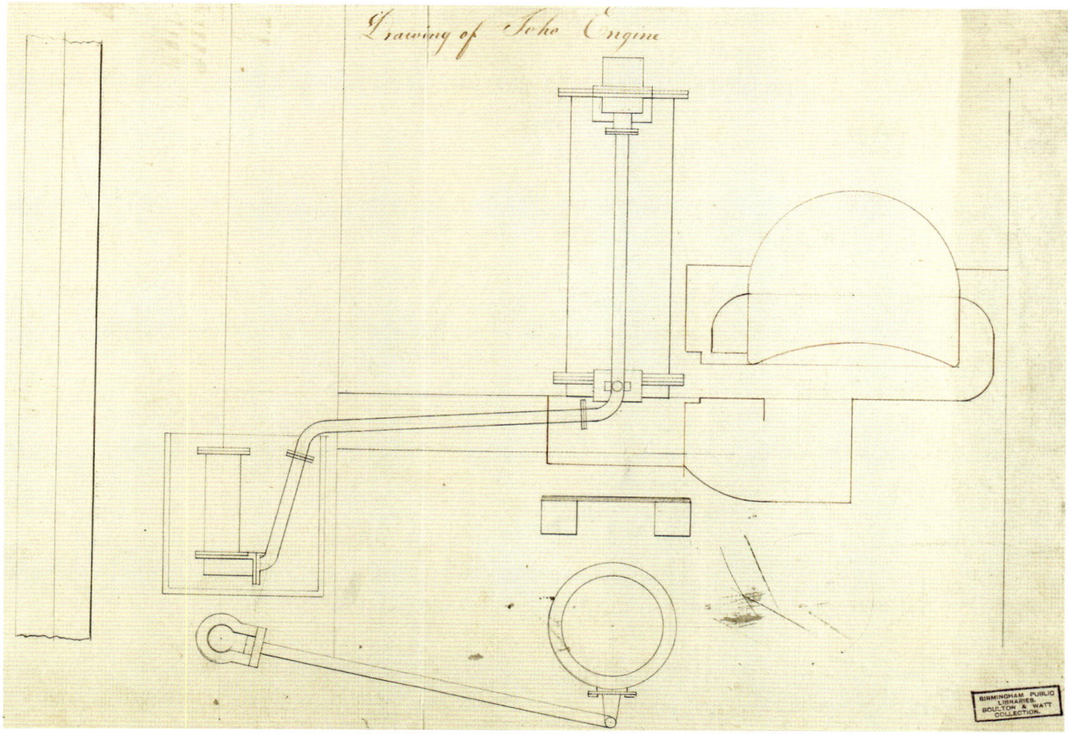

Fig 3.3a
Elevational drawing of part of the 33in Soho pumping engine, 1777.

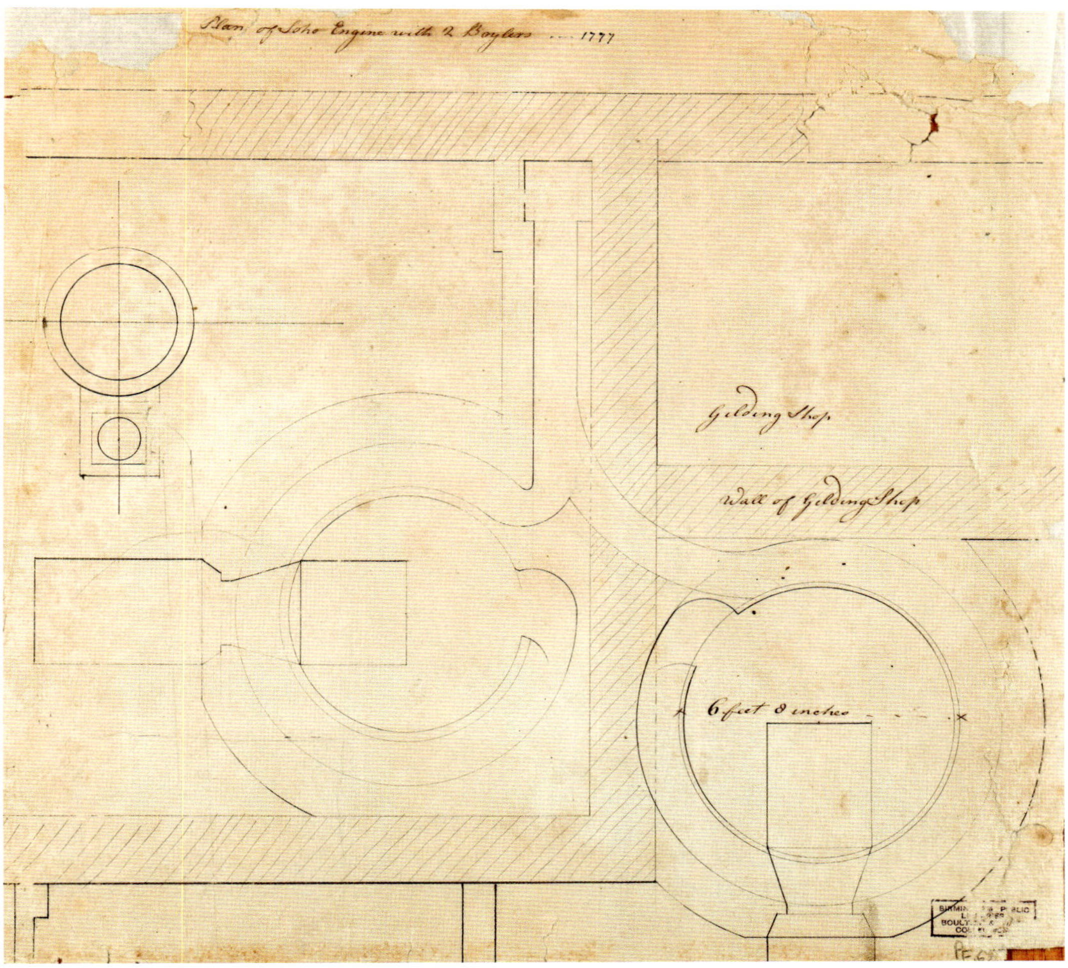

Fig 3.3b
Plan of the 33in Soho pumping engine, showing the boiler proposed to be moved to the outside of the engine house, 1777.

In 1770, Boulton informed James Adam that he had 'two Water mills employd in rolling pollishing grinding & turning various sorts of Laths'.[29] This phrase could be misinterpreted as meaning there were two separate mill buildings at Soho. However, it is more likely that Boulton had in mind Holford rolling mill as well as Soho. In the summer of the same year, 'half of the movements' in Soho Mill were stopped and four horses applied to the gin. Moreover, the water problem was seen by Boulton to be worsening. He claimed that the proprietors of the newly built Birmingham Canal Navigation had intercepted two of the streams that fed his mill: 'When I have no Water my workpeople standing still Murmuring'.[30] But an unexpected surge of water at a mill during a flood could be equally calamitous by damaging machinery and waterworks structures. In May 1773, the flood occurred in the daytime and the mill dam was saved.[31]

Water and steam combined, 1774–7

It is interesting to speculate whether Boulton would have become involved in steam-engine production had his mill been assured of a more copious and reliable flow of water. Immediately below the Manufactory, Boulton could see all his spent mill water filling up Great Hockley Pool, which was then used to supplement the supply to Aston Furnace further downstream. His solution to the problem was the combination of an old idea with a new invention: a steam pumping engine using Watt's condenser. As a technically minded man, he was aware of the Newcomen engine employed principally in pumping water from coal and tin mines. As early as 1766, he had experimented with a model of a Savery engine, but there is no evidence that he actually installed a full-sized Savery engine at Soho, though this has been suggested.[32]

In 1774, the Kinneil engine was brought to Soho and presumably installed on the Great Bank, which had been used for a head of water by the mill, but farther to the south. By April the original block-tin cylinder had been replaced by a cast iron version made by the Wilkinson brothers at Bersham near Wrexham.[33] The foundations of the engine house and the boiler were laid in June and July of that year and building work continued until at least October.[34] It was not until August and September of 1775 that the 'great water pump from J[ohn] Woods' arrived to be installed in the engine house.[35] According to Boulton, the latter measured '12 feet wide, 24 feet long and 18 feet high from the floor to the wall plate of the roof'.[36]

The first working Watt steam engine in the world was intended to pump tail-race water about 24ft (7.3m) back up the slope of the Great Bank.[37] Apart from a new channel from the old tail race to the pump, a new cut may have also been constructed at the top of the pump around the south side of the principal building to connect with what was known as the 'canal'. The latter was a decorative feature running along the whole forecourt, but it also performed the utilitarian duty of bringing water from the mill pool to the opening of the head-race culvert, which took water under the principal building to the mill. As a result, mill water was made to come full circle (*see* Figs 2.10 and 3.5), but the circulation system would not have worked without a reservoir at the tail-race level. This Boulton achieved by building another pond immediately above the existing Hockley Pool, held back by a curving dam that followed the outline of the former bank. The cost was shared equally between Matthew Boulton, as a private individual who purchased the land on the Warwickshire side of the Hockley Brook, enlarging his garden lake, and the firm of Boulton & Fothergill, which benefited from the water.[38] The separation between the new upper pool (3.23 acres, 1.31ha) and the old Hockley Pool (10 acres, 4.45ha) was necessary as the latter provided for Aston Furnace downstream.[39]

In July and August 1777, the original 18in (457mm)-cylinder engine was replaced by a 33in (838mm)-cylinder version, working on the expansive principle, which survived until the last years of the Manufactory. Because of its jerky and violent action, the engine became known as 'Beelzebub'. It did not fit happily into the engine house and, consequently, alterations had to be made to the building.[40] Nevertheless the beam still projected through the roof, and was 'out of the House & beginning to come in' when the pump chain failed in September 1777.[41] More serious damage was done to the engine house in July 1778.[42] The roof and floors were all destroyed but the beam and cylinder survived. It was stated recently that a 'large part of the Manufactory burnt down', disrupting 'the production of engine parts', but this is not correct.[43] In fact, the fire was a blessing in disguise, for Boulton was 'able at last to have the

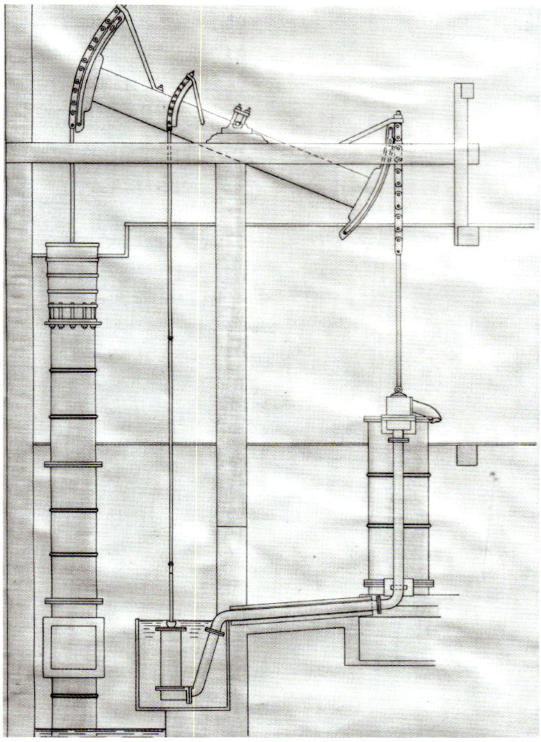

Fig 3.4
Elevational drawing of the 33in Soho pumping engine, produced on its dismantling and transfer to the Science Museum, London, c 1850.

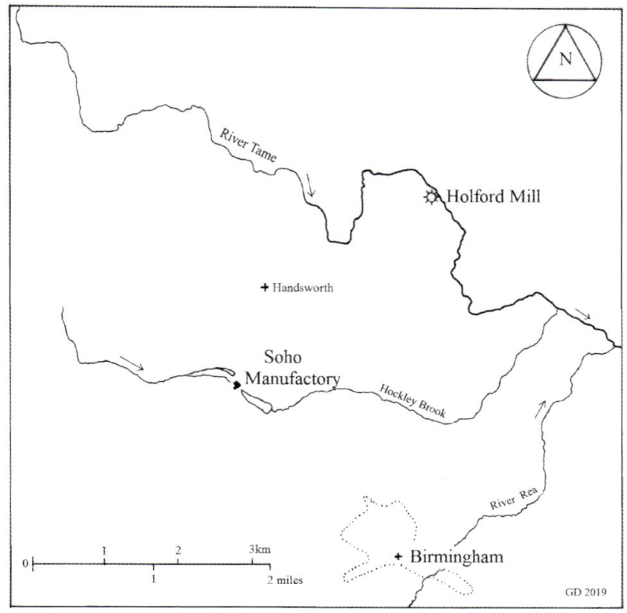

Fig 3.6
Map showing the site of Soho Manufactory and Holford Mill, c 1764–81. The dotted line represents the built-up area of Birmingham at this time.

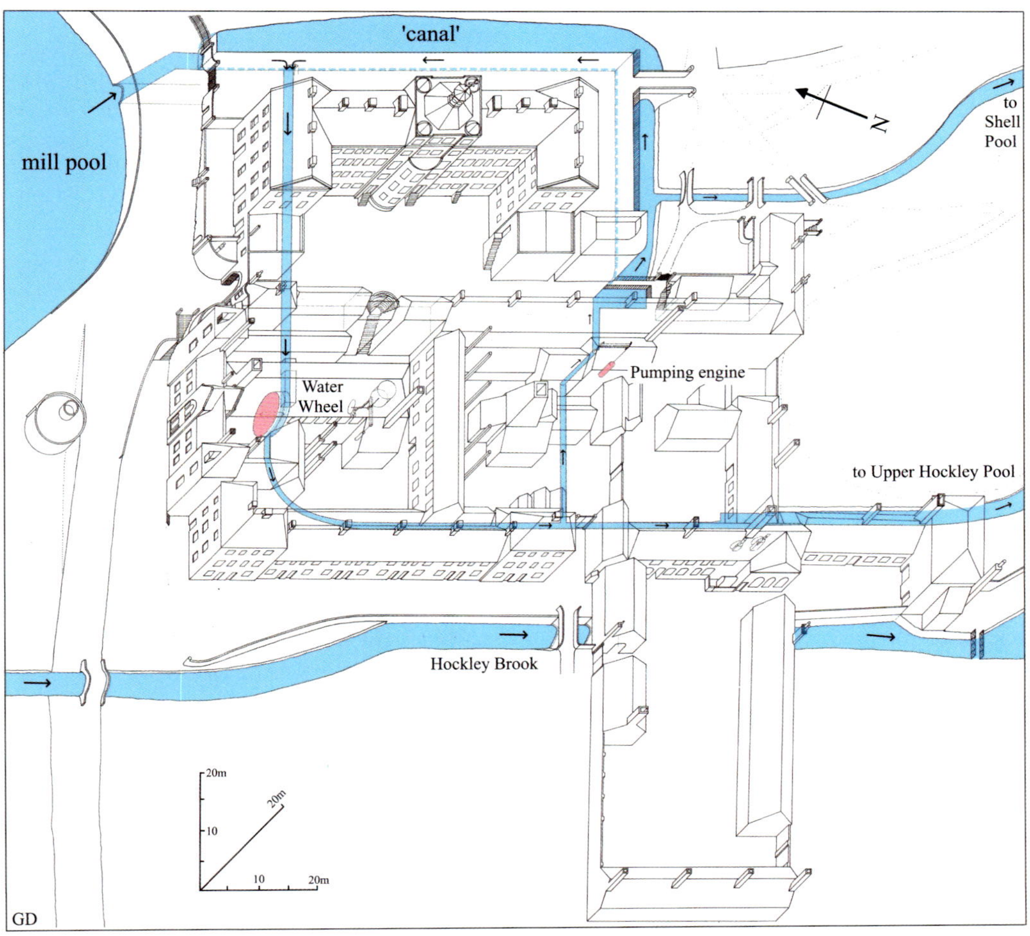

Fig 3.5
Axonometric projection of the Soho Manufactory, featuring the mill waterworks system and the recirculation of water by the Soho pumping engine, c 1805.

engine-house as it should be'.[44] The engine and its building were restored within three weeks, presumably to a more satisfactory design, and 'Beelzebub' came to be known more kindly as 'Old Bess'.

Most of the drawings for these two engines were kept in the upper part of the engine house and the fire destroyed the great majority. There is no known drawing of the first engine, neither of the 18in (457mm) cylinder nor its pump. Three Soho drawings have survived of the 33in (838mm) engine and are reproduced in Figs 3.2 and 3.3. A fourth is to be found at the Science Museum, London, and was probably made shortly before it was dismantled after the sale of the Soho Mint machinery in April 1850 (Fig 3.4).[45] The plan (Fig 3.3b) is useful in that it indicates that the engine house was 17ft (5.18m) wide rather than the 12ft (3.65m) Boulton suggested in his letter of August 1775 cited above. This discrepancy may have been caused by the alterations made to fit in the larger engine. It is also clear that another boiler was installed, this time on the exterior, to provide the extra steam required. The full water-circulation system is illustrated in the perspective in Fig 3.5.

Fig 3.7
Plan of the Holford Mill rolling machinery, 1781.

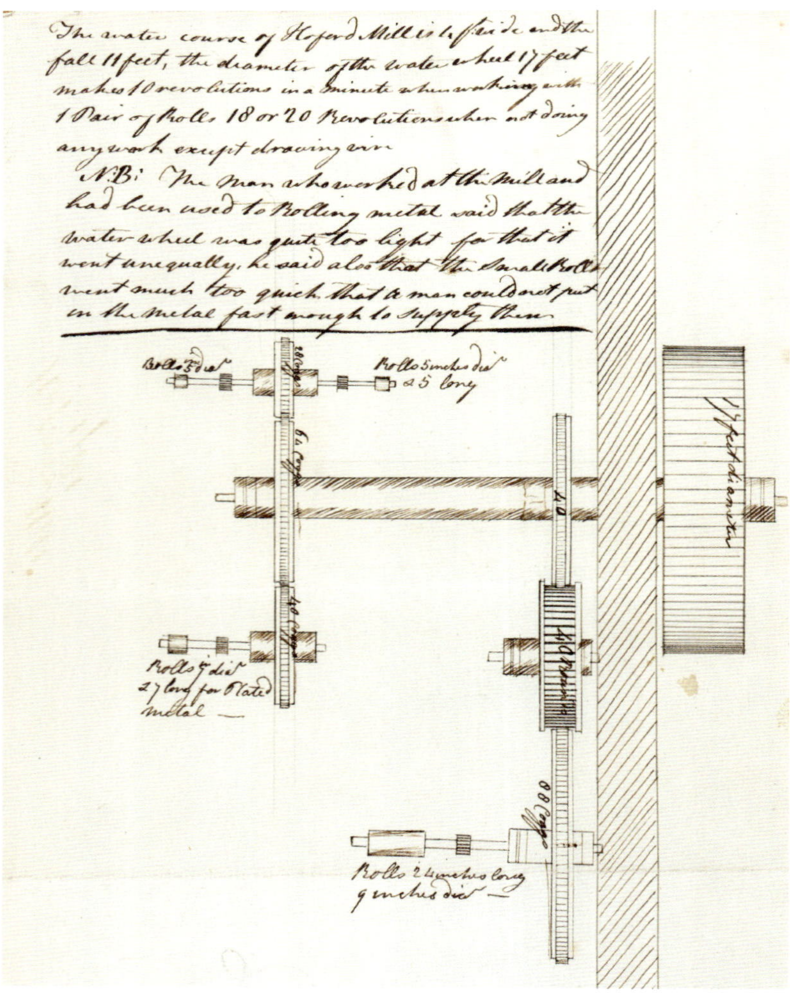

Holford Mill, c 1764–81

Holford Mill was used for fulling cloth in the 14th century and by the 16th century it had become an iron or hammer mill (Fig 3.6). Published accounts of the mill have a gap in its history from the mid-17th century to 1794, a period that includes the Boulton & Fothergill tenancy (*c* 1764–81).[46] It appears that Matthew Boulton was a subtenant of Holford as he had been earlier at Sarehole. Such subtenancies are notoriously difficult to detect as they are rarely preserved in the documentary sources and, consequently, both the Sarehole and the Holford connection eluded early researchers of Soho.

It is evident from a letter of about 1761 from Thomas Moore, the head leaseholder of Holford, that Matthew Boulton was interested in the mill in the early 1760s.[47] The first definite reference to his use of Holford dates from 1764 when rent was paid and new rolls were being ordered from Sheffield.[48] In 1765, various materials, including a large amount of ale, presumably to help lubricate the repair work, were being carried over to the mill.[49] Detailed accounts survive from the period 1776 to 1781.[50]

In April 1780, Thomas Moore indicated that he needed to sell his interest but that he would allow Boulton & Fothergill to remain as long as the lease was still in his possession.[51] Fothergill discussed with Boulton whether to buy the lease for the offer price of £1,000 and concluded that they could 'build a more commodious Mill at Soho for about half that Sum, notwithstanding I could wish we could have the power of the different Mills & watercourses in this neighbourhood'.[52] John Scale, manager of the button business, shared the same opinion: it was better to build a new rolling mill as the 'plated business has suffered very much for want of rolling and is likely to suffer more', though he was less optimistic about the potential cost.[53] The manager of the plated-ware business himself, John Hodges, not surprisingly implored Boulton to build 'a Rolling Mill on the Spot'.[54] Holford was 'very much out of repair' and its inventory was valued at only £60 at the end of 1780.[55] It was abandoned during 1781, but the decision to build a new mill at Soho was not acted upon until 1785.[56] In 1781 a plan of the Holford machinery was drawn showing a 17ft

(5.1m)-diameter waterwheel connected to four sets of rolls, measuring from 5in (127mm) to 27in (685mm) long, the 27in rolls used 'for Plated metal') (Fig 3.7).[57]

Soho Mill, 1776–84

A survey of the whole Manufactory, dated November 1776, reveals that the mill was divided into two rooms: room 89 (the 'Rolling Mill') measuring 16ft × 16.5ft (4.8m × 5.02m), and room 91 ('Turners Mill') measuring 16ft × 15ft (4.87m × 4.57m). Room 90 was 'Turners handing shop' with dimensions of 9ft × 33.5ft (2.74m × 10.21m).[58] A possible arrangement of these rooms is shown in Fig 3.8. Earlier in the same year, a considerable amount of work, including the repair of the wheel with metal straps and new castings, was done on the mill.[59] Two millwrights were employed from May to July 1776.[60] During March 1777, the foreboy was mended and more castings and mill brasses made.[61]

In 1777, the French foreign office sent a spy, De Saudray, an engineer, to Soho, who managed to obtain entry and make some drawings. He observed that, in the mill, a single shaft gave motion to multiple drives for the rolling and polishing of metal and the making of gold and silver plate.[62] Unfortunately, the drawings have not been traced.

In May 1777, the rent of the 'upper part' of the mill was fixed at £100 for the button company, and when the inlaid-button business was added in June 1782, the rent of the 'Lower Part of the Mill was reckoned at £30'.[63] These upper and lower parts were the lapping/polishing shop and the rolling mill respectively, the rents reflecting their relative power or worth at the time. In 1778, Boulton estimated, in relation to the button company, the rental value of his 'two mills' at £100, but it is difficult to judge whether he meant by this phrase the two parts of Soho or Soho and Holford Mills.[64] By 1779–90, the polishing mill was managed by Robert Kimnel.[65] From 1780 to 1781, part of the mill was rented by Watt's copying-machine company to bore and turn rolls.[66]

In 1782, the rolling mill accounts were separately recorded, but little activity was registered between that year and 1784, the cost of two roll frames and patterns being entered in July 1782.[67] In January 1782, Boulton requested James Watt to send two millwrights from Cornwall to mend the waterwheel, which was 'tumbled to pieces', using 55ft (16.76m) of inch-thick deal. As soon as he could, he meant 'to build a new one 20 feet [6.1m] Diameter and 6 feet [1.83m] broad upon the Sole'.[68] The mill had been allowed to get into a serious state of dilapidation, but at this time Boulton was focusing on the exciting possibilities of steam-powered rotary action and, until the technical and patent problems were solved, the mill was given low priority. Perhaps he envisaged his own steam-powered rolling mill; he was certainly encouraging others in this direction.[69] Despite the fact that the Soho sun-and-planet rotary gear had been developed in the infant engine works, Boulton nevertheless rebuilt his mill using water power instead of steam.

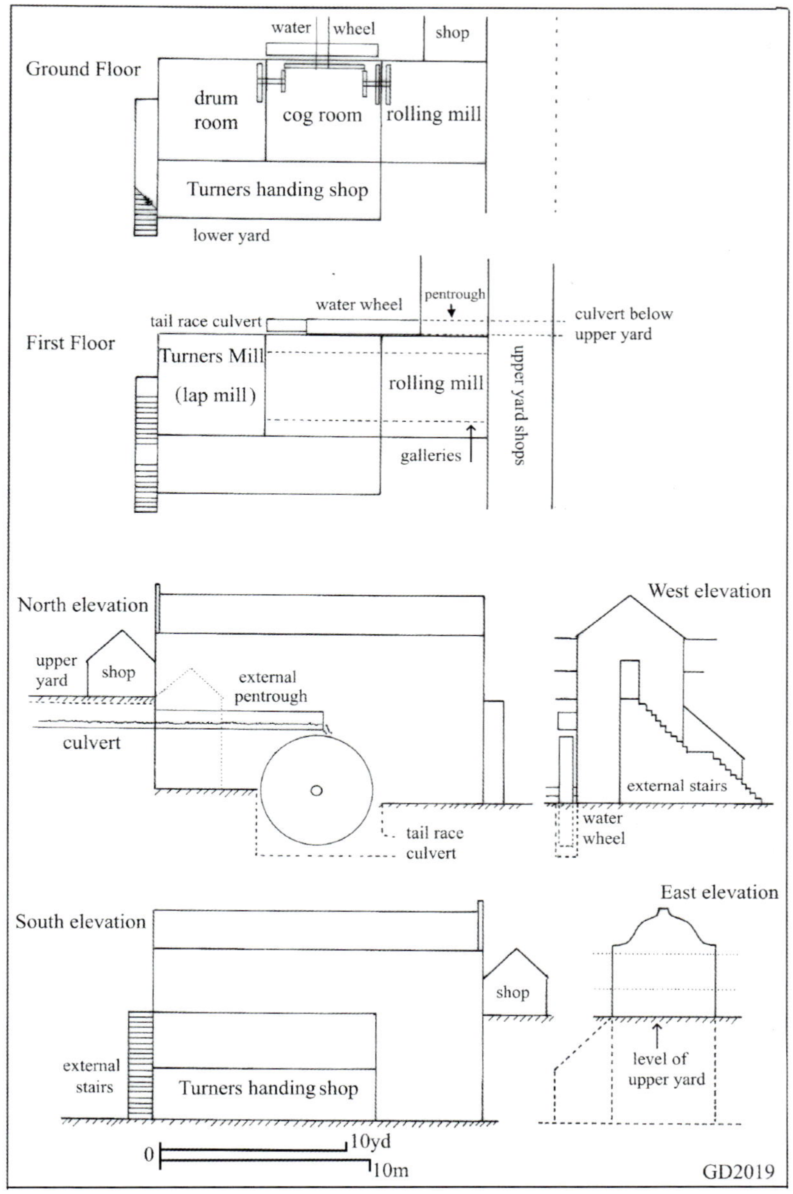

Fig 3.8
Plans and elevations of Soho Mill, c 1776.

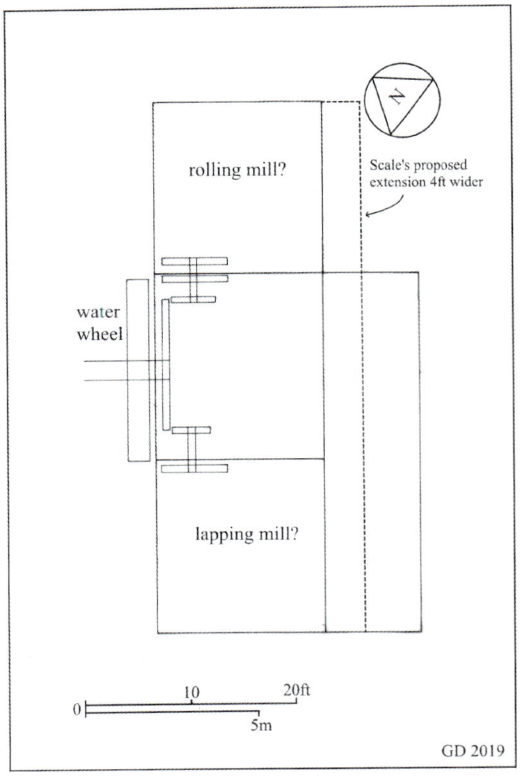

Fig 3.9
Redrawing of John Scale's proposal to rebuild Soho Mill, 1784.

In June 1784, John Scale pressed Boulton for a decision on ordering a new waterwheel.[70] By September, Boulton was suggesting making a temporary repair and delaying until the following spring the start on the new wheel without which 'we shall never gain by our plated trade till we rolle the mettle at Soho'.[71] It was at this stage that John Rennie, a young engineer from Scotland, became involved in one of his first jobs on the path of an illustrious career. From August to September, he made estimates for a new rolling mill.[72] John Scale urged that the bare minimum of repairs be carried out to the old wheel but, more importantly, requested Boulton for an 'opinion about a new building in place of the old one'.[73] Boulton had already considered a plan for a row of laps down the middle of the mill. However, Scale was not keen, as most steel-lapping was done on one side of the lap, making the other side unusable and therefore impossible to let, an important consideration in Scale's mind. He preferred to have a passage running down the middle of the mill with doors leading into heated rooms where 'Lappers and handers' could work alongside each other. He suggested pulling down the old mill and building it on the same orientation but four feet wider. Scale sketched on his letter to Boulton a plan of his proposals, which has been redrawn for Fig 3.9.[74] It shows the waterwheel connected to two sets of major gearing, presumably to the rolls on one side and to the laps on the other. As laps were located on an upper floor and driven by belts on drums below, it is likely that the lap shop was on the side where the first-floor door (with external steps) is shown on the rear perspective of *c* 1768 (Fig 3.10 and *see* Fig 3.8). The mill measured 50ft × 16ft (18.24m × 4.87m) overall and the wheel had a diameter of 17.5ft (5.33m) and a width of 2ft (0.6m).

The second rebuilding of Soho Mill, 1785

Scale's plan for the rebuilding of the mill was not implemented. A more radical idea was adopted, under Boulton's influence and assisted by Rennie, where metal-rolling figured more prominently. The new building was to be over 2.5 times the area of the old mill and built at right angles to the former site (Fig 3.11). Nevertheless, the 'Rolling was a secondary consideration and necessarily on a confined scale – the whole

Fig 3.10a
Detail from a bird's-eye view of the rear of the Manufactory, c 1768, showing the two-storey structure of Soho Mill and its external stairs.

Fig 3.10b
Detail from a bird's-eye view of the front of the Manufactory, c 1768, showing the waterwheel and decorative shaped gable.

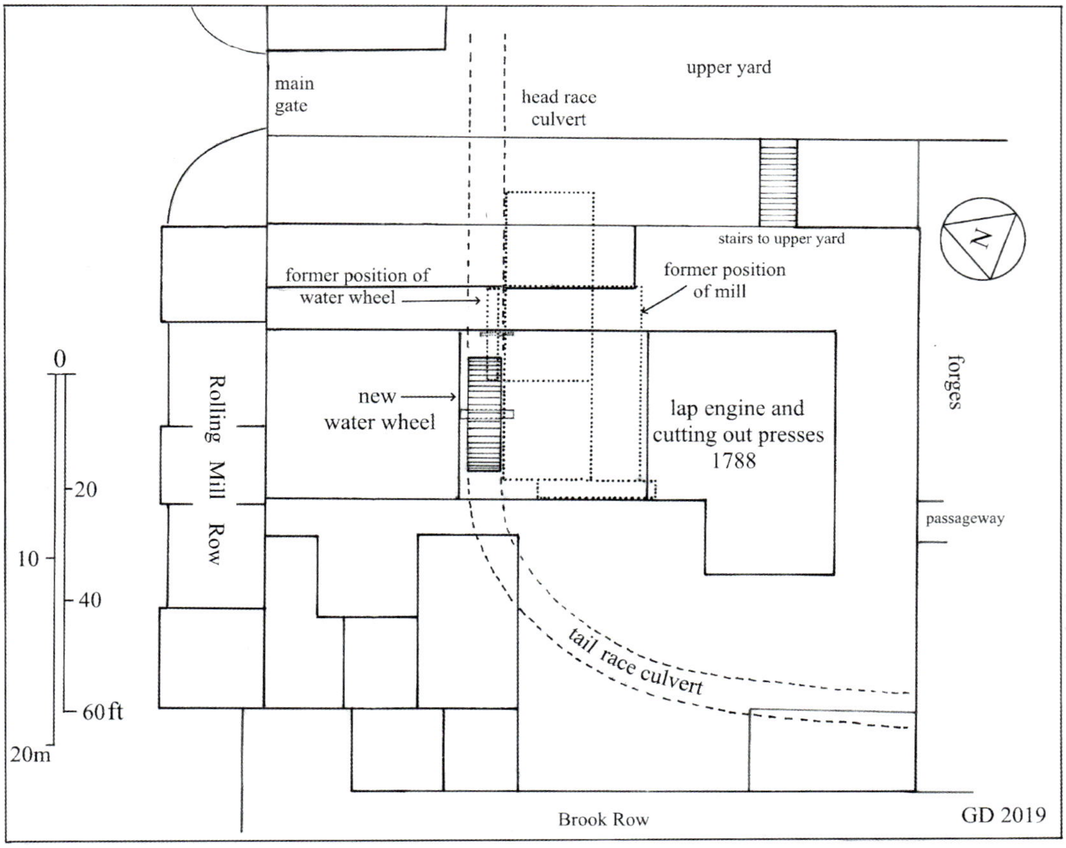

Fig 3.11
Plan of the reconstructed Soho Mill and its environs, 1785, with the earlier mill footprint overlaid.

power of the Mill at that period not exceeding 20 Horses the greater part of which was employed to turn the grinding and polishing Laps with the other Machinery belonging to the Steel and Plated Manufactories'.[75]

By the beginning of August 1785, the foundations of the new waterwheel pit were being laid, and digging them out and taking down the old foreboy had been 'a heavy job'.[76] Rennie left soon after for the Albion Mill, London, and reported to Boulton on 18 August that he had 'got six Millwrights and about 26 Labourers Bricklayers and Carpenters set to work' and had 'since learned that they had got all the Under works finished and the Fly wheel into the mill'.[77] This was not quite true. On 26 August, the 'Large Fly Wheel' was not yet in place, as a depth of 7 feet (2.13m) needed to be dug from under the gate to get it through and it then had to be hoisted over the stamping shop onto the site. The waterwheel shaft was, however, installed.[78] In October, the roof was being erected and it was hoped that the mill would be 'be ready to Polish by Christmas'.[79] The cost of the mill was £1,895 17s 10¼d (Fig 3.12).[80] A value for the building (£2,269 15s 8d) was entered in the ledger for 1787, and

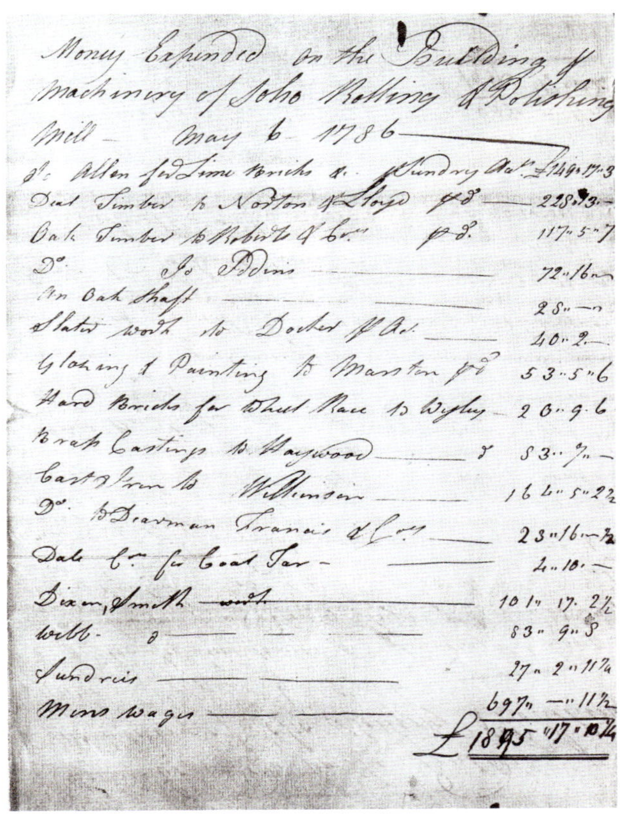
Money Expended on the Building of Machinery of Soho Rolling & Polishing Mill — May 6 1786

J. Allen for Lime Bricks &c. Sundry Acct.	£149.17.3
Deal Timber to Norton & Lloyd pd	228.13.–
Oak Timber to Roberts & Co. pd	117.5.7
Do. Jo Addins	72.16.–
An Oak Shaft	25.–.–
Slaters work to Docker p Acct	40.2.–
Glazing & Painting to Marston pd	53.5.6
Hard Bricks for Wheel Race to Wigley	20.9.6
Brass Castings to Haywood	83.7.–
Cast Iron to Wilkinson	164.5.2½
Do. to Dearman Francis & Co	23.16.–½
Dale & Co for Coal Tar	4.10.–
Dixon Smith work	101.17.2½
Webb Do	83.9.3
Sundries	27.2.11¼
Mens wages	697.–.11½
	£1895.17.10¼

Fig 3.12
John Rennie's building and machinery account for the reconstruction of the rolling and polishing mill at Soho, 6 May 1786.

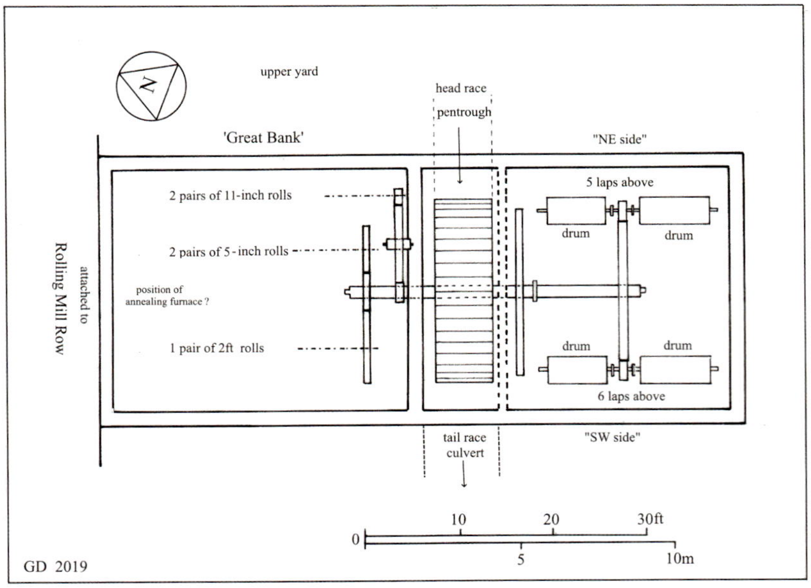

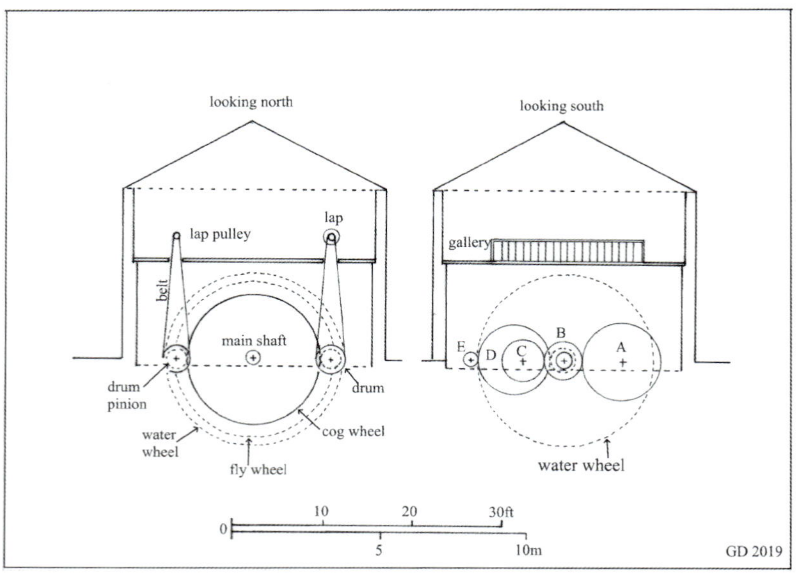

John Rennie's expenses amounted to £27 0s 3½d.[81]

Rent (£100 per annum) for the lapping mill was first collected at about the beginning of May 1786 and £200 per annum for the rolling mill from the beginning of August, suggesting that fitting out of the mill had been completed by this time.[82] However, this is contradicted by the complaints of John Hodges in September 1786 that the rolls were not ready and, as a consequence, such work was still being done elsewhere, 'your hands here in the meantime having little else to do'.[83] It was fortunate that the copper had not yet arrived for the East India Company coining contract.

There are no drawings surviving for this phase, but its basic internal layout can be reconstructed based on detailed experiments that were carried out on the machinery by Peter Ewart in 1786 (Fig 3.13).[84] The waterwheel, now internal and measuring 20ft (6.1m) in diameter and 6ft (1.83m) wide, was centrally placed. On its north side lay the rolling mill, which was open to the roof. It contained five pairs of rolls, a wheel of breaking-down rolls and a wheel of large breaking-down rolls. Of necessity, there would also have been a furnace to heat the metal before it was squeezed in the rolls. On the south side of the waterwheel, aided in its movement by an 18ft (5.48m)-diameter fly wheel, there were two pairs of drums (referred to as 'SW' and 'NE') running five laps and six laps each, respectively. The drums were, presumably, connected to the waterwheel via a large cog-wheel mentioned by Ewart. The laps were situated on the floor above and most likely were belt-driven directly from the drums. There are two definite drawings of the Soho waterwheel, the simplest shown in Fig 3.14, confirming that

Fig 3.13a
Plan of Soho Mill, 1786, showing the new waterwheel powering both rolling and polishing (laps).

Fig 3.13b
Cross sections of Soho Mill, 1786, showing the arrangement for the powering of the laps and the cogs required to run the metal rolls.

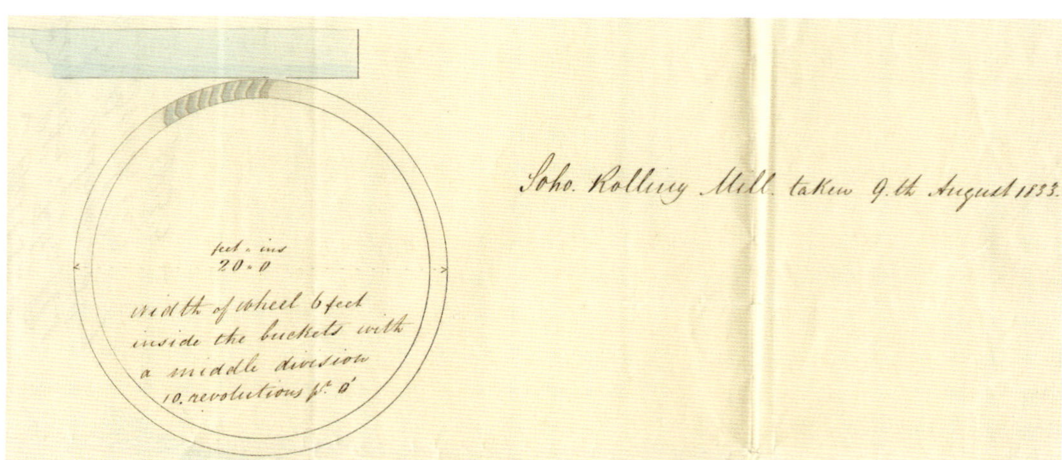

Fig 3.14
Elevation of the Soho Mill overshot waterwheel, 9 August 1833.

in 1833 the 6ft (1.83m)-wide buckets had a central division, presumably for extra support; an unidentified drawing of a 20ft (6.1m)-diameter wheel is possibly a third.[85]

Converting to coinage, 1786–7

During 1786, and especially 1787, Boulton began to consider an alternative and far more intensive use for his rolling mill than the production of sheet metal for plated ware and buttons. He was appalled by the state of the country's coinage and foresaw that, with high-quality dies and an updated technology, he could lead the world in the mass production of coins and medals. A collar to hold the coin to be struck was adopted to maintain consistency and regular form, and the rotary steam engine applied for rapid and regular production. The rolling mill was to stand at the beginning of this process, flattening copper cakes into sheets and then slitting them into strips (*see* Chapter 5).

In 1786, Boulton obtained a contract to produce the blanks for an East India Company coinage. All the processes, except the striking of the coin, were to be carried out at Soho. In September, there were delays in the supply of the copper and the mill was 'slack of rolling', the true reason being the unfinished state of the rolls.[86] At this time, a drum was being installed in the mill to run cutting-out machinery, a brush and two shaking boxes.[87] In the latter half of 1787, 30 tons (perhaps 50,000 pieces) of copper were rolled for the East India Company coinage at the rate of 5 tons (4.5 tonnes) per week, and by June it appears that the blanks were struck for the first time on presses at Soho.[88] It is possible that the power of the mill had been harnessed in these early coin-press experiments. Boulton spent considerable time in perfecting the method of rolling copper to provide a superior finish. This involved, after several hot rollings, annealing, pickling and scouring, and then passing the copper cold through finely turned and polished steel rolls.[89]

The lap engine, 1788

Boulton was determined to obtain the national coinage contract, but any plans to establish steam-powered presses in his own mint would have been frustrated by the low capacity of his rolling mill. This was encumbered by lapping machinery and had never been designed to cope with the heavy demands of copper rolling. It is revealing that, given the availability of his own rotary steam engines, his solution to the problem of insufficient rolling power was to attach an engine to the lapping, rather than to the rolling, end of the mill.

Early in 1788, Boulton had not yet decided on this arrangement and envisaged connecting the steam engine to the waterwheel shaft via a clutch so that the engine and waterwheel could work together or independently, providing 20hp and 27hp respectively. The three pairs of existing rolls could then be replaced by five. Boulton planned the various processes meticulously and expected that the mill would cease work only from midnight to 4 a.m.[90] John Rennie was invited to help plan the new machinery for the mill, and on 8 January he submitted an estimate of cost amounting to £1,327 6s 9d, which he rounded up to £1,400 (Fig 3.15).[91] In the meantime, the last of the East India Company coinage blanks were despatched.[92]

In June 1788, as the mint was being erected on the menagerie garden site, five cutting-out presses, probably operated by hand, were installed in the gallery of the rolling mill.[93] As late as July, Rennie was asking Boulton to decide whether he wanted an extra steam engine to be attached to the rolling mill, since this would influence the new layout. Such a plan had been discussed the previous Christmas (1787) and was preferred by Rennie.[94] Drawings passed to and fro between the two men, but only the correspondence seems to have survived. Boulton sent two schemes: one an adaptation of the 'Christmas plan', which needed four more cogwheels and was more expensive; the other, where a 'train of Rolls was worked by pinions'. Rennie recommended the former.[95] On 14 July, Rennie sent revised drawings of the mill showing the layout of the lap-engine house. The door and window openings in the existing gable were to be used for the drum and flywheel shafts. The engine itself was to be enclosed within an internal wall so that the remainder of the engine house could be freed for other machinery such as drums.[96] On 27 July, Boulton wrote: 'I certainly shall never think of adding another Fire Engine at the warehouse end of the Mill as my Mill will now be sufficiently powerfull when the Laps are turnd by the Engine now building in the great Yard for I believe those laps etc took one third of the power of the Water wheel and consequently the Rolling Mill will have 1/3 more power than at present'.[97]

1058 Cube feet of Oak for frames	@ 4s	£211	8	0d
304 feet deal	1/6d	£22	16	0d
198 feet 6 inch oak plank	1/9d	£14	7	3d
4820 lb of Screw Bolt[s]	5d	£102	10	0d
2 Plum[me]r Block patterns		£2	2	0d
24 Plum[me]r Blocks	14s	£109	18	0d
45 Brasses = 1590 lb	1s	£94	10	0d
Fitting ditto		£6	0	0d
20 Iron Straps and screw bolts = 600lb	4d	£10	0	0d
Making up and fitting up the frames		£128	0	0d
38 1/2 feet of wheel patterns	25s	£48	2	6d
17 Iron wheels = 314 Cwt	15s	£260	5	0d
Fitting arms and drilling		£14	14	0d
102 Screw bolts and ditto = 448lb	6d	£11	4	0d
Hanging ditto wedges etc		£35	14	0d
Gearing etc		£80	0	0d
11 Shafts wit[h] turning = 218 Cwt	16s	£174	16	0d
		£1327	6	9d

Source: LoB, MS3782/13/49/19

Fig 3.15
John Rennie's estimate for extending Soho Mill, January 1788. Rennie's original figure of £1326 was altered to £1327 incorrectly.

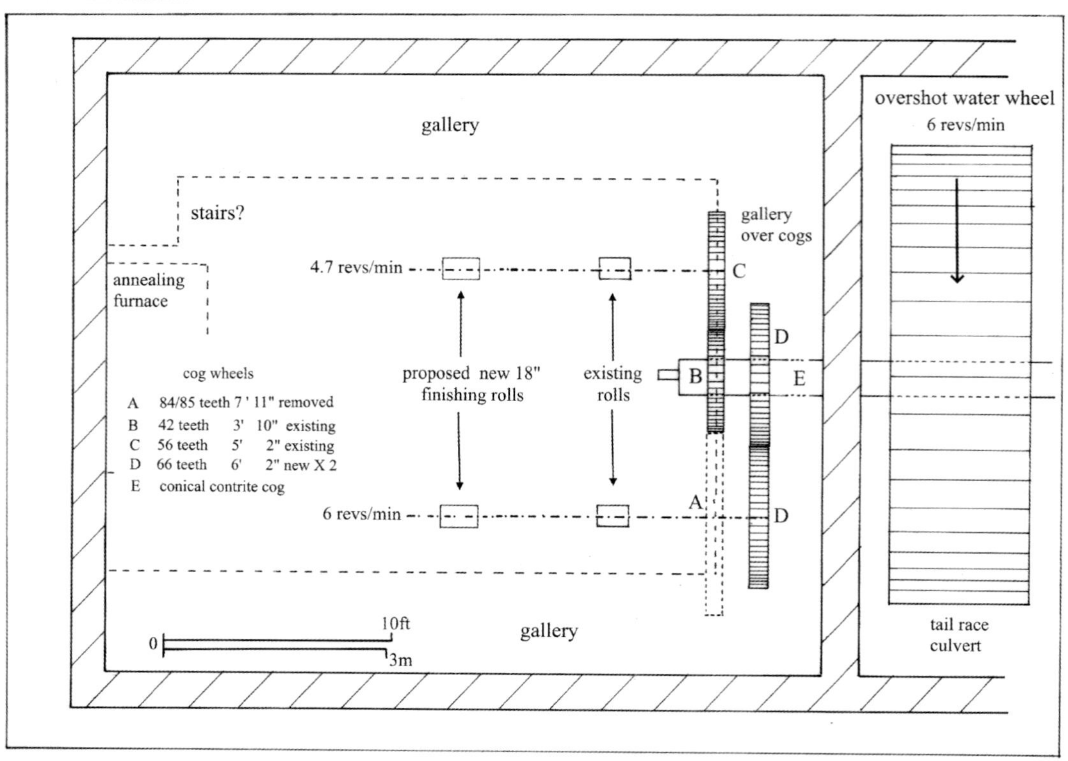

Fig 3.16
Plan of the new arrangement of metal rolls, Soho Mill, 1788.

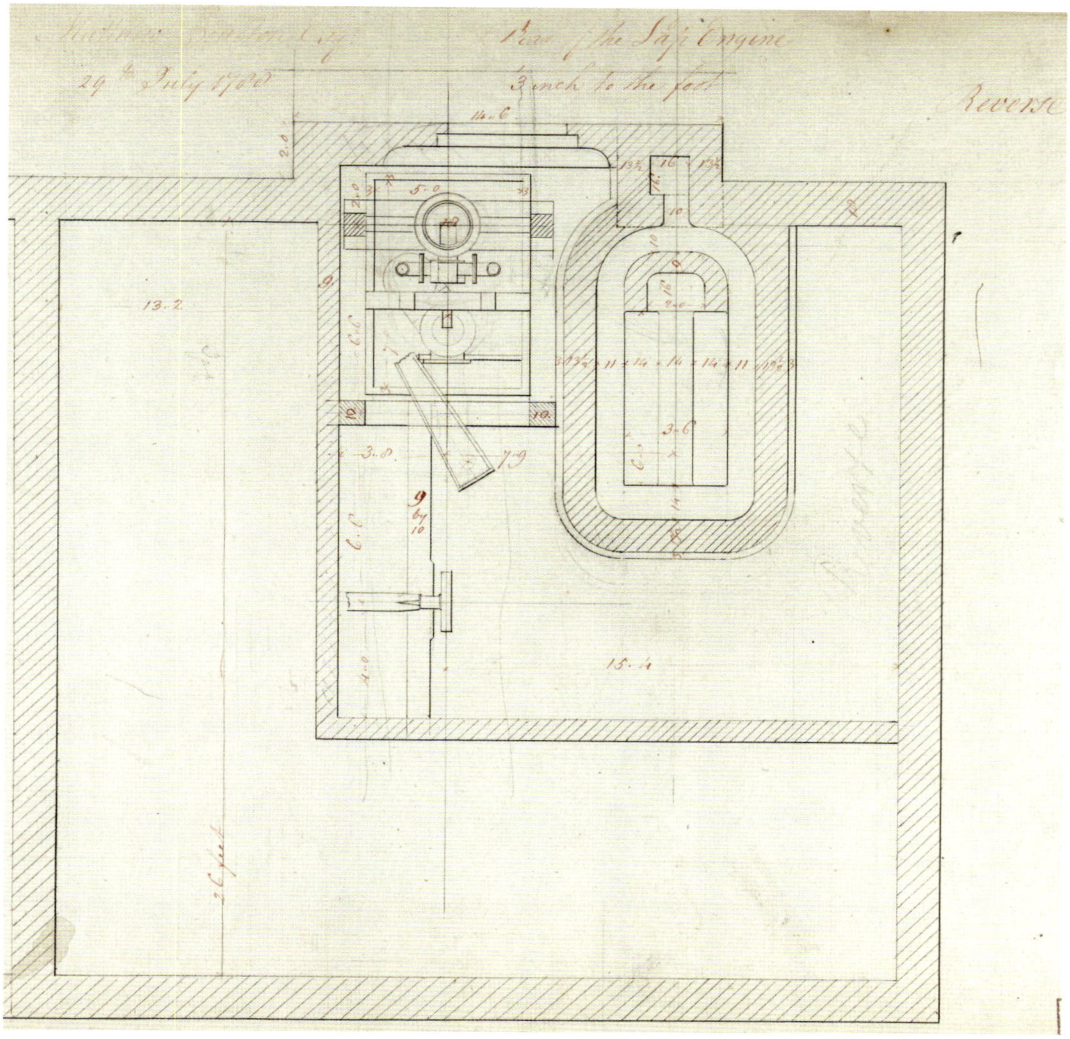

Fig 3.17
Plan of the proposed lap engine with internal boiler, 29 July 1788 (Reverse). Drawings marked 'Reverse' were produced on James Watt's copying machine, thereby reversing the image.

Fig 3.18a
Plan of the proposed coin cutting-out presses, 29 November 1788. These were to be situated on a floor above the lap engine and powered by it (Reverse).

Fig 3.18b
Elevation of the proposed coin cutting-out presses and their connection to the lap engine, 29 November 1788.

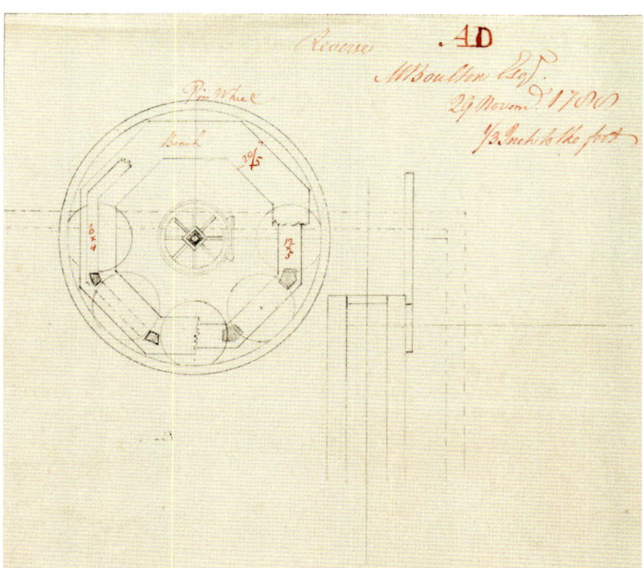

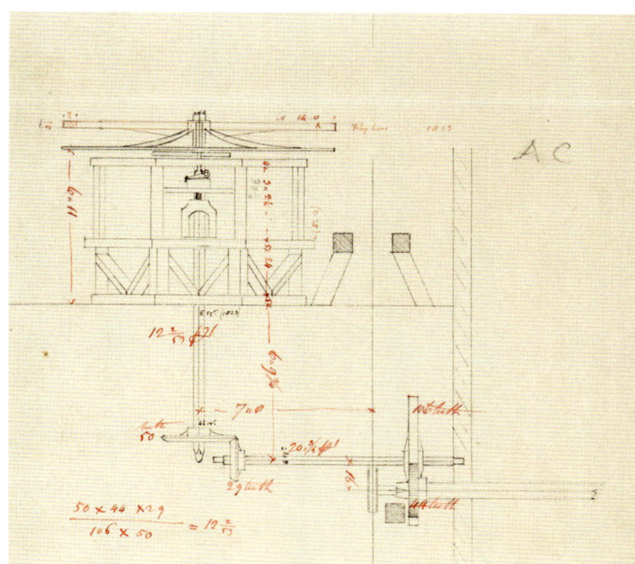

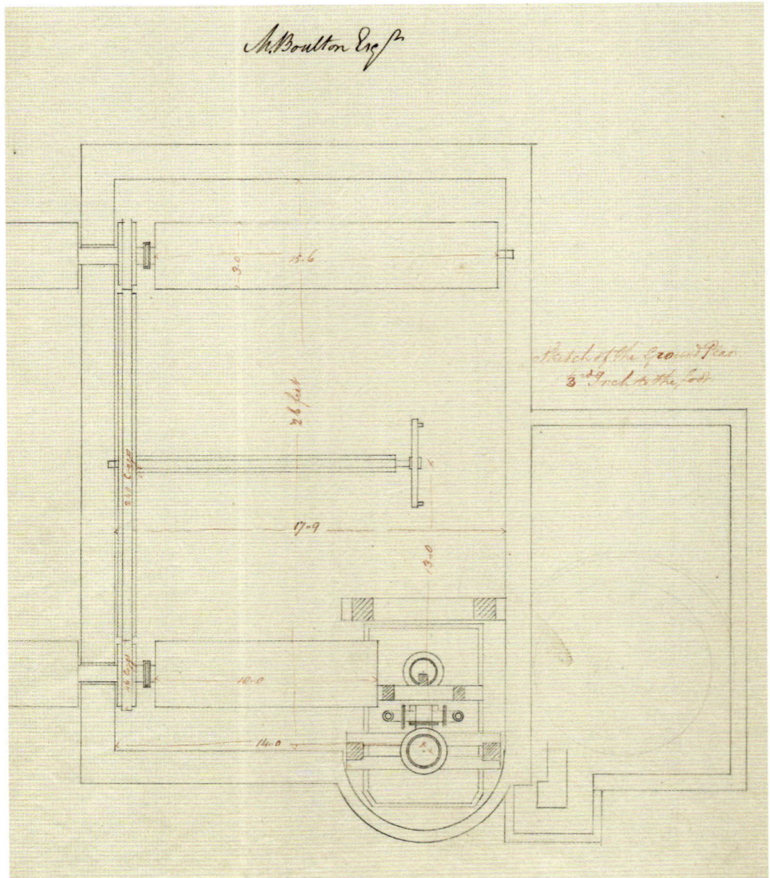

Fig 3.19a
Plan of the lapping mill engine and machinery, not implemented, early 1788.

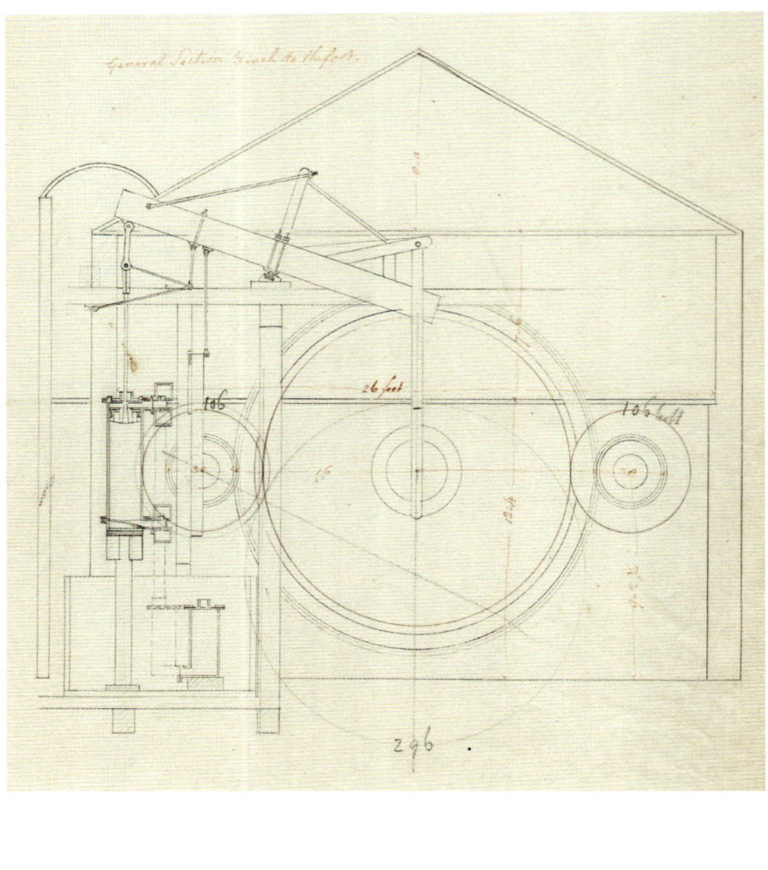

Fig 3.19b
Elevation of the lapping mill engine and machinery, not implemented, early 1788.

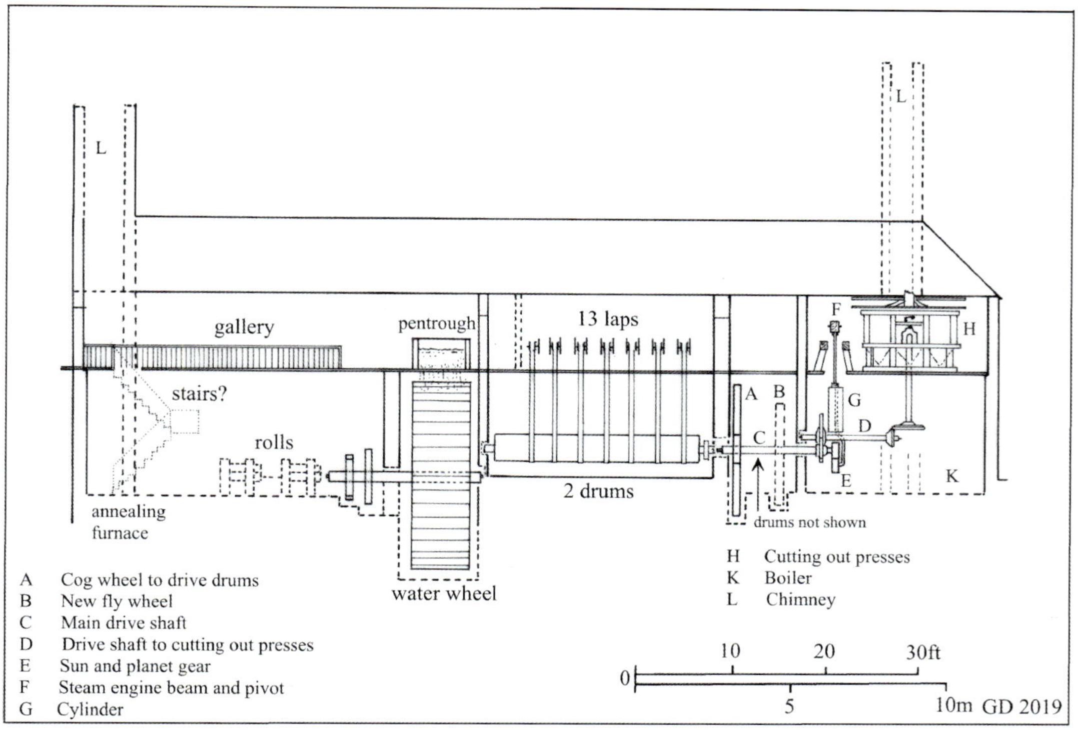

Fig 3.20a
A long cross-section of the completed Soho rolling and lapping mill, 1788–90.

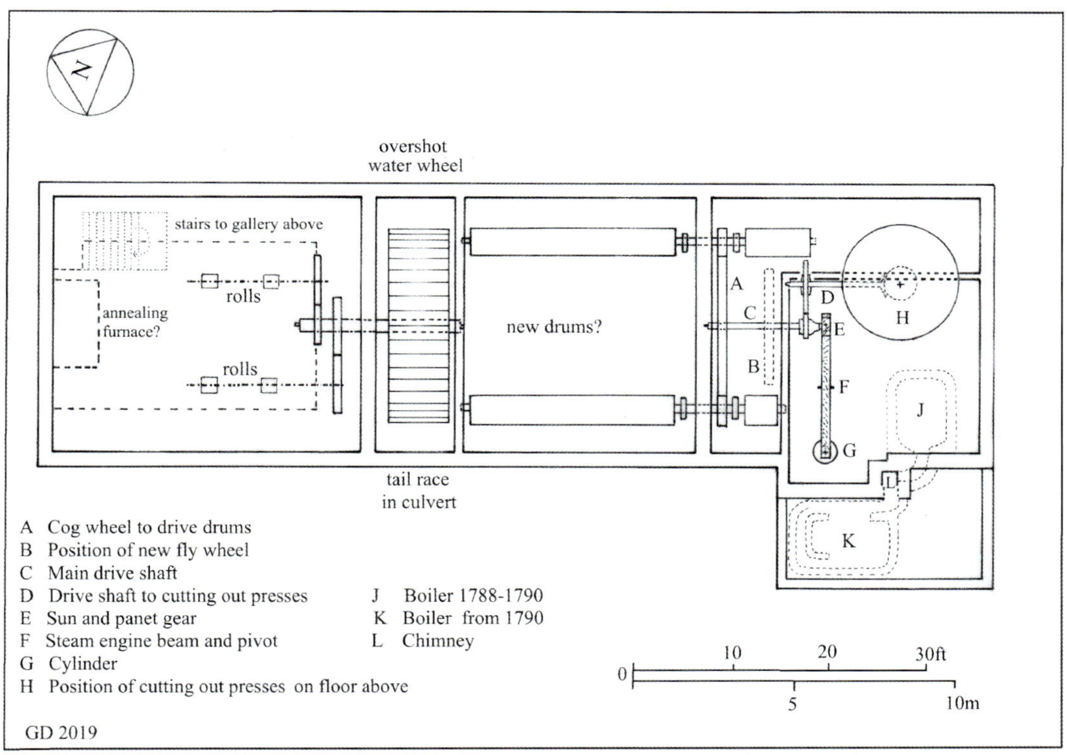

Fig 3.20b
Plan of the completed Soho rolling and lapping mill, 1788–90.

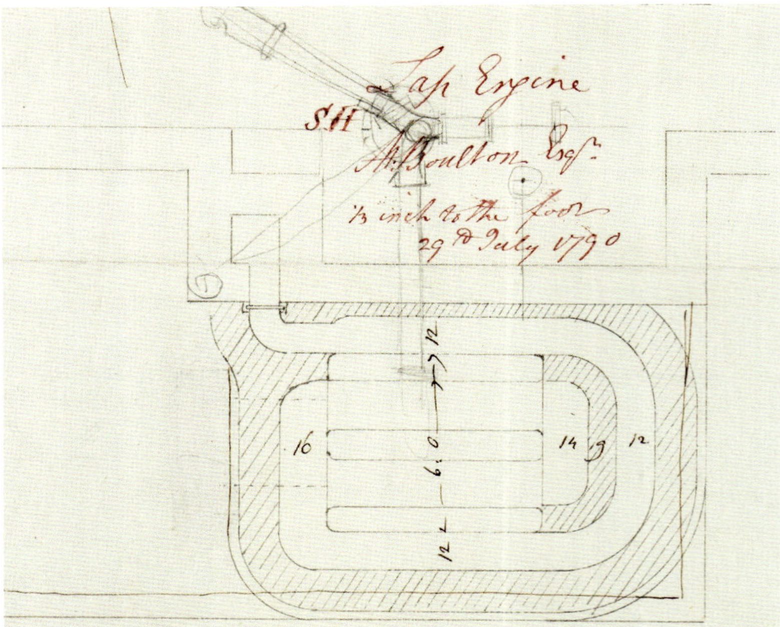

Fig 3.21
Plan of the proposed boiler extending the lap-engine house, Soho Mill, 29 July 1790.

In view of the expense of the new lap-engine house, compromises had to be made in the arrangement of the gearing for the rolls. The alterations are illustrated in Fig 3.16. Two new 18in (457mm) pairs of rolls clutched into the two existing pairs together took up less space than the old arrangement. By 27 July the 'Building for the new Laping Engine & mill' was 'nearly finished',[98] and on 3 August the masons were 'to put the Roof upon the New Engine Laping Mill'. The 18in (457mm) cylinder for the double-acting engine had, however, not yet arrived from Bersham.[99] During all this activity, Peter Ewart made at least his second appearance at Soho (*see* p 52) and Boulton remarked that he seemed to be 'a well behaved proper person'. His work was to be supervision rather than design as there was 'little to contrive'. Despite having reached this stage on 23 October, Boulton implored Rennie to send him more millwrights as there was a great deal of work left to be done at the 'Lapping Mill', and without them it would not be finished before Christmas as he had hoped.[100]

In August 1788, a 'Trial was made of Cutting-out Presses worked by a Steam-Engine'.[101] Plans, dated 29 November 1788, show an eight-place cutting-out press for installation on the upper floor of the lap-engine house and supported by Rennie's internal brick partition below at the drum-floor level.[102] It was to remain there until 1824 when it was refitted with metal parts and sent to the new Bombay mint.[103]

Using a combination of the few plans available (Figs 3.17–3.19) and other documentary evidence, it has been possible to reconstruct the general layout of the rolling and lapping mill as it was at this time (Figs 3.20a and b). A gallery connected the lapping shops with the rolling-mill offices in former workers' houses adjacent to the mill on the north side, and there was probably also a stair descending from it to the rolling-mill floor. The structure apparently extended around both sides of the mill and left the centre free for furnaces and for light to enter by skylights. At the end of July 1790, plans were drawn up for the removal of the boiler from within the lap-engine house and for it to be placed against an outside wall (Fig 3.21).[104] Presumably, it was intended to make more space within the engine house for other activities related to lapping or the cutting out of coin blanks. There is no direct evidence that the work was carried out promptly, but a plan dating from 1792 shows the extension as planned (Fig 3.22).[105]

Steam and water, 1789–1809

The 1780s was the pivotal decade in the history of the mill. Up to this time, lapping and polishing had been the mill's most significant functions and, despite the application of the most modern contemporary technology, the button and plated-ware businesses, which these functions served, were soon to go into long-term decline. On the other hand, the rolling mill, inextricably linked with the mint, was to prosper, driven though it was by the increasingly archaic power of water.

It is not known exactly how the laps were arranged in the two lap shops.[106] In the early part of 1789, there were 26 laps, and on 9 March, 2 'flat' laps were removed and replaced by a brushing machine considered equivalent to 6 separate laps. Later in March, 8 'side' laps were added, making 32 laps plus the brushing machine.[107] After a dispute, an annual rent was charged by Boulton, as owner of the buildings, to the button business, Boulton and Scale, equivalent to 40 laps at £4 4s 0d each, a total of £168. Likewise, the rolling mill was treated as a separate concern and began to pay rent of £200 to Boulton. If any of the Soho businesses required any metal-rolling, they were charged for it on an individual basis by the mill. Boulton claimed that he had spent £3,000 on rebuilding his two mills, £1,800 on the lapping side alone. He also revealed that the cutting-out machine consumed one-third of the lap-engine power.[108]

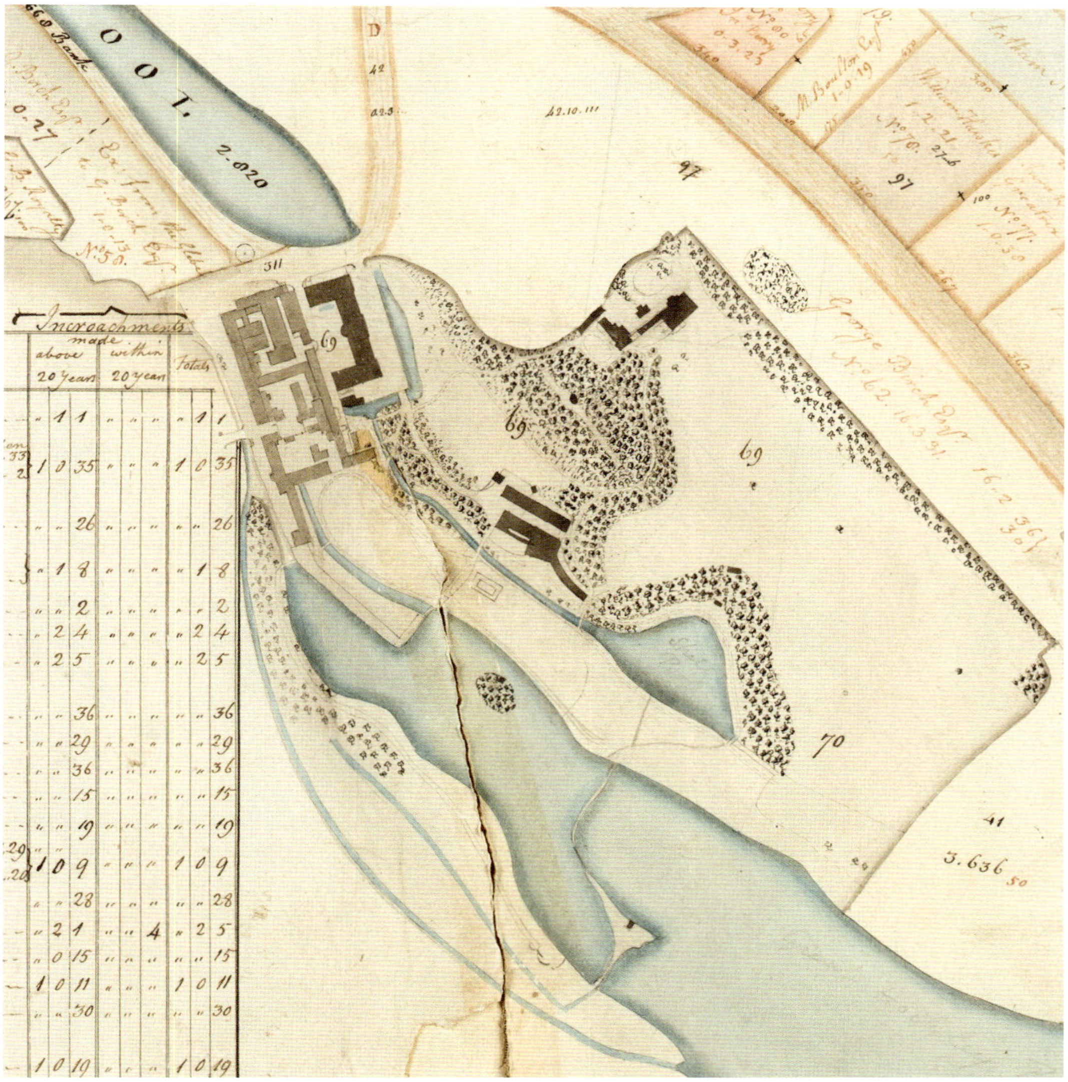

Fig 3.22
Detail from Samuel Botham's map of Handsworth, 1792, showing the extension to the lap-engine house for a new boiler, creating an L shape. Unlike other small-scale maps of this area, this plan of the Manufactory is accurate. The map also clearly shows Boulton's Upper Hockley Pool, created in about 1774 to hold tail race water to be pumped back to the water mill using Watt's engine. The Hockley Brook has been diverted into a new channel but this was abandoned for the extension of the engine works in 1802–4 and the brook returned to the old channel.

A detailed Mint inventory dating from 1790 has survived that lists rooms in various parts of the mill. The cutting-out shop, with six out of eight presses inoperative, also contained two coin-milling machines, one nearly 'finished'. Next door was a workshop, full of tools and equipment, belonging to a Mr Peploe. On the rolling mill side were accommodated the mill gallery, a shaking shop, with its machine already obsolete, two annealing shops and a melting shop. The actual rolling mill was not listed.[109]

The power of the rolling mill was, however, tested by John Southern in 1790. The results were disappointing. When opened, the 'shutless', the sluice at the end of the foreboy over the wheel, could not turn three pairs of rolls, and this under a full head of water (27in [685mm]) in the foreboy. Normally, there was much less water in the foreboy and one pair could barely be turned.[110]

Early in the morning of 24 March 1791, a fire broke out in the 'Cutting out Mill'. Little damage was done as the alarm was quickly raised. The fire was caused by stray sparks from the copper reverberatory furnace in the rolling mill falling through the still-unglazed open skylights of the cutting-out room.[111] In May, a large quantity of idle machinery in the mill was put into a state of readiness: the '8 press[es] in the Cutting-out mill' being made workable and eight hand presses being placed on one side the mill gallery; 'and cleaning metal on the other'.[112] At the beginning of June, a breakage of a cogwheel shaft put an entire stop to work, but the opportunity was taken to desilt the mill pool.[113] Unfortunately, the cast iron replacement shaft found in the engine yard quickly broke and it was decided to cast a new one.[114]

Boulton was most particular about the polished surface of his finishing rolls and in 1794 he

Fig 3.23
List of rooms in Soho Mill, 1809.

Shaking shop
Rough Shaking shop
Cutting out shop
Drilling and Grinding shop
Passage leading to Cutting out shop
Foreby
Vault belonging to Cutting out shop
Old Engine house
Lapping up shop
Pickling shop
Annealing shop

Source: LoB, MS3782/3/37

admitted to John Edwards, a Cornish metal-roller, that, some years previously, he had invented a dressing and polishing machine for rolls using laps that he had kept 'fixt in an underground Building called the Bastile & always kept secret'.[115] Boulton persuaded Edwards to have his rolls dressed at Soho, but the Cornishman was unhappy with the result. Boulton admitted to a lack of supervision as he had not ventured into the rolling mill since the year (1795) had begun, as 'my complaint in my left kidney renders it necessary for me to avoid going up hill and down & therby my own Manufactory is much neglected & I have more work than Health'.[116] The time was fast approaching when Boulton would have to give up his active involvement in many aspects of the Soho Manufactory.

In 1797, John Kellet, the manager of the Mint, visited Aston Brook mill with a view to leasing it for rolling metal. Nothing came of this enquiry, but it is interesting to note that, despite all previous efforts to upgrade the rolling capacity at Soho, there were still times when it was insufficient.[117] The peaks and troughs of demand arrived with alarming unpredictability, however, so there were slack times when the mill cried out for extra work and took in rolling from beyond Soho.[118]

It must not be forgotten that throughout this period and for the following 50 years at least, 'Old Bess', the pumping engine, was used to top up the mill pool. She worked at night so that the rolling mill was ready to work in the morning. It is not known if the sleeping residents of the Soho houses had become accustomed to the noise![119] A few facts from the history of 'Old Bess', one of the two Soho engines displayed at the Science Museum (London), are worth quoting. In 1797, the beam was replaced using the old iron work and the pump barrel re-bored.[120] On 20 July 1800 at 6 a.m., fire broke out near the engine, which had been pumping for an hour. The flames spread to the roof of the engine house and engulfed surrounding roofs, which shed their slates, injuring the firefighters.[121]

The button business, under the partnership of Boulton and Scale, was dissolved in 1796 and, despite subsequent efforts to rejuvenate and reorganise the trade, the use of the lapping mill declined throughout the first decade of the 19th century. Part of the mill was occupied by the latchet company and the plated-ware company for a glass-grinding shop, and this slide was arrested to some extent. The glass-cutting shop was described by Johanna Schopenhauer when visiting England between 1803 and 1805.[122] The grinding wheels were apparently driven from a 'long wooden cylinder' (a drum?) located on the floor of the shop and the cylinder itself moved 'by a steam engine', presumably the lap engine, 'located in the room below'. Information on mill rents from 1777 to 1816 can be used to illustrate the various Soho firms' involvement in lapping and rolling and the relative balance between the two functions, at least as far as the rentals can reliably indicate.[123] On the death of Matthew Boulton, an inventory of the Mint premises was made that included rooms in the rolling mill (Fig. 3.23).[124] Most of these rooms were to continue to belong to the coining business ('MB Mint') until the Mint was demolished in the early 1850s. Gilt- and plated-button manufacture having ceased, the button business, concentrating on steel buttons from 1810, transferred to John Bownas. Only

Fig 3.24
Account of repair work completed at Soho Mill, 1838.

Amount of Sundries...for the erection of new Foreboy, Reparation of Water Wheel, Pit Wheel New Floor to Gallery, etc	£74	16s	7.5d
Vaughan, for New Foreboy	£32	2s	8d
Jones, for Castings	£13	16s	11d
Brown, for Tar White Lead etc	£1	12s	0d
Boulton Watt & Co, for Sundries	£10	8s	11.5d
Wages paid for the above repairs	£47	19s	6.5d
	£180	16s	8.5d

Source: LoB, MS3782/6/185

the plated-ware company, which remained under the control of Matthew Robinson Boulton, paid rent for a number of years directly for the lapping mill, but must have shared space and power with Bownas's steel button company under an unknown financial arrangement.

The years of decline, 1810–50

In October 1815, the waterwheel shaft failed and the rolling mill was reported 'quite at a stand'. John Kellet suggested strapping the shaft with a 12–13in (304–330mm) square timber. The matter was discussed with William Murdoch and William Creighton, who considered that an entirely new timber or cast iron shaft would take too long to find or produce. Creighton suggested a compromise: strapping the shaft with iron and bracing it against the sole of the wheel with a king post. Thus reinforced, the shaft, it was hoped, would 'last long enough to wear out the rest of the Machinery', which indeed it was doing, as the sides of the foreboy also needed replacing.[125]

Further repairs were carried out to metal parts of the waterwheel in 1827 and to its timber components in 1828.[126] Between 1825 and 1829, the lap engine and pumping engine were extensively repaired.[127]

When William V Toney was considering acquiring Bownas's button business in 1832, he only wished to take on the 'The lower part of the mill where the Fire Irons are polished'.[128] This was presumably located either in part of the engine house or in the room adjacent where the drums once revolved to turn the laps on the floor above. He was not interested in the 'upper part' of the mill. The plated-ware company was also up for sale at this time and a prospective buyer was offered the rolling mill. A Mr Chamberlain observed that 'the Rolls were old & too narrow, and the power insufficient for the purposes of the Plate Trade; that consequently the Mill would be an incumbrance upon the concern and they could not take it on'.[129] The consequences of lack of investment over the years were catching up on Boulton's descendants. The plated-ware company was acquired by Messrs Robinson Edkins and Aston and renamed The Soho Plate Company.[130] In the negotiations, it transpired that William Toney's steel trade was paying £230 annually for the lap engine with The Soho

Warehouse	£52	02	11d
Room over Office	£59	10	11d
Grease Room	£12	0	10.5d
Rolling Mill	£1087	9	10d
Rolling Mill Gallery	£58	1	0d
Roll Turning Shop	£239	3	3d
Machinery in Lower Mill	£46	9	8d
Pickling Shop & Shop adjoining	£40	9	1.5d
Smelting Foundry	£19	2	1d
Shop behind Annealing Furnaces	£10	13	07d
Stable & Yard	£53	19	06d
Old Engine	£17	17	0d
Clay Hole	£4	5	4d
Casting Shop	£8	3	9d
	£1709	08	10d

Source: LoB, MS3782/3/41

Fig 3.25
List of rooms with their value in the rolling mill inventory, 1841.

Fig 3.26
List of the rolling mill premises, 1850.

Fourth Day's Sale
Rolling Mills
Pickling House
Roll Turning Shop
Annealing Shed
Rolling Mill
Mill Adjoining
Timber water wheel 30ft diameter [sic, should be 20ft]
Weighing Warehouse
First Floor
Gallery
Three–inch Fir Forebye
Back Yard
Foundry
Pumping Engine House
Pumping Engine with cast iron cylinder 2 feet 6 diameter
Boiler House
Medal or Multiplying Room
End of Forth Day's Sale

Source: LoB, MS3782/119/Folder 6; LoB, Birmingham Miscellaneous F/1-157177; LF 63.13 64034.

Plate Company contributing £80.[131] How the power was actually used at this time is unknown.

Throughout the 1830s and early 1840s, repairs to the rolling mill and the pumping engine, known also as 'the old engine' ('Old Bess') were carried out.[132] In 1835, a major overhaul costing £385 2s 7d was completed on the lap engine.[133] The lap engine is the second of the Soho engines that found its way to the Science Museum (London) and one wonders how much, if any, of these engines on display have their 'original' parts. From the evidence of the accounts, it is likely that many of the parts were replaced several times over their long life. The machine for finishing rolls, which Matthew Boulton had hidden away in his 'Bastile' so many years previously, was at this time located in the rolling mill and it needed repair at a total cost of £88 14s 0d.[134] For 1838, there are detailed reports on the dilapidated state of the rolling-mill machinery.[135] Production of rolled copper for the mint was being halted by the state of the waterwheel shaft, its reinforcing pins breaking. In addition, leaks from the mill-pool dam were such 'that the old Engine can scarsely make head against it, the opperations in the Mill have frequently been obliged to be stopped in order for the Engine to fill the Pool', and the rotten foreboy leaked sufficiently, after the stop gate was shut, to set the wheel in motion. Carrying out these repairs revealed more problems and the extra work that was completed is listed in Fig 3.24. The total cost was £180 16s 8½d.[136] This included the governor, installed in 1805, from the drawing of which the relationship of the wheel to the foreboy can be reconstructed.[137]

In 1841, a detailed inventory of the rolling mill was undertaken and the rooms listed compare closely with those in earlier inventories. This confirms that the cutting-out press had been missing for some time, having been sold to the Bombay mint in 1824 (Fig 3.25). There is also a possibility that some of the workshops, such as the pickling shop, had been transferred to adjoining premises. The once-secret roll-turning shop was situated in the 'lower mill'.[138]

The last years, 1850–63

Over five days, starting on 29 April 1850, the Mint and its contents were auctioned. The fourth day was devoted to the sale of the rolling mill and its machinery. Fig 3.26 is based on the detailed sales catalogue, and some of the most important items of equipment are included. We know, therefore, that a timber waterwheel was still in position at this time, but not when it had finally ceased to work. Its diameter was given as 30ft (9.14m), 10 too many, for it is unlikely that the 20ft (6.1m) wheel recorded in 1838 had been replaced by another larger one in timber. Furthermore, the rolling mill was only 29ft (8.84m) wide (*see* Fig 2.14).

As mentioned in the introduction, the author was initially attracted to work on the Soho Manufactory, intrigued by the fact that a watermill was still functioning in the 1840s where a complete Boulton & Watt steam engine works had been constructed in the very early years of the 19th century. Why had steam power not superseded water power at the rolling mill? The answer is relatively straightforward: once major capital expenditure on mill pool, dam, races, buildings and machinery been completed, running costs remained relatively low as long as the 'free' fuel supply, water, continued to flow. In Soho's case this was much aided by James Watt's pumping engine recycling the tail-race water.

Although the timber waterwheel had operated since 1785 (undoubtedly much repaired), it is unlikely it found a buyer, in contrast to the fate of 'Old Bess', the ancient pumping engine. It was purchased for £48 by a Mr Lewis, who sold it for £58 to Samuel Walker, a metal roller at Heath Mill. A large triangular pool had been created in the early 19th century and he placed it on an island, presumably for display as an old relic rather than for any practical purpose. Samuel Walker then sold it to Messrs Branson and Gwythers, a major Birmingham construction firm based at Belmont Row, which in 1861 donated it to the Science Museum.[139]

Unlike the mint, the rolling mill was not to be demolished soon after the sale as it was useful enough to be leased. It was claimed that Mr Toy put up a rolling mill.[140] Toy certainly took out a lease of the former Soho Plate Company premises and erected a steam engine in the yard between the mill and the principal building, but he did not lease the rolling mill.[141] This was done by Frederick Jenks, a papier-mâché maker, who, in January 1853, agreed to take the 'Upper and Lower Rolling Mills', the lap engine and other adjoining premises.[142] The plan of the Soho Manufactory made about this time shows the 'Upper' and 'Lower Rolling Mill', the former in the position of the original rolling mill and the latter occupying the space on the opposite side of the waterwheel where the drums once ran the laps on the floor above (*see* Fig 2.32). It is not known how the lower rolling mill was powered nor when it was installed. Under the new agreement, Frederick Jenks was to work the lap engine but supply William Toney and his steel button and fire iron business with 3hp at £12 per hp; in another version of the agreement it was to be between 3 and 6hp at £12 per hp.[143]

In early 1854, with 'Old Bess' and possibly the waterwheel removed, the mill pool was filled in.[144] Smiles's statement that he saw 'Old Bess' working in 1857 must be mistaken, unless he meant it was with one of the subsequent Birmingham owners outside Soho.[145] Meanwhile the lap engine was 'working as well as ever' and was constantly employed for the use of William Toney until 28 December 1858, when its main shaft broke. William Toney had intended to close his business only a few days later.[146]

In the late 1850s, the rolling mill at Spring Hill, Birmingham, was built to remove the nuisance that was being caused to the local residents at Soho. In July and August 1859 the new mill was advertised to let.[147] By this time, a William Henry Powell had taken over the Soho Mill and it was he that transferred, along with Alfred Toy, to the new 'Soho Works' in about 1859–60 (*see* pp 38–40).[148] The old rolling mill stood empty for at least another 18 months, but fortunately, in 1861, Matthew Piers Watt Boulton, then living in Great Malvern, donated the lap engine to the Science Museum, London.[149] On 29 May 1862, Aaron Smith agreed to remove 'The Old Rolling Mill', among other buildings, within six months.[150] At the same time, further filling in of the mill pool took place.[151]

It had been just over a century earlier that Ruston and Eaves built their rolling mill beside a windswept warren on Handsworth Heath. A few years later, they were followed by the ingenious Matthew Boulton, but instead of his Manufactory, as might be expected, forming the kernel of a major industrial area, it was the garden around Soho House that was to leave more of an imprint on the local landscape. In the 1860s, Soho Park filled up with the villas of respectable gentlefolk and there was little toleration for the Manufactory in their midst. Today, those stuccoed residences, though decayed, still crown the summit of Soho Hill, but not a trace of the Manufactory nor of its rolling mill is to be seen. Its site is passed by many but appreciated by very few.

4

The Manufactory engine works

The early years, 1775–80

It must be stressed that when the newly established firm of Boulton & Watt began selling their patented steam engine in 1776, the commodity they were purveying was, strictly speaking, an idea or an advantage rather than a piece of hardware. The Soho Manufactory was not immediately converted or extended into an engine works. James Watt decided, and Matthew Boulton perhaps reluctantly agreed, that it would be easier to act as their own agents for the invention, providing only engineering expertise, drawings and skilled erectors. The customer dealt directly with recommended or conveniently placed manufacturers who supplied the required engine parts. In its early years, the firm of Boulton & Watt earned its income by premiums calculated on the amount of coal saved by their engine, i.e. on its advantage over the Newcomen or common engine.[1]

It took many years to fulfil Boulton's original ambition of establishing his own engine works near his own manufactory and beside a canal where he would 'erect all the conveniencies necessary for the completion of the engines and from which manufactory we would serve all the world with engines of all sizes'.[2] It was not until the mid-1790s that the Soho Foundry was established beside a canal in Smethwick, a mile away from the Manufactory. From small beginnings in 1775, an engine works grew up beside the Manufactory, expanding quickly in the early years of the 19th century to complement and support the operations at the Foundry. The Soho Engine Manufactory and the Soho Foundry have been confused by some writers on the subject,[3] and this chapter attempts to clear away some of the misunderstandings, first by analysing how the Soho Engine Manufactory physically developed and, second, by reconstructing its function, plan and buildings at various periods.

The Kinneil engine, which Watt brought down from Scotland in 1773, was erected to serve the Boulton & Fothergill Manufactory, and, more precisely its watermill. It did not form part of the Boulton & Watt premises, although its position was to mark a boundary between the yards of the two firms. The engine raised water 7.3m (24ft) over the Great Bank, which split the Manufactory complex into two basic levels. Before the erection of the engine, this section of the Great Bank had apparently been built over in the preceding years by a range of workshops. They presented a single storey to the principal building and three storeys on the opposite downslope side. The water leaving the top of the pump had to pass through part of this workshop range to reach the canal leading to the mill pool. Some of these workshops came gradually to be occupied by the engine firm.

Even though it had been decided from the outset that income would be obtained by premiums rather than by the direct sale of steam engines, Soho quickly began to produce some of the more specialised engine parts. In theory, this made sense, but inadequate control of work and costs led to low productivity and complaints of high prices. Despite his ambitions, Boulton realised that retreat was necessary before the next major advance: 'we should avoid Manufacturing as much as possable except the Brains, the heart & the lungs of our Engines.'[4] This meant that, for some time, mainly valve containers, or 'nozzles', as they were called, were to be made in the first building constructed by the firm. In August or September 1775, Boulton gave a progress report: 'The new forging-shop looks very formidable; the roof is nearly put on, and the hearths are both built.'[5] The forging shop, costing £110 15s 9d, was located at right angles to the Great Bank workshops and enclosed the southern end of an area that was soon to be the first engine yard. In its centre stood 'Solomon's Temple', which was eventually taken over by Boulton & Watt and used initially as a store.[6]

From 1775 to 1781, Boulton gave a number of Manufactory rooms over to the engine company.[7] These probably lay in the Great Bank range as they were the closest and space was available there. This bank of workshops was then occupied by the newly formed firm of James Watt and Company, producing letter-copying machines patented in 1780 (Fig 4.1).[8] From 1780, the latter firm was paying rents on a number of rooms, some of which had been part of the abandoned clock business (*see* pp 19–20).[9] In September 1780, William Playfair, a new Boulton & Watt employee, proposed that there be only four smiths (two workmen and two assistants) at Soho who would be sufficient to 'forge the work for & fit 10 or 12 Nozzles & do the other little things which is as much as will be wanted next year'.[10] But Playfair could not foresee that rapid expansion of the works to experiment with and develop rotary power was imminent.

Completion of the first engine yard, 1781–9

By July 1781, a model of a crank, the never-to-be-adopted 'ecliptic' or 'swash-plate', had been attached to the 'little engine', Soho's original pumping engine removed from water-pumping duties in 1777.[11] The model and engine may, at this time, have been located in a small workshop attached to

'Shops belonging to Engine Co.'	sq ft
Little forgery Shop by Clock Shop	70
Clock Shop	203
Shop adjoining Webbs	217
Shop over Webbs	217
Thorntons Burnishing Shop	217
Bradburys Color Shop	170.5
Bradburys finishing shop	224.75
Bingleys Shop	457
E Creeds Shop now Roberts	224.75
Halls drtawing room now Mr B[oulton]	240
Hemmings Shop	320
Engine forgery shop	1144.5
Solomons Temple	592
Moors press Shop	195.75
Moors Stamping Shop	195.75
Moors Die Shop	73.5
Bradburys gilding Shop b[e]low	141.5
Bradburys Stair hole	18
Carless Shop	209
Ryleys Casting Shop	276.75
	5408

Source: LoB, MS3782/13/126

Fig 4.1
List of rooms occupied by Boulton & Watt, 1787. Most of the rooms listed at this time were occupied by James Watt and Co., letter copying.

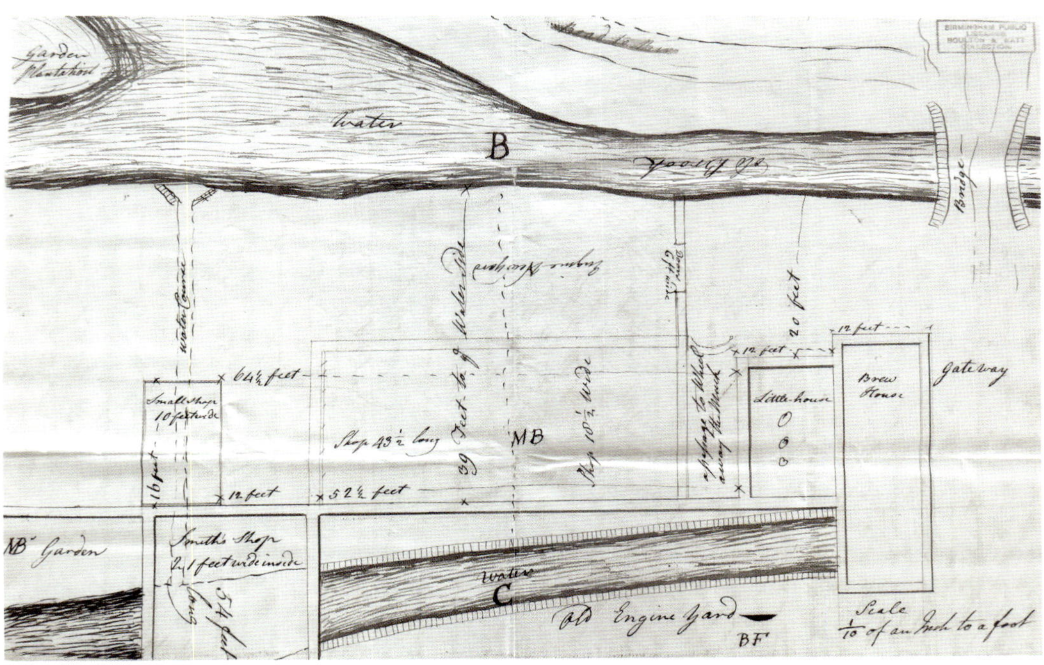

Fig 4.2
Matthew Boulton's plan for the proposed fitting-up shop, 1781. This was to be located between the Hockley Brook at the top of the plan and the mill tail-race water flowing towards and under the Boulton & Watt forging shop of 1775 ('smith's shop').

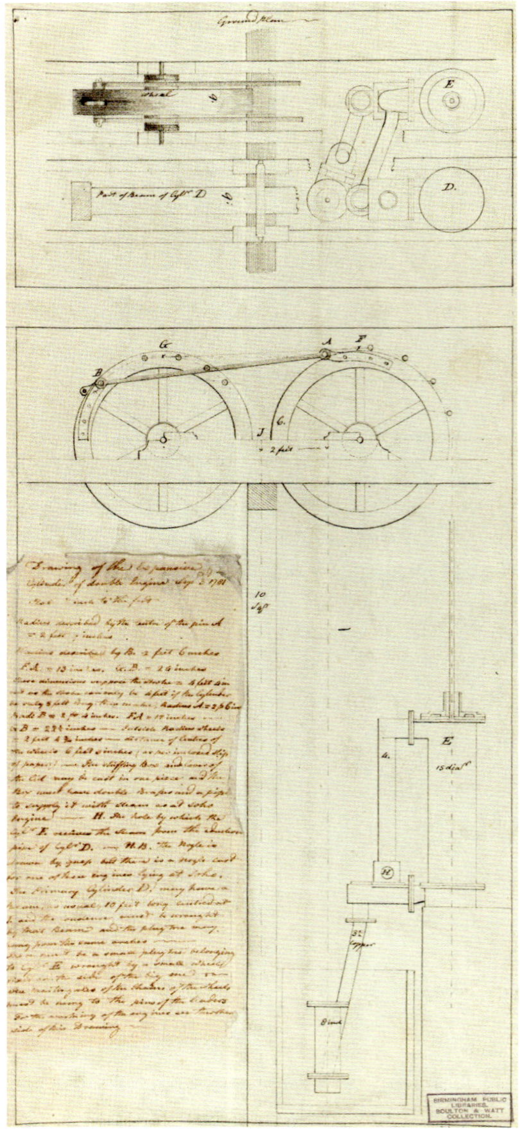

Fig 4.3
Plan and elevation of the two-cylinder compound engine, 3 September 1781.

the west end of the forge and marked on a plan dating from 1781.[12] Here, the engine would have been close to the mill tail race and the supply of water necessary for its operation. This site was later chosen for the main engine house. The plan in question (Fig 4.2), being in Boulton's own hand, is of a type that has rarely survived for Soho, doubly so as it also shows a proposed extension to the works: a building intended 'to fit up Little Engines'. The site lay within his private garden, but he intended to donate the land to the Boulton & Watt Company. The new fitting-up shop enclosed the west side of the engine yard, sandwiched between the open channel of the mill tail race, now within the yard, and the Hockley Brook on the outside. By 27 September, the foundations had been dug by Mr Thomas Elvin who had been engaged to complete the work on his estimated sum of £131 10s 0d.[13] It was actually to cost less than £100.[14] On 30 October, Boulton reported: 'Our new shop is built up to the Wall plate but we wait for the Roof. The double devil with all its Nossells condenser etc is ready to erect as soon as the Shop is tyled'.[15] The 'double devil' was a curious two-cylinder 15in (381mm) compound engine of which Watt sent a drawing from Cornwall to Soho in September 1781 (Fig 4.3).[16] It was arranged by Boulton to be worked either as a compound engine or as two independent engines and was placed at the southern end of the new shop where a boiler chimney could be conveniently erected against the gable. This shop, together with the forge, or smiths shop, erected in 1775, was transferred by Boulton to the Boulton & Watt books so that 'we can all be Cocks of our own dunghill'.[17]

This corner of the Soho Manufactory now became the test bed for two major interlinked advances in steam-engine technology: the double-acting engine and rotative power. The circumstances were not, on the face of it, favourable, as Boulton was immersed in the fractious break-up of his partnership with Fothergill, and Watt was far away in Cornwall supervising the erection of engines. Their absences may explain why the forging shop was bedevilled by drunkenness at this time.[18] Boulton implored Watt to return from Cornwall to test the two 'small engines', i.e. the compound 15in (381mm).[19] Under these circumstances, it is hardly surprising that this engine was not put to work until November, some months after the sun-and-planet gear had been developed. By this time, construction of a house for an entirely new 18in (457mm)-cylinder engine was under way: 'The foundation ... is laid. It is 29ft long and 18 feet broad'.[20] This was an extension to the newly built fitting shop, which contained the compound engine ('Double Engine') and connected the latter shop to the original 1775 forge, but projecting a little way southwards from the forge (Fig 4.4). On this – one of the rare occasions that James Watt involved himself in the design of the firm's buildings – he was eventually overruled by Boulton. Watt ordered 'the walls to be raised 11 feet above ground'. John Buchanan (the Boulton & Watt clerk) complained to Boulton, insisting that the walls should be the same height as the shop adjoining, which contained the compound engine. By 13 November, the matter had been settled in Buchanan's favour through the intervention of John Scale.[21]

On 11 November, John Scale, no technical

man, witnessed the sun-and-planet in operation attached to one of the cylinders of the compound engine; he saw 'the Engine turn a wheel with a steady, regular motion by I don't what you call it, say one wheel running round the other without turning itself' and noted that 'a small tilt and a pair of rolls are intended to be added'.[22] On 13 November, John Buchanan also reported on experiments on the 'Second Engine', presumably the other half of the compound engine, which had been connected to a pump. In the meantime, the boiler for the adjacent new engine house had been installed and the flue was under construction. Contemporary drawings of this building show that the flue was intended to share the chimney already built for the compound engine next door (Fig 4.5).[23] On 13 November, John Hodges, a manager of the plated-ware department, had seen the engine at work and was sufficiently impressed by its performance to suggest that one could be applied in the mill to the rolling of metal for the plated trade.[24] On 26 November, the engine was set to work both a forge hammer and the pump mentioned above, but the hammer helve (oscillating shaft) broke.[25] By 28 November, 'Engine No 2' was again operating and Watt was well pleased with its performance.[26] It is probable that 'Engine No 2' was part of the compound engine as Watt summarised in a letter to Boulton: 'I wrote to you last post of the trial of the hammer ... The present facts are, cylinder 15 inches diameter, and 4 feet stroke'.[27] A drawing of the tilt hammer and pump arrangement survives but is inexplicably dated 8 August 1781, half a year before the sun-and-planet motion illustrated was invented. Dickinson and Jenkins suggested that it was dated a year too early in error and this makes sense in view of the letter evidence. Within a short time, the compound engine was apparently divided into two and each part sold separately.[28]

The house for the 18in (457mm)-cylinder 'up-and-down' engine was probably completed early in 1783. The main purpose of the engine, the first double-acting rotary at Soho, was to test corn-milling machinery, of great potential in the application of rotary power.[29] The other intended use of the new engine, metal-rolling, had also been suggested in late 1782, and John Hodges, manager of the plated business, pleaded with Boulton to apply it at Soho for their 'own Rolling'.[30] The experiments successfully carried out in this part of the engine manufactory led directly to the establishment of the first commercial corn mills powered by Boulton & Watt engines: Chester Corn Mill (January 1786) and Albion Mill, at Blackfriars Bridge in London (March 1786).[31] Steam engines producing rotary power had already been put to use on a commercial basis for the first time on Snow Hill and on Water Street in Birmingham. In about 1780 partners James Pickard established a corn mill and Charles Twigg a metal rolling and gun barrel boring mill.[32] In May or June 1783, the engine was being tested but with no machinery attached (Fig 4.6).[33] The corn-mill machinery was completed in September, although to Watt's exasperation 'they [the millwrights] have multiplied wheels upon wheels until it has now almost as many as an orrery'.[34] On 30 September, an inventory recorded that the engine and corn mill cost £381 1s 10½d, while the first forge engine next door had probably already been dismantled leaving only 'Materials of Engine ..., in Old Engine house valued at £15'. The whole of the Boulton & and Watt inventory was assessed at £1,417 19s 6d.[35] From September to October 1783, however, experiments were being carried out upon a 'forge' engine that was valued at £190 for insurance purposes.[36] It is not certain which engine was powering the forge at this time. To complicate matters, as well as the recently erected 18in (457mm)-cylinder engine and the old compound engine, a new 12in (304mm) sliding-valve engine came into use at this time.[37]

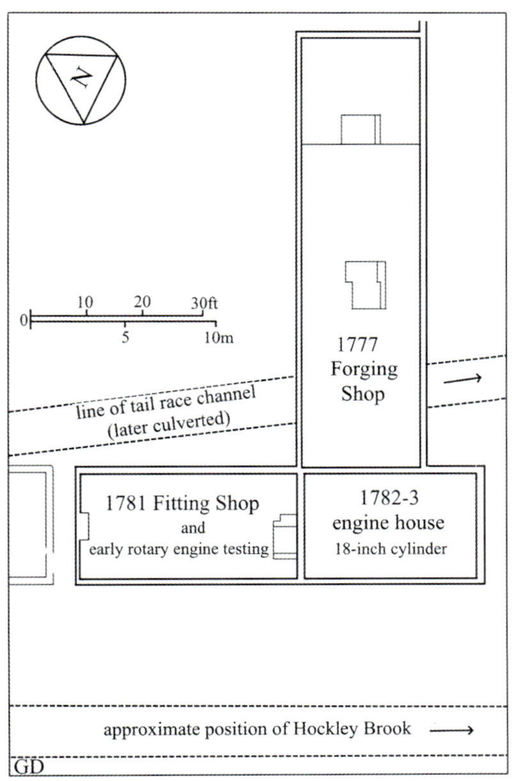

Fig 4.4
Sketch plan of the Boulton & Watt forge and fitting shop, eventually connected by an engine house in 1782–3.

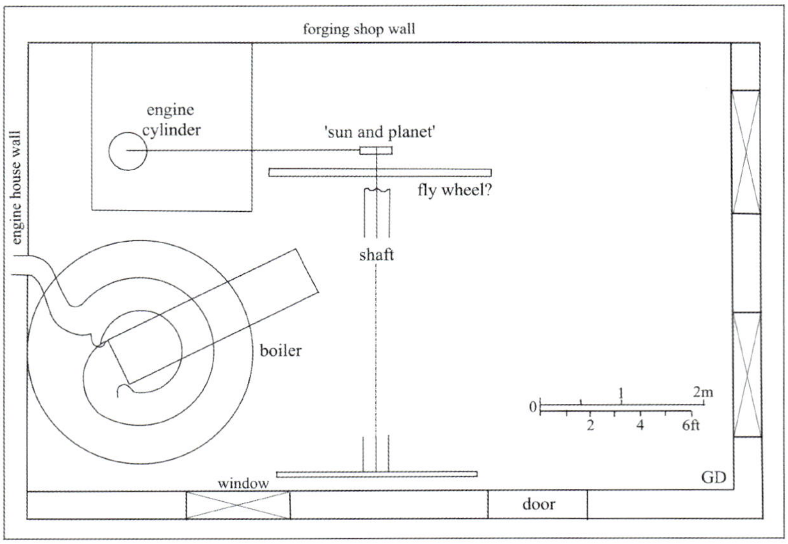

Fig 4.5
Redrawing of the plan of the 18in-cylinder engine house, October 1782.

The whole of the works, buildings, engines and tools were valued at £850 for this insurance, less than the figure quoted above (£1,417 19s 6d) for the firm's own inventory of machinery and equipment of 1783.[38]

On 9 October 1783, experiments were being conducted on both the forge engine and the corn-mill engine. Buchanan hoped to grind corn for customers as soon as these could be found.[39] Five months later, in March 1784, Boulton proudly boasted that 'This Mill ... Grinds Corn for all our Neighbourhood'.[40] It turned one set of 4ft (1219mm) stones making 120 revolutions per minute and grinding 9 bushels (about 327 litres) of wheat an hour. A drawing of the mill machinery at Chester [1785] gives an idea of the appearance of such an installation (Fig 4.7). The Soho 18in (457mm) engine was also connected to a boring machine for pumps, probably located in the original forging shop immediately to the east. All was not at once successful in the milling business, as a baker in Wednesbury in debt to the mill for £40 disappeared to the United States. Buchanan was, however, pleased that their Soho miller, Joseph Boulcott, was a good worker.[41]

The 1783 inventory mentioned above is part of an annual series stretching to 1793.[42] Fortunately, from 1785 the contents are arranged by individual room and it has been possible to identify (with the help of other evidence), first, the location of most of the rooms and workshops in any one year and, second, the manner in which an important expansion phase of the engine

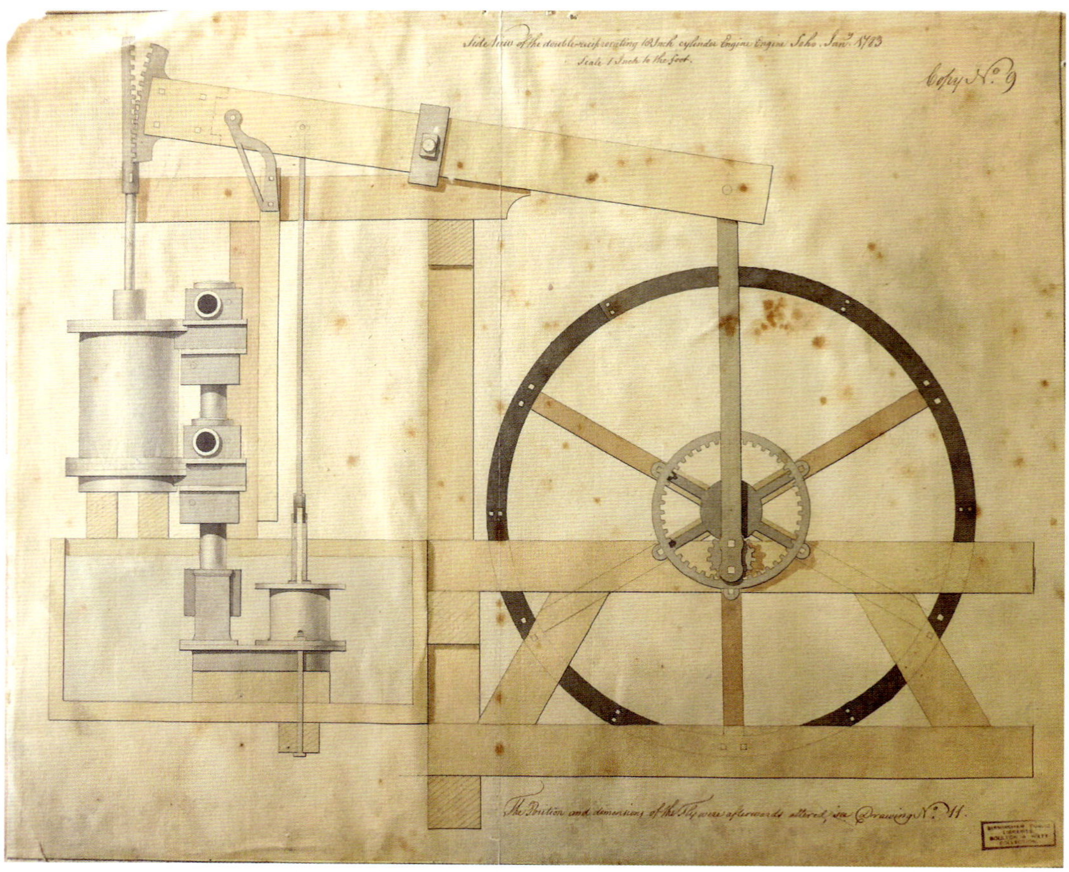

Fig 4.6
Elevation of the double-action 18in-cylinder engine, January 1783.

Fig 4.7
Elevation of the corn-milling machinery at Chester [1785]. At Soho the layout also worked a dressing machine to sort the flour into four grades and another machine that cleaned the wheat before it was ground.

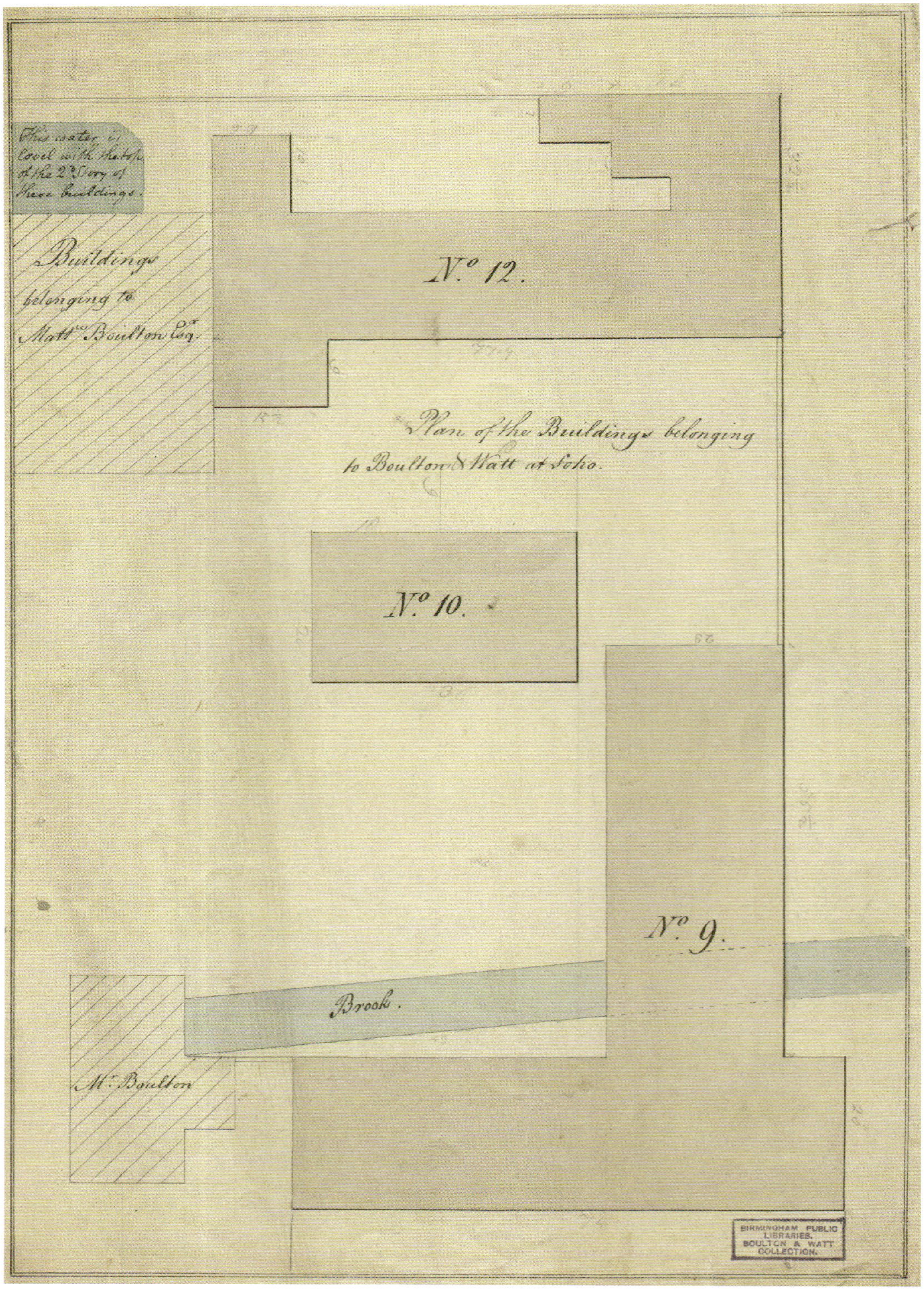

Fig 4.8
Plan of Boulton & Watt engine works, c 1783–5. Building no 12 was occupied by the copying-machine workshops. Building no 9 corresponds with the plan in Fig 4.4.

works was carried out between 1790 and 1792. Two plans form part of the supporting evidence: the first is undated, but was probably made between 1783 and 1785, and the second is part of one dated June 1788[43] (Fig 4.8, *see* Fig 2.14). The *c* 1783–5 plan shows the corn-mill engine house, which was completed in early 1783, a building in the centre of the yard, identified as the 'Temple', used as a store. On the Great Bank, the long block of workshops of the copying-machine company

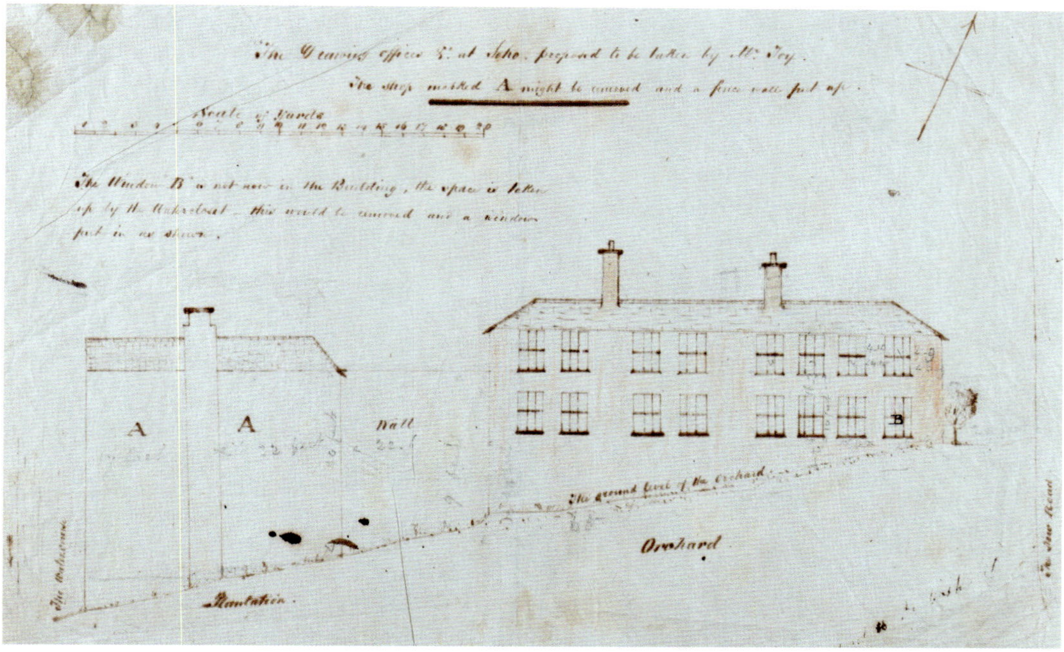

Fig 4.9
Elevation of the drawing office, c 1850.

had buildings attached to the single-storey side facing the top of the bank. On the 1788 plan, however, only one small building, lit by a skylight, is to be seen connected to the top side of the Great Bank buildings. Two years later, the drawing office was constructed on this site, with windows overlooking the Soho lower pool, the relatively new (*c* 1774) upper Hockley pool, to the south. By 1788, the old forging shop had been lengthened eastwards from about 16.7m (55ft) to 22.5m (74ft) and the 'Temple' altered from a rectangular plan to an L plan. The inventories taken between 1785 and 1788 record no new rooms being added during this time, only changes of name, and it could, therefore, be concluded that the forging shop was extended between 1783 and 1785. Cartwright's turning shop, later Samuel Carter's forge (1788), is mentioned for the first time in 1785 and may have occupied this new space. It is interesting that the intriguingly named 'Temple' became 'Solomon's Temple' in 1785 and housed, at least until 1788, the 'Little Engine' (Soho's original 18in [457mm] pumping engine), perhaps for experimental purposes in the extension.

In 1787, a list of 'Engine Co Shops' was compiled; they measured 5,408 sq ft (502.4 sq m) in all (*see* Fig 4.2).[44] In fact, most of the workshops were not used by the engine works of Boulton & Watt but assigned to the copying-machine company of James Watt & Company. The latter occupied much of the Great Bank building, which formed the east range of the engine yard.

Expansion and rationalisation, 1790–2

In the 1790 inventory, dated 30 September, the premises listed differ significantly from those on the previous year's list, reflecting a season of major extensions and alterations.[45] A new drawing office had become a necessity as both the volume of work and the consequent need for plan storage expanded. The only elevation of the drawing office, dating from as late as the 1850s, shows that it was a two-storey structure constructed at right angles to the Great Bank shops at their southern end (Fig 4.9).[46] The lower storey may have accommodated the 'Boulton & Watt' room, mentioned for the first time, and the room for the new clerk, Mr Forman. A newly constructed shop lay empty, but it is clear from the following year's (1791) inventory that it was to be a forge under the charge of Ben Seager. It had been built on the south side of the main engine house, extending down the peninsula dividing the Hockley Brook and the mill tail race. The stores in 'Solomon's Temple' had been divided into an iron and brass 'temple'. A casting shop had been erected with a shop above on the west side of the yard, with a passage separating it from the old fitting shop. This upper storey had also been extended southwards over the fitting shop and was used mainly to hold completed engine parts. In the 1791 inventory, the drawing office was listed as John Southern's, who for many years to come was to supervise its work.

He was also to become one of the firm's principal engineers and helped design the pneumatic version of the coining presses at the Soho Mint in 1797–8 (*see* pp 100–9). Certain rooms cannot be located with any certainty, but by a process of elimination could be found in either part of the Great Bank range or at the end of Ben Seager's new forge. At least two carpenters shops were run by John Smith, and his name is marked on a plan of *c* 1800 within the Great Bank workshops.[47]

In 1797, a carpenters shop is described as being over Seager's, implying that it was at this time in the two-storey end of Seager's range, which was in existence by at least 1796 (*see* Figs 2.16 and 2.17).[48] The *c* 1800 plan just mentioned has the note 'wood shed' at this position. In the summer of 1795, James Watt's copying-machine company expanded its premises and installed the 'little engine', which had undergone a major overhaul.[49] It is possible that this phase of work forced part of the carpenters premises to be located above and at the end of Seager's forge. On 30 September, the builder, Glover, was paid £91 4s 3d 'for New Buildings', which may relate to this work.[50]

By this time the ambitious scheme to build a separate engine manufactory in Smethwick was well under way (the Soho Foundry, Chapter 7). From now on the firm of Boulton & Watt could produce all their engine parts, including, most importantly, the cylinder, and deliver a complete engine to their customers. Annual figures for the production of engines during the years 1786–7 to 1796–7 reflect the original arrangement under which a licence was granted to the customer to build and use an engine, with a few specialist parts supplied from the Manufactory. The yearly totals ranged from 9 in 1794–5 to 30 in 1795–6 and again in 1796–7 (Fig 4.10).[51] In the following year, 1797–8, production of presumably complete engines is recorded at the Foundry for the first time, 10 out of total of 25. From 1797 to 1798, both the Soho sites shared in the assembly of engines, with the Manufactory the modest leader until 1801–2. The years 1802 to 1804 witnessed the most extensive single phase of building at the Soho Engine Manufactory in order to meet increasing demand and to match the casting output of the Foundry with sufficient small, mostly forged, engine parts. The manner in which engine production

Fig 4.10
Steam engine production at the Soho Manufactory and Foundry, 1786–7 to 1804–5.

Year	Total	Manufactory	Foundry	
1786–7	16	16	-	
1787–8	10	10	-	
1788–89	12	12	-	
1789–90	14	14	-	
1790–1	15	15	-	
1791–2	26	26	-	
1792–3	23	23	-	
1793–4	17	17	-	
1794–5	9	9	-	
1795–6	30	30	-	
1796–7	30	30	-	
1797–8	25	15	10	4 increased in power
1798–9	34	19	15	4 increased in power
1799–1800	41	23	18	2 altered
1801–2	52	23	29	
1802–3	48	19	29	
1803–4	41	15	26	
1804–5	32	10	22	

Source: LoB, MS3219/6/127-8, 133

Fig 4.11
Detail of watercolour by John Phillp, showing a steam engine being hauled across Birmingham Heath towards the Manufactory, 1796. The Lower Hockley Pool can be seen in the middle distance.

was divided between the Manufactory and Foundry is not yet fully understood and is beyond the scope of this book. Little attention has been paid to this important relationship and it deserves a separate definitive study. The Manufactory could not assemble complete engines unless the cylinder was delivered overland from the Foundry. A Phillp watercolour, dated 1796, shows six horses hauling a cart loaded with a single engine cylinder (Fig 4.11) towards the Manufactory in the distance. Other castings apart from the cylinders were also heavy, especially the cast iron beams that replaced their timber equivalents around 1800. Smaller engine parts were much easier to move between the two sites.

The new engine yard, 1800–4

The construction of the new engine yard represented the largest single phase of expansion of the engine works at the Manufactory. It also heralded a new era in the organisation of the firm with the arrival of a new generation, Matthew Robinson Boulton, James Watt Jr, and a gifted engineer who was then only slowly emerging into the limelight: William Murdoch. The new firm of Boulton Watt and Sons was formed on 1 October 1794, with Boulton and his son, Matthew Robinson, and Watt and his two sons, James and Gregory, as the partners. In 1799, James Watt Sr finally retired, not unwillingly since he had gradually withdrawn over the years from active involvement in the firm. He relinquished his financial share to his two sons and on 1 October 1799 the firm of Boulton, Watt and Company, Soho, was formed.[52]

Almost immediately, Matthew Robinson Boulton set about rebuilding and extending the engine works across the Hockley Brook into Birmingham parish. The Handsworth Manufactory had been his father's creation and it seemed logical for further proposals and alterations here to fall upon his heir. Moreover, James Watt Jr had already taken a leading role in the establishment of the Foundry independently of his father. This phase of building at the Manufactory is blessed, first, with the unusual survival of several large-scale plans, none of which have been published or apparently even studied before, and, second, remarkable and detailed documentation of the planning and execution of the building scheme. The latter material was introduced by Dickinson and Jenkins to a wider audience in 1927 and then extensively analysed by Roll in 1930.[53]

The pre-war Boulton and Watt scholars did not attempt to identify the author of the documents. Griffiths has recently attributed them to James Watt Jr, but the distinctive handwriting is clearly that of Matthew Robinson Boulton.[54] Roll carried out his researches without reference

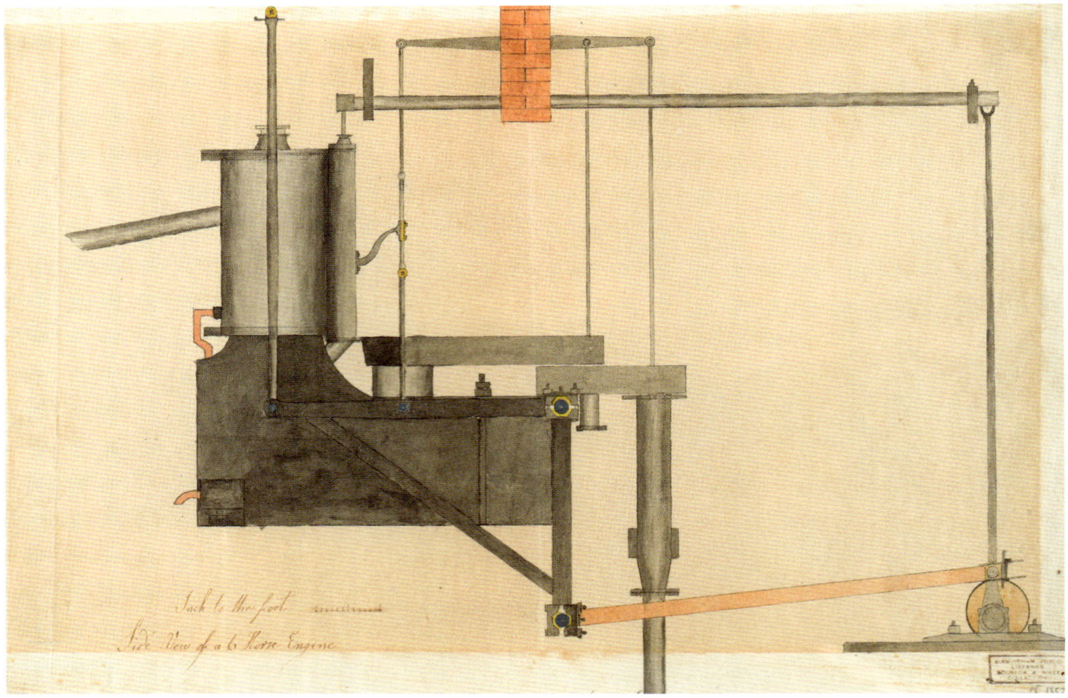

Fig 4.12
Water-coloured elevation of 6hp bell-crank engine by William Murdoch, c 1803.

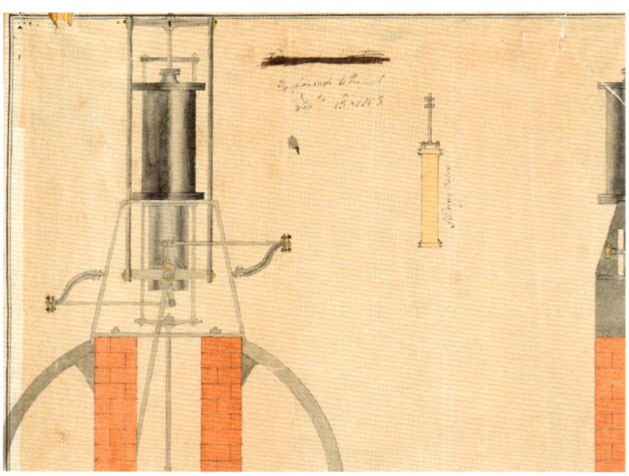

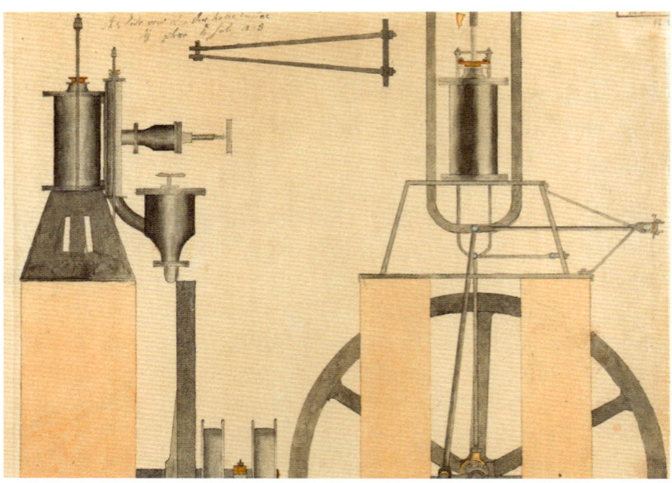

Fig 4.13
Water-coloured elevations by William Murdoch of the 3hp small engine for the great lathe, 13 September 1803.

Fig 4.14
Water-coloured elevations by William Murdoch of the 1hp small engine for the piston-rod lathe, 4 July 1803.

to any mapping, even though the group of Manufactory engine works plans mentioned above was available at the time. Indeed, he asserted that the earliest plan of Soho dated from nearly 50 years after the documents were written and that it was 'impossible to compare the arrangement of the shops on the actual site with the positions ... stipulated'.[55] Although there are still many uncertainties, the documents and plans do permit a broad reconstruction of both Matthew Robinson Boulton's intentions and the actual layout of the engine works achieved.

In December 1801, Matthew Robinson Boulton evaluated the cost of various combinations of the steam engines required at the Manufactory.[56] The choice was between one, two or three engines, all three options costing just over £1,000. In the following year, Matthew Robinson Boulton selected a combination of three engines of 6, 4 and 3hp. This decision was significant, as engines of such a small size were frowned upon by the Soho establishment, particularly by James Watt and John Southern.[57] The small engines, beamless and with slide valves, were conceived and designed by William Murdoch. He had only recently returned to Soho after many years away in Cornwall, and found Matthew Robinson Boulton and James Watt Jr seemingly receptive to his ideas. There are watercolour drawings of little engines by

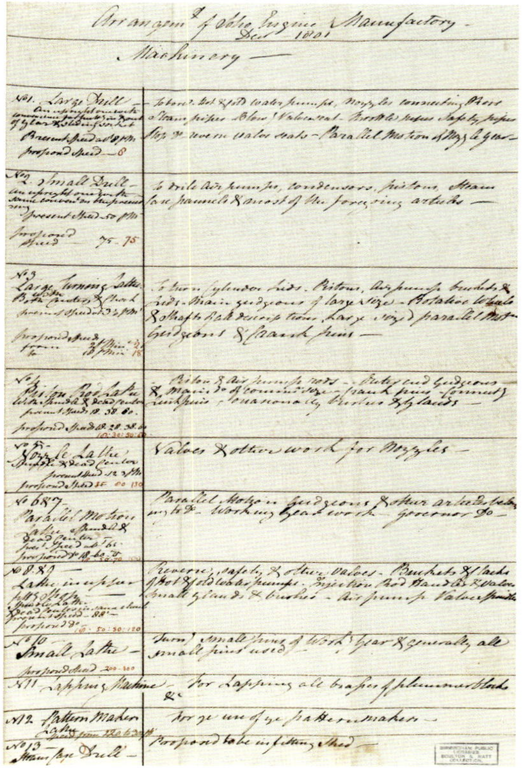

Murdoch himself in the Boulton & Watt collection, which are identifiably those installed at the Manufactory in this period (Figs 4.12–4.14).[58]

The most important document is entitled 'Arrangement of Engine Manufactory Soho ... December 1801' (Fig 4.15).[59] Divided into two parts, it first lists all the machinery, both old and new, with the function of each piece. The second part gives a list of workshops, some to be erected, others to be rebuilt, together with their machinery, the operations undertaken in each and, as Roll recognised, 'most important of all, their relative situation and communications'.[60] Griffiths confused the shops listed in this document with the Soho Foundry premises. As a result, he unintentionally described components being brought out of the Soho engine manufactory in Handsworth and being instantly transported onto the canal at the Foundry one mile away.[61] To add to this confusion, he mistakenly placed the three little engines in question at the Foundry.

The arrangement of workshops proposed by Matthew Robinson Boulton has been mapped in Fig 4.16 and subsequent documents confirm

Fig 4.15a
Matthew Robinson Boulton's table listing the machinery required for the new engine works, December 1801.

Fig 4.15b
Matthew Robinson Boulton's table setting out the arrangement of workshops and machinery for the new engine works, December 1801.

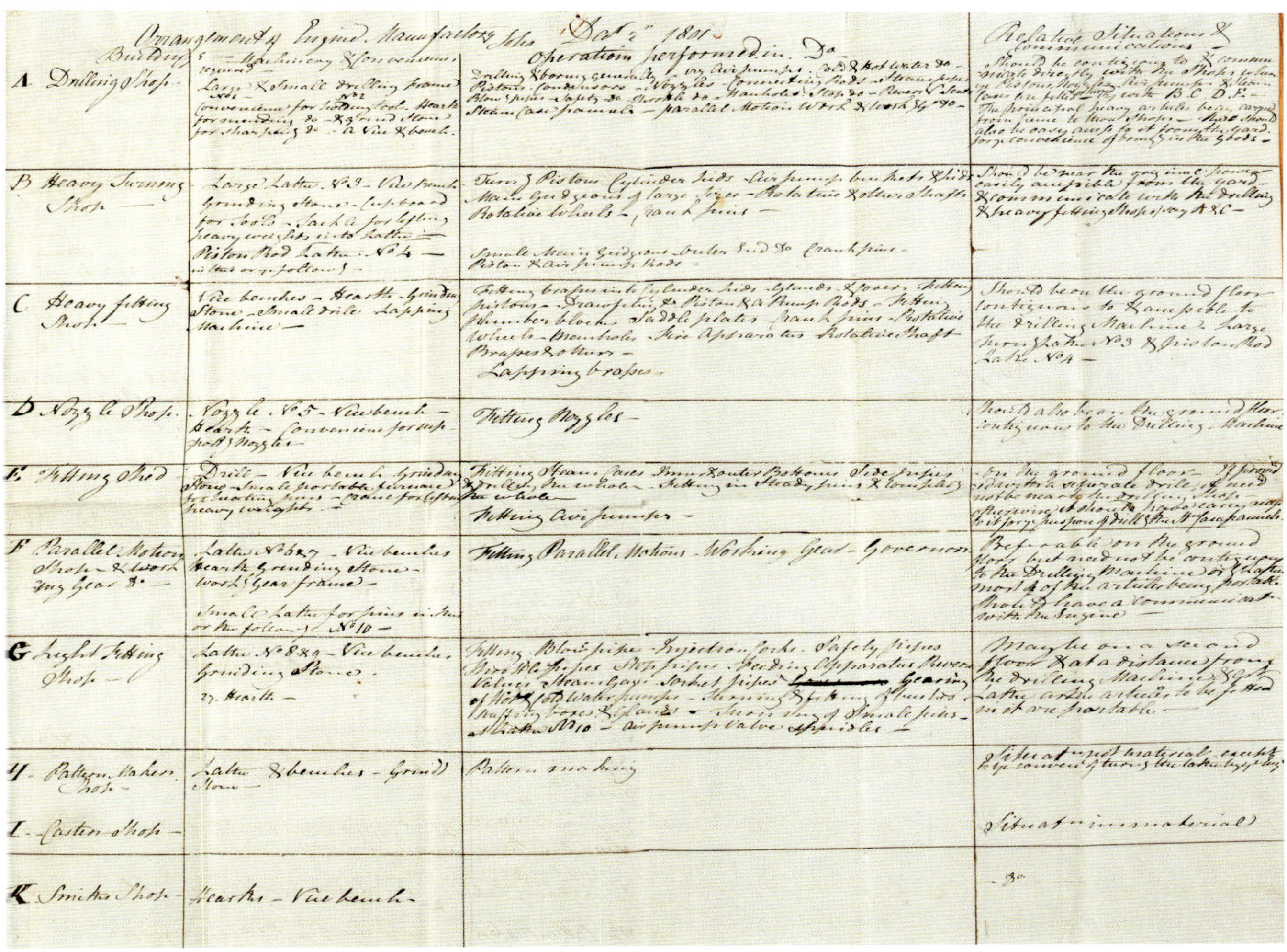

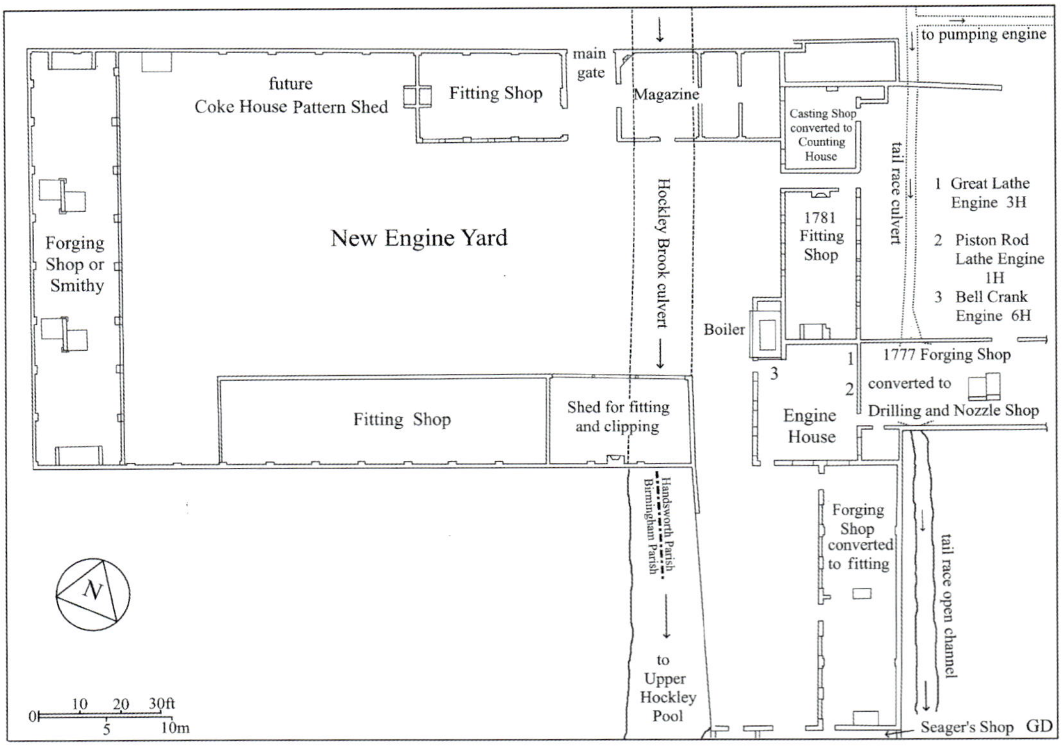

Fig 4.16
Plan of the new engine works at the Manufactory, 1802–4. For the first time buildings are erected beyond the Hockley Brook in Birmingham Parish.

that it was executed more or less as described. Two large-scale plans of part of the engine manufactory show the layout of buildings and machinery in and around the engine house before the construction works commenced in 1802 (Figs 4.17 and 4.18).[62] The engine house contained one beam engine with a cylinder of approximately 15in (381mm) diameter, indicating that the 18in (457mm) corn-mill engine, installed in 1783, had been replaced. The engine powered a complicated array of machinery including the 'Great Lathe' and the 'Piston rod Lathe' in the same room, a small and large drill, a nozzle lathe in the shop adjoining to the east (i.e. the old forge built in 1775), and a parallel-motion lathe in the room to the north (the old fitting shop of 1781) (Fig 4.19). The plan confirms that the engine house had been extended westwards in the direction of the Hockley Brook, removing the boiler to outside.

Work started in 1801:

> At Soho a great addition has been made to the Engine Establishment, by taking in a new Yard from the Common and arching over the brook in front of the old fitting shop [sketch included (Fig 4.20)]. Our intention is not to have any of the heavy casting brought into the old Yard, which will be used for smaller goods. The buildings are only one storey high and are now covering in. With this & the additions at the foundry, we expect to do double the work of last year, which amounted to exactly an Engine per week.[63]

The detailed building accounts appear in the following year, 1802.[64] Work began by clearing and levelling the area of the new yard on the west side of the Hockley brook; this was to be the first time that the Manufactory extended into Warwickshire from Staffordshire. A perimeter wall was raised and a new smithy or forge shop placed against its west side. On the south side, a long fitting shed was erected, leaving a gap between it and the engine house to allow access into the existing narrow yard that lay between the Hockley Brook and Seager's old forge. Meanwhile, this forge was stripped out and converted into the heavy fitting shop. A gate opening into the new yard was made on the north side and separated a newly built fitting shop from a store or 'magazine', the latter connected to the existing casting shop, which itself was converted into a counting house. The casting shop, in turn, was transferred to 'Solomon's Temple', which was considerably rebuilt. The drilling shop, part of the original 1775 smithy, was likewise radically altered, having its yard-side elevation and roof reconstructed and new drilling machines installed.[65] Finally, in this first season of work,

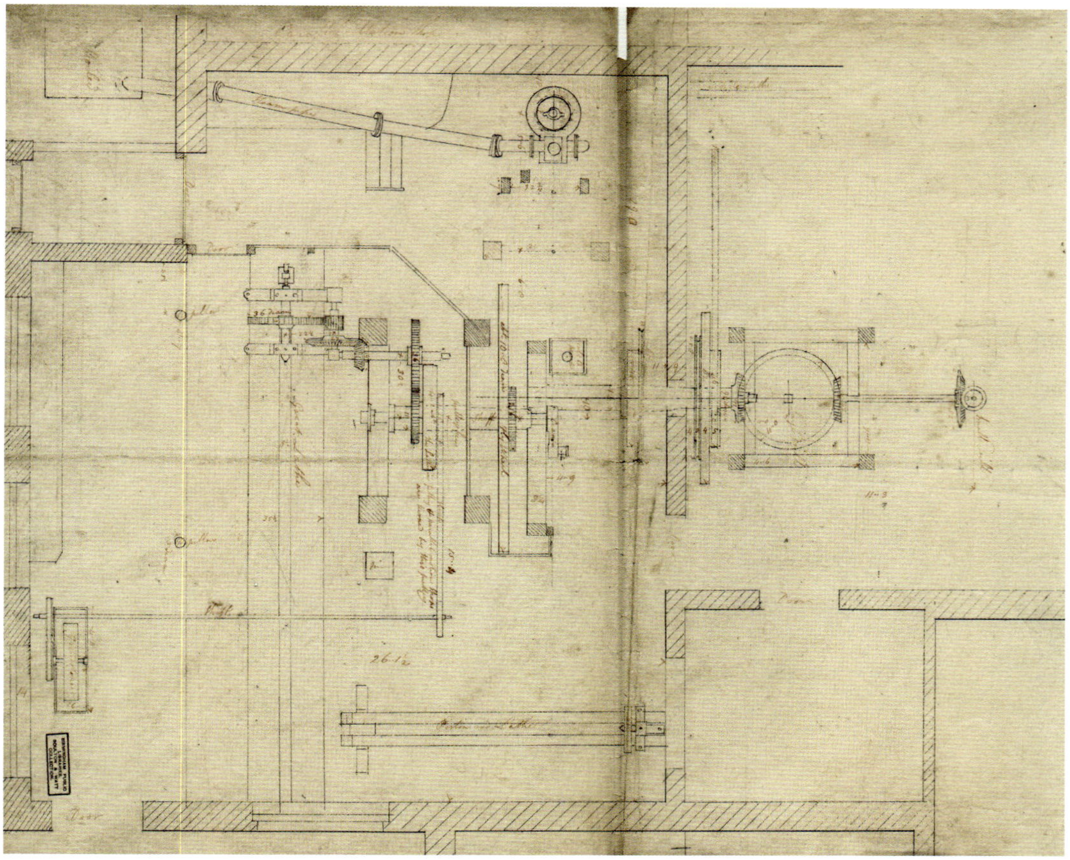

Fig 4.17
Plan of the engine house, late 1790s.

Fig 4.18
Plan of the parallel motion shop, engine house and new forging shop, late 1790s.

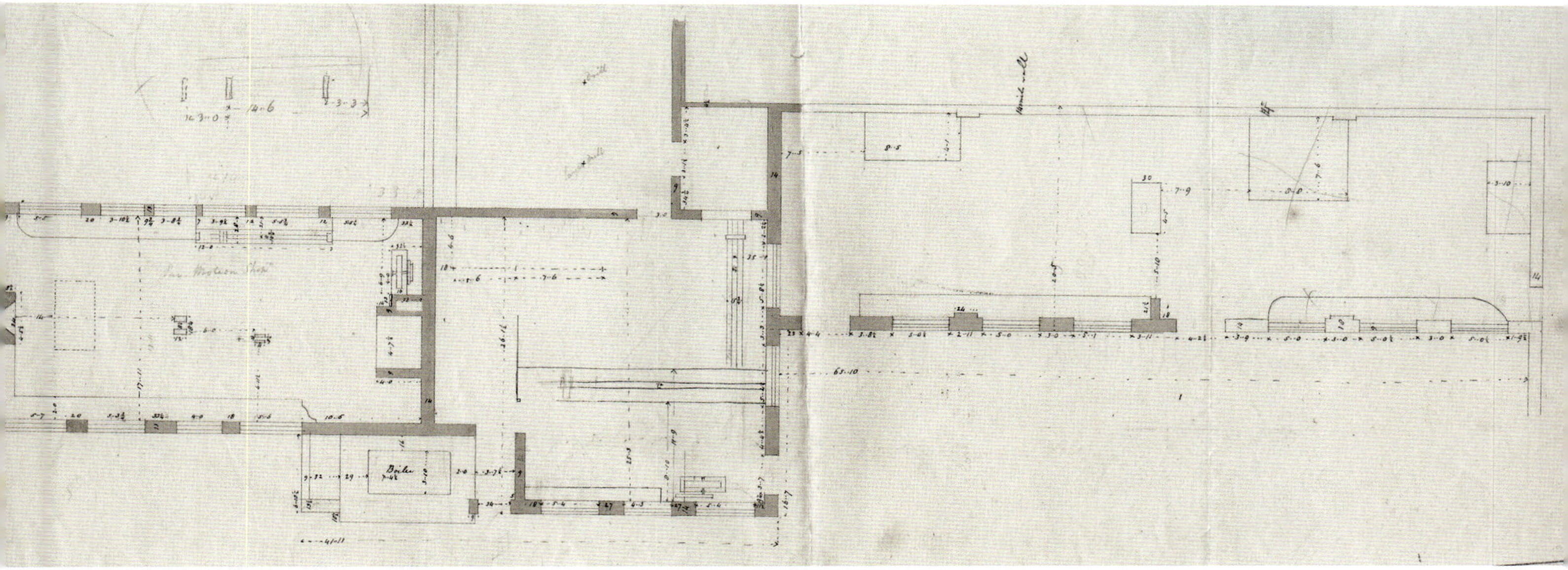

some preparations were made to the building to accept the new 6hp engine.

In October 1802, planning was well advanced for the other two engines. The 3hp engine was intended to power the great lathe, whose position in the engine house remained unaltered. The original proposal for a 4hp engine was eventually changed to a 1hp engine running the piston-rod lathe, which was moved out of the engine house into the drilling shop next door. Both of these engines were to be of the Murdoch beamless type, with cylinders mounted above and directly connected to the main shaft and fly wheel.[66] Working drawings, dating from October and November

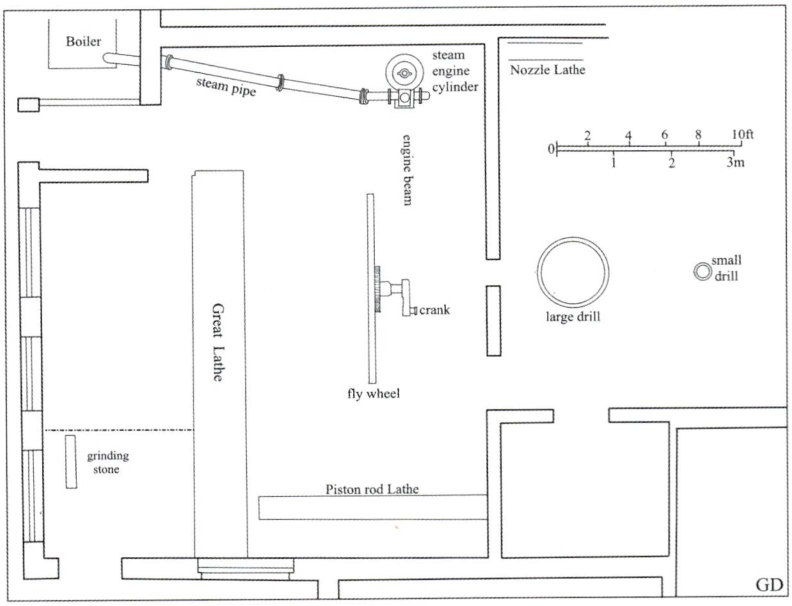

Fig 4.19
Redrawing of Fig 4.17.

1802, of the piston-rod lathe engine have survived (Fig 4.21).[67] The 6hp version was also Murdoch's design but, by contrast, was a prototype of the bell-crank engine. A working drawing, dated 19 June 1802 (Fig 4.22), does not show the cylinder nor does the latter feature in the machinery accounts under 'Engine A 6 horse' as it was called, though there is a Murdoch watercolour of this beamless engine (*see* Fig 4.12).[68] However, the cylinder, measuring 16in (406mm), was indeed manufactured, the engine altogether costing £411 14s 4d.[69] A plan dating from early 1803 shows the position of the three engines (Fig 4.23).[70] Dickinson and Jenkins believed that the bell-crank engine was not produced after 1802, but the 'Engine Book' lists well over 100 of these engines, most built by 1814 and for the West Indies sugar plantations.[71]

The majority of the building work accounted for under the 1803 accounts, made necessary to take the three engines and a new great lathe, took place in the engine house.[72] Its roof was rebuilt and the 6hp engine modified. The old engine was removed after 29 April and the great lathe and piston-rod lathe engines installed in its place.[73] The drive of the piston-rod engine passed through the engine-house wall to a new lathe, which, from this time, was located in its own room made out of a subdivision of the drilling and nozzle shop.

According to the 1804 accounts, comparatively little work was needed to complete the project. Most of the costs were absorbed in finishing off the reconstruction of the engine house and the installation of the three steam engines and great lathe. Never again was there to be such

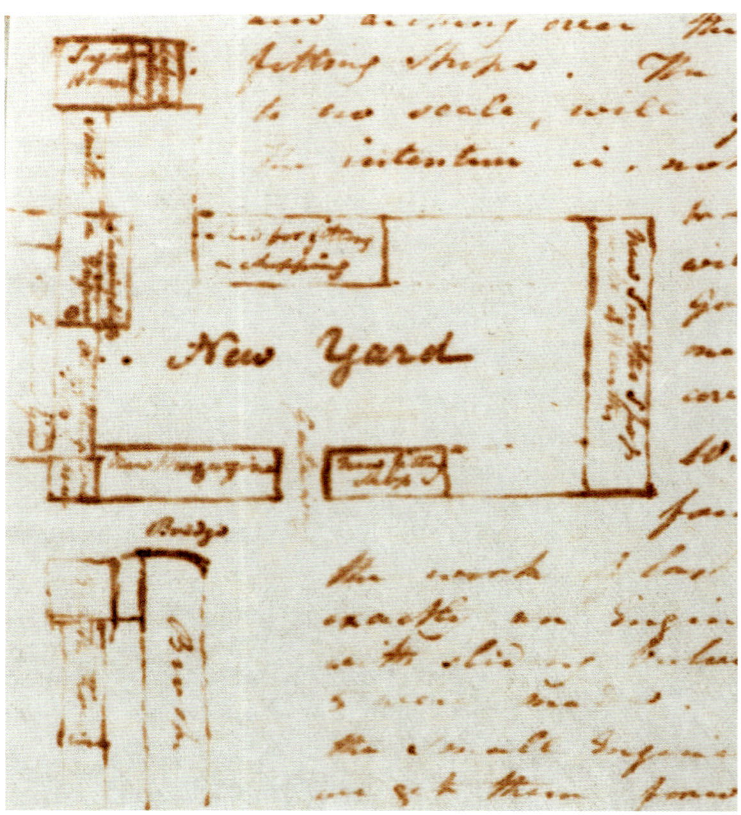

Fig 4.20
Reproduction of James Watt Jr's sketch plan of the engine works from a letter to Gregory Watt, 28 November 1801.

a large extension to the engine workshops or to any other part of the Manufactory. A plan drawn in 1811, based on an earlier plan, shows the extent of the buildings shortly after this major phase of construction was completed (Fig 4.24).[74] Building costs over the three years from 1802–4 were £2,246 18s 10½d, with the heaviest year (1802) at £1,372 15s 15½d. Machinery costs of £1,822 12s 11d peaked in 1803 at £929 15s 4d (Fig 4.25).[75]

Conversion to marine engine works, 1805–50

There are detailed building and machinery accounts for much of this period, and a number of drawings and cross sections, both limited mainly to the years before 1820 and to the area in and around the engine house, survive for the engine works.[76] Much of the building work described in the accounts is, therefore, difficult

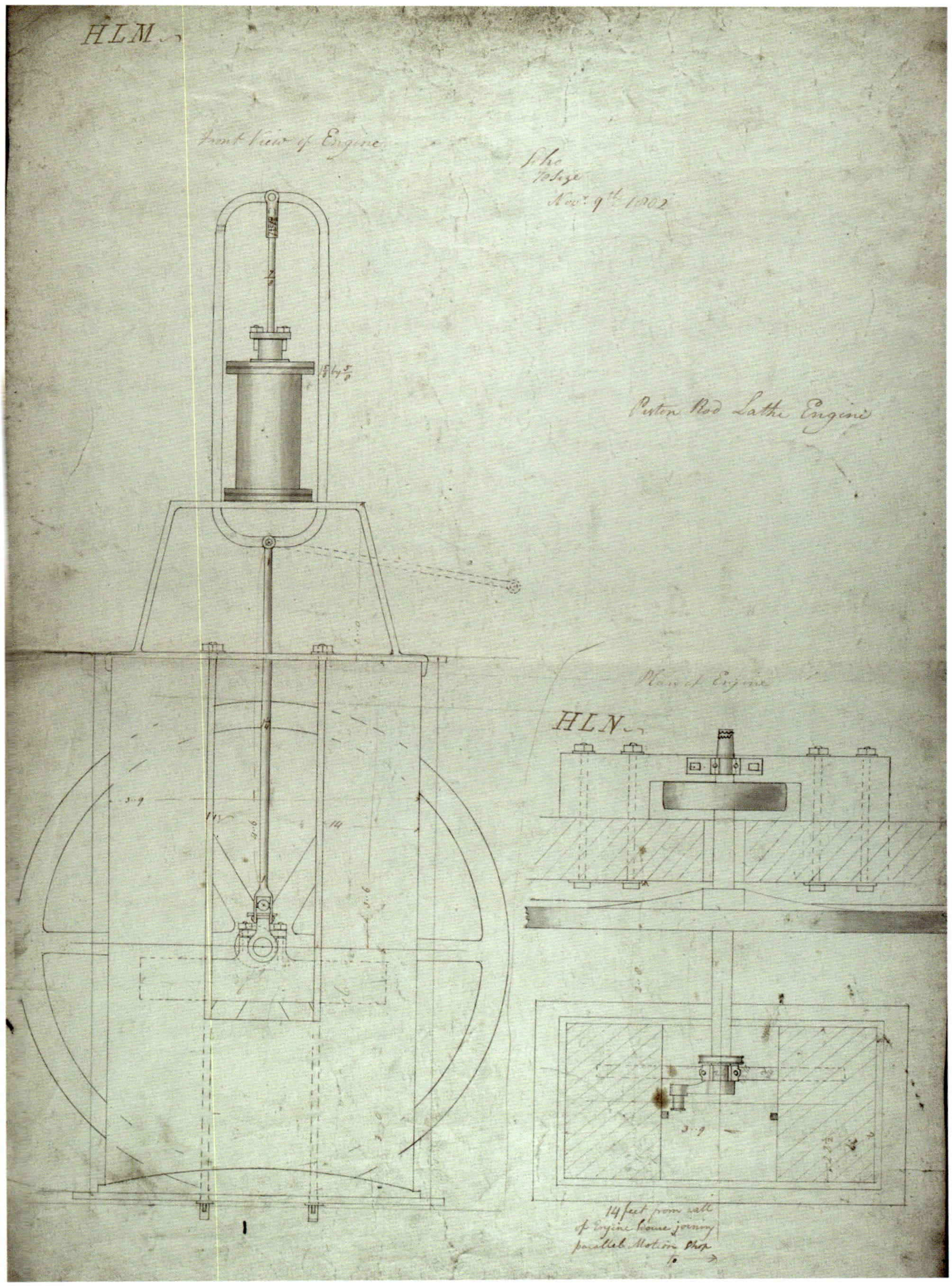

Fig 4.21
Elevation of the piston-rod lathe engine (1hp), 9 November 1802.

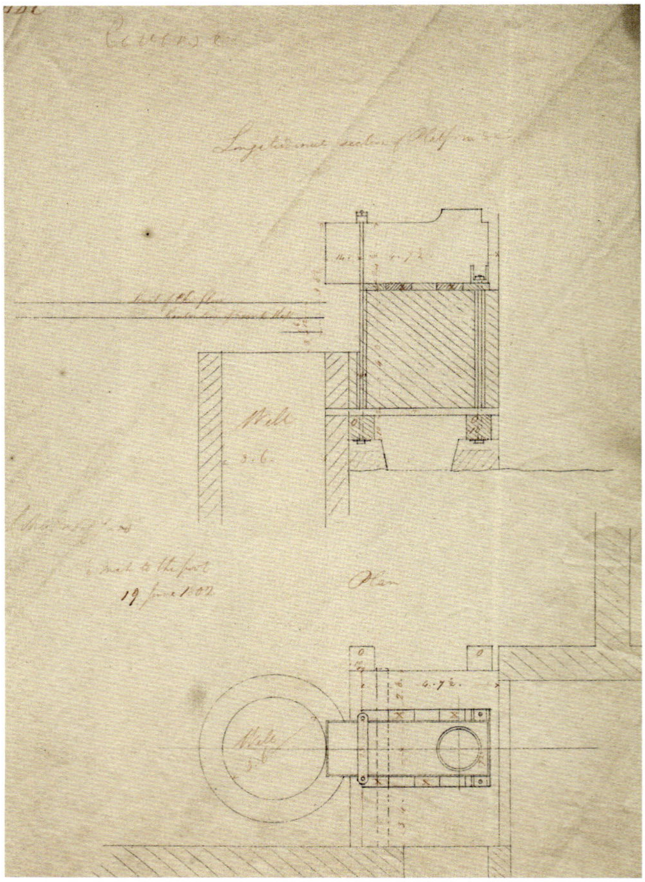

Fig 4.22
Elevation and plan of the block for the bell-crank engine cylinder (6hp), 19 June 1802 (Reverse).

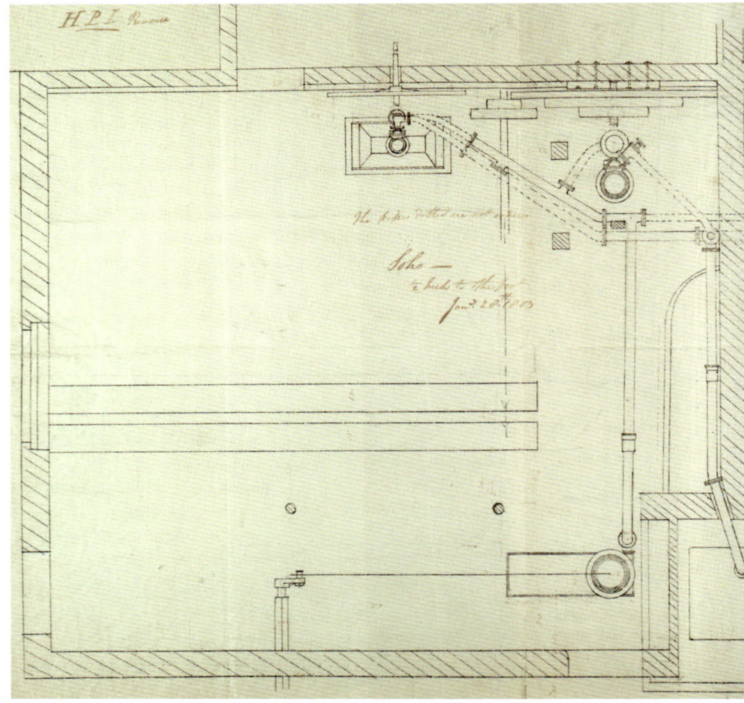

Fig 4.23
Plan of the three Murdoch small engines to be erected in the existing engine house, 28 January 1803 (Reverse).

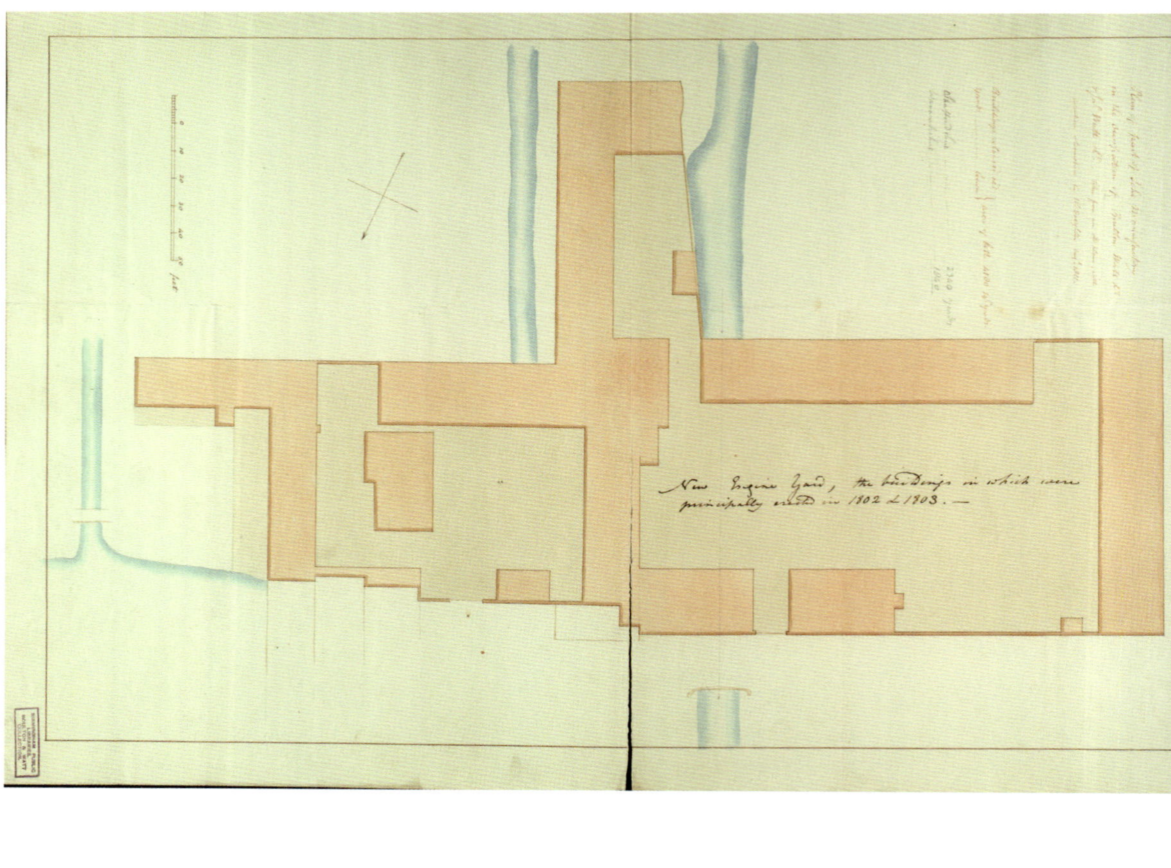

Fig 4.24
William Creighton's 1811 copy of an earlier plan of the Manufactory engine works.

Fig 4.25 Building and Machinery costs, Manufactory engine works, 1802–4.

Buildings	*1802*	*1803*	*1804*	*Total*
Fence wall	92 00 11	-	-	92 00 11
Magazine	223 04 4.5	5 03 01	-	228 07 05.5
Forge Shop	328 10 6.5	7 03 10	5 04 10.5	340 19 03
Samuel Carters Shop	-	7 15 06	11 14 08	19 10 02
Carpenters Shop	-	6 16 04	7 12 00	14 08 04
Drilling shop	194 19 09.5	35 12 01.5	20 08 09	251 00 08
Engine House & Turning Shop	-	250 08 00	115 15 05	366 03 05
Fitting Shed	139 07 11	40 06 00	-	179 13 11
Lower Fitting Shop	-	25 05 09	-	25 05 09
Shop on south side of Gates	100 14 08	-	-	100 14 08
Piston Rod Shop	-	93 18 01.5	1 18 9.5	95 16 11
Casting Shop	68 13 02	17 00 08	-	85 13 10
Privies	17 03 07	-	-	17 03 07
Yard	22 17 08	1 11 03	-	24 08 11
B & W Room and Room adjoining	-	157 10 07.5	-	157 10 7.5
Bridge	78 00 04	-	-	78 00 04
Well near Forge Shop	1 01 08	-	-	1 01 08
Gates	18 15 07	-	-	18 15 07
I Lodge & T Huttons	-	26 06 09.5		26 06 09.5
Room				
Engine A 6 horse	58 14 03	-	-	58 14 03
Passage leading to	-	12 05 07.5	-	12 05 07.5
Boultons Room				
Model Room	-	13 10 09	-	13 10 09
Engine Framing 6 horse	28 10 07	8 06 10.5	-	36 17 05.5
	£1372 15 00.5	£709 01 04	£165 02 06	£2246 18 10.5

Machinery	*1802*	*1803*	*1804*	*Total*
Great & Small Drilling Machines	224 09 08.5	32 11 9.5	-	257 01 06
Nozzle Lathe	60 18 08	21 15 5	-	82 14 01
Lying Shafts	32 06 1.5	-	-	32 06 1.5
Forge Shops	248 04 07	-	-	248 04 07
Seager and Molyneux Lapping Machine in lower fitting shop	17 05 10	-	-	17 05 10
Double Lathe in upper fitting shop	85 07 05	-	-	85 07 05
Bellows Drill Frame in Fitting shed	19 16 02	26 06 08	-	46 02 10
Great Turning Lathe	-	289 08 04.5	69 10 07.5	358 19 00
Piston Rod Lathe	-	116 08 7.5	4 01 00.5	120 09 08
Engine B [3hp]	-	190 08 09	31 07 04	221 16 01
GreatTurning Lathe engine				
Engine C [1hp] Piston	-	98 08 00	-	98 08 00
Rod Lathe Engine				
Engine A 6 horse	-	78 05 04	17 09 05	95 14 09
Grinding Stone in				
Piston Rod Shop	-	16 06 03	-	16 06 03
Drilling Shop	-	12 09 01	-	12 09 01
Upper fitting Shop	-	11 05 05	-	11 05 05
Bellows Piston Rod Shop	-	15 13 02.5	-	15 13 02.5
Apparatus for	-	12 05 03	-	12 05 03
trying nozzles				
Lower Fitting shop	-	8 03 02	-	8 03 02
Apparatus for grinding seats and bonnets of nozzles in drilling shop	-	-	10 04 09	10 04 09
Parallel Motion Lathe additions	-	-	71 15 11	71 15 11
	£688 08 04	£929 15 04	£204 09 01	£1822 12 11

Source: LoB MS3147/9/7, ff. 1-38,42,44-9,52-4,56-60,62-75,129.

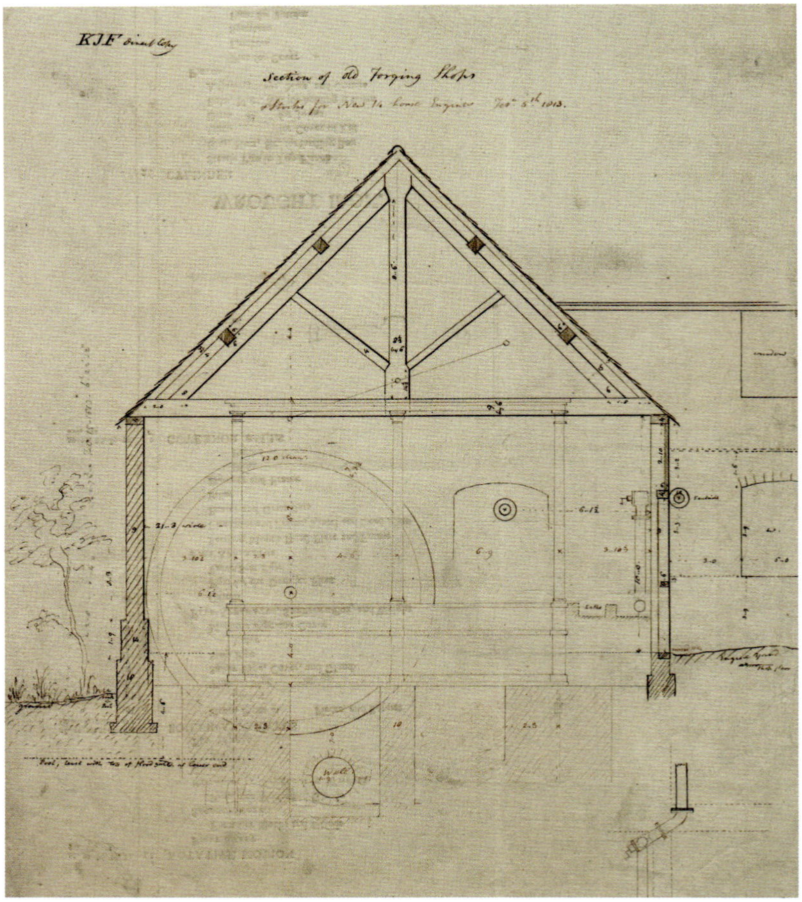

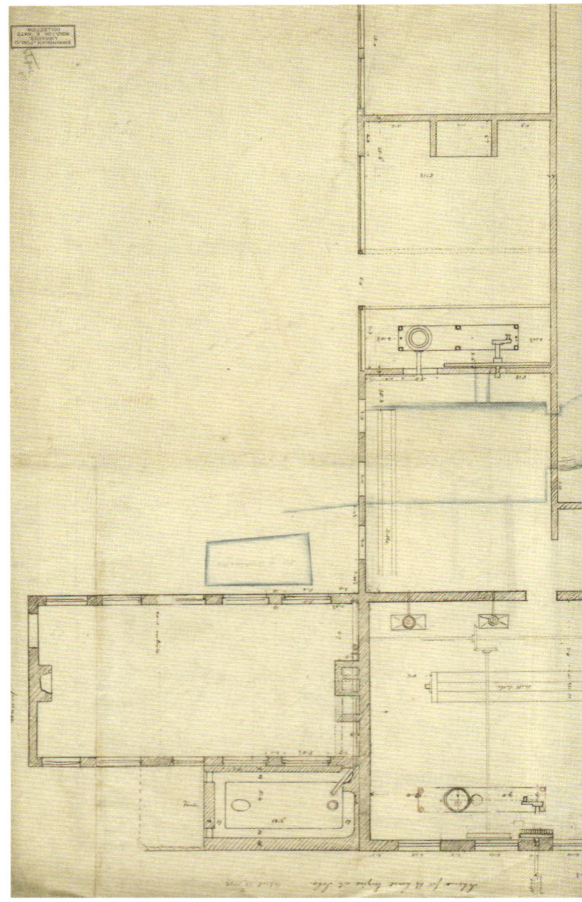

Fig 4.26
Cross section of the old forging shop (1777) showing the stocks (the cast iron columnar framework) for a new 14hp steam engine and the fly wheel, 5 February 1813.

Fig 4.27
Plan of the engine house and adjoining shops showing the stocks for testing 14hp engines erected in the old forging shop and a new 14hp engine to replace the 6hp bell-crank engine, 13 April 1813.

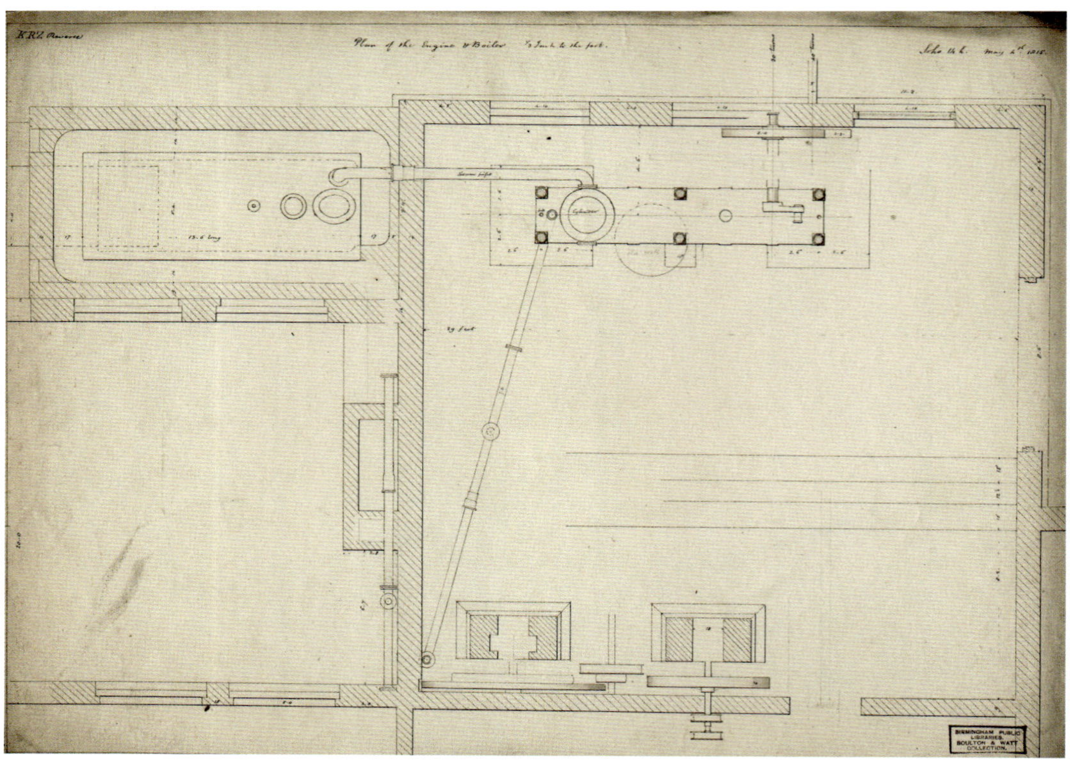

Fig 4.28
Plan of the engine house showing the new 14hp engine and boiler, 4 May 1815 (Reverse).

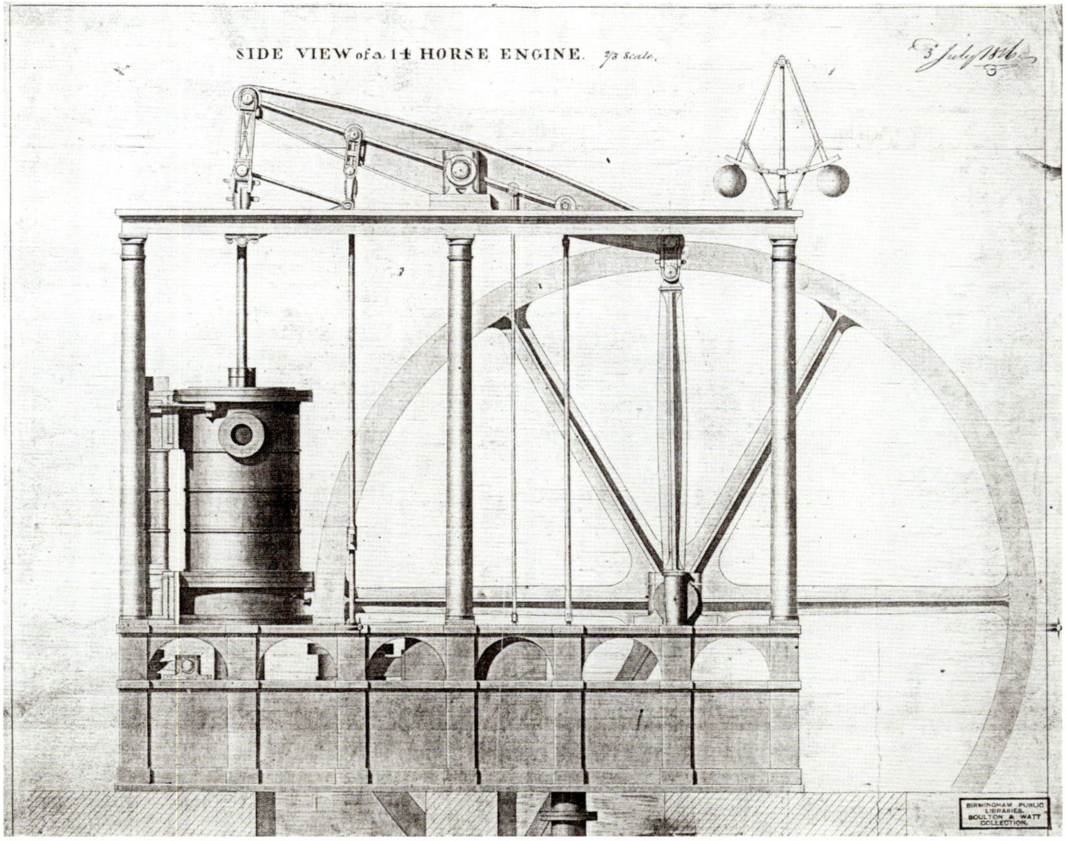

Fig 4.29
Elevation of a typical 14hp steam engine, 3 July 1816.

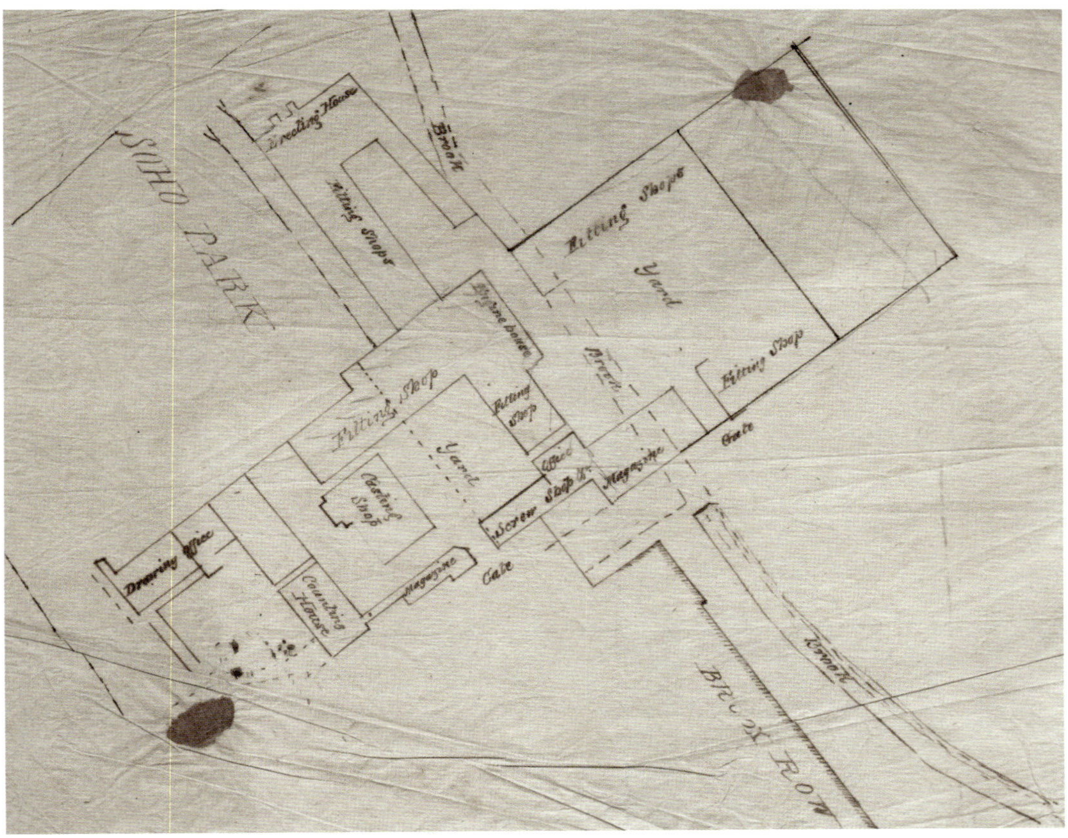

Fig 4.30
Plan of the Manufactory engine works showing the erecting house, n.d.

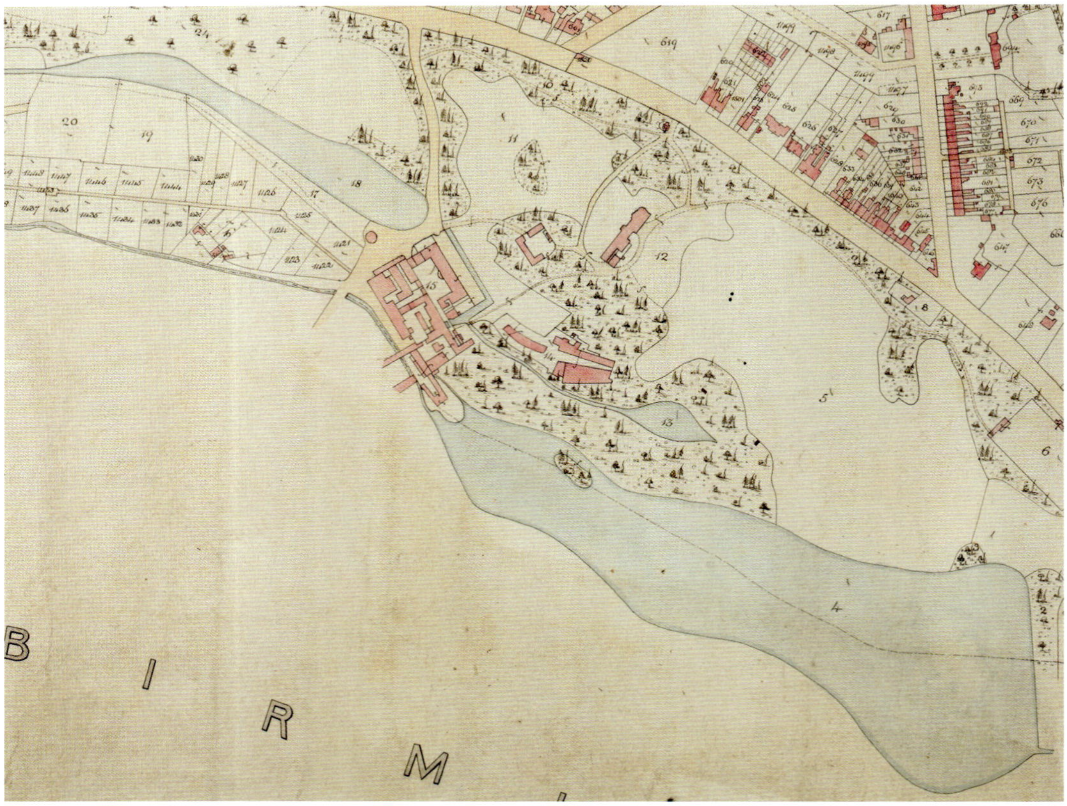

Fig 4.31
Extract from the tithe map of Handsworth Parish, 1843, showing the final extension to the Manufactory engine works on the promontory between the Hockley Brook and the mill tail race. The buildings now return along the Hockley Brook to form a U plan. The dam that separated the Upper from the Lower Hockley Pool has been removed.

Fig 4.32
Magnificent water-coloured plan and elevation of a lathe to be erected in the piston-rod shop (former forging shop 1775), 23 December 1827. The plan includes the adjacent engine house with two surviving small Murdoch engines and the newer 14hp beam engine (1815).

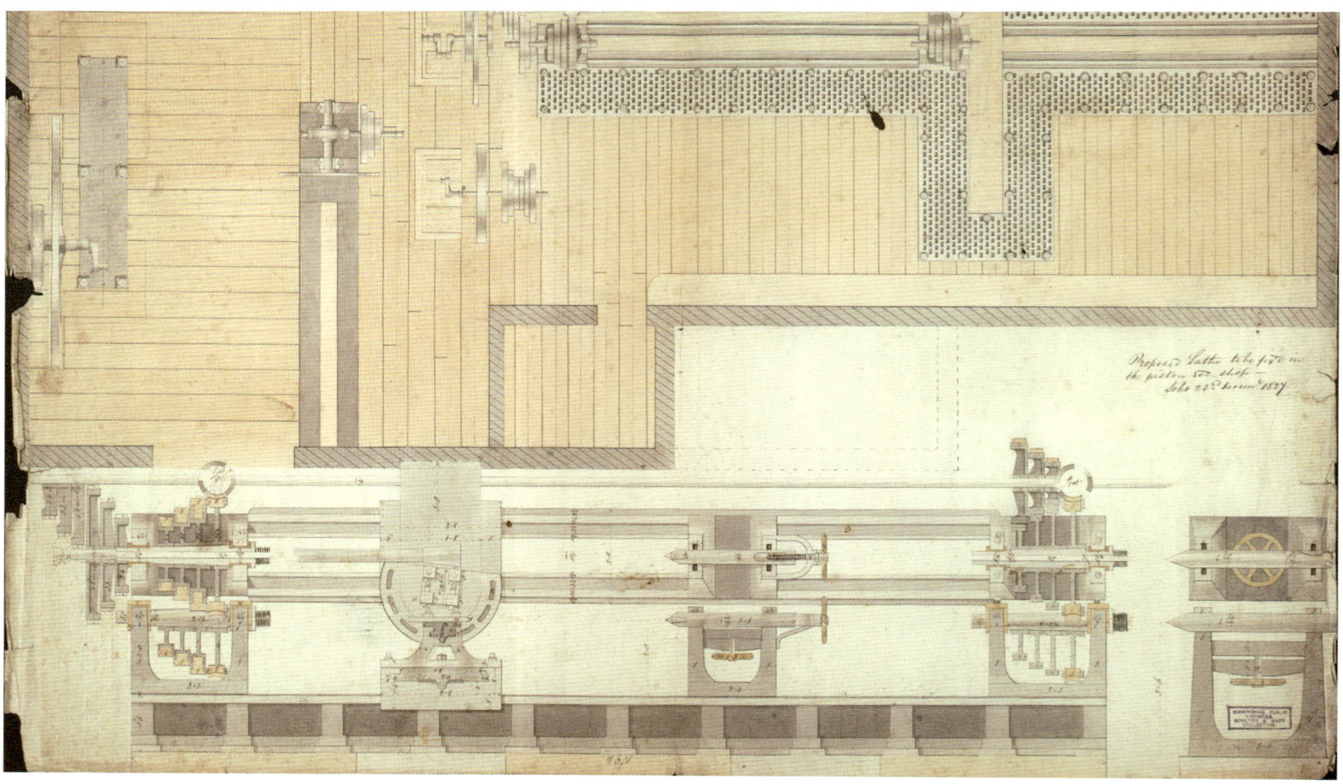

to interpret in terms of changes to the plans and elevations of the buildings. This documentation deserves a detailed study in its own right and only a generalised account can be given here. It is clear, however, that the Manufactory became the main production centre of Bolton & Watt marine engines following the successful trials of their vessel, the *Caledonia*, in August and September 1817. Generally, the Boulton & Watt archive has not been extensively or intensively studied from the time the sons, Matthew Robinson Boulton and James Watt Jr, took over the firm. The exception is Erich Roll's pioneering history of the Boulton & Watt partnership, but his account deals with the first few years only and ends in 1805.[77] The firm of Boulton Watt & Company, Soho, requires a separate, detailed analysis to identify the factors, undoubtedly obsolescence amongst them, that led to the steam-engine works at the Manufactory being demolished at the height of the 'Steam Age'.[78]

In 1807, a wheel-lathe shop was built upon an entirely new foundation, but its location is uncertain. It was probably built in the 'new' yard, for in 1822 a wall was heightened between the wheel-lathe shop and Molyneux's forge, which is known to have stood against the western boundary wall of the yard. In 1813–14, the framework (stocks) for 14hp engines was installed (Fig 4.26). This consisted of a six-column frame for erecting and testing engines of this size and was placed in the 'old forge', the earliest building of the engine works built in 1775. A plan, dated 13 April 1812, shows this proposal and also the replacement of the 6hp bell-crank engine with a new 14hp engine (Fig 4.27). This latter change was not carried out until 1815 (Fig 4.28). The old 6hp engine was repaired, some new parts made, and then sold to Messrs W & E Franklin of Trowbridge.[79] A fine drawing (dated 5 July 1816) of the 14hp six-column engine shows what an elegant machine it was (Fig 4.29).

Subsequently, most development was related to the new business of marine-engine production. In 1818, 'stocks' for 15hp boat engines were erected; an undated map marks the two-storey end of the workshops that ran southwards along the peninsula between the mill tail race and the Hockley Brook – the 'Erecting House'; this is possibly where the boat engines were assembled (Fig 4.30).[80] In 1820, 'Stocks for Boat Engines in the Large Engine House' were constructed. The latter was also called the '10 and 15 H[p] Boat Engine House', not a power house in the normal sense but a place for erecting engines of this type. In 1822–3 and in 1825, further building works took place in the 'Boat Engine House'.[81]

In 1825, a screw shed, and in 1827, a steel magazine, were erected in the old engine yard on its north side against the main Manufactory boundary. The 1827 accounts indicate that there was a workshop ('John Mears') situated over the boat-engine 'shop', that the boat-engine house was newly connected by a shed to a grinding shop, and that the 'Boat Fitting Shop' had been converted to a file shop. These building works, representing the last extension of any significance at the Boulton & Watt works, probably created a U shape out of the range of workshops running southwards along the peninsula to the 'boat engine house'. Few plans survive for this period and none are of a large scale. The 1843 Tithe map for Handsworth is the first to show, although many years after the event, the U plan of buildings on the promontory, with the extension in question facing the Hockley Brook (Fig 4.31).[82] One of the finest Soho machine plans, a watercolour dated 23 December 1827, shows a proposed lathe in the shop farther towards the centre of the main works where the stocks for 14hp engines had been erected in 1813–14 (Fig 4.32). In 1830–1, the original 1hp and 3hp Murdoch engines were replaced by two 3hp engines and continued to run the lathes as before. The casting shop, the old 'Solomon's Temple', was taken down in 1834 and a new brass-casting shop and pattern room erected. Two years later, the accounts cease and there is no detailed information on the engine manufactory buildings for the remainder of their nearly 20-year lifespan.[83]

The last years of the engine works, 1850–3

There is still much research to be done on the last decades of the Soho engine works at the Manufactory. The story of the decline of the Boulton & Watt firm has understandably attracted far less attention than the glamorous ventures of Boulton and Watt Sr, heroes of the so-called 'Industrial Revolution' and leaders of technological innovation in the late 18th century. The move to sell the Mint machinery in 1850 and to demolish its buildings was followed quickly by the abandonment of the engine works, although no member of the Boulton or

Watt families was involved in the latter decision. The new firm that was allowed to use the name, James Watt and Company, had decided to consolidate its operations at the Soho Foundry (*see* Chapter 7). In 1852, most of the machinery of any value was stripped out of the engine works and transferred to the Foundry, in which a large erecting shop had been built in 1847, partially to accommodate it. This building has survived and is now statutorily listed grade II*. A considerable quantity of machinery was moved over to the Smethwick site, including the 14hp and the two 3hp engines, originally installed in 1815 and 1830–1 respectively, 14 lathes, 4 planing machines, and a drilling machine.[84]

The buildings at the Manufactory were demolished soon after. Rate books record the works as void in 1851, omit to mention them in 1852, and note that they were pulled down in 1853.[85] Confirmation of this is to be found in a letter of 15 February 1853 written by the firm James Watt & Company: 'as we have given up the occupation of our premises at Soho as a factory, and it appears to be desirable for Mr [Matthew Piers Watt] Boulton to have use of the ground ... we are ready ourselves to consent to it and will ... dispose of the buildings and clear the ground in accordance with the terms of our lease'.[86] It is likely that the copying-press buildings were also removed in this period. A photograph taken from the Great Bank, dated *c* 1860, shows the main Manufactory buildings still standing, but all the engine works and copying-press buildings that were in the foreground are shown to have been razed to the ground (*see* Fig 2.35).[87] The first Soho manufactory of engine parts was no more. Fortunately, its younger brother, born 20 years later as the Soho Foundry at Smethwick, has in part survived to the present day, unlike any buildings at the Manufactory site.

5

The Soho Mint

As with the Manufactory, there has traditionally been more study of the products of the Mint than of the physical appearance, layout and function of the buildings in which they were made. Lack of research on the buildings may be due in part to the fact that they are not the subject of any known illustrations. The scarcity of Mint building views specifically may, in turn, have been the result of Boulton's secretive attitude towards his new mechanical invention. Indeed, when views of the Manufactory are examined, the Mint can either only be glimpsed at a distance through trees or only be seen at the edge of the depicted view (Figs 5.1, 5.2 and *see* Fig 2.23).

Although there has been work published on the Soho Mint in recent years, it has concentrated on the machinery,[1] on the enterprise,[2] and on production, design and its workers.[3] Both Cooper and Doty touch upon the buildings of the first steam-powered mint in the world, but their accounts on these matters are confusing, even misleading. This is despite the fact that there is a reasonable plan coverage for the Mint, in contrast to the Manufactory, though it is even better for the coining machinery that was exported to mints abroad. Cooper provided a useful historical survey of mint technology in which he refers to the arrangements at Soho as a background to Boulton's important contribution to the development of mechanised coining.[4]

The Mint Company was owned exclusively by the Boulton family: it ran the mint at the Manufactory and exported mints to many countries across the world. The firm of Boulton & Watt made parts for the Mint Company, but only as the principal supplier, and there were, indeed, many other foundries used. Neither the firm, Boulton & Watt, nor its successor after 1800, Boulton, Watt & Company, minted coins, and the latter firm ceased to exist on the death of James Watt Jr in 1848.[5] The Mint Company was wound up by Matthew Piers Watt Boulton in 1850 and there followed the dismantling of the Mint buildings in the early 1850s. Thereafter, James Watt & Company continued to trade at the Soho Foundry in Smethwick in the export of new mints and the resupply of existing ones. Despite the famous name, the firm had no Watt (or Boulton) family connection.[6]

More recently, George Selgin and the author have analysed the physical arrangement of production at the Soho Mint.[7] Selgin, having introduced earlier accounts that misleadingly stressed a linear assembly-line layout, made it clear that the process of making coins, from the rolling of copper to the final minting, took place in a number of buildings scattered through the Mint and Manufactory complex, including the Soho Mill.

The Soho Mint was a product of Matthew Boulton's creative and innovative energy, although he used Boulton & Watt engineers, most notably John Southern, to help him technically and managerially. Later, William Buckle and William Creighton worked for Matthew Robinson Boulton. The latter's contribution to the Soho Mint business has not been appreciated. In fact, Doty unjustifiably belittles his role, inexplicably placing James Watt Jr to the fore.[8] It is certainly worth emphasising that Matthew Robinson Boulton was responsible for the export of the great majority of mints abroad and that he masterminded the reorganisation of Soho Mint buildings and machinery in 1824–6. The actual drawings were produced by William Creighton (*see* Figs 5.25–5.27).

Preparations, 1786–7

The pitiful state of the national coinage, owing to counterfeiting and shortages, must have irked Boulton for many years. It was not until the mid-1780s, however, after the Boulton & Watt

Fig 5.1
Pen-and-ink view of the side of Soho Manufactory drawn by John Phillp, 1796, taken from the bank of the mill pool looking directly at the side of the principal building, behind which other buildings descend steeply down the Great Bank to the right. To the left, and farther away, the Mint buildings are glimpsed above a boundary wall.

rotative engine had been developed and sufficient rolling-mill capacity had been put down, that he could think seriously about steam-powered coining. The technical problem of making coins 'round & all of one size' had also to be solved. However, on a trip to Paris and its mint in 1786, Boulton met Jean Pierre Droz. The Frenchman had recently devised a metal collar, split into six parts, which apparently met this need.[9] Confident that technical obstacles could now be surmounted, Boulton then applied himself to overcoming institutional resistance in the shape of an apathetic government and the vested interest of the Royal Mint in London.

In the meantime, through his agent John Motteux, Boulton obtained a contract with the East India Company to make 18 tons (16 tonnes) of copper coinage for Sumatra.[10] It is clear that Soho was to roll the copper into sheets, cut out, anneal, boil and scour the blanks, mill their edges and then send them to a new mint in French Ordinary Court, London. This was being built with Boulton's advice under the supervision of Richard Jupp, the East India Company's surveyor. The mint was a new building rather than the conversion suggested by Gould.[11] At least two of the four coining presses were manufactured by Anthony Robinson, a Birmingham founder, and sent to London. The building was only finished in December 1786 after much delay.[12] The coining contract was completed in April and May 1787, and another order for 30 tons (27 tonnes) was finished by January 1788.[13]

While he lobbied for the biggest prize, the English national coinage, and worked out the mechanics of applying a steam engine to coin production, the East India Company contracts provided Boulton with valuable practical experience. On 2 April 1787 he wrote to Droz: 'I also intend working the great Presses by a Steam Engine which I have erected in such a manner as to drive or work Ten presses at a time'.[14] Boulton was less than truthful here, as he revealed in a letter two weeks later: 'If Government choose to put the Coinage under the care of me and my friends I will undertake to erect in 3 or 4 months an apparatus sufficient to coin any quantity per day that Government will contract for'.[15] By May 1787, he had a model of a 'means of working 6 or 8 or 10 or any Number of presses without the application of human Labour and so that any one press can be stoped in a Moment'.[16] It is clear that by June some of 'the Copper Coin for the India Company' had been 'press'd at Soho' but this work had certainly not been driven by steam engine.[17] Earlier, in April, Boulton had planned secretly to erect a press in a room and work it by a rod connected to his mill, still only water-powered.[18] In December Boulton was

Fig 5.2
Pen-and ink by John Phillp, c 1796, of the principal building and proposed Latchet (Crescent) Building. The latter, only partly built at this time, obscures the Mint buildings to the left, which were originally part of the 'fairy' farm or menagerie. The coining room and engine house stand well hidden behind.

boasting that 'he hath executed and perfected at very great expense such an apparatus as he is persuaded will enable him to make coin, not only superior in beauty and workmanship to that of any nation in Europe, but manufactured (in consequence of the peculiar construction of his machinery) that the counterfeiting will in a great degree be prevented'.[19] It is difficult to establish the degree to which this machinery was, in fact, wishful thinking or exaggerated public relations. Regardless of the rhetoric, there was a genuine desire to create a new minting technology and place it to work at Soho. But first, Boulton required confirmation from the Treasury that the national coinage was his to produce.

The first Soho Mint, 1788–9

In 1787, a Committee of the Privy Council was finally set up to consider 'the state of the Coins of the Realm'.[20] Boulton was invited to attend in December and this seemed to have been encouragement enough to begin building at Soho. Accounts have survived that itemise work to 'the Building in Garden' (22 December) and 'Getting up the Brickwork Round the money Press' (5 January 1788).[21] Boulton reveals the location of this work to his son at the beginning of February 1788: 'I am building a Mint & new Manufacture for it in my Farm Yard behind the Menagery at Soho'.[22] The buildings in question stood in his garden about 120yd (110m) south-east of the south-east corner of the Manufactory's principal building and enjoyed a fine view to the south over the Upper Hockley Pool (Fig 5.3, marked 'Fish Pond'). Boulton had had them erected from the late 1770s onwards to enjoy the fashionable pleasures of a late 18th-century garden and to pursue his hobbies.[23] Apart from the menagerie, or aviary as it was sometimes called, there was also a tea room, a laboratory and a fossil room. In the end, Boulton seemed less concerned about despoiling his garden buildings by planting a mint within them than about revealing the secrets of his new mint technology by locating it too close to the Manufactory. The site was relatively secluded and development work could progress covertly as John Roberts, one of the engineers involved, assured Boulton in London: 'Not a syllable of the Business shall transpire from me to anyone but J Harrison & I hope you will be quite easy on this point'.[24] At this time, Boulton was thinking of using a 'double 16-inch' [406mm] engine, and one of the most important of the surviving Mint plans

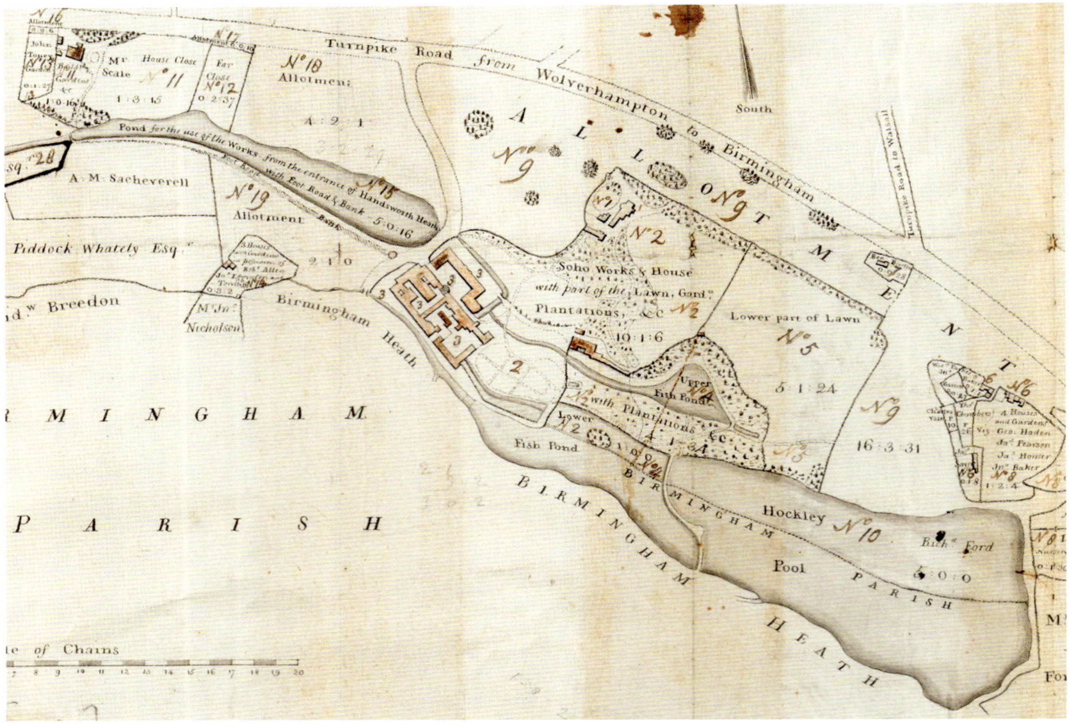

Fig 5.3
Detail from John Snape's map of Handsworth Heath, c 1785. The 'fairy' farm or menagerie lies between the Manufactory and the 'fish pond'.

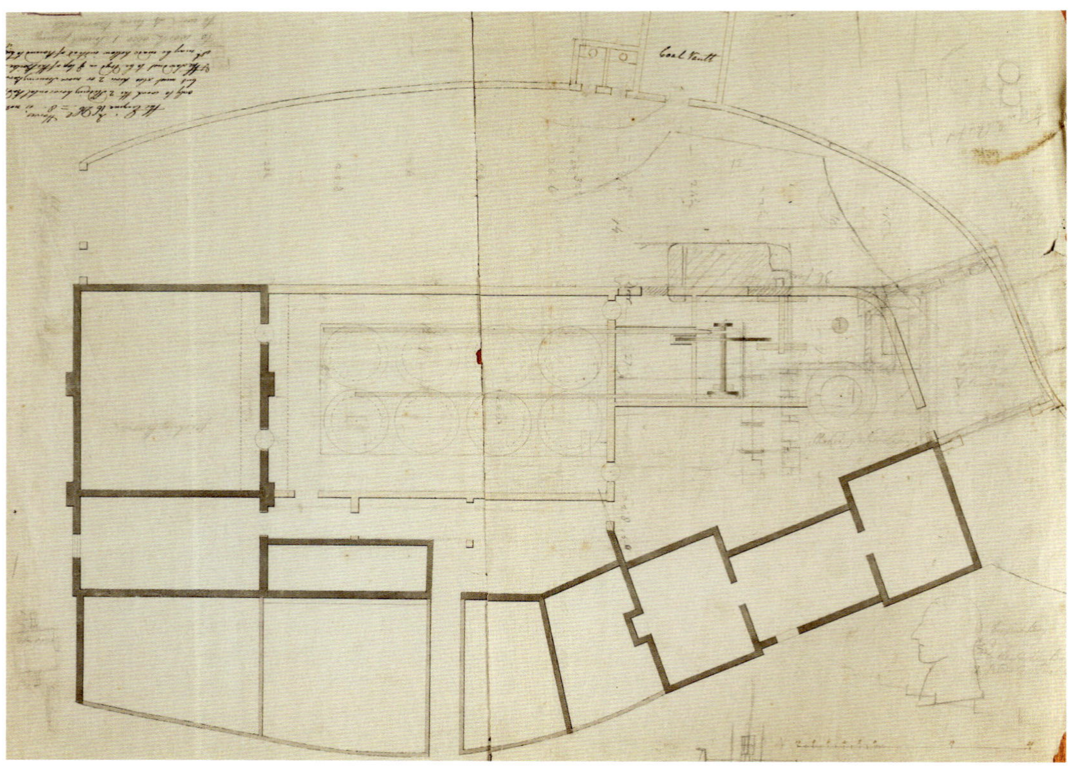

Fig 5.4
Plan of the Mint, c January 1788. The existing farm buildings and menagerie pens are colour-washed dark grey, while the walls of the proposed coining room and engine house are a light buff in colour, but with many alterations added in pencil. The plan has been orientated to accord with the phase drawings in Fig 5.5. It is revealing that the plan is orientated looking from the direction of Boulton's house and not from the Manufactory.

(undated, but probably January 1788) contains a note in Boulton's hand that the 16in (406mm) double-acting engine of 8hp was not only to work two sliding horizontal rods but also two or more scouring barrels (Fig 5.4).[25] The plan may have been the one 'taken' of the 'Ground and Buildings in [Boulton's] Garden' by John Roberts and John Harrison on 26 January and redrafted 'in a proper manner' for Boulton's inspection by Zacchaeus Walker Jr on the following day.[26] Its significance lies in the fact that it records the first application of a steam engine to minting presses and it clearly shows Boulton's existing garden buildings and the newly built mint attached. This building measured 43ft 6in (13.26m) × 27ft 8in (8.46m) in plan and two parallel lines of four presses linking with two 'Slideing horozontal Rods' are sketched as being within it. The rods are driven from the flyshaft of the engine, housed in what seems to be an open enclosure on the south side of the mint. The manner in which the presses were to be put in motion by the sliding rods is uncertain, but many years later both William Murdoch and John Southern laid claim to having suggested 'working Eight Coining Presses by means of a sliding rod connected with the Engine by a Crank'.[27] There is no documentary evidence that this first arrangement was implemented. Sketch plans of this phase and those immediately following can be seen in Fig 5.5.

At the end of January 1788, two small and two large presses were being prepared, and by 5 February 'four more Presses for cutting out' had been ordered.[28] There is some ambiguity as to whether coining presses or cutting-out presses were being installed in these first experiments. According to the 1810 Soho conference: 'A trial was made of Cutting-out Presses worked by a Steam-Engine applied to them thro' the means of a Crank & Sliding-rod, about August 1788'.[29] In June, the steam engine was being installed and four cutting-out presses were placed in the gallery of the rolling mill where they could only have been powered by hand.[30] Nevertheless, three 'large' presses had been delivered, presumably for the coining room. A cross-sectional drawing of the mint, dated 22 July 1788, shows that an air pump was intended to be attached to a single sliding rod via a chain over a large pulley (Fig 5.6)[31] and an undated but probably *c* June 1788, perhaps slightly earlier, plan and cross section presents a more complicated pivoting beam arrangement at the pump (Fig 5.7).[32] The air pump was intended to pull the single rod back, activating eight presses in two parallel but staggered lines 'and was to communicate with the Condenser of the Engine in order to have the Vacuum formed', exactly as shown on Fig 5.7.[33] A plan drawn up later, relating directly to the cross section dated 22 July 1788 mentioned above, has eight presses in the 'staggered-parallel' formation. In addition, the engine is shown moved from the position shown on Fig 5.4 in

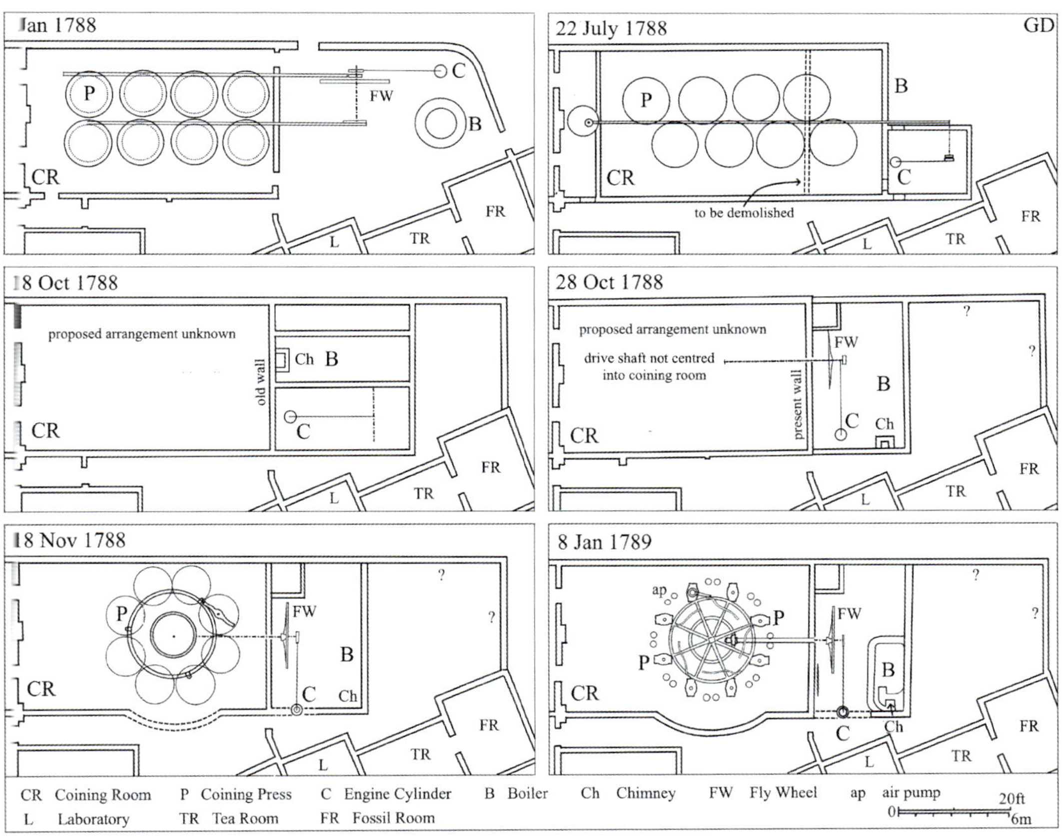

Fig 5.5
Sketch plans showing the development of ideas during the year 1788 for the coining room machinery and position of the steam engine, culminating in the final design in January 1789.

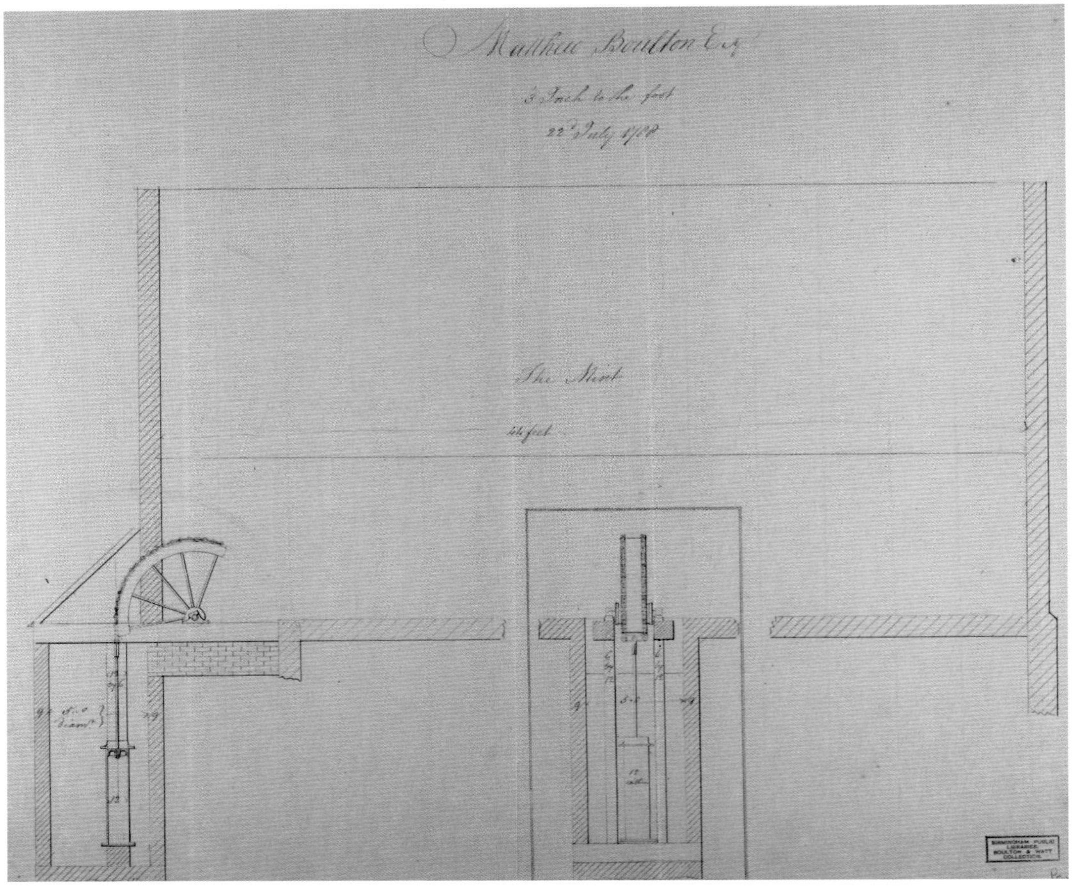

Fig 5.6
Two cross sections of the proposed coining room pulley and air pump, 22 July 1788.

January, turned through 180 degrees, and housed in a narrow and roofed rectangular structure end-on to the minting room (Fig 5.8).[34] Whether an actual move took place is difficult to judge. Several drawings of the engine and engine house in this new position have survived from the period 16 June to 17 July, but work was already well advanced by 18 June on setting up the 16in (406mm) 'little engine'.[35] To confuse matters, another set of plans, dated 18 October 1788, confirm the engine's new position but introduce a nearly square engine house for the boiler and chimney. For the first time, the tea room, fossil room and laboratory are identified on plan, as the engine house was intended to come uncomfortably close to them (Fig 5.9).[36]

While this experimentation was taking place, Boulton had to be away in London much of the time in order to attend the new Privy Council Committee on the Coinage of the Realm. Naturally, he took this opportunity to publicise his new ideas and to lobby for the national coinage contracts. On 30 January 1788, the Committee asked Boulton to provide specimens of his intended coinage.[37] The dies for the specimens were engraved (sunk) by Jean Pierre Droz and 'struck by the Press Mr Droz had constructed at Paris, there being no one in England capable of striking such'. Boulton's fledgling mint at Soho was far from ready. In March and June 1788, Matthew Boulton presented these specimens to the Privy Council Committee.[38] Despite the fact that the Committee offered very little encouragement, Boulton decided to take the risk and continue with the development of his mint. In April 1788, he tried to tempt Droz to Soho: 'I have now begun to build a new Hotel de Monnoye which will be sufficiently large to hold 8 presses.'[39]

From July 1788 until early 1789, no letters survive that discuss the progress of the works on the mint, but drawings demonstrate that a major change of plan and technology took place after 18 October, the last date on which any plans indicate a connecting-rod mechanism. The 1810 conference minutes confirm a significant change at this time:[40] 'In the latter end of 1788 & beginning of 1789 a Press was erected having a Curve attached to its Fly, which was acted upon in rotation by five Pins placed upon the circumference

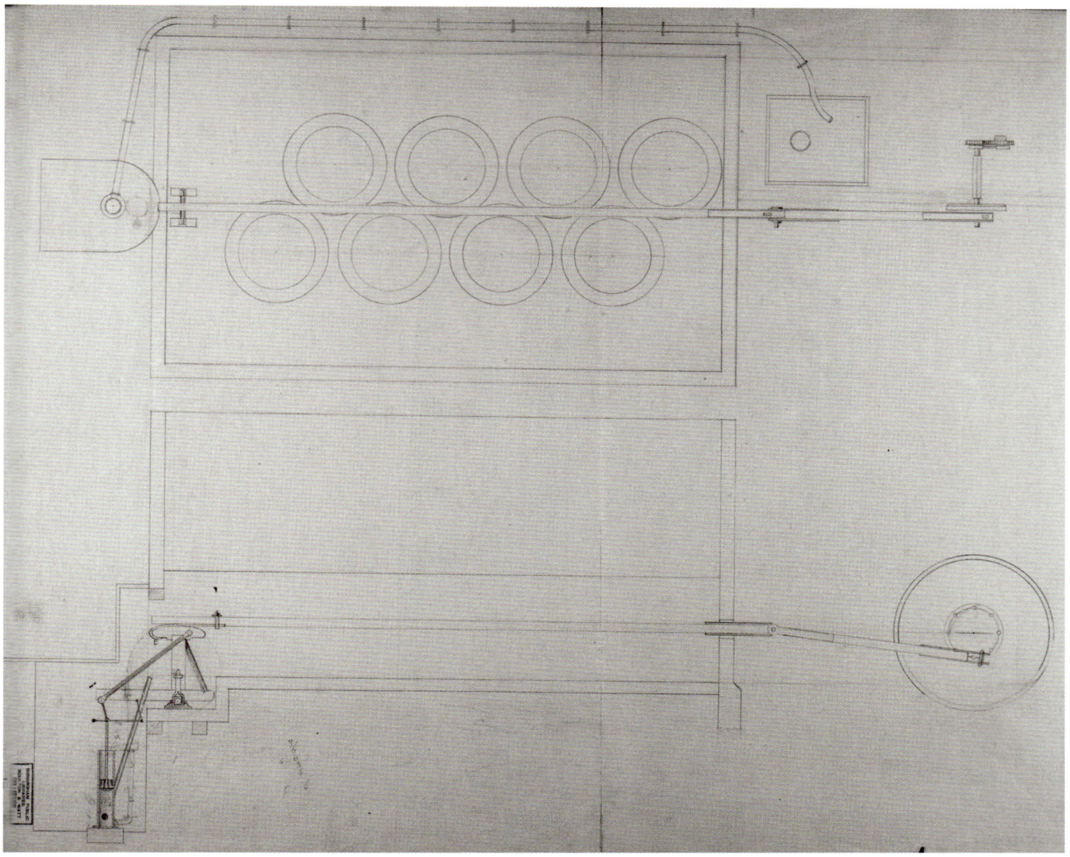

Fig 5.7
Plan and cross section of proposed coining room machinery, c June 1788. The steam engine is located to the right.

Fig 5.8
Plan of the proposed coining room machinery, steam engine and boiler, 22 July 1788.

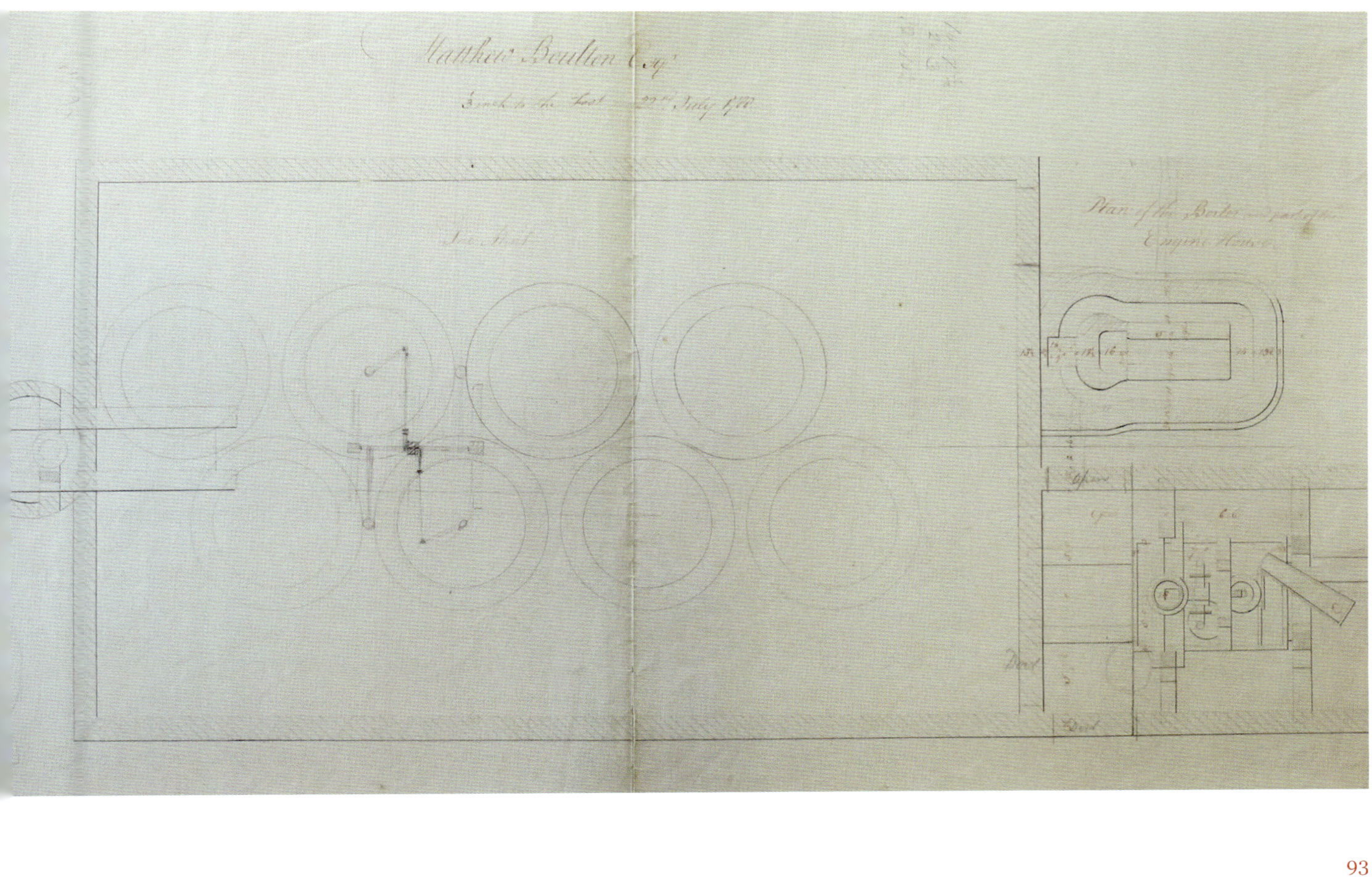

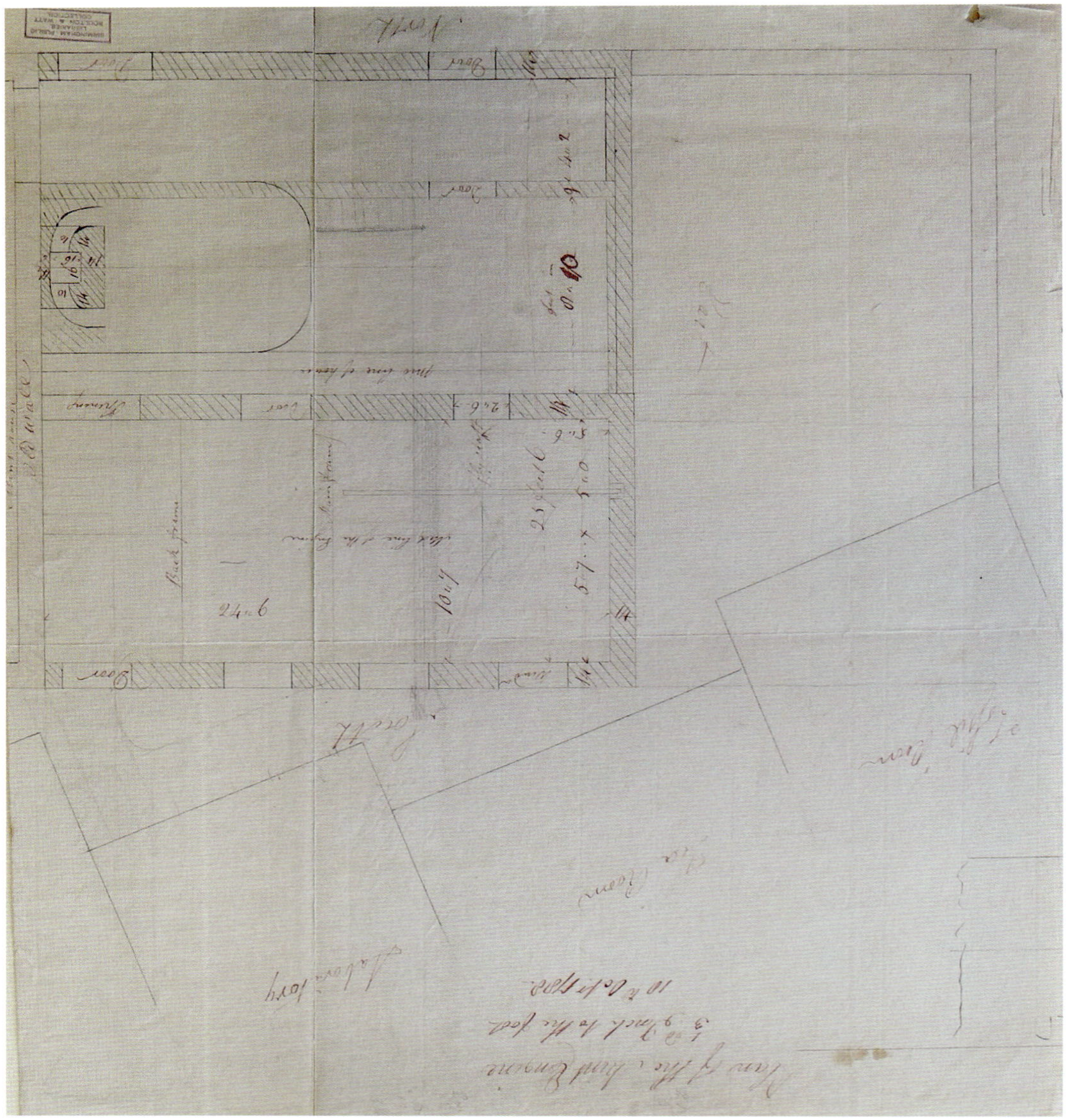

Fig 5.9
Plan of the Mint engine house and boiler room, 18 October 1788. The plan has been orientated to accord with Fig 5.5.

of an Horizontal Wheel put in motion by the Steam-Engine. This method was suggested by Mr Southern.'[41] John Southern was soon to become head of the Boulton & Watt drawing office and it is clear, as mentioned above, that some Boulton & Watt employees contributed at this time to the development of mint technology. Three drawings, dated 28 October 1788, show the engine had shifted through 90 degrees, but with the cylinder staying more or less in the same position (*see* Fig 5.5).[42] The engine house was narrowed to a rectangle, from the rough square indicated on the plans dated 18 October, leaving more space behind the tea room. Significantly, the connecting rod was replaced by a flyshaft entering the coining room and this necessitated moving the boiler and chimney. An important plan, dated 18 November 1788, shows the circular arrangement of presses for the first time, but with three rather than five pins activating the curved flies of the eight presses (Fig 5.10).[43] The pins are attached to a horizontal flywheel and its vertical shaft is connected by cogged and bevelled wheels to a horizontal shaft below the floor driven directly by a 'sun-and-planet' motion. The engine is shown in the same orientation as on the drawings of 28 October, but with the cylinder moved to the main (west) exterior wall to allow the flyshaft to run along the central axis of the minting room.[44] As a result of this shift, a segmental bay had to be added to the coining room to allow for the circulation around the western side of the presses. An earlier, undated plan shows the segmental bay as a

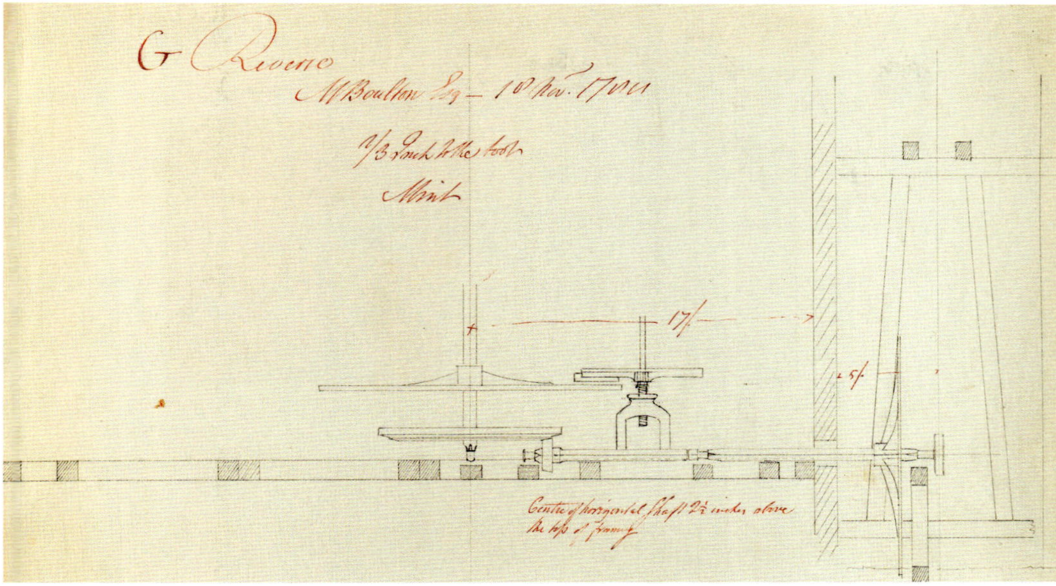

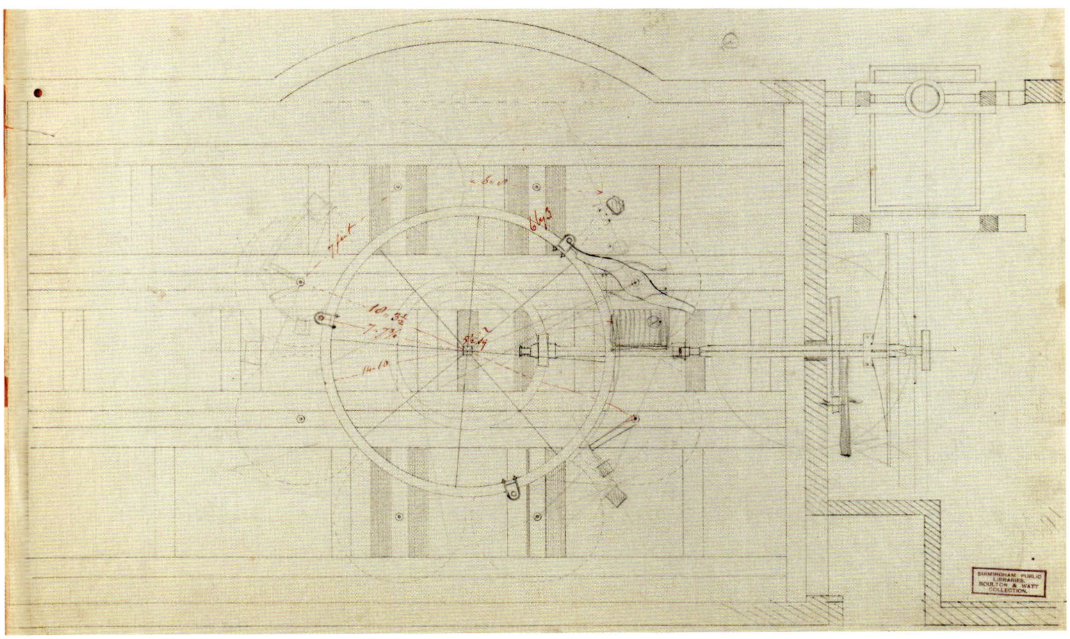

Fig 5.10a
Cross section of the coining room machinery, 18 November 1788 (Reverse). The final design had been conceived.

Fig 5.10b
Plan of the coining room machinery showing presses arranged in a circle, 18 November 1788 (Reverse).

proposal.[45] On 24 November 1788, John Southern was working on the upright shaft of the pin wheel.[46]

James Watt generally took little interest in the Mint and, as discussed above, the business never became part of Boulton & Watt. It was Watt, however, who recommended moving the pins to the arms of the press and the curves to the horizontal wheel after 'repeated Trials' of Southern's original arrangement met with 'various objections'.[47] Very quickly, it was realised that the pin arm and fly had to be separate items engaging at the right moment to impart motion to the screw, but the addition of weights to the fly could not produce a 'smart blow'.[48]

Several other engineers were involved in these refinements, including Peter Ewart and James Lawson, and at the conference 20 years later it proved difficult to disentangle who was responsible for which part of the improvements. One of the most important of these, ascribed to James Lawson, was the fixing of the vacuum pumps to each of the presses, in lieu of weighted flies, to produce the smarter blow, thus introducing a second and different motive power between the mechanics of the press and the steam engine. Thenceforth, vacuum power was to prevail in the Boulton mints.

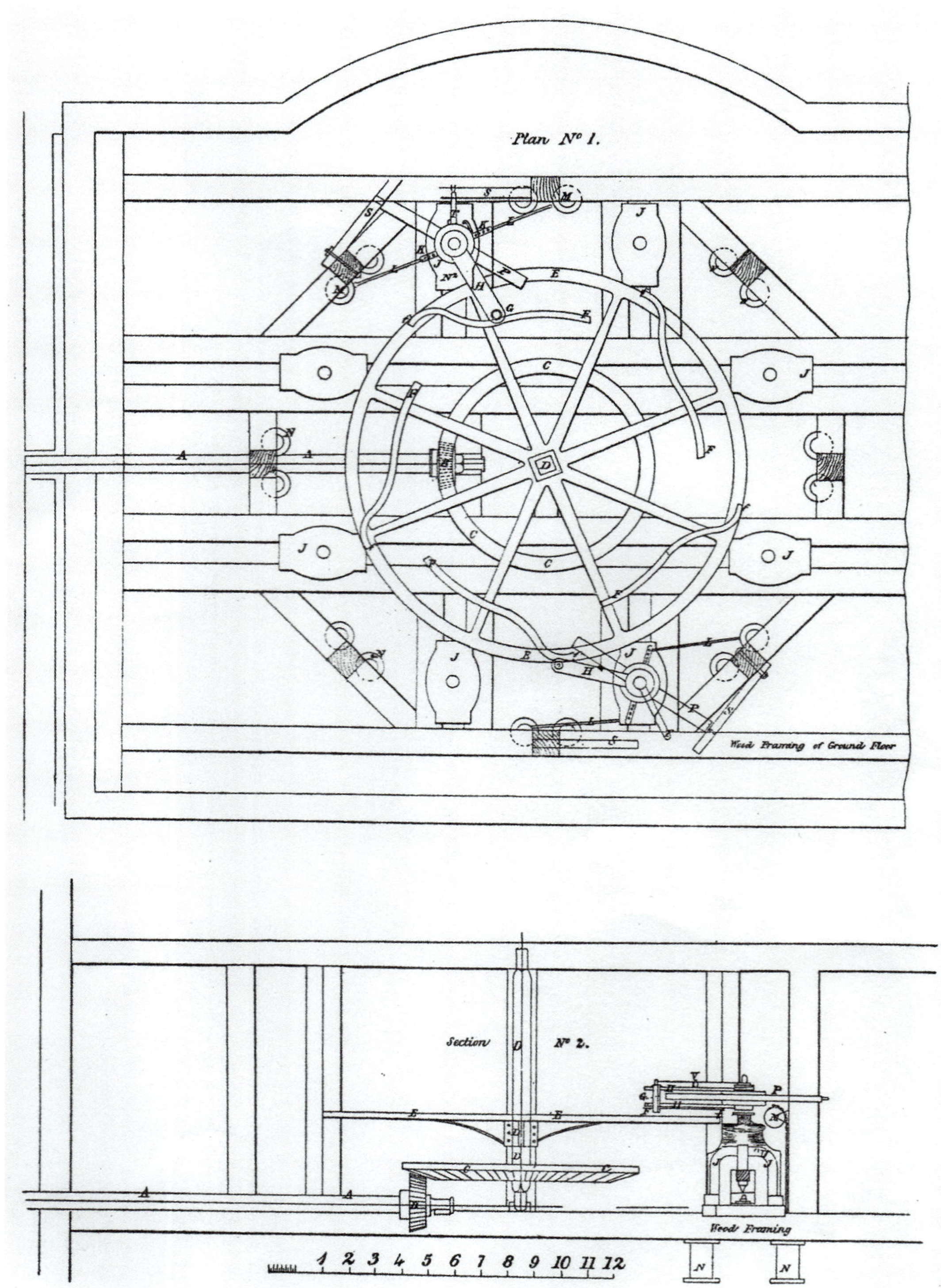

Fig 5.11
Matthew Boulton's patent drawings for steam-engine-powered coining presses, 1790.

Letters have survived from early 1788 chronicling the installation of the presses and later improvements. In late January 1789, the original Southern pin wheel was installed with a press.[49] Within a week or two, Watt's idea of reversing the position of the pins and curves was implemented.[50] On 29 January, Boulton was anxious that the 'disengaging part' should be 'right & properly fixed', perhaps alluding to the separate arm and fly of the one press that seemed to be in position at this time.[51] Several months later, in July, the trial of a 'new Fly' on an 'old press' proved successful: a rate of 55 blows per minute was achieved during these experiments, and Boulton was anxious to have another two presses in operation as soon as was feasible for he still harboured hopes of obtaining a government contract.[52]

The presses were also improved by the provision of a 'layer-in' (first developed for the manual presses supplied to the East India Company in 1786–7), which automatically fed the blanks under the die for coining. At first, the collar used for milling the edges of the coins was Droz's six-section split collar, which was subsequently replaced by a simpler version of Boulton's devising. Droz had been at Soho since about October 1788, but left under a cloud sometime in the summer of 1790 without having delivered the expected technical improvements, which included the multiplication of dies.[53] Another innovation was to make the die twist slightly as it struck the blank, imparting a high polish to the ground of the coin.[54]

By the end of March 1790, Boulton had still not been given a decision on the national coinage. In spite of this, he was loath to release his 'expensive workmen' as it would have been difficult to recruit them again quickly and he would have also risked their revealing the secret.[55] In June 1790, James Lawson sent Matthew Boulton a working 'Model of Mint' and a plan.[56] It is not known whether this plan was used as the basis for the patent for the coining machinery.[57] Lawson was certainly responsible for producing drawings that had to be enrolled with the patent by 8 August 1790.[58] The patent specification drawing is a representation of the coining-press arrangement at the Soho Mint, complete with the added segmental bay, but at this time the building may not have housed all eight presses as shown (Fig 5.11).[59] The publication of the patent coincided with arbitration over the dispute with Droz, driving Boulton into paroxysms of rage and invective and who, Lawson observed, only 'worked hard in adjusting his microscopical nicitiyes'.[60] During this time, Boulton revealed that he 'only intended erecting 6 presses' and that he had actually 'only 4 Erected & 1 for Multiplying [dies]'.[61]

Mint extensions, 1791

In 1791, the mint, which up to this time had only been fit for experimentation and small-scale production, the latter consisting of a few contracts for tokens, coin and medals, was provided with a major building extension.[62] Boulton had anticipated matters in the Soho mill by freeing the waterwheel to turn the rolls only, principally to make the copper sheet necessary for coining. The steam engine installed in 1788 took over the lapping process and it was also connected to a blank-cutting-out machine with up to eight presses in a circle (*see* pp 53–8 and Fig 3.18). This was not ideal as the mill was situated about 110yd (100.58m) from the mint, although Doty considers this 'a logical place ... and an early example of Boulton's tendency to see manufacturing as a linear process'.[63] Doty wrongly assumed that both the rolling of copper and blank cutting-out were contained within the mint. Other minting functions were being performed at the mill, but some of these had to be brought up to the mint site if serious production was to take place. Some had already arrived, as, by the end of 1790, workshops had been established to maintain the presses with a variety of lathes, some powered by the steam engine.[64] The die multiplication shop, or the 'Bastile', as it was called, was likely to have been positioned close to the coining presses, but its location is not certain.

Despite his efforts, Boulton did not obtain the national coinage at this time and so the stimulus for the new building seemed to be the prospect of further private contracts. These materialised in the immediate years that followed and included Soho-made East India Company coinage, the Monneron tokens for the Paris bank, Barbados tokens, Anglesey halfpenny tokens for Thomas Williams, Southampton tokens, and many others.[65]

When it was applied to the contract for the East India Company, the mint machinery at first continually broke down, prompting a redesign. Among other changes, the twist imparted by the die on impact with the coin was abandoned. In April 1791, Boulton boasted about his improvements in a letter to Droz but, in view of the breakdown in their working relationship, did not reveal any details: 'I ... took the sudden resolution to adopt another plan, which I had conceived some months ago & by setting all hands to work I accomplished it in one Week: since which we have worked 20 Hours every day and not made one false blow or broke anything since I changed the principle'. However, these claims cannot be taken entirely at face value given that Boulton was still trying to prove Droz's technical incompetence as compared to his own prowess. Moreover, there are no drawings or other accounts that can substantiate these changes. Boulton reminded Droz that he

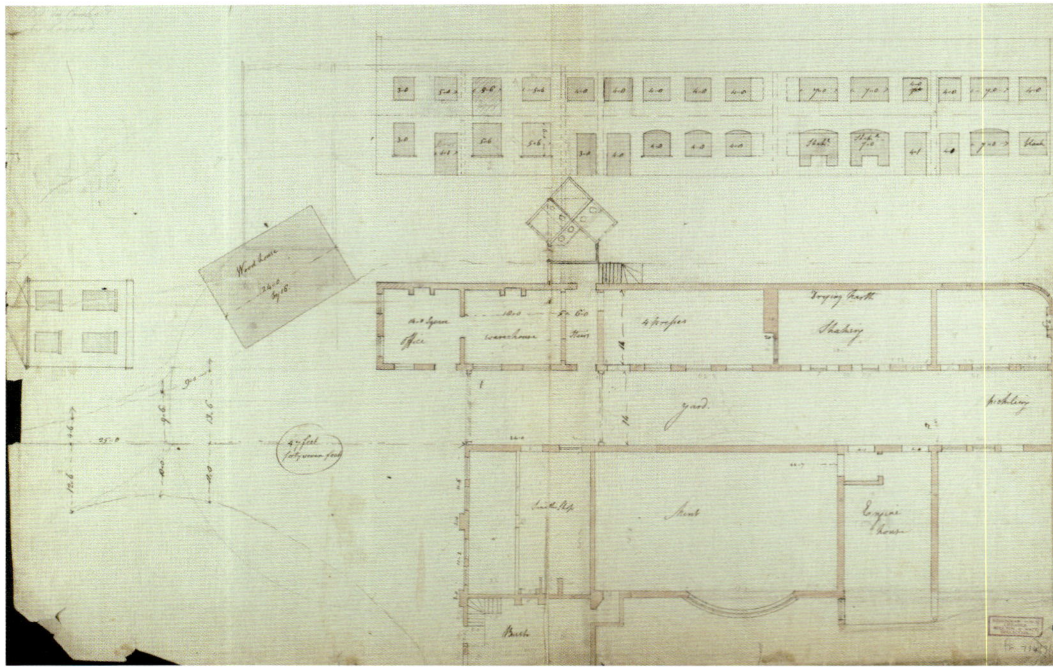

Fig 5.12
Plan and elevation of the 1791 mint extension, a range 14ft (4.27m) wide erected parallel to the existing coining room and engine house and separated by a yard of the same width.

had four presses and that he needed two more to complete the 'whole number intended' and that he could not send an unfinished press to Droz as the latter had requested.[66] By 23 May, the fifth press was nearly ready and the moving of the multiplication press into the mint was being considered to provide the sixth.[67] However, very soon the plan was changed to eight (rather than six) presses as Boulton sent details on the arrangements required to fulfil an impending order: 'We have 6 presses cast from the design of Droz model but we must have 8'. Boulton also sent a sketch plan of the location of the new building but wanted 'a plan of the Mint Buildings & the yard & ground so that I may plan the intended new building.'[68]

The location of the new building was to be east of, and parallel to, the existing mint building and engine house, a site that required some excavation as the land sloped upwards towards Soho House. This work had started by 26 May, and on the following day (Friday) Boulton was promised that the excavation work would be finished by '[Monday night] ready to begin to build'.[69] In answer to an earlier enquiry from Matthew Robinson Boulton, Boulton Sr had explained to his son that he wanted 'to build shops 2 stories high from the wooden house to the end or as far as the Engine House door & even continue them on as far as the North End of the wooden house and remove the wooden house to another spot, & for this purpose the ground must be cut out so as to erect a straight building'.[70] The coin contracts were still by no means certain, and in case they did not materialise Boulton suggested that only a 'back wall to keep the Ground' was built at first.[71]

In fact, it was the 'slow progress makeing the Mint' that made Boulton fear the loss of contracts, and he demanded that 'Every one concerned in the management of the coinage should study morning noon & night how to vanquish difficulties rather than raise them'. Boulton fortunately identified the contracts in these exhortations: '1st the East India order done by Oct[obe]r next the 16 ton of Anglesey done in one month 3d one two or 3 Ton of Southampton [for the firm of Taylor Moody and Company] directly and 24 Ton of half pence about 39 to the lb done every week for one year.'[72] The builder, Charles Glover, was also being reminded 'to drive on with the building' even though Boulton had not yet sent back the promised detailed plan from London.

In a letter written on 7 June 1791, Boulton enclosed detailed instructions, dated 5 June, regarding the mint and, in particular, the new building, as it was unlikely he could 'settle the [drawn] plan before tomorrow or even then'. The yard between the new and the old building was to be 14ft (4.27m) wide, the new shops measuring 13ft 6in (4.11m) internally. They were to contain coin-shaking machines for drying on the ground floor and lathes on the upper floor powered by cords and a double pulley attached to the main flywheel shaft in the mint across the yard. Both shaking and pickling could then be removed from the mill. In addition, on the ground floor there was to be a carpenters shop, a counting house, a storeroom, a smiths shop, a room for four hand cutting-out presses, two 'necessary' houses, and coal vaults. Boulton's proposal to transfer the lap engine to the mint to help power a circle of cutting-out presses was not acted upon.[73] Of great interest was Boulton's instruction to scour the region and to recruit 'some uncorrupted boy[s] from 14 to 20 Years of Age', two for each of his eight coining presses. On 11 June 1791, James Lawson reported to Boulton that 'The place for the new shops is ready but as Booth [a bricklayer] has not yet finished the New Engine Buildings & you are undetermined I think it will be safer to wait beginning to build till you co[me] home'.[74] Boulton had still not returned by 16 June and Glover was reluctant to start the back (retaining) wall until Boulton's plan had finally been determined.[75] Boulton's return from London must have prompted the building works because his son was able to state on 28 October 1791 that 'within the last 3 mo[nths] a new range of shops had been built, Artists brought from Paris, a number of new presses erected, all fill'd with people in full work, a Contract signd of great magnitude & now all is upon the brink of Standing still for want of Copper'.[76] Notwithstanding the problem of copper supply, the new building must have been close to completion in the autumn of 1791. Building accounts show expenditure of approximately £770, with the largest sum (£523) going to Charles Glover. Several other names are mentioned, mostly bricklayers (including the G Booth mentioned above), J Pearson, J Webster and John Smith.[77]

A contemporary plan (*c* 1791) of the building survives with notes in John Southern's hand (Fig 5.12).[78] The elevation shows a two-storey block of 15 window bays, some with segmental heads, divided internally, from north to south, into office, warehouse, stairs, space for four hand presses, the shaking shop, and a room that remained unidentified. The new building was separated from the existing mint by a yard, at the south end of which was an open area assigned to pickling. The shaking shop was situated opposite the engine house and could have taken power from the first part of the main shaft leading to the coining presses, most likely via a tunnel below the yard. The plan accords reasonably closely with Boulton's instructions of 5 June 1791 referred to above.[79]

The September 1995 excavation uncovered the north-west corner of the warehouse in the 1791 building. A brick pit against the yard wall was found to contain the fixings for an unidentified machine, and 20 coin blanks and a minted coin in the later backfill (*see* Appendix 1).

The doldrums, 1792–6

This period at the Mint was characterised by small-scale technological improvements against a background of insufficient orders of the scale and prestige that Boulton desired. The Mint establishment, both as buildings and a workforce, waned as a result. In early 1792, a second air pump was attached to the presses to help dampen the recoil, and the 'rollers' or pins on the press fly arm, which engaged with the curves on the horizontal flywheel, were changed from wood to metal.[80] In March 1792, some brick stoves for bronzing and gilding coins and medals were constructed by Charles Glover on the first floor of the 1791 range over the shaking shop.[81] During this time, only two or three presses were in working order, slowing down and causing difficulties in the production of private tokens for the Monneron Frères of Paris.[82] Their bankruptcy at the end of March, however, meant that Mint workers had to be laid off.[83] In the following months, experiments were carried out for the production of very small coins.[84] On 15 September 1792, Boulton ordered the construction of a 'little water wheel intended for the little new Building at the front of the Menagerey in order to turn the Engraving Lathe'. This was, presumably, the reducing lathe sold to Boulton in 1790 by the Frenchman Jean Dupeyrat, and an important piece of equipment in the production of the coining dies.[85] The position of the 'little new Building' between the menagerie and the canal, which ran to the Shell Pool, can be roughly established, but it is not understood how the waterwheel was powered. Unfortunately, there are no other references to this building or to its waterwheel.

As a result of the underemployment of the Mint workers, Mint buildings and plant, Boulton entered into partnership with the Smith brothers to produce a patent buckle called a 'latchet' (*see* pp 27–8). Many of the rooms of the 1791 workshops were taken over by the new latchet firm and some building work was undertaken. In late 1793, a new stamp shop, presumably for the buckles, was constructed, and it may have been placed at the rear of the 1791 building on the site of short-lived water closets (*see* Fig 5.12).[86] Both James Webster and Charles Glover, who worked together on the 1791 building, were involved in the construction of the stamp shop, although Glover was not paid until October 1795.[87] In April 1794, Glover also took down and rebuilt 'the shop [at] the upper end of the Mint yard' at a larger size,[88] and during the rest of the year he was also involved in work on the 'Buckle shops near the Tea Room', a gallery in these shops, a die shop, and on a 'Silver Room at the back of Mr Browns Acc[omptin]g House'.[89] The buckle shops next to the tea room are probably those mentioned by Glover when one of his workers, measuring up to alter the gallery, was stopped by one of the Smith brothers who suggested removing the roof of the building and raising another shop over the gallery. Glover was unhappy with the idea and complained to Boulton that 'it would produce a great deformity in the Mint Buildings'.[90] Its location was most likely to have been at the rear (east) side of the tea room and immediately south of the engine house.[91] An even bigger job for Glover in 1794 was to begin the construction of the first part of the Latchet (Crescent) Building, a perplexing decision on Boulton's part in the circumstances of underused Mint workshops. Something of the reason may be gleaned from the comment in Glover's letter dated 27 January 1794, suggesting to Boulton a way of resolving 'Mr Smith's' need for more accommodation:

> If you cannot contrive room enough the least and the cheapest in the end would I think be finally to determain on the plan and Elevation of the new shoping intended in the plan we lately leveled up to the Gravel walk where you intended to have a handsome room, and then to build one or two shops & c for Immediate use, in conformity to that plan, reserving the other part until you see it indispensably necessary.[92]

It may be that, in the end, the latchet operation demanded more room than was surplus in the Mint and that Glover's suggestion is the first known reference to the proposed Latchet (Crescent) Building and also its construction in phases.

Within three years of the construction of the 1791 mint building, the buckle (latchet) business was so well established there that when a fire broke out within on 7 February 1794 it was described as being in the 'Buckle Shops' rather than in the mint. The fire began either in the room containing 'the Great presses' next to the shaking shop or in the room above. Workmen prevented the whole of the building from being destroyed and managed to confine the blaze to this central part, the poor mint guard dog being the only casualty (room marked, '4 presses', in Fig 5.12).[93]

At the end of 1794, the Latchet Building was nearing completion, with sash windows being installed and glazed and doors being hung.[94] Building accounts continue into the middle of 1795.[95] It was the junction between the southern bay and the curving wing dating from this phase of construction that was excavated by *Time Team* in April 1996 (*see* Appendix 1). The mid-1790s saw the nadir of the mint operation, with only a third of the space (5946 sq ft/552.38 sq m) occupied by this business and the rest (11,963sq ft/1,111.36 sq m) used by the Latchet Company.[96]

The national coinage and the reorganisation of the Mint, 1797–9

It was not until 1797 that Matthew Boulton finally achieved his ambition of coining for the government, when in March of that year he at last 'signed & seald with the Treasury ... to Coin pence'. The order was for 480 tons (435.5 tonnes) of 1d pieces and 20 tons (18 tonnes) of 2d pieces, with the first delivery of 20 tons to be on 29 May 1797 and 20 tons per week thereafter.[97] He immediately began considering minor modifications to the mint to strengthen it for the massive task ahead.[98] The eight vertical posts of the circular frame that held the presses needed to be replaced and Newbold (Boulton's builder at the time) was called in to advise. In addition, recoil air pumps were required to soften the blow made by the presses.[99]

More radical changes to the machinery were, however, being considered. A hint is given by Boulton in a letter to John Southern on 19 May 1797: 'I hope you have not lost sight of the new Mint for I am persuaded it will be far more compleat & harmonious than the present one, & the more I think of it the more I am pleased'.[100] In the meantime, adjustments to the existing presses were carried out and it was hoped that six would be ready by the second week of June.[101] As negotiations on the government contract took longer than expected, it was not finally signed until 9 May and no coins were delivered on 29 May.

John Southern played a key role in technological developments at this time. In January 1798, Matthew Boulton approved his plan for 'working of Coining Presses by means of a partial vacuum'.[102] One machine was to be tested, and if it proved 'to be a better mode' than the existing means of powering the presses, Boulton was willing to pay Southern £500 for exclusive rights to 'purchase the invention'. It was not until April that we hear of actual experiments being carried out. Much of the correspondence naturally took place between Southern and Boulton. Twelve years later, however, the Soho engineers disputed that the idea was Southern's alone and contended that it had been discussed in another application as far back as 1786 when William Murdoch suggested 'a Plan of working the Pumps of Cornish-Mines by means of a communication being formed between them & a Vessel exhausted by a Steam-Engine'.[103] Southern was incensed at not being given due credit and it is clear that he had just cause. The 1798 correspondence highlights John Southern's vital role in the developments that were reported to Boulton while he was in London trying to extend the government contracts to include halfpennies and farthings.

Changes to the mint machinery were radical. Previously, the steam engine was applied to moving shafts ending with a horizontal wheel with cams or 'curves' that forced up a piston in a cylinder, creating a vacuum. The energy created by the sudden release of the piston on the passing of the cam was transferred to revolve the screw of the press. Thenceforth, the steam engine would be applied directly to the creation of a partial vacuum in a long tube running parallel to the presses. For each press, there was a piston and cylinder attached to the top of the tube. The piston was linked by vertical and horizontal levers to a hollow elongated 'trumpet' attached to the top of the screw and arms of the press. Using the expansion of air let into a partial vacuum below and atmospheric pressure above, the sudden motion of the piston downwards gave impetus to the screw. In addition, a heavy balanced beam, connected to the screw on one side and to a smaller cylinder and piston on the other, helped return the screw to the upper position and reduce the violence of the recoil. The characteristic 'trumpet' on top of the press contained in its hollow interior a thin rod linking the screw with the balanced beam above. The coining presses were no longer arranged in circles but in a line parallel to the straight vacuum tube. However, the cutting-out presses continued to use the old technology with minor refinements and were still invariably arranged in circles. As a result, cutting-out rooms tended to be square and coining rooms rectangular (Figs 5.13 and 5.14).

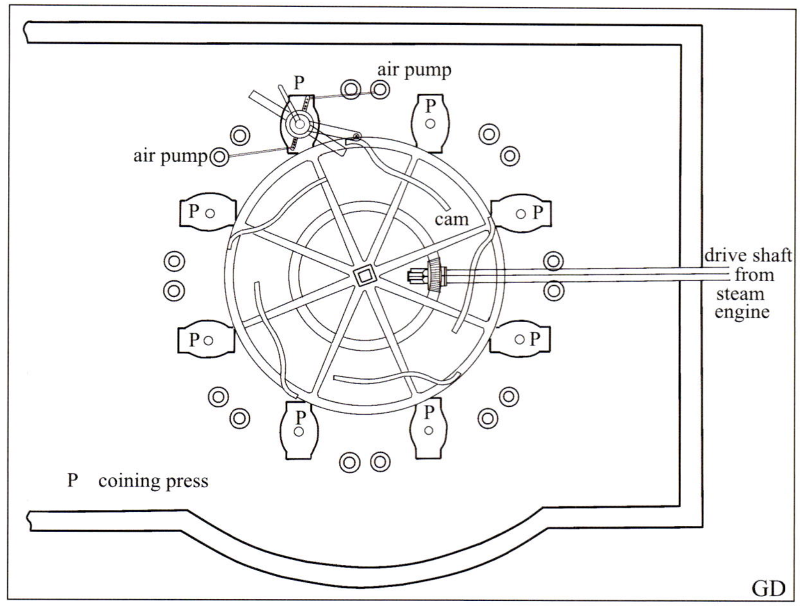

Fig 5.13
The layout of coining presses in the round, 1788–98.

Doty claims that the refitting of the mint was carried out partly to test the new arrangement for a new mint in St Petersburg, Russia.[104] Furthermore, he asserts that the Russians' requirement that coining of different metals be

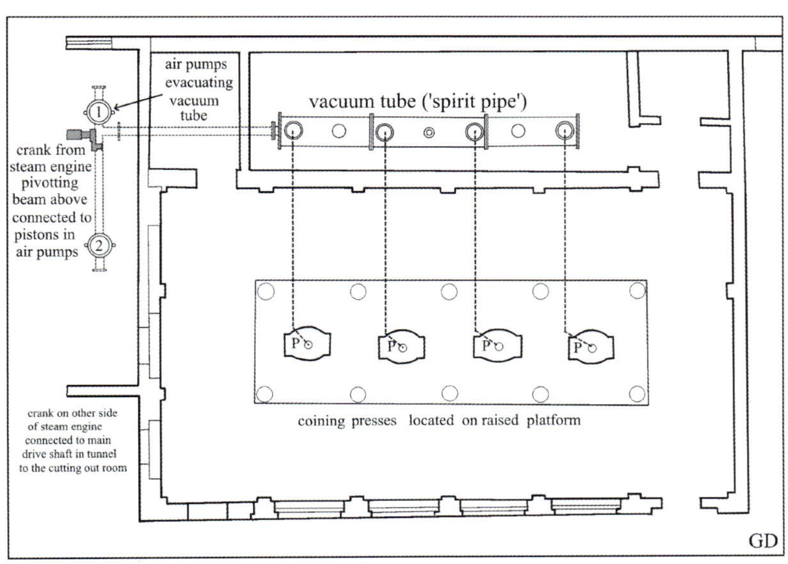

Fig 5.14
The layout of coining presses in line as used from 1798 onwards in all Boulton mints, including the Soho Foundry Mint constructed in 1860.

carried out in different rooms forced the adoption of the vacuum-power technology with presses in a line and capable of being partitioned from each other. The application of vacuum power to coining, however, had little to do with a proposed mint in St Petersburg. The 10-year-old technology was simply inadequate for minting on the grand scale needed for the home currency. The mechanicals quickly smashed themselves to pieces, and John Southern's ideas presented an alternative in which the blow to the press could be better controlled. The linear arrangement of presses sprang directly from the technology – the vacuum tube was straight. Where the blow was not so severe, as in the case of cutting out, the circular arrangement persisted.

On the 23 April 1798, Southern reported on the second trial of the 'Barostat piston'. This was the piston that induced motion to the press's screw and which sat over the vacuum tube. The exact location of the experiment is unknown but, space being a little tight, it may have been close to the engine. As a result, Southern 'could not apply the indicator where I had prepared a hole for it without breaking the sash and one of the ribs of the frame' and test the air pressure in the 'air vessel' (vacuum tube). Although the piston leaked, the trial 'proved much more successful than the first'.[105] Boulton did not merely observe the trials at a distance, as the few undated pages of his detailed notes, calculations and sketches on the working of the 'Barostadt' (or barostat) that have survived clearly show (Fig 5.15).[106]

Also in April 1798, a radical reorganisation of the Mint buildings was under discussion. Boulton had already sketched a layout of eight presses, and from contemporary mapping it is clear that these were to be erected in an area perhaps of former menagerie pens lying to the west of the Mint coining room and adjacent to the north side of the tea-room complex. The January 1788 plan indicates that the walled area here consisted of enclosures open to the sky (*see* Fig 5.4).[107] John Southern was concerned that the eight presses would not fit into the area allotted by Boulton and there would only be room (50ft/15.24m in length) for seven unless the eighth press was to 'infringe on the lapping-up room'. The latter may have occupied the

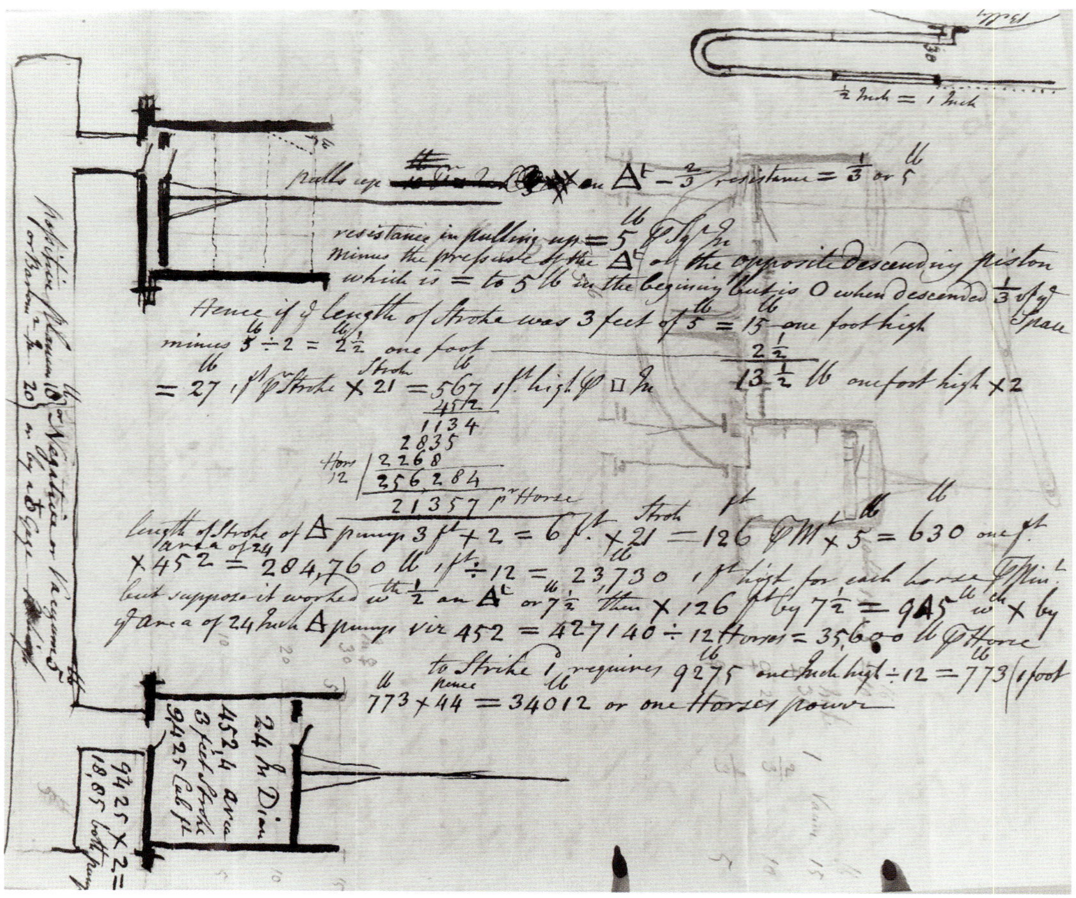

Fig 5.15
Matthew Boulton's sketches of the barostat and calculations of its performance, c 1798.

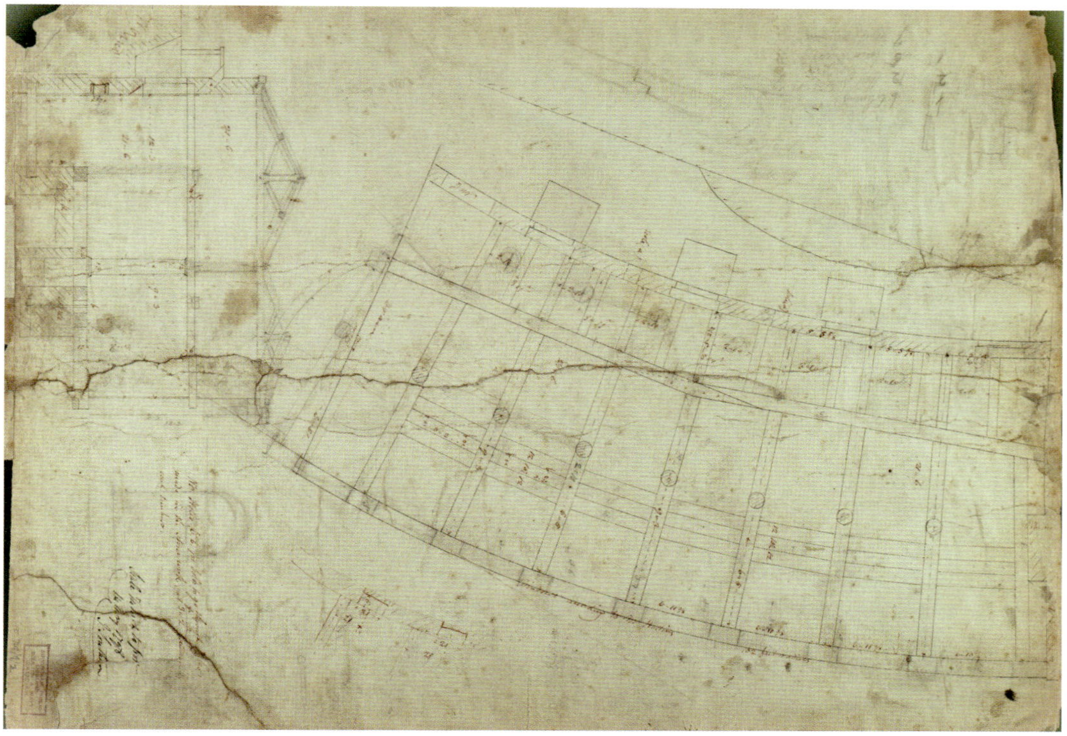

Fig 5.16
John Southern's plan of the new coining room, located in the area of the former menagerie pens and constructed to employ the vacuum-power technology he had a major role in developing, 14 May 1798.

northernmost of the old menagerie pens. Boulton replied that seven would do 'in the new Mint & one or two in the old one, when found necessary' and reminded Southern of the need for 'secrecy', recommending that the experimental equipment should be dismantled as quickly as possible in case any of it should 'be seen by a Sagetious spy'.[108]

In mid-May, Boulton urged Southern via Lawson 'to conclude his Experiments & forward as much as possible the Building & all that is necessary for carrying into effect the new plan of Coinage'.[109] The response to this, although not mentioned in the correspondence, appears to have been a drawing signed by John Southern and dated 14 May 1798 (Fig 5.16).[110] This shows the plan of a slightly curved building of eight bays, one per coining press, following the original arc of the unroofed area of the menagerie. The curved bay of the existing coining room is visible to the east, as is the chimney of the tea room to the south. The eighth press is shown, but it has required the construction of a segmental bay, presumably into the lapping room. The cross section of the building reveals that it was two storeys high, with the first floor at the same height as the yard by the old coining room. This arrangement was determined by the topography of the site, with land falling away westwards. The ground floor, in turn, was at two levels, with a sunken passage 5ft (1.52m) wide running for about 10ft (3.05m) immediately below the old coining-room yard and about 5.25ft (1.6m) below the main floor, which itself was 16ft (4.88m) wide. A row of Doric columns at this level supported the floor above, but this second storey was only about 4ft (1.22) high, as it was only intended to hold the upper part of the mint machinery such as the pivoting balance beams of the presses. Four windows on the side of the old mint yard needed light wells and on the main and highly visible west elevation a series of windows were to be designed 'according to Mr Hollins'.

The Southern drawing, apparently implemented, was a less ambitious version of an original scheme designed by William Hollins in about April 1798. A misfiled and undated watercolour in the Boulton & Watt portfolios of an elevation and cross section is now known to be of the new mint (Fig 5.17).[111] The latter was to envelop both the site of the old coining room and the menagerie pens, altogether 43ft (13.11m) wide and 18ft (5.49m) high. An account for this drawing was dated 6 April [1798].[112] It seems that within a month or so this grand design was rejected, presumably on the grounds of cost, and Southern set to work on his own drawing. There is another undated drawing by William Hollins, which is an attempt to create an imposing and

Fig 5.17
Water-coloured elevation and plan of the new Soho Mint by William Hollins, c April 1798.

symmetrical elevation to the tea room and menagerie complex even before the open pens were rebuilt as a coining room.[113] A payment to Mr Hollins is recorded in 1797 for a drawing of the tea room, which may be the elevation in question.[114] The menagerie was not rebuilt in the way suggested, but it is difficult to determine if any of the remainder of the elevation was implemented. Hollins also advised on the construction of the mint chimney. He was concerned that the considerable vibration produced by the machinery would eventually destroy the stack and suggested using stone cramped together and that 'the form of a Tuscan column' will help 'resist the winds'.[115] There is a drawing of the mint chimney by William Creighton showing a 65ft (19.81m)-tall cylinder on a panelled base, but this is more likely to be the 1825 version, which was clearly intended to have a panelled base.[116]

The new part of the mint building was constructed by Benjamin Wyatt of Sutton Coldfield. During 1798 and 1799, he was involved in a considerable amount of other work at Soho, including the central block of the Latchet (Crescent) Building, new stables, and rebuilding at the house. Building accounts indicate that work on the mint began in May 1798 and continued well into 1799.[117]

At the end of August, drawings for a new 23in (584mm) steam engine were prepared. It was intended not only to replace the existing 10-year-old 16in (406mm) engine, but also to be located in a new position close to the vacuum pipe it was to evacuate in the new coining room. This room was previously used as a workshop and is marked 'Buschs' on the 1791 map (*see* Fig 5.12). The boiler house was to link the outside corner of the mint with a single-storey building belonging to the latchet company (latchelarian shop) and the boiler chimney was to be built against the wall of the latchet shop (Fig 5.18).[118] The steam engine itself is omitted from the drawings, but the sun-and-planet crank is shown attached to a flywheel alone and to no other machinery. The fly shaft may have been applied to moving workshop machinery, but was certainly not involved in the operation of the coining presses. The drawings do not make it clear how the presses were to be operated, and this may have been deliberate for reasons of secrecy (*see* p. 105). All that is shown is a second beam 2ft (610mm) shorter than the engine beam and pivoting nearly 3ft (910mm) higher. The ends of these two beams overlapped and they were apparently connected so that the engine beam was able to pivot the shorter beam above. Drawings, dating from around September 1798, showing only vacuum pumps and pipes have to be used to obtain a fuller picture (Fig 5.19).[119] It then becomes apparent that this second beam was connected to two vacuum pumps, one at either end, the pumps themselves connected beneath by a horizontal pipe that eventually led to the main vacuum tube positioned in the lowermost part of the new coining room. The vacuum pumps were to occupy part of the yard between the old and new coining rooms and, as a result, this was to be roofed over. Two drawings, dated 31 October 1798, show the engine for the first time, but again the vacuum machinery is left out (Fig 5.20).[120] It is assumed that the proposed plans for the steam engine, vacuum pumps and pipes were implemented more or less as shown. A simplified plan of the mint as it was after these alterations were carried out is shown in Fig 5.21. Doty, however, arrived at an entirely different and, as a

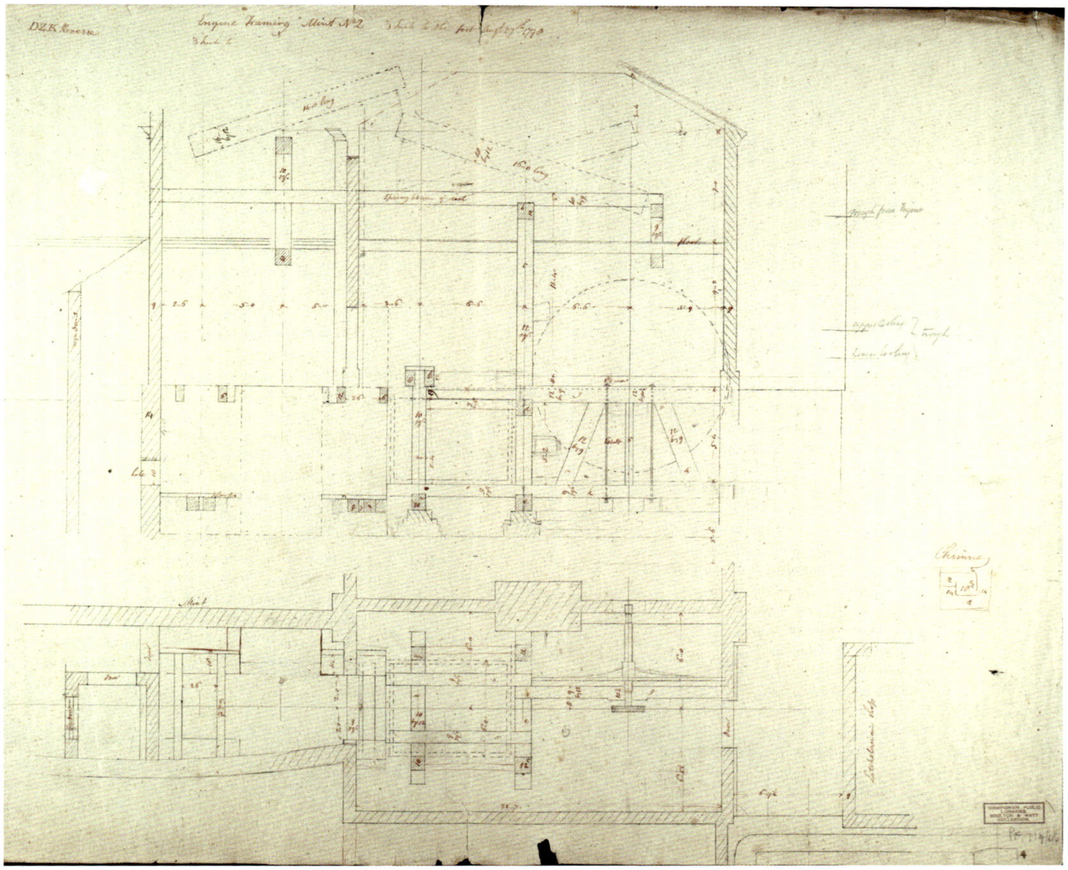

Fig 5.18
Plan and cross section of the new mint engine room, 27 August 1798 (Reverse). The shorter beam pivoted by the engine beam operated two vacuum pumps connected to the main vacuum pipe.

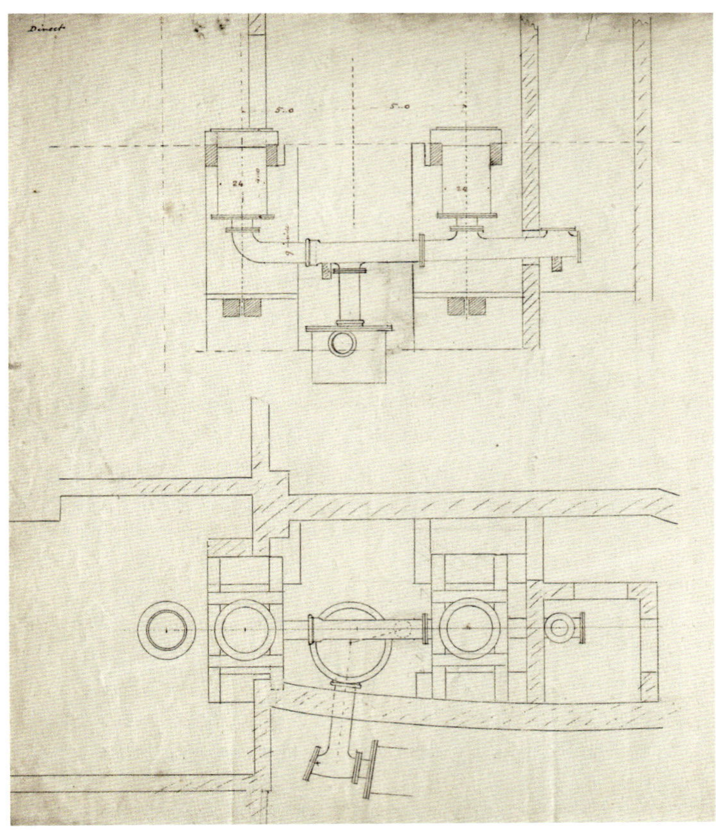

Fig 5.19
Plan and cross section of the vacuum pumps and pipes, c August 1798. The connection to the main vacuum tube leading to the presses was first vertical and then horizontal.

consequence, erroneous layout of the new mint with the steam engine placed on the floor above the coining presses.[121]

In early November Southern questioned Boulton's desire to block a doorway into the new mint from the last remaining (and to be demolished) menagerie pen on the north side because 'the spirit pipes were intended to be taken in there' and he felt that it would be better to leave the door until the pipes had been delivered that way. Secrecy over the pipework was of such concern that Southern was worrying about the best route for this new material to arrive without its being seen.[122] Boulton agreed to delay blocking the door and begged for rapid progress on the 'new Engines'.[123] By 21 November, the framework of the new steam engine was erected and it was hoped to have the engine installed within a month, and the spirit pipes and pumps even earlier, despite the fact that the engine erectors might see the pumps. It is difficult to imagine how the men could have been prevented from seeing them as the nearest pump was only 2ft (610mm) away from the engine cylinder.[124] On 14 December, however, none of the 'spirit pipes' or 'exhausting vessels' had yet been installed.

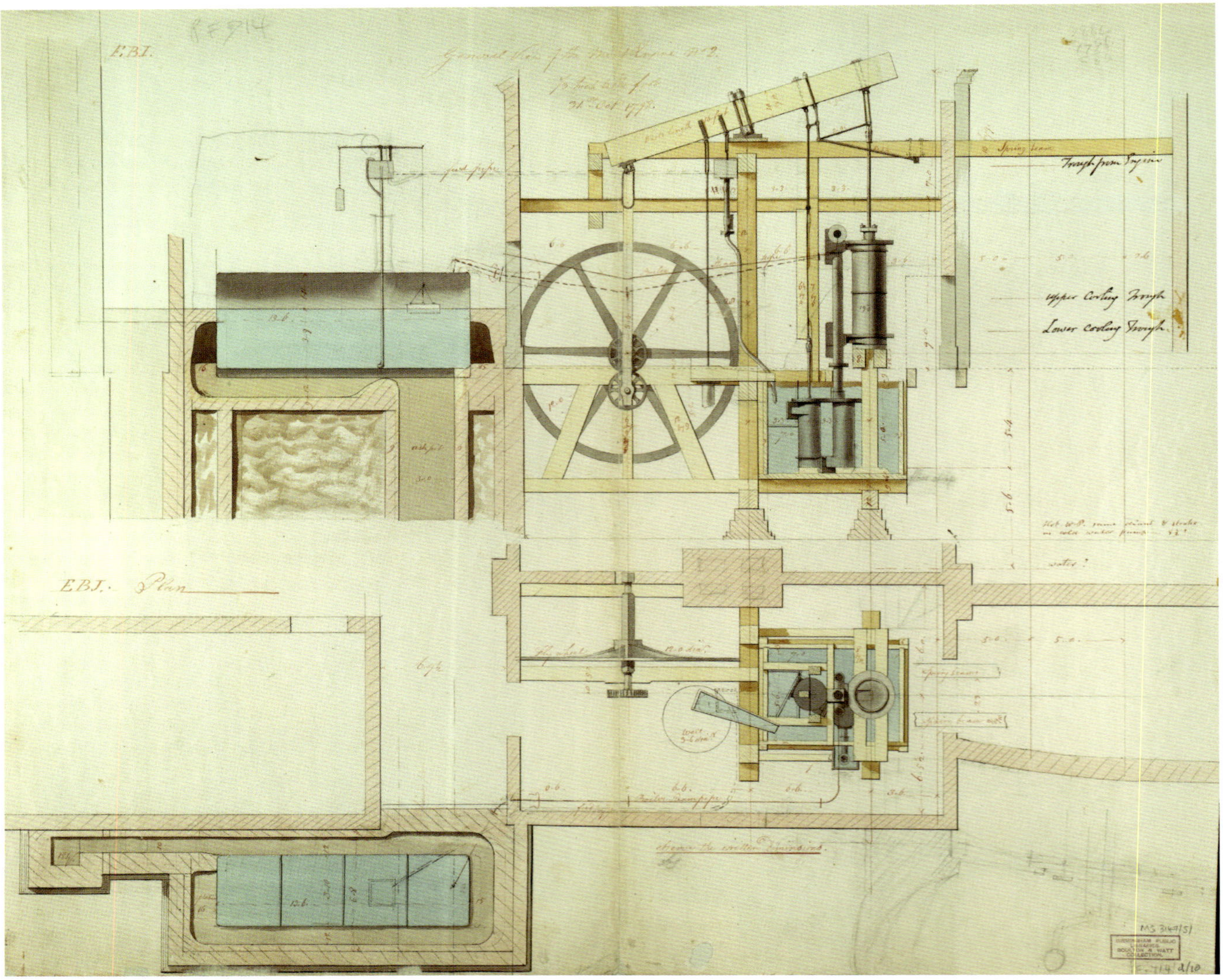

Fig 5.20
Water-coloured elevation and plan of the new mint engine and boiler without its connection to the vacuum pumps, 31 October 1798.

Southern preferred this to be done only after Boulton had returned from London, although he hoped to have the engine working within a week.[125] The steam engine cost £322 18s 4d, excluding the engine house.[126]

There is no further correspondence until February 1799, when we hear about delay in moving presses from the old to the new mint.[127] For the next few months, all effort was devoted to getting the full complement of eight presses working. On 21 February, two presses were tested and worked 'without any quarrel or disagreement'.[128] By 9 March 1799, Boulton was becoming anxious as his coinage contracts were being delayed by the state of the mint and he had not heard whether the first four presses were operating. He wanted the fifth, a new one, to be installed immediately and the shortfall made up by transferring three out of the old mint.[129] On 11 March, Southern regretfully reported that the four presses were not yet operational but should be by that afternoon. He counselled against transferring the old mint presses, as three of the new ones would be ready within a fortnight, but in order to expedite the coinage contracts he suggested that the four new presses in the new coining room and three in the old could be worked together.[130] Southern kept his promise and the four new presses were brought into operation by the morning of 12 March.[131]

Not satisfied with being 'daily tyed to a stake at the House of Commons & baited for 3 hours on the Copper trade', Boulton found time to negotiate the export of his new mint technology to Russia. Preparations had to be made to receive the Russian ambassador, including papering the mint walls and ceiling, painting the former dark green and latter light sky blue,

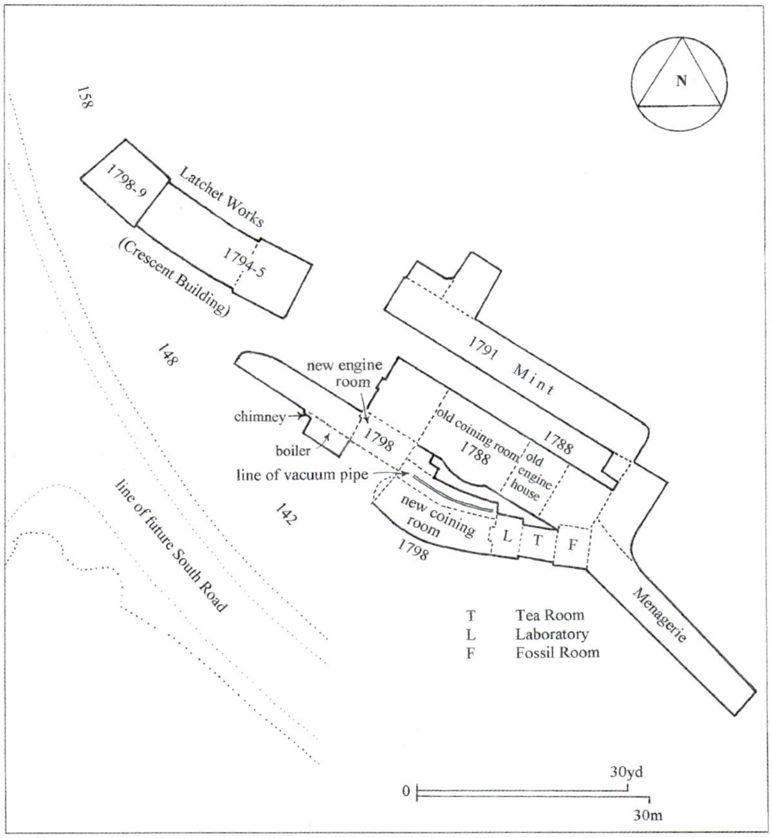

Fig 5.21
Sketch plan of the new mint, 1798.

Fig 5.22
Drawing of the coining press trumpet and ceiling blaze, by John Phillp, 1799.

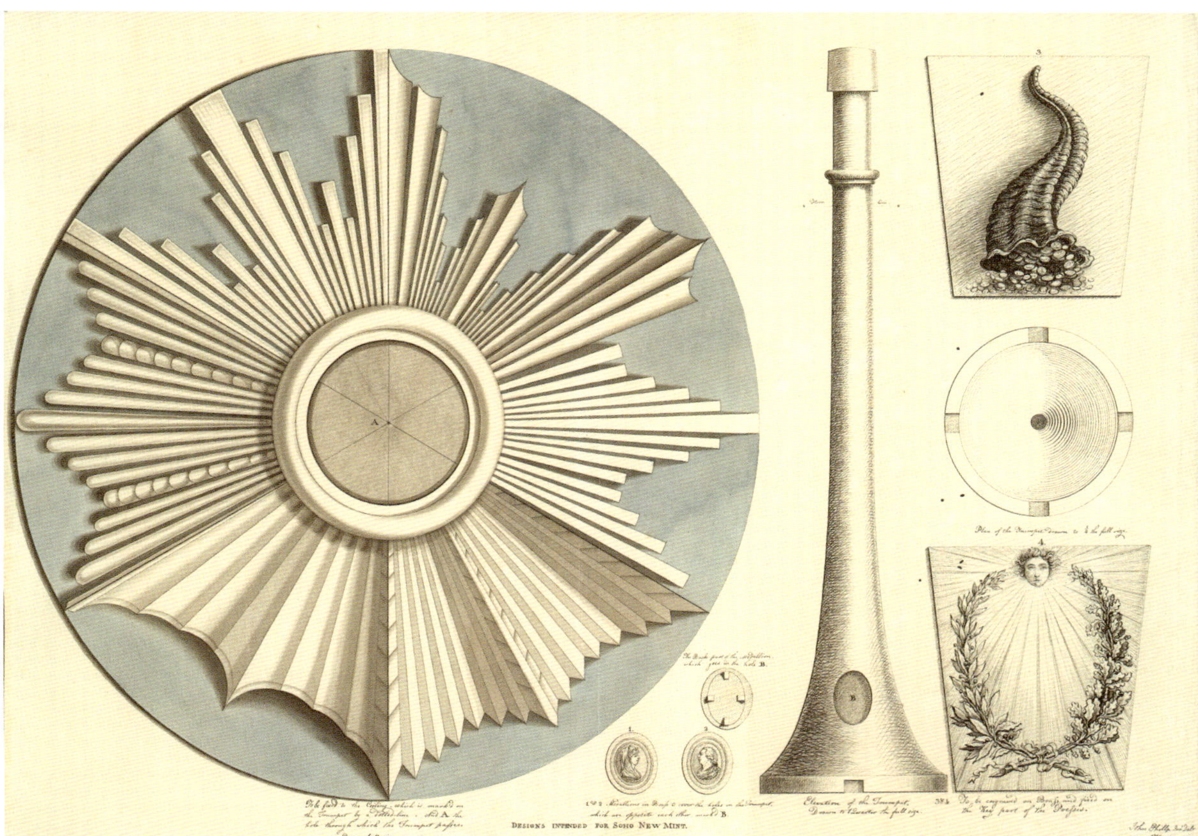

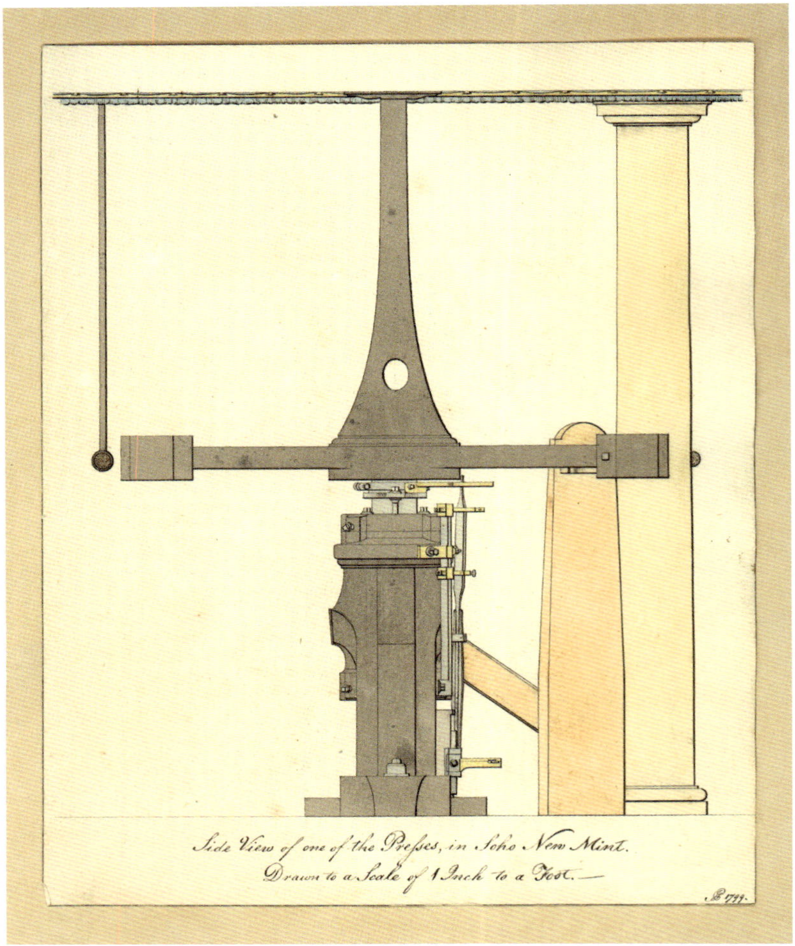

Fig 5.23
Side elevation of a coining press with the trumpet above by John Phillp, c 1799.

giving the doors and windows a coat of stone-coloured oil paint, and erecting decorative iron roses where the trumpets for each press passed through the ceiling.[132] The correspondence of March 1799 provides the earliest available information on the internal appearance of the mint and there is fortunately more material to enhance the picture. John Phillp drew several patterns for a star blaze ceiling rose to surround the press trumpet and designed other more minor decorative features (Fig 5.22). He produced the now only known drawing of a press in the 1798–9 mint (Fig 5.23). He also drew the 1788–97 version of the coin press. The iron wheel that engaged with the curves on the horizontal wheel can be seen below the fly arm of the press (Fig 5.24).

In April 1799, Captain Hankin and the Colonel of the Royal Scots Greys applied to see the mint. Matthew Boulton allowed the visit on condition that they were accompanied by John Southern: 'I wish you would shew it them and enter by the Tea Room takeing care of the Cave door.'[133] The exact function and position of the cave are not known and it was only mentioned once before in the correspondence: 'What ever flue we may think necessary to warm the cave I am persuaded it must be low as the spirit pipes for it will warm upwards & but very little downwards'.[134] It was close to the menagerie entrance to the new mint and near to the level where the

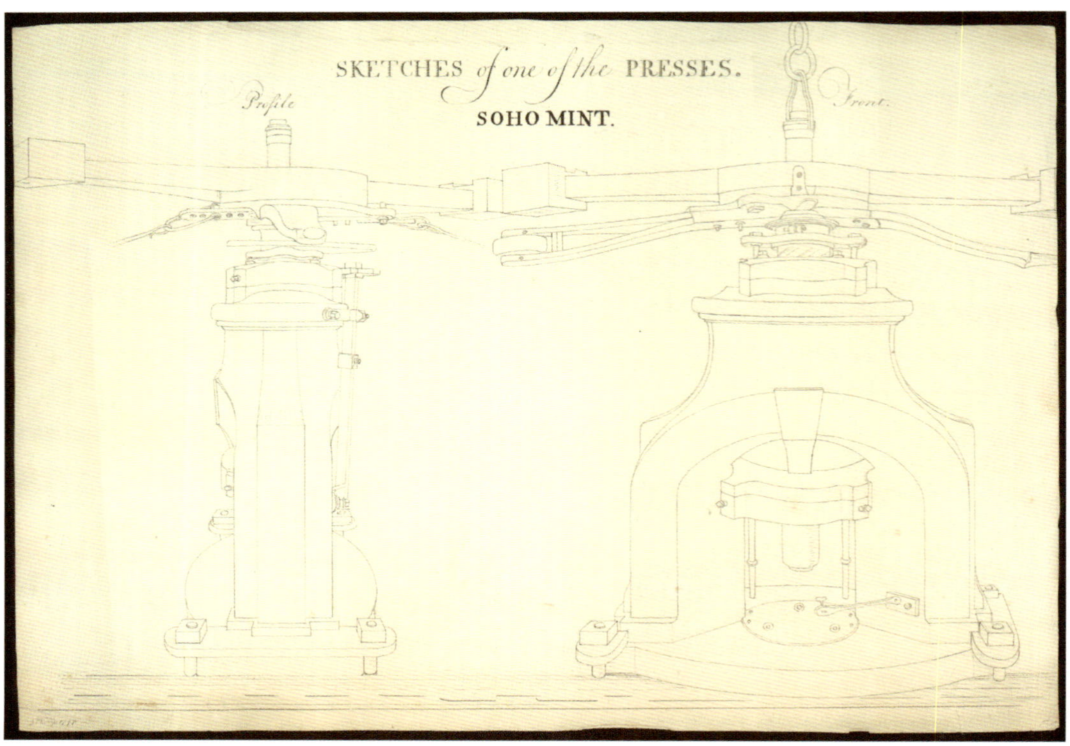

Fig 5.24
Elevations of a press in the original 1788 coining room by John Phillp, 1797.

vacuum pipe ran in the 1.5m-deep trench in the coining-room floor.

On 1 May 1799, John Southern wrote triumphantly to Boulton announcing that all the eight presses were at work at last: '6 on pennies 1 on half pence 1 on farthings'. The presses all working simultaneously were very noisy and Southern intended to festoon the beams with paper curtains to help deaden the echo.[135] The coining room had also only just been painted, but 'final finish in the painting way' was to be undertaken by Cornelius Dixon. On 3 May, Boulton ordered the cessation of halfpenny production because the contract had not yet been signed.[136] The signatures were obtained fairly quickly afterwards so that by the end of 1799 the production of national coinage at Soho stood at:[137]

Twopence	40 tons
Penny	1,226 tons
Halfpenny	526 tons
Farthing	26 tons
Total	1,818 tons

Consolidation and expansion, 1800–10

Boulton had realised his dream of creating the first steam-powered mint in the world, but the next, no less ambitious, step was to sell his new technology abroad. By 1806, he had set up a mint in St Petersburg (Russia) and one in Denmark. The Soho Mint had also produced the national coinage and in technical terms had left the Royal Mint in London far behind. From the government's point of view, this situation was intolerable and the capital's mint had to be updated. In 1805, as Boulton approached 80 years of age, the contract was obtained to install machinery on the Soho model at the new Royal Mint. It must have pleased him to see the antiquated technology, the sinecures and the stifling organisational practices of the country's principal mint swept away.[138] Although further contracts for the national coinage were obtained, it was obvious that these would eventually dry up as the Royal Mint applied Boulton's own machinery to make the nation's pennies. Soho had always produced tokens, commemorative medals and foreign coinage and had now begun to export mint machinery. It was the combination of these activities that allowed it to survive the eventual loss of the national coinage.

The effect on Soho of the growth and diversification of business in the first decade of the 19th century was the expansion of the Mint into premises previously given up. It must be stressed again that the mint business was never part of the firm of Boulton & Watt. It was entirely controlled by Boulton himself and, after his death, by his son Matthew Robinson Boulton, followed for a short time by his grandson Matthew Piers Watt Boulton. The Boulton & Watt Foundry in Smethwick produced many of the heavy mint-machinery castings, but only as contractor to the Mint Company. However, there was more fluidity between the firms in the use of staff, particularly the senior engineers and managers, e.g. John Southern. The mint firm itself, known as 'MB Mint', split originally between two sites, the main coining complex itself and the rolling mill within the Manufactory, then gradually took over space in the Latchet (Crescent) Building as that business wound down during the early 1800s. In fact, the reasons for building the central bay of the Crescent Building in 1798–9 are not clear. It may have produced extra space for the mint business, for in May 1799 the lower storey was appropriated 'to be fitted up with vices'. However, Benjamin Smith of the latchet company refused Boulton the lower story of the older south bay, insisting that it could not be spared.[139] On the other hand, the new mint had caused the abandonment of the original coining room and engine, the latter being afterwards engaged in pumping water for Boulton's garden. On 20 July 1800, a fire broke out and 'the floor & roof of the [old] Engine house were consumed, and also a very small part of the roof of the adjoining lumber room (to the East). No damage whatever has been sustained by the new mint or by the Tea Room. The old mint has also escaped with only a few broken panes.' The old mint engine was described as being 'alive & well after its wasting', with some of the timber work singed by the fire but capable of being repaired in a matter of days. The engine was set back to work on 24 July without the roof being restored.[140]

Comparison of the inventory of *c* 1795 with the 1809 inventory shows that, by the time of Matthew Boulton's death in 1809, the Mint contained over 40 rooms spread over 3 sites, a fourfold increase since the mid-1790s and before the contract for the national coinage had been obtained.[141] The production of latchets ceased in about 1806 and most of the expansion had taken place by taking over the latchet premises, much of it in the original 1791 mint building (*see* pp 99–100). The main Mint complex was entirely reoccupied and a room or two was taken in the then underused Latchet (Crescent) Building.

In January 1810, six months after Boulton's death, the leading Soho engineers met to discuss the past development of the mint machinery and to determine their respective contributions to the process. The conference was not lacking in contention due, most notably, to Southern's assertions that the importance of his role in the whole process had not, he felt, been appreciated. In view of the innovative foment of the previous years, it proved difficult to define each person's role, for ideas had been stirred with all others 'in the simmering Soho pot'. In the event, we should be grateful that the engineers at least made the attempt to identify the ingredients and, as a result, have left a rare account of such a process to aid modern scholarship. They also felt the need to acknowledge Boulton's role for posterity:[142]

> in the whole course of time they were employed by him [Boulton] at the Mint, or consulted on matters relative to it, he was always fully intent not only upon investigating the causes of the difficulties which they had received, but, also in suggesting remedies, in all of which he gave constant proofs of his great knowledge of mechanical & metallurgic parts of the subject. It would be both unjust & ungrateful to his memory were they not to take this opportunity to testify, that, many improvements in the rolling, annealing, & cleaning, of the metals, in the forging, multiplying, hardening & tempering of the Dies, in the construction of the milling & Cutting-out Machines, originated solely with himself: that few, if any improvements occurred in the other parts of the Machinery to which he did not lead, or materially contribute by his suggestions; that the arrangement & methodezing of the whole was exclusively his own; & that to his indefatigable energy & perseverence in pursuit of this the favorite and nearly the sole object of the last Twenty years of the active part of his life, is to be attributed the perfection which he ultimetly attained.

In the shadow of Boulton's death, this may be interpreted as a respectful panegyric, but it can never be denied that the Soho Mint was Boulton's supreme achievement.

The reorganisation and rebuilding of the Mint, 1824–6

The papers of Matthew Robinson Boulton have been little studied and consequently his role as owner of the Soho Manufactory and Mint has not been appreciated. There has been a tendency to dismiss him as a reluctant industrialist who preferred to remain on his country estate at Great Tew, Oxfordshire, allowing Soho to decline. Matthew Robinson Boulton did not inherit the genius of his father but he was, nevertheless, a competent engineer and manufacturer.

Between 1810 and the early 1820s, apparently very little change took place in the Mint buildings and machinery. Detailed records exist for coin production, but they have never been studied in any depth. In 1811, a mint was sold to Brazil and there are documents dating from this time that provide valuable information on the organisation of coin making at Soho.[143] In the early 1820s, Matthew Robinson Boulton obtained contracts to supply mint machinery to both Calcutta and Bombay. It may have proved difficult to furnish both these Indian destinations at the same time, and this is why arrangements were made to export old but refitted Soho machinery to Bombay while new equipment was shipped to Calcutta. It is not known whether Matthew Robinson Boulton already intended to update his mint at this time, as it was over 20 years old, or if the opportunity provided by the Bombay order prompted him to refit Soho. Over the years, improvements had been made to the machinery that was being sold worldwide and there was a need for Soho to catch up with its own latest model. Another incentive for reorganisation may have been the opportunity to consolidate minting operations. Cutting out and some milling were still carried out at this time in the lapping mill, which meant that blanks had to be transported from the manufactory to the mint, an inconvenient and laborious task.

Richard Doty considers that Matthew Robinson Boulton was not particularly interested in refitting the Soho Mint once he had sold the machinery to Bombay. He argues that it was only in the hope of eventually selling a smaller facility to the Republic of Gran Colombia that he placed new machinery in the Soho buildings. According to Doty, the deal fell through and

Matthew Robinson Boulton was left with a mint that he only connected to steam power in the summer of 1831.[144] The detailed evidence for the reorganisation of the Mint from 1824–6, however, does not support the contention that the Soho buildings were only used as a temporary working repository for machinery eventually destined to be shipped to South America. The Gran Colombia scheme was only revealed, however, in July 1826, when the Soho Mint had already been mostly rebuilt and refitted. Matthew Robinson Boulton had been approached by the East India Company to produce 25 tons (23 tonnes) of copper coinage to help train the future Calcutta Mint workmen.[145] Matthew Robinson could not help, explaining that the 'contemplated erection of the Press Room Machinery of my Coining Apparatus has been suspended'. This was because a promised order for coinage from Buenos Aires and Colombia had not materialised, nor had the 'additional inducement' that Colombia would purchase the machinery afterwards. In other words, Matthew Robinson was not willing to contemplate the final fit until orders were forthcoming. The reorganisation of the Mint had been exceedingly expensive, as will be seen below.

Earlier in 1826, however, an entirely different explanation had been given for erecting new machinery at Soho. Again, this was a case of Matthew Robinson Boulton justifying not being able to carry out orders received, the immediate cause being the state of his mint. Owing to the high price of copper and the consequent diminished prospect of obtaining coining contracts, he had chosen this particular time 'for carrying out into effect a long contemplated reorganisation of my Mint Machinery'.[146] In view of the radical nature of the rebuilding that took place in the years 1825 to 1826, Matthew Robinson Boulton's latter explanation is the more convincing. The extent and expense of this work would hardly be justified for some short-term contracts and a temporary home for South America-bound machinery. The reorganisation will be examined in more detail below following an account of the dismantling of the existing mint for Bombay.

In January 1821, Matthew Robinson Boulton estimated that Soho machinery could be refitted for the Bombay Mint at a cost of £8,000.[147] A year later, a detailed specification was drawn up, which included the following Soho equipment: eight coining presses with the wooden balance beam replaced in cast iron; some cast iron shafts; eight cutting-out presses with the top and bottom wooden frame refitted in cast iron and a new ninth press; five milling machines with iron pulleys instead of timber; three shaking machines; the iron parts of three annealing furnaces; the iron parts of four die-annealing furnaces; one multiplying press; and three lathes.[148] It is obvious from this list that the Soho Mint was to be thoroughly stripped out. According to Matthew Robinson Boulton, the eight coining presses and seven of the eight cutting-out presses had been taken up and were nearly refitted by the end of August, but they had all been left in position in case of coinage orders.[149] By 1 December 1823, it was reported that all the coining and cutting-out presses had been refitted and John Robinson, clerk at the Mint, assumed he could not use them usefully to fulfil an order during the time the remainder of the Bombay machinery was being completed.[150] By 1 January 1824, all the coining presses had been taken down except one that was working on an order for the East India Company.[151] In seeming contradiction to the events outlined above, in January 1824 Matthew Robinson Boulton instructed that the cutting-out presses should be removed and refitted.[152] John Robinson informed Matthew Robinson Boulton that this work had already been done and interpreted this instruction as referring to the removal of the coining presses and a milling machine, for Captain Hawkins, the chief engineer responsible for installing the Bombay Mint, was urgently awaiting delivery of all the machinery to London for shipping.[153] It was not until September 1824, however, that the Soho machinery was loaded onto two ships destined for Bombay. Matthew Robinson Boulton was paid £9,576 for the Soho Mint machinery and a further £248 for small alterations carried out by Boulton & Watt.[154]

There is a considerable amount of material, including plans, relating to the reorganisation of the Mint in the years 1825–6.[155] However, these plans cover only a limited area of the buildings and, as a body of information, they bear little comparison to the portfolios of informative drawings available for other mints such as Bombay and Calcutta.[156] The lack of a contemporary plan of the whole site has obstructed an understanding of this important phase in the history of the Mint. Drawings by William Creighton, dating from August 1825, show the important changes to the position of the engine and the coining room (Figs 5.25–27).[157] A new

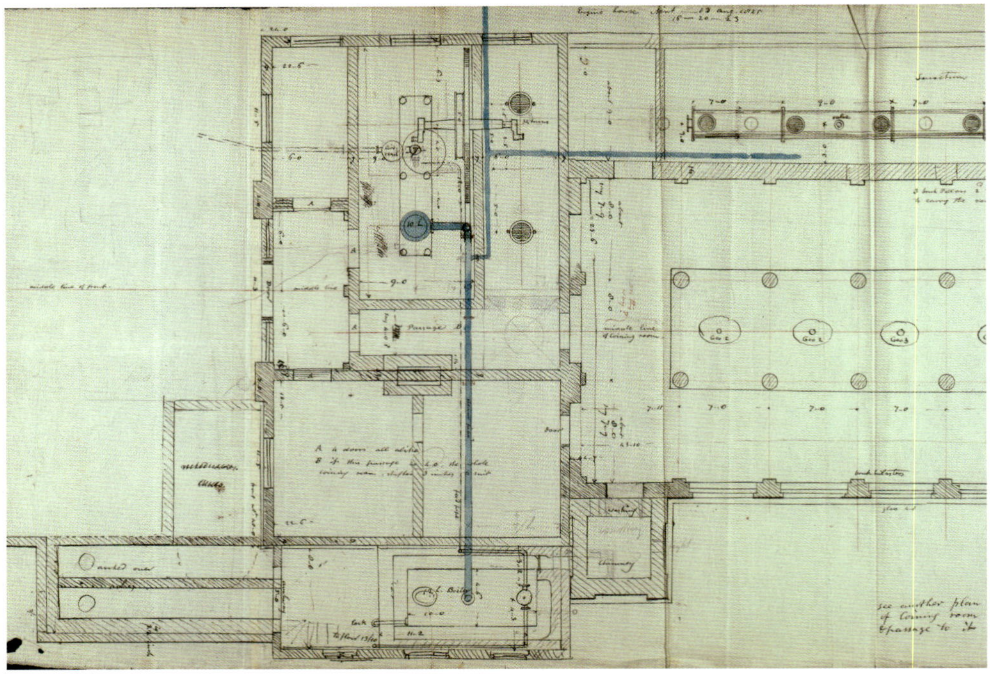

Fig 5.25
Plan of the new mint by William Creighton, 13 August 1825.

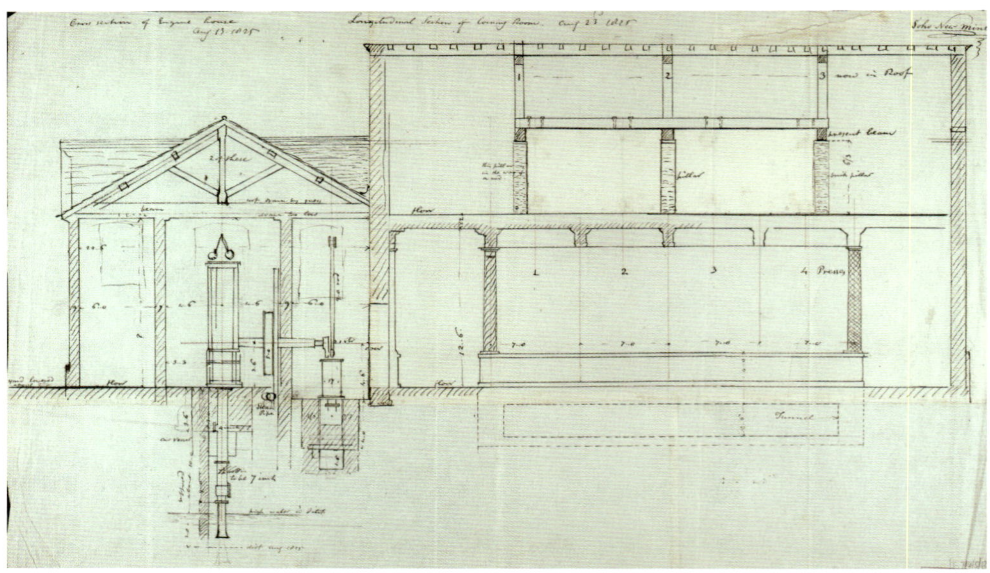

Fig 5.26
Cross section of the new mint by William Creighton, 13 and 23 August 1825.

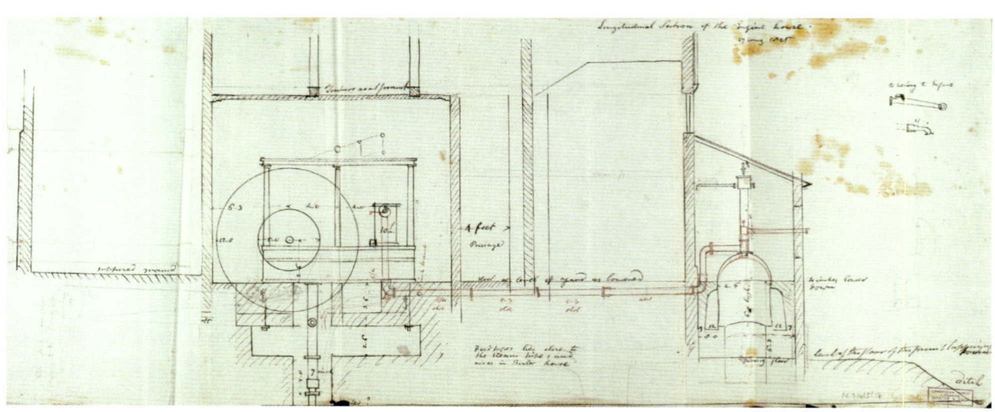

Fig 5.27
Cross section of the new mint by William Creighton, 27 August 1825.

engine was to be installed adjacent to the second mint engine room in the north-east corner of the original mint block, the third and final location. Manufactured by Boulton & Watt, the engine cost the Mint Company £668 7s 0d and had a 19.75in (501mm) cylinder rated at 10hp.[158] A new boiler and chimney were also erected and the mint's second engine of 1798 was dismantled and eventually sold in 1831.[159] In contrast to the three engine positions to this date, the four new presses were to return to the original coining room in use from 1788 to 1797. The plan shows a widening of the room, however, to make space for the vacuum pipe. As could be expected, the presses were to stand in line and parallel to the vacuum pipe. The reduction of presses from eight to four implies a much-reduced capacity but, due to their greater efficiency, perhaps not by the full 50% expected. It is not clear what happened to the second (1798–1824) coining room. The plan shows the corner of the tea room, which had been attached to the south end of the second coining room, but it does not depict the latter. The footprint of the new coining room partly overlapped that of the second in the area of the vacuum pipe, and it can only be assumed that the whole structure had already or was intended to be demolished.

Unlike earlier phases of work at the Mint there are few letters describing progress, but by way of compensation a number of documents have survived that itemise proposed mechanical and building work.[160] The document summarising the building operations relates directly to a plan on which the rooms were given identifying letters. Unfortunately, this plan has been lost, making it more difficult to understand what was intended for the rest of the Mint outside of the engine house and coining room. However, it is clear that a considerable amount of shafting running in tunnels was involved, by means of which all the other machinery was to be powered by the engine.

The crucial factor in the reconstruction of the lost plan was the discovery that a single but lengthy run of new underground shafting was required. Contemporary records suggest that it was intended to be at least 195.5ft (59.59m) long. It was later measured at 210ft (64m) in 1842, and at 203ft (61.87m) in 1850.[161] The same evidence indicates that the shaft ran under 'The Yard' and at one end was connected to a

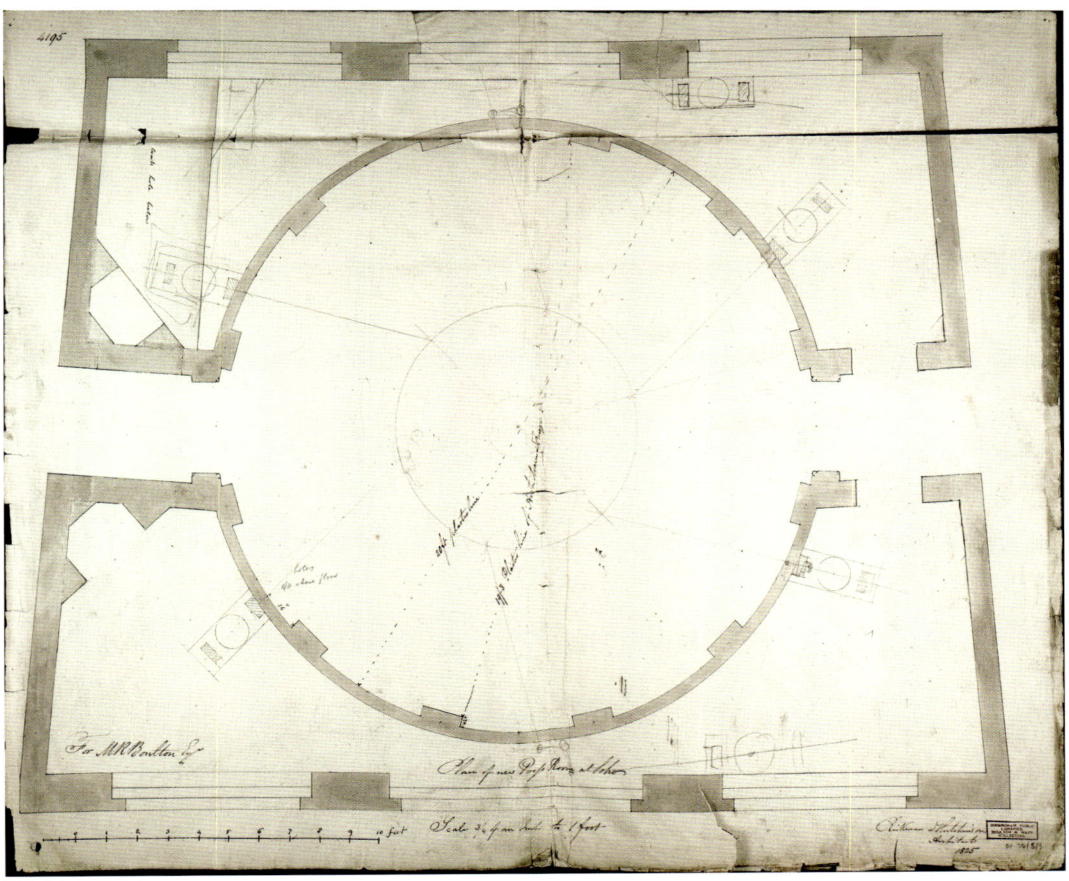

Fig 5.28
Rickman and Hutchinson's plan of the new coin cutting-out room to be located in the central bay of the Latchet (Crescent) Building, 1825.

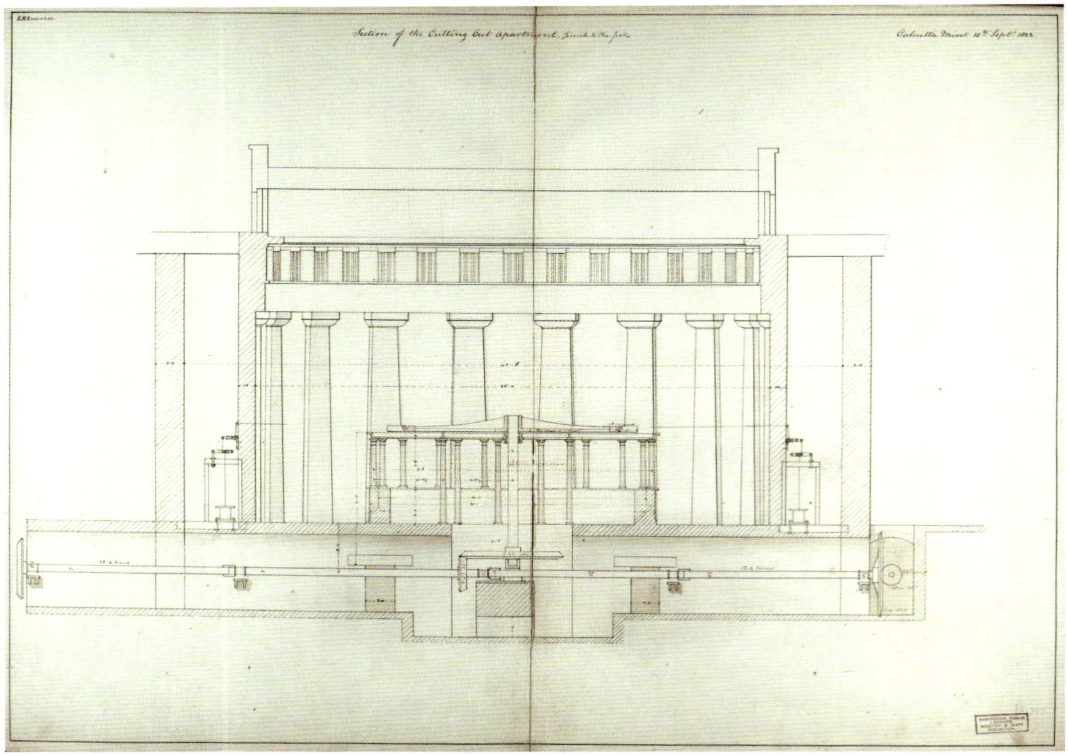

Fig 5.29
Cross section of the massive Calcutta coin cutting-out room, 1822, showing how power was transmitted to it by underground shafts.

water pump and to the machinery of the new cutting-out room at the other. The yard between the original coining room, now to be reused, and the 1791 building seemed the most likely place. Running a 200ft (60.96m) length of shaft in a tunnel down the spine of this yard, only about 100ft (30.48m) long itself, means that the shaft would have to continue northwards and in doing so enter the Latchet (Crescent) Building. Southwards out of the yard was an unlikely direction into the Soho garden. The water pump, which was to serve Soho House, reused the water well in the original 1788 engine house and thus accurately marks where the south end of the shaft was located. The other end, as a result, found itself within the centre bay of the Crescent Building. Having deduced its position and orientation, the location of the 'press room', shown in a plan and hitherto unidentified, became immediately apparent[162] (Fig 5.28). Of added significance is the fact that the plan was drawn by Rickman and Hutchinson, a prestigious architectural practice, whose work at Soho has not previously been known, although the same partnership worked at Great Tew for Matthew Robinson Boulton in 1826–7. No manufacturing buildings have been attributed either to their partnership or to their individual practices.[163] Rickman's son records that in 1826 'Works were carried out at Great Tew for Mr Boulton, and at Handsworth for Mr Watt', presumably at their respective houses.[164]

The plan shows the external wall of the press room to have been trapezoidal, a shape corresponding to the centre bay of a crescent-shaped building. The outside walls enclose a circular wall with buttresses on the inner face. Six vacuum pumps are placed between the circle's outer face and the main exterior wall. There can be no doubt that this plan is of the new cutting-out room of the Mint, the operation at long last transferred from the lapping mill whose old machinery was sold to Bombay; new cutting-out presses were intended. There are no elevation drawings of the Soho cutting-out room and equivalents can be examined for the Mexico City, Bombay and Calcutta mints, the latter two displaying elaborate Classical decoration. The wall buttresses were designed as fluted pilasters supporting an entablature, with the circle of presses within its own cast iron colonnade, and the whole room top-lit (Fig 5.29).[165] It seems that Rickman and Hutchinson were probably employed to design the architectural elements at Soho and not the technology of this important room. The drawings of foreign mints show the shaft entering the room through a tunnel to finish at the very centre in the same arrangement as in the Crescent Building

(Fig 5.30). The Calcutta cutting-out room, with 18 presses, was vast in comparison with Soho with only 6 presses. In 1826, and perhaps not coincidentally, a six-press cutting-out room was ordered for a mint in Mexico City. The order was cancelled and the equipment was eventually sold to Lisbon, Portugal, in 1836.[166] The drawings of the Mexico City cutting-out room provide a good impression of the scale of the same facility at Soho (Fig 5.31).[167] Using the foreign mint drawings as a major source, a three-dimensional reconstruction of the cutting-out room at Soho has been attempted (Fig 5.32).[168]

This placing of the new cutting-out room in the old Latchet (Crescent) Building has major implications for the position of the other minting functions. It is now clear that the southern half of the building, including the end bay, was reorganised to take on the minting functions between cutting out and coining, making use of the shaft from the engine, which ran under the floor. The various machines were connected to it by a system of leather belts and pulleys and their functions included milling, shaking from oil, tubing, annealing, pickling, and dry shaking; there was also a workshop for the maintenance of the cutting-out and milling machines.[169] Blanks that had undergone all these processes were to be conveyed to the main building by small trucks using an inclined plane below the level of the yard on the outward journey and a system of counterweights on pulleys to return. In summary, the Latchet (Crescent) Building was supplied with power for the first time in order to be integrated into the new Mint complex. The documentation also indicates that the north of the building was to be rebuilt, 'raised to a second story corresponding with the other part of the building & roofed with a pediment gable end'.[170] It is not clear whether this proposal related to the end bay or the whole north wing. The only part of the building that had three storeys was the central bay, so whatever was intended would have unbalanced any symmetry, for the south wing had been constructed with two storeys (*see* Fig 2.23).

Confirmation of the orientation of the main shaft within the Mint site is given at the crucial link with the engine. Roughly sketched in pencil, and presumably added not long after 27 August 1825 to the west–east cross-sectional drawing of the engine house, is a 3ft (0.91m) pulley and a pair of smaller tightening pulleys with the line, a long belt wrapping round the pulleys, also marked (Fig 5.33). The belt was also connected to a 5ft (1.52m) pulley on the main crank of the engine itself. The 3ft (0.91m) pulley, put into motion by the engine, revolved the 200ft (60.96m) cast iron shaft and it was placed, as could be expected, below the level of the yard between the new engine house and the 1791 building. The latter was to have its upper storey removed to produce a series of single-storey, powered workshops driven by pulleys attached to the main shaft. A rough plan in pencil with no title can now be identified with the 'New Fitting Shop', otherwise the 'New Workshop', which was to house three lathes, a drill, a grinding stone and a hearth.[171] The screw lathe was to be accommodated in the adjacent shop to the north. At the back of this part of the building, it appears that the rising ground was to be removed and a new retaining wall built to create a passage or 'area', as it was called, around the outside.

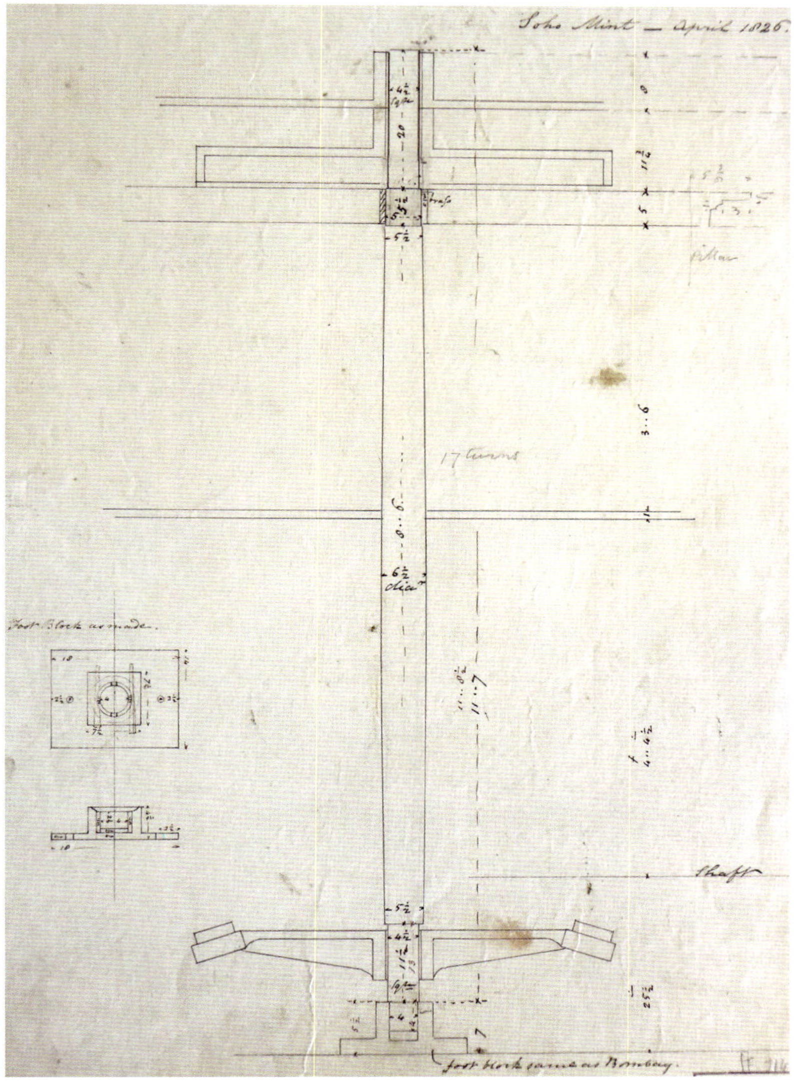

Fig 5.30
Drawing of the vertical shaft for the coin cutting-out room, new Soho Mint, April 1826.

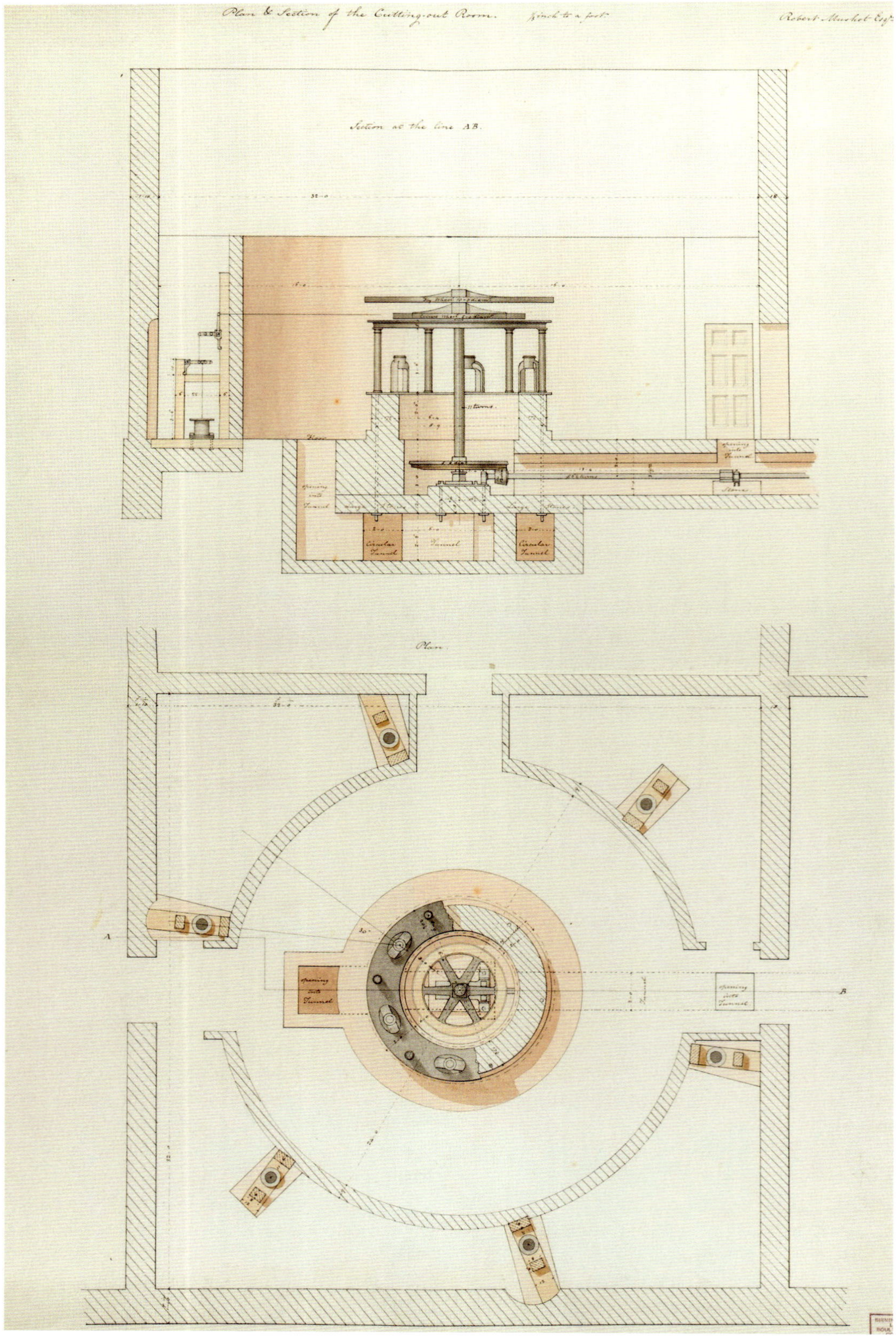

Fig 5.31
Plan and cross section of the Mexico City coin cutting-out room, 21 June 1826.

With the main pieces of the new layout located, an attempt has been made to reconstruct the lost 1825 map (Fig 5.34). This reconstruction formed the working hypothesis for the 1995–6 excavations, which concentrated on the mint and Latchet (Crescent) Building site. A detailed report on the excavations forms Appendix 1, but certain findings will be interwoven here with the documentary evidence in so far as they confirm, expand or contradict the historical account.

Of greatest significance was the discovery of the bottom of the driveshaft tunnel running parallel to the west wall of the 1791 building, traces of which were also found (excavation trench Soho 2). The walls survived to a height of about 1ft 1in (129mm) and ran 1ft 10.5in (571mm) apart under the centre of the mint yard, which, from map evidence, was 14ft (4.27m) wide (*see* Fig 5.12). In the neighbouring garden, the *Time Team* excavation uncovered the important junction between the main tunnel and that leading to the steam engine (excavation trench Soho 3). Two of four large sandstone blocks, which supported the 3ft (0.91m) pulley giving motion to the shaft, had survived. The tunnel here stood to a greater height than in Trench 2 and contained a drain in the floor leading to the engine that may have carried spilt water from the Soho House pump. Another tunnel, entering from the 1791 building, joined with the main tunnel but on the opposite side to the engine. This was identified as the structure for a belt-driven screw lathe located at the northern end of the new 1825 fitting shop (*see* Fig 5.34).

The main levels of the 1825 mint coining room and engine were destroyed during the

Fig 5.32
Cut-away diagram and reconstruction of the cutting-out room machinery, 1824–5.

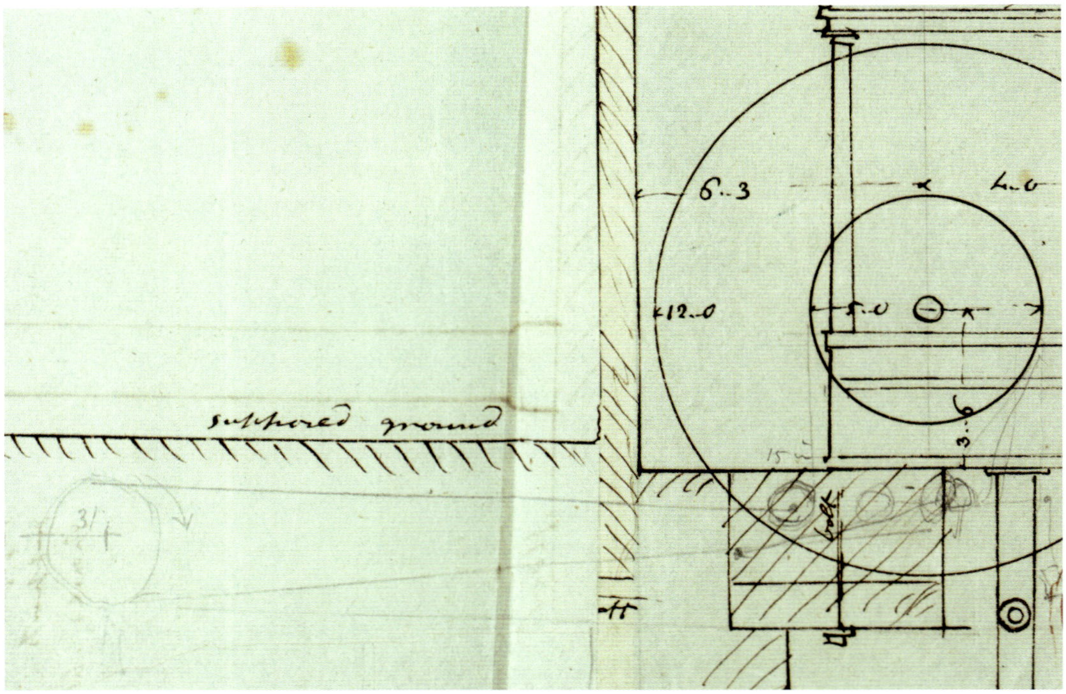

Fig 5.33
Detail of the cross section in Fig 5.27 showing in pencil additions to the connection between the steam engine and the underground drive shaft and main pulley, c August 1825.

Fig 5.34
Plan of the new Soho Mint, 1824–6.

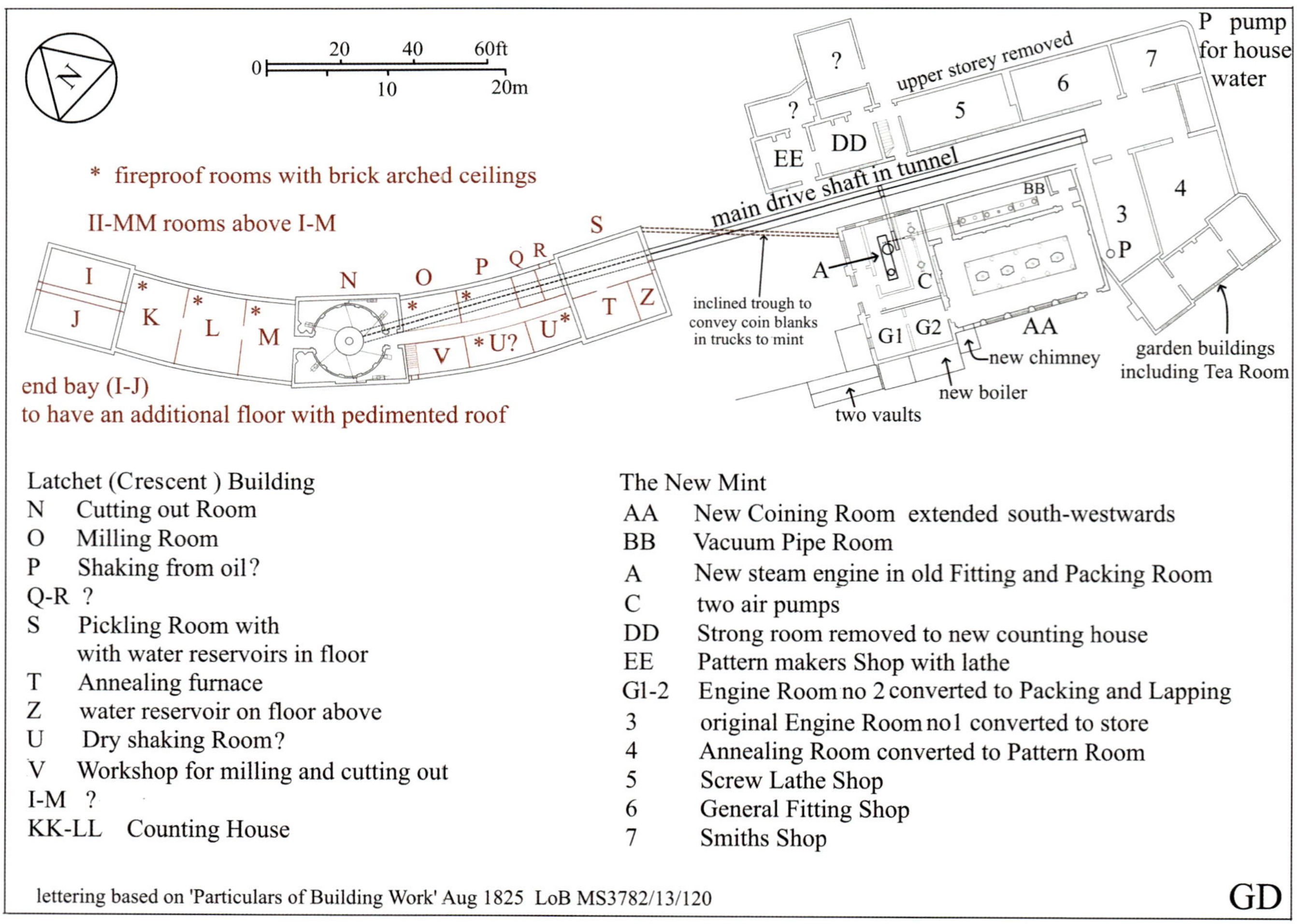

First World War by sand extraction, and attention was focused on the deeper engine pit. Probing found demolition rubble, with large blocks of brick masonry, down to a depth of 8.5ft (2.59m) without reaching any definable bottom, as the rubble continued downwards. This material may have been the remains of the engine well or the adjoining culvert that served it. It is possible that the floor of the well or culvert has survived at a deeper level.

The considerable documentation for the 1824–6 reorganisation merits a study in its own right, and there is only sufficient room here to add a few more chronological details. It must be stressed that Matthew Robinson Boulton, assisted by William Buckle, was intensely involved in the planning of the new mint and much of the documentation is in both their hands. In 1824, it was proposed to have three new engines: one of 40hp for rolling, presumably as a substitute for, or an addition to, the waterwheel, another of 24hp to run the presses and ancillary coining machinery, and the third of 10hp to power the lathes.[172] In the end, Matthew Robinson Boulton made do with one new 10hp engine (*see* p 113). A proposal for a more compact design of the coining machinery itself, using a flywheel instead of weighted fly arms and disposing of the trumpet and balanced beam, was also abandoned (Fig 5.35).[173] With the old machinery removed and on the way to Bombay by autumn 1824, Matthew Robinson Boulton concerned himself with the design of the new lathes.[174] It appears that presses were ordered early on in the process but there was considerable delay before significant activity began in mid-1825, followed by an explosion of documentation in August 1825.[175] Matthew Robinson Boulton reported on the state of the mint in May 1825, not quite accurately, in view of the parts that had still to be ordered:[176]

> The whole [mint] ... was dismantled and transported to Bombay and tho' we have completed the new Machinery by which it is to be replaced, no part is yet put up so as to be in a state of activity. Modifications, for I do not use the much misapplied word of Improvements, have been made in the construction of various parts and considerable alterations must be made in the arrangement of the Buildings to admit of the organisation of the Machinery in the way it is contemplated to be erected.

The main parts of the vacuum apparatus were ordered from the Soho Foundry between August and December 1825.[177] Orders were placed for six cast iron shafts for the main tunnel in August and manufactured around 22 September 1825. Another six were required in January 1826, but for some reason these were made at the Phoenix Foundry, Birmingham, and delivered by 29 March 1826.[178] These six would have been installed under the Crescent Building and run into the cutting-out room. The architects, Rickman and Hutchinson, were paid £5 5s 0d for their plan of the cutting-out room. A drawing with additional details of the 'mouldings at large' has been presumably lost.[179] This appears to have been a sketch of the pilasters, which was left at Soho House for Matthew Robinson Boulton's approval at the end of October 1825.[180] The architects' clerk of works worked for 34 weeks between 12 September 1825 and 6 May 1826 supervising the erection of the cutting-out room.[181]

Fig 5.35
Water-coloured plan and elevation showing the existing and an alternative scheme for the coining press mechanism, 19 April 1824.

A length of about 1.6m of the lowest two courses of the foundation of the front (east) wall of the cutting-out room in the central bay of the Crescent Building was found (Trench 4). There was insufficient left on its own to identify which part it formed of the front elevation (*see* Fig 5.28) and this was roughly achieved by plotting the main machinery shaft, whose end conveniently pointed to the centre of the cutting-out room. The two fragments of the foundation uncovered in Trenches 4 and 5 were sufficient to establish the footprint of the southern wing of the Latchet (Crescent) Building, and logically of the whole building, accepting it was symmetrical on either side of the central bay.

The supply of parts from the Soho Foundry ceased in the summer of 1826 and the rest of the year was taken up with final minor fitting out.[182] Matthew Robinson Boulton made copious but not very legible notes on the planning of work and technical matters illuminating the state of progress to a degree, but unfortunately not readily revealing information on the physical layout of the mint. Sometime in March or April 1826, Matthew Robinson reminded himself to 'Examine and determine as to the best mode of covering in the old press room'.[183] This suggests that the 1798–1824 coining room had indeed been demolished and its remains were to be covered over and perhaps landscaped into the garden.

Identified costs of the Mint amounted to between £6,000 and £7,000, including £2,261 13s 5½d for materials furnished by Boulton & Watt, £668 7s 0d for the Boulton & Watt engine, and £1,205 18s 0½d for the building works (Fig 5.36).[184] This would imply that Matthew Robinson Boulton made a profit on the sale of the old machinery to Bombay (for which nearly £10,000 was received) against the construction of the new mint and its re-equipment. The relatively small net investment was to last another 25 years. By July 1827, however, the mint was not capable of full operation, the coining-press room not yet 'restored since the demolition of it for the Bombay Mint'.[185] Nevertheless, Matthew Robinson confirmed that the 'the other parts of the new Mint here ... have been restored'. Production records indicate that coin blanks (planchets) only, and exclusively for the United States of America, were produced from 1826 to 1830. The rest of the time was occupied supplying Bombay with more equipment and producing the mint for Mexico City, the order for which was unfortunately cancelled due to the financial difficulties of the sponsoring companies Barclay, Herring, Richardson and Company and Baring Brothers and Company.[186] Doty considers that the mint was not re-powered until the early 1830s.[187] Before this time, however, the mint certainly had much new machinery. By the end of 1826, the mint had been rebuilt so that every major operation was capable of being powered by the steam engine. Cutting-out presses had been installed, put into motion via the long underground driveshaft, and hence production of planchets mentioned above was possible. However, coining presses were not to be erected for several years, although the infrastructure of vacuum pumps, vacuum tubes and balancing beams was probably already in place.

In the summer of 1830, it appears that the Mint despatched its first coin order for the island of Guernsey, but it cannot be certain whether this small job was done on steam-powered presses.[188] At the end of 1832, Boulton & Watt were paid £822 9s 2d for 'sundry materials for Soho New Mint part of which are still in the possession of B&W and laying on the common opposite Brook Row'.[189] It is possible that this included some of the equipment that had been necessary to complete the fitting out of the coining-press room. In 1824, five presses were made for the new Soho Mint, but it is not certain what happened to these.[190] In 1833, two more coining presses were manufactured.[191] It is difficult to establish the true state of the coining room in the

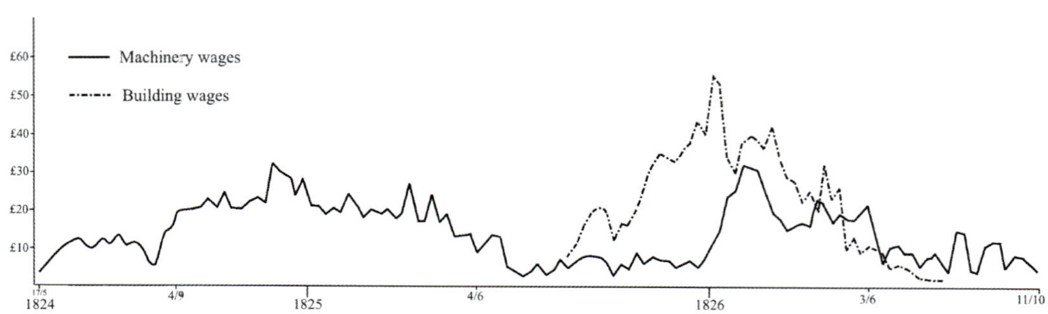

Fig 5.36
Graph of the expenditure on machinery and building wages at the new Soho Mint, 1824–6.

years 1830–5, but certainly coinage production was fitful in this same period. An upsurge in orders from 1835 concentrated attention on the perhaps neglected coining room.

The rebuilding of the coining room, 1835

On 6 June 1835, Matthew Robinson Boulton wrote a memorandum on minor proposed alterations to the machinery in the coining-room roof, reminding himself to 'speak with [William] Buckle relative to the Pneumatic Machinery'.[192] By 29 June, Buckle had provided an estimate for repairs to the roof, including 'Erecting Pneumatic apparatus', altogether coming to £190.[193] The double-pitch roof was 'quite rotten' and Buckle proposed a single pitch, but three feet (914mm) wider, expanding into the yard between the coining room and the fitting shop in the 1791 building. This was to provide more space around the vacuum tube for inspection and repairs. The work was carried out in the same year, but the actual cost (£319 16s 10d) turned out to be over £100 more than the estimate, and Buckle had to provide a breakdown of the bill to justify the increase.[194]

Two Mint inventories have survived, dated 1842 and 1849, which provide valuable information on the content of the various rooms. Most of these can be located, and the main machine rooms are laid out as planned in the 1824–6 reorganisation.[195] In particular, four operational presses are listed as being in the coining room as originally intended. There is insufficient space here to analyse these documents, but they are additionally useful in illuminating the 1850 Mint sale particulars.[196]

The sale and demolition of the Mint, 1850–3

Matthew Piers Watt Boulton inherited the mint business on his father's death in 1842. Although a considerable number of his papers survive, they have been little studied and M P W Boulton remains a shadowy figure. It was in his time that the Manufactory and the Mint were demolished and the Soho estate divided up for residential development. The mint was the first of the buildings to be removed, and the 1849 inventory was possibly prepared in anticipation. By December 1849, the responsibility for the Mint had been transferred to trustees and M P W Boulton wrote to Chubb, his manager, to inform him of the end of the Boulton connection:

> I find it desirable of me to give up all operations connected to the Mint as by continuing them I may be incurring responsibility in case of any accident or damage to the machinery. It will therefore from this time be exclusively under the management of the trustees, who will have charge of keeping it in repair. I do not know up to what time I have been incurring expenses of coals, tin oil etc for the machinery & I should wish to know. But from this time all such expenses on my part will have to cease. For the same reason it will be best that Gozzard should discontinue the making of medals & I shall wish you consequently to write to those parties who have hitherto been supplied by the Soho Mint, informing them of this change, that they may order them elsewhere. The making of dies and in fact all operations connected with the Mint will be in like manner discontinued, so far as I am concerned. I should wish you to apply to the trustees for orders as to the person to be employed in keeping the machinery in order. Mr Jones will give you directions respecting this. I have no objection whatever to the trustees employing Vale, Howard or any of the Mint men now in my employ for this purpose without any additional payment on their part; but it will be best if you should receive formal directions on this head: and that it should be clearly understood that they are so employed under the trustees orders. Employment will be found for the Mint Men during the winter months, in various miscellaneous operations on the estate but in the spring (say about the commencement of March) I shall no longer be able to find them employment with the exception of Charles Howard whom it is my intention to retain at any rate in partial employment as his infirmities render it difficult for him to obtain it elsewhere. It is my present intention to give permanent allowances to Sam Vale (senior) and Jerome and a present to Gozzard as I believe he is well off a permanent allowance is scarcely needed in his case. And I should probably make presents to the others ... I should wish this change generally to be intimated to the men in order to prepare them for it, but you can let them understand that they will hear further on the subject before the change takes place.[197]

It is not known how much of the contents of this fateful letter came as a bombshell to the Mint men and women and how much had percolated through to them by rumour beforehand. Events progressed rapidly, and within five months the contents of the Mint were sold by auction between Monday 29 April and Friday 3 May 1850.[198] As with the 1840s inventories, most of the rooms can be located, but there is additional valuable information on the dimensions of machines, equipment such as shafting and leather belts, and fixtures such as benches and furniture. This information was very useful in helping to interpret the 1824–6 documentation and the findings of the 1995–6 mint excavations (*see* Appendix 1).

There is little definite documentation on the demolition of the Mint, but it appears that this was a prolonged process and not a single event. The chimney stack was felled in 1850 and a strip of copper was retrieved inscribed with the names of workers, including that of Mr Vale, who placed it in the foundation in 1825. His son, Samuel Vale, remembered the event and paid a workman 2s 6d to find the copper memento.[199] A thief was caught stealing lead and glass from the Mint on 18 May 1851 and was prosecuted in December of the same year.[200] In May 1852, a payment was made to workers who had spent three to four days removing the boiler from the Mint and transferring it to the lap engine in the Mill.[201] On 28 May 1853, two workers were paid compensation for injuries sustained 'in the fall of the Mint Buildings' and as late as September in the same year bricks were being cleaned up from an old wall at the Mint to build a bridge and wall near the Manufactory cottages at Brook Row.[202] The gradual erosion of the Mint site was the beginning of the final chapter in the history of the Soho Manufactory site, and the tragedy of its loss, which was palpably felt at the time, can still be appreciated today. However, the mint machinery had been given a new lease of life on two local sites, having been sold to Heatons in Birmingham and James Watt and Company of the Soho Foundry, Smethwick.

Fortuitously, in 1899 four photographs were taken of the remaining visible brickwork on the site. They show the part of the 1791 building where an 'area' or passage was created at the rear in about 1825–6. A high retaining wall was required, cutting deeply into the slope rising to Soho House, and this was the reason that this structure survived (Figs 5.37–40).[203] A small building relating to the use of the site as a timber store a few years before helps confirm the position taken by the photographer as the hut is also marked on the first edition OS 1:500 map. By coincidence, the photographs very closely cover part of the area excavated in 1995–6.

This study would have been very deficient had not a particular item in the 1850 sale found

Fig 5.37
Photo of the Soho Mint site, 1899, looking east. The bank was situated immediately above the 1791 mint building.

Fig 5.38
Photo of the Soho Mint site, 1899, looking north.

Fig 5.39
Photo of the Soho Mint site, 1899, looking south-east.

Fig 5.40
Photo of the Soho Mint site, 1899, looking north-east.

its way into the Birmingham City Archives: Lot 133 'Quantity of working drawings for the machinery at the Royal Mint, the Calcutta, Bombay, Soho, and other Mints'. These drawings were probably acquired by James Watt & Company, the successors to Boulton, Watt & Company, for they all also made another purchase: one of the four Soho Mint presses, which was then transferred to the Soho Foundry. It must be stressed again that at this time the firm was no longer connected to the Boulton or Watt families. In a letter written soon after the sale, James Watt & Company confirmed that 'Messrs Ralph Heaton & Sons of 7 Bath St Birmingham bought two of the Soho coining presses'.[204] James O Sweeney, no doubt influencing Doty, has, therefore, no grounds for assuming that Heatons had purchased all four.[205] The destination of the fourth is, however, not known.

A year later, in 1851, George Lingard of Snow Hill, Birmingham, offered to buy the Soho Foundry press, but James Watt & Company declined, suggesting instead that they could make a new one at a cost of £230.[206] The single press installed at the Foundry, but not necessarily set to work, explains the set of drawings, dated 1850 to 1851, confusingly entitled 'Soho Mint'.[207] The drawings would have been useful when in 1860 James Watt & Company decided to set up a new mint, also confusingly called the 'Soho Mint', in a new building at the Foundry. It is interesting that the original coining press purchased in 1850 was set up at the end of the row of 12 new presses but not connected to the

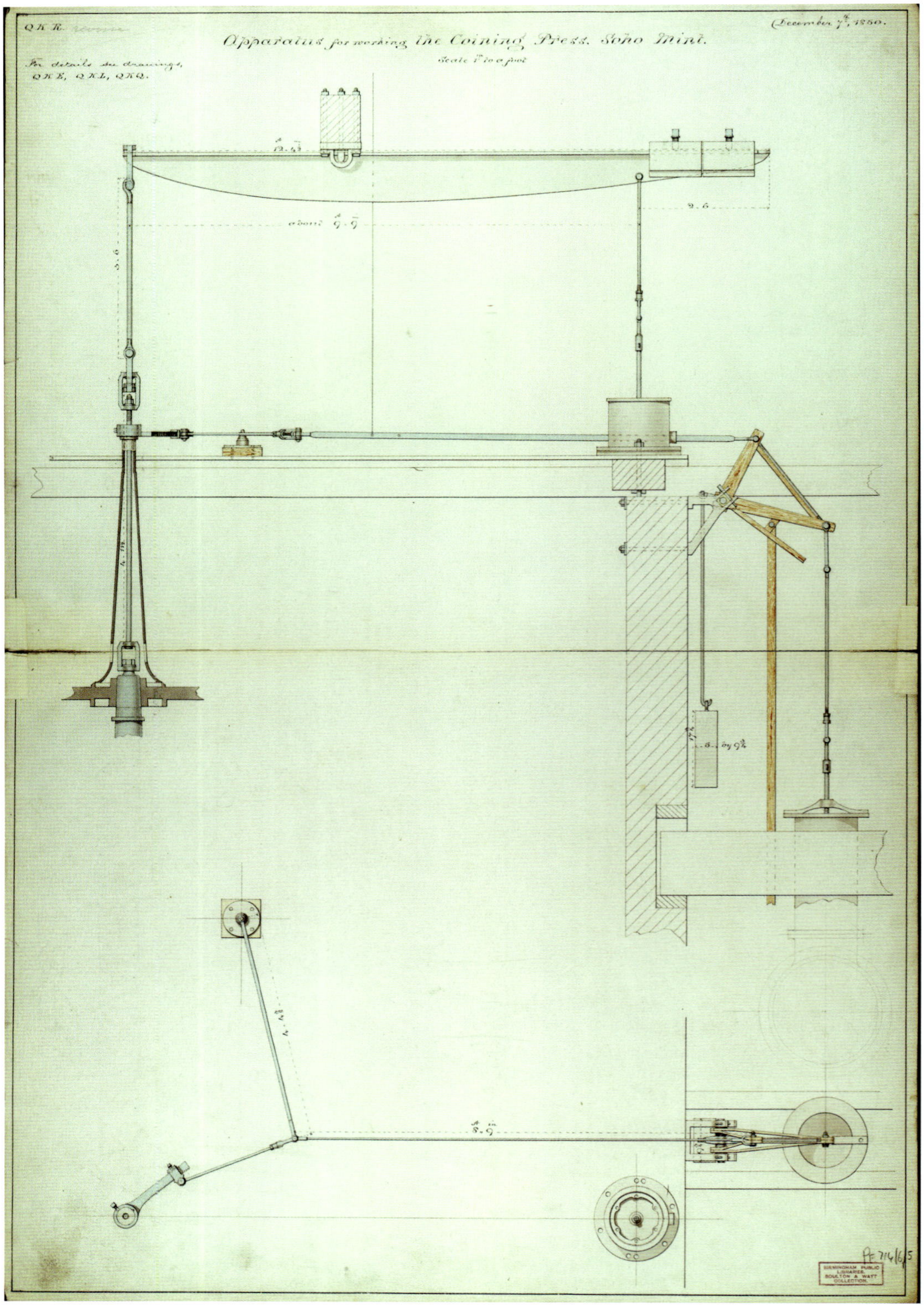

Fig 5.41
Water-coloured plan and elevation of the mechanism that connected the vacuum tube to the coining presses, Soho Mint, 7 December 1850. This was probably drawn before it was dismantled and the press moved to the Soho Foundry, having been acquired by James Watt & Co.

pneumatic machinery. It is not known where it had stood in the previous 10 years.

Most of the Boulton & Watt material, presumably with the old and new mint drawings, was acquired by George Tangye in 1894 on the sale of the Soho Foundry to Avery's and in turn given to the City of Birmingham in 1911. The location of the mint drawings in the Boulton and Watt collection has caused the Matthew Boulton Mint Company to be confused with Boulton &

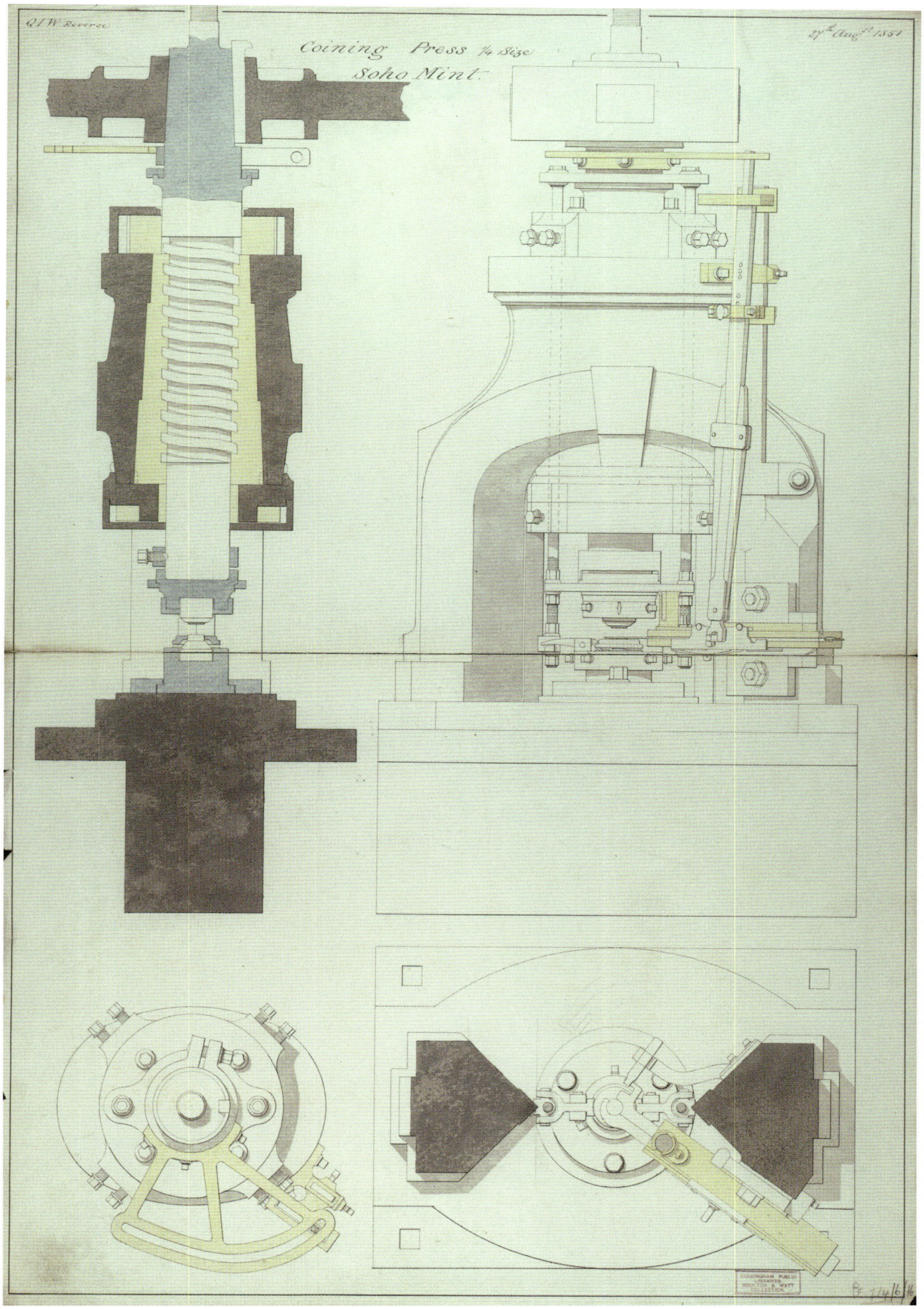

Fig 5.42
Elevations of a Soho Mint press drawn before it was moved to the Soho Foundry, 27 August 1851.

Watt ever since.[208] Fortunately, the new drawings produced by James Watt & Company in the 1850s and 1860s provide the most accurate and detailed depiction of the machinery installed at the original Soho Mint in 1824–6 (Figs 5.41 and 5.42).[209] The use of the name 'Soho Mint' at the Foundry site after 1860 exacerbated the already existing confusion but it is hoped that this study will help others to distinguish between the two sites once and for all.

6

The Soho Manufactory and Mint site: post-demolition history

1850–87

The buildings of the Soho Manufactory and Mint were gradually demolished between the early 1850s and 1863, leaving little, if anything, standing above the ground at the Manufactory. Fragments of wall partially buried in a bank survived at the Mint site (probably part of the 1791 building), but were lost when the area was developed with housing in the early 20th century. The documentary record does not tell us whether the Manufactory and Mint were systematically robbed of their below-ground structures on demolition. As a working hypothesis, it was assumed that this did not happen, as experience shows that the deep below-ground masonry structures associated with industrial sites are not normally removed. On the other hand, there is evidence that attempts were made to sell the material from the demolished buildings (*see* p 40).[1]

Fortunately, a photograph was taken of part of the Manufactory after the loss of the engine works (*c* 1853) and before the remainder was demolished (*see* Fig 2.35). This shows demolition rubble lying heaped over the area where the engine and letter-copying-machine works once stood. The important break-of-slope within the site, which has elsewhere been called the 'Great Bank' for convenience, can be clearly seen, with a range of shopping built into it. It would have been difficult, even dangerous, to remove all of the structure from this feature and it is likely that the retaining wall was left *in situ*. It would also be reasonable to assume that archaeology of the below-bank area would be least prone to erosion by the natural tendency for materials to accumulate there from above and seal the deposits.

The first-edition Ordnance Survey maps at 1:500 and 1:2500 scale (Figs 6.1 and 6.2), published in 1889–90, are the first to show the site in any detail after demolition. Only one building has been erected on the Manufactory site, in a position at the southern extremity of the former engine works. This is connected with a rope walk, an area where rope was manufactured, which Harry Walker Haines had established alongside the Hockley Brook and below the Great Bank.[2] The latter shows as a significant break-of-slope running parallel to South Road from the direction of St Michael's Hill and helps to fix the two main levels of the Manufactory. South Road corresponds with the eastern extremity of the site when first laid out, running along the frontage of the principal building, and the western extremity was defined by the surviving Boulton allotments, which used to lie at the end of the engine works. The Hockley Brook provides another marker, particularly the part shown as culverted, which seems to coincide with its course formerly running below the engine yard. The whole site appears to be treeless and any disturbance after demolition minor.

The Mint site has several structures over it, mostly open fronted, but none belonged to the previous industrial phase. They were used by James Wilson, a local builder who lived at Soho House, for storing timber, and some appear on a series of photographs taken in 1899 (*see* Figs 5.37–5.40).[3] The aspect was wooded, as the Mint stood on the fringes of Soho Park, which had been developed for villa-type housing. An illustration of brick cellars in a bank and of material being carted away may be of the same area; it suggests that some disturbance was taking place at the very end of the 19th century (Fig 6.3).[4] By the early 1880s, housing was

starting to be built on South Road, but such is the length of the road that it was not until the turn of the century that terraced houses (numbers 68–96) arrived in the vicinity of the Soho site.[5]

1887–1903 (Fig 6.4)

By 1903, an L-shaped road had been laid out, replacing the rope walk, on the lower manufactory site. It was called Beech Road but was never developed. However, the Great Bank, which overlooked it, does not seem to have been disturbed. On the Mint site, the timber storage

Fig 6.1
Ordnance Survey map, 1:500 scale, surveyed 1887. The Great Bank is now a prominent feature of the Manufactory site, having been cleared of all its buildings.

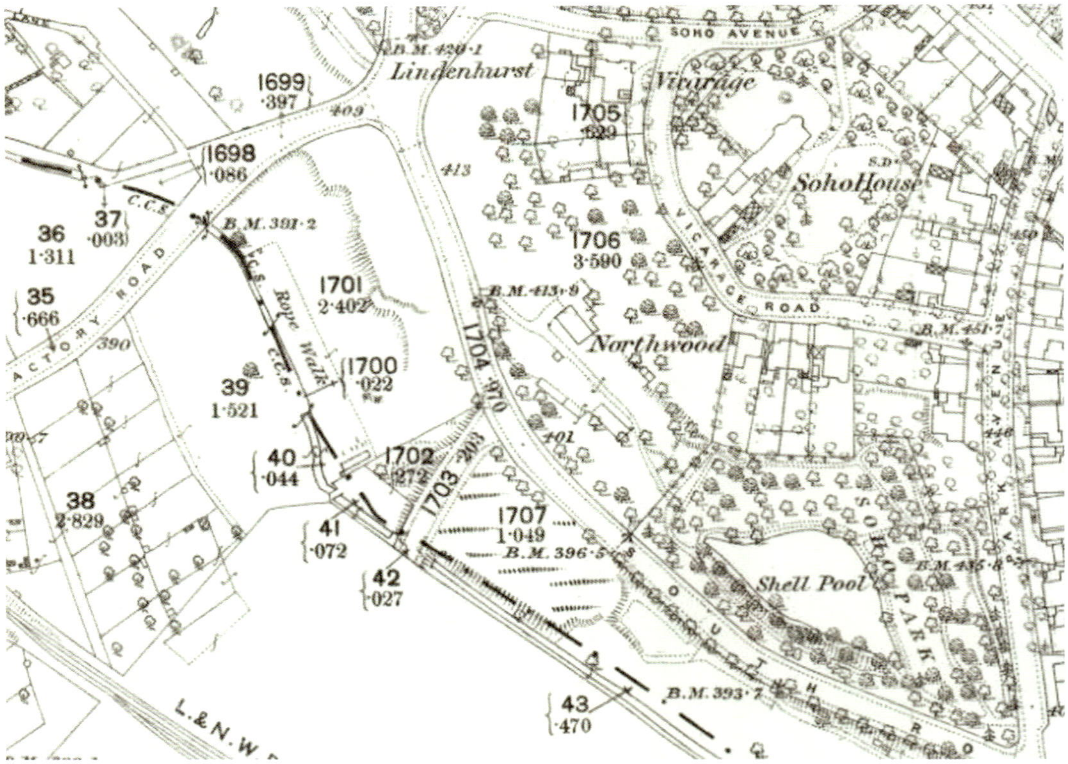

Fig 6.2
Ordnance Survey map, 1:2500 scale, surveyed 1888. The Manufactory and Mint sites are now clear of building and contrast with the well-treed aspect of the former Soho, which has been preserved intact around the Shell Pool. The Manufactory allotments have also survived on the west side of the Hockley Brook.

Fig 6.3
View probably over the Soho Mint site by Alfred Osbourne, 1891, looking towards the built-up area of Birmingham Heath (see *Figs 5.37–5.40*).

sheds have been cleared and the land was being prepared for house plots.

1903–14 (Fig 6.5)

The Ordnance Survey 1:2500 map revised in 1913–14 shows that significant changes had taken place since 1903. Around 1908, a vast quantity of material from an unknown source had been deposited onto both the Manufactory site and the Boulton allotments to create an elevated platform (henceforth known as the 'Great Tip') roughly at the level of South Road and the ground floor of the principal building.[6] This material, 25–30ft (7.6–9.1m) in depth, was dumped from the Great Bank to the Hockley Brook and beyond, effectively sealing the lower Manufactory site. As a result, the Great Bank disappeared from view, but probably survives archaeologically below the existing ground level. A causeway or isthmus connected the two extensive dumps of tipped material crossing above the Hockley Brook culvert. At the beginning of 1909, complaints were made to Willmott, Fowler and Willmott, land agents of the Boulton family, that rubbish being tipped on land adjacent to the Hockley Brook was narrowing, even obstructing, the stream course.[7]

To the north of the Great Tip, a terrace of houses had been built by 1906, descending St Michael's Hill.[8] As the Great Bank would have split the terrace into two main levels, material must have been introduced onto the lower level to create the existing even gradient. As a result, the lower half of the terrace of housing lies on a significant quantity of made-up ground. This has caused some subsidence in at least one of the houses, and boreholes that were sunk in 1996 investigating the cause, but oblivious to this fact, met solid brickwork at a depth of 13ft (4m). This was likely to have been the floor of the rolling mill and was at the level predicted by a cross section drawn by the author before the boreholes were drilled (Fig 6.6).[9] This overburden is undetectable

Fig 6.4
Ordnance Survey map, 1:2500 scale, revised 1902–3. The first terrace houses on South Road have been built in the area of the former Shell Pool and contrast in size with the earlier villa residences in Soho Park above.

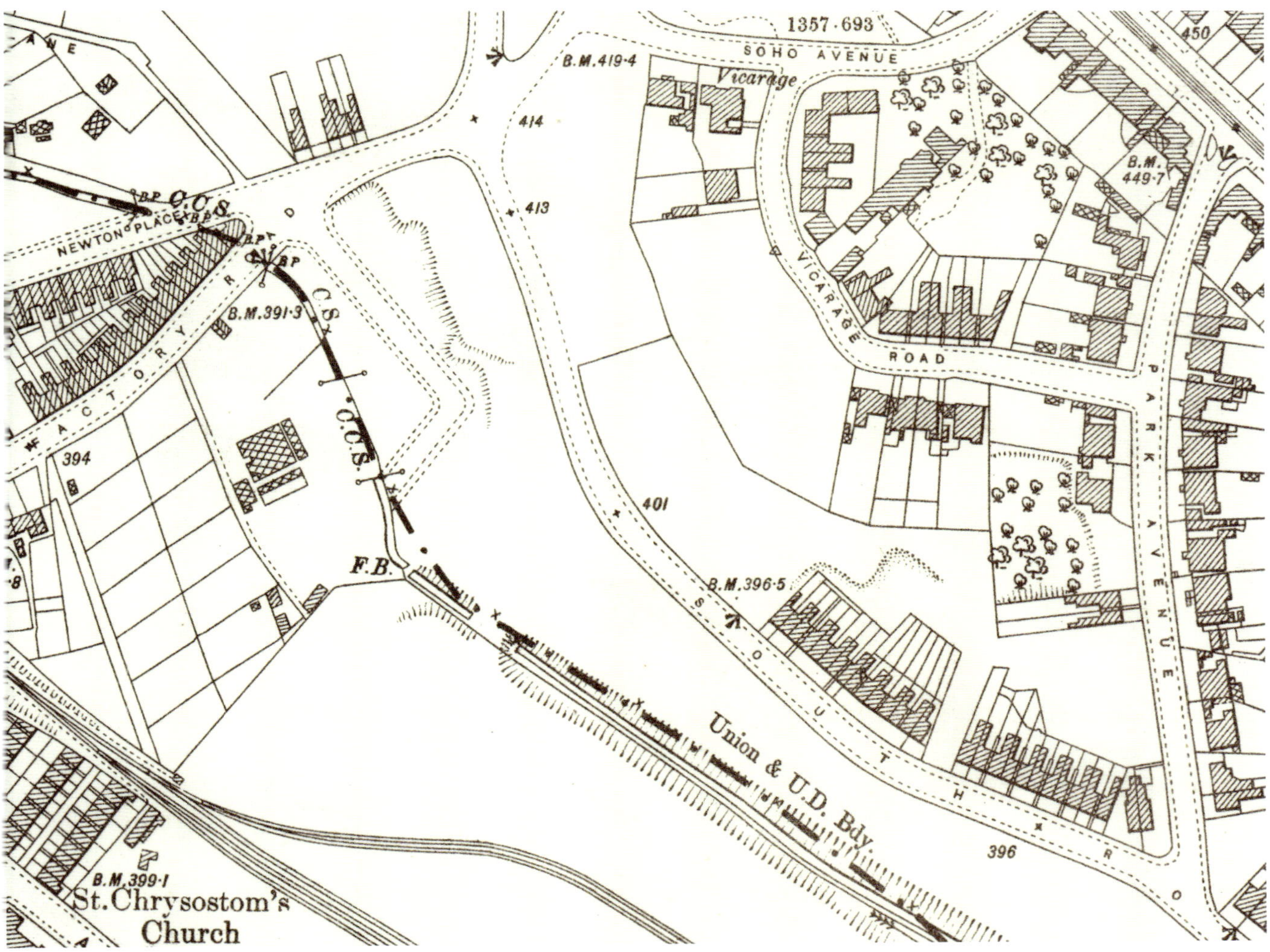

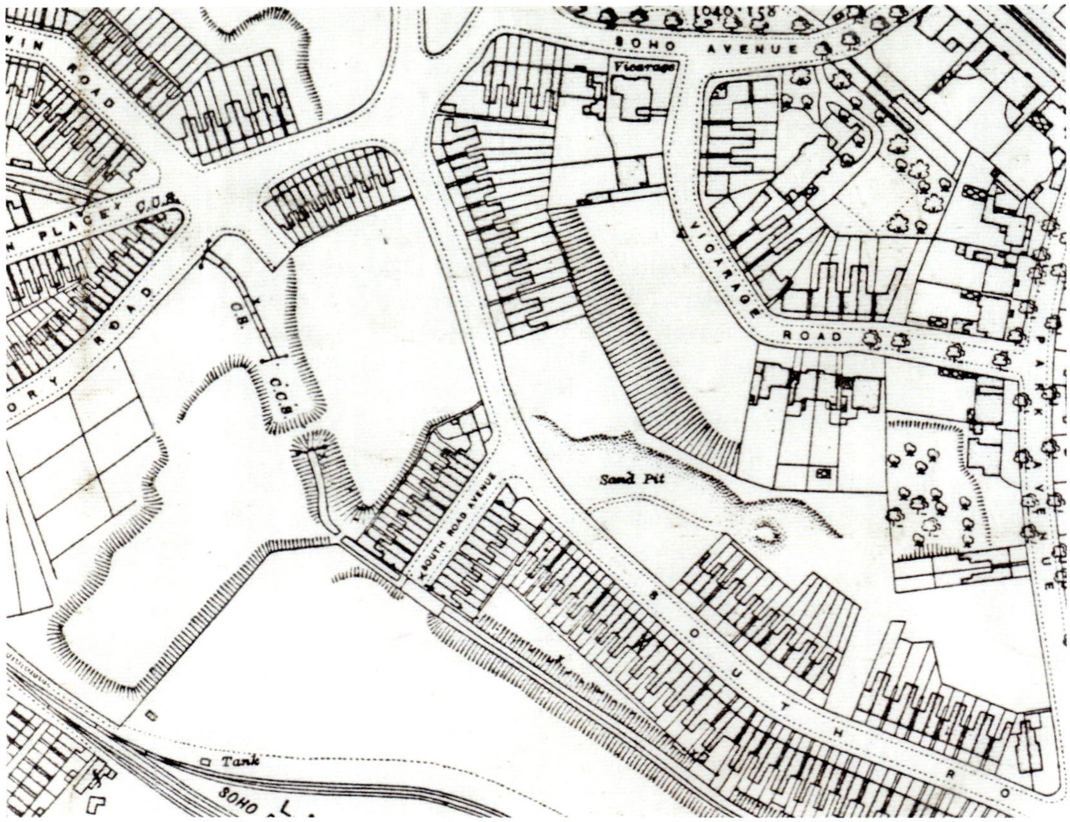

Fig 6.5
Ordnance Survey map, 1:2500 scale, revised 1913–14. South Road had been further built up. Major earth-moving operations have dug out a sandpit on the site of the Soho Mint, created a terrace for Vicarage Road partially encroaching on the Mint site, and deposited a vast amount of material on the site of the Manufactory on either side of the Hockley Brook.

from the direction of South Road, but the edge of the vast dump of material immediately to the south can be seen from Factory Road at the Hockley Brook bridge. It forms a steep bank overlooking the rear of the St Michael's Hill terrace. The construction of this terrace led to the abandonment of the Beech Road scheme and the Great Tip buried the remainder.

In contrast to the sealing deposits laid over the lower part of the Manufactory site, the foundations of the mint were severely damaged before the outbreak of the First World War. A sandpit had been opened up and its working out probably removed many of the surviving mint foundations, including all three steam-engine positions, but fortunately avoided the site of the 1791 building and the Latchet (Crescent) Building. The steep bank created at the working face shows clearly on the 1913–14 revision of the Ordnance Survey map (*see* Fig 6.5) and it

Fig 6.6
Reconstructed elevation of the Soho Manufactory buildings that lay along the present St Michael's Hill (compare with Fig A1.6).

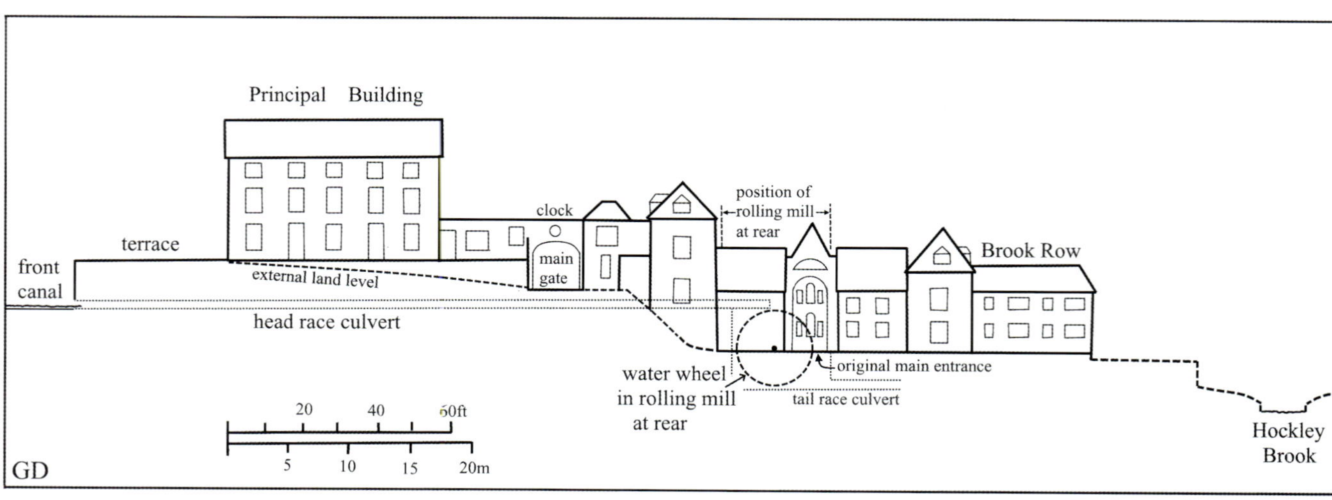

appears not to have advanced significantly after this date.[10] A bank runs more or less in the same position through the gardens of South Road today. The archaeology of the 1798 coining room might have fared better as part of it lay about 10ft (3.05m) below the general level of the mint (*see* pp 100–9).

Some sealing deposits were, however, introduced on part of the Mint site. Much of Vicarage Road had been developed by 1890, but a vacant area of land remained immediately above the site owing to the difficulty of building on the steep slope. Before 1914, a large amount of material was deposited on this area to create a terrace level with Vicarage Road, but at the same time accentuating the bank overlooking South Road.[11] The bottom edge of this tipped bank had crept onto the Mint site, partially burying the 1791 building and, in particular, a rear wing that had once projected into the original slope. By coincidence, this is the area that was photographed in 1899 (*see* Figs 5.37–5.40). Brickwork, no doubt surviving due to its work of retaining the slope at the rear, can be seen. This was probably constructed in about 1825 to enable a passage, or 'area' (as it was called), to be made around the rear wing. All this brickwork now lies buried in the tipped bank, the lower part of which is retained by a blue-brick wall.

The final event of any significance in this period was the construction in 1911–12 of a terrace of housing, numbers 158–190 (evens) on the north-east side of South Road.[12] This terrace lies over the canal, which fronted the principal building and which was filled in when the need for a water supply to the mill ceased in the 1850s. This feature may therefore survive relatively intact and, in particular, the canal wall about 14ft (4.2m) high that retained the terrace on the principal-building side. Not all the houses were built over the canal; numbers 158 and 160 South Road coincided with part of the Latchet (Crescent) Building, but may not have caused its foundations too much damage in their construction. Numbers 162–4 South Road (evens) lay in the area between the canal and the Latchet (Crescent) Building.

The inter- and post-war years (Fig 6.7)

The remainder of the Manufactory and Mint site was built over in this period as a frontage to South Road. In the early 1920s, semi-detached houses, numbers 128–156 (evens), were erected over the sandpit, with numbers 150–6 (evens) directly over the Latchet (Crescent) Building. It has been assumed that this house construction caused some damage to the archaeology as the houses stand on a terrace cutting into the main slope. Nevertheless, the deep below-ground structures of the Latchet (Crescent) Building used as part of the mint after 1826 probably survived. It may be of significance that none of the ground floors of these houses have suspended timber floors but are solid concrete instead, owing perhaps to the presence of masonry foundations that were too much trouble to remove.

In the 1920s, the site of the Manufactory principal building experienced a more mixed development. A number of commercial buildings were erected north of the cul-de-sac South Road Avenue. These premises were owned by E Crowder, a builder and former occupier of the sandpit in the First World War years, later Crowder and Brown. They included a builders shop, yard, a timber store, and a garage, and extended backwards partly over the Great Tip.[13] Two pairs of semi-detached houses, numbers 243–249 (odds), were then built in the remaining gap to the corner with St Michael's Hill. It is difficult to judge on this evidence alone how this building activity disturbed the Manufactory archaeology at the upper level where the principal building stood. The new workshop foundations were obviously deeper than those of the semi-detached houses next door, but fortunately no cellars were constructed. From local oral evidence, it is known that part of the Crowder and Brown frontage had petrol pumps, which were likely to have been fed from underground tanks.

The building plans of the Crowder and Brown premises record the presence of a main sewer, the Hockley Brook sewer, running diagonally across the site from north-west to south-east. This was constructed in 1883, and it was noted on the plans that 'the site is made up ground to a depth of 20ft [6.56m]'.[14] The Birmingham City Council drainage plans in the former City Engineer's Department provided information on levels and its actual course, which seems to be confined almost entirely to the lower Manufactory yards.[15] It is estimated that the level of these yards was approximately 382ft (116.4m) OD, and the sewer invert (bottom) is recorded as running across the site at about 380.4ft (115.9m) OD, in other words slightly

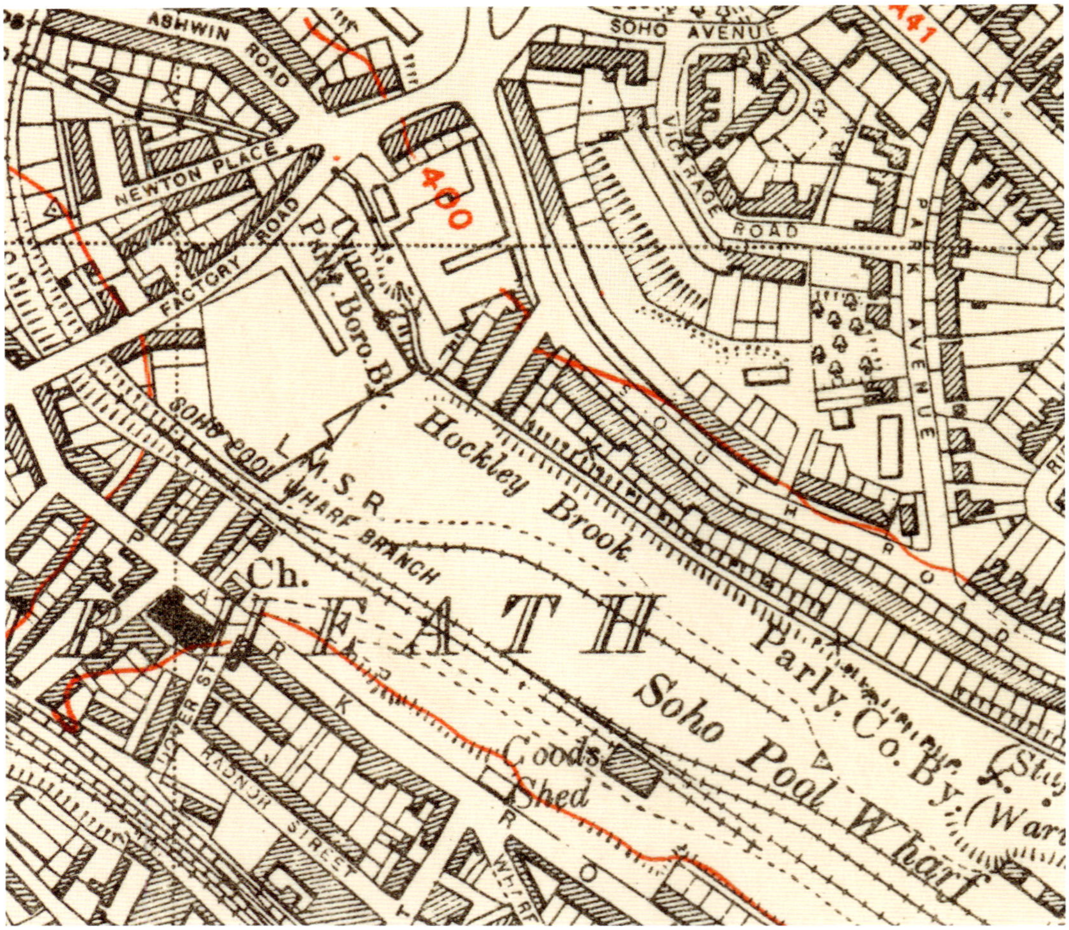

Fig 6.7
Ordnance Survey map, 1:10,560 scale, surveyed 1913–14, with revisions 1938.

penetrating the lower Manufactory yards. There is insufficient information, however, to be precise on these complex historic levels, the margin of error being too great to conclude that the sewer penetrated the yard levels and any foundations of buildings situated in them.

Development along Factory Road does not appear to have disturbed the archaeology of the former Manufactory engine works too greatly. Much of the area had been sealed by the Great Tip and, at an unknown later date, the narrow isthmus that connected its two parts was broadened to create a single raised platform capable of being developed. The Hockley Brook culvert was buried as a result, and this could not have taken place before 1925 when the brook locally was lowered.[16] The former Cheney's brass-lock factory, a distinctive brick building fronting Factory Road, with round arched windows at ground level, was established in the 1920s, and its two-level layout is explained by the presence of the Great Tip over which it was partly built. The access road on its east side leading to the Hive Industrial Estate rises steeply onto the summit of the tip and the rear part of the factory is at this higher level. The main part of the factory lies at street level, however, and to maintain this level from front to back required part of the tip to be cut away in an area very close to the westernmost workshop of the Boulton & Watt engine yard. There is insufficient information on this historic level to determine whether the archaeology of this workshop was disturbed by the removal of the tip. The back wall of the main factory serves also to retain the higher level of the Great Tip. The construction of a factory on the opposite side of the access road to Cheney's appears also to have removed part of the tip and created a floor level much closer to the ground level of the original engine yard in this part.

In the post-war period, the remainder of the Great Tip was built over with industrial sheds, leaving a narrow gap above the short, deep channel of the Hockley Brook. The Brook Works on Factory Road (G&D Steels Ltd, 2017) was constructed over the same made-up ground that underlies St Michael's Hill terrace adjacent. The result of over 100 years of building and

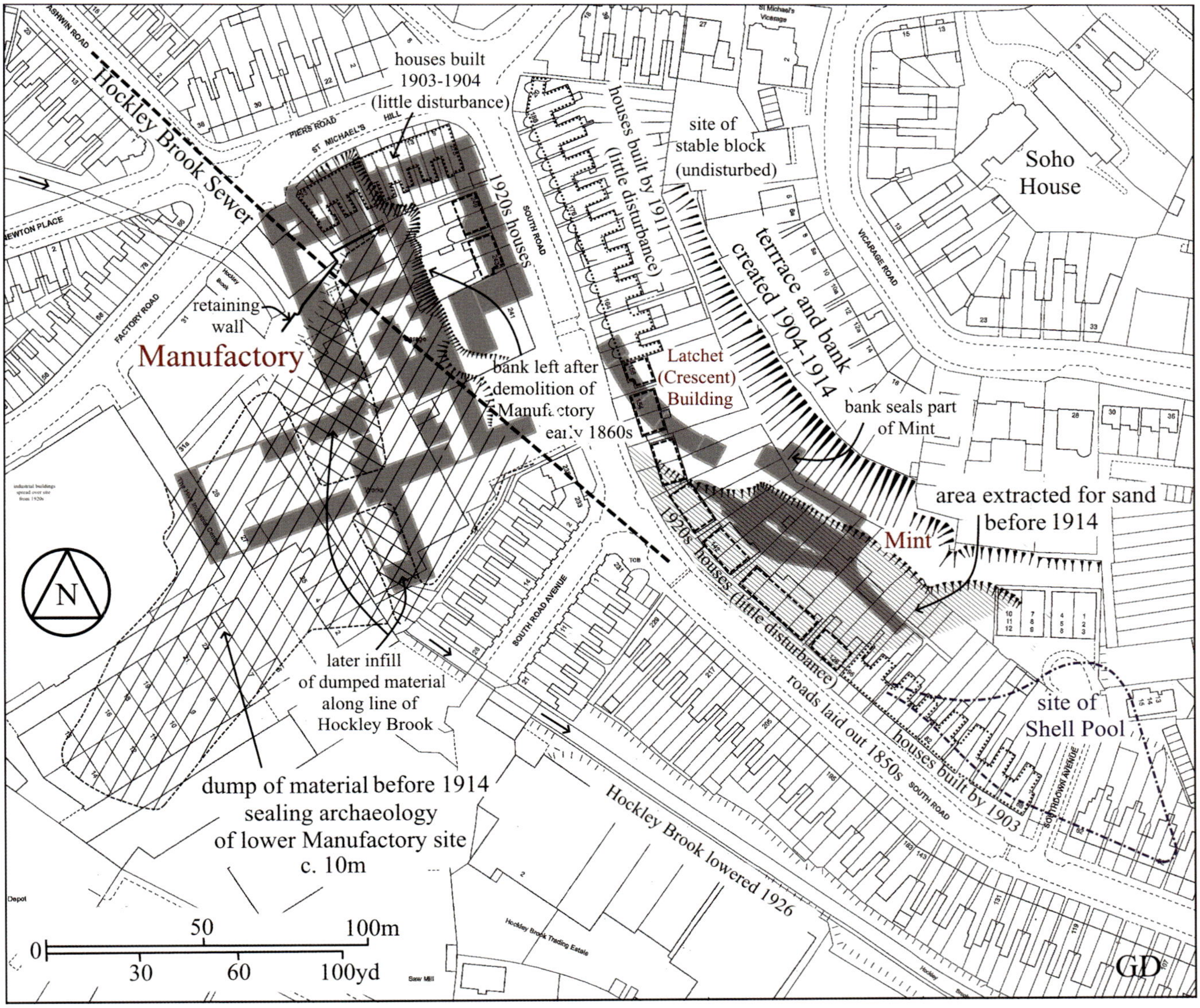

Fig 6.8
The main events affecting the archaeological remains of the Soho industrial buildings.

extracting operations that has created varying degrees of archaeological potential over the site is summarised in Fig 6.8.

Most of the Manufactory archaeology appears to have been preserved, the lower level sealed under 25–30ft (7.62–9.14m) of the Great Tip. From cartographic evidence alone, the upper part of the site upon which the principal building stood is close to the present level of South Road and therefore vulnerable to damage by building operations. Before 1914, much of the archaeology of the Mint was removed by sand extraction, but this destructive operation avoided the 1791 building and the Latchet (Crescent) Building. Part of the latter is built over with housing and a part of the 1791 building has been sealed by tipping from the direction of Vicarage Road.

The archaeological excavations, 1994–6

With nothing visible of the Manufactory and Mint above ground to help, the rich material of the Soho archive enabled the author to produce a 3-D reconstruction of both sites around the year 1805 (*see* Figs 2.26 and 3.5). The ground plan created for this exercise was also used to plot as accurately as possible the location of the buildings on current OS large-scale maps. This inevitably involved a degree of error, as no buildings had survived to be recorded on the earliest OS mapping of 1890 (1:2500 scale). Archaeological excavation in theory could rectify this problem as long as the remains of the Manufactory and Mint had survived below the ground. If so, there was valuable information to be gained on their nature, depth and extent.

In November 1994 the Conservation Team of Birmingham City Council's Planning Department agreed to fund a small excavation where part of the front wall of the principal building had been identified by the author as passing under the forecourt of a factory on South Road. A fragment of this wall was found, but it could not be recognised as such at the time within the small trench it was found. A planned extension to the excavation was not permitted.

The author then pursued other means of progressing the physical investigation of the site. The townscape of factories, houses and gardens was not an easy one in which to conduct archaeological excavations, particularly where there would be no areas cleared prior to any redevelopment. Fortunately, in the early 1990s an archaeological programme, *Time Team*, broadcast on Channel 4, had established itself as a means of investigating potentially interesting archaeological sites. The Soho Manufactory and Mint, famous for its association with Matthew Boulton and James Watt, was an attractive proposition for the programme, but it would be breaking entirely new ground in venturing into a built-up townscape and into industrial archaeology for the first time. *Time Team* were used to working in rural locations where unsuccessful trenches could be abandoned and the archaeology moved to another part of the field. This was not an option in Handsworth back gardens and factory forecourts (*see* Figs A1.24 and A1.25). In these circumstances, the map plotting and documentary research that had been carried out was essential. The analysis in this chapter of the events that took place at the site since demolition in the mid-1850s could prevent digging in areas where buildings had been entirely removed, such as for sand extraction, or buried under tens of metres of dumped material (the Great Tip). Despite the detailed preparatory work and the consequent identification of a number of potential trench sites, *Time Team* was wary of committing to the Soho site without more certainty of what might be found. The programme makers, therefore, agreed to fund a small trial excavation at the site of the mint in one of the rear gardens on South Road. This took place in September 1995 and successfully located part of the 1791 mint building (*see* Fig 5.12). The *Time Team* producers were duly convinced and filming was organised to take place over Easter in the following year, 1996. In the meantime, in October 1995 a small extension to the trial trench dug the month earlier revealed that the brick tunnel (1824–6) that contained the drive shaft for all the mint machinery had also survived, its level preserved in neighbouring gardens. There were sufficient gardens at our disposal where owners were not concerned about their transformation by archaeological excavation.

A detailed report and mapping of the archaeological excavations is contained in Appendix 1. For the more general reader, there follows a summary of the main findings following the six trench positions, Soho 1 to Soho 6. In view of the difficulties of the site, the excavations at Soho were not conducted in the usual manner of a *Time Team* programme in this period, with trench positions often decided during the three days of filming after a group discussion of the protagonists. A research design was prepared identifying both the objectives of the excavations and the location of trenches, enabling an immediate start to be made with only three days available.[17]

Soho 1

The front wall of the principal building (1765–7) at cellar level was identified near its southern end. It was set back slightly from the back of a footway line on the west side of South Road below the forecourt to industrial premises. Most of the principal building lies under the front gardens and houses on this side of South Road and at the corner with St Michael's Hill, a much smaller part within the industrial premises themselves.

Soho 2

Part of the 1791 mint building was located at the top end of the garden of 144 South Road, together with the lower part of the brick tunnel constructed in 1824–6, which contained the main drive shaft heading towards the coin cutting-out room situated in the central part of the former Latchet (Crescent) Building.

Soho 3

This trench in the upper part of the garden to 142 South Road uncovered the continuation of the main drive shaft tunnel at its junction with an offshoot to the steam engine installed in 1824–6. The main drive shaft had been powered by means of a belt-driven pulley connected to the engine. Apart from the lower part of the walls and floor of the tunnel, the massive stone blocks that supported this main pulley also survived. Another smaller offshoot tunnel marked the position of a smaller pulley and belt drive heading into the refitted 1791 mint building.

Soho 4

A small fragment of the lowermost three courses of the central bay of the Latchet (Crescent) Building, which contained the 1824–6 coin cutting-out room, was revealed. The brickwork lay immediately below the patio slabs in the garden of 154 South Road.

Soho 5

Another section of the drive shaft tunnel and the southern end of the Latchet (Crescent) Building that had been converted into part of the mint in 1824–6 was discovered in the garden of 150 South Road. As a result, the position of both the Latchet Building and the orientation of the drive shaft tunnel were fixed accurately for the first time.

Soho 6

An attempt was made to find the deep well below the steam engine that provided its water supply, its precise position determined from the drive shaft pulley foundations in Soho 3. Sand extraction in the early 20th century had destroyed the engine room and its foundations. Below patio slabs in the garden of 142 South Road, only demolition rubble was found. It was probed to a depth of 2.6m but no evidence of the well structure was found.

7

The Soho Foundry

Location and site (Fig 7.1) main foundry centred at SP 03418883

The Soho Foundry lies approximately one mile (1.6km) north-east of the centre of Smethwick in the Borough of Sandwell in a central part the West Midlands conurbation. It was situated in the northern part of the ancient parish of Harborne – Smethwick Township. The Soho Foundry was historically linked to the Soho Manufactory (demolished 1850–60s), which stood about a mile (1.6km) to the east in Handsworth parish, now part of Birmingham. The Birmingham/Sandwell boundary passes within a quarter of a mile (0.4km) of the site.

The Boulton & Watt buildings lie within a site owned today by Avery Weigh-Tronix, originally W T Avery Ltd, the well-known weighing machine manufacturers. The present site covers an area of 20 acres (8.1ha) (assembled by 1895), compared to the 17–18 acres (6.8–7.2ha) of the first Boulton & Watt acquisition. It lies between Foundry Lane to the north and east, the Birmingham Canal and the railway line from Wolverhampton to Birmingham New Street station to the south-east and south, respectively, and the site of the former Smethwick gasworks (now a scrap metal yard) to the west. The local environment is almost entirely industrial, though an island of residential property abuts the south-east boundary.

Origins

The origins of the Foundry lie in the method by which Boulton & Watt steam engines were produced in the first two decades after 1775, the first year of James Watt's patent for a steam engine with a separate condenser, and in the expiration of the patent itself in 1800. In essence, Boulton & Watt were not the manufacturers of their steam engines but purveyed the right to build a steam engine according to their patent.[1] This right took the form of a premium paid to Boulton & Watt based upon a calculation of coal consumption saved compared to the less efficient Newcomen engine. The purchasers of this right were sent drawings of the engine but were then obliged to seek their own manufacturers. As part of the service, an engineer from Boulton & Watt was sent out to help erect the engine once all the parts had been made and delivered to site. One of the most important components was the cylinder, which had to be accurately bored for the engine to work efficiently. Boulton & Watt usually recommended the Wilkinson brothers, William and John (of Bersham near Wrexham, Wales), considered to be the best manufacturers of engine cylinders in the country, to supply this part.

In 1795, the Wilkinson brothers quarrelled, with the unfortunate consequence that the Bersham Ironworks were closed. The closure was the immediate cause of the decision taken by Boulton & Watt to build their own cylinder-casting and boring mill on a canal-side site in Smethwick. In the longer term, the expiration of his patent in 1800 would have allowed anyone thereafter to build a steam engine to Watt's design. Boulton & Watt therefore needed to be able to manufacture all the component parts of their engine so that they could offer to supply a whole engine and erect it on site. In this way they could stay ahead of any future competition. In fact, the firm had already begun small-scale production of some of the smaller, specialist engine parts at the Manufactory.

Another event gave added impetus to the foundation of the first purpose-built steam-engine manufactory in the world. In 1794, James Watt Jr (b 1769), Gregory Watt (b 1777) and Matthew Robinson Boulton (b 1770) were brought into the firm under the style of Boulton, Watt & Sons. They brought with them fresh enthusiasm, energy, and the capacity to take on new ventures. James Watt Sr had rarely shown interest in the detail of manufacture and was gradually withdrawing from the business to his home at Heathfield House (now demolished) in Handsworth. Matthew Boulton, living on-site in Soho House, was occupied on many fronts and with his latest project – the mechanised production of coinage at the Soho Mint – in particular. With Matthew Robinson Boulton increasingly taking on responsibility for his father's complex of enterprises at the Soho Manufactory, it fell to James Watt Jr to take the lead in the establishment of the Soho Foundry. A résumé of the other Soho businesses based principally at the Manufactory is provided in Chapter 8.

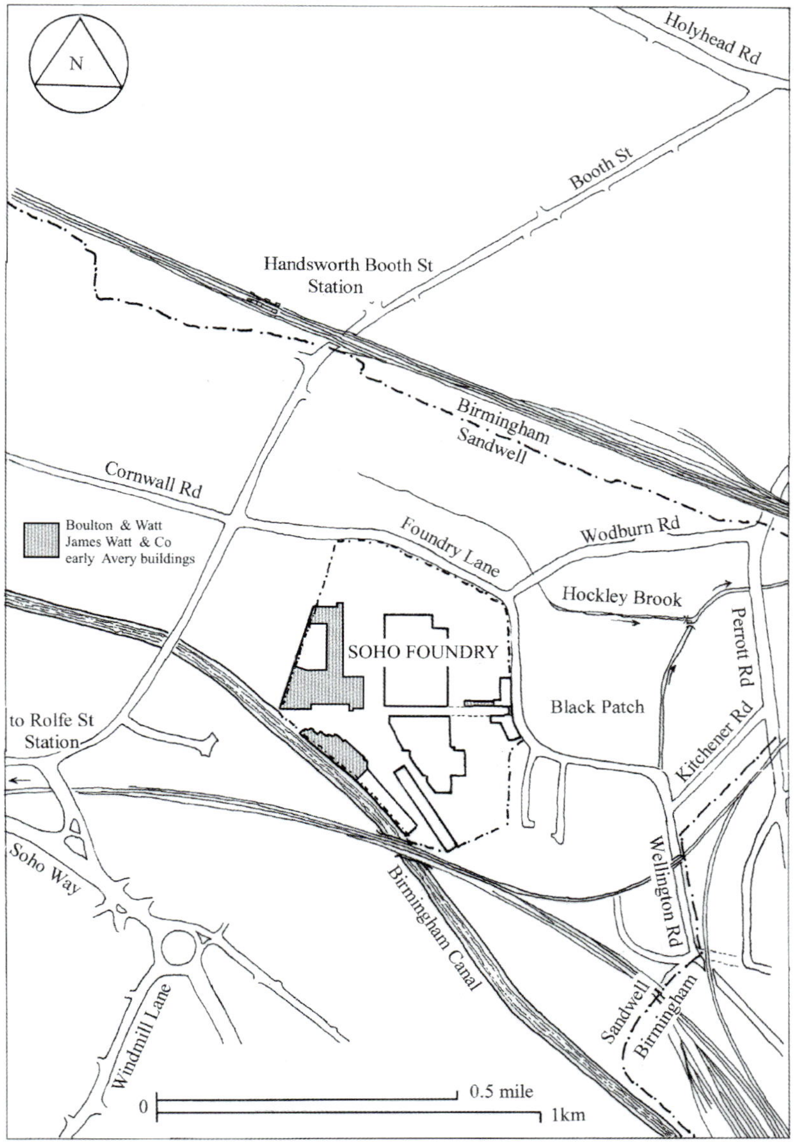

Fig 7.1
Plan of the present environs of the Soho Foundry.

Phase 1: The foundation of the foundry, 1795–9 (Fig 7.2)

Phase 1A: May 1795–August 1798

On 3 May 1795, James Watt Jr wrote to James Lawson (a Boulton & Watt engineer): 'We are beginning to consider seriously about erecting a foundry & boring mills ourselves.'[2] On the same day James Watt Jr wrote to his father:

> Mr Southern has suggested an [idea] which I think is worth consideration ... Query whether we had not better get the Cylinders cast by them & bore them ourselves with our present little Engine. The present Large Lathe might be converted at no great expence into an occasional boring Mill & the tools would serve at the other establishment should it ever take place ... It will be well before our patent dies a natural or violent death, to have our establishment for making engines put on a superior footing to our competitors. Mr S[outhern] will sketch out his ideas of the proposed addition & they will be sent up for your & Mr B[oulton]'s consideration.[3]

John Southern was a Boulton & Watt engineer and head of the drawing office at the Manufactory. His drawing of a boring machine has survived (Fig 7.3).[4] It is evident that Southern had suggested a temporary set-up at the Manufactory pending the 'new project'. This proposal was quickly dropped and the idea of separate establishments revived. On 10 May, Southern's drawing was sent to James Watt in London with a 'description of the proposed boring Mill to be worked by the present little engine'. It is clear that James Watt Jr had put the building of a foundry to one side for the time being, but he continued to work on the establishment of the boring mill.[5] A site for the mill had been found in Smethwick, about a mile (1.6km) away from the Manufactory in Handsworth, by the side of the Birmingham Canal on land belonging to George Kennedy. The canal-side site would allow easier and cheaper carriage of raw materials to, and finished goods from, the proposed works. John Southern was not confident that the little engine was powerful enough to work the mill, and on 6 June 1795 James Watt Jr wrote to William Wilkinson whom he was beginning to use as a consultant engineer (against the interests of William's brother, John):

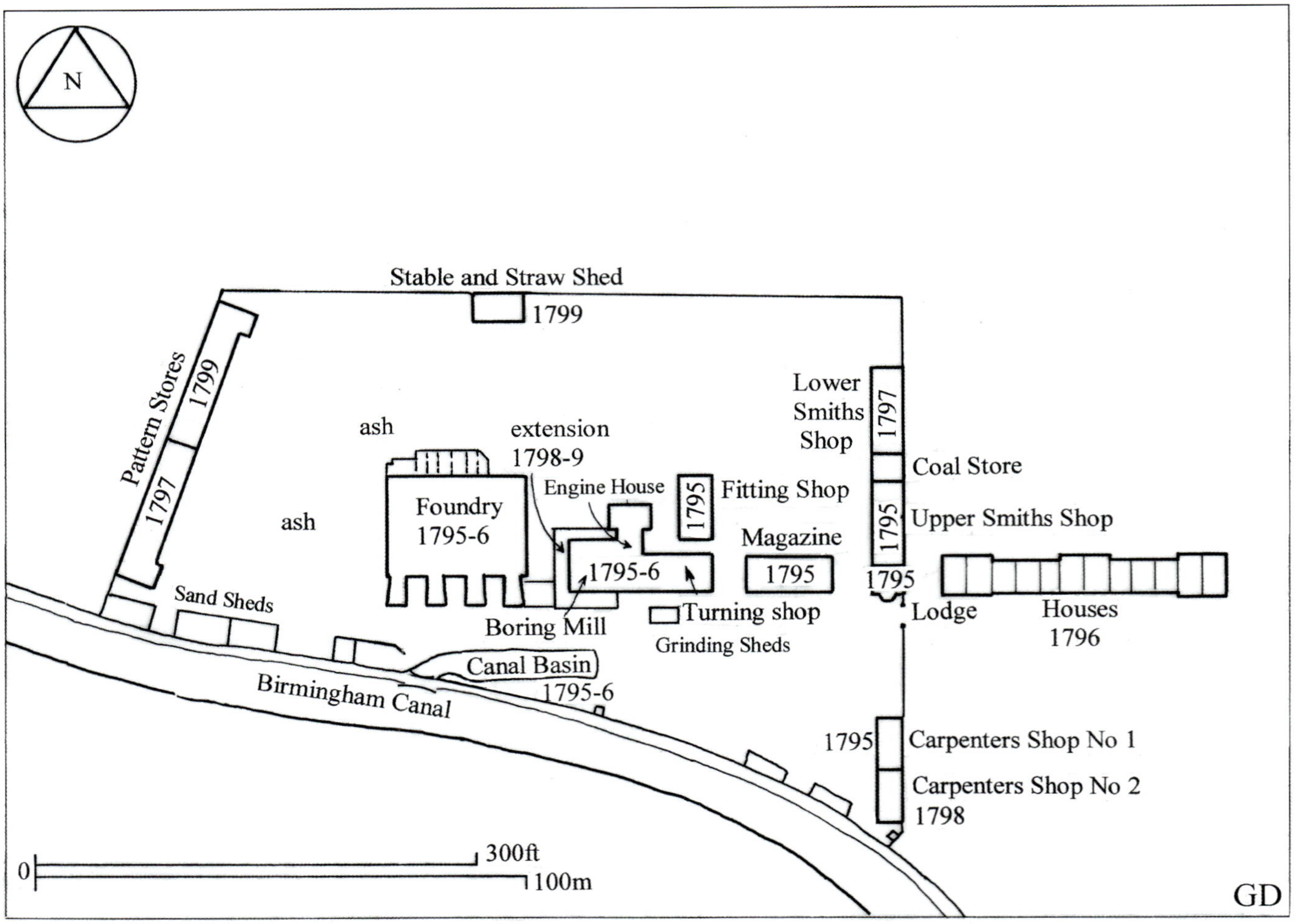

Fig 7.2
Soho Foundry, phase 1 plan, 1795–9.

> I now beg leave to remind you of your promise to give us a sketch of a small foundery and Boring Mill. We are going <u>immediately</u> to a 9 horse Engine for the latter, as we find it impossible otherwise to get through with our Orders. Whether or not we add a foundery to it, will depend upon future contingencies, at present we shall only go on with the Boring Mill. But we wish it to be erected in such a way as may be convenient for the Foundery if it ever takes place.[6]

At this point, James Watt Jr had changed his mind about the proposed site and was looking at the south side of the canal opposite George Kennedy's land and away from the tow path, but this idea was not to last. It was clear, however, that whatever site was chosen a 'side cut or dock' would be required.

James Watt Jr advocated vertical boring, and on 8 June 1795 sent 'Peter Ewart's plan for Perpendicular Boring' to Matthew Boulton in London.[7] Peter Ewart was a young engineer employed by Boulton & Watt. The alternative to Ewart's plan was horizontal boring as practised at Bersham, and James Watt Jr left the decision between the two methods to be made by his father and Matthew Boulton. In the meantime, negotiations with George Kennedy on the land purchase focused on an area of 17 acres (6.88ha) back on the north side of the canal (Fig 7.4).[8] Watt Jr was relying on his father to provide the purchase money for the land, which was to be repaid from the future profits of the works, and sought his and Matthew Boulton's 'determination as soon as possible that no time may be lost in beginning the erections'.[9] Matthew Boulton replied on 11 June that the price (£1,338 15s 0d) being asked was too high and that £1,100 should be offered instead.[10] He expressed his preference for horizontal boring and requested that Peter Ewart make 'a drawing of the best horizontal plan he can devise' so that a quick choice of method could be made. The seniors eventually chose

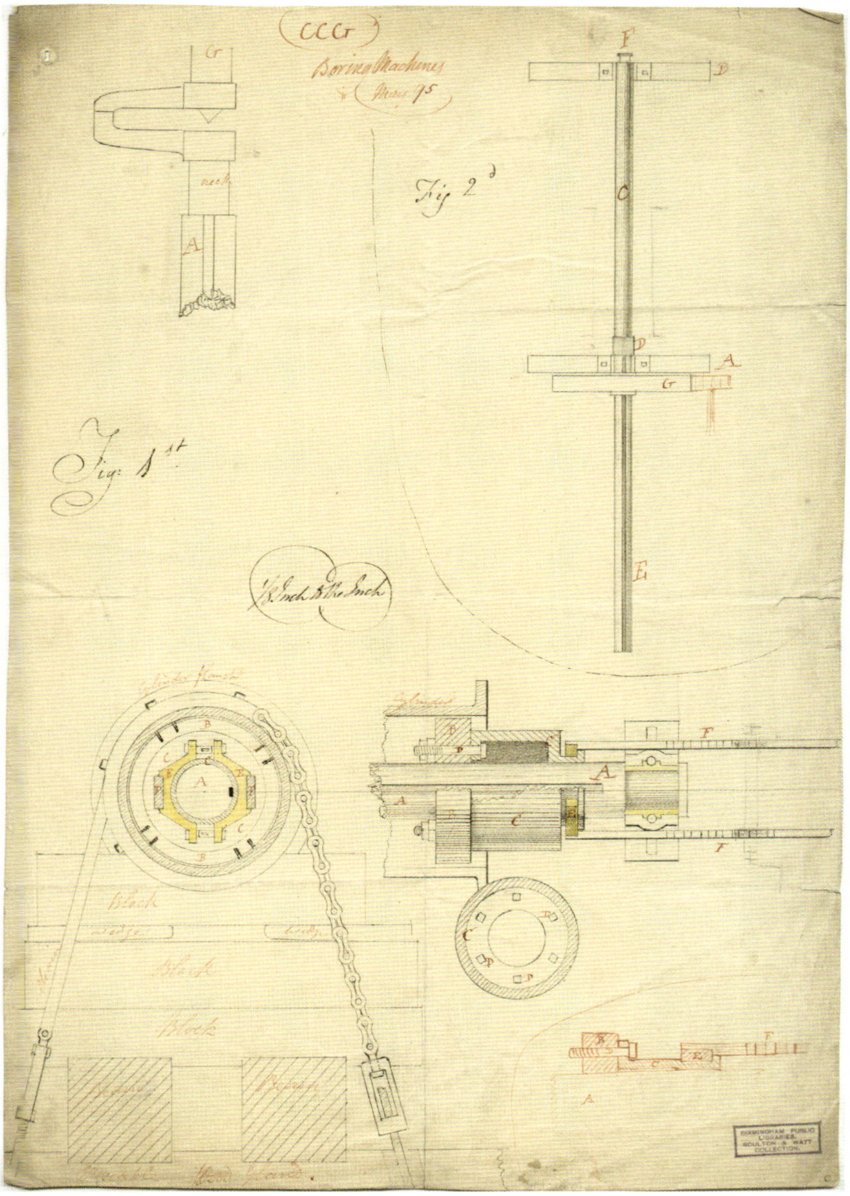

Fig 7.3
Drawing of the boring machinery, May 1795.

the horizontal method, perhaps influenced by Ewart's still surviving drawing of the vertical-boring machine, which would have necessitated major below-ground structures.[11]

Mr Kennedy seems to have won in the haggle over the price of his land and by 15 July James Watt stated that he had 'bought Land value £1,340'.[12] In fact, the actual conveyance took place on 26 and 27 August 1795.[13] James Watt provided all the finance and instructed his attorney to prepare a lease to Matthew Boulton, Matthew Robinson Boulton, and James Watt Jr for 500 years at a rent of £65 15s 0d per annum.[14] It was covenanted that, on the payment of £1,318 by the parties to James Watt, the freehold would be conveyed to them. The newly purchased estate measured 18.25 acres (7.38ha) and occupied an area between the canal to the south, Foundry Lane to the north, and Mr Whately's (Wheatley's) land and Rabone Lane to the west.[15]

Sometime in July or early August 1795, it was decided to add a foundry and other buildings to the site.[16] On 14 August, James Watt Jr received an important letter from William Wilkinson, whose advice had clearly been sought on the layout of these new works. The newly purchased land fell approximately 30ft

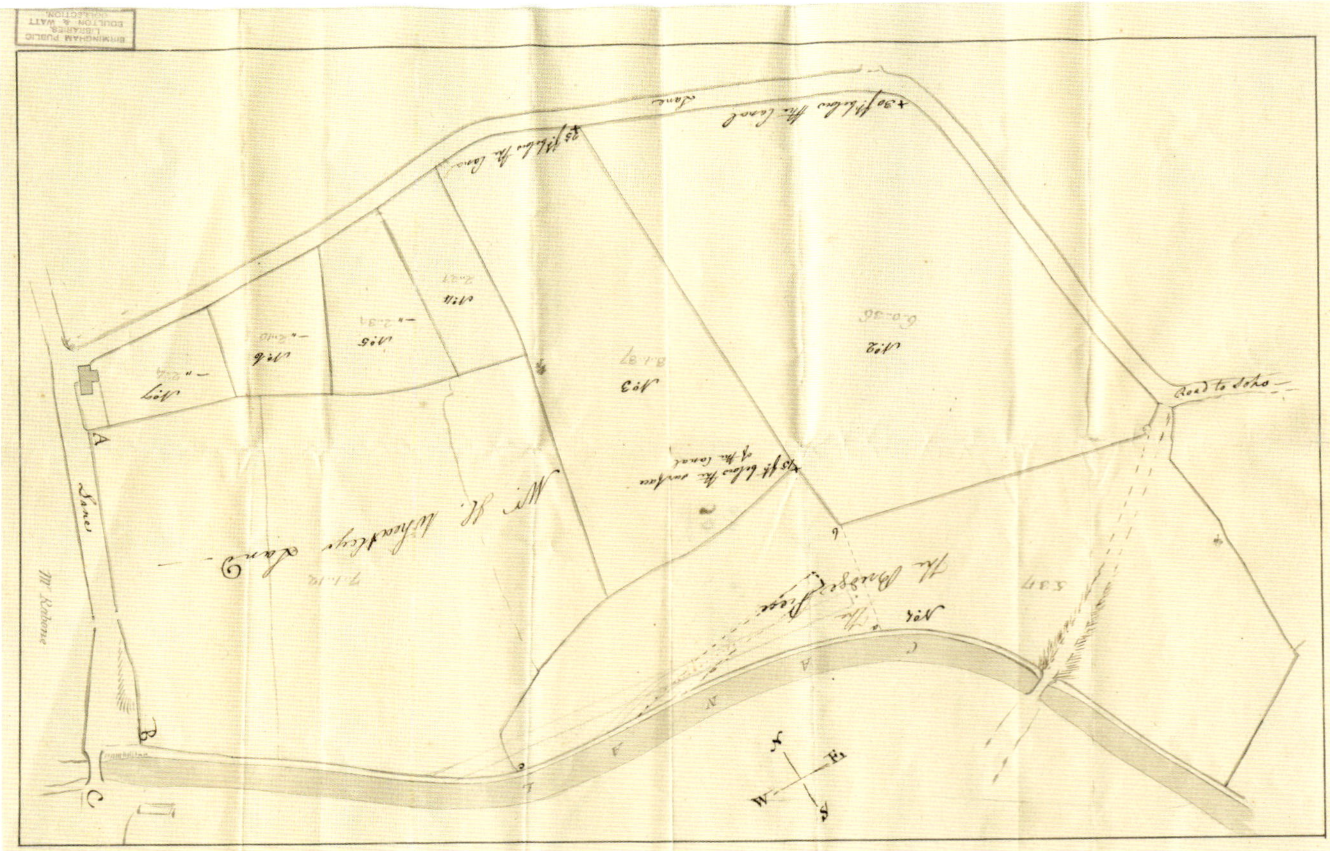

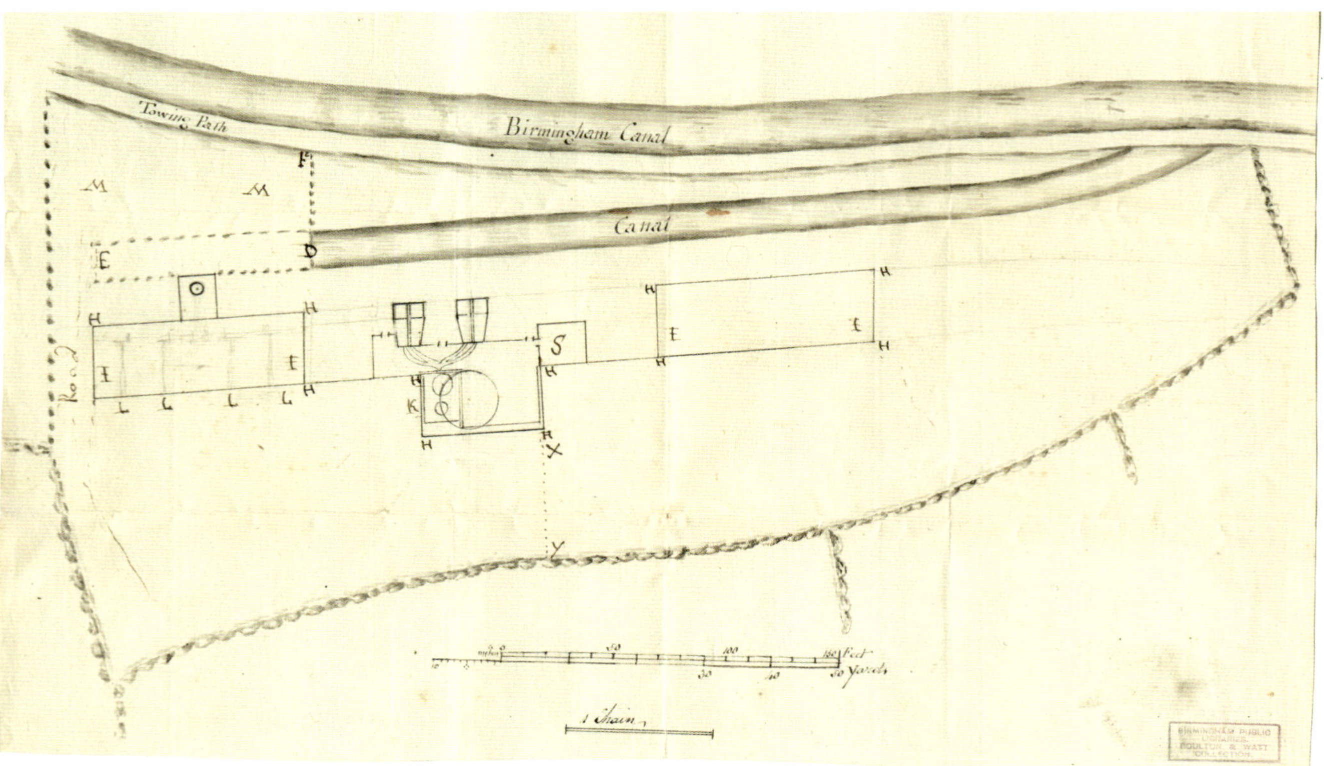
Towing Path
Birmingham Canal
Canal
Feet
Yards
1 Chain

(9.14m) from south to north and east, a feature that Wilkinson exploited in his proposal for the Soho Foundry layout. He drew a plan with all the buildings, foundry, boring mill and workshop to be located in the field called 'Bridge Piece', immediately alongside the canal (Fig 7.5).[17] He then suggested that the foundry should be built with its floor 18in (45cm) above the level of the canal and that the boring mill should be placed adjacent to the foundry on the east, 7.5ft (2.2m) below the level of the canal,

> which will leave a difference of 9 feet between the Two Levels of the Ground. My Motive for this is to render the Labour more easy in the Manufactory. By this means the level in the Boring Frames at LLLL will be level with the door at K through which the Cylinder will come when Cast.

It was always intended that a canal basin would be constructed, access to a canal having been a prime motive for the selection of the site. This is clearly shown on Wilkinson's drawing, though it is longer than the arm that was actually built. With the bottom of the casting pit in the foundry at the same level as the boring mill, the arduous task of lifting heavy cylinders out of the pit in which they were cast was eliminated. They would only then have to be trundled the short distance from the foundry to the boring mill. The position and levels of the boring mill and the foundry relative to one another are essentially Wilkinson's concept and his crucial role in the planning of the Soho Foundry has been identified by Gale.[18]

The designs for the Soho Foundry were not, however, entirely dependent on Wilkinson since a layout for the boring mill and engine house was in preparation before his proposal arrived. In August 1795, Boulton & Watt produced drawings of this building, which differed from the scheme submitted by Wilkinson.[19] The engine and boiler houses projected north from a broad, single-storey boring mill to the west and a two-storey range of narrower workshops attached to the east (Fig 7.6). The engine was intended to power both the boring machines and the lathes and drills in the workshop. The workshop range was usually called the Turning Shop but was also known by many other names including Piston Rod Shop and Nozzle Shop.

Similarly, Wilkinson's plan for a large building containing workshops to the west of the foundry was not carried out. In August, drawings of a smiths shop were prepared; this was to be located with another identical block against the eastern boundary wall of the factory site.[20] The foundry itself was not placed in the centre of Bridge Piece but as far west in the field as was practically possible. Wilkinson's recommendation that a portion of Henry Whately's land west of the original purchase should be acquired to allow more room around the foundry was, however, acted upon (Fig 7.7). By March 1796, the irregularity in the shape of the original site had been ironed out through an exchange and purchase of land with Whately, which resulted in the straight western boundary surviving to the present day.[21]

Wage accounts provide an accurate record of the commencement and progress of work on the buildings.[22] The construction of the boundary wall was started on 3 August 1795, followed by the beginning of work on the smithy (forging

Fig 7.4 (opposite)
Plan of the Soho Foundry estate purchased in 1795.

Fig 7.5 (opposite)
William Wilkinson's proposed layout plan for the Soho Foundry, August 1795, the Birmingham Canal and canal arm being built on the south side of the site.

Fig 7.6
Plan, elevation and cross sections of the boring mill and turning shop, August 1795.

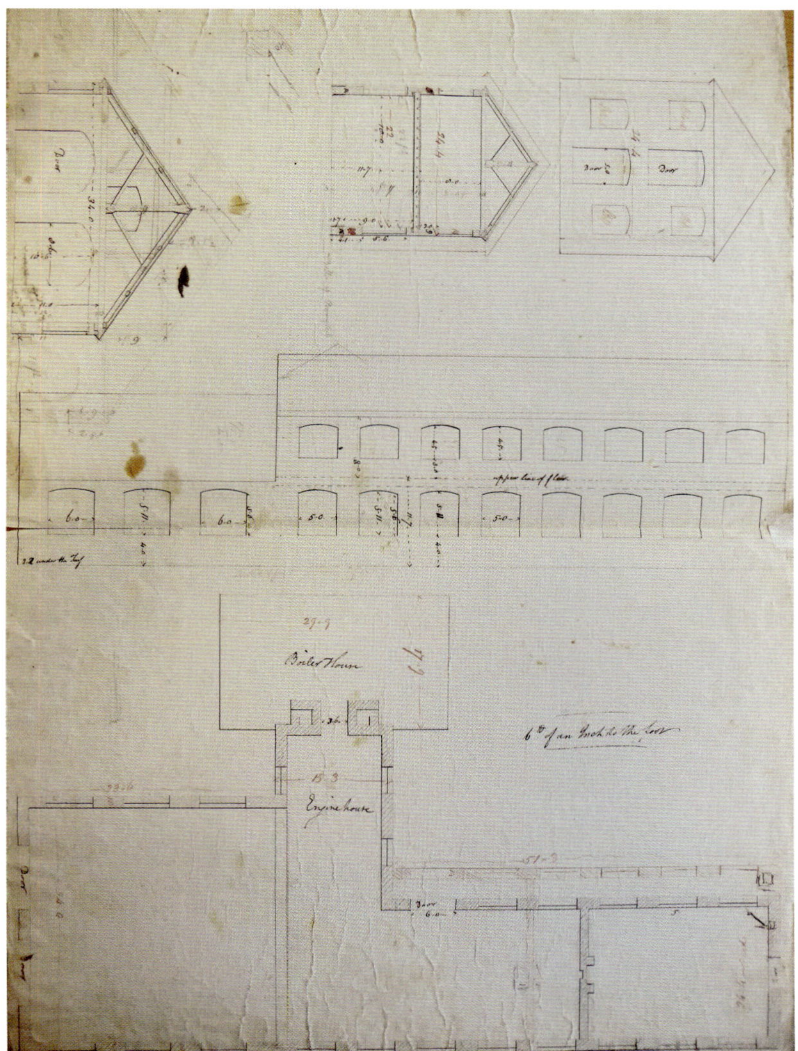

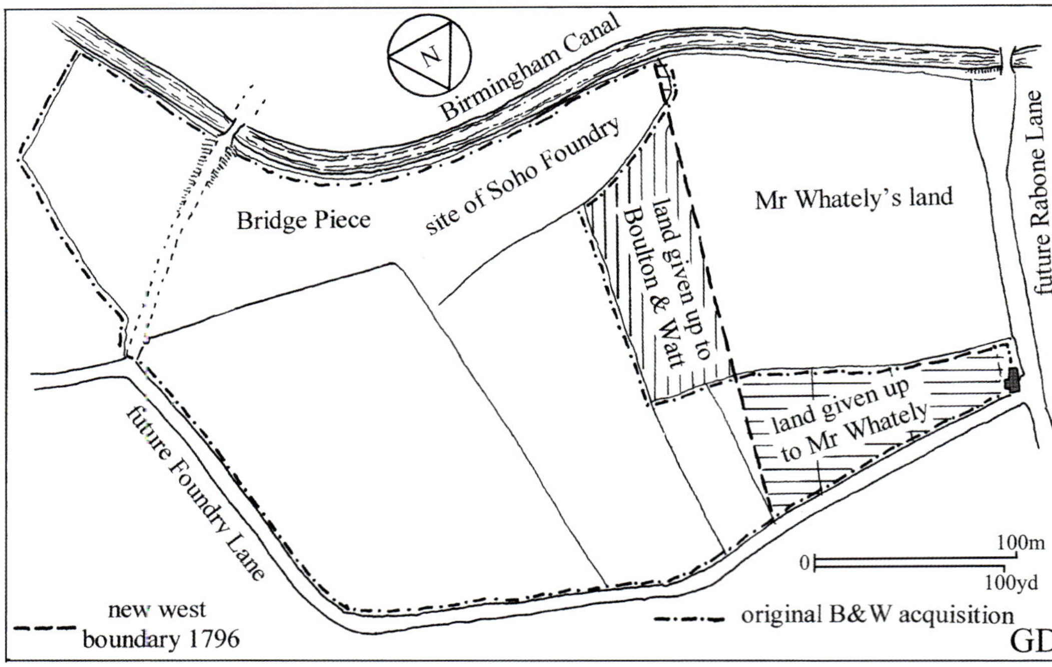

Fig 7.7
Plan of the Soho Foundry estate showing exchanges of land, 1796, creating the present west boundary of the site.

shop), the lodge, the carpenters shop and the boring mill on 29 August.[23] The smithy contained a hearth on each of the north and south gable walls and a larger hearth on the east wall, with a bellows room projecting outwards beyond the main building (Fig 7.8).[24] The west elevation of the smithy into the yard was intended to have an open timber frame with a wide central entrance, but this elevation was not built as intended (*see* Phillp drawing, Fig 7.9). The lodge was attached to the south end of the smithy.[25] The carpenters shop, too, was built against the east boundary wall and on the same alignment as the smithy, but positioned further south near the canal. It was a five-bay, two-storey building with a central door on the west elevation facing the yard.[26] There were no windows on the east elevation.

The construction of a particular building could be interrupted by other priorities. An important decision was made, perhaps late in August or early in September 1795, to build the foundry that season. Six drawings of the foundry were made on 7 September, but none have survived.[27] On 14 September, James Watt Jr wrote to John Southern in Newcastle:

> we are going on pretty well in the common jog-trot way, except in the new buildings where we are going on at full gallop & hope to have the Brickwork completed this week. Should that be the case we shall make a dash at the foundery this Season.[28]

The drawings may have been made obsolete by James Watt Jr's advice to Southern the following day that the foundry should be 60ft (18.29m) square:

> I told you yesterday that we should make a dash at the foundry this season. 60 ft. sqr. is the size we propose. Please to give your ideas upon the subject of the stoves Cyl[inde]r Pit &c & the abstract of your observations upon the founderies in the North. You must let us have them soon, as we are commence [sic] our operations immediately, not to lose this astonishingly fine season.[29]

On 15 September, James Watt Jr wrote to his father giving a detailed report on progress at the Soho Foundry. James Watt had little natural inclination for matters of business and the letter reveals his reluctance to be drawn into the venture despite having provided all the capital:

> Our Boring Mill, Blacksmiths Shop, Lodge and Carpenters shop are all ready for covering in. The Dock too is finished all but the bridge and our Walls are nearly all up. We hope from this specimen that you will give us some credit for activity & that you will not be angry with us, if the success of our past exertions induces us to go beyond the line originally proposed and to finish the foundery this year.
>
> Eight very good master bricklayers now upon the point of standing still, 300,000 spare bricks, the finest weather I ever remem-

> ber, the prospect of saving a whole year, and fresh orders coming in every day are inducements enough ... We propose making the Foundery 60ft Square & taking Wm Wilkinson's advice about it.[30]

On 17 September, a drawing of the magazine (the store for materials such as iron and brass) was completed and a start was made on the building in the same week (Fig 7.10).[31] This magazine was a seven-bay, two-storey building with both an external and an internal staircase, and it was placed east of the turning shop on an east–west alignment. This respected the orientation of the intended main roadway through the Soho Foundry. The roadway had not yet been laid out, but its east–west direction was already

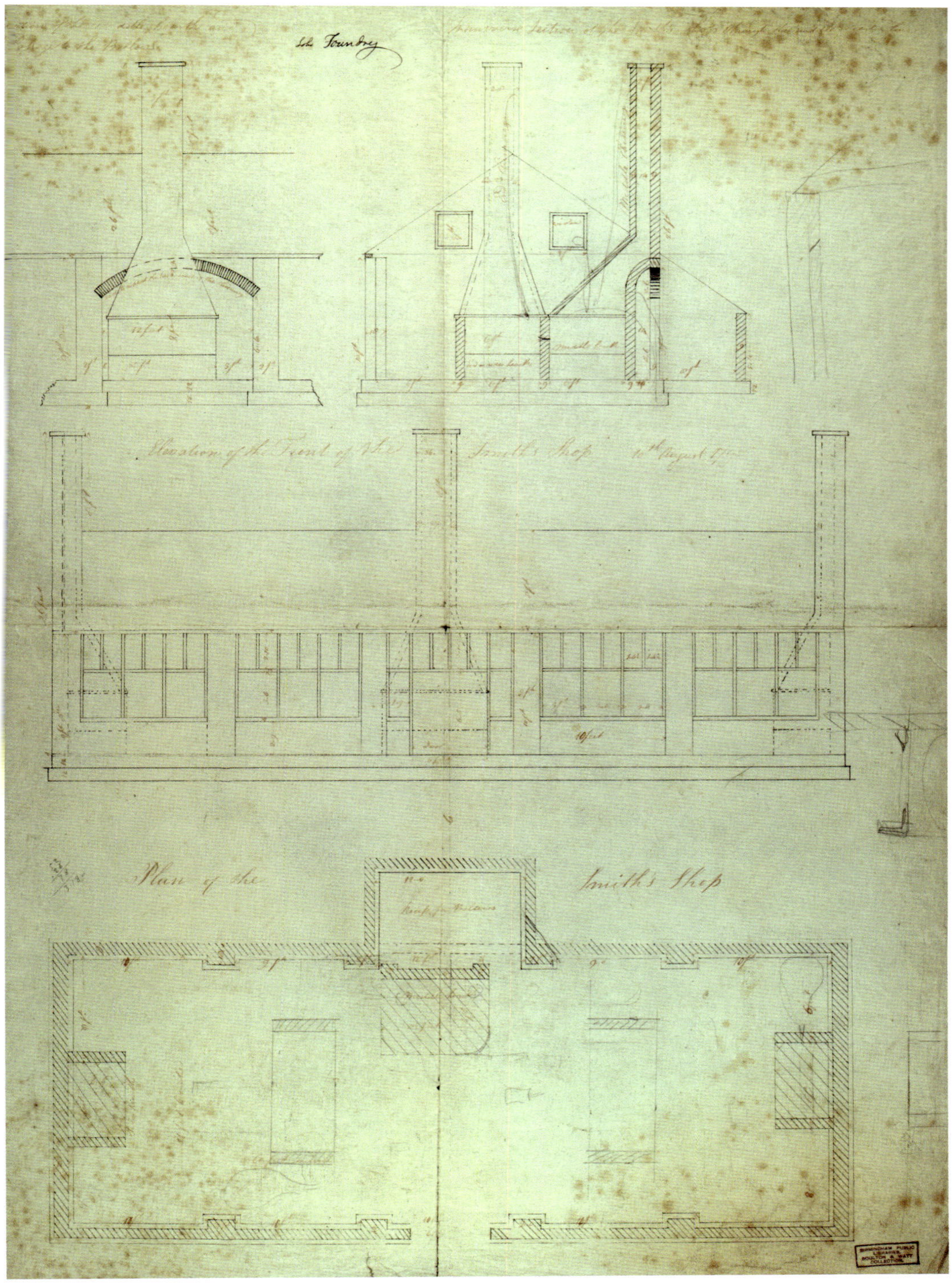

Fig 7.8
Plan, elevation and cross sections of the smithy, 10 August 1795.

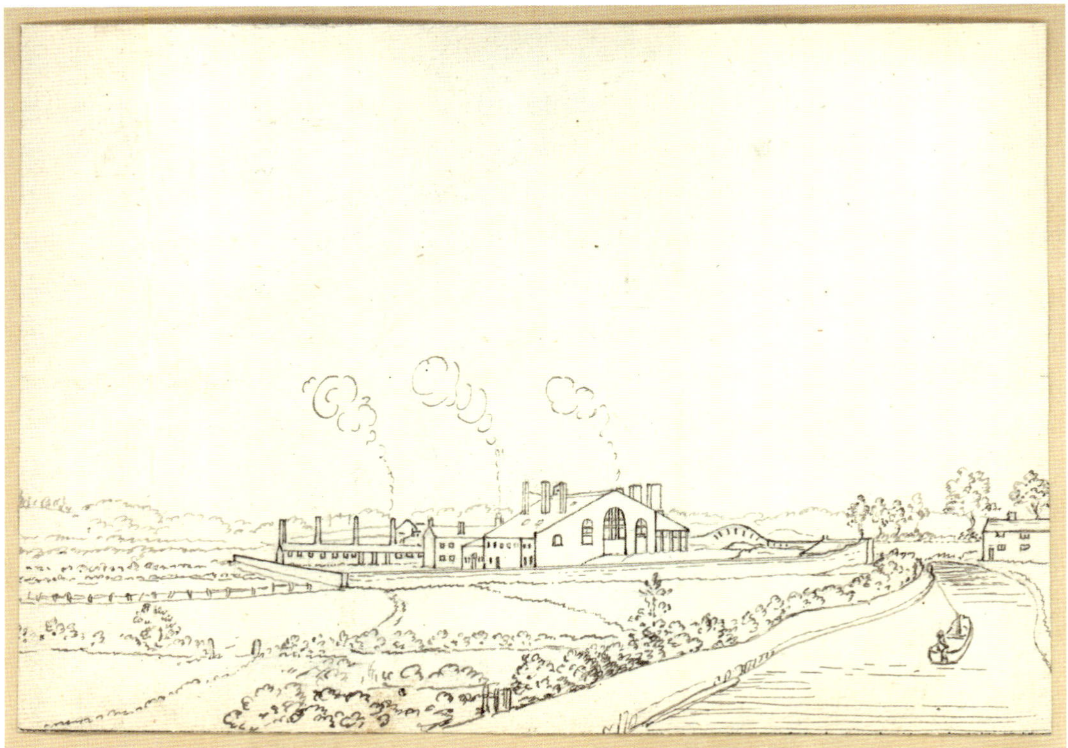

Fig 7.9
Pen-and-ink drawing of the Soho Foundry by John Phillp, taken from the Birmingham Canal bank looking south-east, 1797.

fixed through the location of the lodge (and main entrance to the works) on the eastern boundary of the site.

On 19 September, an additional 700,000 bricks were purchased, and Matthew Robinson Boulton asked Southern to check the price of crown glass in Newcastle as the Stourbridge makers were unwilling to supply it.[32] It was estimated that 1,700 'squares' of eleven sizes were required. On the following day, Matthew Robinson Boulton reported to Southern: 'The beautiful season is highly favourable to our building schemes & I assure you we are not wanting in our exertions to employ it to the best advantage'.[33] On the same day, Matthew Boulton was less positive and felt the need for a rallying call:

> I expected the Men would have worked the Dock this Day as the neck of it can be more conveniently done on a Sunday but was disappointed. See, mark, learn & inwardly digest the Foundry as we now have Bricks enough to do anything that the season will allow.[34]

With the aid of two of Wilkinsons' Bersham staff, Gilbert Gilpin and Abraham Storey, the latter soon to be appointed as the first foundry manager, the plan of the foundry was almost ready by 24 September. The details were sketched by James Watt Jr and described to his father (Fig 7.11):

> I sketched down the result as under a a a a are four air furnaces, situated as near together as the men can work the fires for the conveniency of running from all four into the Cyl[inde]r pit (d), which is placed as near to them as possible to prevent the metal cooling. By this means it is removed 10ft from the end of the foundery but a passage of 10 feet wide, arched over is to be left at (b) to convey the Cylinders into the boring Mill. The building is to be 80 feet long by 40 feet wide. The stoves will be placed upon the opposite side to the air furnaces in order to leave the end of the foundery (f) entirely for castings in green Sand, which should not be mixed with the dry sand, which will be managed in the middle part of the building. There will be two cranes; one at (o); the other not yet determined. Additional air furnaces may if wanted be built along the Wharf side as represented by the dotted lines. A shed will be carried from the roof upon the side where the stoves are & the space under it appropriated to mixing up Loam &c, which may be conveyed in to the Cylinder pit by passage (c).[35]

In fact, the foundry was built 95ft long and 46ft wide (28.96m by 14.02m), based on the only detailed plan that has survived. It must date from soon after 24 September, for work on the building began on 7 October (Fig 7.12).[36] The drawing is of the lower ground level and of a longitudinal cross section. It shows the bases of five air furnaces attached to the external face of the south wall and the positions of another possible three. It is important to emphasise that there was an extra storey on the north elevation of the foundry because of the fall in the land. (For convenience, this extra storey will be called 'lower ground' and the main foundry floor 'upper ground'). A series of five compartments, each 20ft (6.1m) wide, stretched the full length of the external face of the north wall at lower ground level. The three central compartments were inaccessible, probably built solely to support the rooms on the upper ground floor, which contained the sand-drying stoves. The compartments on either side of the central three were accessible from the yard outside. The compartment on the east might originally have been used for mixing loam, since a passage connected it directly to the casting pit. A broader passage, 12ft (3.66m) wide, led eastwards from the casting pit towards the boring mill.

On 24 September, Matthew Boulton reported to James Watt:

> You'l be astonished to see what progress our young men [their sons] have made with the building, every shop warehouse & Boreing Mill being now nearly ready for roof. Except the Foundry which I find will require one Year after it is begun before it will be in a state of business.[37]

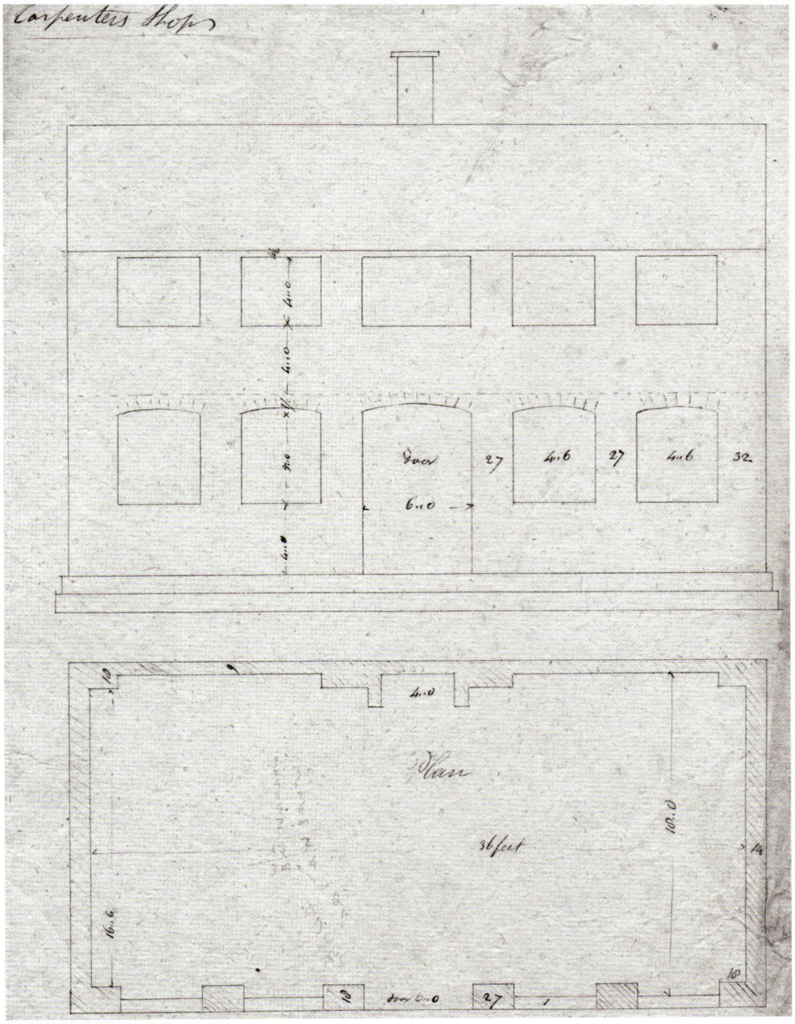

Fig 7.10
Plan and elevation of the carpenters shop, c 1795.

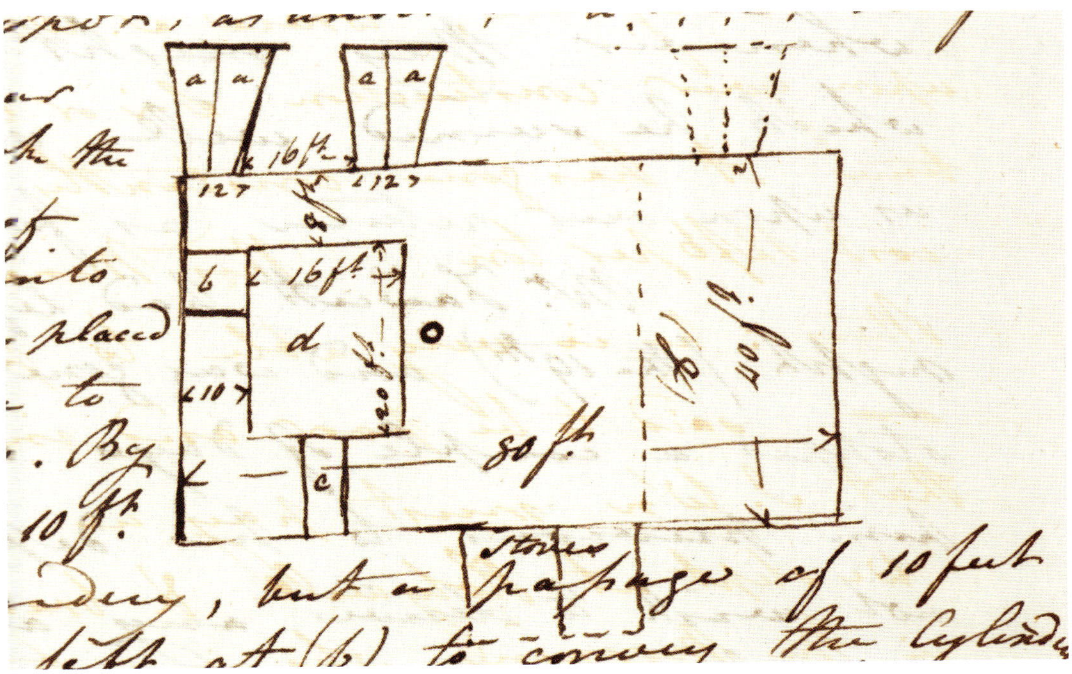

Fig 7.11
James Watt Jr's layout plan for the main foundry building, 24 September 1795.

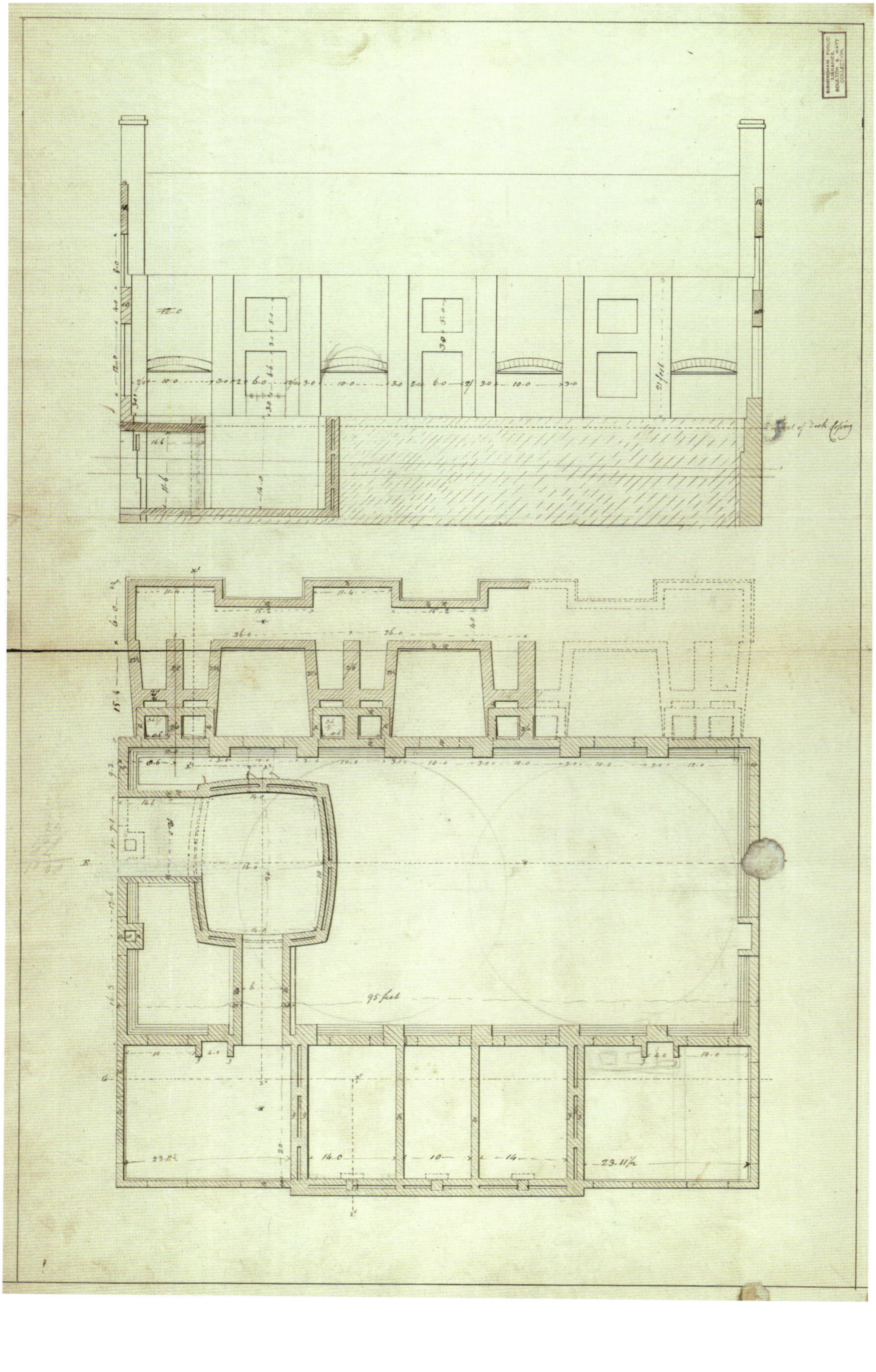

Fig 7.12
Plan and cross section of the main foundry building, c 1795.

In the following six months, while the foundry was being built, a considerable effort was expended on earth-moving and levelling.[38] The deep excavations for the foundations of the air furnaces had to be backfilled. Despite the natural advantages already offered by the local topography, the south side of the site for the boring mill still had to be excavated up to 6ft (1.83m) into the falling ground to put the building on a level with the lower ground floor of the foundry. A retaining wall was built 10ft (3.05m) from the south elevation of the boring mill, creating a sunken yard reaching ground level at the east end.

On 26 October 1795, James Watt Jr admitted that there had been 'a great many Drawbacks about our foundery, but we have now got the foundations compleated & are nearly up to the level of the Wharf ... Our other buildings are for the most part, roofed in'.[39] Two days later, he complained about the weather: 'The wet weather is a great hindrance to our getting on with the foundry, as we cannot make our bricklayers stick to their work, we still however do not despair of finishing it this season, unless the frost sets in sooner than usual'.[40] It was at about this time that the construction of the fitting shop, where the engines were assembled from their separate parts, was started. It was placed a few yards to the north of the turning shop and orientated north–south. Five bays long and two storeys high, it contained a hearth on the north side and central doors in the east and west walls. The south bay of the building was without a first floor, apparently to accommodate 'moveable wooden frames' designed by Ewart for the fitting of parallel motions and working gears.[41]

At the end of October, James Watt Jr declined an offer from William Wilkinson to take a share in the Bersham works, for 'we have launched out too widely in our infant works at Smethwick to be able to recede, having already laid out upwards of £2000, which sum will be nearly doubled before the year expires'.[42] Watt Jr thanked William for his advice on the Soho Foundry and admitted almost apologetically that 'in general we have disposed the works differently so as to suit the peculiarities of our business'. Nevertheless, in mid-November, Wilkinson's advice was sought on the form of the cupola and, more particularly, on the air furnace's chimney stacks, which were being built at the foundry and had reached 15 or 16 feet (4.57–4.88m) in height. He was also asked to supply drawings.[43] Matters had not gone well as the newly cast iron beams supporting the stacks did not fit together properly.[44] The recent wet weather had been replaced by frost, but this was not seen as an obstacle. On 16 November, William Wilkinson replied providing a plan and giving details of the Bersham cupola, which had no chimney 'as the Men clean it out by Standing upon it'.[45] His drawing was based on his brother John Wilkinson's patent of 1794.[46] James Watt Jr then drew his own version, sending it to William for his approval. The design consisted of a double cupola that would fit into the remaining 10ft (3.05m)-wide rectangular space at the west end of the south wall.[47]

On 20 December, James Watt Jr reported that 'we are getting on the roof of the foundry, which we hope to have ready for the slates before Xmas day'.[48]

1796

It was to be the end of January before the foundry roof was fully covered and the delay caused the postponement of the opening ceremony.[49] The rearing feast took place on 30 January 1796 and the address was given by Matthew Boulton. The newspaper report of 2 February 1796 in *Aris's Gazette* has been quoted at length by Dickinson.[50] There is only room here to repeat a few of Boulton's words:

> I now come as the Father of Soho to Consecrate this place as one of its Branches, I also come to give it a name & my Benediction. I will therefore proceed to purify the walls of it by the sprinkling of wine and in the name of Vulcan & and all the Gods and Godesses of Fire and Water, I pronounce the name of it *Soho Foundry* – May that name endure for ever & let all the people say amen.

Little did he know how long the name would endure (and confuse).

The newly established Soho Foundry found it difficult to recruit workers as the required skills, particularly for such a large and innovative enterprise, were in short supply. The skills shortage affected all operations from foundry-men (such as moulders and casters) to engine fitters and turners:[51] 'After advertising and using various means we have been unable to supply our deficiency & several Engines are now lying in the yard for want of hands to put them together'.[52] The Wilkinsons' troubled foundry at Bersham was an obvious source of supply and Abraham Storey was eventually poached to become the foundry manager.[53] Other workers also followed Storey to the foundry from Bersham.

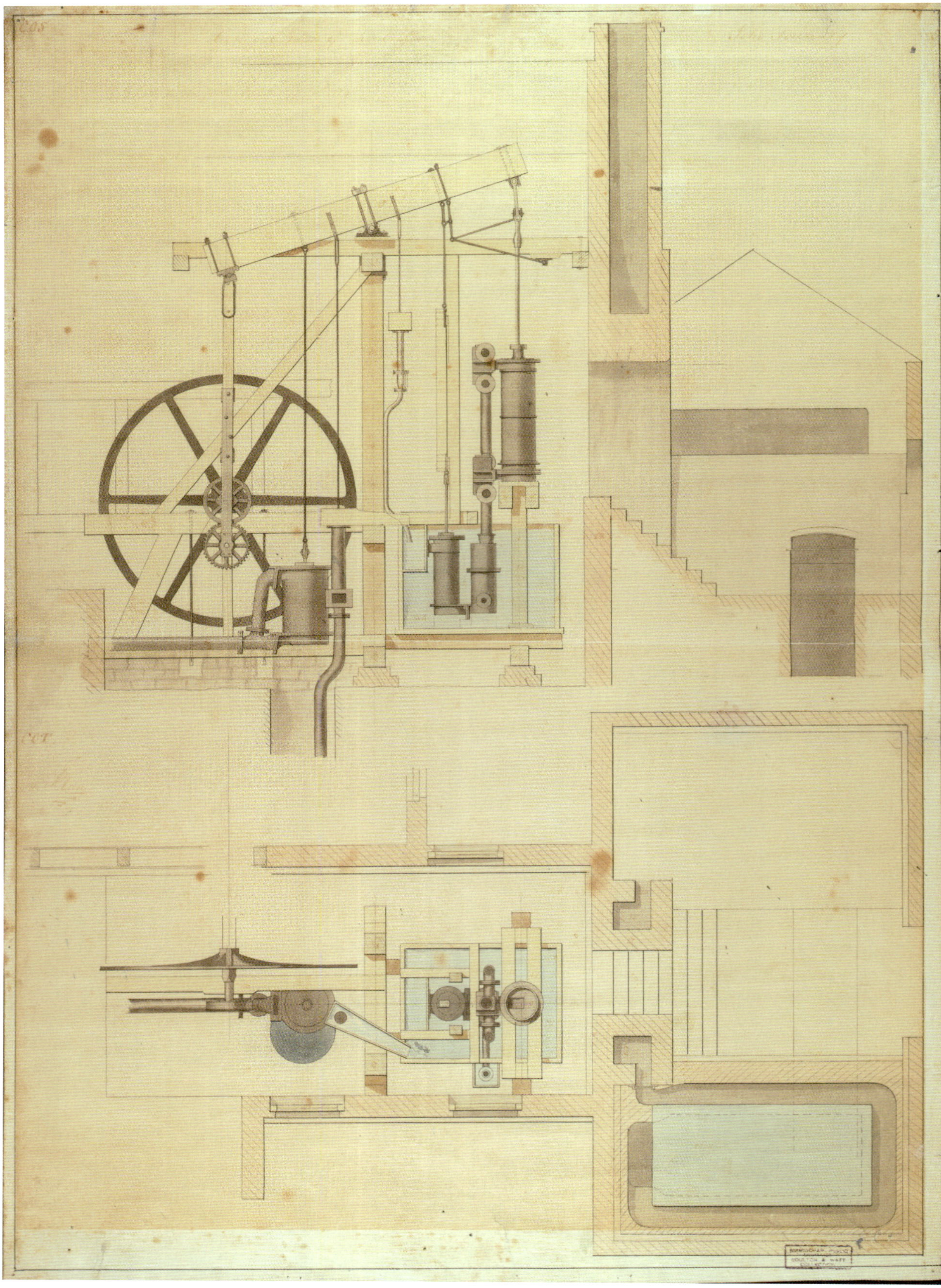

The major role played by Peter Ewart in the design of Soho Foundry buildings and machinery in these early months was identified some time ago.[54] Ewart was heavily involved in the design and installation of the boring machinery and was given the task of recruiting some 'pupils' ('eleves') to assist an apprentice in the erection of the steam engine for the boring mill and turning mill.[55] In February 1796, several detailed engine drawings were made and most of these have survived (Figs 7.13 and 7.14).[56] They show a standard Boulton & Watt rotary beam engine with a 20in (508mm) cylinder rated at 14hp and a sun-and-planet gear. Apart from powering the boring mill on one side and the lathes and drills in the turning shop on the other, the engine was also connected to a blowing cylinder 28in (711mm) in diameter, which provided blast to the cupola in the foundry. The drawing was sent to Peter Ewart around 8 March.[57]

Houses were considered necessary to attract workers, such as charge-hands and clerks, to the Soho Foundry. Although plans had been drawn in October 1795, building work did not begin until March 1796 when more plans were made.[58] The later plans show a row of eight two-storey cottages flanked at each end by a pair of three-storey houses with hipped roofs. These were built immediately outside the main gate on an east–west alignment on the north side of the road leading from Foundry Lane. The terrace was demolished by Avery's in the late 1890s.

It appears that one air furnace was commissioned in March 1796 when requests went out to supply pig iron.[59] The first castings were modest affairs, as James Watt Jr admitted: 'We ... are going nimbly at the foundery, where we have one furnace at work and we are already able to cast – Grate Bars!'[60] He was less positive a few days later:

> we are under the necessity of taking off some of the best men from their ordinary work to employ them in getting forward the Machinery for the new foundry where our progress is by no means adequate to our expectations.[61]

Little progress was being made two months later when James Watt Jr, away on business, requested a report. Ewart was also away and the completion of the steam engine for the boring mill and turning shop awaited his return. The erection of cranes in the foundry was going slowly. The boundary wall was 6ft (1.83m) high all around and the houses at each end of the terrace had their roof cover on.[62]

On 20 June 1796, there was great excitement as the first engine part, a nozzle (valve), was cast. Unfortunately, there were no lathes in the turning mill to fit them and no prospect of having them for many months because of their intended 'uncommon construction'.[63]

There are a few undated small-scale site plans that were drawn in 1795 and early 1796 to show the buildings intended to be constructed, and they are reasonably reliable as a

Fig 7.13 (opposite)
Water-coloured elevation and plan of the boring mill steam engine, c 1796.

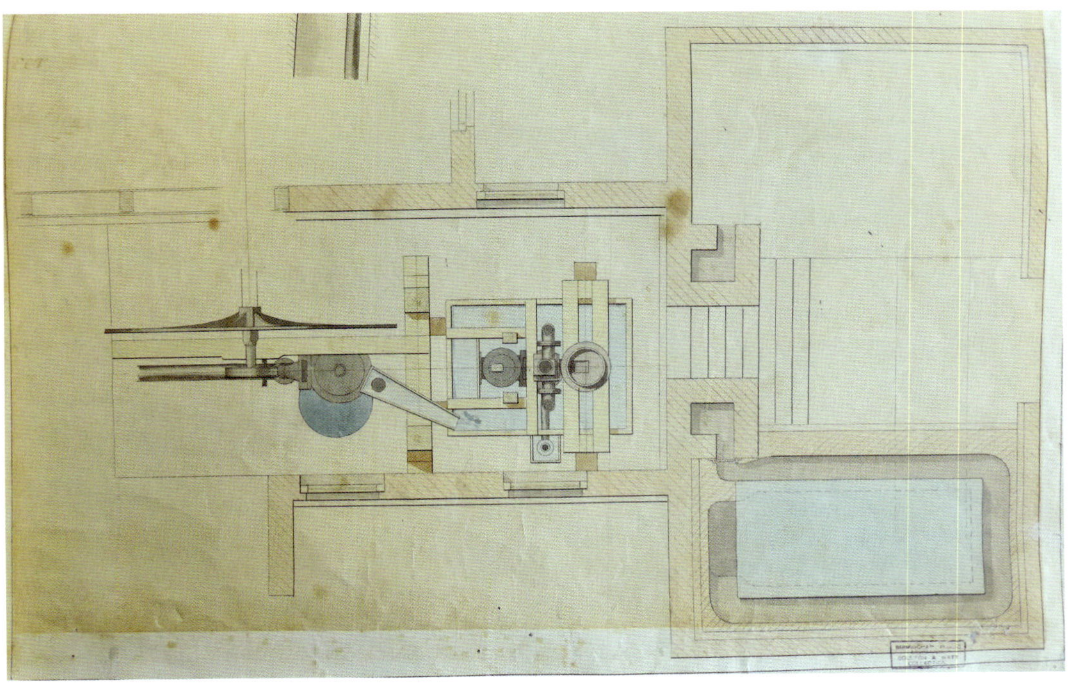

Fig 7.14
Extract from the plan of the boring mill engine demonstrating fine draughtsmanship, c 1796.

record for the actual Soho Foundry layout completed by mid-1796 (Fig 7.15).[64] A larger-scale plan fills in useful details such as the tunnel beneath the air-furnace stoking holes, which was entered from the west side of the foundry by a long descent between two parallel walls (*see* Fig 7.32). Another plan (Fig 7.16) identifies the individual buildings – the upper part of the magazine (F) was to be used as a counting house and the eastern half of the turning mill (G) was to contain a pattern turning shop on the first floor and a magazine on the ground floor. The other half (H), closest to the engine, was intended for the turning and drilling shops on both floors.[65] This disposition of functions in the building was quickly rearranged.

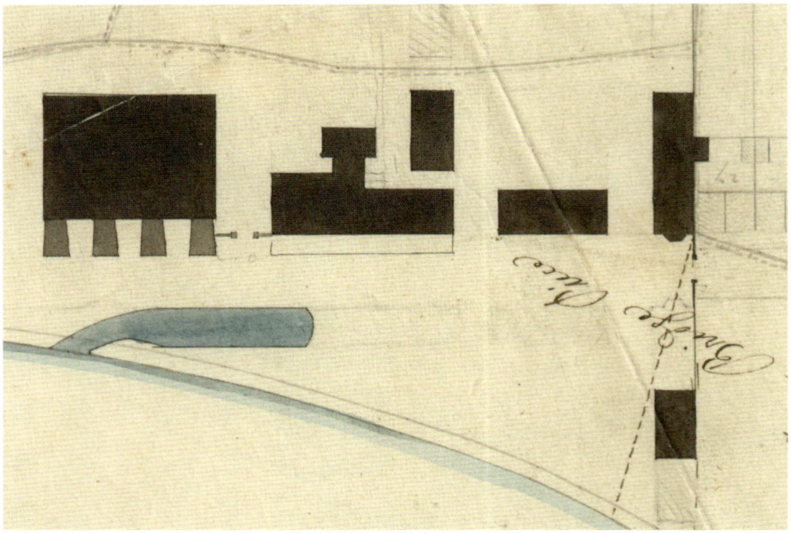

Fig 7.15
Extract from a water-coloured plan of the Soho Foundry and surrounding fields, c 1795–6.

In July 1796, slow progress on the foundry fit-out was blamed on the push to finish the houses, a surprising priority. Greensand castings (small items) could be made, but it was to be two months (September) before the casting and boring of a cylinder took place.[66] All this expenditure on buildings was making James Watt (the main creditor) nervous and his son felt compelled to reassure him:

> All the buildings which have hitherto been erected there do not amount to more than £7 & 8000 and the whole will be completed for £1 to 2000 more, which will go out very gradually. It is not our intention or wish to erect any new buildings for the present and I believe we may safely say that all upon the premises are of absolute necessity.[67]

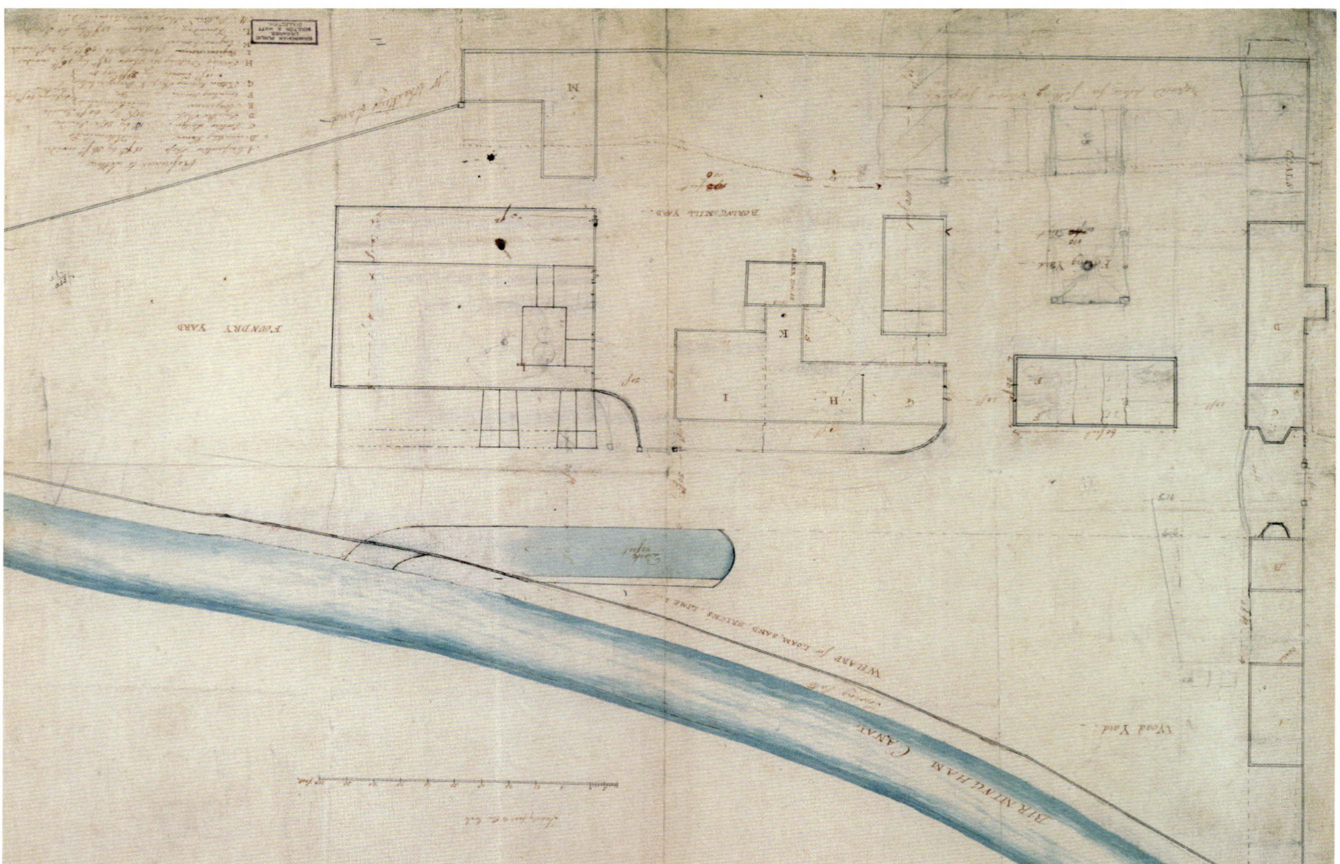

Fig 7.16
Extract from a plan of the Soho Foundry, c 1795–6.

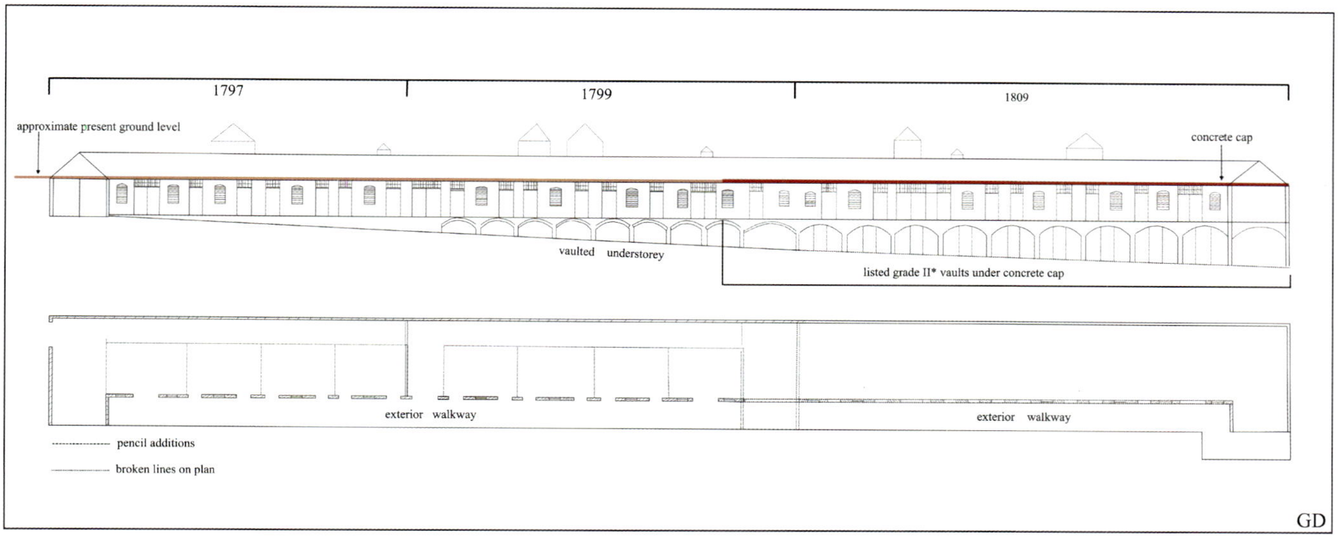

Fig 7.17
Overdrawing of an elevation and plan of the pattern stores, 1797, 1799, 1809. The upper storey was entirely removed by Avery's, and most of 1799 vaults lie buried beneath the existing ground level. The listed pattern vaults lie under a concrete cap and are accessible via tunnels (see Fig 7.83).

James Watt Jr also claimed that 23 engines had been finished in the year so far, to be followed by 9 or 10 more based on orders in hand before the 12 months were finished. If these figures are correct, then – given the circumstances – this was a staggering achievement.

On 15 September 1796, Peter Ewart wrote to James Watt Jr in Cornwall that the boring mill was 'improving considerably in point of progress, for which to be sure there is great room'.[68] The likelihood of boring in this month was obviously receding. James Watt Jr's assurances to his father that no more building was planned were not shared with Ewart, who asked 'whether the pattern house is to be begun upon'. The pattern stores were actually built between March

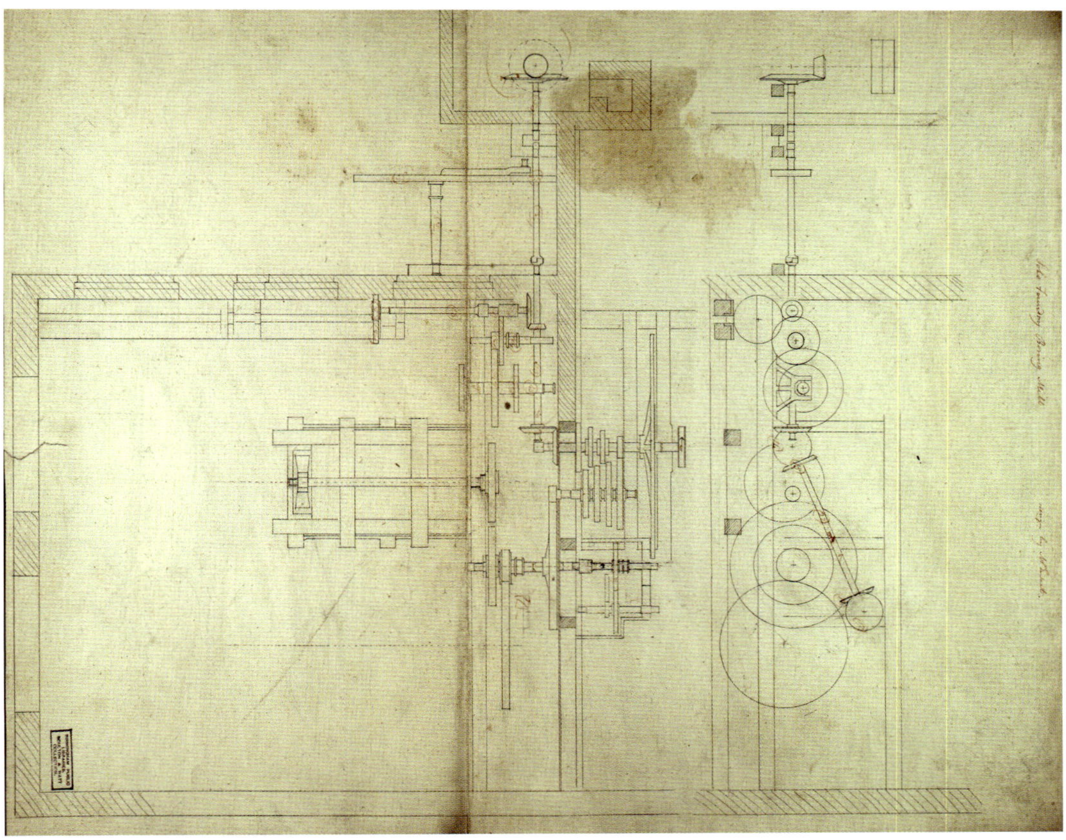

Fig 7.18
Elevation and plan of the boring mill machinery by Peter Ewart, 1796, demonstrating the complex interlinking of numerous cog wheels.

and September of the following year, 1797.[69] Being erected against the west boundary wall, this was the first major building not to respect the cardinal points of the compass, and it determined the orientation of other buildings that followed, creating a discontinuity of layout at the west end of the site. Later extensions to the pattern stores helped maintain the original ground slope, while the immediate area was being raised by the dumping of ash from the foundry furnaces (*see* Fig 7.2). The first pattern stores were single storey, and a plan and elevation has survived attached to drawings of later extensions (Fig 7.17).[70]

It was not until 1 December 1796 that the boring of the first cylinder (for a 16hp engine) began in the boring mill, but unfortunately did not proceed satisfactorily.[71] The vibration experienced during boring was to be the cause of much frustration and annoyance over the next two and a half years, and the equipment was eventually replaced. Peter Ewart designed the original horizontal boring machine and his drawing has survived (Fig 7.18).[72]

The plan and section show a complex system of interlocking toothed spur wheels and bevels connecting from the crank on the engine: the sun-and-planet gear had presumably been quickly replaced. Apart from powering a single boring machine and a lathe in the boring mill itself to the west, the engine also drove an angled shaft to the ceiling above and to the east. There are extant drawings (dated 24 March 1797) of the shafts that led from here, via a pair of drills, the full length of the turning mill to the outside of the east wall. At this point, the shaft turned through 90 degrees and (it is assumed) headed north to the fitting shop (*see* Fig 7.2). A drawing (dated 21 July 1797) of an internal elevation by the east door in the fitting shop shows two drills, one on the ground storey and the other on the floor above, but driven by belts internally.[73] The date of these drawings suggest when the line shafting and the machinery it powered were installed through these workshops.

1797

Illustrations of the Soho Foundry are rare and only two have survived from this early period. The first, by William Creighton, is dated 1797 (Fig 7.19), but there is evidence that indicates it was more likely drawn in 1796; the second, by John Phillp (*see* Fig 7.9), was probably drawn in 1797. Creighton's view, described as 'from the E' (erroneously altered to 'SE'), is from the north-east and is dominated by the foundry, with the rest of the premises partly obscured by the east boundary wall. The upper smithy is the only building shown against the boundary wall; the lower smithy was not built until September 1797 at the latest.[74] Although the construction of the row of houses outside the main gate had begun in March 1796, Creighton's note ('houses built here') suggests that he had finished the view before they were completed. There is no north boundary wall in the view and the ground is shown as being very uneven, the result of the considerable movement of earth during the construction of the foundry. All this suggests a date of 1796 rather than 1797. The foundry presents its distinctive east gable with three windows, one obscured by a tree (*see* Fig 7.86). The upper and lower ground storeys can be seen clearly on the north elevation, with the blank part of the elevation corresponding to the drying stoves within. The central chimney on the north pitch of the roof relates to the drying stoves and suggests that the hearth sat on the junction between the main part of the building and the north outshot. The two flanking chimneys rise above hearths (function unknown) situated in each of the two lower-ground-floor rooms (*see* Fig 7.12).

Phillp's pen-and-ink drawing shows the view from the canal bank towards the north-west of the site. Again, the foundry dominates the scene, but this time the west rather than the east gable is shown. The additional storey on the north elevation and in the north outshot can be seen clearly, together with the bank of earth between the two external ground levels. In contrast to Creighton's view, the central part of the north elevation appears to have windows in the upper ground storey but the same three chimneys on the north roof pitch are shown. The outshot for the air furnaces on the south side appears to be open-sided supported by columns or posts. Both the 1795 and 1797 smithies are visible against the east boundary wall, with the space in between used as a coal store, and the north boundary wall is complete. The work that took place in 1797 to support the new furnaces for the drying stoves against the north elevation (*see* p 154) is not shown, so the view was probably drawn in the spring or early summer of 1797.

Despite the fact that the boring mill machinery was vibrating excessively when at work, James Watt Jr was grateful for Ewart's 'assistance in forming the general plan of the works particularly the Foundery, and ... superintendance of the execution of the buildings and all

Fig 7.19
William Creighton's drawing of the Soho Foundry from the north-east, 1797 erroneously described as from the south-east (see Figs 7.86 and 7.87).

their details' for which he was paid £280.[75] Watt confirmed to Ewart that the boring shaft was 'dithering' (vibrating) in one of the drive wheels and in the cutter and that various remedies were being tried to stop it. Although matters had improved, at the beginning of February William Wilkinson was invited to visit Soho and suggested a number of alterations to the mill, including a new socket for the cutters and the removal of a wooden pinion.[76] These made little difference to the vibration and it was concluded that the problem lay either in the wheel that drove the boring rod or in the strength of the rod itself.[77] It is significant that it was at this time that James Watt Jr first raised the possibility of using a worm screw (endless screw) to communicate the motion. This was essentially William Murdoch's idea and it ultimately provided the remedy.

Peter Ewart was mortified by the reports from the boring mill and suggested first that the cause of the problem might be the weakness of the rod and then that it might be movement in the socket holding the cutters.[78] At the end of March, with Murdoch at the Soho Foundry, it was decided to fit a worm screw worked by bands to the new shaft lathe and a drawing of the worm screw has survived.[79] Leather bands instead of the cog wheel drive were applied to the boring rod but were later removed as this made little difference. Despite the lack of results, James Watt Jr was gracious to Ewart, since he acknowledged that 'the whole band of schemers participate in the disgrace'. In turn, Ewart admitted that worm screws were 'certainly a good thing' but should be made of steel to counter the great wear and friction entailed in working the rod.[80]

The first Soho Foundry inventory to have survived is dated 31 March 1797 and gives the value of buildings and machinery in each department and in the establishment (which included buildings and machinery serving the whole works; for example: the lodge, the offices, cranes, or the drainage system). The boiler department and the gas plant and buildings were added in the first decade of the19th century.[81]

Table 7.1 Value of buildings and machinery, 31 March 1797

BUILDINGS			
Establishment	£1,908	3s	9.0d
Foundry	£3,025	8s	10.5d
Fitting	£1,111	15s	6.5d
Smithy	£546	11s	11.0d
	£6592	00s	01d
MACHINERY			
Establishment	£497	7s	11.0d
Foundry	£1,161	8s	5.5d
Fitting	£1,855	9s	6.5d
Smithy	£298	1s	5.5d
	£3,812	7s	5.0d
Grand Total	£10,404	7s	6d

Source: LoB, MS3147/9/15

The foundry had been the most expensive building to construct, but the fitting department and its troublesome boring mill had cost more for machinery. In addition the 12 house built outside the main gate had cost over £2200.

In June 1797, it was decided 'to send all the present shafts and wheels [in the boring mill] to the Melting pot and replace them with others of at least twice the strength'.[82] By this time, straps had been successfully substituted for cogs, and the long horizontal shaft connected to the drills had also been put into operation. At the end of August, Murdoch departed for Cornwall and left

William Harris as 'substitute in getting on with the new Machinery, of which much remains to be undone for want of hands'.[83]

By June also, the foundry cupola was at work melting nearly a ton (1,016kg) per 12-hour day.[84] The Foundry was not to be solely engaged in the business of making steam engines, since a large amount of work would come from the mint business Matthew Boulton had established with his son. This not only produced coins but also sold coining machinery to other mints across the world, and the Foundry contracted for the production of the machinery. As early as July 1797, the older Boulton wrote that the firm had 'cast One Great Coining Press this day at the Foundry'; the press was intended for his new mint at the Manufactory.[85]

The stoves that had been built in the outshot on the north side of the foundry to dry the moulds had proved unsatisfactory and over the summer and autumn of 1797 they were rebuilt.[86] This first involved lengthening a vaulted brick arch, which may originally only have been a short structure occupying part of the lower-ground-floor room on the east side of the foundry (*see* Fig 7.12).[87] A brick arch here was a sensible way of providing a convenient link with the narrower vaulted tunnel leading to the large casting pit. It appears that the arch was extended westwards, removing three compartments to support the new stoves immediately above on the upper ground floor. This new work did not include the lower-ground-floor room on the west (*see* Fig 7.12). The new arch, however, could have provided direct access into this room, thus connecting the whole of the north lower ground level of the foundry. The large tunnel under the foundry today appears to originate in this work. It was extended a few years later in 1801–2 and will be called the 'Great Arch' for ease of identification.

Associated with this work, detailed in the Soho Foundry accounts dated September and October 1797, was the construction of five small vaults ('arches') orientated north–south immediately against the north wall of the foundry and the newly constructed Great Arch inside.[88] A sixth space left largely uncovered was vaulted later. The reason for these vaults, which have survived to the present day, seems to be directly related to the drying stoves. Judging by the position of the three chimneys, the original hearths for the stoves appear to have been placed on the wall dividing the main foundry from its north outshot, the stoves themselves projecting into the casting floor area (*see* Figs 7.9 and 7.19). A more convenient position for the hearths was on the exterior north wall of the outshot, but this

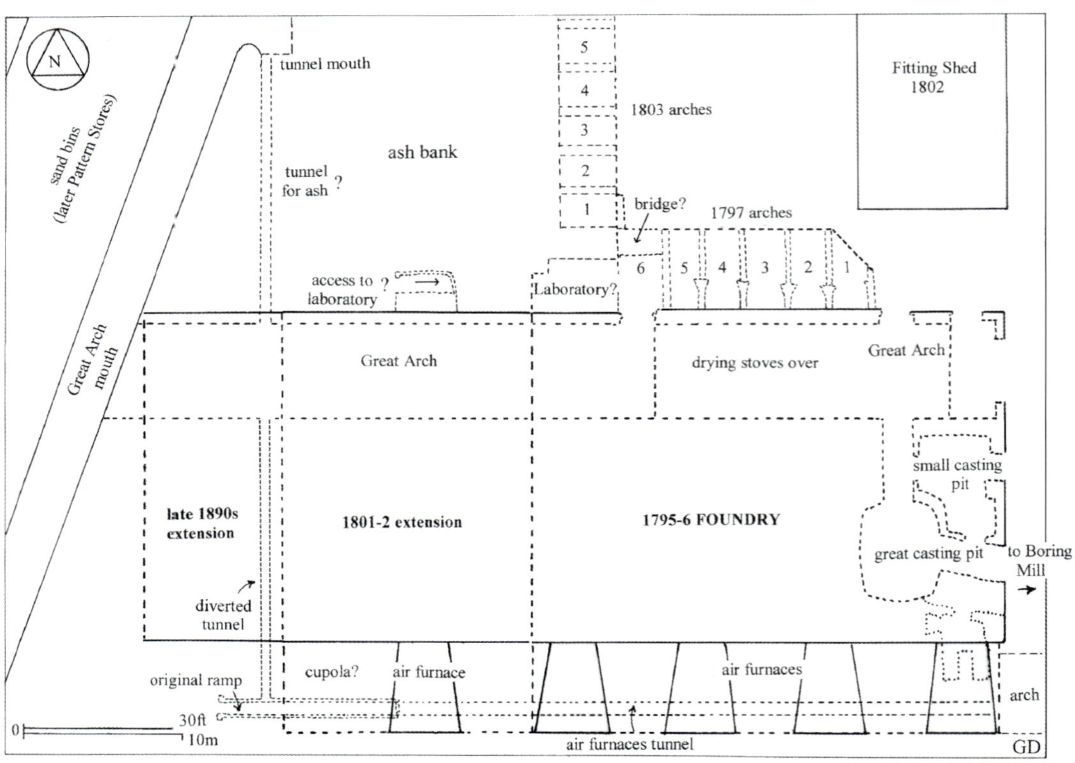

Fig 7.20
Plan of the main foundry building, showing the position of the tunnels and vaults.

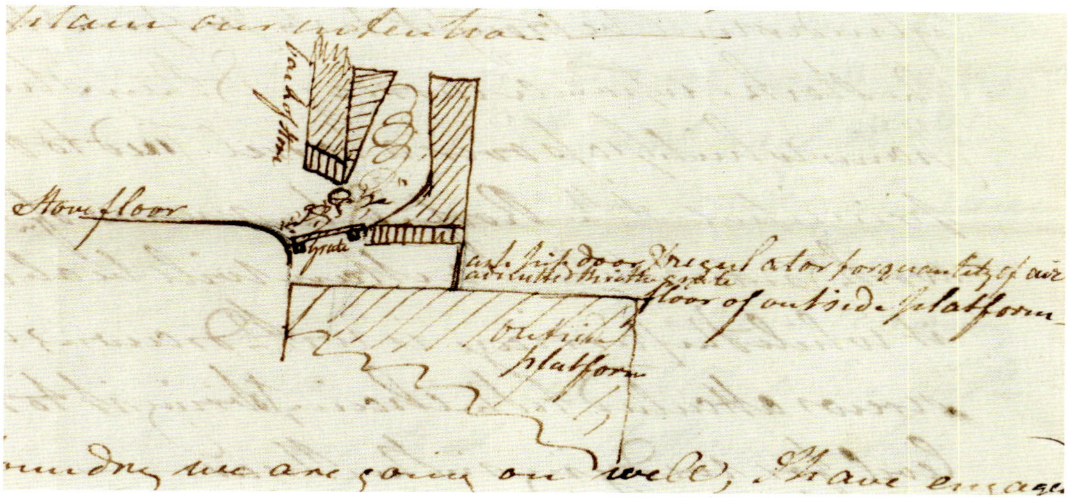

Fig 7.21
Matthew Robinson Boulton's sketch of a drying stove hearth, 13 October 1797.

was a storey above the ground level outside. The solution adopted was to construct an elevated external access to the back of the hearths from which ash could be removed (Fig 7.20). It appears that a flat platform (approximately 9ft/2.74m × 19ft/5.79m) was constructed and supported by the five small arches or vaults, which could then be used for storage. To help in stoking, the platform was lower than the upper ground level in the foundry so that the five supporting arches were lower than the Great Arch on the other side of the foundry wall. In October 1797, Matthew Robinson Boulton drew a cross section of such a stove standing on its 'outside platform' (Fig 7.21).[89] By this time, the ash dump had probably reached this area and the raised platform could be connected westwards directly to it. The platform can be seen in Fig 7.22 against the north foundry wall, depicted in a light-grey wash in contrast to the darker grey of the main building. Another platform, apparently with a vault supporting it, orientated east–west, appears on the plan immediately west of a gap, a yet-to-be-covered sixth vault. A west entrance to this seventh vault is shown against the proposed foundry extension. The design of the entrance gives the impression that it was to be dug into the ash deposit in the form of a ramp or stairs. A 'bridge' across the open gap of the future sixth vault connected the main platform to the ash deposited on the north side of the east-west platform (*see* Figs 7.20, 7.22 , 7.89). The vault below the latter was probably William Murdoch's laboratory in which he installed the retort in

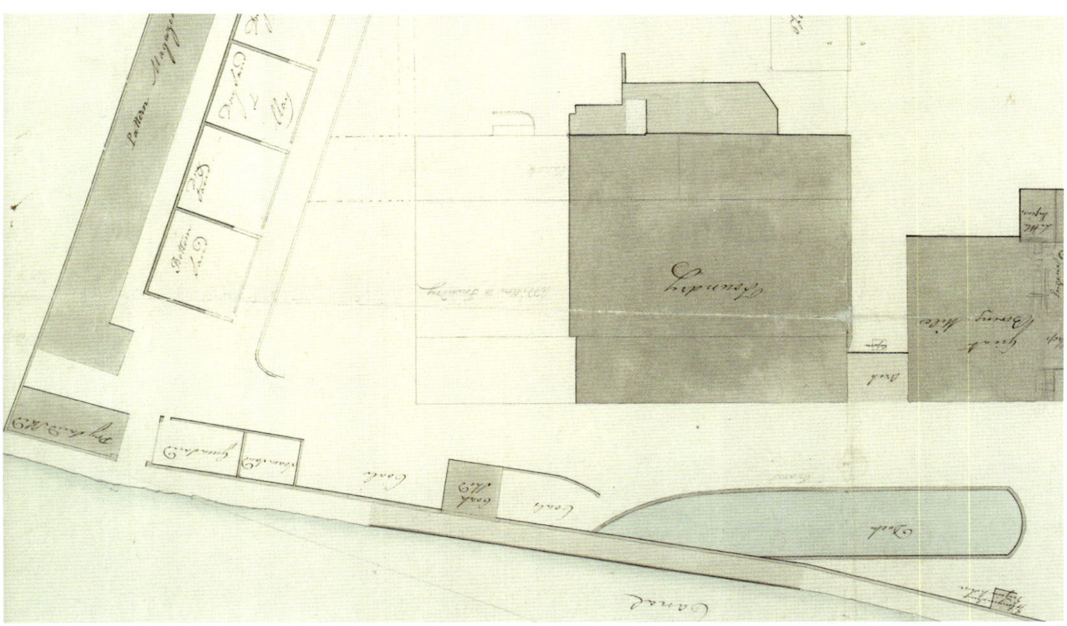

Fig 7.22
Extract from a water-coloured plan of the Soho Foundry, c 1800, with pencil additions for the 1801–2 extension and related structures.

December 1798 that first provided the gas to illuminate the foundry (*see* p 158).

Another inventory was taken on 30 September 1797, providing a useful list of buildings and the machinery they contained.[90] Little of note that had been built to date had escaped the correspondence between the principals, except the second smithy (lower smiths shop), erected, like the first, against the east boundary wall, leaving a space in between to store coals under a shelter. The inventory provides a useful baseline, since the formal Soho Foundry building and machinery accounts were begun on the same day.[91] Their fortuitous survival provides the great majority of information on the development of the Soho Foundry over the next 50 years or more. The correspondence between the principals, which has proved to be so revealing up to this point, was to peter out within a few years.

On 9 November 1797, Matthew Robinson Boulton reported to Watt Jr that 'the different undertakings at the foundry which I mentioned as being then in hand are finished & to our satisfaction. The effect of the new fire places to the stoves exceeds our expectations'.[92] However, the boring mill problems had not been resolved.

The cylinder pit that is marked on the early plan (*see* Fig 7.12) was first recorded in the

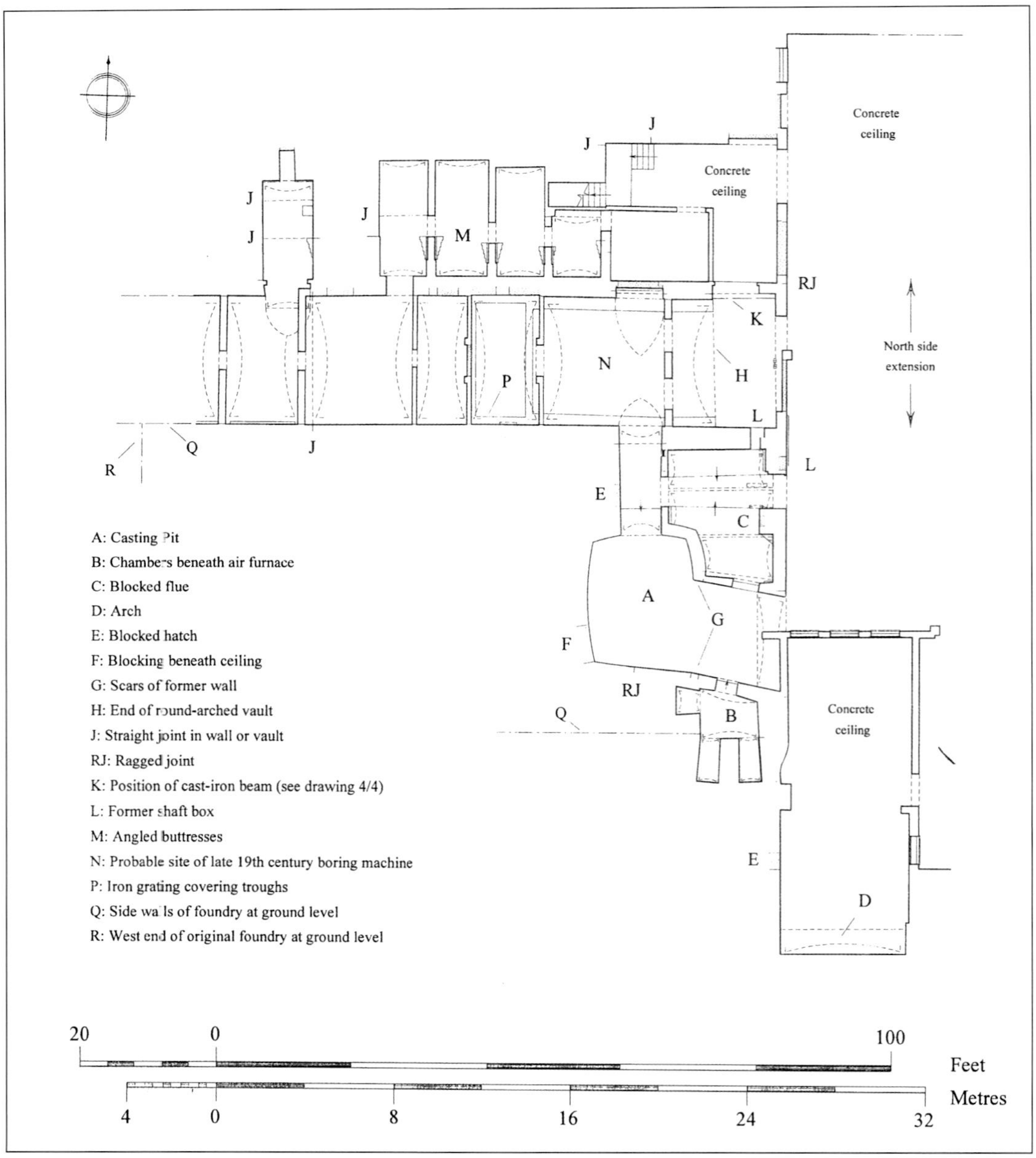

Fig 7.23
Plan of the lower ground floor of the main foundry building, 1996.

1797 accounts, but was likely constructed in the previous year, with a vaulted tunnel north to the original Great Arch and another leading east out of the building towards the boring mill. This was always known as the 'large cylinder pit' since a 'small cylinder pit' was constructed at roughly the same time. The small pit needed only 14 iron plates as a cover in comparison to 26 for the large pit.[93] Both these adjacent chambers still survive (Fig 7.23 and *see* Fig 7.20).

1798

Despite the other improvements carried out at the Soho Foundry, on 17 February 1798 Peter Ewart admitted that he would find some of his 'handiwork very deservedly in great disgrace'.[94] On 7 March, James Watt Jr requested Ewart to attend a meeting after Murdoch had returned from Cornwall to 'proceed to final judgement upon the Boring Mill machinery and completion of the large rod and new apparatus'.[95] Straps had been applied to almost all the machinery, but it was taking night and day for a week to bore a cylinder of moderate size (31hp, *c* 13in/330mm) or two air pumps. Murdoch was extremely reluctant, however, to leave Cornwall and his commitments there.

Phase 1B: New boring machinery, buildings and gas, September 1798–December 1799 (*see* Fig 7.2)

By 1 September 1798, James Watt Jr had issued instructions to build a new carpenters shop south of the existing one against the east boundary wall. This was to accommodate the pattern makers who, up until then, had occupied the upper storey of the boring mill, uncomfortable tenants considering the fire hazards posed by the steam engine and the lathes and drills.[96] Timber storage was also to be removed to the new shop. It was proposed to turn the patternmakers' lathes by 'one of the small model engines'. The work proceeded quickly and on 16 September Watt Jr wrote to his partner:

> The new Carpenters Shop is built & roofed in but not slated. No news of Murdock. It will not be safe to delay the extension of the Boring Mill any later this season. I have therefore settled with Southern, a plan the most con-

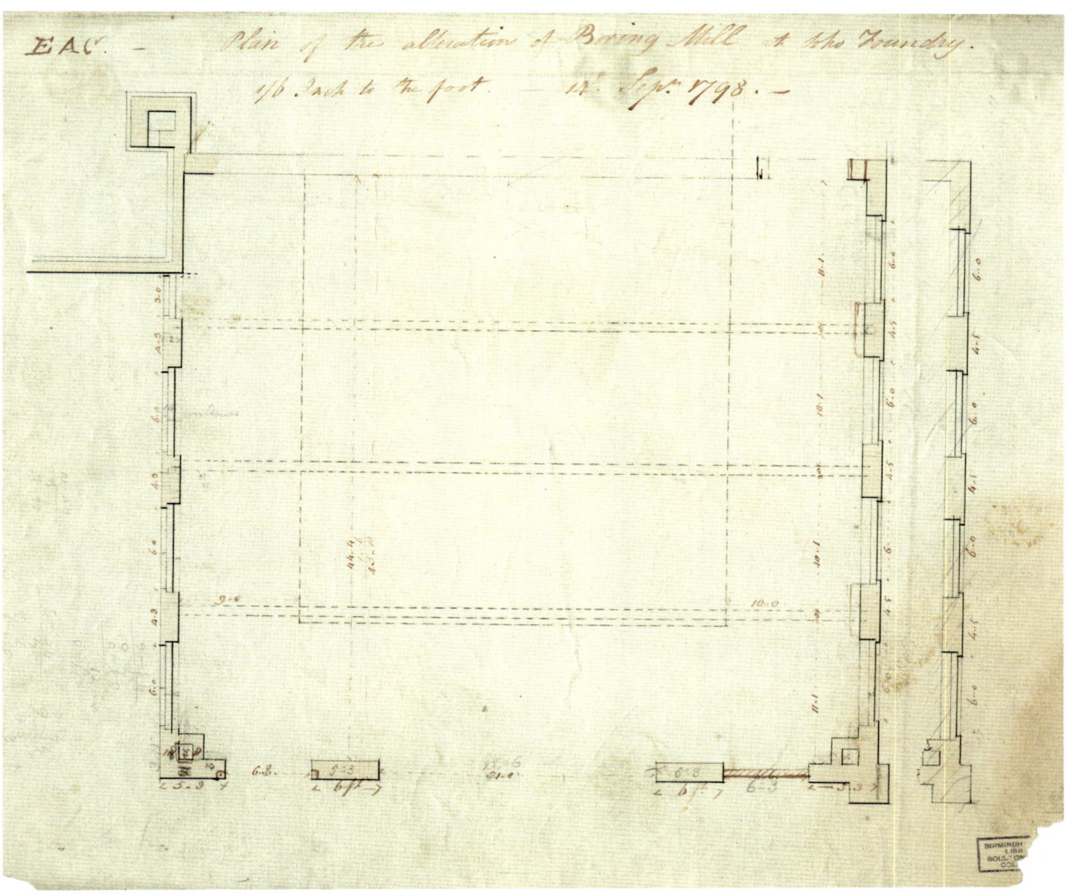

Fig 7.24
Plan of the extension to the boring mill, 14 September 1798.

> venient & the least expensive we could devise & intend getting the brickwork done without further loss of time. The interior arrangements may wait Murdock's coming, if there is any chance of that event taking place ... It is very mortifying after all our expence & trouble to have our works thus incompleat and so little prospect of their being rendered perfect before the termination of the patent. I am really of the opinion we ought to wait no longer than the end of this year, at all events, for Murdock. It is folly to be throwing away the best years of the patent.[97]

Southern's drawings, dated between 14 and 17 September 1798, have survived and show that the boring mill was to be extended 9ft (2.74m) northwards, 11ft (3.35m) westwards and 10ft (3.05m) southwards to make room for the new machinery that Murdoch was to design (Fig 7.24).[98] The boring mill was effectively rebuilt to accept entirely new engines and machinery.

By 9 November, the new carpenters shop had been whitewashed and arrangements were being made to move the pattern makers from 'their dangerous situation' as soon as possible, leaving the lathe in position until the boring mill was complete.[99] Murdoch eventually arrived and set about the long-awaited task. He proposed two schemes for the boring mill machinery, one based on cogwheels, the other on the worm screw. James Watt Jr was indifferent as to which was selected, as long as everything was made significantly stronger than the existing set-up. It is likely, therefore, that Murdoch made the decision in favour of the plan based on the worm screw, his personal preference.

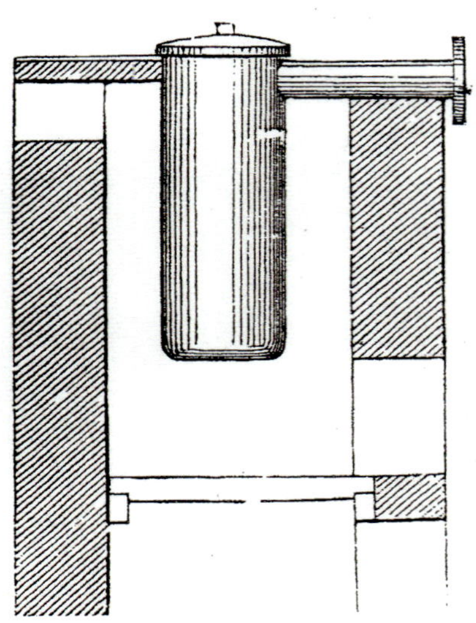

Fig 7.25
Drawing of William Murdoch's retort as installed in 1798, probably in his laboratory.

While he had been in Cornwall, Murdoch had experimented with gas lighting and, despite the urgency of the work on the boring mill, was determined to develop his ideas further. He managed to have small gas retorts set up in the 'Soho Foundry laboratory' and these were fitted on 12 December 1798.[100] The laboratory was probably situated in the seventh vault or arch mentioned above, attached to the north side of the foundry and lying to the west of the five arches supporting the platform for the drying stoves and the sixth, yet to be vaulted over (*see* Figs 7.20 and 7.89). The structure was already in existence in 1798, since the first mention of the laboratory is the account for the installation of two furnaces for Murdoch. The costs are listed under the Establishment Department machinery account.[101] The actual construction of the laboratory was probably included in the Foundry building accounts for 1797.[102] The laboratory was described as being 'in Arch under Foundry for Furnaces'[103] and in later accounts the five arches were identified by their proximity to it – 'Under Arches near Laboratory'.[104]

Murdoch left an account of these events but, unfortunately, was not precise about their location:[105] 'In the year 1798, I removed from Cornwall to Messrs Boulton and Watt & Co's works for the Manufactory of Steam Engines at the Soho Foundry and then constructed an apparatus upon a larger scale [than in Cornwall], which during many successive nights was applied to the lighting of their principal building [the Foundry]'. James Watt Jr added a little more detail when recalling the event in 1809: 'He [William Murdoch] constructed a retort of iron with a tube from it about thirty of forty feet in length, and to the end of it he applied the burners of various dimensions, and gave light during the night time to one of the buildings of the Soho foundery'.[106]

Thirty or 40ft (9.1m–12.1m) of pipe would only have brought the gas into the north-west corner of the foundry on the west side of the drying stoves. The foundry manager had an office that might have been located in this corner. It could have been the first room at the Soho Foundry to have been lit by gas.

The apparatus Murdoch used is illustrated in Fig 7.25 and was small enough to fit in the vault.[107] The fact that the retort is so precisely drawn in Samuel Clegg Jr's book on the making of gas is good evidence that his father, Samuel Clegg Sr, at least saw the equipment. Samuel Clegg Sr was apprenticed to Boulton & Watt and articled in 1800, but the relationship had soured by mid-1803.[108] He left the firm in some disgrace to forge his own illustrious career in gas lighting, probably taking with him the drawings of the Soho Foundry gas equipment published by his son in 1841. Tradition has it that Clegg was Murdoch's assistant in the gas experiments and this was the obvious opportunity to observe the equipment at close quarters. It is interesting to note, therefore, that two great pioneers of gas lighting probably worked together in the small vaulted laboratory at the Soho Foundry. In 1812 and 1816, the laboratory still contained four retorts weighing between 30lb (13.6kg) and 50lb (22.6kg).[109]

The 1798 experiment represented the first illumination of industrial premises anywhere by means of a permanent gas installation. More progress might have been made at this time but for the pressing need to solve the problems of the boring mill. The day before the retorts were fitted in the laboratory, the new worm drive in the boring mill had been set in motion:[110]

> This morning Murdoch's screw commences its active operation in this life ... M R Boulton, Mr Southern and the other man – Midwifes are attending the delivery. The gestation has been rather a painful one to Murdock.

It is clear that the worm drive had been inserted into the existing machinery only for the time being, though 'the performance of the screw gives perfect satisfaction'.[111] Matthew Robinson's long letter of 15 December describes in detail the new plan that was quickly adopted after much deliberation. Several drawings exist of the

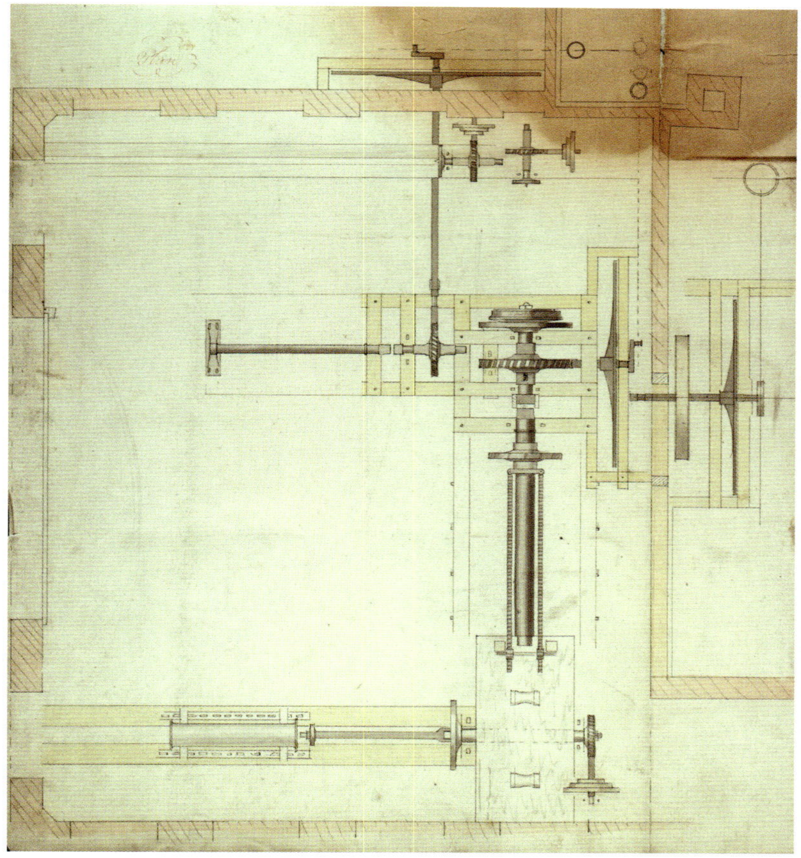

Fig 7.26
Water-coloured plan of William Murdoch's boring machinery, also showing the position of the small engine cylinders in the top right-hand corner of the drawing, c 1798.

Fig 7.27
Water-coloured elevation of William Murdoch's boring machinery, demonstrating its use of the worm screw, c 1798.

scheme and there are various versions of those dated 31 December 1798, some of which were probably sent to James Watt Jr in London (Figs 7.26 and 7.27).[112] The greatest change was to introduce two small beamless engines each running a boring machine. These were to be located in the westernmost of the two boiler houses (which might never actually have contained a boiler) (Fig 7.26, nos 2 and 3 on the plan). One engine had a long connection to a crank and fly wheel close to the existing beam engine. The crank turned a shaft with a worm screw and the largest of the boring bars, orientated north–south. The other engine was closer to its crank, which, in turn, was further away from its worm screw. This powered a small boring rod orientated east–west. It was also intended to install two lathes, one on the north and the other on the south side of the mill below the windows. The west wall had a large doorway through which the cylinders arrived from the Foundry casting pit. It appears that this plan was largely implemented (Fig 7.28).

Murdoch designed the small beamless engines and the installation in the boring mill coincided with a growing countrywide demand for them. James Watt Jr perceived their value, although his father and John Southern were prejudiced against them.[113] On 9 January 1799, James Watt Jr stated confidently that 'There seems little doubt that Orders for these Small Engines will be numerous'.[114] He was anxious to give the job of fitting them to William Harrison, who would be paid by the piece and given the two shops in the fitting department, probably those recently vacated by the pattern makers. Matthew Robinson Boulton responded positively, having discussed similar plans with Murdoch, and agreed to encourage Harrison and work on Southern's 'doubts and scruples'.[115] Southern could not devote much time to the scheme, however, as he was heavily involved in the new mint at the Manufactory, which was under development at this time using his ideas on vacuum power.[116]

It was decided to have a new boring rod made at Low Moor Foundry near Bradford. Murdoch's visit there had convinced him of the need to 'separate the different [boring] operations', as the Yorkshire ironworks was planning the same.[117] The separation of boring operations should not be interpreted as the division of the various processes involved in boring, but the transfer of machinery from a single, overloaded engine and drive system to the two new little engines each with its own gearing and drive shafts. The plans of Murdoch's scheme were sent to James Watt Jr in London and he quickly agreed to 'the

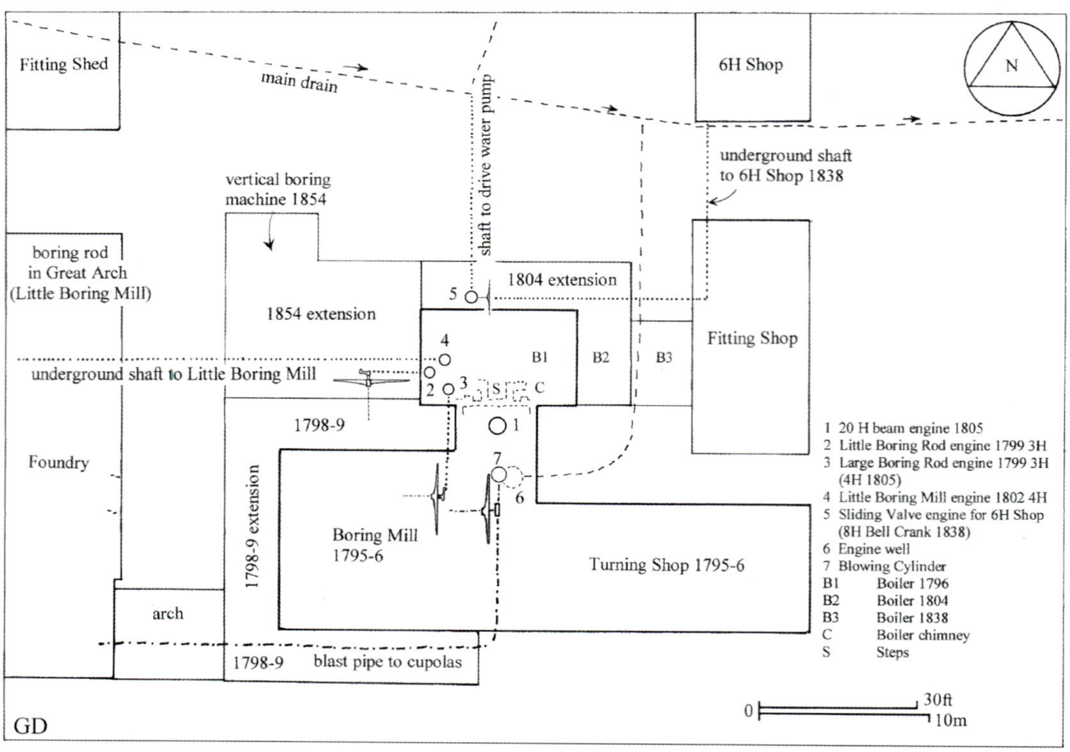

Fig 7.28
Plan of the boring mill and turning shop showing the position of steam engines.

principle of a separate Engine and therefore they may get ready with all speed'.[118] Matthew Robinson Boulton was also keen to get started, since Murdoch was feeling the pull of Cornwall. He wanted 'the benefit of Murdoch's super vis-tendance [supervision]' and could keep him at the Soho Foundry while 'the construction of the Boring Mill' was 'his principal hobby horse'.[119] Throughout February, Southern's office produced drawings of the little engines but, unfortunately, none have survived.[120] The engines had the piston rod connected to a cross head, which, via a pair of side rods, moved a pair of bell cranks pivoted on a large cast iron block upon which the cylinder stood. The bar connecting the two bell cranks could drive a crank directly or, by means of a long rod, move a crank at some distance, as in the boring mill. A contemporary drawing of the steam pipes and pipes to the condenser shows the exact position of the two cylinders and also reveals that they shared the beam-engine condenser.[121] The cylinders were 11.75in (298mm) in diameter, had a 2ft (600mm) stroke, and were rated at 3hp.[122] A successor bell-crank engine, illustrated in Figs 7.44 and 7.45, was still in operation at the Soho Foundry in 1895.

A cheap supply of Rowley Rag (flagstones) was used for the floor of the boring mill and these may still survive below the present brick floors on the site of the mill.[123] In March, work on the boring machinery was seriously delaying orders, and James Watt Jr considered it 'very desirable indeed that Murdoch should defer his departure until the little Engines are got to work, which cannot be effected in less than a couple of Months ... it would not be prudent to let any part of it be fixed by any other person'.[124] However, it appears that, on balance, it was more important to pacify the old Cornish customers than to attract new customers, and Murdoch was released for a few months. One of the little engines meant to drive the little boring rod was partly fitted waiting for him to fix it in position. The 'plate' (cast-iron block) for the engines to stand upon had been cast and the fixings for the bell crank were ready. The frame for the great boring rod was complete and a consignment of Rowley Rags was 'on the spot'. James Watt Jr concluded that no 'other time will be fitter than the present for the alteration, which I think may be so managed as not to stop the little rod more than 3 or 4 days'. On 16 April, this rod suffered an accident without serious damage.[125]

By 1 May, the boring rod, weighing 3 tons 13¼ cwt (3.39 tonnes), was finally on its way from Low Moor.[126] In Murdoch's continued absence, the little boring engine was set to work and by 20 May was performing well.[127] By 24 May, Murdoch had returned and set about laying down the frame for the great boring rod.[128] On 10 June, James Watt Jr reported at length to the young Boulton:[129]

> At the Foundry Murdoch has much improved the little engine. On Friday the 31st of May sentence was passed upon the old boring Machinery & immediate execution took place. Since that time there has been a requisition of labourers, carpenters & masons in the Boring Mill. The Framing is laid and the masonry going forward with vigour. We shall certainly have the little boring rod at work in the course of a fortnight ... I wish now to submit to you the propriety of commencing this season such further erections about the foundry as seem necessary to its completion.
>
> 1st to continue the present pattern shop to the bottom of the yard. This cannot be delayed any longer without great inconvenience; we are brimful nay overflowing with patterns. It may be a question whether it would not be proper to carry it two storeys high, as I fear we must come to that at last with the whole of the range.
>
> 2nd to build by contract 12 more houses – you are, as well as myself, so fully aware of the advantages of making the men comfortable & keeping them free from contamination, that I need say no more on this head.
>
> 3rd A shed for the fitting Yard, to keep our cast iron and other heavy goods under; where they may be protected from the weather & so arranged as to be easily got at. The shed to be built on brick pillars & slated over ...
>
> 4th a stable in the field.

James Watt Jr was not in the habit of resting after major exertions, but his partner was less enthusiastic about maintaining momentum:[130]

> I can only say that my aversion to the further use of bricks and mortar makes me desirous of avoiding every any erection of them where not indispensable ... six houses would supply the present want ... The facility of getting at & removing the Patterns appears to be a principal consideration ... and should not be relinquished for a trifling addit[iona]l expence. A second storey I should apprehend would on this account be objectionable as the

Fig 7.31
The blocked arch of the ash disposal tunnel constructed in the Great Arch, c 1801–2.

water that had been heated by the main beam-steam-engine condenser, now having to do extra work for the two small boring mill engines.

It was about this time that a plan of the Soho Foundry was produced, with existing buildings colour-washed and identified. The plan was then used to mark the position of proposed buildings (Fig 7.30).

1801

It was not until 1801 that work began to extend the seven-bay foundry by 52ft 6in (16m) on the west, making the whole building 147ft 6in (44.9m) in length (*see* Figs 7.20 and 7.30). This was the equivalent of four extra bays of the original building (13ft 6in/4.1m each), but an 1834 drawing of the foundry shows only three bays added to the original seven (Fig 7.31).[140] It is likely, therefore, that three broader bays were built, each 17ft 6in (5.3m) in length.

Significant new subterranean structures were associated with the foundry extension. Ash from the furnaces had originally been tipped on the west side of the foundry from a narrow tunnel that ran from east to west under the ash pits of the air furnaces (Fig 7.32 and *see* Fig 7.20). From the tunnel mouth, long parallel walls contained the ramp up to the newly tipped ground level. The extension was built over part of this structure, the rest abandoned (*see* Fig 7.22). Under the extension, the ramp was roofed over and connected to a new tunnel that ran north through the dumped ash immediately outside the west wall of the foundry extension. This tunnel intercepted a new section of the Great Arch at right angles (*see* Fig 7.31). The narrow tunnel continued northwards through more of the ash to emerge after about 558ft (170m) at the original untipped ground level (*see* Fig 7.20). The new part of the Great Arch continued westwards for about 130ft (40m) through the ash beyond the foundry extension and emerged via a much wider opening at the original ground level opposite new sand bins. This tunnel mouth was set in a new long wall retaining the ash. The wall ran parallel to the pattern stores and the sand bins and eventually turned sharply east to accommodate the mouth of the new ash tunnel.

In this way, the basic tunnel structure at the foundry was established (*see* Fig 7.20). The Great Arch was used to move sand from the bins and patterns from the stores to the casting pits. Beyond the narrow tunnel mouth to the north, there must have been a ramp by which ash was gradually deposited in a northerly direction, creating a bank level with the upper ground floor of the foundry.

An estimate for a total of £1,829 was sent to James Watt Jr on 9 June 1801; this was accepted and work began soon after, continuing into 1802.[141] The foundry extension contained a new stove for drying moulds and an air furnace, although two of the latter were originally planned.

A second row of eight houses was started on 29 August 1801 and completed on 27 February 1802.[142] These were situated east of the earlier row and five of them survive to the present day. The builder James Smith's bill was disputed by Matthew Robinson Boulton since he apparently built the houses 'one foot short of the Stipulated height'.[143] Drawings and a specification of these 'club' houses, as they were called, have survived.[144] The two larger surviving houses attached to the west side of this row were built in 1808–9 (*see* p 171) (Fig 7.33).[145]

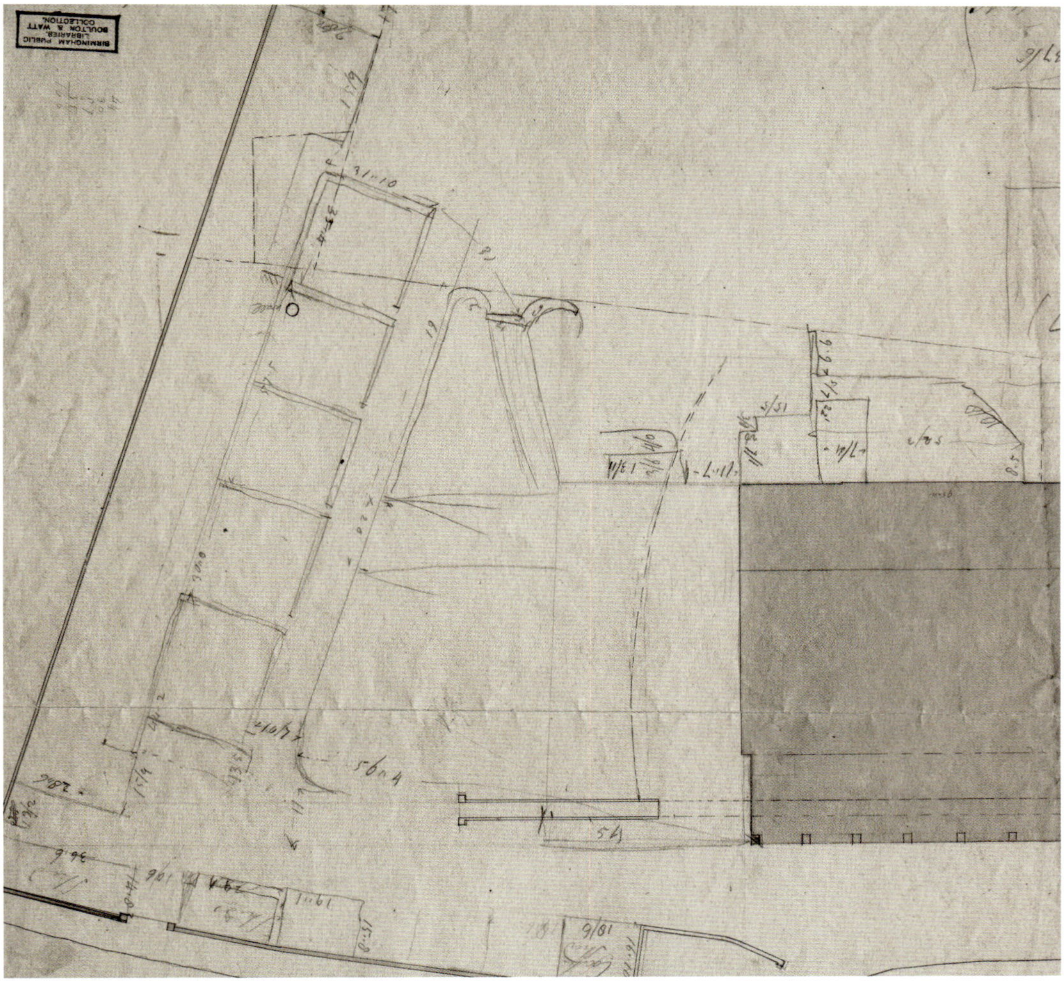

Fig 7.32
Extract from a plan of the Soho Foundry with pencil additions, c 1796.

Fig 7.33
The surviving terrace of foundry workers' houses. The pair at the end in which William Murdoch is reputed to have lived date from 1808–9, while the smaller cottages towards the entrance arch were built between 1801 and 1802.

1802

The most significant event in 1802 was the resumption of the experiments with gas lighting and the re-illumination of the foundry. Little had happened since Murdoch's short-lived experiment in 1798, but Gregory Watt's witnessing of Lebon's demonstration in 1801 prompted a revival of interest in gas lighting at the Soho Foundry.[146] A new retort was probably placed in the laboratory. It was made on 17 February 1802 and fitted and first used on about 20 February to light the foundry.[147] In March 1802, to celebrate the Peace of Amiens, the Soho Manufactory was illuminated with gas produced from two small retorts placed in existing fireplaces in houses at each end of the principal building.[148] However, the elaborate decoration on the façade was illuminated by oil lamps. Unfortunately, a tradition has emerged that the building was entirely lit by gaslight at this event. It is not known how many times the foundry was lit in this way in 1802, but experiments continued throughout the year and by 1803 an apparatus was installed to illuminate a larger area of the Soho Foundry site.[149]

Boring capacity was increased in 1802 with the installation of a third boring rod in the Great Arch at the east end of the foundry. Known as the little boring mill, it was placed in the same position as the later one illustrated in *The Engineer* in 1895, as two surviving drawings confirm (Figs 7.34 and 7.35 and *see* Fig 7.90).[150] The little boring mill would have effectively blocked access from the Great Arch to the casting pit. A longer route around it was made in the new part of the Great Arch, where a tall archway gave on to the exterior between the laboratory to the west and the five vaults to the east (*see* Figs 7.20 and 7.89). The route skirted the vaults and turned the north-east corner of the foundry to reach the doorway in the east wall leading to the casting pit. It is possible that the widened doorway, observable today, dates from this period. The new boring rod was powered by its own Murdoch-designed 4hp bell-crank engine in operation about December 1802 and costing £119 12s 2d.[151] The new engine was installed alongside the other two little engines on the north side of the boring mill (*see* Fig 7.28). This required a long shaft from the bell cranks to connect to the worm drive on the new boring machine. The crank connected to the long drive shaft can be seen in Fig 7.34. The direct route would have passed through the little casting pit, turning at right angles via cogs through the Great Arch wall to reach the boring machine. The shaft was probably therefore placed below ground.

The shed proposed in June 1799 by Watt Jr to store engine parts was finally erected in

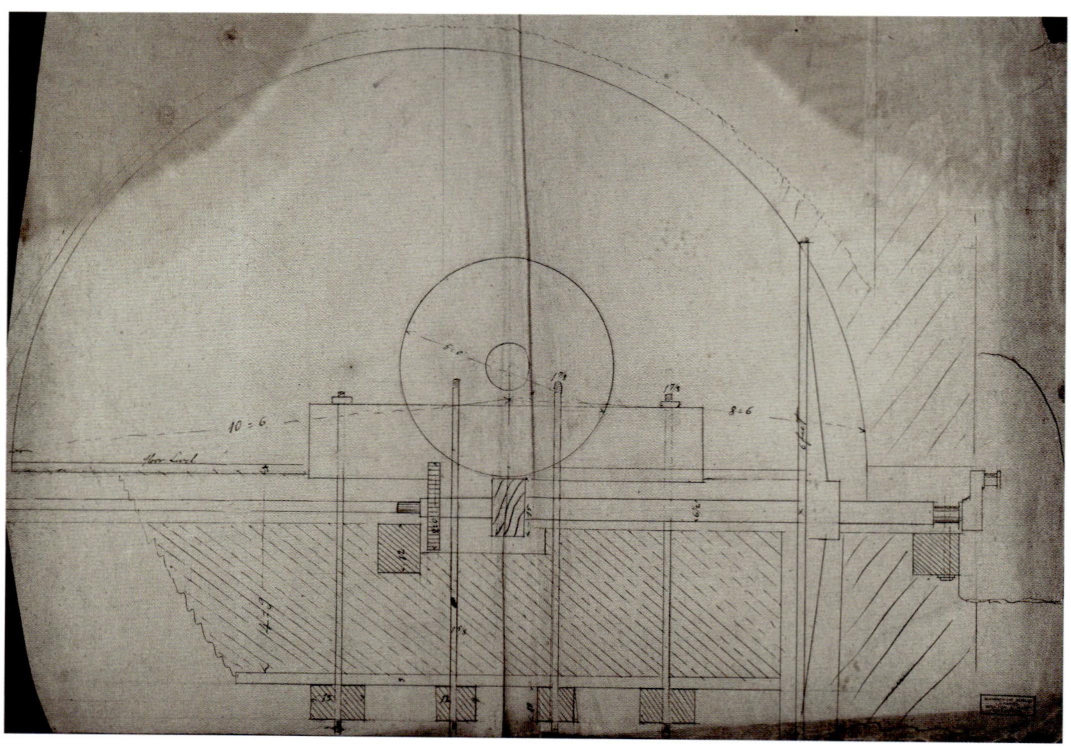

Fig 7.34
Elevation of the boring mill machinery that was inserted into the Great Arch, c 1802 looking eastwards.

1802.[152] Known either as the fitting shed or the erecting shed, it was orientated north–south and was positioned about 7yd (6.4m) north of the little boring mill in the Great Arch close to the row of five vaults. In 1802, a small foundry was erected against the canal arm to the south-west of the main foundry. Its exact purpose is not known.

Phase 2B: The completion of the first yard

1803

Sometime in the spring of 1803, the construction of a new workshop was started. Orders for engines were pouring in, particularly for the small bell cranks, and extra space was needed to fit them:[153] 'We are now doing them [all engines] at the rate of one per fortnight, and as there are 17 orders in all on hand, it will be the end of February [1804] or say 8½ months before the whole can be completed if the new shop does not in the meantime afford some extra facilities'. On 8 June, James Watt Jr reported to his brother:[154]

> Our own Engine house here is undergoing a complete metamorphosis, and we are adding a new Engine and Shop to the Foundry Establishment, the latter 134 ft long is now roofing in. It is intended for the Fitting of little Engines and I hope will enable us to get on with at least one per week which will scarcely enable us to meet the present demand. Some other alterations of minor importance are going on there which I hope will be finished in the course of the summer, and if it should afterwards be found expedient to add a shed for making boilers & a Counting House, that establishment will have reached, what I should vote to be its ne plus ultra.

The fitting shop, known as Harrison's shop after a principal charge-hand fitter (or, alternatively, as the 6H shop after the steam engine that powered it; H was the convention used for 'horsepower' at the time by Boulton & Watt) was actually about 106ft (32.3m) in length not 134ft (40.84m) as Watt Jr claimed. It was orientated north–south, continuing the line of the 1795 fitting shop, but with a space in between. Its north end coincided with the north boundary wall.[155] It was powered by its own 6hp bell-crank engine, which was placed in a northward extension of the little engine house (*see* Figs 7.28 and 7.44).[156] Based on a 16in (406mm) cylinder, the engine cost £320 4s 7d. It was set to work in January 1804 but, being some distance away, it is not known how the engine powered the actual shop.[157] Four lathes and one drill were also installed, along with a boiler to test the engines.[158] This compares with the three lathes and one drill

Fig 7.35
The later large horizontal boring machine in the Great Arch, engraved in 1895.

already working in the fitting shop and the nine lathes and two drills in the turning shop. The little engine house was also extended eastwards and northwards to wrap around the original boiler house (*see* Fig 7.28).

Another important decision was made in 1803. Up to this date, boilers had been made – most of them probably at Mr Horton's Foundry – off the premises, and Boulton & Watt wished to gain control of the quality and supply by manufacturing boilers themselves.[159] Thus, a new and fifth department was created: the boiler-making shop. This was placed at right angles to the north end of the new 6H shop. Its long north wall probably shared the north boundary wall with the 6H shop. It was longer and broader than the latter and stretched almost to the east boundary wall.[160]

In 1803, another set of small vaults (seven in number) was constructed on a north–south orientation within a new wall retaining the east side of the ash dump. The furnace ash deposit was now confined by walls to the west and east (*see* Figs 7.20 and 7.29). The new vaults were set at right angles to the five built against the north wall of the foundry in 1797. They were probably built for storage. The seven vaults were incorporated into the 1847 erecting shop and survive to the present day (*see* p 179 and Figs 7.36 and 7.48).[161]

1804

Watt Jr had been desperate for a counting house at the Soho Foundry for some time and in 1804 the long-held plan to build it on the south side of the main gate was realised.[162] Occupied by a growing number of clerks and their accounting and letter books, it would act as the administrative centre for the site. The counting house was aligned north–south against the east boundary wall, leaving a space between it and the carpenters shop. Its north gable end faced the gate, with a bay window mirroring the one on the porter's lodge on the opposite side of the access road. A plan, incorporating two alternative elevations, survives, showing a two-storey, three-bay building with a hipped roof. The floor was to be fireproof, presumably to protect the paper records. Much of the Boulton & Watt collection was amassed and maintained in this building.[163]

Another cupola had been erected in the foundry extension in 1803. The blowing

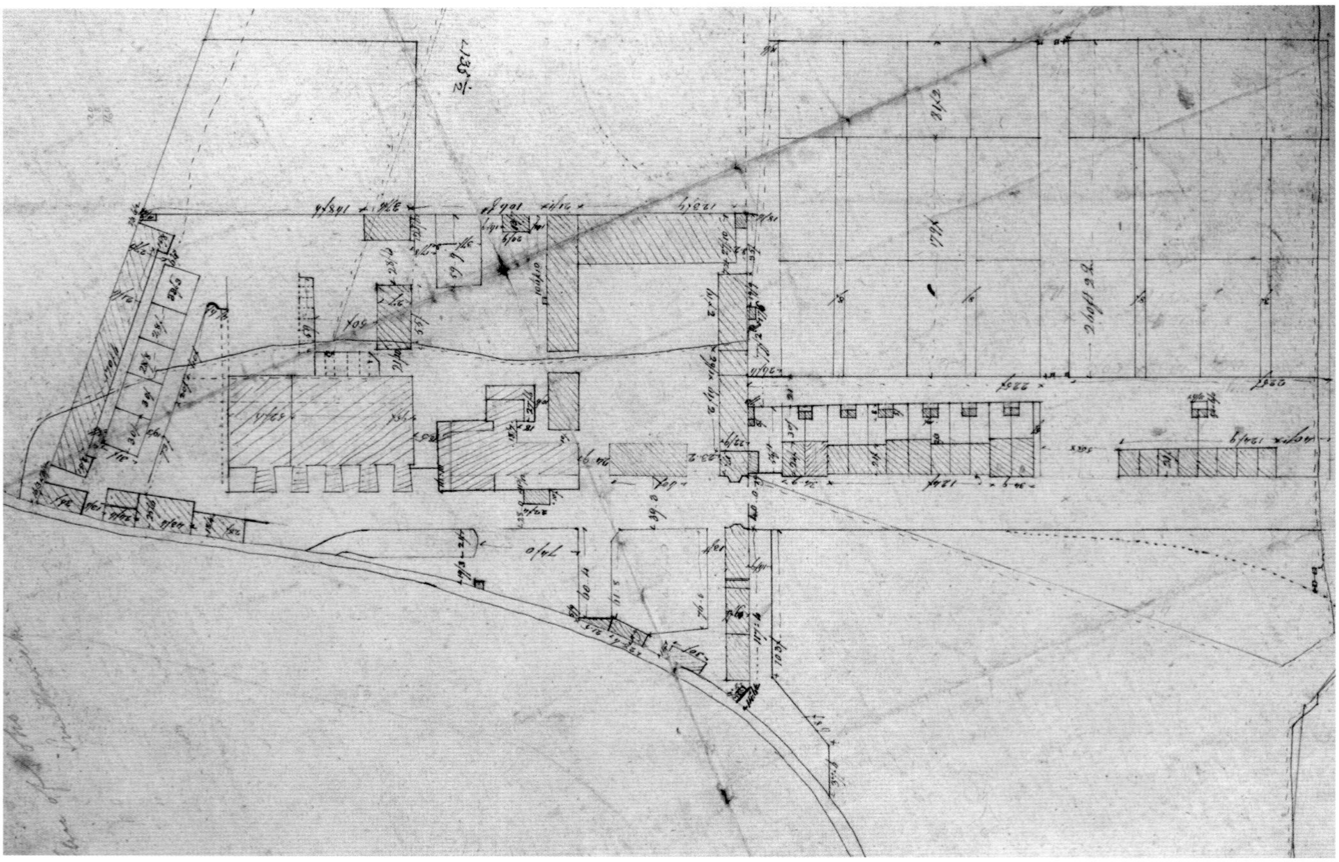

Fig 7.36
Plan of the Soho Foundry, c 1808.

cylinder was worked by the beam engine and provided blast to the original cupola. The cylinder was replaced in 1804 by a larger model for which a drawing exists.[164] The old cylinder was to be used to blow the new cupola in the little foundry.[165]

In the years 1802–4, Matthew Robinson Boulton masterminded a major extension of the engine works at the Soho Manufactory (*see* Chapter 4). This was probably built to cope with the extra demand for engines that prompted the construction of the new 6H shop at the Soho Foundry. The division of work established between the Soho Foundry and the Manufactory is not yet precisely understood, but extant documentary material would allow an analysis to be undertaken.

1805

The year 1805 was another important year at the Soho Foundry as gas lighting was installed in a number of buildings and the production of gas equipment was set up in the boiler shed.[166] The first factory that Boulton & Watt supplied with gas plant was Philips and Lee's cotton mill in Salford in 1805. The firm was the first of about ten customers over the next few years.[167] The site plan dating from about 1800 that had been amended to at least 1805 marks 'Gasom[r]' at the east end of the boiler shed (*see* Fig 7.30).[168] This could be interpreted as being the position of the foundry gasometer with the retorts adjacent, although it is clear that in 1812 this was the place where gasometers were manufactured.[169] According to the Soho Foundry Building and Machinery accounts, the plant (such as gas retorts and gasometers) was constructed at least three years before any dedicated building, suggesting the borrowing of existing Soho Foundry structures or a position in the open air.[170] The location of this early equipment has not been determined, and the position of the first dedicated gas building, a retort shed constructed in 1809–10, is also not known.

At the Soho Foundry the engine house, boring mill, Murdoch's room on the first floor of the turning shop and the office (counting house) all had gas installed in 1805. This would make them the first *group* of industrial premises in the world to be properly and permanently lit by gas. It is not known when exactly in the year this historic event occurred. Samuel Clegg claimed that he had lit the first mill with gas, Henry Lodge's mill at Sowerby Bridge, near Halifax, two weeks before Boulton & Watt's installation at Phillips and Lees's mill in Salford.[171] If there is any truth in Clegg's claim, then it would have been in mid-December, as William Murdoch reported from Salford that 50 lamps had been lit by New Year's Day, 1806.[172] Later in the same year at the Foundry, when there were three retorts and three gasometers, gas lighting had been extended to the fitting shop and the parallel motion shop, adjacent to Murdoch's room in the turning shop.[173]

In 1805, the 14hp beam-engine cylinder in the boring mill was replaced by a 23.75in (603.25cm) cylinder rated at 20hp.[174] Considerable building work accompanied this change, including raising the roof of the engine house.[175]

1806–8

From 1806 to 1808, there was relatively little investment in buildings and machinery. The upper and lower fitting shop became known as the nozzle and working gear shop and the coppersmiths shop.[176] The first yard, which extended from the canal arm to the north boundary wall, had filled with workshops, but James Watt Jr's hope (expressed a few years previously in 1803) that no more buildings would be needed was ill-founded. At the end of this period a plan with dimensions added was produced of the Soho Foundry site, which included allotments that had been laid out at the rear of the two terraces of houses (Fig 7.36).

Phase 3: The expansion northwards, 1809–16 (Fig 7.37)

Phase 3A: The pattern stores, houses and gas

The busy years of the first decade of the 19th century had produced an avalanche of patterns that quickly overran the existing storage space. In 1809, it was decided to extend beyond the north boundary, almost doubling the length of the existing storage range. Eleven new bays were added altogether in 1809. The 'new pattern shed' was two-storey and continued the form of the phase built in 1799.[177] It was built against the west boundary wall and the lower ground level consisted of a series of vaults supporting a narrower storey above and a fronting walkway. The previous phase's end bay, which broke forward over a timber floor, was cut back; the bay at the north end of the new extension broke forward in the same fashion, but this time over a

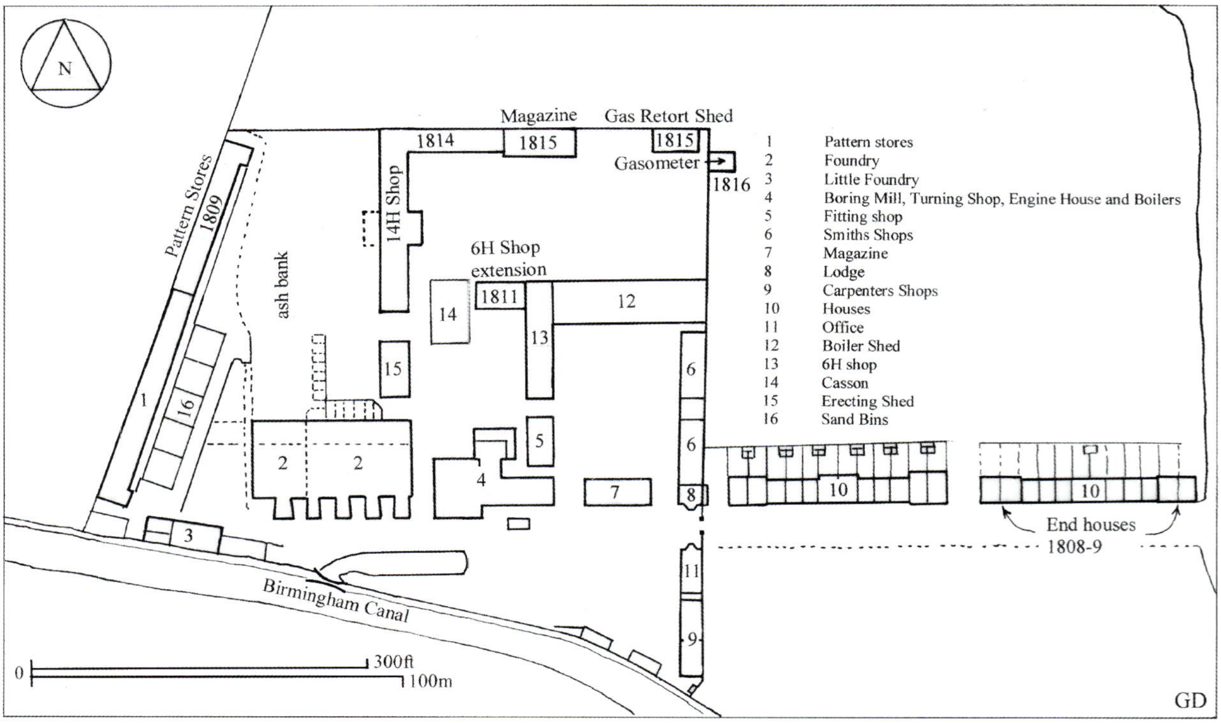

Fig 7.37
Soho Foundry, phase 3 plan, 1809–16.

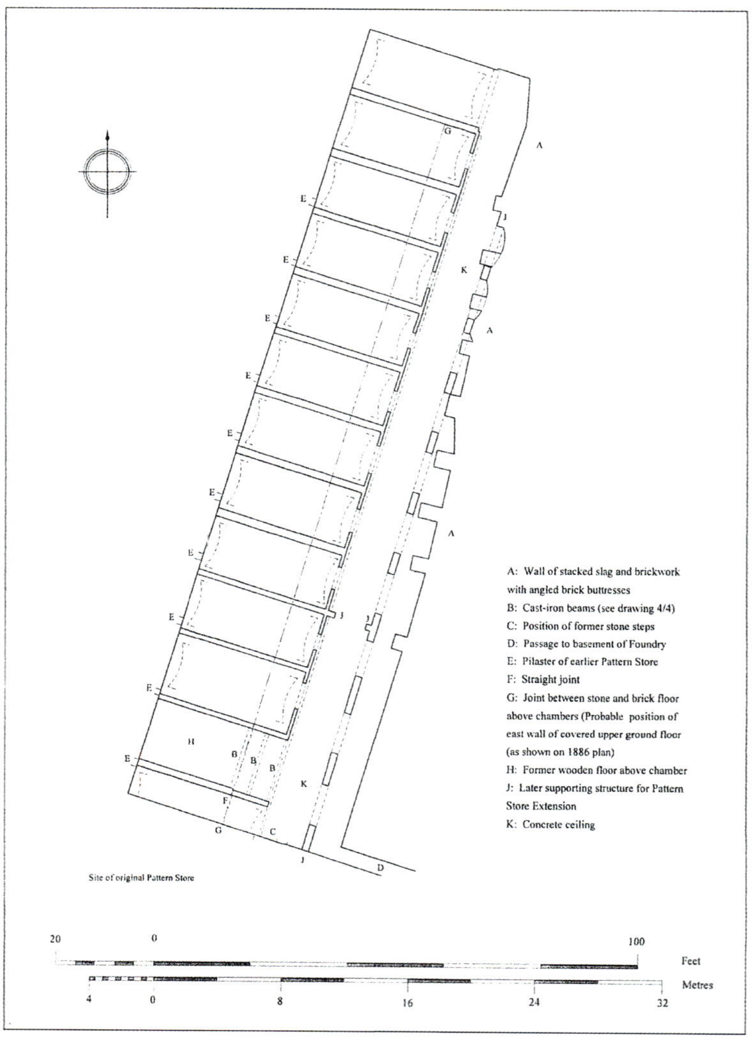

Fig 7.38
Plan of the northern end of the pattern store vaults, surveyed in 1996, the remainder to the south buried in the ground (see Figs 7.17 and 7.91).

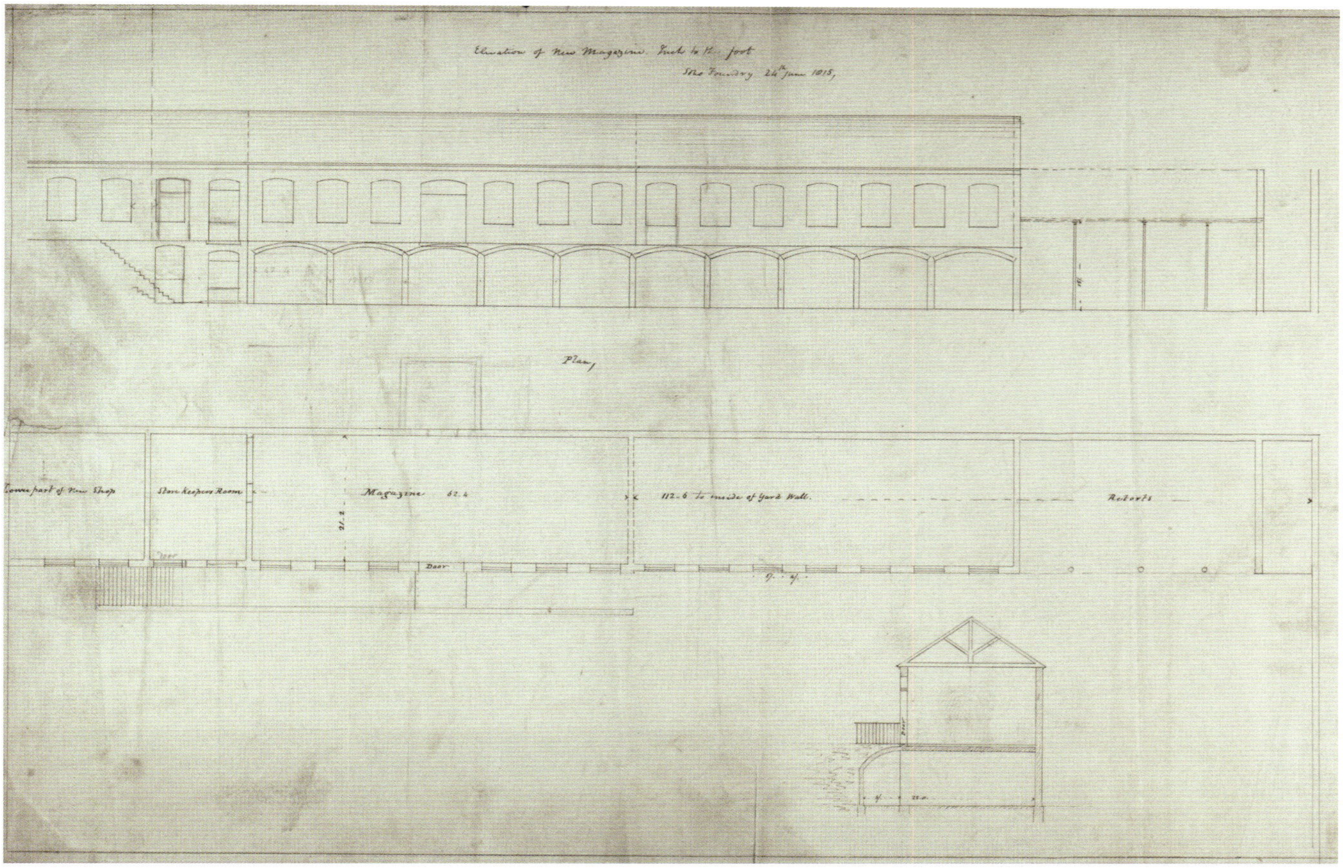

Fig 7.39
Plan and elevation of the new magazine, 24 June 1815.

vault. These brick vaults have survived to the present day. A few unmarked and undated drawings of this phase have also survived and clearly show how the vaults increased in height northwards as the land fell (*see* Figs 7.17 and 7.91).[178] One elevation has each of the vaults identified as storage for particular items; loam patterns, for example, were to be kept in the second and third arches from the south. The Royal Commission on the Historical Monuments of England (now Historic England) surveyed these vaults in 1996 (Fig 7.38).

The row of eight houses built in 1801–2 had two more houses added at each end. Work started in April 1808 and finished in November 1809.[179] Drawings for these four houses reveal that alternative designs were considered.[180] They had a more generous footprint and storey height than the existing eight but were relatively plain, the only decoration a string course at the level of the first-floor window sills. The hipped roof over each pair provided two architectural 'stops' to the row. The two houses built at the west end of the row have survived; one of these (number 13) was occupied by William Murdoch for a time (*see* Fig 7.33).

It is less easy to understand how the gas plant at the Foundry was developed as no drawings of the buildings have survived, though a portfolio of equipment has come to light.[181] As mentioned above, a retort shed was built in 1809–10; this was followed by a gasometer shed in 1812.[182] Their locations are not known, but the gasometer shed, like the larger one built after it, may have been placed outside the east boundary wall for safety reasons (*see* p 170). In 1812, only one retort was making gas and it had developed a hole in the same place as the two others that had presumably been abandoned.[183] John Murdoch (son of William) requested the installation of a second, for he suspected the hole had been caused by the strain of a single retort having to supply all the gas for the works. In 1815, the retort shed was demolished and the retort equipment moved to a new building, and in the following year the gasometer shed was taken down and a new 'gasometer house and pit' built. A retort house is shown on a drawing, dated 24 June 1815, planned to be built against a new magazine some 115ft (35m) north of the old boundary wall and near the north-east corner of the new boundary wall (Fig 7.39).[184] This appears to be the site of the retort shed built in 1815. The gasometer house and pit were built immediately outside a new section of the east boundary wall, an extension of the old east wall joining the new north wall. In September 1816, the new gasometer pit 'was secured on the outside' and filled for the first time for testing.[185]

Phase 3B: The 14H shop and magazine, 1814–15

In 1814, there was a further encroachment into the area beyond the former north boundary wall with the construction of one of the largest workshops on the site. It was known as the '14H shop', since it was intended for the fitting of 14hp engines. This type of engine was designed to stand on a separate cast iron block, and six classical columns connected by an entablature supported the beam.[186] It was typical of the Boulton side of the partnership to combine art and technology, although James Watt Jr was also a well-educated and cultured man.

The 14H shop was L-shaped, the main part aligned north–south, continuing the orientation and width (30ft/9.14m) of the 1802 fitting/erecting shed. At a distance of 20ft (6.01m) from the fitting shed, it stretched 165ft (50.29m) to the new north boundary wall and required the demolition of the 1797 stable and straw shed. These dimensions have been calculated from the surviving fabric and later maps, for much of this section of the building survives. The other part of the 14H shop ran west–east for about 68ft (20.73m) and was 21ft (6.4m) wide. The fall in the ground eastwards allowed a basement (lower ground) room to be constructed at its east end. This east end is shown on a plan and elevation of the magazine that was built up against it on the same line in the following year (1815) (*see* Fig 7.39).[187]

The building costs of the 14H shop alone were £2,389 6s 10d.[188] A 16in (406mm) 6hp engine of the independent-block type – costing £523 7s 7d – was installed, using the new A frame.[189] This pattern of cast iron frame was used to support the beam.[190] The engine and boiler were positioned at the junction between the two parts of the shop so that machinery in both sections could be conveniently powered.[191] There are no extant drawings of this engine. Other machinery installed in the shop at this time included a small and a large drill, four small lathes and a large lathe, and a screw machine.[192]

In 1815, a magazine for the fitting department was built on an east–west alignment and joined to the east end of the east–west range of the 14H shop. Fortunately, there is a drawing (dated 24 June 1815) that reveals that the magazine was similar in form to the pattern stores (*see* Fig 7.39). Instead of exploiting the fall in the ground to the north, it took advantage of the slope downwards to the east. The upper floor of the two-storey magazine was level with the 14H shop at the west end; the lower storey was composed of brick arches or vaults, ten in all. This storey was at ground level at the east end but at the west end a flight of about 18 steps led down from the higher ground level. A 6ft (1.83m)-wide open passageway was intended to run in front of the arches, with a wall retaining the ground to the south. It was proposed to arrive at the main door to the upper storey via a short bridge from the retaining wall. It is clear that there was a break-of-slope about 10ft (3.05m) high on a roughly north–south line near the east end of the passageway.

By the end of this phase another large yard at the lowest level of the site had been completed. The buildings on the north side, part of the 14H shop, magazine and retort house, were intended to have entirely enclosed it, but it is likely that the eastern half of the magazine was not built as intended leaving a gap. The magazine and the retort house would then have required a length of boundary wall between them. Further to the west, ash tipping may have extended by this time into the space between the pattern stores and the west side of the 14H shop. It is not known how the ever-increasing deposit of material in this area was confined on the east side. It is possible that the ash deposit never reached it. On the west side, the wall had a distinct batter, being constructed of large fragments of clinker holding back material above the access-way to the lower ground level vaults in the pattern stores. This sloping clinker wall can still be seen today. At this time, the access-way varied in width between 7ft (2.13m) at the north end and 45ft (13.72m) at the south near the sand bins.

Visitors were only very occasionally allowed into the Soho Foundry and so contemporary travellers' accounts are rare. In 1814, J C Fisher – accompanied by James Watt Jr – was privileged to see the works:[193]

> The works are completely enclosed by a high wall and consist of several separate buildings, each of which is many hundreds of feet in length. The most important are the foundry, the pattern shop, and the new workshop.

> Four furnaces produce enough molten iron to enable castings to be made up to a weight of 200cw[t]. The plant containing the stores for drying moulds is situated opposite the foundry. The space between these two buildings forms a pit in which the largest cylinders are cast upright. The sand for the moulds is dug on site.

James Watt Jr also showed him the gas plant and his description is the only contemporary one known:

> The coking – strictly speaking the distillation of – the coal takes place in two large furnaces. The separation of the gas from the bitumen and other substances takes place in two other containers nearby. The gas is conveyed in pipes from the containers into two iron holders with a capacity of 3,000 cubic feet of gas. These holders – closed at the top – are open at the bottom but are sealed by the crater in which they stand.
>
> In order to show me how the installation worked Mr Watt [Jr] had the counting house cleared, and then he lit the gas. The light on each desk came from glass lamps containing four jets. It burned brightly without an odour. No one has yet made public the method by which the smell of the gas can be removed and the blue part of the flame eliminated, but many attempts to do this have been successful.

Gas-lit premises were still a singular novelty at this time.

Phase 4: Further expansion northwards and eastwards, 1823–38

Phase 4A: The blowing engine, new smithy, boiler shop, gasworks and pattern turning shop, 1823–4 (Fig 7.40)

In 1821, Joshua Field visited the Soho Foundry and drew a schematic plan that captured the basic layout more or less correctly (Fig 7.41).[194] His account is illuminating (though he saw no gas lights!):

> The Foundry is a large rather dark building having 3 double wood cranes along the middle with about as many air furnaces placed rather outside the building having their tapping & dipping holes inside the large doors in the wall between these furnaces, so stoking is outside the foundry. The cupolas are at one end blown by a cylinder worked by an engine of ab[ou]t 20 Horses power of old construction. This engine also works various machinery grinding &c, – there are 4 or 5 boring bars & each is worked by a small bellcrank engine except the large one which is I believe worked by the large engine but as the bar was not at work could not see. In one room the cylinders of 4 Engines of about 4 horse each stand close together coming about 2 feet through an iron floor. Underneath they each work a fly wheel by a bell crank which drives the boring bars & lathes; the man at the bar stops the engine to stop the bar. These engines have neither air pumps or condensers (except one which is now cast of[f]) but have an eduction pipe leading to the condencer of the great Engine and so are necessarily dependent upon it but one having an air pump that can be attached they work without the large one.

This is an accurate description of the foundry, boring mill and small engine room. The large bar was, however, probably not worked by the beam engine but by its own little engine. The engine – with its own air pump – was the 6hp bell-crank for the 6H shop. A well was built for this engine in 1806.[195]

A new building programme began in 1823 and was probably related to the production of the marine side-lever engine for land use. The boat-engine business had begun only a few years previously and was experiencing competition with Maudslay, Sons and Field of London.[196]

In 1823, the boiler house for the 6hp engine in the 14H shop was nearly all pulled down and a 10 and 20hp boiler erected in a new house.[197] The gas retort house and gasometer shed were demolished, the gas retorts moved for the final time in the history of gas-making at the site. This was not to be the last major revamp of the actual gas plant and machinery, however, so the gasometer and retorts surviving into the 20th century were not built by Murdoch (d 1839), as has often been claimed. The removal of the retorts and gasometer to another location was caused by the need to expand the boiler-making facilities and to provide blowing capacity in workshops outside the foundry for the first time. The construction of new gas-plant buildings caused the site boundary to be shifted northwards again, with the retort house and gasometer house alongside one another, the latter fitting into the new north-east corner of the boundary

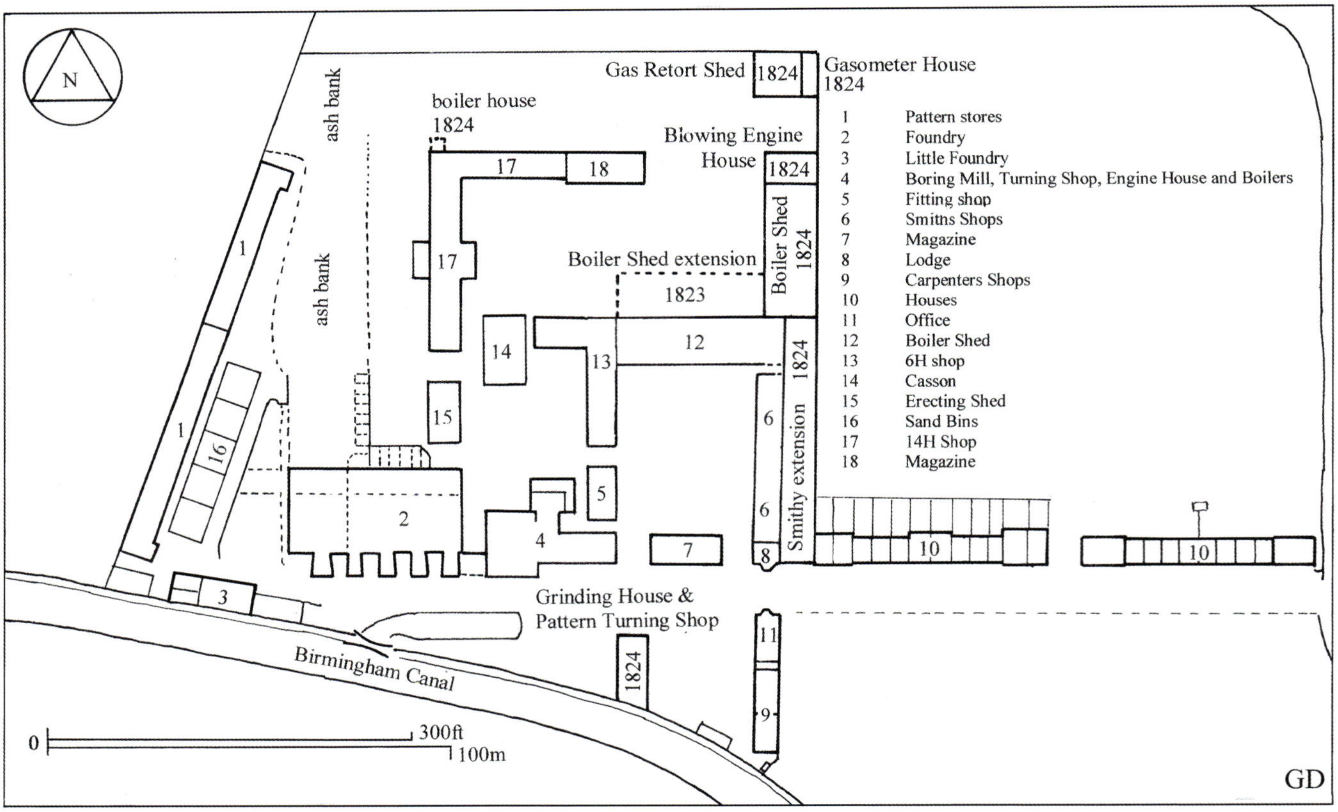

Fig 7.40
Soho Foundry, phase 4A plan, 1823–4.

wall. The advance of the north boundary was initially limited to the eastern part of the site but, in 1828, a new north boundary wall 22ft (6.7m) high and 375ft (114.3m) long was constructed along the full length of a new line from the west boundary to the east boundary.[198] This wall marked the northern limit of expansion until the early 20th century.

In 1824, the east boundary was also moved about 24ft (7.32m) eastwards to allow the construction of a broad boiler shed measuring about 110ft (33.53m) × 47ft (14.33m), orientated north–south. It incorporated a blast chamber at its northern extremity, the site of the former 1816 gasometer pit. In the previous year, the 1803 boiler shed had undergone a major rebuild and extension with 'back wings', but the nature of these large changes is not yet clearly understood.[199]

On 22 May 1823, William Murdoch Jr mused that he had little chance of 'swilling sea air' that season 'thanks to Boiler Making & Boiler shed buildings now going on with'.[200] In October, James Watt Jr expressed his regret that, although construction work may have been complete, full production of boilers was not possible owing to labour shortages: 'We are making

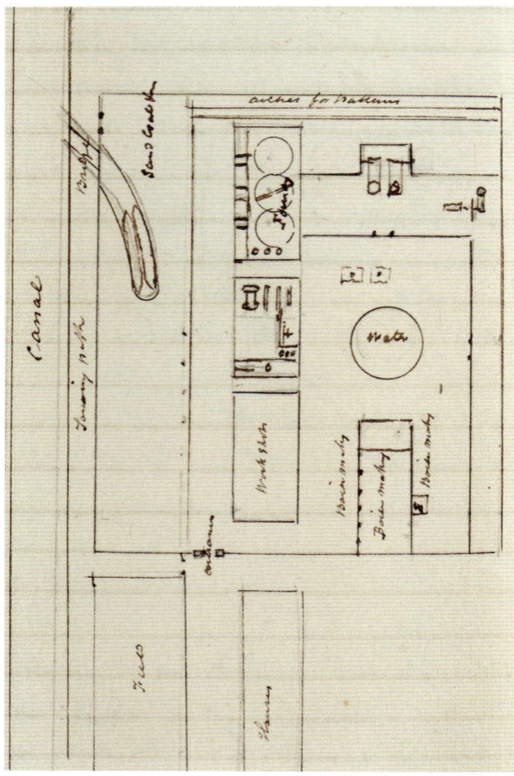

Fig 7.41
Plan of the main foundry building by Joshua Field, 1821.

additions to the punching machinery and notwithstanding the advanced season, going on with further building but we hardly contemplate any assistance from them before the spring'.[201]

The south end of the new boiler shed against the east boundary was joined to the new part of the smithy, which was also undergoing a major extension eastwards in 1824. The old smithy was more than doubled in width from 22.5ft (6.86m) to nearly 50ft (15.24m). Two drawings are extant that show clearly that the old smithy was to be left standing, and that the extension was to be 6ft (1.83m) higher.[202] This allowed light into the new building through a glazed clerestory above the eastern wall plate of the original shop. The 1795 length of east boundary wall below was demolished and cast iron columns erected instead.

In 1824, a blowing engine was installed immediately north of the site of the 1816 gasometer house as an extension of the new boiler shed. The engine was of the 8hp six-column type and directly operated three blowing cylinders. It had been constructed in 1817 but was not commissioned until the autumn of 1824.[203] A drawing, dated 29 June 1824, shows a

Fig 7.42
Engraving of the blowing engine, 1895. Note the classical architecture adopted to support the main structure.

Fig 7.43
The blowing engine, 1895.

regulating cylinder high in the corner of the room. From here, the blast entered the new boiler shed where the blast reservoir occupied and reused the former gasometer pit. The blast was then directed south to the hearths in the boiler shed itself and in the smithy, to a hearth in the 14H shop, and even as far as a new blast furnace in the crank shed, which was being converted at this time from the 1802 fitting/erecting shed.[204] The engine and blowing cylinders survived into the late 19th century and are shown in an engraving and photographs (Figs 7.42 and 7.43). The east wall of the blowing engine house was built on the new east boundary of the site.

In 1824, a new building containing a grinding house and pattern turning shop was built on a north–south orientation between the main east–west road and the canal and on the site of a former paint shop dating from 1804.[205] The grinding shop had previously been located close to the south side of the turning shop. The orientation of the canal caused the south gable of the new building to be sharply angled. A tunnel was probably constructed from the beam engine in the boring mill to bring power along a shaft to the two grinding stones installed in the new grinding house. Also in 1824, the 20hp beam engine in the boring mill was converted to 24hp.[206]

Phase 4B: 1829–38

For the first time since its establishment, the Soho Foundry suffered trading losses in the years between 1829 and 1831, but matters improved during 1833 and 1834.[207] Between 1829 and 1832 the turning shop was reorganised; the piston rod shop on the ground floor and the parallel motion shop and William Murdoch's shop on the first floor were opened into one large upper and one large lower shop.[208] Some lathes were repaired, others replaced, and new drive gearing introduced.

In 1834, the foundry – the first building at the Soho Foundry to be lit by gas – was supplied with new gas lighting. The gas plant used by Murdoch in the laboratory in 1798 and in 1802 to illuminate the foundry was crude and quickly become obsolete. A plan of the 1834 gas installation has survived and shows a supply brought from the 14H shop to the north of the foundry (*see* Fig 7.46). A single gas light illuminated the

Fig 7.44
Engraving of the 10hp bell-crank engine in the boring mill, 1895.

Fig 7.45
The 10hp bell-crank engine, 1895.

boring rod in the Great Arch below the foundry (the small boring mill). The plan shows that the foundry was a 10-bay building at this time.[209]

In 1838, the 1804 6hp engine that powered the 6H shop and boiler shed machinery was ordered to be replaced by another bell-crank engine rated at 8hp (upgraded to 18hp, *see* p 181) (*see* Fig 7.28). This survived until 1896 and was featured in an illustrated article in *The Engineer* in 1895 (Figs 7.44 and 7.45). The 8hp engine was connected to the 6H shop by a new underground shaft tunnel. From the engine, the tunnel first went east to enter the nozzle and working gear shop (the former fitting shop) and, once in the building, turned through a right angle northwards.[210] Covered with five iron plates, it then crossed the yard to the 6H shop.[211] The new engine was not installed until 1839 and cost £453 0s 11d.[212] Although no drawings for it have survived, there is one extant for the third boiler added to the two already existing (9 Feb 1838). These served the new 8hp engine, the three other little engines, and the beam engine.[213] The east–west section of the shaft tunnel ran immediately north of the row of boilers and their ash pits (*see* Fig 7.28).

The new boiler house almost completely filled the space between the nozzle and working gear shop on the east and the existing boiler houses and the small engine house on the west. In 1838, significant changes were made to the nozzle and working gear shop, including the demolition of two hearths and the construction of two new ones, one of these on the wall next to the new boiler house.[214]

Phase 5: The transition from Boulton & Watt to James Watt & Co: consolidating on one Soho site and expanding southwards, 1840–53 (Fig 7.47)

In 1840, Matthew Robinson Boulton withdrew from the partnership and James Watt Jr became the sole owner of the firm known as Boulton Watt & Co, although there was no longer any Boulton connection.[215] Matthew Robinson Boulton died in 1842 and James Watt Jr's advancing age and occasional illness prompted the search for new partners, energies and finance. Two of the Soho Foundry managers, James Brown and Gilbert Hamilton, were rewarded with 2/12 shares each and a 3/12 share was sold to Henry Wollaston Blake, a London businessman. James Watt Jr himself retained a 5/12 share in the company. James Watt Jr died in 1848, and the firm ceased to be known as Boulton Watt & Co. The new firm was permitted to use the name of James Watt & Co in order to retain familiarity and prestige in a difficult trading period. The new partners had already taken control of the business, and major decisions on future development had been made before James Watt Jr's death. The attitude of Watt Jr to these momentous changes is not known.

Since the reconstruction of the engine works at the Manufactory in 1802–4, engine production had essentially been divided between the two Soho sites. This had not been efficient, with cylinders cast at the Soho Foundry having to be transported to the Manufactory to be fitted. The investment in the Manufactory side of the business, and the Boulton & Watt family connection with these buildings, ensured that the firm continued to operate two sites a mile apart while

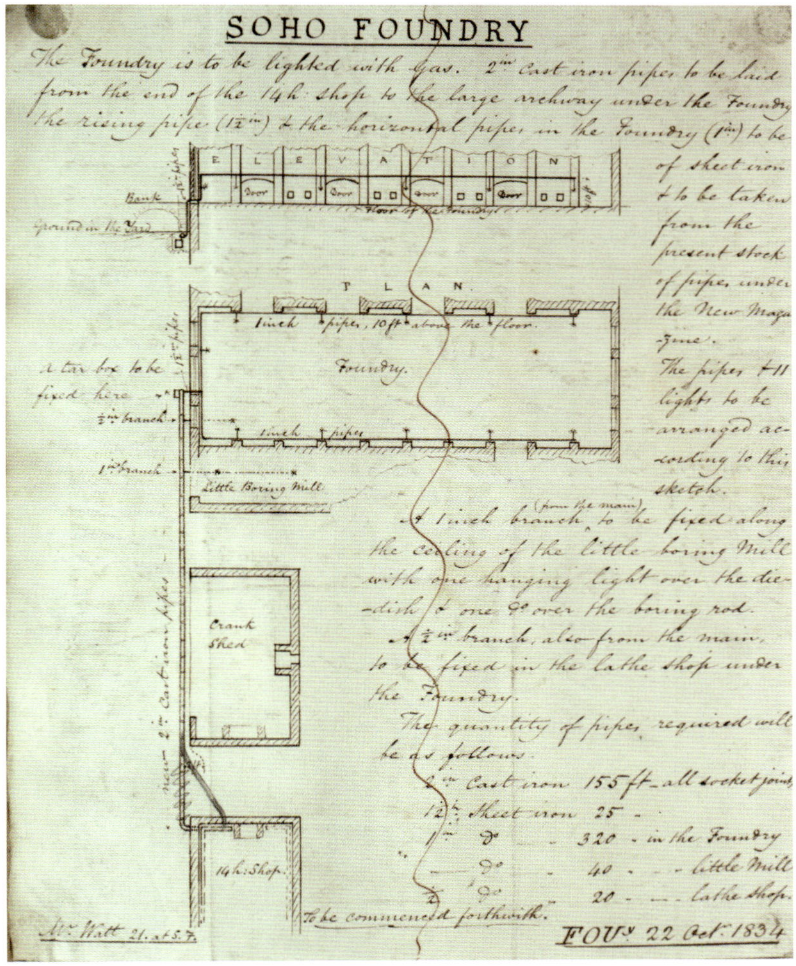

Fig 7.46
Plan of the foundry, crank shed and part of the 14H shop showing the proposed gas lighting, 22 October 1834.

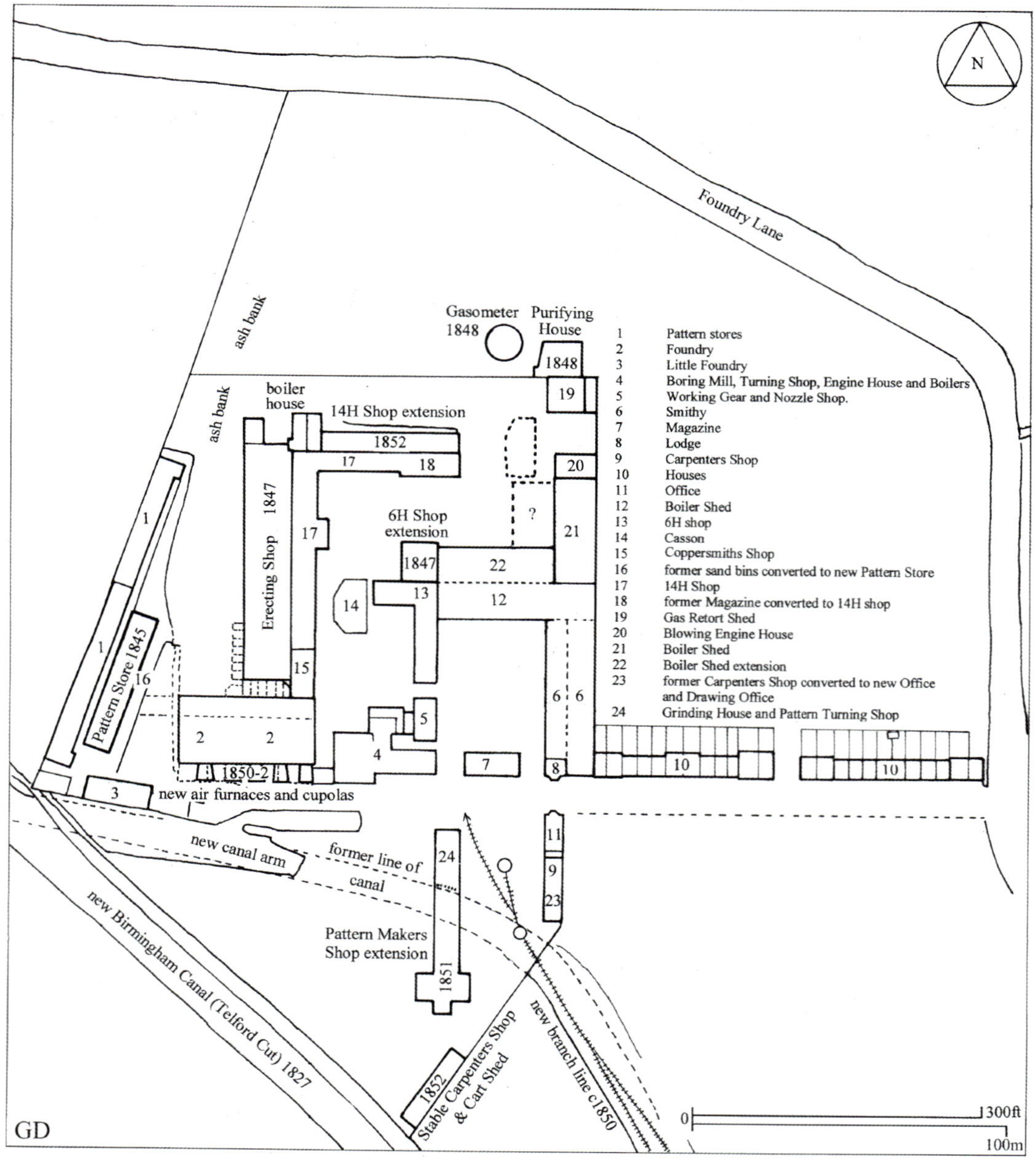

Fig 7.47
Soho Foundry, phase 5 plan, 1840–53.

Matthew Robinson Boulton and James Watt Jr were alive. It is not known exactly when the decision was made to consolidate onto one site and close the Manufactory engine works. With increasing competition, there was no room for sentiment towards the site where the first James Watt steam engine was put to work and where the application of rotary motion to this engine had been developed. The Soho Foundry was expanded in preparation for the consolidation of the works.

In 1845, the sand bins situated at the west end of the main foundry building were converted into a range of pattern stores, with openings on the east side opposite the ash-retaining wall and the mouth of the Great Arch (*see* Figs 7.20 and 7.30). The original form of the pattern stores is not known, and they may have been only a single storey in height. The stores were altered in 1851, and again sometime later, creating a single lofty room two storeys in height and lit by roof lights. A timber-boarded gallery supported by cast iron columns carried the upper storage level.[216] The lower part of this building has survived to the present day, but below ground, having been filled with material up to the level of the main foundry. The ground-level openings, though now blocked, are still visible in the

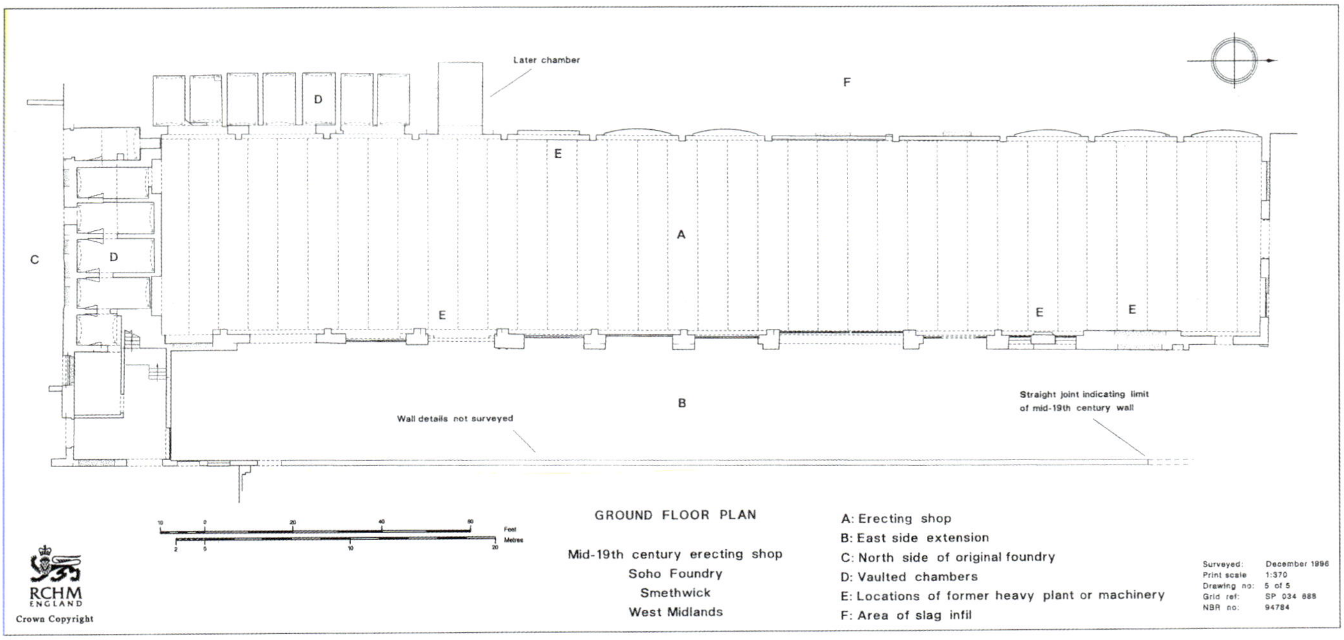

Fig 7.48
Plan of the 1847 erecting shop, 1996.

tunnel linking the Great Arch with the vaults of the 1809 pattern stores. In the late 1890s, Avery's re-fronted these arches in order to support their new foundry extension above and may have incorporated some of the upper part of the pattern stores in their new buildings.

In 1847, a new erecting shop was constructed – the largest single building on the site to date – measuring 253ft (77.11m) × 50ft (15.24m) (Figs 7.48 and 7.49).[217] The new building was orientated north–south and positioned so that the two rows of small vaults on the north side of the foundry built in 1797 and 1803 could be incorporated. The openings of the six vaults built in 1797 faced into the building along its south wall. The vaults built into the ash bank in 1803 looked into the south end of its long west wall. The remainder of this wall was built against the ash bank and its lower part may have predated the erecting shop. Above are two tiers of windows. The east wall was built against the north–south range of the 14H shop and the crank shed. A series of arches were constructed to join the old and new shops together. Above the arches on the east wall are two tiers of windows matching those on the west wall. An iron roof was manufactured by H Smith of Vulcan Forge, West Bromwich. It cost £1,132 3s 6d, just less than a third of the full cost (£3,742 11s 4d) of the building. The price was based upon the area of both pitches of the roof, a 'square' (100 sq ft/9.29 sq m) costing £8.[218] Smith's men began assembling the roof at the end of

Fig 7.49
The 1847 erecting shop looking south, 1997.

Fig 7.50
The 1847 erecting shop looking south, 1895; a scene of recent abandonment, eerily still.

August.[219] Photographs taken in 1895 show the present roof and, since the structure is unlikely to have been replaced before then, the 1847 roof is almost certainly the one still in existence today.[220] New and reused machinery from the Manufactory was placed in the shop to aid the erection of engines that had become progressively bigger during the 19th century. This impressive building with its early iron roof survives almost intact today. The 14H shop and the fitting shed, by 1834 a crank shed, were also joined for the first time and made into a new fitting shop. In 1852, the former crank shed was converted into a coppersmiths shop.

An extension measuring approximately 40ft (12.1m) square to the 6H shop was also built in

Fig 7.51
The 18hp side-lever engine, 1895.

Fig 7.52
The gasometer constructed in 1848, frequently ascribed to William Murdoch, who died in 1839; now demolished.

1847 onto the north side of both the 1803 6H shop and an extension dating from 1811.[221] It obliterated the 1816 blacking shop and its 1834 chimney.

1847 was a busy year: the 8hp six-column blast engine, installed in the blowing engine house in 1824, was uprated to 12hp.[222] In 1848, the year of James Watt Jr's death, the 8hp A-frame engine was taken out of the 14H shop and sold to I H Machu of Bunhuill Row, St Lukes, London.[223] It was replaced with an 18hp engine that had been made in 1834 but not used.[224] The latter was known as a side-lever marine engine for land, and cost £715 14s 11d. It was needed to power not only the enlarged 14H shop but the new adjacent erecting shop. The engine survived at least until 1895, the year it was photographed (Fig 7.51).

The gasometer, frequently and erroneously attributed to Murdoch, was probably built in 1848 by a Mr Richardson nine years after the former's death.[225] The new gasometer was unhoused for the first time since possibly the very earliest years of gas plant at the Foundry. Circular in shape (the earlier ones having been rectangular or square), it was placed beyond the north boundary wall on ground raised by the dumping of foundry ash (Fig 7.52). As well as the gasometer, Richardson supplied new retorts, but these were installed in the existing 1824 retort house. Purifying apparatus was built against the outer face of the north boundary wall and housed a year later in 1849. In 1848, gas lighting was extended to the new erecting shop and the boiler sheds and in 1851 to the new part of the 14H shop and the new pattern shop (*see* p 182). In 1852, the old gasometer house was converted for the use of the file cutters who had come over from the Manufactory engine works.

In 1850, four old air furnaces in the foundry were demolished and a new reverberatory furnace and cupola were erected in their place. In the following year, a large cupola was added and, in 1852, three more air furnaces.[226] All of these furnaces appear to have been constructed in the lean-to on the south side of the foundry and to the west of the earliest air furnaces (Fig 7.53). A pit for casting engine condensers was built within the foundry in relation to these new furnace positions, but its exact location is not known.

This period was important for the introduction of the railway to the Soho Foundry (*see* Fig 7.47). In 1826, Boulton & Watt had purchased the land between the old and new lines of the Birmingham Canal, but the line of the abandoned old canal remained in the ownership of the canal company, isolating their 1826 purchase. It was not until 1846 that the abandoned line of the canal was acquired by Boulton, Watt & Co, providing for the first time an opportunity to expand the Soho Foundry site southwards. In

Fig 7.53
The main foundry building, 1895.

1848, the firm agreed to convey a section of the original 1826 purchase to the Birmingham, Wolverhampton and Stour Valley Railway Company for their main track. In exchange, the railway company would lay down a branch line to the Soho Fcundry along the line of the abandoned canal.[227] The line entered the site on its new south-east boundary just south of the carpenters shops. The boundary continued in a straight line to the new canal. Part of the old canal was retained to continue the link to the private canal arm cut to serve the Soho Foundry in 1795–6. Another section of the old canal line provided another basin.

Fig 7.54
The 14hp engine, 1895.

In 1851, one of the first buildings to be erected south of the abandoned canal was a south extension to the pattern makers' shop built in 1824. A rough outline plan of about this time (1851) shows the building terminating in a cross wing.[228] Its length was increased by approximately 145ft (44.12m). In the same year, the 1798 carpenters shop (No 2) was converted into offices with a drawing office above and a managers and clerks offices below.[229] Previously, the drawing office had been located at the Manufactory. House number 1 in Foundry Row was made into a cashier's office. In 1852, a stable, carpenters shop and cart shed were erected against the new south-east boundary wall near to the canal.

At the north end of the site, the east–west range of the 14H shop and magazine was doubled in width. The magazine had been absorbed into the 14H shop a few years before in 1846. The new range was supported on brick vaults, forming a basement, as in the former magazine. Access to the vaults was gained by a ramp descending from the level of built-up spoil on the north side of the building. From 1852, the new shop was worked by a six-column 14hp beam engine that from 1815 had powered the engine-works machinery at the Manufactory. Although there are no drawings of the engine in its Soho Foundry setting, there are several from the Soho Manufactory dating from 1815.[230] The engine was also photographed in 1895 (Fig 7.54).

Two other small engines each of 3hp from the same engine room in the Manufactory were transferred to the Soho Foundry and set up in an extension to the boring mill engine house west of the existing little engine house. At least one of these was connected to a new boring rod. These engines dated back to 1802–4. They were early versions of the beamless table-top variety designed by Murdoch (*see* Chapter 4). In 1852–3, in addition to the engines, 4 planing machines, 14 lathes, 1 circular saw, and 1 drilling machine were transferred from the Manufactory and erected in a number of shops, both old and new, at the Soho Foundry.[231] Preparations for this move began in October 1850.[232]

This considerable phase of building was conducted in a period of poor trading and therefore large capital outlays on buildings and machinery were not matched by income from sales. In May 1849, 19 men were discharged and 30 men had their wages reduced.[233] In June 1850, further efforts were being made to lower expenditure on the workforce.[234] In these circumstances, there could be no question of maintaining both Soho sites. In April 1851, James Watt & Co announced:[235] 'Messrs James Watt & Co. beg to inform their friends and the Public that their Business will in the future be conducted at their principal Establishment, at Soho Foundry, Smethwick. Their offices at Soho, Handsworth, are now closed in consequence of this new arrangement'.

A dramatic but desolate view of the Soho Foundry, belching smoke from it chimneys, partnered by the Muntz metal works on the opposite side of the canal at French Walls, is impressionistic; the foundry had no chimney so tall, but it conveys the fortress-like quality of the boundary walls (Fig 7.55).

Fig 7.55
Engraving of the Soho Foundry from the north-west, mostly hidden by high walls to the left, with Muntz's Metal Works to the right on the other side of the canal, which cannot be seen, late 1840s?

Phase 6: James Watt & Co, 1853–95 (Fig 7.56)

Although maps at reliable scales (Figs 7.57 and 7.58) covering a wider area than the Soho Foundry site help to some extent, the lack of any building and machinery accounts for the period 1853–95 makes it difficult to establish a chronology of development. In view of this and the limited space that can be devoted to the post-Boulton & Watt period, a listing (Table 7.2) rather than a historical account has been undertaken. This has been organised into Foundry departments and, where possible, dates have been assigned. The numbers in brackets refer to building listed on Fig 7.56.

Table 7.2 James Watt & Co developments, 1853–95

Establishment	
before 1878	No 1 carpenters shop (*ex* foundry) converted to check office, fire engine house, and storeroom above (9)
before 1878	Parallel motion shop, Murdoch's shop, and drill shop below (*ex* fitting) converted into stores (4b)
n.d.	Network of railway lines developed through yards and into shops
n.d.	Bar iron and steel and metal stores on east side of smithy and south of steam hammer shop (projecting into gardens)
Foundry	
after 1860	Brass foundry north side of strip foundry
n.d.	Tunnel from fan in boring mill to cupola in foundry
n.d.	Extension to pattern makers shop on west side facing mint
after 1878	File cutters shop (*ex* 1824 gasometer house) converted to two-storey pattern store
1876	Lifting gear installed over 12in (304.8mm) boring rod in Great Arch under foundry (little boring mill)
Fitting	
1854	The 1799 3hp and 4hp bell-crank engines in the little engine house dismantled and broken up
1854	The 8hp bell-crank engine in the little engine house upgraded to 10hp
1854	Extension to boring mill on north side for vertical boring machine to be used for cylinders for the ship *Great Eastern*
c 1854	Original boiler house demolished, separating remaining two boilers from boring mill; new chimney
before 1878	The two 3hp table-top engines transferred from the Manufactory are removed
before 1878	Nozzle and working gear shop (*ex* fitting shop) converted to boiler fitting shop (subsequently converted to stores E ground floor and B&W Museum first floor, see Boiler department below) (5)
n.d.	24hp beam engine in boring mill uprated to 30hp
Smithy	
after 1859	Steam hammer shop with extension eastwards from smithy into allotment gardens
c 1865	12hp blast engine house and room over built against north side of 1824 blowing engine house
1865	New fan for blast
Boiler	
n.d.	Major extension of boiler-making sheds on north side to create the most extensive single production space on the site (12)
n.d.	Raising roof over part of boiler shed; painting of large advertisement 'James Watt & Co Engineers Soho Foundry' on same
before 1878	Nozzle and working gear shop (former fitting shop) converted into boiler fitting shop (subsequently converted to 'E store' with B&W Museum on first floor) (5)
New Mint Department	
1860	Soho Foundry Mint built against canal boundary
c 1860	Brass strip shop constructed against west side of main foundry building

Sources: LoB, MS3147/9/1; MS3147/10/76–77; Sandwell Municipal Borough Council, Board of Health Map of Smethwick 1857; Sandwell Community History and Archives Dept, Richard Clarke's map of Harborne 1859.

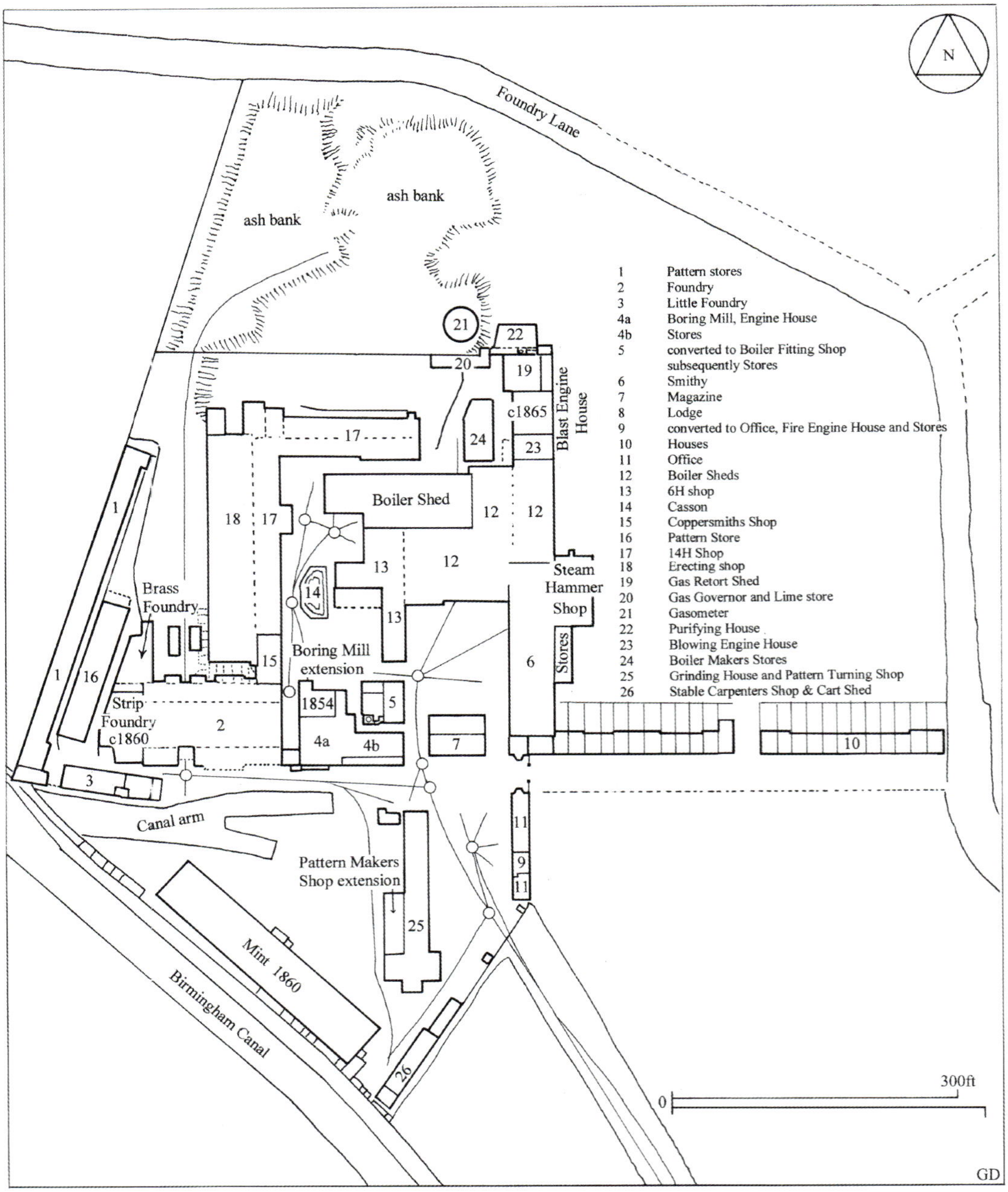

Fig 7.56
Soho Foundry, phase 6 plan, James Watt & Co, 1854–95.

Trading conditions improved in the late 1850s with the introduction of new engine designs, including the high-pressure types against which James Watt and his son had maintained a long-standing prejudice.[236] James Watt & Co. supplied engines for ships (the most famous being Brunel's *Great Eastern* in 1854), waterworks, breweries, textile factories and mints. In 1860 the firm felt sufficiently confident to build its own mint using Matthew Boulton's technology, which dated back to the turn of the century (*see* pp 193–6).[237] James Watt & Co. had inherited the Boulton & Watt patterns, which had presumably been kept on the site in the ever-expanding stores. A rare documented visit to the Soho Foundry describes the pattern stores:[238]

> The pattern shops are very considerable ... All these capacious rooms are packed to repletion with wood patterns for every imaginable description of machine casting ... Although these patterns may be counted by tens, if not hundreds of thousands, they are so methodically arranged that any single limb of a machine on which the dust of half-a-century has accumulated could be picked out in a trice by the intelligent superintendent of this department.

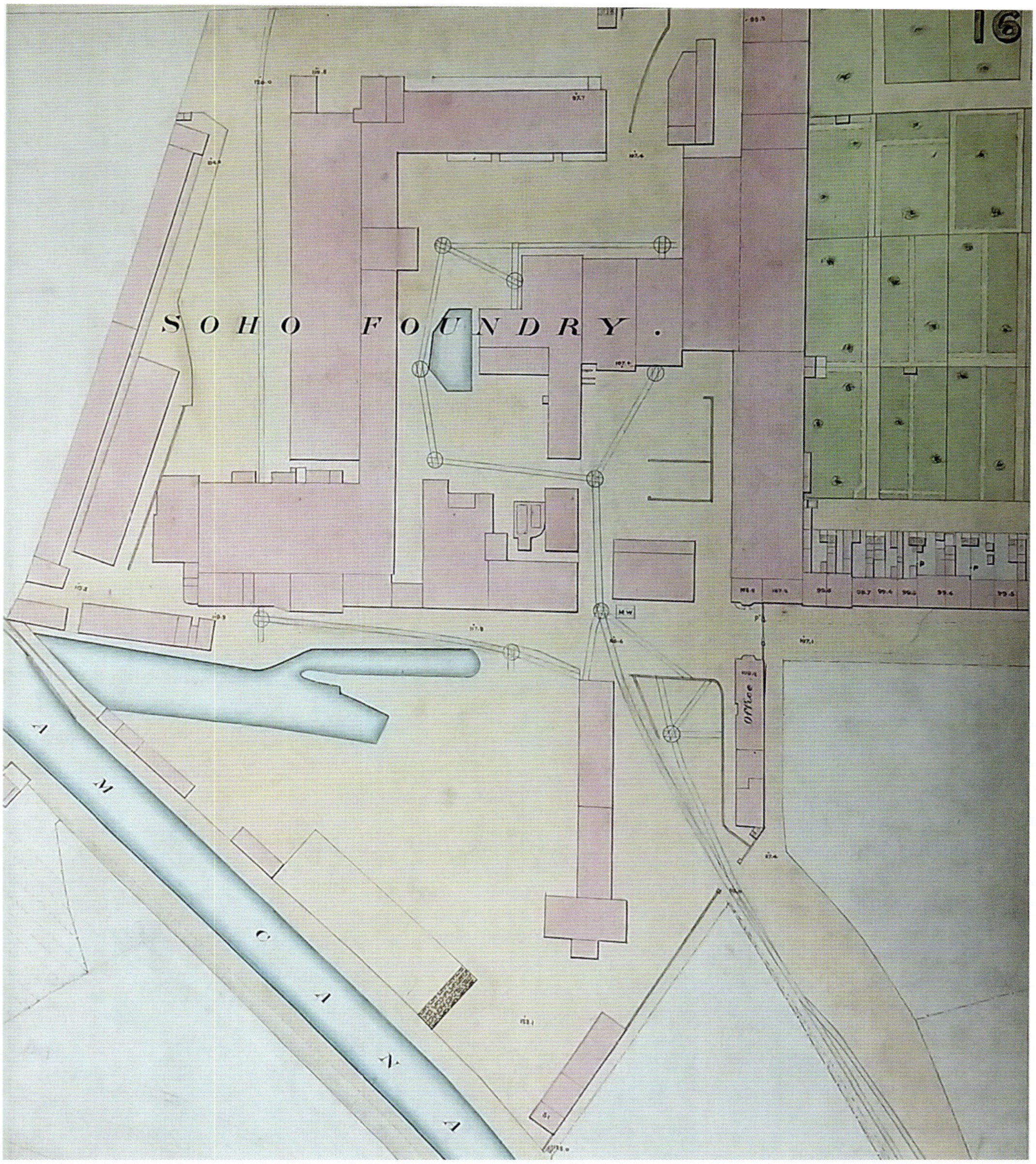

Fig 7.57
Extract from the Board of Health plan of Harborne, 1857, providing the most accurate plan of the Soho Foundry and its environs in this period.

The account indicates that, at this time, only half of the upper storey of the 1797–1809 pattern stores remained.

The author was impressed by the erecting shop: 'a splendid building, probably unsurpassed for its purpose in the kingdom', but he found the foundry 'fitted up in the ordinary way', except for wooden cranes. His description of the Soho Foundry was of a 'quaint and old-fashioned [establishment] ... seeming to have been erected piecemeal, parts being added on the requirements of an expanding trade demanding additional space'.[239]

The reason for the eventual demise of the firm in 1895 is hinted at here. The buildings had been extended but, with the exception of the erecting shop, never comprehensively rebuilt. Again, although there had been some modernisation, there had also been a reluctance to throw away old and obsolete machinery. Perhaps veneration of Boulton, Watt and Murdoch and their achievements hindered rather than inspired innovation. In 1892, an engineer visiting the Soho Foundry was struck by the unnecessary decoration and polish on the engines: 'You are old fashioned people aren't you ... You won't get work unless you advertise and canvas for it'.[240] The firm could no longer rely on its reputation – there were too many competitors with up-to-date working practices.

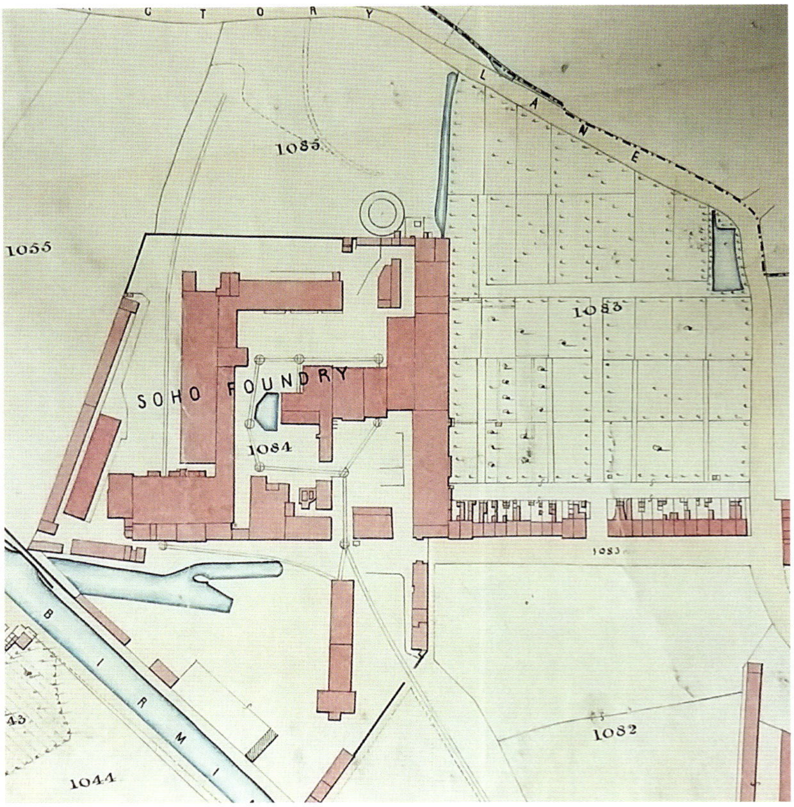

Fig 7.58
Extract from Richard Clarke's map of Harborne, 1859.

Summaries of building and machinery accounts reveal that there was little investment in the years after 1855. The value of buildings and machinery rose from £82,667 in 1848 to £105,087 in 1855. Thereafter, the total was £115,998 in 1894, an increase of only £10,911 over a 39-year period.[241] The partners mortgaged the premises for £15,000 in 1873 and borrowed a further £10,000 in 1880. The £25,000 total was reduced to £20,000 in 1883, but from this time onwards the debt could not be shifted.[242] The mortgagees foreclosed on the loan and brought about the sale of the premises in 1895. W & T Avery's purchase price of £19,500 was short of the sum required to pay off the mortgage. The goodwill and the patterns sold for £2,000 made up the difference. H W Blake, the only surviving partner at this time, died in relative poverty in 1899.[243] Since the £25,000 loan had not been invested in the plant to any great extent, it can only be assumed that it helped service trading losses.

Although the Soho Foundry was advertised for auction and catalogues published in May 1895, the property was withdrawn and W & T Avery Ltd submitted an offer, which was accepted.[244] By then, Avery's were a well-known firm of weighing-scale manufacturers whose origins lay in Moat Lane and in Digbeth, Birmingham.[245] They had premises in many of the largest towns in the country and needed to move out of their cramped buildings in the centre of Birmingham.

The printed particulars for the sale are extremely important in understanding the layout of the Soho Foundry at this time.[246] They include the first extant large-scale plan of the site with the function of all the buildings marked for the first time for nearly 100 years (Fig 7.59). The material is too extensive to be analysed here but it would be useful to list the steam engines (no change from 1878) and some of the machinery (Table 7.3).[247]

Table 7.3 Steam engines and main machinery, 1895

	Type	*Cylinder size*	*Location*
1	30hp beam engine	13in (330mm)	Boring mill
2	10hp bell crank	16in (406mm)	Boring mill
3	18hp side lever	26in (660mm)	14H shop
4	14hp beam engine	22in (559mm)	14H shop
5	12hp beam engine	24in (610mm)	Blowing house
6	?hp horizontal engine	13in (333mm)	Blowing house adjacent
7	?hp horizontal engine	29in (737mm)	Mint
8	?hp horizontal engine	29in (737mm)	Mint
9	8hp portable engine	9in (229mm)	In shed adjacent to 6H shop

58 lathes
6 horizontal planing machines
3 wall planing machines
5 radial drilling machines
7 vertical drilling machines
3 horizontal boring mills
1 vertical boring mill
6 wall drilling machines
2 countersink drilling machines
4 shell drilling machines
3 slotting machines
6 shaping machines
4 screwing machines
5 punching and shearing machines
3 steam hammers

Source: 1895 Sale Particulars[248]

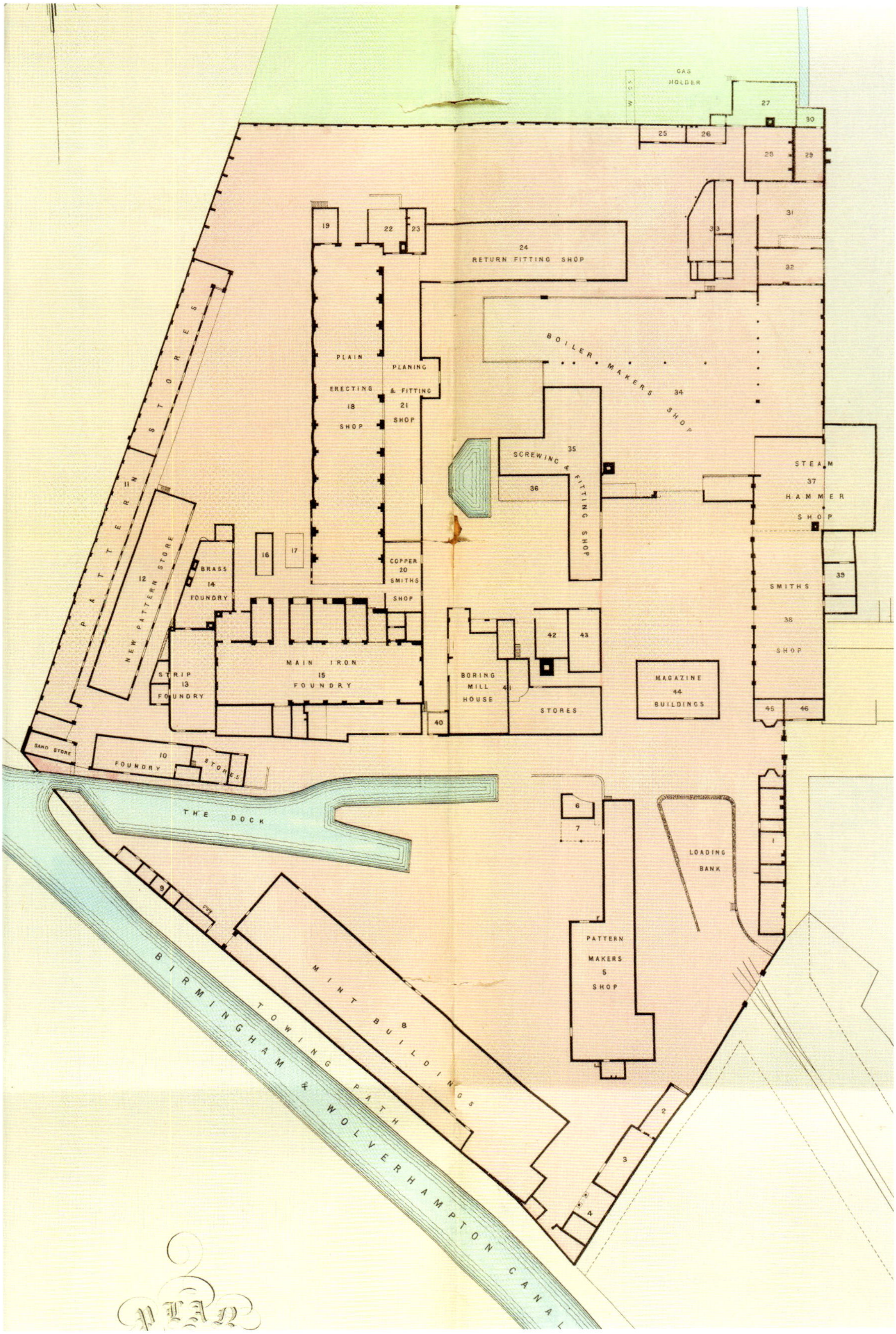

Fig 7.59
Plan of the Soho Foundry from the 1895 sale catalogue.

Fig 7.60
Engraving of the large face plate lathe in the erecting shop, 1895.

Fig 7.61
Engraving of the heavy slotting machine in the erecting shop, 1895.

Fig 7.62
Engraving of the vertical boring machine in the erecting shop, 1895.

The sale attracted considerable attention in the engineering world because of the connection with Boulton, Watt and Murdoch and the survival within the works of many curiosities from their era. George Tangye (of the great Cornwall Engineering Works, which stood not far to the west of the Soho Foundry) purchased the firm's records. These were eventually donated to Birmingham Reference Library to become the Boulton & Watt collection. But for this material – and the fact that Avery's did not carry out their original intention 'to dismantle almost the whole of the vast whole buildings ... and erect new shops' – this chapter could not have been written.[249]

A series of important articles about the Soho Foundry appeared in *The Engineer* in the remainder of 1895 and into 1896.[250] At first *The Engineer* was scathing:

> One feels, in fact, like being in a museum ... It is a curious rambling old place, badly arranged from a modern point of view, and the tools are all old, both in existence and design. How these works contrived to exist as

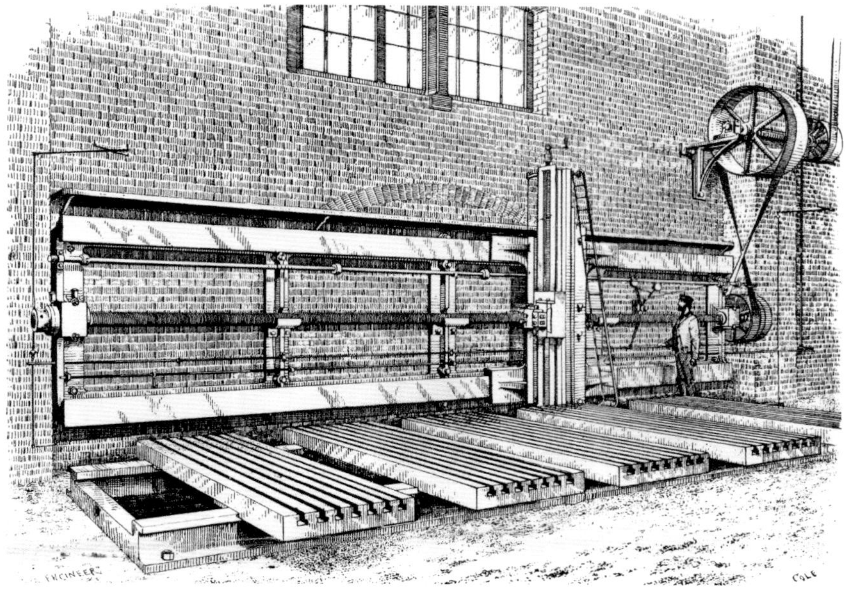

a factory, and compete with other modern establishments up to as recently as last Saturday, is something of a puzzle to us.[251]

However, by the next article four months later the tone had changed from disdain to a recognition of the historical significance of this industrial museum:

But these tools are so full of interest, so remarkable in many respects, and so valuable as showing the progress of invention in special departments that we have deemed it desirable to send our special draughtsman to Soho to make such drawings as will suffice to place on record the details of mechanism, every particular of which would be lost to the outside world.[252]

These are the first known illustrations of Soho Foundry machinery and have fulfilled their original purpose. All but one of the machine locations have been identified, some where the building or fabric to which it was attached still survives. There is insufficient space here to analyse the detailed information in these articles, but the majority of the engravings have been reproduced (Figs 7.60–7.65 and *see* Figs 7.35, 7.42, 7.44).

Apart from the engravings, a photographic survey of the Soho Foundry was very fortunately commissioned (probably by George Tangye) during this time, resulting in over 90 photographs of the exterior and interior of buildings and of individual machines.[253] All but a few locations have now been identified, but the detailed analysis of their content would require a separate study. A small number of the photographs

Fig 7.63
Engraving of the large pillar radial drill in the erecting shop, 1895.

Fig 7.64
Engraving of the large planing machine in the erecting shop, 1895.

Fig 7.65
Engraving of the large vertical boring machine in the boring mill, 1895.

Fig 7.66
The 1847 erecting shop and the lower 14H shop attached, from the east-south-east, 1895.

Fig 7.67
The large face plate lathe in the north-east corner of the 1847 erecting shop, 1895.

Fig 7.68
The south-west corner of the 1847 erecting shop, showing the arches to the vaults, 1895, those to the right embedded in the ash bank.

Fig 7.69
The boring mill, 1895.

Fig 7.70
The 14H shop looking south, 1895.

have been selected for those buildings that are still standing (Figs 7.66–7.70 and *see* Figs 7.43, 7.45, 7.50, 7.51, 7.53–7.54).

Twice in 1909 and once in 1919, *The Engineer* featured the Soho Foundry in a short series of articles (commemorating the centenaries of Matthew Boulton's and James Watt's deaths respectively), which supplement the information contained in the 1895 articles.[254] Apart from featuring the principal managers and engineers and some individual machines, important material describes the layout of the fitting department, including the 6H shop, the 14H shop and the erecting shop.[255]

The survival of the Soho Foundry

The first edition of the OS 1:2500 (surveyed 1886) map captures the full extent of the Boulton & Watt and James Watt & Co buildings a decade before they were acquired by Avery's in 1896 (Fig 7.71). The second edition (revised 1902) records the major changes that the firm had made in converting an antique steam-engine manufactory into a weighing machine factory (Fig 7.72). Despite the work of authorities such as Gale and Roll, until the last two decades there was little understanding of what had survived of the buildings of the Boulton & Watt and James Watt & Co era and, particularly, of the earliest years at the turn of 19th century. The Avery demolitions were substantial, but it is clear that a great deal of the engine manufactory fabric still exists, even from the 1790s and 1800s, which is extremely rare for buildings with a combination of this age, function and significance. The losses and survivals are mapped on Fig 7.73. From reading any guide to sites of industrial archaeology, it is immediately apparent how few steam-engine manufactories are listed for the whole country.[256] For many years it was understood that only the offices of Boulton & Watt's 'famous' Soho Foundry had survived.[257] This listed terrace of houses at the main entrance was a distraction from the fact that much more of the Soho Foundry was still standing farther into the site. In 1992 the Monuments Protection Programme Step 1 Report on the Iron and Steel Industry, which included foundries and boring mills, entirely omitted the site.[258]

The demolition of the Soho Manufactory and Mint in the 1850s and early 1860s emphasises how precious is the survival of the Smethwick part of the site, a fact that was appreciated only when the buildings were threatened with demolition in 1996. Up to this time the only buildings and structures listed were the remaining part of a terrace of houses, including Murdoch's cottage, the gateway and gates to James Watt's Heathfield House in Handsworth and, off site, the towpath bridge on the Birmingham Canal.[259] With pressure coming from several quarters, the main foundry building and the 1847 erecting shop were listed by the Department of National Heritage in June 1996.

Sandwell Council invited the Royal Commission on the Historic Monuments of England to survey the site and in late 1996 they produced written reports and the first measured drawings of the Foundry (Fig 7.74).[260] These significantly advanced our understanding of the site but they were unfortunately interpreted as the final authoritative word on the subject, when in fact they should have been regarded as only the beginning of a major project of measured survey, field work and documentary research. In April 1997, an application was submitted to demolish the remainder of the buildings not statutorily listed. These included the Soho Foundry mint (*c* 1860) and the remaining pattern stores (1799–1800 and 1809). Further research was conducted by the author to establish their historical significance. With the help of Smethwick Local History Society, a campaign was organised to save these buildings from demolition, which resulted in the addition of the pattern stores to the statutory list and the regrading of all the buildings to grade II*. It was appreciated that listing was only the first stage and that the reuse of the buildings was the only viable way forward. This, in turn, could only take place guided by further research, survey and archaeological investigation.

Before this could take place, the Soho Foundry mint was threatened with demolition as it had not been statutorily listed (Fig 7.75). Sandwell Borough Council commissioned the author to conduct documentary and a desk-top archaeological study of the building to establish its historical and technological significance.[261] This work was much aided by a comprehensive series of plans for the installation of the mint machinery in 1860.[262] The conclusion was that the Soho Foundry mint was the only surviving building in this country that contained minting machinery that followed the design originally used at the Soho Mint in Handsworth from 1798 to 1799 (Fig 7.76). It was also clear from the plans that the foundations of the machinery were, as expected, deep and robust and unlikely to have been removed when Avery's converted the building to a smithy around the years 1896–7. Accordingly, Sandwell Borough Council commissioned the University of Leicester Archaeological Unit to carry out an evaluation excavation within the building.[263] Three trenches were opened up in the summer of 2000 in the coining room, engine room and boiler room. The state of excavation was found to be excellent, finding, for example, the masonry support of one of the 13 coining presses and the base of the channel that contained the vacuum tube that ran

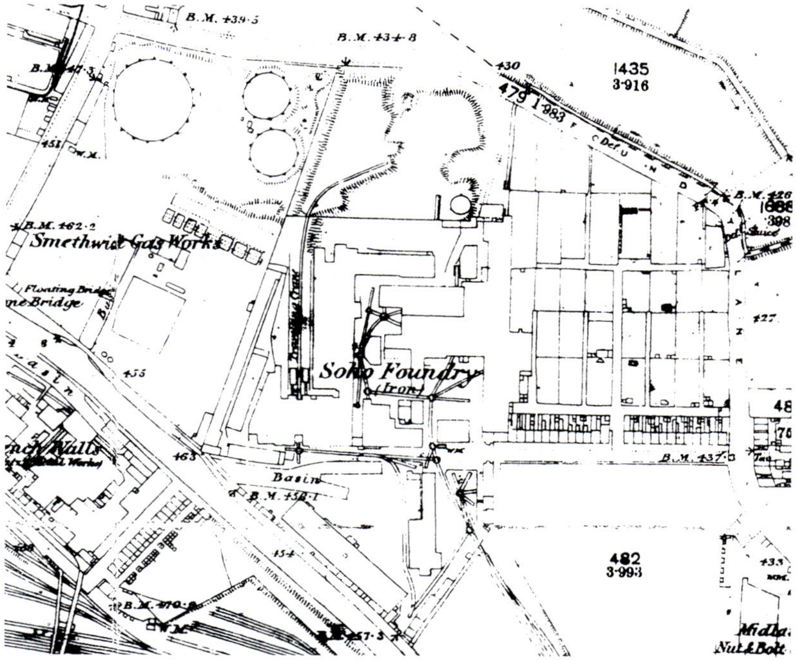

Fig 7.71
Ordnance Survey map, 1:2500 scale, surveyed 1886.

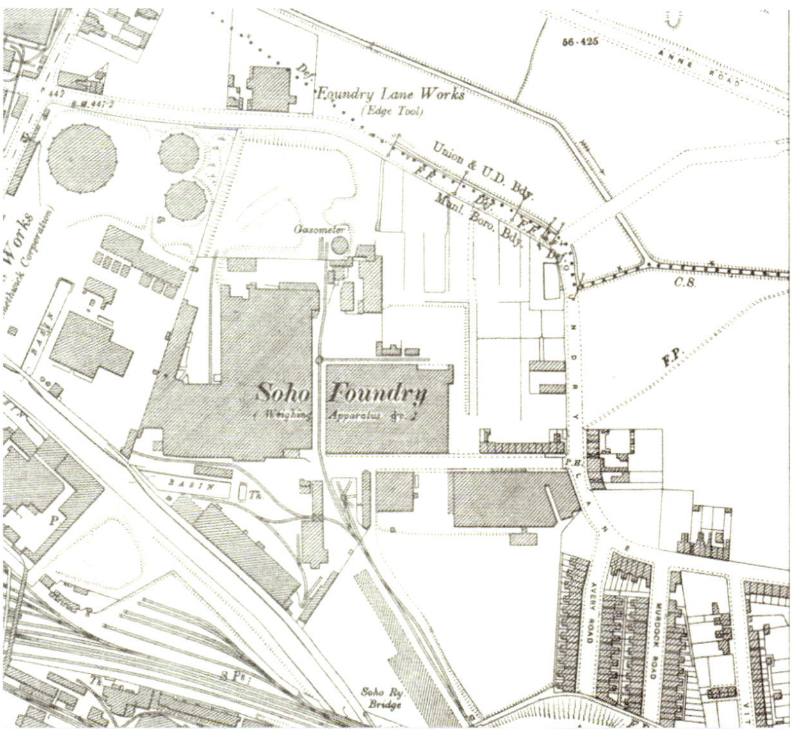

Fig 7.72
Ordnance Survey map, 1:2500 scale, revised 1902.

Fig 7.79
Photo of the roof protection over the main foundry building, 2009. The 1847 erecting shop and the heightened 14H shop in front are attached to its north side and continue for some distance off photo to the right.

Fig 7.80
The 1809 pattern stores, 1895. The patterns have been tossed into lower ground floor access way and lie against the battened wall retaining the ash bank. This area is now to be found at the end of the tunnel leading from the Great Arch.

substantially extended by Avery's in the late 19th and early 20th centuries.[270] It was concluded that they were of less architectural and historical importance. 'Therefore, where their removal might facilitate the preservation of earlier buildings, and contribute to a greater understanding of the Soho Foundry, demolition should be considered' (Fig 7.78).[271] The final part of the Conservation Plan (Phase VI) was completed in October 2003 and borrowed freely and in parts verbatim from the previous reports.[272]

In 2004 Avery buildings (1897–1900) that had been constructed against the east side of the 1847 Erecting Shop and 14H shop were demolished. As a result, the name, 'James Watt & Co', could again be seen painted in white letters onto the north gable of the 1847 erecting shop. Here, in 1896, Boulton & Watt buildings, including the boring mill and engine house, the magazine, the 5H shop and boiler sheds, had been demolished to make way for them (*see* Fig 7.73).[273]

The Boulton & Watt Foundry had continued to deteriorate during the first decade of the 21st century and it was agreed in 2006 that a temporary roof should be erected over this building to protect it from wind and weather while a new use was yet to be found.[274] Expenditure of over £700,000 was jointly funded by Historic England (then English Heritage), Sandwell Metropolitan District Council and Avery Weigh-Tronix. The work did not take place until 2008. Roof sheeting was laid over a massive scaffolding framework and presents a dramatic picture for train passengers on their journey from Birmingham New Street station to Smethwick Rolfe Street and beyond (Fig 7.79).

Associated with the temporary roof works was more demolition of Avery buildings, this time on the west side of the site. These were the two-storey pattern stores (1897) suspended over the surviving vaults of 1809 Boulton & Watt pattern stores and the light foundry built between 1904 and 1919, connecting with Belfast roofs the 1847 erecting shop and the Avery pattern stores. It was to be the first time since 1897 that the Boulton & Watt pattern store vaults saw the light of day (*see* Fig 7.91). This was to be for a short time only, however, as a new concrete slab was suspended above them at the former foundry floor level for their protection (Figs 7.80 and 7.81). Again, they can only be inspected at the end of a long tunnel that starts in the Great Arch in the main foundry building.

Summary

The surviving fabric of the Soho Foundry complex can roughly be divided into two categories though these are not mutually exclusive:

1. Standing buildings and structures, including tunnels and vaults.
2. Below-ground buried structures and associated archaeological deposits.

Buildings (Figs 7.82, 7.83)

Demolition in the early Avery period (1895–*c* 1905) has taken its toll and the standing buildings now comprise:

- a The foundry with its extensions westwards and lower ground level (the Great Arch, vaults and casting pit).
- b The 1809 pattern stores at basement level.
- c The 1845 pattern store at basement level.
- d The 1847 erecting shop and attached shopping eastwards.
- e The 1860 Foundry mint.
- f The terrace of cottages at the main entrance (early 19th-century).
- g Tunnels and vaults at lower ground level that connect a, b, c, and d.

In 2008 the gatehouse and associated office buildings at the main entrance built by Avery's in 1925 were listed grade II.

Buried archaeology (Fig 7.84)

The footprint of the buildings of the Boulton & Watt and James Watt & Co period (1795–1895) is the basic frame for establishing any archaeological potential, but also included should be the roadways, yard areas, pools, the former canal and canal basin, and spoil. Such is the nature of industrial structures that many of them are robust and lie deep below ground out of harm's way. Some of these buildings have been demolished and have been built over in the Avery period and are therefore unavailable for archaeological investigation. Evaluation excavation can take place where demolition has left the site clear or within the standing buildings themselves, but the latter sites are not available for the time being for health and safety reasons. Listed below are the most important of the individual sites.

Fig 7.81
Photo taken in 2008 of the 1809 pattern stores upper level, the timber upper storey removed by Avery's. The arches below have their openings facing left towards the massive wall retaining the ash bank. This is partly obscured by brick arches that supported the Avery pattern stores, now demolished. All is now plunged back into darkness under a concrete cap laid at upper ground level above the arches on the left (see Figs 7.91 and 7.92).

Fig 7.82
Oblique aerial photo of the Soho Foundry, September 2020. Scrap metal from Sims Metal bordering west side of the Foundry has collapsed onto the concrete cap constructed over the B&W pattern stores.

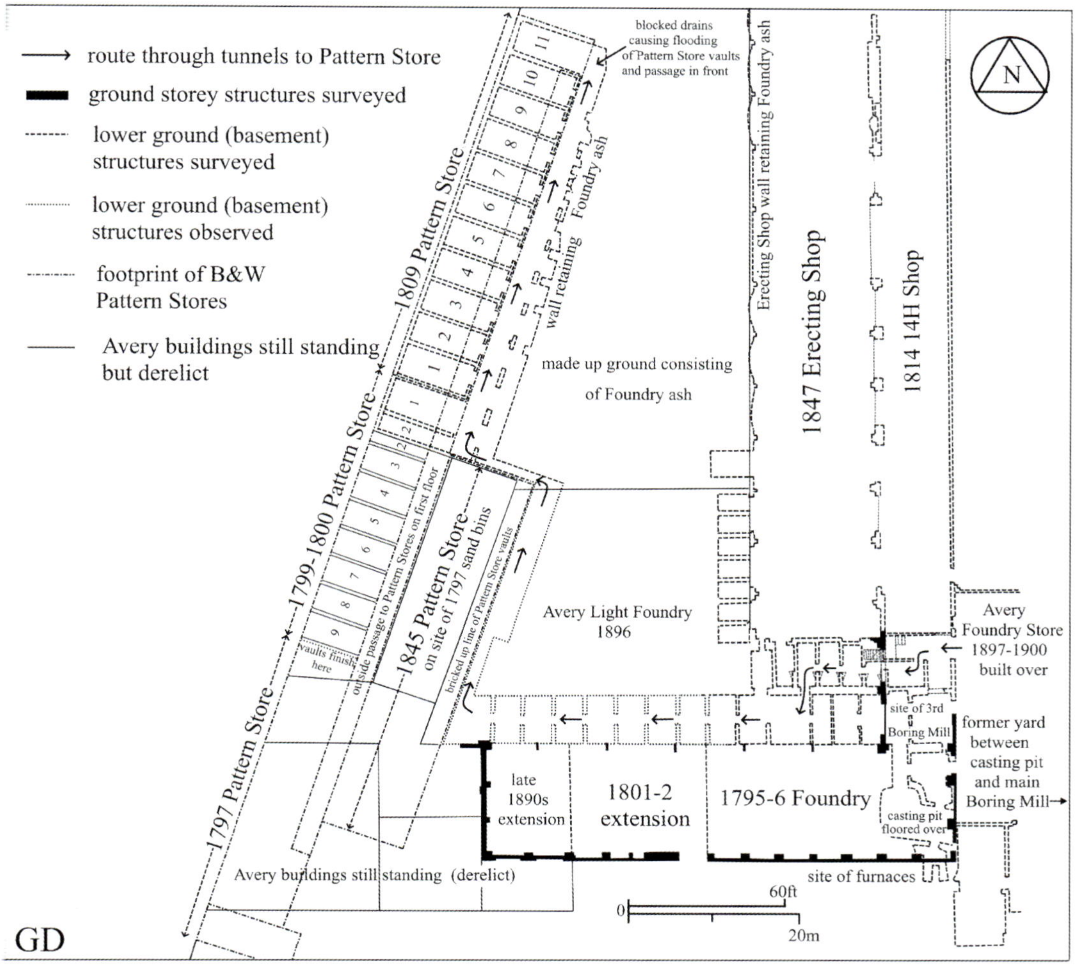

Fig 7.83
Plan showing the the Great Arch and connecting tunnels in relation to existing and lost buildings.

A Open-air sites

i The boring mill, turning shop and engine house (1796–1800).
ii Fitting shop (1795).
iii Small foundry (1802).
iv 6H shop (part) (1803) and extension (1811).
v 14H shop (east–west wing) (1814, 1852).
vi Gasometer (1848).
vii Canal basin (1795–6).
viii Grinding house, pattern turning shop (1824), extension (1851).
xi Culverts for drainage, water supply to steam engines and other uses, underground steam and gas pipes, the Casson (pool).
x Ash spoil (1795–).
xi Abandoned line of Birmingham Canal.

B Sites within Boulton & Watt and James Watt & Co buildings, subject to Health and Safety requirements.

i The foundry (1795–6, 1801–2, 1860).
ii The pattern stores (1797, 1799–1800).
iii The erecting shop (1847).
iv The 14H shop attached on east side (north–south wing) (1814).
V The Soho Foundry mint (1860).

C Sites within Avery Weigh-Tronix buildings and site

i Porters lodge (1795).
ii Carpenters shops (1795, 1798).
iii Smithy (1795, 1797, 1824).
iv Magazine (1795).
v The first terrace of houses (1796).
vi Office (1804).
vii Boiler sheds (1809–16, 1823, 1824).
viii Blowing engine house (1824).
ix Gas retort shed and gasometer house (1824).
x Gas purifying house (1848).

Fig 7.85
The south elevation of the main foundry building, 1996.

Fig 7.86
The east gable and south elevation of the main foundry building, 1996. The groups of three vertical brick scars on the south elevation represent the position of the demolished air furnaces. The large blocked round-headed windows and oculi once lit the casting pits at this end of the building. In the late 1890s Averys replaced the steeply pitched roof with Belfast trusses, removing the top of the gable.

Fig 7.87
The interior of the main foundry building looking east, 2018. The brick structure was built over the position of the casting pits. To the left the timber boxes shroud the scaffolding towers which support the present temporary roof.

Fig 7.88
The 'James Watt and Co' painted sign on north gable of the 1847 Erecting Shop, 2018. It was previously obscured by the Avery's weighbridge shop, now demolished. The former Boulton & Watt 14H shop, heightened by Averys, runs parallel to the Erecting Shop to the left and was extended at the same height by Averys to the right.

Fig 7.89
Vault (no 6) on north side of the main foundry building off the Great Arch, 2001; this was once an open passage with a bridge over at the far end. Vault no 5 lies to the right and within the wall to the left is possibly William Murdoch's laboratory (see Fig 7.20).

Fig 7.90
The east end of the 'Great Arch' at the site of the little boring mill, 2006 (see Figs 7.34 and 7.35)

Fig 7.91
The 1809 Pattern Store vaults, 2008. The vaults gradually increase in height away from the viewpoint taking advantage of a downward slope. Unfortunately the drainage at the far end has been blocked for some time and in 2008 the demolition of the Averys' Pattern Stores above brought down rubble and rubbish into the water.

Fig 7.92
The battered wall made of waste clinker supporting the ash bank, 2008. In the late 1890s it was strengthened by Averys with massive brick buttresses and the arches supported their new Pattern Stores above (now demolished). This wall stands opposite the Pattern Store vaults.

Fig 7.93
The 1847 erecting shop looking south, 2018 (see Fig 7.50 for the scene in 1895).

Fig 7.94
The 14H shop looking south, 2018. Sharing the wall on the right is the 1847 erecting shop, which was once lit by a middle tier of windows, now blocked. Averys heightened the left-hand-side wall of the 14H shop and raised a new Belfast roof over. A top tier of windows above the Belfast roof continues to light the erecting shop.

8

The significance of the three Sohos

Introduction

The study of the three Soho sites leads ultimately to one question: how significant were the technical processes, methods of organisation, and the buildings in which they were contained to the nature and momentum of the Industrial Revolution of the late 18th century? Giving an answer is fraught with difficulty, not least because the Industrial Revolution itself as a concept is notoriously hard to define. There is not even agreement that such a transformation actually happened. This is not the place, however, to analyse this recent, complex debate, but if any attempt is to be made to place the Manufactory in its economic and technological context, an outline of the main issues is necessary.[1]

Among those who accept that there was an Industrial Revolution in Britain, it is now generally agreed that it took place in different regions at different times and that its nature varied from place to place. The over-concentration by scholars in the past on the cotton and iron industries has been much criticised.[2] It is contended that this traditional approach has distorted our perception of the economic and technological changes that took place in the 18th and 19th, centuries, thus obscuring the major part played by small-scale domestic industry: the heroic, male-orientated domain of large factories with their powered machinery has overshadowed the role of small workshops and women in the workforce.[3] Likewise, economic historians have been traditionally obsessed by macroeconomics, population growth indices, capital formation, productivity and the like. This approach has also been challenged, as it tended to ignore regional variation and the inventiveness and adaptability of local communities. However, in the justifiable attempt to revise the orthodox view of the Industrial Revolution, there was always a danger that 'the baby would be thrown out with the bathwater' and this is exactly what happened: a school of thought emerged that asserted there had, in fact, never been an 'Industrial Revolution' – instead, slow continuous growth and continuity had prevailed.[4] The concept of 'gradualism' ousted the idea of a revolution. Not surprisingly, the new orthodoxy was as untenable as the old, as anyone who has studied 18th- and 19th-century Britain closely could easily appreciate. From the perspective of Soho and Birmingham, 'the current wave of writing which seeks to iron out the industrial revolution to a trivial rate of British economic growth' seems absurd.[5] One has only to examine the phenomenal rates of growth of Birmingham's population, which trebled between 1750 and 1801 and quadrupled in the next 60 years to 1861.[6] Reformulating these same statistics, the population of Birmingham increased by a factor of 13 between 1750 and 1861. This rate of growth was not sustainable by a predominantly agricultural society and could only be an expression of the dramatic economic changes that were taking place in Britain during this time, still best described by the battered (but not obsolete) term, the Industrial Revolution.

The notion of factory production, also of immediate relevance to Soho, has undergone similar problems of definition and revision. Despite the complexities and, at times, the elusiveness of the concept of the 'factory', it would be difficult to carry the discussion further without it. Ure considered that machinery and power were essential elements of the factory system.[7] Mantoux also claimed that machinery gave factories their special character, distinguishing them from manufactories, whose principal mode of production was the division of labour. He was, however, more circumspect, preferring to see the manufactory merge gradually and imperceptibly into the factory system: 'different moments in the course of one and the same evolution'.[8] Tann dispensed with these distinctions altogether and held that the fundamental characteristics of the factory system were the concentration of the means of production, with or without powered machinery, alongside requisite organisational changes.[9]

In the analysis of significance, the Soho Manufactory and Mint will be treated separately from the Soho Foundry. Although several of the themes discussed are common to both sites, the Foundry had a sufficiently distinct origin and function to justify this approach. Much of the discussion in the first section will be dominated by the Manufactory as a whole and reference to the Mint as an individual enterprise will appear as appropriate. The evidence from eyewitnesses is of value here, usually recorded in diaries following their visit to the works. Thus current opinion and reaction with the benefit of direct observance can augment and complement our own view of the Soho phenomenon studied with the advantage of hindsight.

The Soho Manufactory and Mint

The size of the Manufactory

There is no doubt that the Manufactory was a large establishment. Contemporary accounts describe between 400 and 1,000 workers in employment, the most frequent figures quoted being in the range 600–700.[10] The true total at any one time is difficult to establish, as there are no contemporary lists of all the employees, but it certainly was not static, perhaps averaging 600 and fluctuating in line with trading conditions. Numbers also had a general tendency to increase as the Manufactory expanded from a watermill and a few workshops in the early 1760s to its maximum size in the early 1820s after several extensions of the engine works. In 1776, there were 132 rooms and workshops listed (just over 32,000 sq ft/2,972.8 sq m).[11] At their maximum extent, the Manufactory buildings covered an area, including courts, of about 90,000 sq ft (8,361 sq m). By contrast, the hardware trade in the town of Birmingham, two miles distant, was characterised by much smaller units of production, the workshops rather than the factory, so that Soho stood out as an extreme. 'There are no large and crowded factories such as abound in the other districts', remarked a factory inspector in 1843.[12] It was not until the mid-19th century, however, that other enterprises in Birmingham reached the totals of over 500 employed by Soho.[13] As late as 1835, only 5 out of 43 cotton mills in Manchester, within archetypal factory territory, employed between 400 and 700 hands.[14]

Matthew Boulton, the great salesman, may be excused his hyperbole in claiming he had the largest hardware manufactory in the world, but a French visitor wrote before 1782 that Soho was 'une des manufactures les plus etendues de la Grande Bretagne ... Six cent personnes sont occupées ... dans une vaste edifice tres bien construit' (one of the most extensive manufactories in Great Britain ... Six hundred people are employed ... in a spacious, well-constructed building).[15]

The size of the Soho Manufactory reflected one of the fundamental characteristics of the factory system: the concentration of the means of production.[16] This concentration may have been forced on Boulton in the very early years to avoid the inefficiencies of production at two separate sites. Thereupon, in true Boulton style, exigencies were quickly translated into grand ambition, and the scale of the new buildings surpassed anything that had been known previously in the Birmingham toy trade. Although many of the processes at the Manufactory were labour-intensive, this does not dilute the fact that Soho was a factory from about the mid-1760s. Concentration of the means of production demanded basic changes in organisation even if little machinery was involved. This was certainly the case at Soho in the earliest years when power was contained within the watermill alone. Organisational changes, such as the introduction of the division of labour, were equally characteristic of the factory system and prevailed at the Manufactory.

Specialisation and the division of labour

Although the Soho Manufactory was not the first to divide production into specialised tasks, what distinguished it from many other enterprises in the hardware and engineering trades was the degree to which division of labour was applied. Yet there was still opportunity for some of the most talented craftsmen and women in the country to display their skill in, for example, the manufacture of ormolu and silverware. Not all work was reduced to the dull, repetitive activity so typical of later mass production techniques.

alongside the Manufactory. But he was not happy just to see his Soho Mint successfully at work; the whole world deserved to have good coinage. Considering the difficulties of transporting heavy equipment across the globe in sailing ships at this time, it was a remarkable achievement to have exported and set up steam-powered mints in such far-flung places as St Petersburg (Russia), India and Mexico. Much of this effort was to fall upon the shoulders of Matthew Robinson Boulton, whose accomplishments as an engineer and exporter of technology have not generally been appreciated.

Among the better-known names is John Rennie, who established his career helping to design the new rolling and lapping mill at Soho, introducing cast iron gearing, which had been rarely used before, and went on to help set up the Albion Mill, the first steam-engine driven corn mill. William Murdoch is best known for inventing gas lighting and applying it at the Soho Foundry. He is less well known for his role in designing the machinery to go into the major extension to the engine works at the Manufactory in 1802–4. Here, in the mid-1770s, had been established the world's first steam-engine works, admittedly for the manufacture of only a limited number of small parts. Murdoch installed two small engines to his own design, which were the earliest known working versions of the table engine, patented in 1807 by Henry Maudsley.

The number of technological 'firsts' registered at Soho may never be fully counted. It is worth quoting James Watt's own words from his memoir of Boulton: 'To enter into all the various mechanical improvements which have been due either to his own invention or to his fatherly patronage is beyond my powers; of some I may never have heard, & others may have slipt my memory'.[34]

The Manufactory buildings

Most of the buildings at the Manufactory had a utilitarian function and appearance. Though there is little detailed surviving evidence of their structure, it is likely that the basic envelope consisted of brick walls, pierced by cast iron or timber windows where needed, and timber-truss roofs covered in slate or plain tiles. Late 19th-century photographs of the Foundry indicate that the building techniques employed there were, on the whole, traditional.[35] These comments would apply to the workshops, forges, engine houses and watermill situated below and behind the principal building, except for 'Rolling Mill Row', where an effort seems to have been made to create a more than commonplace façade in the very early 1760s. It is not unexpected that visitors marvelled at the contents, 'the prodigious number of different tools ... the mechanical inventions ... superior in multitude, variety, and simplicity from those of any manufactory in the known world'.[36] The buildings themselves, except for their scale and number, were hardly distinguishable from any other industrial premises at the time.

The same cannot be said for the principal building, designed by the architect William Wyatt, which commanded attention even during construction. Known early on as 'the mansion', it was (according to Jabez Fisher) 'like the stately Palace of some Duke'.[37] The desired effect had been achieved on Boulton's visitor, whose comments on the canals in the Soho gardens – that they answered 'the *Dulce* as well as the Utile' – could equally apply to the principal building. In the 18th century a small number of factory owners such as Josiah Wedgwood and Richard Arkwright were concerned with aesthetics, none more so than Matthew Boulton. Another need was satisfied by the 'movement towards a conscious architectural style': that of the social aspiration of nouveau riche entrepreneurs to be accepted by the old order who already possessed their elegant Georgian country homes.[38] By the mid-19th century, the desire of manufacturers to apply the latest architectural style had decreased sharply. Factories tended to be located in urban areas with their owners escaping to the countryside to set up residence. In the demolition of the principal building in 1863, there was lost not only a classic exercise in English Palladianism, but also an exemplar of the social and aesthetic aspirations of a new class of entrepreneurs.

The housing built by Boulton at the Manufactory has received little attention in the literature. All the dwellings were constructed in the 1760s and were located in four places: in the terrace called Brook Row, in parts of Pool Row or Rolling Mill Row, and in two wings of the principal building.[39] The housing was interlocked with the industrial premises and did not form a distinct residential quarter. It is not known for whom the houses, totalling about 22, were originally intended.[40] Considering the size of the workforce, even as early as the 1760s, only a very small minority could have been housed on-site. Most had to travel, presumably on foot, moments in the course of one and the same evolution'.[8] Tann dispensed with these distinctions altogether and held that the fundamental characteristics of the factory system were the concentration of the means of production, with or without powered machinery, alongside requisite organisational changes.[9]

In the analysis of significance, the Soho Manufactory and Mint will be treated separately from the Soho Foundry. Although several of the themes discussed are common to both sites, the Foundry had a sufficiently distinct origin and function to justify this approach. Much of the discussion in the first section will be dominated by the Manufactory as a whole and reference to the Mint as an individual enterprise will appear as appropriate. The evidence from eyewitnesses is of value here, usually recorded in diaries following their visit to the works. Thus current opinion and reaction with the benefit of direct observance can augment and complement our own view of the Soho phenomenon studied with the advantage of hindsight.

The Soho Manufactory and Mint

The size of the Manufactory

There is no doubt that the Manufactory was a large establishment. Contemporary accounts describe between 400 and 1,000 workers in employment, the most frequent figures quoted being in the range 600–700.[10] The true total at any one time is difficult to establish, as there are no contemporary lists of all the employees, but it certainly was not static, perhaps averaging 600 and fluctuating in line with trading conditions. Numbers also had a general tendency to increase as the Manufactory expanded from a watermill and a few workshops in the early 1760s to its maximum size in the early 1820s after several extensions of the engine works. In 1776, there were 132 rooms and workshops listed (just over 32,000 sq ft/2,972.8 sq m).[11] At their maximum extent, the Manufactory buildings covered an area, including courts, of about 90,000 sq ft (8,361 sq m). By contrast, the hardware trade in the town of Birmingham, two miles distant, was characterised by much smaller units of production, the workshops rather than the factory, so that Soho stood out as an extreme. 'There are no large and crowded factories such as abound in the other districts', remarked a factory inspector in 1843.[12] It was not until the mid-19th century, however, that other enterprises in Birmingham reached the totals of over 500 employed by Soho.[13] As late as 1835, only 5 out of 43 cotton mills in Manchester, within archetypal factory territory, employed between 400 and 700 hands.[14]

Matthew Boulton, the great salesman, may be excused his hyperbole in claiming he had the largest hardware manufactory in the world, but a French visitor wrote before 1782 that Soho was 'une des manufactures les plus etendues de la Grande Bretagne ... Six cent personnes sont occupées ... dans une vaste edifice tres bien construit' (one of the most extensive manufactories in Great Britain ... Six hundred people are employed ... in a spacious, well-constructed building).[15]

The size of the Soho Manufactory reflected one of the fundamental characteristics of the factory system: the concentration of the means of production.[16] This concentration may have been forced on Boulton in the very early years to avoid the inefficiencies of production at two separate sites. Thereupon, in true Boulton style, exigencies were quickly translated into grand ambition, and the scale of the new buildings surpassed anything that had been known previously in the Birmingham toy trade. Although many of the processes at the Manufactory were labour-intensive, this does not dilute the fact that Soho was a factory from about the mid-1760s. Concentration of the means of production demanded basic changes in organisation even if little machinery was involved. This was certainly the case at Soho in the earliest years when power was contained within the watermill alone. Organisational changes, such as the introduction of the division of labour, were equally characteristic of the factory system and prevailed at the Manufactory.

Specialisation and the division of labour

Although the Soho Manufactory was not the first to divide production into specialised tasks, what distinguished it from many other enterprises in the hardware and engineering trades was the degree to which division of labour was applied. Yet there was still opportunity for some of the most talented craftsmen and women in the country to display their skill in, for example, the manufacture of ormolu and silverware. Not all work was reduced to the dull, repetitive activity so typical of later mass production techniques.

Division of labour can be viewed from a technical and a managerial point of view. In the former, a manufacturing process, such as the making of a button, is broken down into a number of tasks, each performed by an individual worker and each forming a link in a chain from raw materials to finished product. At Soho, there was much evidence of the specialisation of production, reflected, for example, in the wide variety of workshops in the button-making business: the burnishing shop, soldering shop, chasing shop, forging shop, and cutting-out shop to name but a few.[17] Visitors were impressed that, 'instead of employing the same hand to finish a button ... they subdivide it into as many different hands as possible ... Thus a button passes through fifty hands, and each hand perhaps passes a thousand in a day'.[18] 'Each workman has only a very limited range, so that he does not need constantly to change his position and tools and by this means an incredible amount of time is saved'.[19]

The management of labour employed in such great numbers – and assigned to so many different crafts and jobs – created both problems and opportunities. The Manufactory was not one vast building with goods moving along a fixed production line; it was more a series of discrete workshops or rooms through which products followed a much less easily defined geographical course. Most of the Soho workers were organised within these workshops, which were often named after a foreman to whom they were immediately answerable. So, for instance, in the button business in about 1788, among others there were Otley's burnishing shop, Thickbroom's forging shop, and Jerom's stamping shop.[20]

In Mantoux' classic definition of the manufactory, capital and labour were separated, and this was indeed the case at Soho where only Boulton and his senior partners (e.g. Fothergill and Watt) were capital investors.[21] The Soho workshop system was very dependent upon the assiduousness and integrity of the employees and waged foremen, particularly when Boulton and his partners were so frequently away from Soho. With no middle tier of management 'to hold the fort', abuses occurred, encouraged by the fact that much work was paid on a day rate. For example, John Scale complained to Boulton: 'Sanders goes on very slowly in the pearl cutting out shop & I am sure he will do no good until he has it piece work'.[22] Scale himself promised to 'cut out' for a half-day to establish a piece rate, but the perennial problem at Soho – with its vast range of products – was the lack of standardisation, which prevented reliable piecework rates being determined. Joshua Field observed as late as 1821 at the engine works that 'The regular parts of the engine are given piece work but some parts cannot and all new work is day work'.[23] The real picture was more complicated, as Roll's analysis of the wages and labour conditions in the engine yards shows, but what is missing from the Soho archives is the workers' perspective and viewpoint.[24] Generally, information on working conditions, industrial relations, and on the organisation of production at the workshop level is difficult to find.

It would be misleading to suggest that the Manufactory was predominantly staffed by highly skilled craftsmen, albeit engaged in narrow bands of work. The division of labour was intended to create simple, routine and repetitive tasks, and the consequent deskilling allowed the Soho firms to exploit the cheap labour of women and children. Boulton had no qualms about employing youngsters to attend the various machines, such as the coin presses, but it appears that this practice was not as prevalent in the Manufactory as it was in other contemporary establishments.[25] Another observer remarked that, 'The work becomes so simple that, five times in six, children of six and eight years of age do it as well as men, and each from ten pence to eight shillings a week'.[26] It may be assumed that women generally undertook more menial tasks – commanding a position in wage labour between the children and the unskilled men – but evidence for this is scanty. It is known, however, that they did skilled work as lappers in the mill.[27]

It comes as no surprise that, as well as its scale, the very organisation of work impressed visitors. One of the most perceptive and eloquent, Jabez Maud Fisher, described it thus: 'The whole Scene is a Theatre of Business, all conducted like one piece of Mechanism, Men, Women and Children full of employment according to their Strength and Docility ... a little Army of all ages'.[28] Though not novel, what he saw had little precedent.

Diversification

The Manufactory astonished all with its range of products. In view of this diverse output, Soho was more akin to an industrial complex than to a single factory. It must be said that the choice of products was almost entirely due to Boulton's aspirations and ambition, and it is unlikely that a large factory making Birmingham toys would have acquired a steam-engine business and mint by the end of the 18th century under anyone else's direction. In this diversity, Boulton was well ahead of his time, as most existing factories were devoted to a single or a closely related range of goods such as cotton cloth or ceramics. The wide spectrum of products also meant that economic booms and slumps could be smoothed out and the complete failure of a business dependent on a single product avoided. For many years, the profits from the engine business sustained Boulton's other Soho concerns such as the plate and button companies.[29] Whether Boulton's multiplicity of interests had commercial durability as the prime aim is doubtful. They were more likely the consequence of his personality: a craving to experiment, discover and innovate. Fisher's eloquence encapsulates his restless character:

> like many other great Men he has his hobby horse. He is scheming and changeable, ever some matter on the Anvil to divert his attention from a steady pursuit of some grand object. He is always inventing, and by the time he has brought his Scheme to Perfection, some new Affair offers itself. He deserts the old, follows the new, of which he is weary by the time he has arrived at it. This Volatility prevents him from becoming very rich.[30]

An immense number of articles were produced at Soho, but selecting only a few should give a reasonable impression: buttons, buckles, chains and boxes in all variety of metals, ormolu vases and clock cases, silver and silver-plated candlesticks, tureens and bowls, coins and medals, letter- and drawing-copying machines, and last – but not least – steam engines for pumping water, driving machinery, and powering boats and ships. More comprehensive listings of just his metal-ware products can be found elsewhere, but is no wonder that when Josiah Wedgwood visited Soho in 1767 he recognised Boulton as 'the most complete manufacturer in England in metal'.[31] Soho products could be found in the palaces of kings and empresses, on the tables of the urban middle class, in the counting houses of businesses, in factories, mills and mines, and in the pockets or purses of every citizen. The Birmingham toy trade had a reputation for tawdriness and poor quality. Boulton, using the Soho production techniques and the network of contacts he built up among the nobility, changed the toy trade image so that high quality could be purchased relatively cheaply but, it must be stressed, still at a price that only middle-class and aristocratic customers could afford.

The variety of Soho wares was produced in a complex of partnerships and firms discussed in Chapter 9. Diversification of production, managed by an elaborate commercial organisation, is more reminiscent of a large modern national or multinational company. By the turn of the 19th century, Boulton had created a prototype for such an enterprise, albeit imperfect. His genius consisted of an ever-shifting vision of what was feasible and what could be made, and the Soho Manufactory, as the physical manifestation of this genius, occupies an important place in the history of manufacturing.

Technological advance and innovation

Soho is most frequently remembered as the place where James Watt's steam engine was developed and represents, therefore, a potent image in steam-engine folklore and mystique. Watt's condenser was undoubtedly innovatory, along with subsequent advances such as the parallel motion and rotary steam-power applications. This story has been told many times before and need not be recounted here,[32] but it is worth repeating that the first Watt engine to do any practical work was installed at Soho to recycle mill water. Watt's invention of the first practical letter-copying machine and its production at Soho is often overlooked.

Soho was a hotbed of invention associated with many distinguished engineers of the Industrial Revolution. Boulton himself was a practical and ingenious man:

> the first Inventor of the inlaid buttons, & the first who applied a mill to turn the Laps ... and a shaking box put in motion by the mill ... was also a thought of Mr B[oulton] ... In the method of forming the rollers or cylinders which laminate the metal [in the rolling mill] & in other points connected with it much merit is due to Mr B[oulton].[33]

Matthew Boulton immediately saw the practical applications of rotary steam power and was the first to test steam-driven forge hammers and corn-grinding machinery in a corner of the infant engine yard. Then, with his assistants (most notably John Southern), he perfected presses for coining and cutting out blanks and built the first steam-powered mint in the world alongside the Manufactory. But he was not happy just to see his Soho Mint successfully at work; the whole world deserved to have good coinage. Considering the difficulties of transporting heavy equipment across the globe in sailing ships at this time, it was a remarkable achievement to have exported and set up steam-powered mints in such far-flung places as St Petersburg (Russia), India and Mexico. Much of this effort was to fall upon the shoulders of Matthew Robinson Boulton, whose accomplishments as an engineer and exporter of technology have not generally been appreciated.

Among the better-known names is John Rennie, who established his career helping to design the new rolling and lapping mill at Soho, introducing cast iron gearing, which had been rarely used before, and went on to help set up the Albion Mill, the first steam-engine driven corn mill. William Murdoch is best known for inventing gas lighting and applying it at the Soho Foundry. He is less well known for his role in designing the machinery to go into the major extension to the engine works at the Manufactory in 1802–4. Here, in the mid-1770s, had been established the world's first steam-engine works, admittedly for the manufacture of only a limited number of small parts. Murdoch installed two small engines to his own design, which were the earliest known working versions of the table engine, patented in 1807 by Henry Maudsley.

The number of technological 'firsts' registered at Soho may never be fully counted. It is worth quoting James Watt's own words from his memoir of Boulton: 'To enter into all the various mechanical improvements which have been due either to his own invention or to his fatherly patronage is beyond my powers; of some I may never have heard, & others may have slipt my memory'.[34]

The Manufactory buildings

Most of the buildings at the Manufactory had a utilitarian function and appearance. Though there is little detailed surviving evidence of their structure, it is likely that the basic envelope consisted of brick walls, pierced by cast iron or timber windows where needed, and timber-truss roofs covered in slate or plain tiles. Late 19th-century photographs of the Foundry indicate that the building techniques employed there were, on the whole, traditional.[35] These comments would apply to the workshops, forges, engine houses and watermill situated below and behind the principal building, except for 'Rolling Mill Row', where an effort seems to have been made to create a more than commonplace façade in the very early 1760s. It is not unexpected that visitors marvelled at the contents, 'the prodigious number of different tools ... the mechanical inventions ... superior in multitude, variety, and simplicity from those of any manufactory in the known world'.[36] The buildings themselves, except for their scale and number, were hardly distinguishable from any other industrial premises at the time.

The same cannot be said for the principal building, designed by the architect William Wyatt, which commanded attention even during construction. Known early on as 'the mansion', it was (according to Jabez Fisher) 'like the stately Palace of some Duke'.[37] The desired effect had been achieved on Boulton's visitor, whose comments on the canals in the Soho gardens – that they answered 'the *Dulce* as well as the Utile' – could equally apply to the principal building. In the 18th century a small number of factory owners such as Josiah Wedgwood and Richard Arkwright were concerned with aesthetics, none more so than Matthew Boulton. Another need was satisfied by the 'movement towards a conscious architectural style': that of the social aspiration of nouveau riche entrepreneurs to be accepted by the old order who already possessed their elegant Georgian country homes.[38] By the mid-19th century, the desire of manufacturers to apply the latest architectural style had decreased sharply. Factories tended to be located in urban areas with their owners escaping to the countryside to set up residence. In the demolition of the principal building in 1863, there was lost not only a classic exercise in English Palladianism, but also an exemplar of the social and aesthetic aspirations of a new class of entrepreneurs.

The housing built by Boulton at the Manufactory has received little attention in the literature. All the dwellings were constructed in the 1760s and were located in four places: in the terrace called Brook Row, in parts of Pool Row or Rolling Mill Row, and in two wings of the principal building.[39] The housing was interlocked with the industrial premises and did not form a distinct residential quarter. It is not known for whom the houses, totalling about 22, were originally intended.[40] Considering the size of the workforce, even as early as the 1760s, only a very small minority could have been housed on-site. Most had to travel, presumably on foot, from the surrounding scattered settlements and hamlets and from Birmingham two miles away. Nevertheless, the housing may have acted as an incentive to attract certain workers put off by the isolation of the new works. Later records generally indicate that more senior staff, such as foremen and clerks, were allocated the accommodation for which a rent was paid. James Watt Jr and Matthew Robinson Boulton are known to have lived at the Manufactory early in their Soho careers. It is interesting that in the late 1790s, soon after the Foundry was built at Smethwick, a terrace of housing was added. Allotments were also provided for the live-in employees both at the Manufactory and at the Foundry.

Much work needs to be done to establish the true purpose of the Soho housing and whether its function changed over time. Until this is carried out, it will be difficult to assess the contribution of Soho to the history of industrial housing. What is certain, however, is that housing for workers was rarely provided by manufacturers in the Birmingham area where small workshops rather than factories predominated. Employees were expected to walk to such small establishments from their own homes, regardless of distance. Elsewhere in the country, where there were large mills, particularly in isolated areas, a number of socially minded owners provided housing and other facilities for their workers. Well-known 18th-century examples include Richard Arkwright's Cromford Mill, Derbyshire, Robert Owen's New Lanark Mill in Scotland, and later, in the middle of the 19th century, Titus Salt laid out an almost small town of workers' terraces at Saltaire adjacent to his woollen mill north of Bradford.

Power

Tann's definition of a factory as a place where the means of production was concentrated (with or without powered machinery, but necessitating organisational changes) is the one most applicable to the Soho Manufactory. From 1761 to 1775, the only power source was a waterwheel, which, for the most part, ran lapping and rolling machinery. The power was contained within the mill itself, a relatively small building, and the great majority of workshops and rooms relied on hand- or foot-driven machines. Watt's steam engine, installed in 1775, provided no extra power directly for machinery but, in pumping water back to the waterwheel, allowed the mill to work for longer hours. Boulton was not the first to have water circulated in this way, a Newcomen engine being used for this purpose at Coalbrookdale in 1742 and at Carron in the 1760s.[41] He was nevertheless the first to use a Watt engine in this manner.

In 1779, Pickard's Mill – not far away at Snow Hill in Birmingham – was apparently the first in the world to apply a steam engine to rotary motion using a crank, with Boulton & Watt a close second.[42] It was not until the early 1780s that a steam engine began to run machinery directly at Soho, originally for experimenting with rotary motion. The experimental engines gave way to a permanent source of steam power to run lathes in the engine works. In 1802–4, a single engine was replaced by three small engines distributing power in four directions from the centrally placed engine house, but only within the Boulton & Watt premises. In 1788, a steam engine had been installed at the watermill to run the laps and a cutting-out machine, but, as with the waterwheel, its power was transmitted no further than the mill. In the same year, a steam engine was applied to the coin presses in the mint. For the next 50 years, the five steam engines, the pumping engine and the waterwheel provided the sources of power, but most of the processes at the Manufactory (as in the 1760s) relied on human effort. Only in the 1850s was another steam engine erected at Soho in the yard immediately behind the principal building.

Although the Soho Manufactory is one of the places synonymous with the Watt steam engine, it is both revealing and ironic that in this great factory the concentration of the means of production was not accompanied by a corresponding diffusion of powered machinery. This exemplified the nature of the metalworking industry in the Birmingham region, based predominantly on small workshops, where steam power was relatively unimportant until the 1830s.[43] Consequently, few Boulton & Watt engines were sold in the immediate area. Soho was exceptional in size, but its button and plated-ware trade was best suited to the production methods of workshops (albeit integrated) where mechanisation appeared to make little impact. Another factor may have been Boulton's lack of interest after about 1790 in the trades just mentioned, though they had originally given rise to the Manufactory. Put simply, powering coin presses interested him more than mechanising button and buckle stamps.

A new wonder of the world

The Soho Manufactory was regarded by many as a new wonder of the world, or rather a wonder of the new industrialising and technological world. Even Jabez Maud Fisher, one of the most perceptive and expressive of the Soho visitors, was groping for superlatives to describe what he saw: 'In Short the busy Scene is to[o] great for Description. Tis wonderful, astonishing, amazing'.[44] Such views must be taken seriously, as many of Boulton's guests were members of the old order: aristocratic and educated classes who might have felt a disdain for mechanics and manufacturing. Nevertheless, the travel diaries of the late 18th and early 19th century record the awe that visitors felt on being conducted around the Manufactory. J C Fisher wrote, 'I was dumfounded at what I saw. No description could do justice to the building in which these works are housed'.[45] Soho was added to the itinerary of many a gentlefolk's tour of the country for very good reason, and if the Manufactory had survived to the present day it would certainly be thronged with visitors.

In the late 18th century, the Manufactory was one of the largest industrial complexes in the country.[46] At the extremity of size for any industry and region, Soho represented an extraordinary concentration of the means of production for the period. This scale of enterprise meant that division of labour, not unusual in the toy and hardware industries of the Birmingham region, could be taken to hitherto unknown limits. Furthermore, the division of labour in these metal trades did not necessarily reduce the skill required by workers. Remarkable extremes were witnessed at Soho, from the highly skilled craftsmen in silver and ormolu to young boys feeding coin presses with blanks. The Manufactory comfortably embraced this spectrum of skill but, by the turn of the 19th century, it stood at an important transition point. From then on, factory production would increasingly deskill the workforce, converting tool users to mere attenders of machinery.

The Manufactory's large size came partly from the need to accommodate the production of a bewildering variety of products. Coining needed new mint buildings, and the slow evolution of steam-engine production required an ever-growing engine works. The wide product range was the brainchild of one man, Matthew Boulton. Consequently, the Soho Manufactory was held under one management or, more strictly speaking, by a complicated set of partnerships with Boulton at the hub. This organisational structure foreshadows the large industrial conglomerates or corporations of a later age producing a bewildering variety of products and services. Such companies are not necessarily located on one site and here again the existence of a separate production unit at the Soho Foundry anticipated modern industrial complexes.

There is no doubt that Soho brought together some of the most talented and innovative minds of the late 18th century. It distinguished itself by an impressive list of technological 'firsts' that led the way in many engineering fields and contributed significantly to the momentum of the Industrial Revolution. Engineers trained at Soho went on to forge eminent careers of their own. What is less easily understood is how this innovative energy was eventually spent when, as the 19th century progressed, Soho gradually slipped behind its competitors to end ignominiously in close-down and demolition.

In the past the buildings at the Soho Manufactory and Mint have been little studied. An attempt has been made here to rectify these matters, but there is still much that is not understood. For example, it is not yet known whether innovative building practices were used – the evidence suggests that they were not. On the other hand, the principal building was a grand exemplar of its age and genre; when 'Dulce' and 'Utile', quoting Jabez Fisher, were closer companions; when a factory on the heath was made to resemble a mansion on a country estate.[47] Without doubt, had the Manufactory survived to the present day, it would be one of the most visited industrial monuments in the country. The buildings would be as much an attraction as the story of the tools, machinery and engines that led the world on the engineering and metallurgical front for so many decades.

The Soho Manufactory was not the first factory, but it was one of the earliest and was famed as the biggest in the Birmingham area for some time. Its combination of products was, however, unique and therefore did not provide an obvious model for future industrialisation in the region. Many of its component parts, however, exerted much influence over subsequent developments both in the hardware and engineering trades. Soho was, in fact, like a huge imperfectly cut diamond: rarely found at this size and with a pattern of facets nearly impossible to reproduce. Many, but not all, of the facets shone brilliantly, casting influence in all directions. The 'Soho diamond' could not have been fashioned without Matthew Boulton, but, conversely, the man stood at an important conjuncture in industrial history that provided hitherto unavailable opportunities. In both generating and being impelled by the wave of advances brought about by contemporary industrialisation, the Soho Manufactory quickly transcended its origins as an overgrown toy and hardware workshop.

The Soho Foundry

The first purpose-built steam-engine manufactory in the world

The Soho Foundry was conceived and founded by the Boulton & Watt partnership in 1795 as an integrated engineering works dedicated to the manufacture of steam engines. This was a pioneering venture of fundamental importance, for in this period the engineering industry had barely developed. Before 1795, the various stages that can be identified in the production of a steam engine, e.g. melting, casting, boring, turning and drilling, fitting/assembly/erecting, were carried out, if at all, on a small scale in furnaces, foundries, forges and workshops scattered around the country. Locational factors – such as sources of fuel, raw materials and power (usually water) – caused this dispersion and, not surprisingly, fragmented ownership. Where larger-scale operations managed to develop, they made a variety of products. Steam engines had only been powering machines from about 1783 and initially rarely drove boring rods, lathes and drills. Engines were normally erected for the first time at the allotted site, out of parts of variable quality made in any number of different places. The Boulton & Watt solution to this expensive and time-consuming process was to make all the engine parts in their own manufactory, assemble as many as possible there and deliver the engine to the purchaser, who was then required to organise relatively little for its reception on site. Many products were already made this way, certainly at the Soho Manufactory; the novelty (necessitated by circumstances) consisted in the application of such techniques to the making of a complex engineered artefact such as a steam engine. Fortunately, the conjunction of events that precipitated the creation of the Soho Foundry was matched by a combination of technological and engineering advances that made the whole venture at least feasible. Matthew Boulton would have wished to have done it this way in 1769 just after he first met James Watt, but his idea was far ahead of the technological capability of that time. Even 25 years later, some of the best engineers in the country struggled to perfect the new Soho Foundry machinery.

The Soho Foundry was thus the first purpose-built engine manufactory in the world. It was to be followed by competitors, some of whom wished to take advantage of the expiry of the Watt patent. There was no greater immediate rival than Matthew Murray of the Round Foundry, Holbeck, Leeds. He established his engineering works a matter of months after the Soho Foundry to make flax-spinning machinery and general castings, but was soon producing steam engines. A report on the Round Foundry claimed it was the 'sole significant survival of the first generation of specialist engineering foundries' since the Soho Foundry retained 'almost no original features above ground'.[48] Clearly this is not the case, as has been demonstrated above, but the claim is not surprising in view of our knowledge of the industrial archaeology of early engineering works only 20 years ago. Fortunately, in recent years our understanding of the two most important first-generation engineering foundries (Soho Foundry and Round Foundry) has been radically enhanced.[49] This is warning, however, that many more such sites, established after the Soho Foundry and the Round Foundry, may await discovery.

With our knowledge as yet incomplete, it is difficult, therefore, to establish the relationship, particularly within the context of the physical form, layout, and machinery and power systems, between the Soho Foundry and the many later steam engine firms and general engineering concerns. Some of the most important of these firms include Maudslay, Sons and Field (London), James Nasmyth (Eccles, near Manchester), Joseph Whitworth (Manchester), the Carron Works (Stirlingshire), and the Neath Abbey Works (Glamorganshire) and its sister concern the Perran Foundry (Cornwall). This list does not include the great locomotive works that do survive such as Robert Stephenson's factory in Newcastle and the Great Western works in Swindon. Whatever the nature of the descent from the Soho Foundry, there is no doubting the international significance of the site as the 'founder' of a great lineage in which Britain was pre-eminent in the world for much of the 19th century.

The association with the illustrious names of Boulton and Watt and the workplace of many of the great engineers of the Industrial Revolution

It is no coincidence that the first purpose-built steam-engine manufactory in the world was founded by the leading steam-engine firm, Boulton & Watt. The company attracted many engineers (for example, William Murdoch, John Southern and Peter Ewart) who, in devoting their working lives to the firm, made a name for themselves in their own right. The buildings were not merely workshops and places for the manufacture of products, but also laboratories for innovation and experiment. Great minds endow places with greatness and, conversely, celebrated places can inspire ingenuity and creativity.

The sons of Matthew Boulton and James Watt are less well known and their contribution has often been dismissed, but it is clear that James Watt Jr masterminded the creation of the Soho Foundry – no mean achievement. He was ably assisted by his business partner, Matthew Robinson Boulton, who (in turn) completely rebuilt and extended the engine works at the Soho Manufactory between 1802 and 1804.

Both partners were heavily dependent upon William Murdoch, whose supposed inability to compose a fine phrase in correspondence, and his straightforward and unsophisticated manner, meant he remained backstage, and willingly so, in the commercial, social and political milieu that the senior partners needed to frequent and to foster. These apparent social deficiencies were easily overcome by an engineering genius and inventiveness. On many occasions, William Murdoch was begged to return from his work at other engines in the country in order to solve a technological problem at the Soho Foundry, which remained at a standstill awaiting his appearance. These engineers benefited from the cross-fertilisation of ideas. It is little known that it was John Southern, no slouch as an inventor, who first suggested the use of permanent tanks for the storage of gas.

William Murdoch and the first factory in the world to be lit by gas

The Soho Foundry is synonymous with the very earliest experiments in gas lighting and the production of gas-lighting equipment on a commercial basis. In fact, it was the first factory in the world to be lit with gas generated in a fixed retort. Gas lighting was one of William Murdoch's great achievements, and the laboratory where he conducted experiments has been provisionally identified pending confirmation by archaeological investigation. Murdoch had begun experiments in Cornwall in the 1790s and transferred them to the Soho Foundry on his return in 1798, lighting part of the foundry. A little later, in 1802, the Peace of Amiens was celebrated at the Soho Manufactory by the illumination of the front of the principal building. A myth has arisen that all the illumination was produced from coal gas, but the truth is that only two lights (called 'Bengal lights') were produced from small retorts such as those tried in the foundry laboratory. In contrast to the Soho Foundry, the Soho Manufactory was not known to have been lit by gas. William Murdoch was beaten by a whisker in lighting the first industrial premises outside Soho. His supposed assistant in the Soho experiments, Samuel Clegg, set up on his own in 1805 and in the same year installed a gas-making plant at the cotton mill of Henry Lodge at Sowerby Bridge near Halifax. Two weeks later, Boulton & Watt illuminated the larger cotton mill of Philips and Lee at Salford.

Thereafter, until 1814, Boulton & Watt produced gas-making plant in the Soho Foundry for about 20 firms, and they were front runners with Samuel Clegg, by no coincidence another son of Soho, in the production and installation of gas-making equipment. The direction that Boulton & Watt chose, the installation of private plant at factories that could afford the cost, was not, however, to be the way forward in the longer term. Public supply, from a large independently located gasworks through pipes buried in the street, began in 1812 with the establishment of the Westminster Gas Light and Coke Company in London.

The association with the Soho Manufactory

The association of the Soho Foundry with the illustrious Soho Manufactory endowed the site with an instant celebrity, but, unfortunately, brought about much confusion. After the demolition of the last Manufactory building in 1863, the Soho Foundry stood alone as a monument to the Boulton & Watt achievement. It is important to stress that the survival of buildings at the Soho Foundry is made doubly significant in view of the loss of all the buildings above ground at the earlier enterprise.

The Soho Foundry and engine works at the Manufactory were inextricably linked in production and organisation. Further research, however, is required to establish a more detailed knowledge of this relationship and how it may have changed over time. What is clear already is that the closure of the Manufactory engine works in the early 1850s heralded a major expansion at the Soho Foundry. Room was made for many of the Manufactory engines and machinery with relatively little being abandoned.

The development of steamships

Although Boulton & Watt were not the first to install a steam engine in a boat, in 1804 they adapted a bell-crank engine and sent it to Robert Fulton in America to be used on a boat that first 'sailed' on the Hudson River in 1807. Production of marine engines began in earnest in 1817 with the purchase of the vessel *Caledonia*, which was used for trials involving a side-lever engine. The success of a voyage across the North Sea and up the River Rhine provided good publicity and generated a large number of orders.

The Boulton & Watt marine-engine business was one of the most important in the country during the 19th century. Its most celebrated contract, for which an extension to the Foundry boring mill was built in 1854–5 to house vertical-boring machinery, was for the screw engines of Brunel's ship *Great Eastern*. Although the *Great Eastern* did not become the greatest passenger ship in the world as Brunel had intended, it did successfully lay the first transatlantic radio telegraph cable.

An early producer of mint machinery

In 1788, Matthew Boulton established at the Soho Manufactory the first steam-powered mint in the world. The mint was radically redesigned in 1798–9 with the help of John Southern, and in the following decades mint machinery based on the new design principles was exported across the whole world to (for example) Mexico, Russia and India. The firm of Boulton & Watt acted as subcontractors to the Mint Company in the production of mint machinery, such as coining and cutting-out presses and milling machines, and most were made at the Soho Foundry. It was not unusual for any foundry to take on general work. The patterns for the mint machinery were stored in the Foundry pattern stores, which were inherited by James Watt & Co in 1848 after the demise of the company of Boulton & Watt. These patterns enabled James Watt & Co to continue mint machinery production after the Mint Company was dissolved at the Manufactory in 1850. Matthew Boulton's grandson, Matthew Piers Watt Boulton, closed the Soho Mint in 1850 and all the contents were sold. One press and its attendant parts was purchased by James Watt & Co, owners of the Soho Foundry, though it was not immediately used. In 1860, James Watt & Co built a new mint at the Soho Foundry based on the Boulton model. The fact that they called it the Soho Mint has contributed to the confusion between the two Soho sites. Further study is needed to reveal whether the Soho Foundry Mint is the only building in the world still standing that contained Boulton & Watt minting machinery.

The Soho Foundry in Midlands industrial history and archaeology

The Soho Foundry is one of the most important historical and archaeological sites in the West Midlands conurbation, exemplifying a region forged by industry. Given the number of iron-making sites and engineering works in the West Midlands in the 18th and 19th centuries, remarkably few have survived to the present day. The last 30 years have been particularly destructive, and without a systematic survey more sites will disappear unrecorded. There is only one early site comparable to the Soho

Foundry in the region: the grade II* listed Stourbridge Ironworks of Foster, Rastrick and Company. It dates from 1820–1 and is famous for producing in 1828 the first locomotives to run on a commercial railway in North America and in the Midlands.[50] It is a rare, surviving, second-generation engineering works in the region, helping to emphasise the uniqueness of the pioneering venture of the Soho Foundry.

The great archive of the Industrial Revolution – the Boulton and Watt Collection, Matthew Boulton Papers and the James Watt Papers

It goes without saying that without the massive Soho Archive lodged in the Library of Birmingham little of this book could have been written. The existence of this record confers a significance that embraces all three Soho sites. In its own right the Soho Archive constitutes one of the most important international collections on the Industrial Revolution and its aftermath. The depth and width of the material is astonishing and not restricted to Soho alone: the Boulton & Watt steam engine portfolios, for example, often provide the only surviving plans of a factory or industrial premises in this country or abroad. This book has inevitably used only a small proportion of the information that has been collected on the three Soho buildings.

The treasure that is the Soho Archive allows a multidisciplinary approach, demonstrating that the barriers that still exist between the study of archaeology and documentary history are, in many cases, unnecessary and constraining, hampering the efficacious study of material history.

Appendix 1

The archaeological excavations, 1994–6

Introduction

The Manufactory and Mint were comprehensively demolished in the mid-19th century, leaving few traces standing above ground in the years that followed (*see* Figs 5.37–5.40). Thanks to the preservation of the various Soho archives, detailed research has been able to reconstruct the appearance and function of the buildings. Two vital questions, however, still remained:

1 Had the archaeology of the Soho Manufactory and Mint survived below ground?
2 If so, would these remains contribute to our understanding of this nationally important industrial site?

The archaeological investigations, however, had further related research and planning aims:

a To locate the main buildings of the Soho complex as accurately as possible in the present built-up area.
b To establish whether the archaeological remains confirmed, supplemented or contradicted the documentary evidence, or provided entirely new information.
c To demonstrate the potency of combining

Fig A1.1
Location plan of archaeological excavations, Soho 1–6.

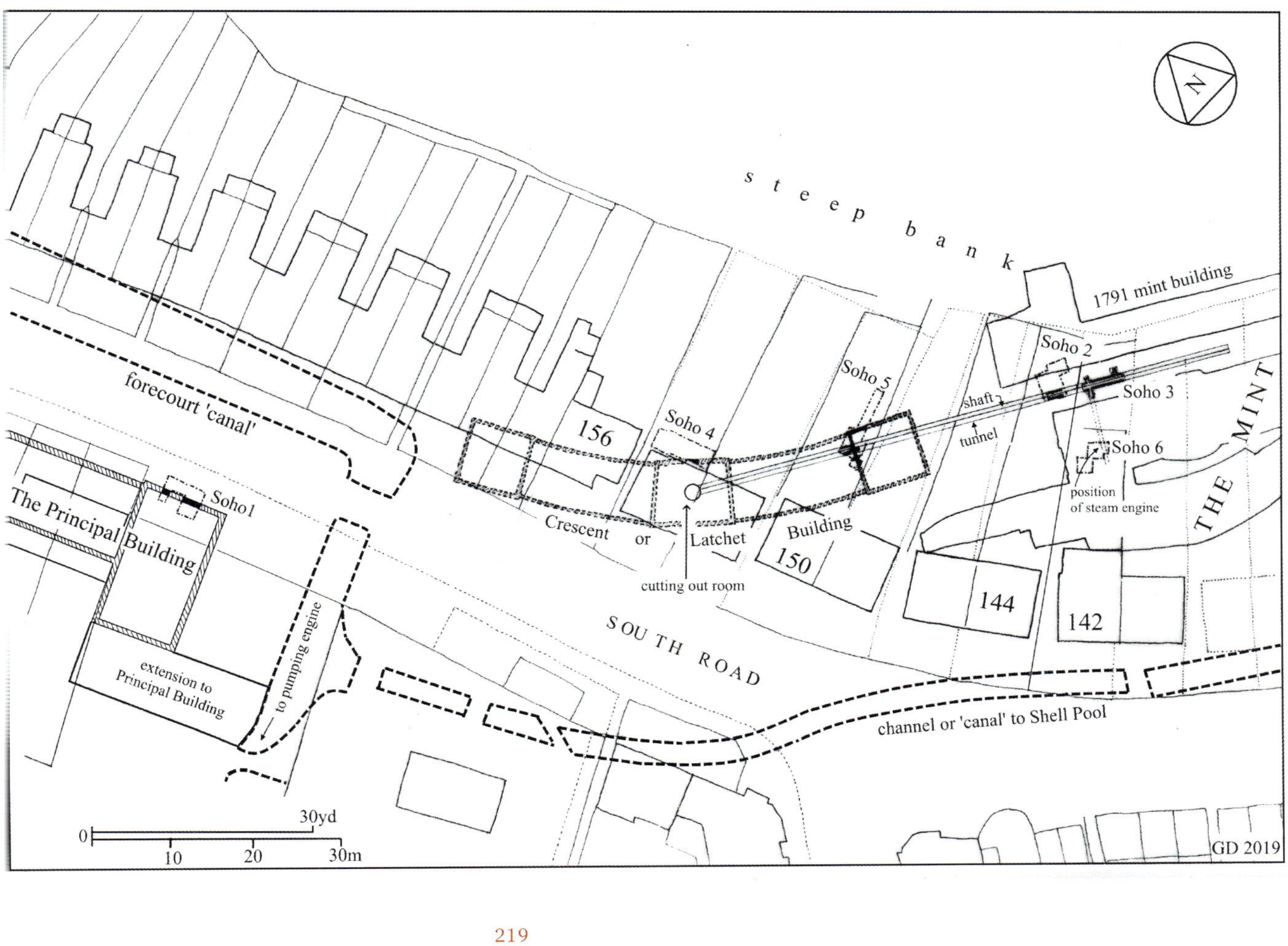

the archaeological and documentary approach to the study of the material past.

d To determine the depth, loss and state of preservation of the archaeological deposits.

The Soho excavations, 1994–6 (Fig A1.1)

Altogether six sites, designated Soho 1–6, were excavated. Soho 1 divides into Soho 1a and Soho 1b, the latter being a re-excavation. Soho 2 divides into 2a, 2b and 2c (Fig A1.25).

Soho 1a: The principal building (SP 05188903)

Objectives

The main aim of this excavation was to locate the south-east corner of the principal building in order to fix the position of the whole Manufactory complex. Overlaying the reconstructed plan of the Manufactory on the latest large-scale OS map suggested that this corner coincided with an open frontage to a factory unit at 241 South Road, but there was still a margin of error due to the inaccuracy of the early Soho estate maps. An advantage in choosing this corner, however, was the presence of cellars with concomitant deep foundations less vulnerable to robbing out on demolition or to disturbance by later building. These cellars underlay the accommodation end bays. The Board of Health map (1850–5) (*see* Fig 2.21) also indicated that the newly laid-out estate road, later to become South Road, in its first length used the terrace between the canal and the principal building. The line of the latter and the edge of South Road were, therefore, roughly coincident. The excavation had secondary aims of establishing the depth and state of preservation of the archaeological deposits.

This excavation, funded by the Conservation Team of Birmingham City Council, took place in November 1994. It was conducted by the former Birmingham University Field Archaeological Unit under the supervision of L A Jones and assisted by Mark Allen. Two trench positions had been agreed with the proviso of opening a third. The following account is based on the BUFAU report and my own observations.[1]

Description

Two trenches, Trench 1 and Trench 2, were opened. Trench 1 measured 2m × 1m and lay at right angles to the public footway; Trench 2 measured 1m × 1m and was dug against the public footway (Fig A1.2).

Trench 1 (Fig A1.3)

The trench was dug to a depth of 1.25m where it met natural geology (1007), a yellow-brown sandy clay. The south side of the trench coincided with the concrete casing of a petrol tank, which had cut into a distinct layer of demolition rubble containing whole red bricks (220mm × 105mm × 65mm) and broken bricks, fragments of green-grey slate, pinkish-white mortar and plaster all mixed in a reddish-brown sandy matrix (1004). This demolition layer in turn overlay the natural clay (1007) and a construction trench that had been cut into it to a depth of approximately 800mm (F1). In plan, it ran as a linear feature across the width of the trench and roughly parallel to the footway and building line. Within F1 were the remains of a brick wall (F2, 1006) standing at a maximum height of 0.45m and six courses of brick (220mm × 105mm × 65mm). The fill of F1 (1005) was yellowish-brown sand and gravel with pinkish-white mortar and a few brick fragments.

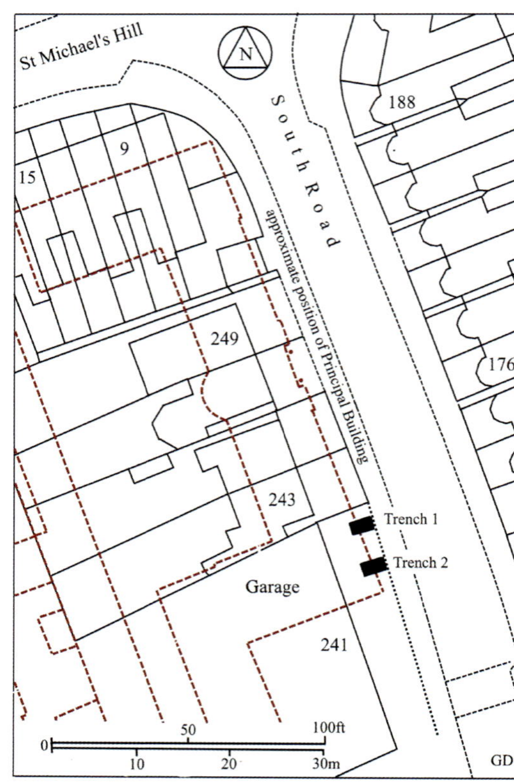

Fig A1.2
Location of trenches 1 and 2 of Soho 1, with outline of the principal building.

Trench 2

This trench was confined to a metre square alongside the footway, owing to the presence of the concrete top of a petrol tank, and was dug to a depth of about 1.2m where it encountered the same natural as in Trench 2. The limited amount of section that was available as a result was difficult to interpret and will not be discussed further.

Finds

Some 19th-century pottery was recovered from Trench 1 (1004) and brick, mortar and roof slate were sampled from the same layer.

Interpretation

Part of the wall (F2) found in Trench 1 ran in the expected direction parallel to South Road along the front terrace of the principal building. It was not possible to interpret this as the front wall, however, owing to the small size of the trench, which was not extended. Confirmation of its position in the building had to await the *Time Team* excavation (Soho 1b below).

The material sampled gave some information on the construction of the principal building. The bricks were fired to a consistent orange-red, which would have given the building (were it not rendered) a distinctive tone. However, the evidence for either a brick or stucco finish is inconclusive. Fragments of grey-green slate found support the documentary references to Westmorland slate being delivered by sea and then via the Severn to Bewdley.[2]

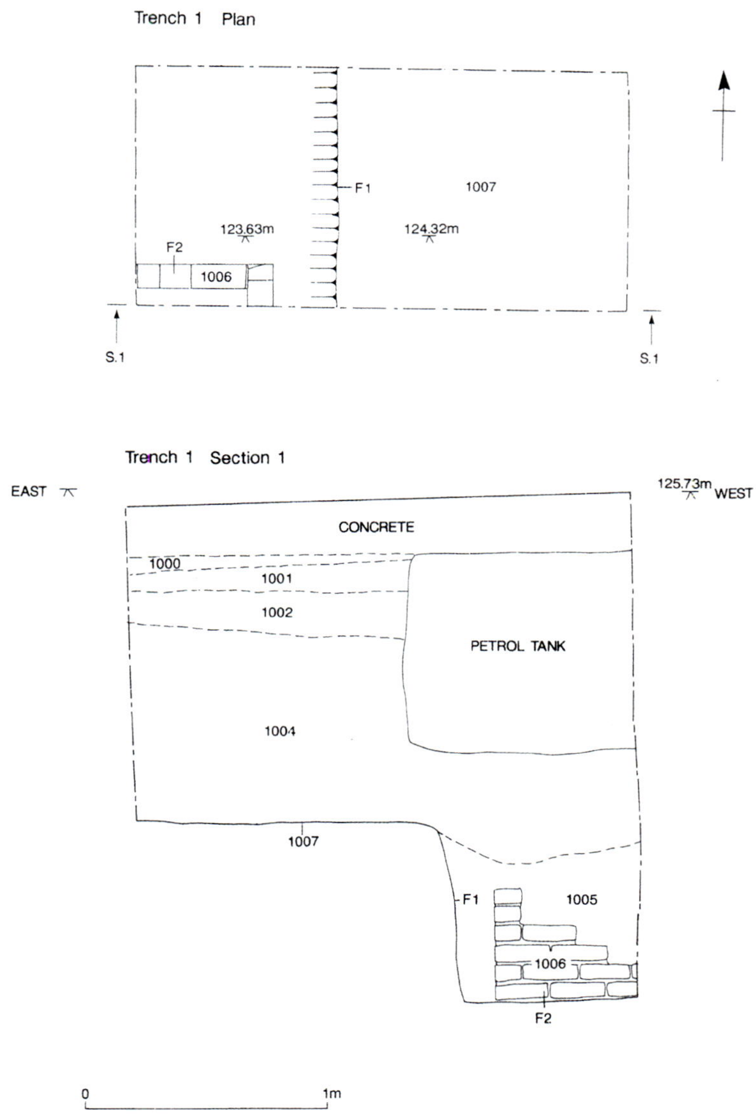

Fig A1.3
Soho 1a, cross section and plan.

Soho 1b: The principal building, *Time Team* 1996 (SP 05188903)

Objectives (Fig A1.24)

The Soho 1b excavation was undertaken to achieve the original aims of Soho 1a, which is to locate the corner of the principal building. A larger area of the forecourt around Trench 1 was opened up but avoiding the obvious constrictions around Trench 2.

Description (Fig A1.4)

The trench measured 5.4m × 3.3m and, at its maximum, was 2.3m deep. On plan, the largest feature was the petrol tank, which was a metal cylinder mostly encased in concrete (F1): the visible casing measured 2.3m × 1.7m, with its longitudinal axis at right angles to South Road. The south side of the trench revealed the concrete wall of a second tank, the one that restricted Soho 1a, Trench 2. The more significant feature was a brick wall (F2) that ran below and between both tanks. It was composed of red brick (215mm ×105mm × 60mm) bonded irregularly in a white mortar, and a length of about 1.8m was exposed. At its highest point, it stood 1.78m below the ground and at the lowest 2.28m, a difference in height of 0.5m or about seven courses of brick. The wall was situated in a construction trench cut into the clay natural (1007), the top of which was about 1.1m below ground, nearly 0.7m above the highest surviving part of the wall. The fill of the construction trench (1005) between the wall (east side) and natural was not

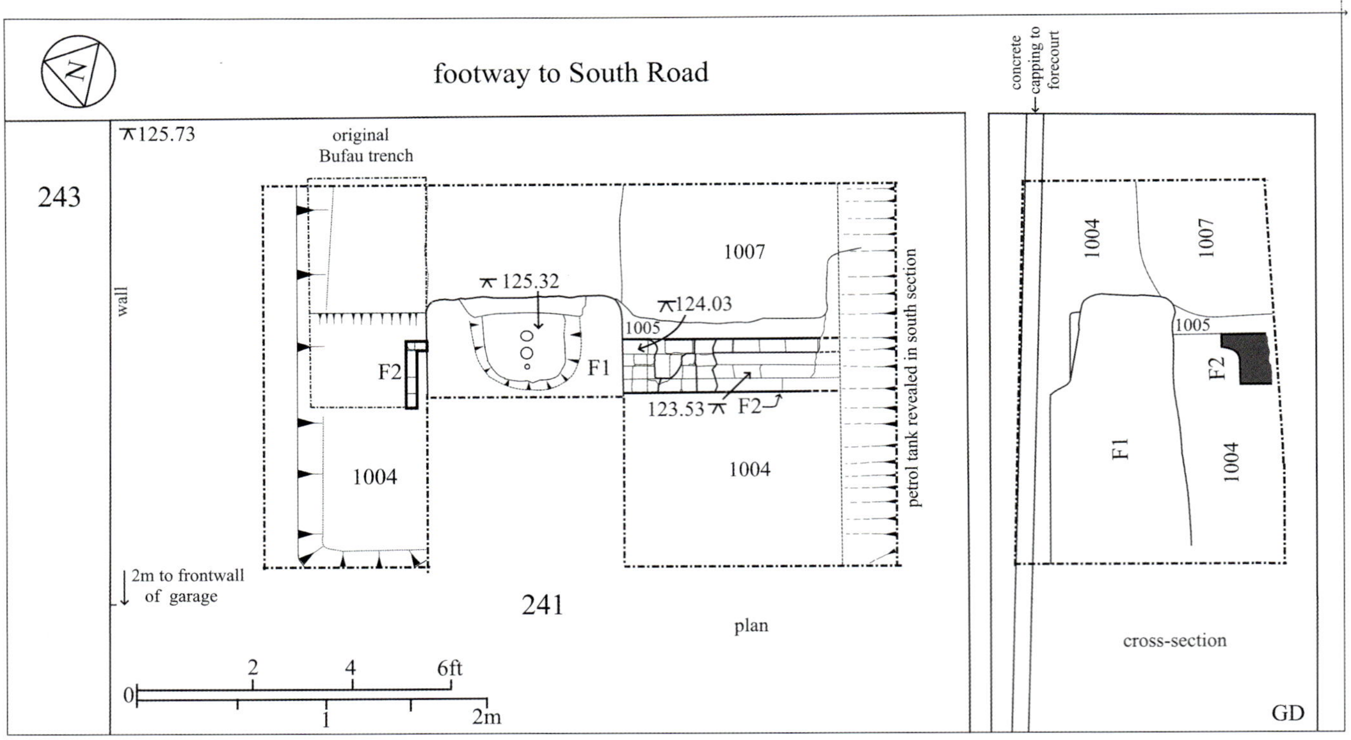

Fig A1.4
Soho 1b, cross section and plan.

removed. The west side of the wall was lime-washed and the area between the wall and the west side of the trench was filled with demolition rubble (1004) containing complete and broken red bricks, grey-green tile and pinkish-white mortar. This demolition rubble had been removed to an approximate depth of 2.3m below ground level. It was probed further with the aid of the excavator bucket, which descended at least another 0.5m without any obstruction. The bottom of this material was not found. The rubble was very loose and mobile and it was decided to backfill temporarily to just below the level of the lowest part of the wall. The demolition rubble underlay the petrol tanks and was cut by them and, in turn, overlay the natural to the east of the wall. The need to restrain the sides of the trench, and restricted time limits, prevented a more detailed recording of the section above the demolition rubble and below the concrete capping of the site, a depth of about 0.45m.

Finds

There were no finds in this trench.

Interpretation (Fig A1.5)

The substantial wall (F2) is interpreted as being the front wall of the Manufactory principal building. It was found retaining clay natural on one side (east) and containing demolition rubble on the other (west) in what was a cellar compartment located under the accommodation wing at the south end of the building. The wall continued downwards to an unknown depth and was lime-washed on its inner face, as might be expected. Estimating for a working hypothesis a depth of a further 1.8m into the demolition rubble, the cellar floor might be encountered at about 3.1m below ground level, so that that the highest and lowest section of its front wall stand at approximately 1.3m and 0.8m respectively above this assumed floor level. The wall and the construction trench in front of it line up exactly with the same features (F2 and F1) that were found in Soho 1a, Trench 1, confirming their function. Accordingly, the features and the contexts have been given the same numbers. On the other side of the petrol tank in Trench 1, the wall survived to a slightly higher level (1.6m below ground level) than in this Trench 1b (1.78m below). The presence of undisturbed demolition rubble above the top of the wall and below the petrol tank means that the insertion of the latter did not cause any further demolition of the wall, which was robbed to its present height when the principal building was taken down in 1863.

The Board of Health Map (*c* 1850–5) (*see* Fig 2.21) indicated that South Road was laid out against the front elevation of the principal building. It is now evident that its front wall was farther westwards, about 2.2m from the

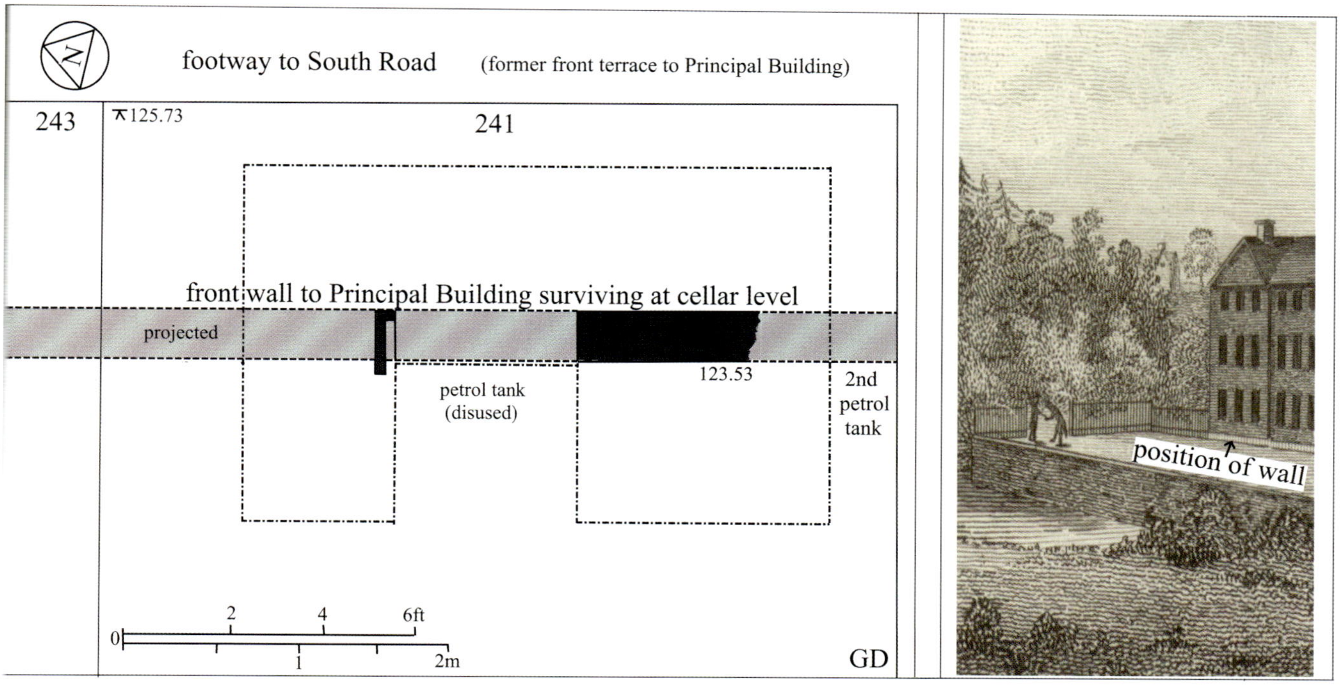

back of the footway line, and lies within the frontages of commercial and domestic premises on this side of South Road; this strip is clear of any buildings except for one domestic garage. The south corner of the principal building was not found, owing to the presence of the second petrol tank. It is estimated that the corner was located about 10m south from the boundary between the house at number 241 and frontage of the commercial premises at number 243 South Road. This calculation is based on the known length of the principal building (54.5m), the north corner of which, with its walled enclosures, could not have projected into Piers Road/St Michael's Hill, the successor to the road that ran between the north side of the manufactory and the mill pool. There remains, however, a small margin of error in the alignment of the principal building and the Manufactory complex north to south.

Fig A1.5
Soho 1b, interpretation plan.

Fig A1.6
Soho 1b, interpretation cross section of principal building and environs.

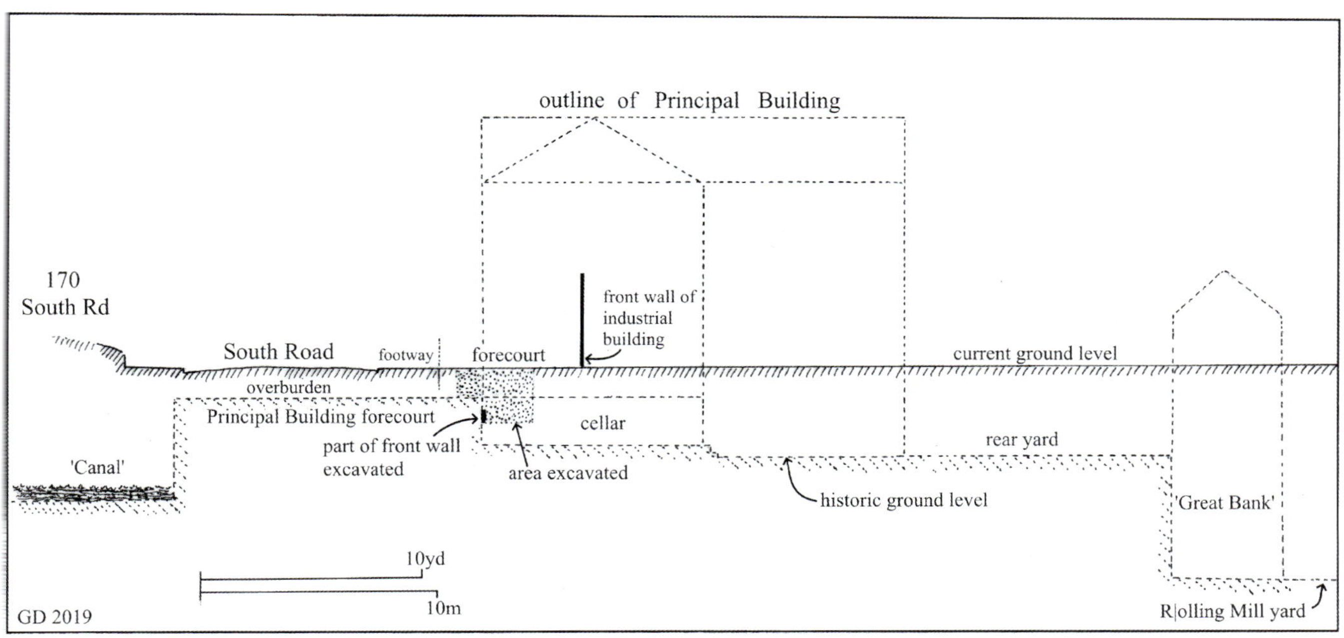

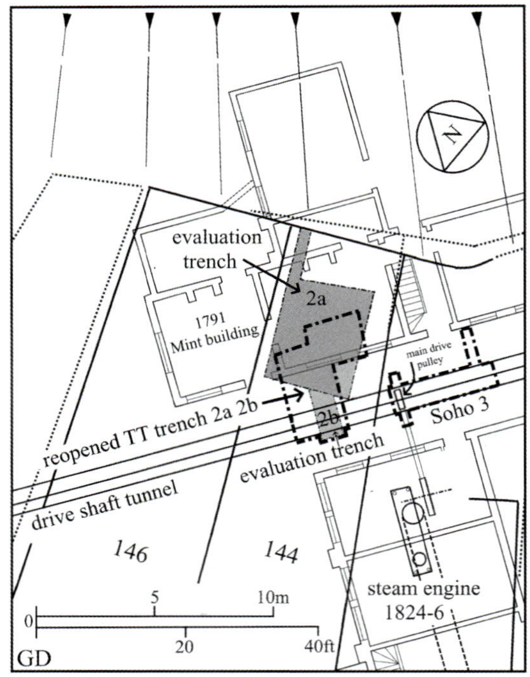

Fig A1.7
Soho 2a and 2b, location of trenches and position of 1791 mint building.

In addition, the depth of deposit has been established. This is good news for the preservation of the archaeology of the principal building (Fig A1.6). The natural geology under the forecourt was found between 1.1m and 1.3m below the ground surface, and it is possible that its valuable top surface was robbed. It was sealed by at least 0.7m of identifiable principal-building demolition rubble, covered by later tipping, and topped by the contemporary concrete, paving and tarmac surfaces. A small area forms front gardens to numbers 243–249 (odds) and number 275 South Road. Where there were cellars, the depth of deposit increases significantly, and cellar floors may lie over 3m below present ground levels. The rear gardens of numbers 243–249 (odds) and the interior of number 241 roughly maintain the level of the street over the former lower rear yard of the principal building. Here the depth of deposit would approach 4m.

Soho 2a: The 1791 mint building, *Time Team* evaluation

Objectives

Initially, there were two main aims of this excavation: the first was to locate the 1791 mint building, thereby fixing the position of the main Mint complex, and to test the hypothesis that this had survived the sand extraction that took place before 1914 (*see* Fig 6.5): the second was to demonstrate to the producers of the *Time Team* programme that there was great potential at this site despite the technical difficulties of working in suburban gardens and on factory forecourts in the search for industrial archaeology. The modest resources influenced the choice of site: uncultivated, bare soil was ideal, and this was found during a reconnaissance in the garden of 144 South Road and in the required position above the steep bank (assumed to be the edge of the sandpit) that ran through the local gardens. The evaluation took place in September 1995.

Description (Figs A1.7–A1.9)

An area 5m × 4m was opened up, lying roughly centrally between the two long garden boundaries and between 1.6m and 2.0m from the rear brick boundary and retaining wall. For convenience, north-west will be north, south-east will be east. The main stratigraphy was found to be both simple and shallow: it consisted of garden soil, which formed a wedge-shaped deposit varying in depth from approximately 100mm to 600mm. Immediately underlying most of the garden soil was a thin layer of grey-black coal ash on average 50mm, which, in turn, overlay the natural, golden-red sand.

A number of features were cut into this stratigraphy. F1 was a brick-built rectangular pit (cut into natural) measuring 2m × 1.5m × 0.6m and, on average, seven courses of bricks deep. The bricks were red (210–230mm × 115–125mm × 40–50mm), set in a grey-white lime mortar, and laid in a rough stretcher bond. There were two levels to the floor, differing in height by a single brick course, the two higher levels flanking either side of the central lower floor. Piercing the east and west wall at the upper floor levels were two pairs of mortices, 200mm × 200mm in section, and traces of timber survived in the west wall slots. Laid against the north and south walls were single skins of brick, which were not bonded to the main structure. The south wall in question was built slightly away from the main south wall, and in the narrow gap in between was found, after this wall was removed, a number of coin blanks. More blanks were located in the lowest level of main fill of the brick pit. Two long iron bolts (with their nuts still attached) were discovered – seemingly *in situ* – in the centre of the small bays of the lowest floor level. They had been fixed to the now rotted timbers that had been held by the mortices in the brickwork.

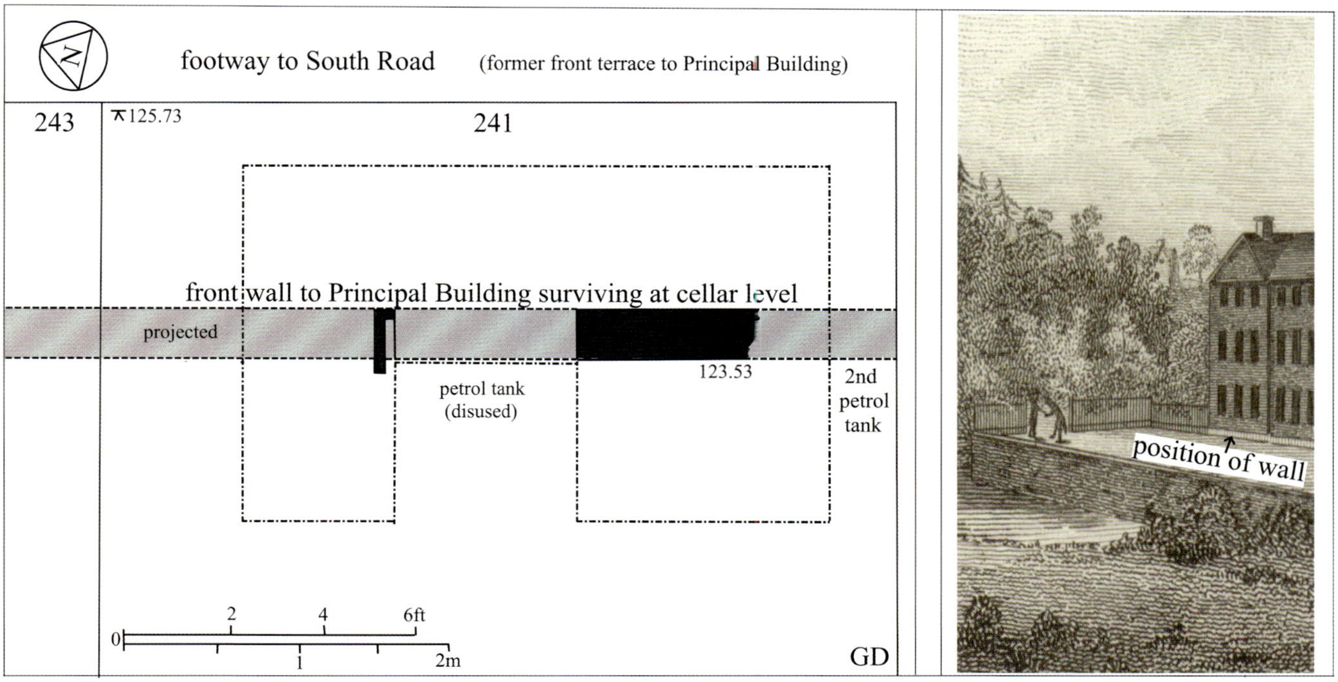

back of the footway line, and lies within the frontages of commercial and domestic premises on this side of South Road; this strip is clear of any buildings except for one domestic garage. The south corner of the principal building was not found, owing to the presence of the second petrol tank. It is estimated that the corner was located about 10m south from the boundary between the house at number 241 and frontage of the commercial premises at number 243 South Road. This calculation is based on the known length of the principal building (54.5m), the north corner of which, with its walled enclosures, could not have projected into Piers Road/St Michael's Hill, the successor to the road that ran between the north side of the manufactory and the mill pool. There remains, however, a small margin of error in the alignment of the principal building and the Manufactory complex north to south.

Fig A1.5
Soho 1b, interpretation plan.

Fig A1.6
Soho 1b, interpretation cross section of principal building and environs.

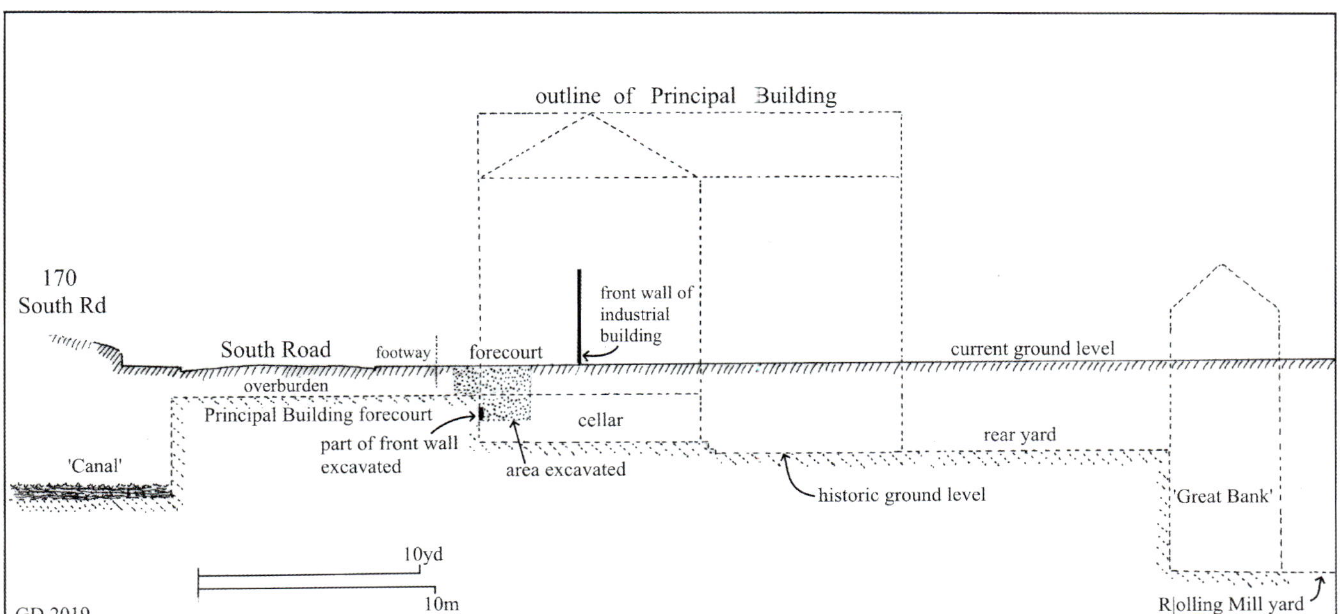

In addition, the depth of deposit has been established. This is good news for the preservation of the archaeology of the principal building (Fig A1.6). The natural geology under the forecourt was found between 1.1m and 1.3m below the ground surface, and it is possible that its valuable top surface was robbed. It was sealed by at least 0.7m of identifiable principal-building demolition rubble, covered by later tipping, and topped by the contemporary concrete, paving and tarmac surfaces. A small area forms front gardens to numbers 243–249 (odds) and number 275 South Road. Where there were cellars, the depth of deposit increases significantly, and cellar floors may lie over 3m below present ground levels. The rear gardens of numbers 243–249 (odds) and the interior of number 241 roughly maintain the level of the street over the former lower rear yard of the principal building. Here the depth of deposit would approach 4m.

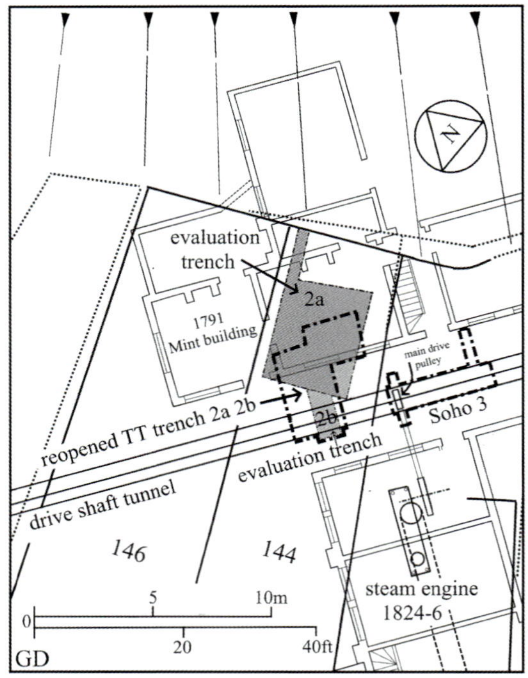

Fig A1.7
Soho 2a and 2b, location of trenches and position of 1791 mint building.

Soho 2a: The 1791 mint building, *Time Team* evaluation

Objectives

Initially, there were two main aims of this excavation: the first was to locate the 1791 mint building, thereby fixing the position of the main Mint complex, and to test the hypothesis that this had survived the sand extraction that took place before 1914 (*see* Fig 6.5): the second was to demonstrate to the producers of the *Time Team* programme that there was great potential at this site despite the technical difficulties of working in suburban gardens and on factory forecourts in the search for industrial archaeology. The modest resources influenced the choice of site: uncultivated, bare soil was ideal, and this was found during a reconnaissance in the garden of 144 South Road and in the required position above the steep bank (assumed to be the edge of the sandpit) that ran through the local gardens. The evaluation took place in September 1995.

Description (Figs A1.7–A1.9)

An area 5m × 4m was opened up, lying roughly centrally between the two long garden boundaries and between 1.6m and 2.0m from the rear brick boundary and retaining wall. For convenience, north-west will be north, south-east will be east. The main stratigraphy was found to be both simple and shallow: it consisted of garden soil, which formed a wedge-shaped deposit varying in depth from approximately 100mm to 600mm. Immediately underlying most of the garden soil was a thin layer of grey-black coal ash on average 50mm, which, in turn, overlay the natural, golden-red sand.

A number of features were cut into this stratigraphy. F1 was a brick-built rectangular pit (cut into natural) measuring 2m × 1.5m × 0.6m and, on average, seven courses of bricks deep. The bricks were red (210–230mm × 115–125mm × 40–50mm), set in a grey-white lime mortar, and laid in a rough stretcher bond. There were two levels to the floor, differing in height by a single brick course, the two higher levels flanking either side of the central lower floor. Piercing the east and west wall at the upper floor levels were two pairs of mortices, 200mm × 200mm in section, and traces of timber survived in the west wall slots. Laid against the north and south walls were single skins of brick, which were not bonded to the main structure. The south wall in question was built slightly away from the main south wall, and in the narrow gap in between was found, after this wall was removed, a number of coin blanks. More blanks were located in the lowest level of main fill of the brick pit. Two long iron bolts (with their nuts still attached) were discovered – seemingly *in situ* – in the centre of the small bays of the lowest floor level. They had been fixed to the now rotted timbers that had been held by the mortices in the brickwork.

Fig A1.8
Photo of Soho 2a trench.

Fig A1.9
Soho 2a and 2b (2c), plan.

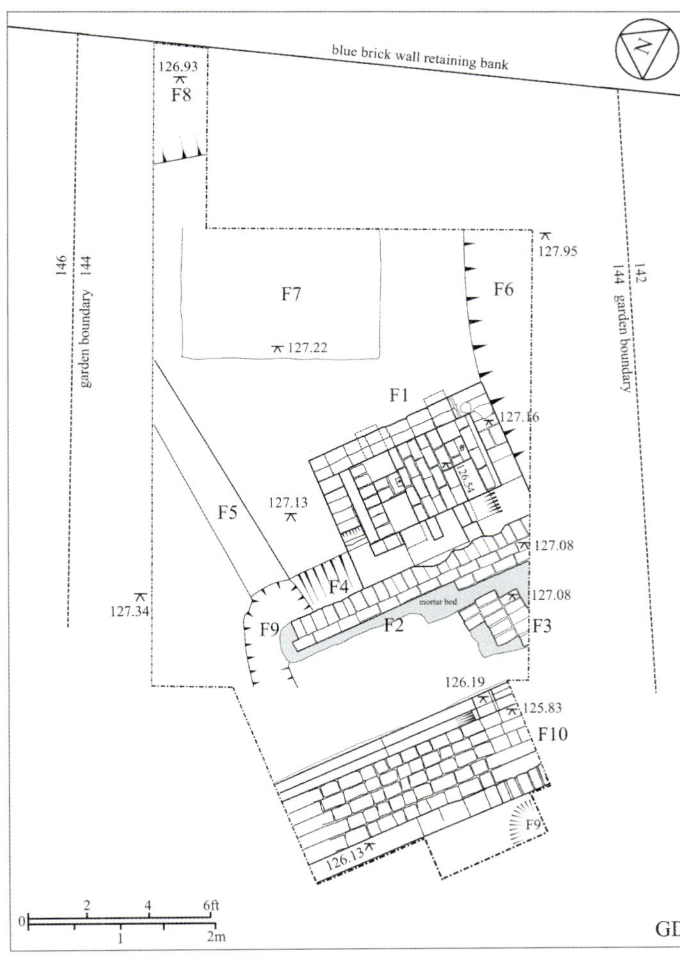

The west wall was three bricks thick (3 × 4½in), while the other walls were two; the exposed top courses of the latter were worn and smoothed. Feature F2 butted up against the west side of the brick pit and consisted of three courses of blue engineering bricks, two angled on either side of a horizontal course, arranged to form a shallow drain. The bricks were laid on a mortar bed. Butting up against part of the west side of F2 was part of a red-brick pavement (F3), also laid on a mortar base?

Feature F4 was a straight cut (700mm × 450mm and up to 100mm deep) into natural. It had been filled with small fragments of compacted grey-white lime mortar. A deep animal burrow (F9) cut into the natural sand at the roughly right-angled junction between F4 and a longer (2.3m) linear cut forming a shallow trench (F5), which continued on into the north section. F5 measured between about 400mm and 500mm wide and was cut between 100mm and 200mm into the natural. It had also been filled with small fragments of compacted grey-white lime mortar. F6 was a pit filled with demolition rubble consisting of broken red brick and grey-white lime mortar fragments. F7 was a rectangular pit that had several phases of fill. F8 was a pit measuring 1.1m × 0.55m, filled with mortar fragments.

Finds

Eighteen copper discs and one disfigured East India Company Sumatra coin of 1803 were discovered in the lowest level of fill in the brick pit (F1). The discs were of three diameters: a) the smallest size, 10mm (4 in number); b) medium size, 25–29mm (6 in number); and c) the largest size, 55mm (8 in number). A crescent-shaped copper clipping was also retrieved from the same context. Two heavily rusted iron bolts (with nuts attached) were discovered in the vertical position also in the fill of F1. They were about 370–380mm long, one with a small piece of timber still attached in the lower part between two metal stays.

Interpretation

The structures uncovered were interpreted as being part of the 1791 mint building and specifically the end (north) room. The latter interpretation was to change in the light of the later *Time Team* excavations at Soho 3. The building had been thoroughly demolished, leaving features that were either cut deeply into the natural or laid immediately upon it. The shallow construction trench for the walls was backfilled with mortar rubble and, in turn, was sealed by the very shallow layer (017) that separated the garden soil (001–003) and the natural sand (021) across the whole excavation. This extensive thin grey-black ash layer (017) may represent a destruction phase, a burning of materials immediately after demolition, or a later deposit related to the use of the site as a timber store. A possible original floor level of the building survives in only a small area, represented by a brown plaster layer (016) and white mortar (015). Significantly, there is only a small difference in level between the latter, interpreted as the remains of a solid internal floor, and the supposed yard level (top of F3). Demolition seems to have been accompanied by systematic removal of all wall courses, made easy by the shallowness of the foundations. During this destruction phase, a pit (F6) was dug within the site of the original building and filled with demolition rubble. This pit extends further south beyond the excavation. F7 is interpreted as a late 20th-century rubbish pit.

Features F4 and F5 were interpreted as being the shallow robber trenches of the front (west) and end wall of the 1791 mint building. Unfortunately, their junction had been disturbed by an animal burrow or tree root (F9). Feature F8 was thought to represent the rear wall of the building, giving the room a width of 5m; however, on the 1791 plan the room measures 4.2m (*see* Fig 5.12). Feature F1 is considered to be a machine pit (but of unknown function) that had been built integral with the front wall of the building. As a consequence, the front wall survived in the excavated area only where it coincided with the pit. The two pairs of mortices and the small amount of wood surviving within one of them represent two horizontally laid structural timbers, 200mm square, to which the two iron bolts were fixed in the vertical position. It is not known whether these bolts at their upper end were attached by means of the nuts, which had been screwed back onto them, directly to machinery or to a metal plate. The top of the bolts as found roughly coincided with the top of the inserted, single-course-width north and south walls, which may then have supported a cast iron plate, acting as a machine base. The coin blanks and the one faulty minted coin probably found their way into the pit by accident, possibly by dropping or by floor-sweeping. In 1791, the end room of the building was intended to be an office and the presence of a machine pit could only be explained by a subsequent change of use (*see* change of interpretation, Soho 2c below). Feature F2 represents part of a drain that ran in the yard immediately outside the front wall of the building, and was probably laid to catch storm water from the eaves of the roof. Feature F3 may be part of a more extensive yard surface.

Soho 2b: The mint shaft tunnel, 1824–6

Objectives

There is no single overall plan of the extensive reorganisation of the mint in 1824–6, and a number of the plans that have survived relate to particular rooms or areas that were difficult to identify. The key to a fuller understanding of this reorganisation was to locate the underground shaft and its tunnel that were installed in this phase and which ran for more than 70m (200ft) through the site. Once the analysis of the documentary sources had determined its location within the yard between the 1791 building and the main Mint complex, and heading towards and into the former latchet works, many of the hitherto unrecognisable pieces of the jigsaw fell into place (*see* pp 110–21). By coincidence, the supposed line of the tunnel passed close to the western edge of excavation Soho 2a in an area close to the back face of the 20th-century sandpit. Could the tunnel have possibly survived the destructive extractions that had already removed much of the main Mint complex? Was the tunnel buried deep enough in the sandy natural? A plan of a proposed workshop with lathes was eventually identified as showing part of the 1791 building and depicted the centre-line of the tunnel lying about 1.2m (4ft) from its front (west) wall and the tunnel floor approximately the same distance below ground.[3] Rough pencil sketches on a cross-section drawing of the proposed steam engine (*see* Figs 5.27 and 5.33) suggested that the tunnel was closer to the front wall by 0.3m (1ft) but roughly the same depth (1.2m 4ft).[4] It was decided to extend Soho 2a by a small amount down the presumed slope of the former sandpit (westwards) to establish whether the tunnel had survived.

Description (Fig A1.10)

In October 1995 the author, assisted by Dillon Close, opened a trench (2.4m × 1.2m) from an existing known feature of Soho 2a (F2, the blue brick drain) downslope and aligned at right angles to the front (west) wall of the 1791 building and F2. The trench was dug into a steep slope. At about 1.5m west of F2 and 1.2m below the level of the same feature, the centre line of a brick-constructed feature (F10) was found. It consisted of a brick floor 0.57m wide lying between two parallel walls (two courses wide) standing from just over two courses high (0.15m) to just over four courses high. In one part of the upslope eastern wall the outer second skin of brick survived to 0.52m. The bricks were hand-made reds (220mm × 115mm × 70mm) in lime mortar and heavily stained with a black deposit. They were laid in an irregular stretcher bond. The brick structure continued north and south into both sections of the trench and was found cut into natural (b004), a clean and loose orange sand. A small pit, F11, was cut into the natural in the south-west corner of the trench.

In the section facing north, a steeply sloping wedge of demolition rubble filled the remains of the tunnel, layer 2004b being more dense than 2003b. These were overlaid by a rapidly widening and sloping wedge of compacted soil and white lime-mortar fragments (2002b). A garden soil (2001b) formed the topmost layer. A small section of orange sandy natural (2005b) was detected below the brick floor (F3) and its mortar bed.

Finds

Two ferrous objects were found in context 2003b: a much corroded and flattened section of a tube, and a less corroded round block of iron or steel. The latter was a coin die measuring about 67mm in diameter and about 46mm in thickness. A broken (but almost complete) crucible was also recovered from the same context.

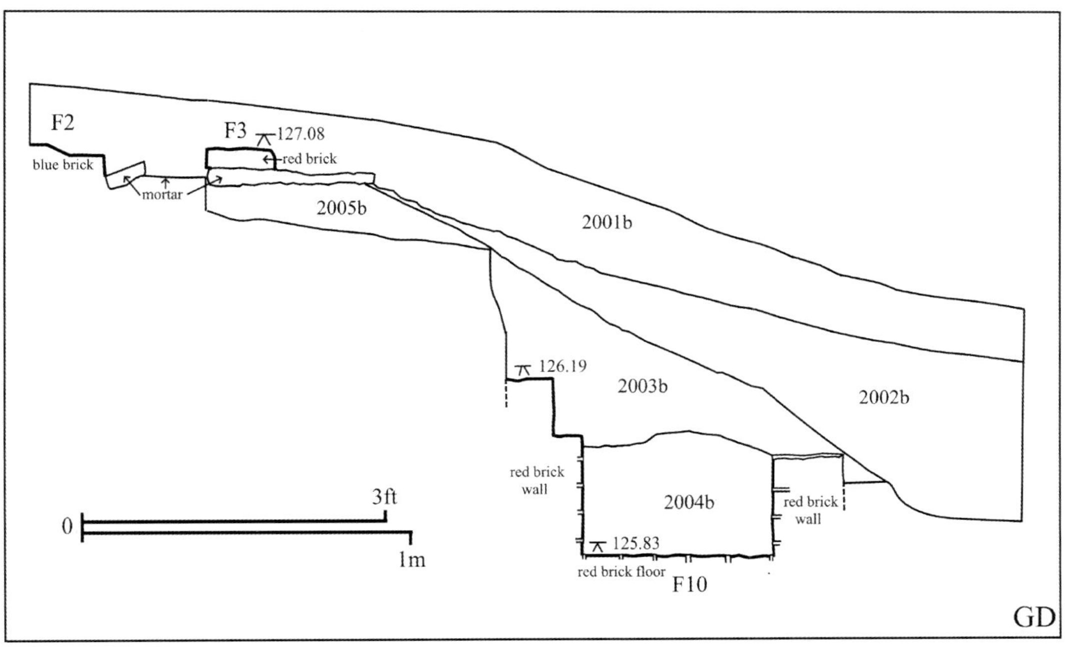

Fig A1.10
Soho 2b, cross section facing north.

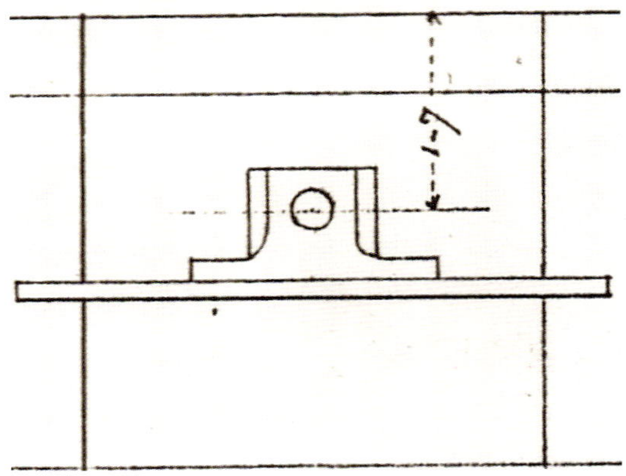

Fig A1.11
Tunnel and support for a drive shaft, cross section, Calcutta Mint, 9 February 1823.

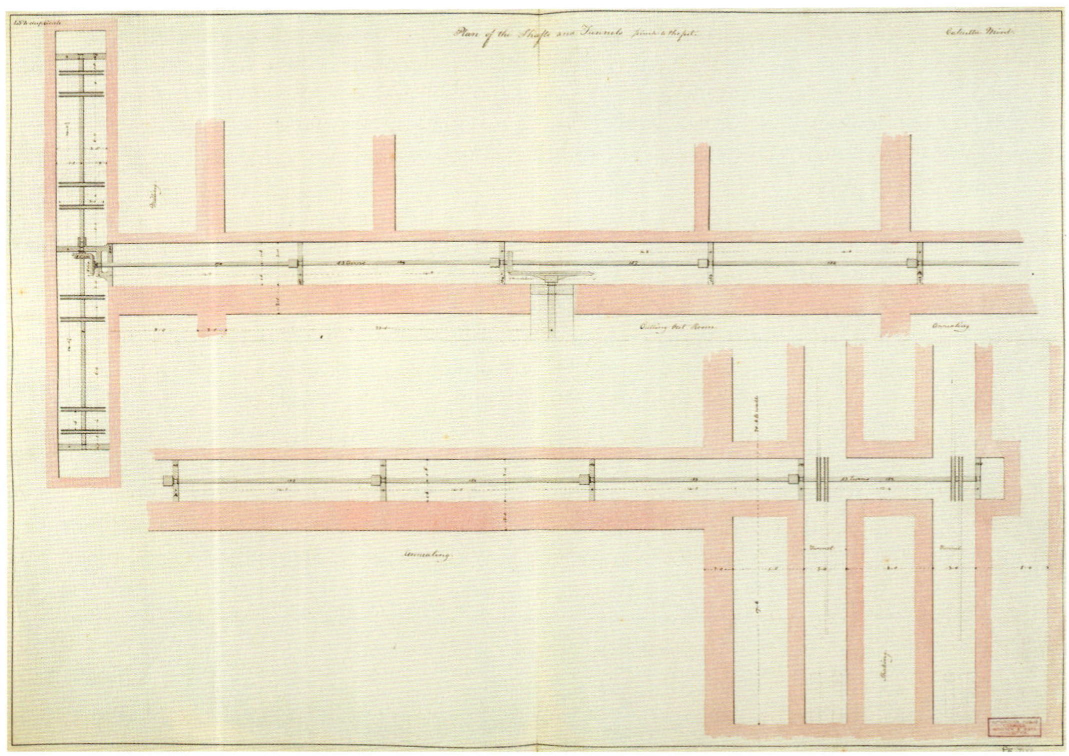

Fig A1.12
Plan of drive shaft tunnels, Calcutta Mint, [1822–3].

Interpretation

The brick feature F10 is considered to be the lowermost part of the tunnel that contained the revolving cast iron shaft linking the mint steam engine to various machines such as lathes, drills and milling machines, all installed in the period 1824–6. It was found at the expected depth (1.2m) below the assumed level of the yard, but its centre-line was at a greater distance (2.0m rather than 0.9m–1.2m) from the front wall of the 1791 building than anticipated. The survival of this feature is remarkable considering how close sand extraction had come to removing it entirely in this particular area.

The yard was 4.2m (14ft) wide (*see* Fig 5.12) and so the driveshaft tunnel would have taken almost a centre-line along it. This central course was probably accidental as the shaft, first and foremost, had to aim for the centre of the cutting-out room in the former Latchet (Crescent) Building. The tunnel was estimated to be about 0.9m high with a vaulted soffit. The cast iron shaft itself was composed of a number of separate sections joined together by clutches and supported on a similar number of bearings built into the side walls (Fig A1.11). Inspection chambers were provided to gain access to the bearings and clutches, which were situated close to each other for convenience. The shafts were listed in the 1850 sale of the Mint machinery. Each weighing about 800lb (362.8kg), it is likely that they had been removed from the tunnels by the demolition of the vaulted soffit. No drawings survive of the Soho structures, but a realistic impression of their appearance can be gained from the drawings of the Calcutta Mint (Figs 5.29 and A1.12).[5]

The discovery of the tunnel was important, as it supported the hypothesis set up on the basis of documentary research. In addition, it supplied evidence for the location and orientation of the Mint complex, together with a pointer to the centre of the cutting-out room in the Latchet (Crescent) Building. It provided a unique glimpse into the system of power transmission that was used extensively in all other mints exported by the Boultons across the world. The tunnel was a remarkable survival in the suburban garden environment in which it was found. Moreover, the line of the tunnel was to be the guiding axis for most of the *Time Team* excavations.

Soho 2c: The mint driveshaft tunnel, 1824–6, *Time Team*

The *Time Team* excavations took place over three days at Easter 1996.

Objectives (Figs A1.26 and A1.27)

Re-excavation of part of Soho 2a and all of Soho 2b was undertaken to locate what had been assumed to be the corner of the 1791 building (144 South Road). Knowing this fixed point would enable the position of the steam engine to be fixed and, as the driveshaft tunnel ran parallel to the west wall of the 1791 building, its alignment would give a direction northwards to the cutting-out room. Soho 2b was also extended north to help fix the orientation of the tunnel more reliably.

Description

The extension of Soho 2b north revealed 2.2m of tunnel in all. The newly exposed portion showed the same physical characteristics as were found in the original Soho 2b excavation: a complete brick floor, and walls on either side surviving on average to three courses.

Reinterpretation

The findings of Soho 3, however, altered the conclusion that the end of the 1791 building had been found in Soho 2a and in the re-excavation. (*see* Soho 3 below). It was not the end room that had been located, but the next room south, marked as a warehouse on the 1791 plan (*see* Fig 5.12). The result was a dramatic shift of the position of the whole of the main Mint complex and the Latchet (Crescent) Building about 4.2m (14ft) northwards through the gardens and houses of South Road. The north-west corner of the 1791 building was to be found in the garden of 146, rather than the garden of 144 South Road.

Soho 3: The mint driveshaft tunnel, 1824–6, *Time Team*

Objectives

On the understanding that the north-west corner of the 1791 building had been found in 146 South Road, compilation of plan evidence indicated that the crucial junction in the driveshaft tunnel with the steam engine was to be found in the adjacent garden to the south (142 South Road). This junction would provide a pointer to the position of the steam engine itself. Excavating a further section of tunnel would also provide information on its state of preservation and, in particular, whether the robbing on demolition was consistent throughout its length. On the other hand, the excavation would prove whether later sand extraction had entirely removed the tunnel.

Description (Fig A1.13)

It might be helpful here to describe how the working hypothesis on the position of the 1791 mint building had to be discarded: a trench 3m × 1.3m was initially opened in the garden of 142 South Road along the presumed line of the tunnel southwards to intercept the connection to the steam engine from the west side. This T junction was calculated to have been approximately 9.5m from the north-west corner of the 1791 building. The tunnel walls quickly emerged as they stood higher than in the garden of 144 South Road, but no link to the steam engine was found in the expected position. On the other hand, a narrow side tunnel was discovered close to this position, but on the east side heading into the 1791 building. The excavation was extended a short distance southwards without result. There was little doubt that the driveshaft tunnel and the 1791 building had been uncovered, but it was now necessary to question exactly which part of the building had been found in Soho 2a and c. If it were not the end of the building (the north-west corner) that was providing the datum point, then it may have been the next cross wall, the first internal wall south in the building. The end room measured 4.2m (14ft) square and consequently the steam-engine junction was perhaps 4.2m (14ft) farther north along the tunnel. This area had not yet been excavated, so an extension northwards was made to include it. Very quickly large blocks of stone on either side of a T junction with a narrow tunnel leading

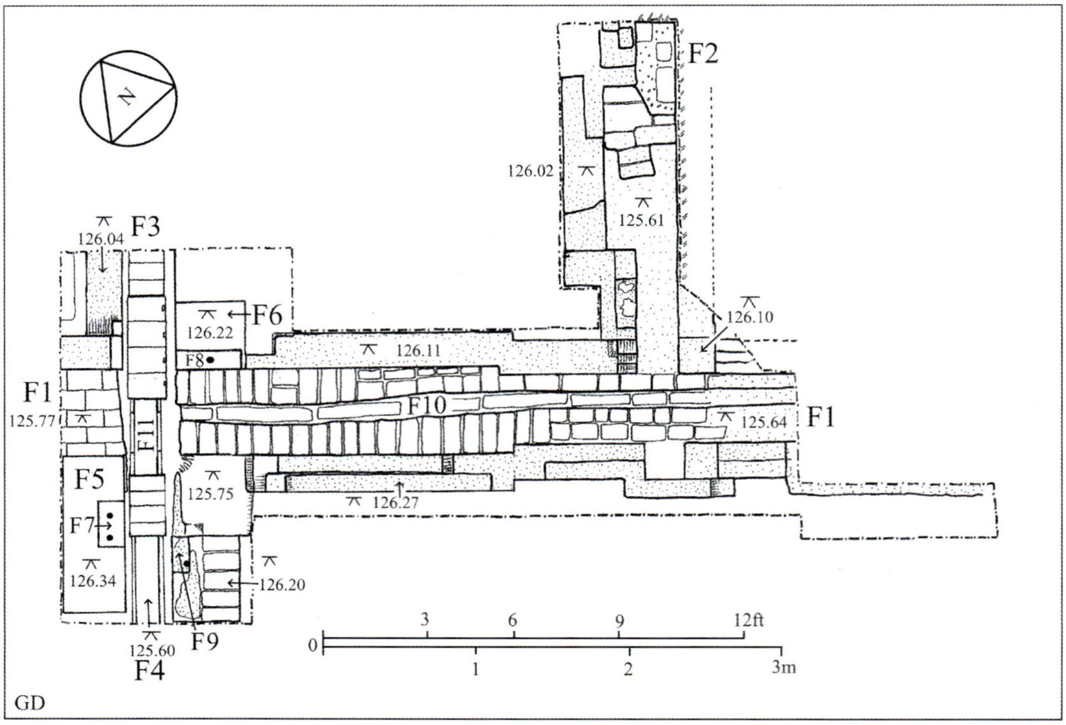

Fig A1.13
Soho 3, plan.

westwards were found. As a result, the position of the whole Mint site and the Latchet (Crescent) Building shifted northwards by 4.2m (14ft) from the original position assumed after the Soho 2a excavation.

The enlarged trench measured 4.8m × 1.3m, having three short right-angled offshoots, two opposite each other (*see* Fig A1.13). The width of the trench was excavated into a gradient of about 1 in 2.5, sloping downwards from east to west. A brick trough (floor and two side walls) (F1) ran the whole length (4.8m) of the trench. The east wall stood above the brick floor between a maximum height of 670mm and a minimum of 400mm. The west wall stood to a maximum height of 520mm, but for the majority of its length it was 300mm high. As a result of the slope of the ground surface, the stratigraphy was shallow (80mm–280mm) in the long section above the west wall and considerably deeper (700mm–1200mm) in the east long section. The stratigraphy consisted of almost entirely garden soil, demolition rubble and redeposited or disturbed natural. The brick trough widened from 450mm to 670mm about 1.8m from the south end of the trench. Its floor was found between 0.9m and 1.2m below the sloping ground surface.

Three structures connected to the driveshaft tunnel at right angles. At about a metre from the south end of the main trench a brick trough (F2) about 300mm high and 260mm wide linked from the east side. It was excavated for a length of 2.3m and increased in width to 500mm at about 700mm from the junction. At about 0.5m from the north end of the main trench a cross junction of two more offshoots was found (F3 and F4), defined principally by two large blocks (F5 and F6) of stone standing diagonally opposite each other. Cut into their top surface were rectangular notches still containing the stubs of iron fixings (F7 and F8). The largest block stood on the north-west corner occupying almost all of one side of this offshoot, the block being 800m long and 600m high; the west offshoot was excavated for about 1.1m from the junction with the main trough. The south-west block was apparently missing, but brickwork further into the offshoot revealed a notch (F9) and an iron stub in its upper surface. The notch in the brickwork was not, however, situated directly opposite the notch in the stone block, but was lower by 130mm, at almost the same level as the notch in the south-east-corner stone block. Defined by both brickwork and stone, the width of both the offshoots, west and east, was about 300mm, just over half the width of the main trough. The north-east corner of the junction was composed of brickwork, but showed no notch, having survived to a level below the other three. The offshoot on this side was excavated for a length of 800mm from the junction with the main trough and restricted on health and safety grounds by the depth of stratigraphy (1.2m) lying over the built structures.

A channel (F10) about 150mm wide and 50mm deep ran (though not exactly in a straight line) approximately down the centre of the brick floor of the main trough. At the cross-junction, this connected to a U-shaped channel made of individual fired bricks, some which were covered with plain clay roof tiles (F11). This channel ran along both the east and west offshoots, that to the west having a slope downwards of about 1 in 20. There was no channel in the brick floor in the short section (400mm) of the trough (F1) between the cross junction and the north end of the main trench.

Finds

One copper coin blank, about 31mm in diameter and 4mm thick, was found in the demolition rubble of the east offshoot trough (F2) at the south end of the trench.

Interpretation (Figs A1.14 and A1.28)

The brick-built trough (F1) is another part of the tunnel (F10) found in Soho 2b and c, a most important section as here power was transmitted from the steam engine to the machinery via the drive shaft. The cross junction, with its heavy stone blocks, represents the link to the steam engine where a 3ft (910mm)-diameter pulley fixed to the driveshaft was turned by means of a leather belt attached to a 5ft (1.5m)-diameter pulley driven directly off the steam engine (Fig A1.14). The leather belt, 56ft (17m) long and 5in (0.12m) wide, was accommodated in the narrow tunnel running off west, and this points directly to the former position of the steam engine (approximately 5m away), the foundations of which were destroyed by sand extraction in the 20th century. The function of the side tunnel running off to the east in the opposite direction is unknown. The pulley could only hold one belt and there may have been another alongside that drove a machine located in the 1791 building. The length of the tunnel leading into this building was not established owing to the depth of the excavation. It seems too long merely to accommodate the 3ft (910mm) pulley, which would only have penetrated the side tunnel for a distance of 150mm, leaving at least 600mm unoccupied. The three notches in the stone and brickwork are likely to be the fixing points for an iron frame to hold the bearings of the 3ft (910mm) pulley. This frame would need to have been extremely robust considering the stresses that it needed to withstand in holding steady the pulley, which drove over

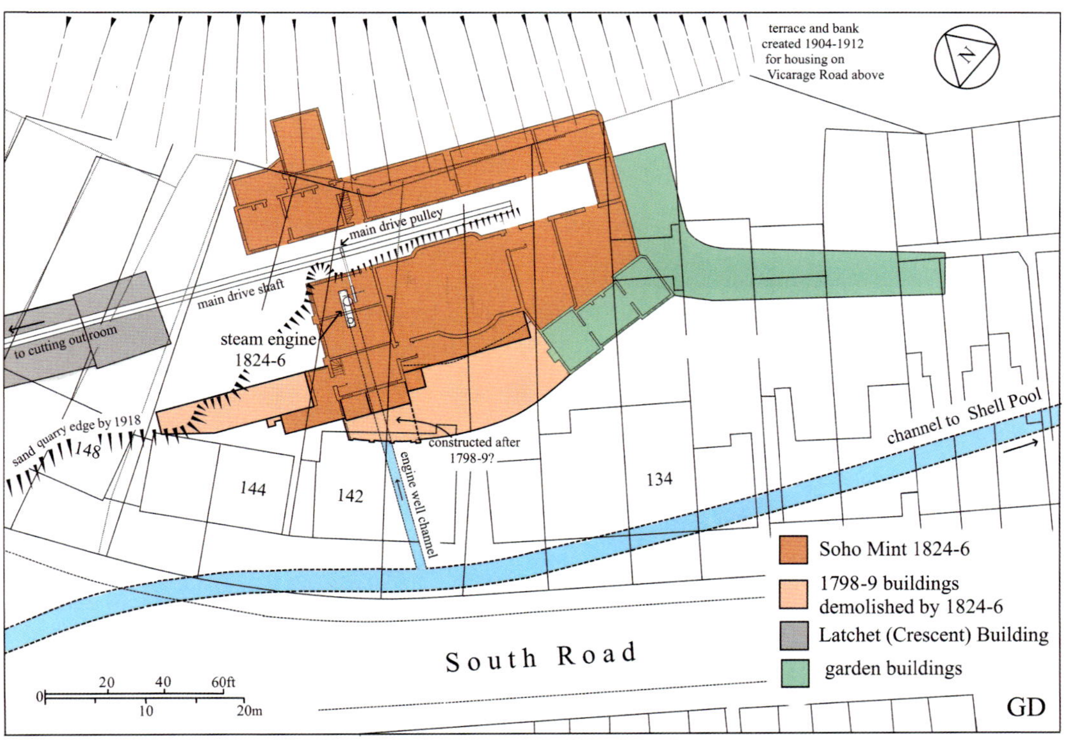

Fig A1.14
Mint buildings and associated water courses overlaid on current OS plan.

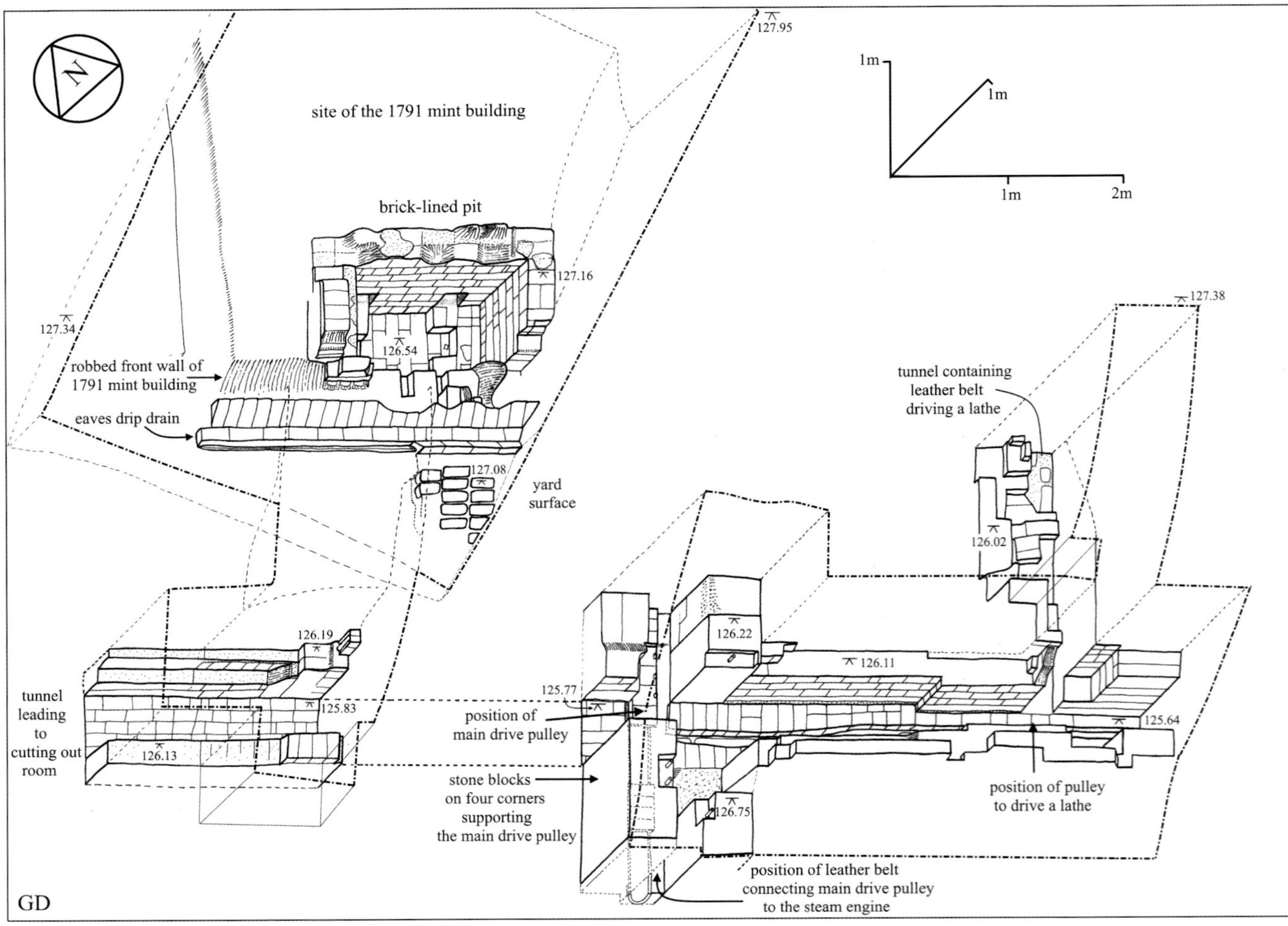

Fig A1.15
Soho 2 and 3, axonometric drawing.

70m (200ft) of cast iron shaft and attached machinery. The configuration of this frame cannot easily be determined from the surviving three bearing points.

The separate brick structure leading off east at the southern end of the excavation is interpreted to be a tunnel leading to a machine, and specifically a grinding stone. This conclusion could not be drawn from the archaeological evidence alone, but once it was understood that the main tunnel here is south of the link to the steam engine, then documentary sources are available to indicate what machinery was attached to this part of the shaft. Plotting the excavated layout of the tunnels onto the plan of the 1791 building (*see* Fig 5.12) has the side tunnel in question entering tightly into the corner of a room marked '4 presses' adjacent to the room with the stairs. It is known that this room was to be converted into 'The New Fitting Shop' with lathes, a drill and a grinding stone, the latter 'in an Iron Trough to be worked by a strap coming from a pulley on the outside in a tunnel under the floor'.[6] An unlabelled sketch plan dated *c* 1825 clearly relates to the conversion of this room, for it shows lathes and a drill in plan and elevation.[7] Significantly, a grinding stone is placed in the north-west corner of the room in exactly the same position that the excavated side tunnel would have entered it. This plan shows the main shaft in the yard outside, but not the tunnel itself. The grinding-stone pulley is not marked on the plan but only on the sketch elevation. It is important to note that the shaft has been drawn too close to the building (1.2m instead of 2m) and it is possible that the line to the centre of the cutting-out room in the Latchet (Crescent) Building had not yet been surveyed accurately.

The junction to the steam engine marked a significant difference in the character of the tunnel. To the south it had a drainage channel running along the centre of the floor, to the north none at all. The water was directed into the steam-engine pulley tunnel and probably drained into the engine well. It is known from documentary evidence that the shaft south of the steam-engine pulley measured about 17.6m (58ft) in length, ending with a pulley that drove a pump located at the first steam-engine well (1788–98). This water was pumped uphill to Soho House. It is possible that leakage from the system was disposed of by the tunnel drain. Water also drained from the side tunnel opposite the steam-engine tunnel and this may have been constructed purely for this purpose.

One of the most important results of the excavation was the accurate fixing of the position of the main Mint complex within the back gardens on the east side of South Road. The depth of the archaeological deposits and structures has been established, along with their state of preservation. The latter varies even within short distances along the tunnel, but it is remarkable how the tunnel (perched as it was in the back slope of the sandpit) survived the sand extraction of the last century. It is fortunate that this is the point where sand extraction halted. For clarity, the relative position of the Soho 2 and Soho 3 excavations, and the structures within them, have been plotted in an axonometric projection (Fig A1.15).

Soho 4: The Latchet (Crescent) Building (cutting-out room), *Time Team*

Objectives

The plotting of the position of the Latchet (Crescent) Building, based on 19th-century small-scale maps, suggested that the centre bay (which became the cutting-out room for the Mint in 1825–6), was located partly under the gardens and partly under the houses numbered 152–4 South Road. The gardens were well tended and their owners not keen on having them disturbed, but the patio of number 154 (the level of which was higher than the corresponding area of number 152) was made available and there was a possibility that archaeological remains had survived better there than next door. It was hoped that enough of the distinctive structures of the cutting-out room might survive to fix the position of the building despite the restricted area to be investigated (Fig A1.29).

The Soho 2c and Soho 3 excavations provided a more accurate direction for the tunnel heading and ending at the cutting-out room. The tunnel was plotted with ranging rods and found heading towards the back elevation of number 152, but the shifting of the position of the whole site northwards by 4.2m as a result of Soho 3 brought the centre of the cutting-out room into the rear of house number 154.

Description (Fig A1.16)

A rectangular area 7.2m × 2.0m was cleared of concrete slabs and excavated to a maximum depth of about 280mm, but on average to only half of this depth, which was the top of natural, a yellow-orange clay (4001). With such a shallow stratigraphy the archaeology consisted almost entirely of features or structures cut into the natural. These were linear (4003), circular (4012), square (4010) and irregular (4007). A section of brickwork 1.6m long and 0.7m wide with a straight edge (4020, F1) emerged at an angle of about 25 degrees from the rear wall of the house. The bricks (210mm × 105mm × 60mm) were orange, hand-made and laid in a whitish lime

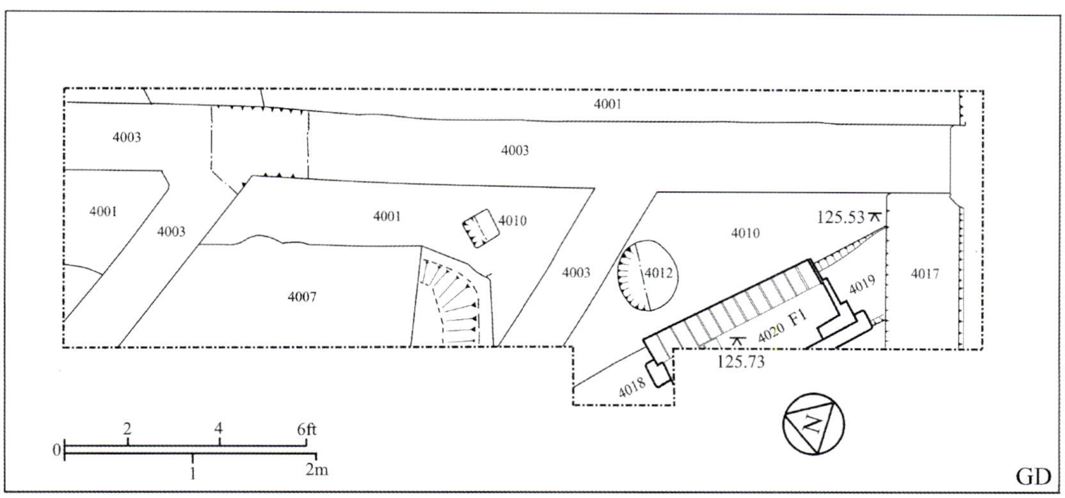

Fig A1.16
Soho 4, plan.

patios were terraced into the existing ground level and there is a chance of a greater depth of archaeological deposit surviving in the gardens that rise to higher levels to the south.

The assemblage of bone blanks may relate to a dump of rubbish from the main Manufactory complex, but it is more likely that they were produced within the Latchet (Crescent) Building after latchet production ceased in about 1808. The building was underused from about the latter date to 1824 when it taken over by the Mint.

Soho 5: The south end of the Latchet (Crescent) Building, *Time Team*

Objectives (Fig A1.25)

It was always intended to excavate two parts of the Latchet (Crescent) Building in anticipation of finding a recognisable part of the cutting-out room in the centre and the south end of the building itself. In theory, this would have provided sufficient information to both create an accurate plan of the building and to fix its position in the present townscape. As mentioned above, and as a result of the Soho 3 excavation, the position of the whole Mint site (including the Latchet (Crescent) Building) shifted northwards by 4.2m (14ft) from the position initially assumed after Soho 2a. The position of the Latchet (Crescent) Building itself had to be swivelled a few degrees west on the axis of the south-east corner of the building in order to align with the wall found in Soho 4 (Fig A1.19). As a result, the south end bay appeared to lie in the gardens of 148 and 150 South Road, with the south-west and south-east corners entirely in number 148. The garden of number 150 was available and it was decided to cut a trench along the long axis of the garden in the hope of intercepting the end bay diagonally. The area chosen as having most potential fortunately formed part of the main garden of the house, lying above the patio and house terrace that was suspected to have caused damage to the local archaeology. There was an opportunity, therefore, of assessing the depth and state of preservation of the archaeological deposits in an area that had probably escaped the activity of 20th-century sand extraction and subsequent house building.

In the testing of the hypothesis outlined above, an additional but unexpected uncertainty was created by the discovery of a mismatch between the Ordnance Survey 1:1250 map of the gardens of the South Road houses and the plan that was emerging from the *Time Team* EDM[8] survey conducted by Stuart Ainsworth.

Description (Figs A1.20–A1.21)

A trench, measuring 8.5m × 1.0m, was excavated running along the south boundary of the garden. During the excavation, the west end of the trench was widened to between 1.7m and 2.0m in the area where brick walls were found. The depth of excavation averaged approximately 1m, reaching a maximum of about 1.4m.

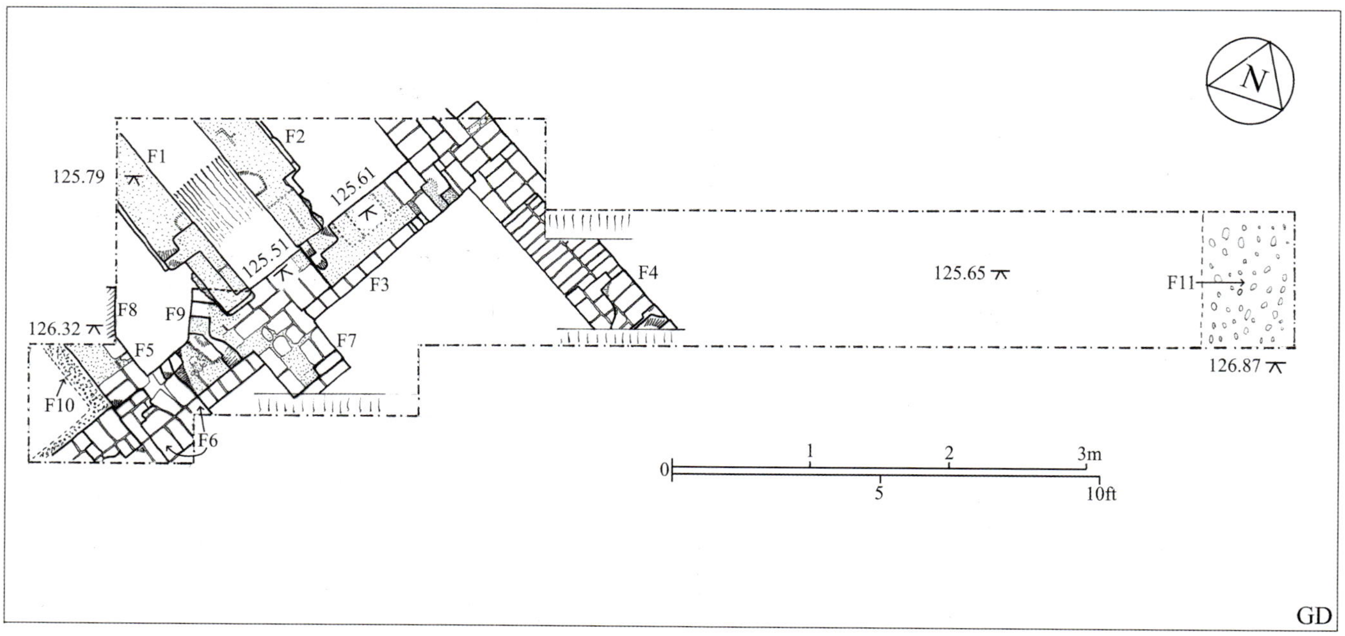

Fig A1.20
Soho 5, plan.

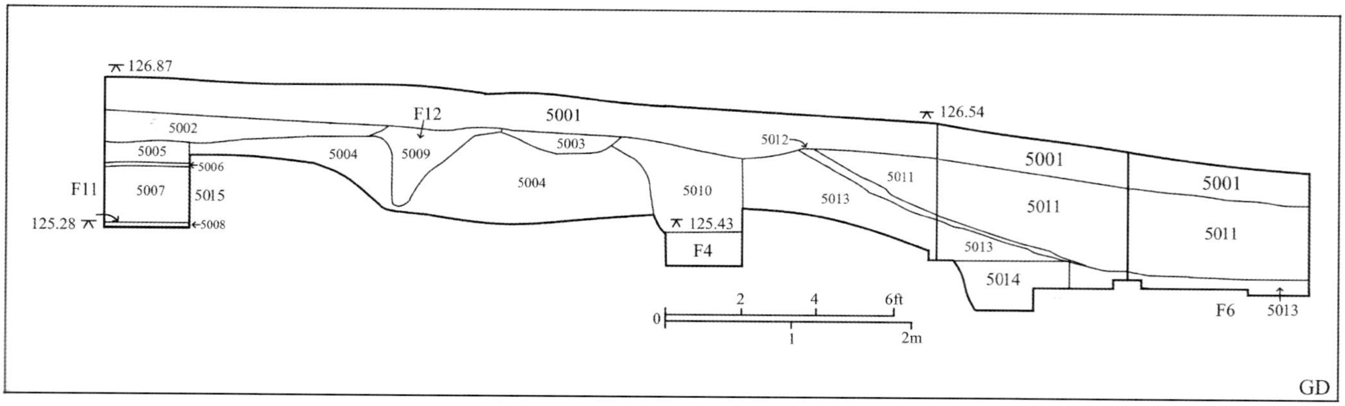

Fig A1.21
Soho 5, cross section north facing.

Running diagonally across the western extremity of the trench were two parallel walls (F1, F2) 460mm apart. Their top was found about 700mm below the surface and only their lowermost three courses of brickwork had survived. Their position and alignment coincided with the projected line of the shaft tunnel. The two parallel walls were three courses wide, narrowing to two just before crossing over another brick wall (F3) more or less at right angles. The latter provided only a 'toehold' support before the two parallel walls finished abruptly. The supporting wall was three courses wide, broadening to four, and contained a 'buttress' (F7) on its south side approximately 450mm square. On the north side, brickwork (F9) could be seen extending from this wall at 45 degrees to disappear under F1. At about 900mm to the east and in the narrower part of the trench, the top of a brick wall (F4) four courses wide was located between 1.0m and 1.4m below the ground surface. This appeared to be parallel to the pair of walls (F1, F2) mentioned above and to intercept F3 at right angles within the section. All the bricks were orange-red, varying around 200mm × 105mm × 50mm within a creamy white mortar.

Immediately after the filming, it was decided to extend the trench to uncover more of the brick foundations. Features F3 and F4 were found to intersect and form part of the same structure, the brickwork being tied together. Feature F4 continued northwards four courses in width beyond the junction but was set back (westwards) by the length of a brick (200m). Feature F3 continued westwards, and at about 700mm from F1 intercepted (and was keyed into at right angles) a brick wall three courses wide (F5). At the point that F5 ran into the vertical section of the trench, the brickwork (F8) turned 45 degrees and, as a result, it could be seen in the face of the section. This angle of brickwork was about 350mm in length and was found to be parallel to the other 45-degree 'buttress' (F9) on the north side of F3, which lay partly below F1. Feature F9 was found to be triangular in plan, with each face about 350mm long, the same as F8. In line with F5, there appeared to be brickwork tied in and continuing southwards of F3, but there was insufficient of this structure exposed to determine whether this was another wall or merely a buttress similar to that found at F7, 450mm to the east.

In plan, natural (a light grey-buff sandy clay) (5015) appeared at both extremes of the trench. At the west end it was cut into by F10, a narrow construction feature between 80mm and 160mm wide following the perimeter of walls F5 and F3. At the east end, a pit (F11) had been cut into the natural. In the remainder of the trench as far as wall F4 the excavation did not reach natural, leaving up to 200mm of deposit above it. Natural was also exposed between walls F1 and F2.

In vertical section between the natural (5015) and the garden soil (5001), the stratigraphy above most of the area of the brick walls was composed of a single layer between 500mm and 800mm in depth (5011) containing broken orange-red brick and white-yellow mortar in a sandy orange or grey matrix. A thin layer of black coal fragments (5012) separated 5011 from 5013, consisting of a black sandy soil. There was slightly more complex layering and horizontal gradation east of wall F3 to the end of the trench and a more significant humic content. An asymmetrical pit (F12) cut into 5004, a black sandy material, was itself filled with ash (5009). It appeared in the south section but not the north. Pit F11 stretched across both sections and was filled with layers of black sand (5005,

5007) separated by a thin layer of ash (5006) and its bottom (1.2m below the ground surface) was lined with river-washed pebbles (5008).

Finds (Fig A1.27)

Six copper coin blanks (one of which was unusually thick at 6mm) were found in 5011 and a thin (3.5cm × 3cm) brass plate bearing an impressed elephant design was found in 5008. Two bone button blanks were also recovered.

Interpretation (Fig A1.22 and Fig A1.30)

The small extensions to the trench uncovered sufficient additional brick walling to identify positively which part of the Latchet (Crescent) Building had been discovered. It was concluded that wall F3 was the north wall of the southern bay. From map evidence, the end bays and central bay were slightly wider than the curving parts of the building that connected them (*see* Fig 2.24). This slight narrowing of the building was clearly evident at the junction of wall F3 and the east wall (F4), where it might be expected, and measured a full-length brick – 200mm. The very first part of the presumed curving east wall continued northwards into the vertical section. This wall survived to a height of five courses at its extreme southern end and it is assumed that the lowermost courses of the wall foundations had been encountered, although it was not determined how many courses were buried below the excavated level.

Wall F5 was interpreted as being the eastern wall of the passageway that ran down the centre of the curving sections of the building. The space between this wall and the front elevation F4 coincided therefore with the first of the curving rooms. At this foundation level, it measured 2.46m in width, narrow by workshop standards. Walls F3, F4 and F5 date to the original construction phase of 1794. Features F8 and F9 are interpreted to be the foundations of a corner fireplace. Fireplaces such as these (but on a larger scale) can be seen on the Rickman and Hutchinson drawing of the cutting-out room (*see* Fig 5.28). The 1824–6 conversion of the building necessitated the removal of several of the corner fireplaces and it is apparent that the same happened in this room to enable the shaft tunnel to be constructed.

By coincidence, about half of the width of the building (3.8m) had been revealed by extending

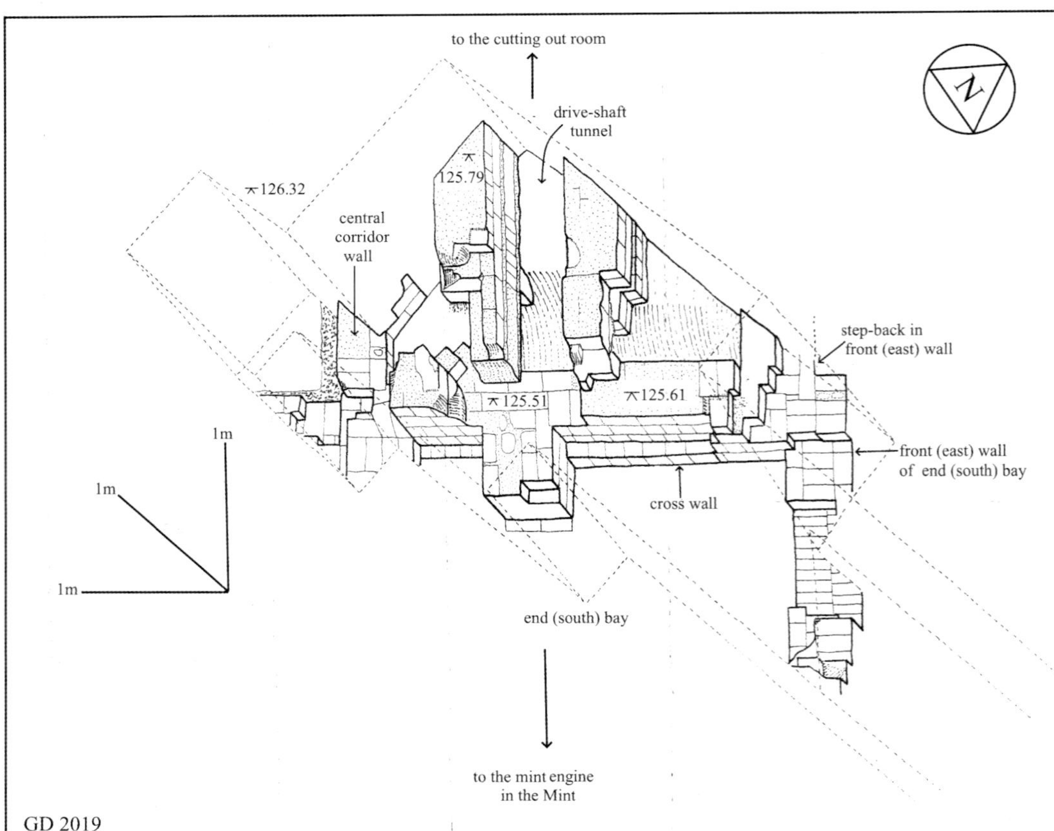

Fig A1.22
Soho 5 axonometric drawing.

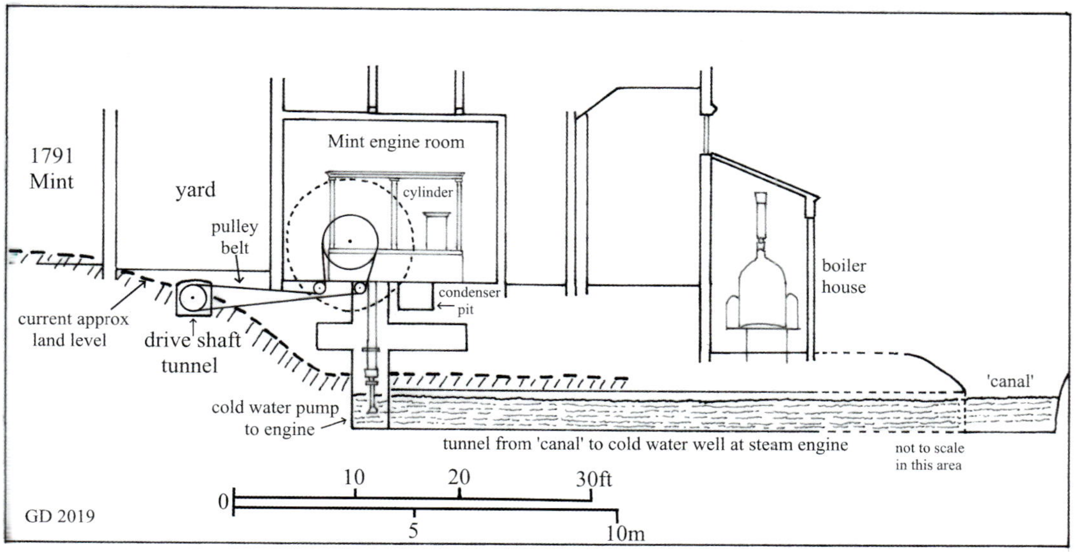

Fig A1.23
Interpretative cross section showing the position of the mint buildings, steam engine and power shaft tunnel in relation to current ground level
(*see* Fig 5.27).

the trench westwards. The purpose of F6 and F7 is not clear; they may have been buttresses or the foundations of a fireplace or hearth located in the large end-bay room. They are tied in with the brickwork of F3 and appear to belong to the primary phase of this building dating to 1794.

Walls F1 and F2, however, belong to the reorganisation of the mint in 1824–6 when the shaft tunnel was inserted into the building and which, by coincidence, met the walls in this part of the building at right angles and ran down the centre of the first curving room on the east side of the building. Unlike in Soho trenches 2b, 2c and 3, the tunnel had lost its floor, but it is possible to determine its position from the projecting line of mortar visible on the inside of both walls between the first and second brick course. This would also have allowed the floor to have been laid directly over wall F3. The OSD height of 125.59m is roughly the same height as the bottom of tunnel in Soho 3 and 4. The tunnel was approximately 3ft (900mm) high with the shaft within running about 2ft (600mm) below the the Latchet (Crescent) Building floor (*see* Fig 5.31).

As a result of this excavation, it is evident that the tunnel was robbed out completely in one place at least where it entered the south end bay from the direction of the cutting-out room. Based on the evidence of three small excavations, it is apparent that there are significant differences in the amount of this structure surviving. All three of the excavations of the tunnel found its demolition material undisturbed. The bottom of the tunnel and the top of the surviving Latchet (Crescent) Building walls are approximately 900mm below present ground level. If the tunnel floor was approximately 900m below the floor of the building, then two conclusions can be drawn: first, the present ground level and the historic ground level are roughly the same and, second, the walls of the building below ground were robbed to a depth of about 900mm, leaving only a few courses of brick. A considerable depth (500–800mm) of plaster, mortar and brick rubble, clearly deriving from its demolition, lay above the area of the building excavated.

On the exterior to the east of the east elevation (wall F4) the deposits are interpreted as being the relatively undisturbed forecourt. They are cut by the robber trench for wall F4 and the ash layer may have been a late surface treatment. The material may have been derived from the original construction phase, but over time it appears to have acquired a humic content from being colonised by vegetation. Dug into this forecourt surface were at least two pits, one at least used for rubbish, though not necessarily intended as such; the full extent of this feature was not established.

The most significant outcomes of this excavation were the identification of walls that are only known from a sketch plan of the Latchet (Crescent) Building (*see* Fig 2.24), the drawing of a more reliable plan in the light of these discoveries and those of Soho 4, and the accurate fixing of this building footprint within the present townscape of gardens and houses around South Road (*see* Figs A1.18–A1.19).

Soho 6: The steam engine well, *Time Team* (Fig A1.23)

Objectives

The sand extraction of the early 20th-century had destroyed much of the main Mint complex, in particular the coining and engine rooms. However, it is possible that the very deepest structures associated with the engine installed in late 1825 to early 1826 might have survived. The upper part of the garden of number 142 South Road corresponded roughly with the Mint yard level, and much of the remainder of the garden lay approximately 2.5m below the slope in the garden assumed to be the last working face of the sandpit itself. The cross section of the Mint engine (*see* Fig 5.27) showed the well that provided water to the engine descending to at least 3.3m below Mint yard level. A culvert brought water to the well from the channel, which linked the main canal fronting the principal building with Shell Pool. The top of the culvert is drawn on the very bottom edge of the cross section and the scale may have been compressed to fit it in. Making no allowance for this factor, and estimating that the culvert was 900mm deep, the total depth of the well from Mint yard level may have been about 4.2m (13.8ft). Removing 2.5m by sand extraction would, in theory, still leave approximately 1.7m of the lowest part of the well and its connection to the culvert.

It was decided to excavate the area of the well. The Soho 3 excavation found the tunnel that led at right angles from the main shaft tunnel to the engine, thus providing a direction to the latter. Using a combination of maps, it was known that the engine well was 7m west of the west wall of the 1791 mint building.[9] A small adjustment northwards of about 900mm had to be made, as the tunnel led directly to the pulley attached to the south side of the engine rather than to the engine itself.

Measuring from the wall unfortunately coincided with a breeze-block retaining wall holding the upper part of the garden. It was not sensible to excavate in this position and it was decided to move the intended trench down the line of the culvert that led to the well in the hope of finding this structure.

Description

A trench, 2.1m east of the engine well and measuring 2.4m × 1.2m, was excavated to a depth of about 1.2m. At this level, it encountered brick rubble and an L-section piece of iron. A limited area (approximately 1.2m × 0.8m) of the trench north of the angle iron was probed to a depth of 2m and some of the brick rubble removed. It was found that this rubble continued downwards below this level and was loose with cavities. After the filming, the same restricted area 1.2m × 0.8m was probed to a depth of 2.6m. The material consisted almost entirely of loose brick rubble, some of it quite large in size. The largest piece was found in the side of the trench below the angle iron and appeared to be the corner of a wall, one side of which was curving. The excavation could go no further for health and safety reasons, but it was clear that the brick rubble, loose with large cavities, continued downwards.

An exploratory excavation measuring 1.6m × 1.6m was dug with its south-east corner intersecting with the north-west corner of the trench above. This position was chosen from the results of the radar survey of the garden, which identified an anomaly (*see* p 241). However, this excavation did not proceed further because of pressures to carry on with other trenches where the archaeological potential – based on documentary evidence – was felt to be greater.

Finds

Only demolition rubble and 19th-century pottery fragments were encountered. One piece of roof tile, light-grey in colour and 10mm in thickness, may have come from the 1788 or the 1791 mint building. A blob of white lime mortar still protected the nail hole.

Interpretation

It was expected that, from the current garden level, it was a minimum of 1.7m to the bottom of the well and culvert. However, large pieces of brickwork were being found at 2.4m and it was observed that this continued downwards. The edge-of-plan (*see* Fig 5.27) distortions alluded to above may mean that the bottom of the well and culvert was much further down than anticipated and that the demolition rubble found was either the remains of the mint or of the culvert. What is clear, however, is that the sand extraction must have encountered the deep and robust foundations off the main Mint complex and almost entirely removed them, an operation that might have caused a frustrating delay in operations. The metre or thereabouts of a sandy soil that was dumped over this area perhaps derived from later sandpit operations or levelling for the construction of houses.

The depth of the brick rubble is significant in being more than 2.6m and deeper than found in any of the other Soho excavations. Masonry related to the engine well and culvert does not seem to have survived undisturbed through these levels, but below 2.6m there still may be brickwork *in situ*. Without more extensive excavation, unfeasible in the South Road back gardens, the nature, depth and extent of this deposit will not be properly understood.

Radar survey

During the *Time Team* excavations at Easter 1996, a radar survey was carried out in gardens at the rear of 142–54 South Rd, in the carriageway itself at the junction of South Road and St Michael's Hill, and on the forecourt of 241 South Road. Although one of the petrol tanks in Soho 1b was detected, initial scepticism that the technique would yield meaningful results was confirmed by the inability of the radar survey to identify the position of the second petrol tank, together with any of the course of the Mint driveshaft tunnel. It was decided not to devote major resources to excavating features identified by the survey, and only a small trench was dug in the garden of 142 South Road.[10]

The significant findings and their implications for the future

The position of three main industrial buildings at Soho, of which there are no standing remains, have now been established: the Manufactory, the Mint and the Latchet (Crescent) Building, the Manufactory accurately in an east–west direction and its orientation north–south narrowed to a metre or so. As the Mint was also attached to 'garden' buildings in Boulton's Soho Park, the position of these has also been established: the menagerie, fossil room, tea room and laboratory.

Significant remains of masonry foundations and below-ground structures have been located and their levels surveyed. With no extant contemporary plan of the 1824–5 Mint driveshaft tunnel, the excavations proved the theory of its location derived from documentary sources. Combining archaeological and documentary investigations demonstrates the greater effectiveness of this approach to study of the material past.

The depths of sealing deposits that lie over the site have been determined in many places and indicate the great variation in vulnerability of the archaeological remains to potential disturbance. The thinnest deposits are encountered in the rear gardens on the east side of South Road, but these areas are unlikely to be redeveloped or built upon to any significant extent in the foreseeable future.

The larger part of the Manufactory below (west of) the Great Bank lies buried under a massive dump of material up to 20ft (6.56m) that effectively prevents the archaeological remains from being disturbed. There is a greater chance of the industrial premises here being redeveloped, but the depths involved between the Great Bank and the Hockley Brook may preclude the need for archaeological investigations required as part of any new planning permissions.

The industrial/commercial buildings fronting South Road, however, lie over the site of the principal building and provide the greatest opportunity and potential for future archaeological work, should redevelopment take place.

Conclusion

Because of the robustness of industrial archaeology and the clear objectives set at the beginning – against the background of painstaking documentary research – the results achieved by the *Time Team* excavations were exceptional despite the limited time available. Our understanding of the Soho Mint and Manufactory site has, as a consequence, progressed significantly, not the least in providing an accurate position of the buildings for the first time. Birmingham and Soho were given national media coverage, a major fillip to the perception of the importance of the industrial archaeology of the West Midlands conurbation.

Fig A1.24
The environs of Soho 1b, searching for the principal building of the Soho Manufactory, 1996

Fig A1.25
The environs of the Soho Mint and the Latchet (Crescent) Building. On the extreme left is the excavation of Soho 2a and 2b (2c) at the Soho Mint. To the right of centre the excavation in the garden has revealed the drive shaft tunnel and part of the Latchet (Crescent) Building, 1996 (Soho 5).

Fig A1.26
The re-excavation of Soho 2a and 2b (2c), the latter providing an orientation for the continuation of the drive shaft tunnel in the garden to the left and its assumed connection to the steam engine, 1996.

Fig A1.27
The re-excavation of the drive shaft tunnel in Soho 2b (2c), looking towards the site of the Latchet (Crescent) Building, 1996.

Fig A1.28
The drive shaft tunnel as excavated in Soho 3. At the far end can be seen one of the four large stone blocks that anchored the main drive shaft pulley driven by the steam engine positioned on the left. In the foreground an off-shoot tunnel indicates the position of a smaller pulley which powered a lathe in the 1791 Mint building to the right. In the distance the Soho 2b (2c) trench can be seen continuing the line of the drive shaft tunnel, 1996.

Fig A 1.29
Soho 4. In the foreground the parallel walls form the lowest part of the drive shaft tunnel. To the right, the tunnel (now entirely removed) entered the southern bay of the Latchet (Crescent) Building and headed on towards the Soho Mint (Soho 2b (2c) and Soho 3), 1996.

Fig A1.30
Soho 5. The remarkable survival below patio slabs of the front wall of the cutting out room in the central bay of the Latchet (Crescent) Building, 1996.

Appendix 2

The Soho businesses

As emphasised in the Introduction, this book is not intended to be a business history of the Soho enterprises. This would be a major undertaking in view of the number of firms involved and, although each could justify a separate study in its own right, their complex interrelationships would also need to be taken into account. The author eagerly awaits any effort on the part of scholars in this direction. Nevertheless, any analysis of the physical development of the Soho buildings and their power systems is helped by an understanding of the complex business structure in which they were created. This summary outline of the Soho businesses is presented as an aid to readers of this book, but also, it is hoped, to alleviate as much as possible the confusion that is apparent in the literature between one Soho firm and another, what each produced and in which buildings.

The complex network of partnerships and firms based at Soho came eventually to reflect the vast range of products that was produced. Figure A2.1 illustrates this evolution by means of individual time lines, but only the principal concerns are shown and there is still a considerable amount of research to be done both on the structure of the individual firms and on their interconnection.

Boulton & Fothergill

In 1759, Matthew Boulton inherited his father's toy business (based at Birmingham and Sarehole mill), in which he had been a partner for the previous nine years. In 1761, he transferred much of the business to Soho, but retained his Birmingham premises until 1765. On 24 June 1762, while still building at Soho, he entered into a partnership with John Fothergill, who was brought in for his knowledge of the foreign markets and mercantile skills. Boulton's share of the capital included the buildings, tools and materials.[1] The firm of Boulton & Fothergill was not a great success financially, reaching the brink of ruin on a number of occasions. It ceased trading on 31 December 1781 amidst mutual acrimony, and Fothergill died in June 1782 insolvent and embittered. Arbitration followed and under the award dated 29 July 1782 Boulton received the Manufactory as compensation for Fothergill's debt of £19,284 against the old firm.

Towards the last years of Boulton & Fothergill, a number of other partners were introduced: Charles Wyatt, son of John Wyatt (the inventor), was admitted to the button business from at least January 1776 to January 1777, replaced by John Scale to June 1782. Francis Eginton, better known as a painter of stained glass, was partner in the silver-plated and ormolu goods business from at least January 1776 to about September 1778.[2]

The button companies

The structure of these minor partnerships foreshadowed the manner in which Boulton organised the button and plated-ware businesses after Fothergill. He now considered himself as sole and private owner of the Manufactory, and he was to charge rent for any concern setting up within it, even if he had a financial stake as was invariably the case. In 1782, Boulton entered into a new partnership with John Scale forming the button company. Scale died in 1792, whereupon his sons, John and George, took over their father's position until the partnership of Boulton and Scale was finally dissolved in 1796.[3] In 1801, the button company was divided into two partnerships: Matthew Boulton & John Bownas (steel buttons) and Matthew Boulton & William Nelson (gilt and plated buttons), but the arrangement

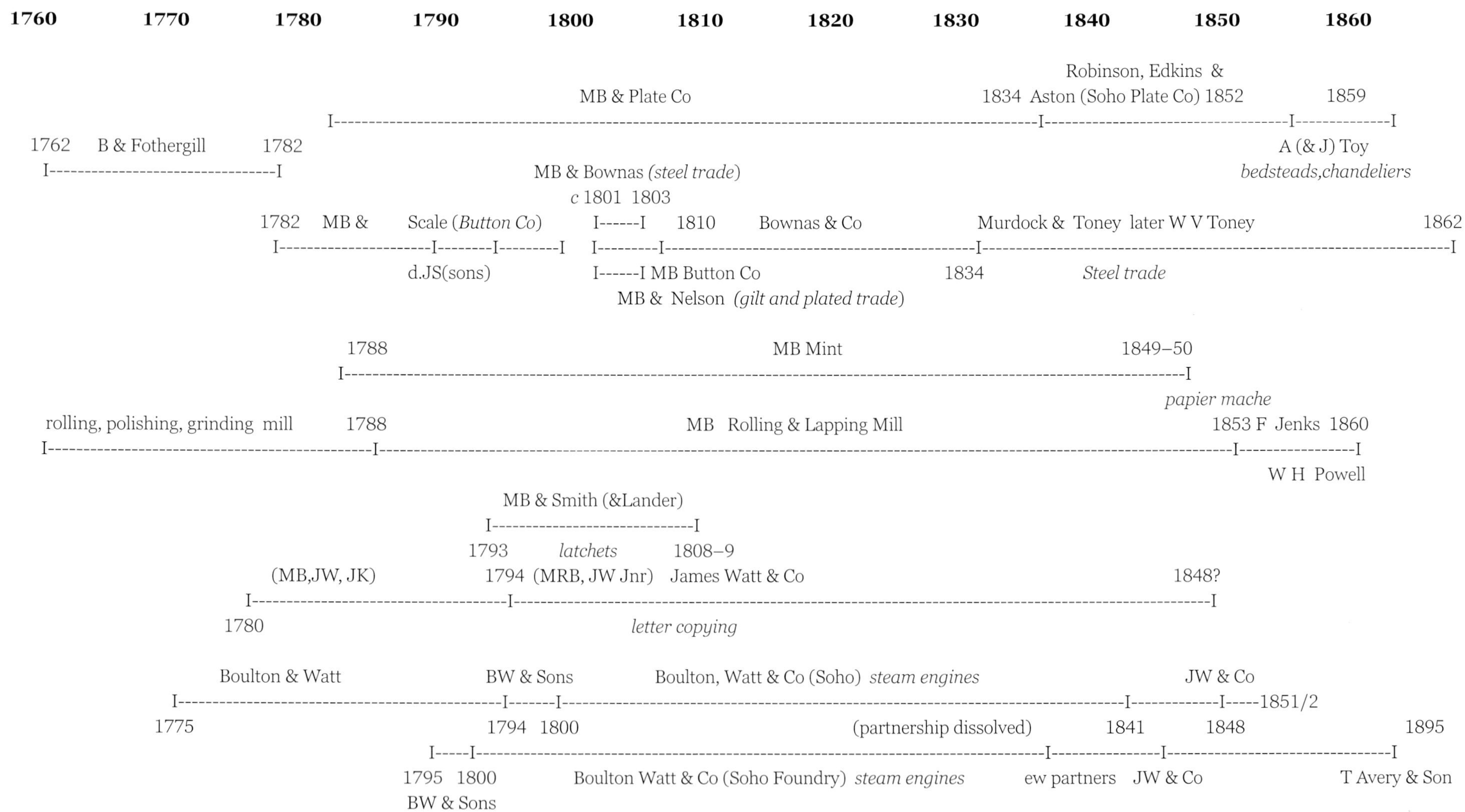
1760
1770
1780
1790
1800
1810
1820
1830
1840
1850
1860
Robinson, Edkins &
MB & Plate Co
1834 Aston (Soho Plate Co) 1852
1859
1762 B & Fothergill 1782
A (& J) Toy
bedsteads,chandeliers
MB & Bownas *(steel trade)*
c 1801 1803
1782 MB &
Scale (*Button Co*)
1810
Bownas & Co
Murdock & Toney later W V Toney
1862
d.JS(sons)
MB Button Co
1834
Steel trade
MB & Nelson *(gilt and plated trade)*
1788
MB Mint
1849–50
papier mache
rolling, polishing, grinding mill
1788
MB Rolling & Lapping Mill
1853 F Jenks 1860
W H Powell
MB & Smith (&Lander)
1793
latchets
1808–9
(MB,JW, JK)
1794 (MRB, JW Jnr)
James Watt & Co
1848?
1780
letter copying
Boulton & Watt
BW & Sons
Boulton, Watt & Co (Soho) *steam engines*
JW & Co
1851/2
1775
1794 1800
(partnership dissolved)
1841
1848
1895
1795 1800
Boulton Watt & Co (Soho Foundry) *steam engines*
ew partners
JW & Co
T Avery & Son
BW & Sons

lasted only until 1803.[4] In 1804, the Matthew Boulton Button Company was formed; it survived until December 1809 when – a few months after his father's death – Matthew Robinson Boulton sold the business to John Bownas.[5] In 1820, John Bownas died insolvent, leaving his brother Edward to sort out the creditors of the former Messrs John Bownas & Company.[6] Matthew Robinson Boulton distrained the company's tools and stock-in-trade for arrears of rent. The 'Steel Trade', as the button business was subsequently to be called, appears to have been retained by Matthew Robinson Boulton until he sold it in 1832 to the cousins, William Vickers Toney and William Murdoch; the latter was the grandson of the illustrious William Murdoch, who made such an important contribution to the firm of Boulton & Watt (*see* Chapter 7).[7] After 1840, William Toney took over the business on his own, trading in steel buttons and fire-irons at the Manufactory until the latter's demolition in 1862–3.

The plated-ware companies

The history of the plated-ware business after 1782 follows simpler lines. In this year, Matthew Boulton created a separate firm under the management of William Bingley, which, from July 1782 to November 1783, was entered into the accounts as William Bingley & Company.[8] Thereupon, it was called the Matthew Boulton & Plate Company and, on the whole, was more profitable than the button company. It was not until 1834 that Matthew Robinson Boulton disposed of it to John Robinson, Samuel Edkins and Thomas Aston, who began trading as the 'Soho Plate Co'.[9] The latter company vacated Soho in about 1850 and plated-ware manufacture finally ceased; in September 1852, a lease of the same premises was made out to Alfred Toy, who also leased Soho House. It was, however, James Toy & Son who were listed in the trade directories as general brass founders and manufacturers of metal bedsteads and gas chandeliers.[10] These activities caused much nuisance to the newly built villa owners on Soho Hill, and in late 1859 Alfred Toy was removed from Soho to the new Soho works at Spring Hill, Birmingham.[11]

The Mint company

The Mint business, known as MB Mint, began at the Manufactory in the mid-1780s and in 1788 moved into existing garden premises, which subsequently expanded into the Soho Mint. It was directly controlled by Matthew Boulton, for whom it was a passion, and was never organised through partnerships. Matthew Robinson Boulton took over the business on his father's death in 1809 and used the firm of Boulton & Watt as a subcontractor to manufacture many of the coining-machinery parts for export. Matthew Piers Watt Boulton inherited the business in 1842 after his father's death, but closed the Mint in late 1849. When the Mint contents were auctioned in the following year, the firm of Heaton's in Birmingham purchased three presses but the fourth went to the Soho Foundry, which was by this time in the ownership of the firm of James Watt & Company. In 1860, they set up another mint (also to be called the Soho Mint) at the southern fringe of the Foundry site against the Birmingham canal (*see* Chapter 7).[12]

The rolling and lapping mill

The rolling and lapping mill originally formed part of the firm of Boulton & Fothergill. When this partnership was dissolved in 1781, the mill became Boulton's personal estate and its power was thenceforth rented out to the various Soho companies, the heaviest users of the lapping part being Boulton & Scale and Matthew Boulton & Plate Company. Rolling metal – most notably copper – became important for coining from the mid-1780s, and from 1787 to 1789 the ledgers record the 'Rolling Company at Soho'.[13] Eventually, the rolling function of the mill became absorbed into the coining business, but survived the demolition of the Mint. The rolling facility was taken over in 1853 by F Jenks (a papier-mâché maker) and then by W H Powell until about 1860 before its demolition in 1862–3.[14]

The latchet company

In about 1792, Boulton began a partnership with the brothers James and Benjamin Smith to produce latchets, a flexible type of shoe buckle. A new building was constructed between the Mint and the Manufactory and part of the lapping mill was rented. The latchet business, as Matthew Boulton & Smith, lasted until about 1808–9 as buckles went quickly out of fashion.[15]

Fig A2.1 (opposite) A time-line diagram of the main Soho businesses

Boulton & Watt and its successors

The most renowned partnership at Soho, that between Matthew Boulton and James Watt, was forged on 1 June 1775, a few days after Watt had extended his original 1769 patent for another 25 years by an Act of Parliament. It has been stressed many times – but the point is worth making again – that the firm of Boulton & Watt in its early years acted as engineering consultants and did not produce steam engines. Boulton was always keen to do the latter but was held back by Watt. It was not until the period 1795–1804 that the firm at both its Soho sites made and assembled all their steam-engine parts. In October 1794, Matthew Robinson Boulton, James Watt Jr and the latter's brother Gregory entered the firm, which was restyled Boulton, Watt & Sons.[16] On 4 July 1800, James Watt senior gave up his then small stake and Boulton, Watt & Company, Soho was formed. On the death of Gregory Watt in 1804, James Watt Jr succeeded to his share, and when Matthew Boulton died in 1809, Matthew Robinson Boulton inherited his father's portion. At this point, therefore, James Watt Jr and Matthew Robinson Boulton became sole partners, each holding a half share of the firm.

A parallel business structure had been created at the Soho Foundry so that by 1809 the same partners had equal shares in Boulton, Watt & Company, Soho Foundry.[17] A new agreement of 4 July 1810 stipulated that after 31 years or sooner the partnership could be dissolved, but allowing only each side and no outsider to bid for the assets.[18] In 1840, on these terms, James Watt Jr reluctantly became sole owner of the Soho engine businesses, having made the higher valuation and not knowing that Matthew Robinson Boulton had deliberately undervalued. His higher bid of £30,000 was paid to Matthew Robinson Boulton, and it was agreed to retain the name Boulton, Watt & Company so long as James Watt junior remained with the firm. In 1841, he found the new partners he was seeking in H W Blake, James Brown and Gilbert Hamilton. The name Boulton, Watt & Company was retained until James Watt Jr's death in 1848, when it was altered to James Watt & Company. A few years later, the firm decided to abandon the Manufactory site and consolidate at the Soho Foundry. It is important to realise that no member of the Boulton or Watt families was involved in this decision and that in 1850 Matthew Piers Watt Boulton (Matthew Robinson Boulton's son) sold one press from the Soho Mint to James Watt & Company at the Foundry. Ten years later the firm established a new mint using the 60-year-old Boulton & Watt technology, confusingly called the Soho Mint, but best referred to as the Soho Foundry Mint.[19] By 1880, H W Blake was the sole surviving partner and in 1895, due to his own financial difficulties, sold James Watt & Company to W & T Avery (weighing-machine manufacturers), who remain to this day in possession of the Foundry site, having been absorbed into the much larger international firm of Avery Weigh-Tronix.

The letter-copying business

The original James Watt & Company was formed on 20 March 1780 to produce the letter-copying machines invented and patented by James Watt. The machines could also be used for plan copying, many produced in the drawing office at the Manufactory and which survive in the engine portfolios of the Boulton and Watt collection.[20] The partners were originally James Watt, Matthew Boulton, and James Keir. In 1794, when the patent expired, Keir retired and the elder Boulton and Watt withdrew, handing the business over to James Watt Jr and Matthew Robinson Boulton as partners with equal shares in the firm. Watt Jr designed a portable version that could be opened up to form a writing desk. Production of this labour-saving device continued at the Manufactory until at least 1841 and perhaps only ceased in 1848 when James Watt Jr died. Its buildings seem to have been demolished along with the engine works in about 1853.

Appendix 3

Biographies

These biographies are provided as a guide to the contribution of the major figures in the development of the buildings and power systems of the three Soho sites, the principal theme of this book. Readers are directed to more comprehensive biographies available in published books, the Dictionary of National Biography and the internet.

Matthew Boulton (1728–1809)

There is no doubt that the Soho enterprises would never have come into being without Matthew Boulton. This Birmingham-born manufacturer established the Soho Manufactory in 1761 on Handsworth Heath at the site of a recently established watermill to manufacture hardware products, such as buttons and buckles. In 1765–7 he built the Palladian principal building to diversify into plated and silver ware. In 1774 James Watt and his improved steam engine arrived from Scotland and the famous partnership was born. Owing to the inadequate water supply, Watt's steam engine was put to work recirculating water to the mill, but Boulton saw that there was a market for selling Watt's power source. In 1775 and 1781, workshops were added to the Manufactory to produce small engine parts, a modest beginning to the engine works, greatly expanded by Boulton's son, Matthew Robinson Boulton, in 1802–4.

In 1788 Boulton established the first steam-powered mint in the world on a separate site a short distance from the Manufactory, its peculiar layout the result of being hidden within the 'fairy farm' or menagerie he had established in his park. He also rebuilt his watermill, with a rotary engine powering the laps or polishers so that the waterwheel could be employed exclusively in turning the metal rolls to flatten copper into sheets for coinage. The mint was greatly expanded in 1797–9 to produce the national coinage, employing radically different machinery relying on vacuum power, produced by a new steam engine. Typically restive and seeking novelty, in 1794 Boulton established a separate works near the Manufactory to produce 'latchets', a springy removable buckle. This venture failed by 1806 owing to changing fashion. With the help of his son, Matthew Robinson Boulton, the Manufactory had reached more or less its maximum size by 1805, four years before his death.

Matthew Robinson Boulton (1770–1842)

The son of Matthew Boulton and his second wife, Ann, Matthew Robinson Boulton became a partner in the firm, Boulton, Watt & Sons in 1794. In this role he designed the layout of the expanded Manufactory engine works in 1802–4, as part of the project for establishing the production of complete steam engines commenced at the Soho Foundry, Smethwick in 1795. He had seen William Murdoch's beamless small engines successfully installed at the Soho Foundry in 1799 and used the same in his refitted engine house at the Manufactory. Matthew Robinson also took over the mint business after his father's death in 1809 and completely rebuilt the Soho Mint in 1824–6, incorporating the existing redundant Latchet (Crescent) Building and finally completing its original crescent-shaped design. In 1840 Matthew Robinson withdrew from his partnership with James Watt Jr in the Boulton, Watt & Co business and died two years later.

In 1815 he had purchased the Great Tew estate in Oxfordshire and claims that he had retired for the life of a country gentleman are not fully justified in view of his continuing heavy involvement in the mint business. By 1834 he had, however, completely relinquished his interest in a large part of the Manufactory premises devoted to the button and plated-ware business, leasing them to non-family partnerships. His extensive papers in the Soho Archive have been little studied and we await a measured assessment of his life in a comprehensive biography.

Matthew Piers Watt Boulton (1820–94)

Matthew Piers Watt Boulton was the third child and first son of Matthew Robinson Boulton and his wife, Mary Anne. He inherited the mint business in 1842 and ownership of the manufactory and mint buildings, but his father had already given up his partnership in Boulton, Watt & Co and responsibility for its premises both at the Foundry and Manufactory. Outside of the Soho world, Matthew Piers Watt Boulton is better known as a classicist and inventor, particularly the aileron, patented in 1868, some 36 years before it was first employed in manned flight. Reclusive and financially secure, he was more interested in pursuing a life of study and writing as a philosopher-scientist, his mind attracted to subjects other than managing the Soho businesses. In 1850 he put up the contents of the Soho Mint for sale, after which the buildings were demolished in the early 1850s. In 1853 he witnessed the demolition of the engine works and letter-copying premises at the Manufactory. They had been leased to James Watt & Co, which had decided to consolidate on one site at the Foundry. In the early 1860s, under pressure perhaps, he had the rest of the Manufactory demolished including the iconic principal building, the last to be brought down in early 1863. Matthew Piers Watt Boulton had already begun to develop Soho Park for middle class villa housing, its new residents complaining of the clamour and smell emitted from the industrial buildings. Illustrious Soho had lasted little more than a hundred years.

William Creighton (1778–1831)

Born in the Kendal area, William Creighton was apprenticed in 1792 to the firm of Boulton & Watt and after 1800 was employed as an engine fitter and agent, and from about 1815 as head of the Drawing Office at the Soho Manufactory. Early in his apprenticeship in 1797 he drew one of the few known views of the Soho Foundry (*see* Fig 7.19). In 1825 he produced the important set of Soho Mint plans that were crucial in informing the archaeological excavations at the site in 1995–6 (*see* Figs 5.25–5.28). The pencilling in, presumably his, of an underground pulley on the original inked cross section led to the discovery of the long tunnel that contained the drive shaft (*see* Fig 5.33).

Peter Ewart (1767–1842)

Peter Ewart was an engineer apprenticed to John Rennie, whom he assisted in the erection of the new rolling and lapping mill at the Manufactory. In 1786 he carried out experiments on the new waterwheel to test its efficiency. He returned in 1788 to supervise the erection of the lap engine and may have helped in setting up the first Soho mint. From 1796 to 1798 he was engaged by Boulton & Watt to set up the boring mill at the Foundry. He had originally suggested a vertical boring machine, but this idea was abandoned for the horizontal arrangement. His drawing of the machinery has survived (*see* Fig 7.18), but it did not prove to be successful, the main problem being that a single beam engine was expected not only to power the boring machine, but also lathes and drills. Efficiency was lost through the friction of a great number of cogged wheels and leather straps. In 1798 the solution was provided by William Murdoch in dedicating a single small engine to a boring machine.

Gilbert Hamilton (1803–82)

Gilbert Hamilton joined the drawing office as a draughtsman in about 1821 and took over its management a short while after the death of William Creighton in 1831. When James Watt Jr was left in sole charge of the firm of Boulton, Watt & Co in 1840, he decided to take on new partners, Gilbert Hamilton and James Brown, another Boulton & Watt employee. Each was given a 2/12 share, another 3/12 awarded to Henry Wollaston Blake, a London businessman, James Watt Jr retaining the largest 5/12 share. On the death of Watt Jr in 1848, the other three took over the firm, renaming it James Watt and Co. It appears that Gilbert Hamilton took the strain of supervising the erection of the Soho Foundry Mint in 1860, although the decision to build was probably made by the partners jointly.

They had also probably earlier initiated the construction of the massive erecting shop in 1847 and the gasometer in 1848, frequently misidentified as William Murdoch's.

William Murdoch (1754–1839)

After arriving at Soho in 1777, Murdoch was employed by Boulton & Watt as an engine erector and spent much time in Cornwall. He was a restless genius inventor, however, continually experimenting beyond the world of engineering, in which he excelled. He is credited with the invention of the sun-and-planet rotary gear that enabled Boulton & Watt to circumvent the crank patent. His pioneering design of small beamless engines was introduced in the Soho Foundry boring mill in 1799, which had previously been bedevilled by problems of vibrating boring rods and the friction of a multitude of cogged wheels and leather belts. Each small engine was dedicated to a boring machine and power was transmitted at junctions in the shafting by another of his inventions, the worm screw.

Busy though he was, at the end of December 1798 had had manged to light the foundry with gas piped from a retort placed in his laboratory. In 1802 his experiments with gas lighting were resumed and the foundry was lit once more. By 1805 the system was successfully extended to several more foundry buildings, encouraging Boulton & Watt to take up the business of selling gas plant to other manufacturers.

Matthew Robinson Boulton witnessed the successful adoption of Murdoch's small engines at the Foundry. In 1802–4 he decided to install another three in the existing engine house as part of the major refurbishment and expansion of the engine works at the Manufactory. James Watt's beam engine was removed and replaced by two table-top and one bell-crank engine (*see* Figs 4.12–4.14).

John Rennie (1761–1821)

This renowned Scottish mechanical and civil engineer masterminded the rebuilding of Soho Mill in 1785, turning it round by 90 degrees and greatly expanding its size. A new waterwheel of 20ft (6.1m) was installed, driving rolls on one side and polishers (laps) on the other. At the same time he was engaged by Boulton & Watt to help set up the first commercial steam-powered corn mill at the Albion Mill, London.

John Southern (c 1758–1815)

Born in Derbyshire, John Southern came to Soho in 1782 to assist James Watt and proved to be an able and inventive engineer. This despite Watt's wish that he give up music on taking up his new position. He worked as both a draughtsman and engine erector, taking on the supervision of the new drawing office built about 1790 at the Manufactory. In 1785 he surveyed a water-powered rolling mill in King's Norton, then outside Birmingham, for its owner, Thomas Dobbs, who had decided to purchase a Boulton & Watt engine to aid his waterwheel. It was installed in 1787, one of the earliest rotary steam engines adopted in the Birmingham area. The venture was not a success, Dobbs refusing to pay the premiums, and the engine was removed in 1793. This did not deter John Southern from marrying Cordelia, Dobbs's eldest daughter, in the same year.

Southern's hand can be seen on many of the early Boulton & Watt engine drawings, but his major claim to fame, largely unrecognised to date, is his application of vacuum power to run coining presses. The first 1788 mint primarily used mechanical power, with the presses arranged in a circle, but the blows imparted to the coins shook the framework to pieces. Southern proposed that the steam engine attached by pumps should be used to create a vacuum in a tube. This was to be placed alongside the presses, now necessarily arranged in a line. A complicated system of linkages aided by additional small vacuum pumps gave motion to each of the screws of the presses. It was Southern's invention that powered all the subsequent Boulton mints erected at the Tower of London and overseas. Southern died in 1815 and never saw its wider application both in the reorganised Soho Mint of 1824–6 and much later at the new mint established in 1860 at the Soho Foundry.

He is buried in the Dobbs family vault situated near the south door of King's Norton church.

James Watt (1736–1819)

Unlike his partner, Matthew Boulton, about whom far fewer words have been written, James Watt was little involved in the development and construction of industrial buildings. In 1782, on the rare occasion when it is known that Watt proffered advice on the height of the intended engine house at the Manufactory, he was overruled. From 1780 his new copying-press company was accommodated in Boulton's existing buildings. In 1795 he did, however, purchase the canal-side land in Smethwick on which the Soho Foundry was built.

Far more important was his contribution to the power systems introduced at the Manufactory, where in 1775 the first working James Watt steam engine in the world was put to work returning water to the rolling and polishing mill. Replaced by a larger cylinder, 'Old Bess', as she was known, survived to the very end of the Manufactory and was rescued by the Science Museum in London, where it remains on display (*see* Fig 2.11). It was in the new engine house mentioned above that in 1782 and 1783 Watt's double-acting and rotative engines using the sun-and-planet gear were first tested. They were applied in the first instance to tilt hammers and corn milling machinery. In 1788 rotative engines were installed at the Soho Mint and in the lapping mill, which was also saved by the Science Museum (*see* Fig 2.13). The 'lap engine' also powered Boulton's cutting-out presses for coin blanks.

James Watt had much improved the steam engine, but inventive genius can also be narrowed into a channel that does not easily look forward. As far as Watt was concerned, the future remained the beam engine, and it took another genius in the firm of Boulton & Watt, William Murdoch, to realise that there was a ready market for small, beamless engines. It was these that were installed in 1802–4 by Matthew Robinson Boulton in the refurbished engine room at the Manufactory engine works. The beam engine had one more use, however, when in 1824–6 the third and last steam engine was put to work by Matthew Robinson Boulton in his rebuilt mint.

James Watt Jr (1769–1848)

James Watt Jr was the eldest son of James Watt, by his first wife, Margaret. In 1794 James, his brother, Gregory, and Matthew Robinson Boulton were taken into the new firm, styled Boulton, Watt & Sons. Within a year a start had been made on the first purpose-built engine manufactory in the world, which Boulton and Watt seniors had little to do with except to preside at the opening ceremony and buy the land, respectively. It was James Watt Jr who took the major role in masterminding and planning the whole enterprise, initially calling on William Wilkinson to advise on a layout. He obtained help again to overhaul the malfunctioning boring mill. Recalling William Murdoch from Cornwall, he allowed him the opportunity of installing his recently invented small engines, aware of but, in the end, undeterred by his father's stubborn attitude to any design but a beam engine.

As the principal in the management of the Soho Foundry, he oversaw its massive expansion between the years 1795 and 1848 (*see* Figs 7.2, 7.29, 7.37, 7.40, 7.47). His partner, Matthew Robinson Boulton, could concentrate his effort on the Soho Manufactory and Mint, and in particular the engine works there. When Matthew Robinson Boulton withdrew from the firm in 1840, James felt the need to take on new partners (*see* Gilbert Hamilton above). It is probable, therefore, that in 1847, a year before Watt Jr's death, the initiative to construct the impressive erecting shop (grade II*) lay with these partners.

William Wilkinson (1744–1808)

The Wilkinson brothers of Bersham, near Wrexham, Wales, were considered to be the best manufacturers of engine cylinders in the country, and Boulton & Watt relied on them until 1795 when William and John (1728–1808) quarrelled and the Bersham Ironworks closed. James Watt Jr had received his early technical education at Bersham and it was to William that he turned for advice on the layout of the proposed Soho Foundry. William must have visited the greenfield site and realised that the slope of the land could be exploited to aid the movement of heavy newly cast cylinders to the rolling mill. The map he produced is rare and important historical document (*see* Fig 7.5).

When William died in 1808, he appointed James Watt Jr as the guardian of his young daughters.

William Wyatt (1734–80)

Architects were not needed for most of the utilitarian Soho buildings, but when Matthew Boulton decided to add a plated-ware manufactory he engaged William Wyatt, son of Benjamin Wyatt (1709–72) and brother of the better known, Samuel Wyatt (1737–1807). The building he designed, perhaps with the help of his brother, reflected the pretensions and ambition of Matthew Boulton. The principal building (1765–7), as it was called, dominates the most common view of the Soho Manufactory, a Palladian mansion housing workshops, warehouses, showrooms and staff accommodation. William Wyatt's relationship with Boulton must have been strained to the limit as the original estimate of costs had risen fivefold by the time the final account was settled. Boulton went on to employ other members of the Wyatt family at Soho House, but not William.

Another architect of the Wyatt dynasty, William's cousin, Benjamin (1755–1813), built the central bay of the Latchet (Crescent) Building in 1798, but the name of the original designer of the whole classical composition is not known.

Abbreviations

As used in reference to correspondence

GW	Gregory Watt
JS	John Southern
JW	James Watt
JWJ	James Watt Jr
MB	Matthew Boulton
MRB	Matthew Robinson Boulton
WW	William Wilkinson
BMT	Birmingham Museums Trust
LoB	Library of Birmingham, Archives and Collections

Notes

Chapter 1

1 In a pioneering study of the Boulton & Watt engine portfolios, Tann published plans of the Soho Manufactory, Mint and Foundry, but with no analysis of their content: Tann 1970, 78, 80, 90. Likewise Delieb and Roberts reproduced plans, now lost, of the much-illustrated Palladian 'principal building' at the Soho Manufactory without commentary on their significance: Delieb and Roberts 1971, 28, 30–1. Listings of workshops at the Soho Manufactory are provided by Goodison in his monumental work on ormolu, but their physical arrangement is not attempted: Goodison 2002, 23–5. Roll's important study of the Boulton & Watt firm and its organisation analysed some of the documentation relating to the layout of the intended extension of the engine works at the Soho Manufactory, but concluded that the actual arrangement could not be established: Roll 1930, 168–78, plates at 316. In his important paper, Gale recognised the contribution of William Wilkinson, the Bersham ironmaster, to the original layout of the Foundry, but his analysis with plans was limited to the earliest years of the establishment: Gale 1961, 73–87. His sketch map of the Soho Foundry phases has needed considerable adjustment, but he was the first to publish a plan of the Soho Foundry in 1895, on the eve of its sale to W & T Avery: Gale 1948, 38, 48. Doty, in his chapter devoted entirely to the development of the Soho Mint, published neither any of the plans available in the Soho archive nor discussed how the three fundamental reorganisations of the mint were physically laid out: Doty 1998, 23–73; *see* Chapter 5. Preceding this book, any detailed analysis of the physical arrangement of the three Soho sites can be found in the author's three articles published as part of the Matthew Boulton bicentenary celebrations (*see* Bibliography, Published Articles).

2 Gale's attempt to eliminate the confusion between the Soho Manufactory and Mint has in many cases fallen on deaf ears: Gale 1961, 73.

3 Copper cake is the raw form of the smelted copper delivered to the rolling mill to be rolled into sheets.

4 Biographical summaries are provided in Appendix 3.

5 The Manufactory was established on Handsworth Heath nearly two miles from the main centre of population, Birmingham; the Foundry is on the Birmingham Canal in Smethwick in an area where the population was almost entirely scattered.

Chapter 2

1 Library of Birmingham, Archives and Collections (subsequently LoB), MS3782/12/1, 66, MB to J H Ebinghaus, 2 March 1768.

2 'Toys' were small metal domestic and personal goods designed for ornament or adornment.

3 Jones 2008, 55–6. Goodison recites many contemporary visitor accounts that marvelled at the wide range of goods and the specialist production methods for which the Manufactory soon became famous (Goodison 2002, 22–6). Most attention by scholars has been given to the luxury hardwares such as ormolu (Goodison 2002) and silver and plated ware (Delieb and Roberts 1971). The button and buckle trade awaits a definitive work.

4 LoB, 324197, lease from John Wyrley to Ruston and Eaves, 3 Feb 1757.

5 LoB, MS3782/60/265, 'Case between B[oulton] and F[othergill]'.

6 Pelham 1963, 79–82; Pelham 1964, 503–4.

7 LoB, MS3782/60/265.

8 Recited in a mortgage of the Soho estate dated 13 Dec 1766, LoB, MS2294.

9 Birmingham University Collections, Wyatt Papers 20, Letter from John Wyatt to an unknown friend, 29 Aug [1762].

10 The principal building was the large Palladian-style frontage building, constructed in 1766–7, which dominates most of the views of the Manufactory (see pp 11–17); see also, Demidowicz 2013, 67–83.

11 The actual direction was north-east, but for convenience east will refer to north-east, south to south-east etc.

12 LoB, MS3782/1/19, 49, 66–7: J Fothergill to Mr Montreal, 4 Jan 1763; J Fothergill to Guadalupe, 15 Jan 1763; J Fothergill to Montreal, 6 Jul 1763.

13 Recited in mortgage, 13 Dec 1766, LoB, MS2294.

14 Cule 1935, 6–7.

15 LoB, MS3782/12/85/204, William Wyatt to MB, 16 Sep 1763.

16 LoB, MS3782/1/34, 235; MS3782/1/16, 11, Boulton & Fothergill to John Perchard, 18 Aug 1764.

17 LoB, MS3782/12/60/34, J Fothergill to MB, 14 Dec 1765.

18 LoB, MS3782/12/20; MS3782/12/60/265, Memorandum by MB [1766].

19 LoB, MS3782/12/20.

20 Ibid.

21 LoB, MS3782/12/85/211, William Wyatt to MB, 29 Dec 1766.

22 LoB, MS3782/12/20.

23 LoB, MS3782/1/16, 107, MB to Samuel Wyatt, 26 Apr 1765.

24 LoB, MS3782/1/16, 138–9, MB to Woolley & Hemming, 19/20 Jun 1765.

25 LoB, MS3782/12/60/38, John Fothergill to MB, 21 Dec 1765.

26 LoB, MS3782/1/16, 158, MB to John Lewis Baumgartner, 13 Jul 1765.

27 LoB, MS3782/1/16, 149–50, MB to William Rigg, 2 Jul 1765; MS3782/12/60/20, MS3782/12/60/22, J Fothergill to MB, 3 and 5 Nov 1765.

28 LoB, MS3782/12/72/1, John Scale to MB, 12 Nov 1765; LoB, MS3782/60/25, J Fothergill to MB, 9 Nov 1765.

29 LoB, MS3782/1/16, 250, John Fothergill to MB, 12 Nov 1765.

30 LoB, MS3782/12/60/37, John Fothergill to MB, 19 Dec 1765; LoB, MS3782/12/60/34, John Fothergill to MB, 14 Dec 1765.

31 LoB, MS3782/1/16, 339, MB to Nathaniel Jeffrys, 8 Mar 1766.

32 LoB, MS3782/12/85/211, William Wyatt to MB, 29 Dec 1766.

33 LoB, MS3782/12/1, 66.

34 See mortgage, 13 Dec 1766, LoB, MS2294.

35 Cule, 10–17.

36 LoB, MS3782/12/1, 30, MB to J H Ebinghaus, 28 Oct 1767.

37 MS3782/85/211.

38 Jones 1985, 20–4, 35–6.
39 LoB, MS49/76, 59, *Batiment vu par devant* (Timmins Collection).
40 LoB, MS3782/12/23/131, William Jupp to MB, 25 May 1769 enclosing invoice for work Dec 1767–Oct 1768.
41 Connor 1984.
42 See mortgage, 13 Dec 1766, LoB, MS2294.
43 Cule, 28, 37.
44 LoB, MS3782/12/20.
45 Smiles 1904, 22–61; Dickinson 1935, 45–122; Dickinson 1937, 75–88.
46 MS3782/12/20.
47 LoB, MS3782/1/23/13; MS3782/6/3, 151.
48 LoB, MS3782/12/76/110, MB to JW [JW's endorsed date: end Aug/Sep 1775].
49 LoB, MS3782/1/5.
50 Goodison 1974, 104–8; Goodison 2002, 192–6.
51 Memoir of Matthew Boulton by Keir 1947, 6–7; Dickinson 1937, 58–9.
52 LoB, MS3782/1/3, 223, 3 Dec 1776.
53 LoB, MS3782/13/126, Inventory Nov 1776.
54 Dickinson and Jenkins 1927, 121–2.
55 Dickinson 1937, 108–9, appendix II.
56 LoB, MS3782/1/4, 467.
57 LoB, MS3147/3/5/42, MB to JW, 11 Sep 1781 plus enclosed plan.
58 LoB, MS3147/5/1447.
59 LoB, MS3782/2/13, Soho Inventory 1782.
60 LoB, MS3782/12/102/1, 'Inventory of the several pieces of Buildings of the Soho Manufactory', 16 Dec 1783.
61 LoB, MS3782/12/102/6, 'Particulars of the Houses & Workshops & Mills of Soho' [*c* 1789].
62 LoB, MS3782/12/60/189, 191, John Fothergill to MB, 10 and 12 Apr 1780; LoB, MS3782/12/72/28, John Scale to MB, 10 Apr 1780.
63 LoB, MS3782/1/2, 202; LoB, MS3782/2/1, 12.
64 LoB, MS3782/12/72/53, John Scale to MB, 7 Sep 1784; LoB, MS3782/13/49/10, John Rennie Expenses *re* Rolling Mill work 1784–6.
65 LoB, MS3782/12/72/59–60, John Scale to MB, 3 and 8 Aug 1785.
66 Boucher 1963, 8–9, 79–80.
67 Dickinson 1937, 133–5.
68 Selgin 2011, 280–1.
69 Dickinson 1937, 136–8.
70 LoB, MS3782/12/66/106, John Roberts to MB, 27 Jan 1788.
71 Dickinson 1937, Fig 5, 141; Patent 8 Jul 1790, no 1757.
72 LoB, MS3782/12/108/53, 28–9; LoB, MS3147/3/12/1, MB to J W Edingburg, 8 Jan 1788; LoB, MS3782/13/49/20, John Rennie to MB, 4 Jul 1788.
73 LoB, MS378212/108/53, 6–7.
74 LoB, MS3782/12/66/1, James Lawson Journal, 22 Jan 1789.
75 National Library of Scotland, MS19824, 6–7, MB to John Rennie, 3 Aug 1788.
76 LoB, MS3147/5/1447.
77 LoB, MS3782/12/102/6.
78 LoB, MS3147/9/8, inventories 30 Sep 1790, 1791, 1792.
79 BMT, Phillp album, 11b, 23.
80 Ibid., 19.
81 LoB, MS3147/5/714c.
82 Gale 1961, 76; Ince 2000, 5.
83 LoB, MS3782/12/106/3.
84 LoB, MS3782/12/106/37, 'Case of Smith' [Boulton memorandum].
85 LoB, MS3782/12/106/38, 'The Mint and its Shops' [Crescent Building costs]; LoB, MS3147, MB to JW, 9 Feb 1794.
86 LoB, MS3782/12/40/1, MB to C Glover, 1 Jan 1795.
87 LoB, MS3782/3/1, 102; LoB, MS3782/6/97, 103–14; LoB, MS3782/6/92.
88 LoB, MS3147/4/145, Day Book Drawings 1786–1841.
89 LoB, MS3782/6/92.
90 LoB, MS3782/12/106/38.
91 Ibid.
92 LoB, MS3782/12/106/37.
93 LoB, MS3782/2/4, 256–9.
94 LoB, MS378212/46/341, Notice to Benjamin Smith and James Smith, 29 Oct 1807.
95 LoB, MS3782/13/120, Particulars of the Builders Work, Aug 1825.
96 Dickinson 1937, 148; LoB, MS4282, MB to JS, 6 Mar 1797.
97 LoB, MS4282, MB to JS, 19 May 1797.
98 LoB, MS3147/5/714d.
99 LoB, MS3782/12/66/92–3, JS to MB, 21 Nov 1798, 14 Dec 1798.
100 LoB, MS3782/12/66/101, JS to MB, 1 May 1799.
101 LoB, MS3782/12/59/190, William Cheshire to MB, 30 May 1799.
102 LoB, MS3147/4/110; MS3147/5/713.
103 LoB, MS3147/9/25.
104 LoB, MS3147/5/1444, Plan of the engine house prior to reorganisation, not dated [before 1802].
105 LoB, MS3069; B&W 529.
106 LoB, MS3069/13/3/86; Loggie 2011, 296–7.
107 LoB, MS3782/2/4, 204; MS3782/13/126, 14, 15, 18.
108 LoB, MS3782/13/126, 21.
109 LoB, MS3782, 184, 209.
110 LoB, MS3782/13/91/2–3.
111 LoB, MS3147/5/1447 [Plan of engine works *c* 1800 with proposed yard in pencil].
112 LoB, MS3782/13/91/20.
113 LoB, MS3782/2/4, 256–9.
114 LoB, MS3782/2/4, 268–9, 288, 297, 305, 313, 341; LoB, MS3782/13/136 [MBP284/136].
115 LoB, MS3782/13/126, 21, 25.
116 LoB, MS3782/2/4, 341; LoB, MS3782/8/12, 20.
117 LoB, MS3782/13/126, 'Inventory of Tools, Utensils & other Goods the property of M R Boulton ... June 1820'.
118 LoB, MS3782/13/126, 122, 'Inventory of the Stock and Tools belonging to the Steel Trade at Soho taken May 16, 17, 22 & 25 1832'.
119 LoB, MS3782/13/126, 115.
120 Griffiths 1992, 320–9.
121 LoB, MS3782/12/27/25, MB to MRB, 25 Sep 1788.
122 Tann and MacLeod 2016, 228–43.
123 LoB, MS3782/13/139.
124 LoB, MS3782/3/146, MRB to J Moseley, 23 Jan 1826.
125 LoB, MS3147/4/132.
126 LoB, MS3147/5/714e, plan and cross sections of the Soho new mint by William Creighton, 13 and 23 Aug 1825.
127 LoB, MS3782/255, MRB to Joseph Thompson, 31 Jul 1826.
128 LoB, MS3782/3/22, 110, 112–13, 126, 134, 149–50, 167.
129 LoB, MS3782/3/22.
130 LoB, MS3782/5/1447 [Plan of the engine company shops, with extensive pencil additions showing new yard – shaded plan, not titled or dated (1790s)].
131 *Whites Directory of Birmingham* 1855, vol 2, 533. Although the firm used the name James Toy, it was in fact Alfred, the son, who was the active member at the time, leasing the Soho premises.
132 LoB, MS3147/5/674.
133 LoB, MS3147/1/51, 273; MS3147/3/135, f 528 James Watt & Co to Alfred Toy, 16 Sep 1852; MS3147/3/135, f 537 James Watt & Co to Alfred Toy, 22 Sep 1852; MS3147/3/135, 546, James Watt & Co to James Toy and Son, 30 Sep 1852; MS3147/3/132 ff 85, 88; MS3147/4/12, 25 Sep 1858, Calculations *re* J Toy engine.
134 LoB, 157177, 'A Catalogue of the Valuable Machinery and Plant of Soho Mint ... 29 April, 1850'.
135 Ballard, Loggie and Mason 2009.
136 *The Engineer*, 2 Jul 1858.
137 LoB, Benjamin Stone Collection, 14/33/A–C, photographer: Mr Osborn.
138 LoB, MS3782/6/182.
139 Gale 1961, 83.
140 Staffordshire Record Office, D564/16; LoB, MS3782/6/182, 210.
141 *Building News*, 2 Jan 1863.
142 *Birmingham Daily Post*, 8 Jan 1863.
143 LoB, former reference MBP 472, packet of letters including Fred Thynne to Matthew Piers Watt Boulton, 4 Dec 1849: current reference not found.
144 OS 1:2500 editions, surveyed 1902–3, 1913–4; OS 1:10,560, surveyed 1913–14, revised 1938.

Chapter 3

1 In the Birmingham area the term mill was used consistently to describe buildings with water-powered machinery, some of which could be aided by steam engines (e.g. corn mill, rolling mill, blade mill, fulling mill). It was not applied to the machinery on its own. In the medieval period 'two mills under one roof' referred to two wheels and its attendant cogs and wheels within a single building, but this use is not encountered in the 18th and 19th centuries.
2 Bennett 1937, vol i, 58–9, 62–3, 88–90, 131, 148–52; LoB, Bickley, vol v, ff 311, 318.
3 Pardoe 1975, 39–40.
4 Bennett 1937, vol i, 152.
5 Shaw 1801, 118.
6 LoB, MS3782/12/60/265.
7 Bennett 1939, vol ii, 132–7.
8 LoB, MS3782/1/34, f 72.
9 LoB, MS3782/12/60/265.
10 LoB, 324197.
11 Charles Robert Autograph letters Collection, Haverford College library, Haverford, PA, USA, Matthew Boulton to Timothy Hollis, 2 Feb 1761.
12 LoB, MS3782/12/60/265; Shaw, 118.
13 Dickinson 1937, 203.
14 Anon 1885.
15 Birmingham University, Wyatt Papers/20, John Wyatt to [a friend] 29 Aug [1762].
16 LoB, MS3782/1/40, John Fothergill to Mr Guadalupe, 15 Jan 1763.
17 LoB, MS3782/60/26, John Fothergill to MB, 12 Nov 1765.
18 LoB, M3782/60/20,22,33, John Fothergill to MB, 3, 5 Nov, 11 Dec 1765.
19 LoB MS3782/1/34, ff 129, 183, 208, 263; MS3782/1/8, f 23.
20 LoB, MS3782/1/16, f 10, MB to Moses Oppenheim, 18 Aug 1764.
21 LoB, MS3782/1/16, f 188, MB to Messrs John Cottrell & Company, 31 Aug 1765.
22 LoB, MS3782/1/8, ff 121, 124–5, 128, 130, 134.
23 LoB, MS3782/12/20.
24 LoB, MS3782/1/16, f 218, MB to Moses Oppenheim 5 Oct 1765.
25 LoB, MS3782/1/8, ff 210, 214, 218, 222.
26 LoB, MS3782/1/8, f 145, 11 Jan 1766.
27 Dickinson 1937, 202.
28 Shaw, 11; Dickinson 1937, 202.
29 LoB, MS3782/12/2, f 29, MB to James Adam, 1 Oct 1770.
30 LoB, MS3782/12/2, f 34, MB to Thomas Gilbert, 2 Feb 1771.
31 LoB, MS3782/12/72/13, John Scale to MB, 27 May 1773.
32 Dickinson 1937, 75–6; Shaw, 11.
33 Hills 2005, 52–3.
34 LoB, MS3782/1/23/13.
35 LoB, MS3782/12/76/110, MB to JW [Watt's endorsed date: end Aug/Sep 1775].
36 Respectively, 3.66m, 7.32m and 5.49m; LoB MS, MB to Burton Wilbie, 15 Aug 1775.
37 Although the engine was installed to do practical work, of necessity many experiments were carried out on it in order to improve its performance, which in the early days was disappointing. These are described in some detail by Dickinson and Jenkins 1927, 107–10 and Hills, 52–6.
38 LoB, MS3782/6/3, f 194.
39 LoB, MS3782/12/108/68.
40 Smiles 1904, 212, quoting letter JW to MB, 4 Aug 1777.
41 LoB, MS3147/3/1/17, MB to JW, 13 Sept 1777.
42 LoB, MS3147/3/2/6, MB to JW, 11 July 1778; Dickinson and Jenkins, 122.
43 Griffiths 1992, 92.
44 Smiles, 212.
45 Pers. com., Ben Russell Science Museum; 1850 Sales Catalogue – LoB, 157177.
46 Dilworth 1976, 18–19; Stephens 1964, 255.
47 LoB, MS3782/12/25/13, Thos Moore to MB, 13 Jul [1761].
48 LoB, MS3782/1/8, f 88; MS3782/1/37, ff 8, 134, MB to Benjamin Huntsman, 9 Aug, 26 Nov 1764.
49 LoB, MS3782/1/8, ff 104, 108, 112, 117–8, 121, 123, 125.
50 LoB, MS3782/1/3; MS3782/1/1; MS3782/1/4; MS3782/1/2.
51 LoB, MS3782/12/25/13, Thos Moore to John Fothergill, 8 Apr 1780.
52 LoB, MS3782/12/60/189, John Fothergill to MB *c* 10 Apr 1780.
53 LoB, MS3782/12/72/28, John Scale to MB, 10 Apr 1780.
54 LoB, MS3782/12/63/15, John Hodges to MB [1780]; MS3782/12/63/28, John Hodges to MB, 6 Apr 1782.
55 LoB, MS3782/12/60/189, John Fothergill to MB, *c* 10 Apr 1780; MS3782/1/4, f 475, 30 Dec 1780.
56 LoB, MS3782/1/2.
57 LoB, MS3147/5/1460.
58 LoB, MS3782/13/126.
59 LoB, MS3782/1/3, f 53, 7 Mar 1776.
60 LoB, MS3782/1/3, ff 119, 135; MS3782/1/1 ff 37–8.
61 LoB, MS3782/1/3, f 301.
62 Harris 1986, 7–57, reprinted in Harris 1992, 158, 168–9.
63 LoB, MS3782/13/126.
64 LoB, MS3782/12/72/121, MB to John Scale, 18 Sep 1778.
65 LoB, MS3782/12/93/52, 57.
66 LoB, MS3782/1/4, f 467.
67 LoB, MS3782/2/1, f 12.
68 LoB, MS3782/1/4, f 114; MS3147/3/6/20, MB to JW, 9 Jan 1782.
69 LoB, MS3782/12/5, f 5, MB to Mr Henderson, Feb 1781; MS3782/12/6, f 16, MB to Chas Wyatt, 28 Feb 1781.
70 LoB, MS3782/12/72/51, John Scale to MB, 24 June 1784.
71 LoB, MS3147/3/8/25, MB to JW, 2 Sept 1784.
72 LoB, MS3782/13/49/10.
73 LoB, MS3782/12/72/53, John Scale to MB, 7 Sept 1784.
74 Ibid; it was drawn over part of the letter he had already written.
75 LoB, MS3782/13/49/124.
76 LoB, MS3782/12/72/59, John Scale to MB, 3 Aug 1785.
77 LoB, MS 3782/13/49/6, John Rennie to MB, 18 Aug 1785.
78 LoB, MS3782/12/72/61, John Scale to MB, 26 Aug 1785.
79 LoB, MS3782/13/49/9, John Rennie to MB, 8 Oct 1785; LoB, MS3782/12/72/62, John Scale to MB, 10 Oct 1785.
80 LoB, MS3782/13/14, account dated 6 May 1786.
81 LoB, MS3782/2/1, f 73; LoB, MS3782/13/49/10.
82 LoB, MS3782/2/3.
83 LoB, MS3782/12/63/43, John Hodges to MB, 23 Sept 1786.
84 LoB, MS3782/12/141, 10 May 1786.
85 LoB, MS3782/13/83; the current reference to 'Mr Boulton's Water Wheel at Soho' has not been identified; former location: B&W Misc Box 6 Mint Engines, Power Transmission; the possible third drawing of the Soho water wheel is at MS3147/5/146.
86 LoB, MS3782/12/74/129, Zach Walker to MB, 21 Sep 1786.
87 LoB, MS3782/12/74/121, Zach Walker to MB, 28 Sep 1786.
88 LoB, MS3782/12/32/105, Thomas Greenhow to MB, 23 Jun 1787; MS3782/12/32/157, Thomas Greenhow to MB, 12 Oct 1787; MS3782/12/32/163, Thomas Greenhow to MB, 27 Oct 1787.
89 LoB, MS3782/12/32/206; MS378212/33/20.
90 LoB, MS3782/ 12/12/108/5, loose note in notebook.
91 LoB, MS3782/13/49/19; LoB, MS3147/3/12/1, MB to James JW, 8 Jan 1788.
92 LoB, MS3782/12/33/12, Thomas Greenhow to MB, 20 Jan 1788.
93 LoB, MS3782/12/66/110, John Roberts to MB, 18 Jun 1788.
94 LoB, MS3782/ 13/49/20–21, John Rennie to MB, 4, 9 Jul 1788.
95 LoB, MS3782/13/49/23, John Rennie to MB, 15 Jul 1788.
96 LoB, MS3782/13/49/22, John Rennie to MB, 14 Jul 1788.
97 LoB, MS3782/12/6, ff 231–2, MB to John Rennie, 27 Jul 1788.

98 LoB, MS3782/12/6, f 231, MB to John Rennie, 27 Jul 1788.
99 National Library of Scotland (NLS), MS19824, 6–7, MB to John Rennie, 3 Aug. 1788.
100 NLS, MS19824/10, MB to John Rennie, 23 Oct 1788.
101 LoB, MS3782/13/20, Minutes of a conference held at Soho, 7 Jan 1820.
102 LoB, MS3147/5/714b; LoB, M3147/4/145.
103 LoB, MS3782/13/58/67, John Robinson to MRB, 27 Jan 1824.
104 LoB, MS3147/5/714b, 29 Jul 1790.
105 LoB, 608098A, Plan of Handsworth Heath ... surveyed by Samuel Botham, 1792.
106 LoB, MS3782/12/102/6.
107 LoB, MS3782/2/3, ff 114–5; LoB, MS3782/12/72/76, John Scale to MB, 20 May 1790; LoB, MS3782/12/72/79, John Scale to MB, 28 May 1790; LoB, MS3782/12/72/132, John Scale to MB, 'Rents 1 Jan 1790'.
108 LoB, MS3782/12/3, f 11, MB to Thos Wilson, 14 Apr 1789; LoB, MS3782/12/8 f 74, 'To Scale Rent of Mills'.
109 LoB, MS3782/13/141.
110 Ibid.
111 LoB, MS3147/15/4, MB to JW, 24 Mar 1791.
112 LoB, MS3782/13/36/56, MRB to MB, 27 May 1791; LoB, MS3782/13/36/58, MRB to MB, 4 Jun 1791.
113 LoB, MS3782/12/57/49, MRB to MB, 4 Jun 1791.
114 LoB, MS3782/12/66/18, James Lawson to MB, 13 Jun 1791; LoB, MS3782/12/57/51, MRB to MB, 16 Jun 1791.
115 LoB, MS3782/12/39/274, MB to J Edwards, 3 Oct 1794.
116 LoB, MS3782/12/40/128, MB to J Edwards, 18 Apr 1795.
117 LoB, MS3782/12/42/44, John Kellet to MB, 9 Mar 1797.
118 LoB, MS3782/121/46/166, John Kellet to MB 19 May 1801.
119 BMT, Soho House, copy of memoirs of Samuel Vale.
120 LoB, MS3782/12/66/79, John Southern to MB, 9 Apr 1797.
121 LoB, MS3782/12/58/97, W B Brown to MB, 21 Jul 1800.
122 Michaelis-Jena and Merson 1988.
123 LoB, MS3782/2/3; LoB, MS3782/2/4.
124 LoB, MS3782/3/37.
125 LoB, MS3782/13/12/121, John Kellet to MRB, 21 Oct 1815; MS3782/13/51, Zach Walker to MRB, 6 Nov 1815.
126 LoB, MS3782/3/46, ff 42–3.
127 LoB, MS3782/3/46, ff 2–3, 33.
128 LoB, MS3782/13/126.
129 LoB, MS3782/13/91/92–3.
130 LoB, MS3782/13/136 [MBP284/165], Circular letter from MRB, 1 Jan 1834.
131 LoB, MS3782/13/136 [MBP284/214], Report, Dec 1833.
132 LoB, MS3782/6/185, ff 10–11, 15, 22, 30–1, 34, 69–71, 101, 110.
133 LoB, former reference MBP436, Box B5 2, Accounts, Sept 1835; current reference not found.
134 LoB, MS3782/13/141, 27 Nov 1835.
135 LoB, MS3782/ 13/120, 'The causes of stoppage in supplying the Mint ...', 7 Nov 1838; '... the cause of additional Expense in the Repairs of the Rolling Mill ...', 19 Nov 1838, both by W H Remmett.
136 LoB, MS3782/6/185, f 71.
137 LoB. MS3147/5/1460.
138 LoB, MS3782/3/41.
139 Science Museum, file on 'Old Bess' and lap engine; part of report, 10 Jan 1862, quoted in Dickinson and Jenkins, 123. The report states in error that the engine was sold in 1848, two years too early. 'Derrington Pool', was likely the enlarged pool used by Heath Mill, situated in Deritend.
140 BMT, Soho House, copy of memoirs of Samuel Vale. He has been identified as Alfred Toy.
141 LoB, MS3782/6/182, Memorandum re tenancy of Alfred Toy at Soho, 29 Sep 1852.
142 LoB, MS3782/11/31, Memorandum of Agreement, Dec 1852 [previously MBP267/18; LoB, MS3782/6/182; LoB, MS3782/11/31?, Agreement, 24 Jan 1853 [previously MBP267/22].
143 MS3782/11/31?, Agreement, 7 May 1853 [previously MBP267/20, 23].
144 LoB, MS3782/11/17, Document *re* filling in of Pool Mar–Apr 1854 [previously 454]; Staffordshire Record Office, subsequently SRO, D564/16, account entry, 15 Apr 1854.
145 Smiles, 212.
146 Science Museum, London, file on lap engine.
147 LoB, MS3782/6/182, f 170; *Midland Counties Herald*, 7 July–4 Aug 1859.
148 SRO, D564/15, account entries 1858–9.
149 Science Museum, London, file on lap engine; Cherbourg House, which he rented, has recently been converted into retirement flats.
150 LoB, MS3782/6/182, f 210.
151 SRO, D564/16, account entries 1862–3.

Chapter 4

1 Dickinson 1937, 81, 90–6.
2 LoB, MS3219/4/66/1, MB to JW, 7 Feb 1769; Dickinson 1937, 81–2; Robinson and Musson 1969, 62–3.
3 Dickinson and Jenkins 1927, 275–7; Griffiths 1992, 293, 298.
4 LoB, MS3147/3/12/1, MB to JW, 6 Sep 1777; Dickinson and Jenkins, 264–5.
5 LoB, MS3782/12/76/110, MB to JW [end of Aug/Sep 1775]; LoB, MS3782/1/3, f 223.
6 LoB, MS3782/13/126.
7 LoB, MS3782/1/5, ff 179–80.
8 Dickinson and Jenkins, 50–1.
9 LoB, MS3782/1/3, f 223, entry 3 Dec 1776; LoB, MS3782/1/4, f 467.
10 LoB, MS3782/12/26/63, William Playfair to MB, 30 Sep 1780.
11 Dickinson and Jenkins, 156, Fig. 23.
12 LoB, MS3147/ 3/5/42a–b, MB to JW, 11 Sep 1781.
13 LoB, MS3147/3/5/46, MB to JW, 27 Sep 1781.
14 LoB, MS3147/3/6/4, MB to JW, 13 Jan 1782.
15 LoB, MS3147/3/5/55, MB to JW, 30 Oct 1781.
16 Dickinson and Jenkins, 124–5, 160–1, Figs. XXIII and XXIV.
17 LoB, MS3147/3/5/58, MB to JW, 13 Nov 1781.
18 LoB, MS3147/3/6/25, MB to JW, 26 Mar 1782, LoB, MS3147/3/6/2, MB to JW, 19 Apr 1782.
19 LoB, MS3147/3/6/20, MB to JW, 27 Mar 1782.
20 LoB, MS3782/12/27/76, John Buchanan to MB, 24 Oct 1782.
21 Ibid; MS3782/12/27/88, John Buchanan to MB, 13 Nov 1782.
22 LoB, MS3782/12/72/46, John Scale to MB, 11 Nov 1782.
23 LoB, MS3147/5/1340.
24 LoB, MS3782/12/63/30, John Hodges to MB, 14 Nov 1782.
25 LoB, MS3782/12/78/67, JW to MB, 26 Nov 1782.
26 LoB, MS3782/12/27/92, John Buchanan to MB, 28 Nov 1782; LoB, MS3782/12/74/70, Z Walker Sr to MB, 28 Nov 1782.
27 LoB, 3147/3/84, JW to MB, 28 Nov 1782.
28 Dickinson and Jenkins, 161, Fig XXXIII.
29 'Double-acting' in the sense that a power stroke was delivered both on the up- and downstroke was quite distinct from the earlier 'double cylinder' engine.
30 LoB, MS3782/12/63/30, John Hodges to MB, 14 Nov 1782.
31 Skempton 1971, 53–73; LoB, MS3147/5/8, MS3147/5/1369; Bill Whitehead, *pers. comm.*
32 John Townley, *pers. comm.*, lecture notes and forthcoming, 'Wasborough and Pickard – the birth of rotative motion by steam power'. These relatively little-known establishments could claim to be the first rotary steam-engine-powered mills in the world.
33 Muirhead 1854, vol ii, 175–6, letter no. 243, JW to Mr G. Hamilton [May or Jun 1783]); 167, letter no. 232, JW to MB, 3 Dec 1782.

34 Muirhead, vol ii, 177, letter no. 245, JW to MB, 5 Sep 1783; 177–8, letter no. 246, JW to MB, 14 Sep 1783.
35 LoB, MS3147/9/8.
36 LoB, MS3147/26/9.
37 LoB, MS3147/5/1346.
38 LoB, MS3147/9/8.
39 LoB, MS3782/12/28/67, John Buchanan to MB, 9 Oct 1783.
40 LoB, MS3782/12/8, f 125, MB to Mr Pradueux?, 6 Mar 1784.
41 LoB, MS3782/12/29/50, John Buchanan to MB, 5 Jul 1784.
42 LoB, MS3147/9/8.
43 LoB, MS3147/5/1447, 'Plan of the Buildings belonging to Boulton & Watt at Soho'; LoB, MS3147/5/1447, 'Ground Plan of Buildings belonging to the Works at Soho ... standing on lease to Mr Boulton' by J A Smith, Jun 1788 plan.
44 LoB, MS3782/13/126.
45 LoB, MS3147/9/8.
46 LoB, MS3782/20/4.
47 LoB, MS3147 [Plan of Soho Engine Manufactory with new yard added in pencil *c* 1800].
48 BMT, Phillp album 11b, 23, 1796; LoB, MS3147/1/32.
49 LoB, MS3782/13/39/142, JWJ to MB, 5 Jun 1795; LoB, MS3782/13/39/143, JWJ to MB, 7 Jun 1795.
50 LoB, MS3219/6/133, JWJ Ledger – entries for engine manufactory 1786–1801.
51 LoB, MS3219/6/3.
52 LoB, MS3219/6/13.
53 Dickinson and Jenkins, 275–7; Roll 1930, 169–88.
54 Griffiths, 298.
55 Roll, 177.
56 The documentation, all in MRB's hand, is lodged at MS3147/9/25.
57 Dickinson and Jenkins, 170, 296.
58 LoB, MS3147/5/1379.
59 LoB, MS3147/9/25; see also Roll, end plates.
60 Roll, 171.
61 Griffiths, 293.
62 LoB, MS3147, B&W Misc Box 8 Soho Foundry and Manufactory [Plan of engine house, scale 1:24; Plan of parallel motion shop, engine house and ' new' forging shop, scale 1:72].
63 LoB, MS3219/6/7, JWJ to GW, 28 Nov 1801.
64 LoB, MS3147/9/7.
65 LoB, MS3147/9/25, 'Memo of the different sorts of work wanted to complete the projected New Machinery at Soho March 1802 ...'; 'Memo of sundries wanted to complete the alterations of the Buildings & machinery of Soho Engine Manufactory March 10th 1802'.
66 LoB, MS3147/9/25, 'Proposed plans for the construction of the new Machinery projected for Soho Engine Manufactory, Oct 1 1802'; 'Memorandum of the different pieces of new Machinery projected for the Engine Manufactory at Soho, Oct 1 1802'.
67 LoB, MS3147/5/1444, 'Section of 6 Inch Cylr Engine Soho Machinery HMA, 15 Oct 1802'; 'Piston Rod Lathe Engine Soho Front View Plan Soho HLM, HLN Reverse [two versions], 9 Nov 1802'; 'Side View of Piston Rod Lathe Engine – Soho HLO Reverse, 9 Nov 1802'.
68 LoB, MS3147/5/1352a.
69 LoB, MS3147/4/266, ff 61–3, 22 Jun 1802.
70 LoB, MS3147/5/144, 'Soho 28 January 1803'; MS3147/9/7.
71 Dickinson and Jenkins, 172; LoB, MS3147/1/51; Ince 2000, 28–30 and Appendix One.
72 LoB, MS3147/9/7.
73 LoB, MS3147/9/25, 'Projected additions & alterations in the Great Lathe shop with their order and their execution'.
74 LoB, MS3147/5/1447, William Creighton's copy of an earlier plan of the Boulton & Watt premises updated, Aug 1811.
75 LoB, MS3147/9/7.
76 Ibid; MS3147/5/1445.
77 Roll.
78 A major contribution to this complex issue has been made by Laurence Ince in his study of stationary-engine production at both Soho factories from 1796 to 1896.
79 LoB, MS3147/5/797; LoB, MS3147/3/110; LoB, MS3147/, B&W 561 Engine Order Book no 8 1811–15.
80 LoB, MS3782/20/4.
81 LoB, MS3147/9/7.
82 LoB, 1843 tithe map for Handsworth.
83 LoB, MS3147/9/7.
84 LoB, MS3147/9/2.
85 LoB, Birmingham Rate Books, All Saints Parish, 1851–3.
86 LoB, MS3147/3/136, between 47–8, James Watt & Co to Messrs Pearce and Thynne, 15 Feb 1853.
87 'The End of the Soho Works', *The Engineer*, 2 July 1858.

Chapter 5

1 Cooper 1988.
2 Doty 1998.
3 Tungate 2009a, 80–8; Tungate 2009b, 185–200; Tungate 2013, 179–98; Symons 2009a, 89–98; Symons 2009b, 170–84.
4 Unfortunately, a number of misconceptions, old and new, detract from the Soho account. Cooper shows a picture of the Manufactory, the standard Eginton view of the principal building of about 1800 (Fig 1.3a) and states that these were the premises of Boulton &Watt where the Mint was reorganised in about 1840. He further claims that a plan dating from 1850, which he also reproduces, is of these same premises. The Manufactory was, in fact, owned by Matthew Boulton and his heirs, and the firm of Boulton & Watt occupied only a part where it operated a steam engine and copying-machine works. The latter buildings are not visible in the 1800 view of the principal building. In fact, the 1850 plan dates to about 1860 and is of the Soho Foundry Mint a mile away, where a new establishment was set up by James Watt & Company. A reorganisation of the Boulton mint at the Manufactory did take place, but about 15 years earlier in 1824–6; Cooper, 123–6, 132–7, 211–14 and Figs 231 and 232.
5 Unfortunately, Doty repeats Cooper's error and also describes the Soho Mint as a Boulton & Watt enterprise: Doty, e.g. 17, 23, 44–6 and throughout the book.
6 The partners were Henry Wollaston Blake, Gilbert Hamilton Jr and James Brown; Ince 2000, 35.
7 Selgin 2011, 79–119, particularly 90–1. Selgin corresponded with the author before publication; Demidowicz 2009a, 116–31; Demidowicz 2009b , 101–5. Cooper, 123–6, 132–7, 211–14.
8 Doty, 18; James Watt Jr hardly appears in this account of the Soho Mint.
9 Memoir of Boulton by Watt 1809, reprinted in Dickinson 1937, 206.
10 Gould 1969, 270–7; LoB, MS3782/12/71/36, 38, John Motteux to MB [1786], 10 Jul 1786.
11 Gould, 271; LoB, MS3782/12/31/105, R Jupp to MB, MB to R Jupp, 4 Sep 1786; MS3782/12/108/53, f 6.
12 LoB, MS378212/74/121, Z Walker Sr to MB, 28 Sep 1786; MS3782/12/31/160, Benjamin Morris to MB, 15 Dec 1786.
13 LoB, MS3782/12/71/48, John Motteux to MB, 4 Mar 1787; LoB, MS3782/12/71/46, John Motteux to MB, 17 Apr 1787; LoB, MS3782/12/71/47, MB to John Motteux 20–1 Apr 1787; LoB, MS3782/12/32/105, 163, Thomas Greenhow to MB, 23 Jun 1787, 27 Oct 1787; LoB, MS3782/12/32/189, John Harrison to Mr Greenhow, 5 Dec 1787.
14 LoB, MS3782/12/15, f 108, MB to J P Droz, 2 Apr 1787.
15 LoB, MS3782/12/6, ff 98–9, MB to John Vivian, 16 Apr 1787.
16 LoB, MS3782/12/6, f 92, MB to J P Droz [May 1787].
17 LoB, MS3782/12/32/105, Thomas Greenhow to MB, 23 Jun 1787.
18 LoB, MS3782/12/6, f 148, MB to unknown person, 23 Apr 1787.

19 LoB, MS3782/13/118A, Minute by MB, 20 Dec 1787.
20 Dickinson 1937, 137.
21 LoB, MS3782/7, partially catalogued (former reference MBP474/74, Bundle Misc bills 1788–1795).
22 LoB, MS3782/13/36/19, MB to MRB, 8 Feb 1788.
23 Ballard, Loggie and Mason 2009, 13–14.
24 LoB, MS3782/12/66/106, J Roberts to MB, 27 Jan 1788.
25 LoB, MS3147/3/12/2, MB to JW, 25 Jan 1788; LoB, MS3147/5/714a.
26 LoB, MS3782/12/66/106, John Roberts to MB, 27 Jan 1788.
27 LoB, MS3782/13/120, Minutes of a Conference held at Soho on 7 January 1810; the 1810 conference, whose minutes are so helpful in explaining these early experiments, was held to investigate John Southern's then recent claims that his contribution to the development of the Mint was undervalued.
28 LoB, MS3782/12/66/106, John Roberts to MB, 27 Jan 1788; LoB, MS3782/12/66/108, John Roberts to MB, 5 Feb 1788.
29 LoB, MS3782/13/120, 1810 conference minutes.
30 LoB, MS3782/12/66/110, John Roberts to MB, 18 Jun 1788.
31 LoB, MS3147/5/714a.
32 Ibid.
33 LoB, MS3782/13/120, 1810 conference minutes.
34 LoB, MS3147/5/714a.
35 LoB, MS3782/12/66/110, John Roberts to MB, 18 Jun 1788; LoB, MS3147/5/714a [8 Plans 16 June–17 July 1788].
36 LoB, MS3147/5/714a.
37 LoB, MS378212/33/29, MB to the Committee, 6 Mar 1788.
38 LoB, MS3782/13/118A.
39 LoB, MS378212/15, f 108, MB to J P Droz, 14 Apr 1788.
40 The conference was organised to identify the engineers and their contribution to the development of the mint machinery.
41 LoB, MS3782/13/120, 1810 conference figures.
42 LoB, MS3147/5/714a.
43 Ibid.
44 Ibid.
45 Ibid.
46 LoB, MS3147/4/145.
47 LoB, MS3782/13/120, 1810 conference minutes.
48 LoB, MS3782/13/118A; LoB, MS3782/12/66/5, James Lawson to MB, 1 Jun 1790.
49 LoB, MS3782/12/66/1.
50 LoB, MS3782/12/66/3.
51 LoB, MS4282, MB to John Southern, 29 Jan 1789.
52 LoB, MS4282, MB to John Southern, 4 Jul 1789; LoB, MS3782/12/66/4, MB to John Southern, 6 Jul 1789; LoB, MS4282, John Southern to MB, 6 Jul 1789.
53 Pollard 1968, 241–52.
54 LoB, MS3782/13/118A; LoB, MS3782/12/66/5, James Lawson to MB, 1 Jun 1790.
55 LoB, MS3782/12/62/83, MB to Samuel Garbett, 29 Mar 1790.
56 LoB, MS3782/12/66/5, James Lawson to MB, 1 Jun 1790.
57 British Patent No. 1757, dated 8 Jul 1790: LoB, MS3782/17/1.
58 LoB, MS3147/3/14/11, MB to JW, 16 Jul 1790.
59 Dickinson 1937, Fig 5, 141.
60 LoB, MS3782/12/66/6, James Lawson to MB, 3 Jun 1790; LoB, MS3782/13/36/47, MB to MRB, 13 Jul 1790.
61 LoB, MS3147/3/14/6, MB to JW, 6 Jul 1790.
62 Apling 1968, 308–16.
63 Doty, 35, 44.
64 LoB, MS3782/120/57, Inventory of Property belonging to Coinage account taken 31 December 1790.
65 Gould; Hawker, 'Eighteenth-century Token Notes from Matthew Boulton's Letters; the Glasgow Halfpenny', *Seaby Coin and Medal Bulletin*, 833 (Sep 1988), 199–204; 834 (Oct 1988), 227–30; 843 (Sep 1989), 200–2; 844 (Oct 1989), 227–30); Margolis 1988, 102–9; Powell 1977, 28–29; Margolis 1990, 200.
66 LoB, Matthew Boulton Papers (MBP) 306/21 (not recatalogued), MB to J P Droz, 19 Apr 1791.
67 LoB, MS3782/12/66/9, J Lawson to MB, 23 May 1791.
68 LoB, MS3782/13/36/64, Resolutions MB to MRB, 16 May 1791.
69 LoB, MS3782/12/66/10, J Lawson to MB, 26 May 1791; LoB, MS3782/12/66/11, J Lawson to MB, 27 May 1791.
70 LoB, MS3782/13/36/56, MB to MRB, 27 May 1791.
71 Ibid.
72 LoB, MS3782/13/36/58, MB to MRB, 4 Jun 1791; Apling, 311.
73 LoB, MS3782/13/36/60, MB to MRB, 7 Jun 1791.
74 LoB, MS3782 12/66/16, J Lawson to MB, 11 Jun 1791.
75 LoB, MS3782/12/57/51, MRB to MB, 16 Jun 1791.
76 LoB, MS3782/12/9/8, f 9, MRB to Thomas Wilson, 28 Oct 1791.
77 LoB, MS3782/3/1, f 6.
78 LoB, MS3147/5/714; this plan has already been published by Tann but misdated to *c* 1800; Tann 1970, 89.
79 LoB, MS3782/13/36/60, MB to MRB, 7 Jun 1791.
80 LoB, MS3782/12/66/22, J Lawson to MB, 21 Jan 1792; MS3782/12/66/23, 23 Jan 1792; MS3782/12/66/21, 29 Jan 1792; LoB, MS3782/12/66/35, John Southern to MB, 30 Jan 1792; LoB, MS3782/13/120, 1810 conference minutes.
81 LoB, MS3782/13/36/64, MB to MRB, 21 Mar 1792; MS3782/13/36/66, MB to MRB, 25 Mar 1792; MS3782/12/66/27, J Lawson to MB, 29 Mar 1792; MS3782/12/57/59, MRB to MB, 2 Apr 1792.
82 LoB, MS3782/12/66/26, J Lawson to MB, 26 Mar 1792; Margolis 1988, 106–7.
83 LoB, MS3782/13/36/67, MB to MRB, 4 Apr 1792; MS3782/3/36/72, MB to MRB, Apr 1792.
84 LoB, MS4282, MB to JS, 13 Apr 1792; MS3782/13/36/87, MB to MRB, 15 Sep 1792.
85 Pollard 1971, 311–17.
86 LoB, MS3782/3/1, ff 6–7; MS3147/5/714c.
87 LoB, MS3782/3/1, f 102.
88 LoB, MS3782/12/106/27.
89 LoB, MS3782/6/92.
90 LoB, MS3782/12/39/3, C Glover to MB, 7 Jan 1794.
91 LoB, MS3782/6/92.
92 LoB, MS3782/12/39/34, C Glover to MB, 27 Jan 1794.
93 LoB, MS3147/3/17, MB to JW, 9 Feb 1794.
94 LoB, MS3782/12/39/35, C Glover to MB, 26 Dec 1794.
95 LoB, MS3782/12/106/27; MS3782/3/1, f 85.
96 LoB, MS3782/12/106/37.
97 Dickinson, 148; LoB, MS3782/13/118A, Memorandum by MB, 10 Apr 1797.
98 LoB, MS4282, MB to JS, 6 Mar 1797.
99 LoB, MS4282, MB to JS, 7 Apr 1797; LoB, MS3782/12/66/79, John Southern to MB, 9 Apr 1797.
100 LoB, MS4282, MB to JS, 19 May 1797.
101 LoB, MS3782/12/66/81, JS to MB, 5 Jun 1797.
102 LoB, MS3782/13/120, MB to JS, 17 Jan 1798.
103 LoB, MS3782/13/120, 1810 conference minutes.
104 Doty, 86–7, 164.
105 LoB, MS3782/12/66/88, JS to MB, 23 Apr 1798.
106 LoB, MS3782/13/141.
107 LoB, MS3782/12/66/90, JS to MB, 25 Apr 1798.
108 LoB, MS4282, MB to JS, 27 Apr 1798.
109 LoB, MS4282, James Lawson to JS, 11 May 1798.
110 LoB, MS3147/5/714d.
111 Ibid; it was identified as such in 1997.
112 LoB, MS3782/6/96, f 94, 'Design and elevation of Mint finished sketch 10s 6d'.

113 Ballard, Loggie and Mason, Fig 7, 14; LoB, MS1682/8/1, 'Elevation of Tea Room, Aviary etc. Soho'.
114 LoB, MS3782/6/96, 25 Mar 1797.
115 LoB, MS3782/12/43/128, William Hollins to MB, 13 Jul 1798.
116 LoB, MS117631, MSS of W Creighton of Birmingham, 462.
117 LoB, MS3782/6/16, ff 98, 107; MS3782/6/95; MS3782/6/97.
118 LoB, MS3147/5/714d.
119 Ibid.
120 Ibid (Fig 5.21).
121 Admitting this was odd, he explained it away as 'an economical arrangement' that 'worked well with the new method of powering the coining machinery'. The arrangement never existed, however, and the analysis of the Soho Mint drawings reveals that the steam engine was installed in an existing room adjacent to the new coining room (Doty, 55); Doty's assertion that 'we are reduced to guesswork' is, therefore, incorrect, in view of the survival of drawings lodged at LoB, MS3147/5/714d.
122 LoB, MS3782/12/66/91, JS to MB, 8 Nov 1798.
123 LoB, MS4282, MB to JS, 10 Nov 1798.
124 LoB, MS3782/12/66/92, JS to MB, 21 Nov 1798.
125 LoB, MS3782/12/66/93, JS to MB, 14 Dec 1798.
126 LoB, MS3147/4/258, ff 397–402.
127 LoB, MS3147/3/21/4, MB to JW, 6 Feb 1799.
128 LoB, MS3782/12/66/94, JS to MB, 21 Feb 1799.
129 LoB, MS4282, MB to JS, 9 Mar 1799.
130 LoB, MS3782/12/66/96, JS to MB, 11 Mar 1799.
131 LoB, MS3782/12/66/97, JS to MB, 12 Mar 1799.
132 LoB, MS4282, MB to JS, 19 and 22 Apr 1799.
133 LoB, MS4282, MB to JS, 22 Apr 1799.
134 LoB, MS4282, MB to JS, 9 Mar 1799.
135 LoB, MS3782/12/66/101, JS to MB, 1 May 1799.
136 LoB, MS4282, MB to JS, 3 May 1799.
137 Dickinson 1937, 152.
138 Crook and Port 1973, 452–60.
139 LoB, MS3782/12/59/190, Wm Cheshire to MB, 30 May 1799.
140 LoB, MS3782/13/39/81, JWJ to MB, 21 Jul 1800; MS3782/13/39/82, JWJ to MB, 24 Jul 1800.
141 LoB, MS3782/12/106/37; MS3782/3/37.
142 LoB, MS3782/13/120, 1810 conference minutes.
143 LoB, MS3782/13/141.
144 Doty, 66.
145 LoB, MS3782/3/255, MRB to Sir George Robinson and to Joseph Thompson, 31 Jul 1826.
146 LoB, MS3782/3/146, f 278, MRB to J Moseley, 23 Jan 1826; see also LoB, MS3782/3/146, f 274, MRB to Samuel Moore, 14 Jan 1826.
147 LoB, MS3782/13/139, f 7.
148 LoB, MS3782/13/139.
149 LoB, MS3782/13/139, MRB to Capt. Hawkins, 27 Aug 1823.
150 LoB, MS3782/13/58/67, John Robinson to MRB, 1 Dec 1823.
151 LoB, MS3782/13/24/189, MRB to John May, 1 Jan 1824.
152 LoB, MS3782/ 8/59/3, MRB to John Robinson, 26 Jan 1824.
153 LoB, MS3782/13/58/67, John Robinson to MRB, 27 Jan 1824.
154 LoB, MS3147/4/109; MS3782/13/40.
155 LoB, MS3147/5/714e.
156 LoB, MS3147/5/707a–d; MS31475/708a–c.
157 LoB, MS3147/5/714e.
158 LoB, MS3147/9/7.
159 LoB, MS3147/5/318–19.
160 LoB, MS3782/13/120, Summary of the progress of Builders work, Aug 1825; Summary of the progress of Mechanists work, Aug 1825; Details of Mechanists Work, Aug 1825.
161 LoB, MS3147/4/109, items 23 Aug 1825, 10 Dec 1825; MS3782/3/42–4, 21; MS3147/10/74, 24.
162 LoB, MS3147/5/714, Plan of new press room at Soho Scale ¾ of an Inch to 1 foot, Rickman & Hutchinson Architects 1825.
163 Colvin 1995, 812–17.
164 Rickman 1901, 35.
165 LoB, MS3147/5/707a–d; MS3147/5/708a–c.
166 LoB, MS3782/13/111; MS3147/3/451/33–39, B&W Box 13/2.
167 LoB, MS3147/5/711.
168 Aston and Taylor 1998, 113–15.
169 LoB, MS3147/5/714e; LoB, MS3782/13/120, Details of the Mechanists Work, Aug 1825.
170 LoB, MS3782/13/120, Particulars of the Builders Work, Aug 1825.
171 LoB, MS3147/5/714e.
172 LoB, MS3782/13/141.
173 LoB, MS3147/5/714e.
174 Ibid, six drawings of lathes, MRB to G Hamilton, 21 Oct 1825; 'New Mint Arrangements Lathes', 23 Sep 1824.
175 LoB, MS3782/3/174; LoB, MS3147/4/132; LoB, MS3147/1/50; LoB, MS3782/13/120, Aug 1825 documents.
176 LoB, MS3782/13/68/58, MRB to George Rennie, 26 May 1825.
177 LoB, MS3147/4/109.
178 LoB, MS3147/1/50, f 350; MS3147/3/213, 29 Mar 1825.
179 LoB, MS3147/5/714e.
180 LoB, MS3782/13/58/86.
181 LoB, MS3782/13/13/25/33, Rickman & Hutchinson bill, 1826.
182 LoB, MS3147/1/50.
183 LoB, MS3782/13/151/34.
184 LoB, MS3782/13/120, Soho New Mint 1824.
185 LoB, MS3782/13/2, MRB to [Capt Hankins], 22 Jul 1827.
186 LoB, MS3782/13/111, Mexican City Mint Box [previously MBP412].
187 Doty, 66.
188 LoB, MS3782/3/22.
189 Ibid, 26 Dec 1832.
190 LoB, MS3147/1/50, 1, 8 May, 14, 18 Oct, 8 Nov 1824.
191 LoB, MS31471/51, 10, 19 Jun 1833.
192 LoB, MS3782/3/210.
193 LoB, MS3782/13/18/148.
194 LoB, MS3782/13/120, Expenses incurr'd in Erecting the Pneumatic Apparatus at Soho Mint, Nov 30 1835.
195 LoB, MS3782/3/42–45.
196 LoB, 157177, 'A Catalogue of the Valuable Machinery and Plant of Soho Mint ... 29 April 1850'.
197 LoB, MS3782/11/25/124, MPWB to Chubb, 11 Dec 1849.
198 LoB, MS3782/119/Folder 6; LoB, Birmingham Miscellaneous F/1-157177; LF 63.13 64034.
199 BMT, copy of memoirs of Samuel Vale.
200 LoB, MS3782/11.
201 Ibid.
202 Ibid.
203 LoB, Photographs, H5/164–7.
204 LoB, 3147/3/134, James Watt & Co to Mr Webster, 31 Aug1850.
205 Sweeney 1981, 12; Doty, 69.
206 LoB, 3147/3/135, James Watt & Company to George Lingard, 3 Jul 1851.
207 LoB, 3147/5/714f.
208 LoB, 3147/5/707–716.
209 LoB, 3147/5/714f–g.

Chapter 6

1 *Building News*, 2 Jan 1863.
2 LoB, Handsworth Rate Book 1882.
3 LoB, Handsworth Rate Books 1882, 1886.
4 Dent 1894, 256.
5 LoB, Handsworth Rate Books, 1899, 1901.
6 Not shown on OS 1913 edition at 1:1250 scale used for the National Land Valuation, LoB.
7 LoB, BCH/AE/1/1/10, Handsworth Public Works Committee Minute book, 1908.
8 LoB, Handsworth Building Plan 3495; Handsworth Rate Book 1906.
9 Griffin Mellors and Associates, pers. comm.
10 Edgar Crowder, a builder, operated the sandpit in the war years but appears not to have advanced the working face any considerable distance. LoB, Birmingham Rate Books 1915, 1918.
11 LoB, 1913 edition of the Ordnance Survey 1:1250 map for Land Valuation.

12 LoB, Handsworth Rate Books 1911, 1912.
13 LoB, Birmingham Building Plans 3063 (1920), 32786 (1921), 38828 (1925).
14 Jones 1984, 46; LoB, Birmingham Building Plan 38828 (1925).
15 Current location unknown.
16 Former Birmingham City Engineers Department Drainage Plan 4988A, Nov 1925.
17 Demidowicz and Molyneux 1996.

Chapter 7

1 The name, Boulton & Watt, will normally be used to describe the firm rather than the two individuals. In essence, decisions made either as individuals working together or as partners in the firm would be difficult to distinguish.
2 LoB, MS3147/3/89, JWJ to James Lawson, 3 May 1795.
3 LoB, MS3147/3/89; MS31473/45/17, JWJ to JW, 3 May 1795.
4 LoB, MS3147/5/1448.
5 LoB, MS3147/3/45/19, JWJ to JW, 10 May 1795.
6 LoB, MS3147/32/23, JWJ to WW, 6 Jun 1795.
7 LoB, MS3782/13/39/31, JWJ to MB, 8 Jun 17950; MS3147/5/1379.
8 LoB, MS3147/3/45/26, JWJ to JW, 10 Jun 1795.
9 Ibid.
10 LoB, MS3147/3/18/3, MB to JWJ, 11 Jun 1795.
11 LoB, MS3147/5/1379.
12 LoB, MS3147/3/89, JW to Mrs Matthews, 15 Jul 1795.
13 Lease and Release, Avery title deeds, at Avery Weigh-Tronix.
14 LoB, MS3147/3/89, JW to Mr Bedford, 24 Aug 1795.
15 LoB, MS3147/3/89, JWJ to Mr Bedford, 15 Jul 1795.
16 The foundry building (main casting shop) will be referred to as the foundry or the main foundry building in contrast to the term, Soho Foundry, which will apply only to the whole site and its buildings.
17 LoB, MS3147/3/537/12a–c, WW to JWJ, 14 Aug 1795.
18 Gale 1961, 78.
19 LoB, MS3147/5/1454, plan, elevations and sections of the boring mill and turning shop, with various alterations, Aug 1795; MS3147/5/1449, 'Section of the boiler house & chimney, 10 Aug 1795, Soho Foundry CHW'; 'Section and plan of the engine and boiler houses, 16 Aug 1795'; MS3147/4/145.
20 LoB, MS3147/5/1454.
21 Avery title deeds at Avery Weigh-Tronix.
22 LoB, MS3147/8/1.
23 Gale 1961, 77.
24 LoB, MS3147/5/1454.
25 Ibid.
26 Ibid.
27 LoB, MS3147/4/145; identified by letter codes, CIN, CIO, CIP, CIQ, CIR, CIS. The letter codes were recorded in this B&W drawings office book as each drawing was commenced.
28 LoB, MS4282, JWJ to JS, 14 Sep 1795.
29 LoB, MS4282, JWJ to JS, 15 Sep 1795.
30 LoB, MS3147/3/45/33, JWJ to JW, 15 Sep 1795.
31 LoB, MS3147/5/1454; LoB, MS3147/8/1.
32 LoB, MS4282, MRB to JS, 19 Sep 1795; also quoted at length in Ince 2000, 5–6.
33 LoB, MS4282, MRB to JS, 20 Sep 1795.
34 LoB, MS3147/3/18/5, MB to JW, 20 Sep 1795.
35 LoB, MS3147/3/45/34, JWJ to JW, 24 Sep 1795.
36 LoB, MS3147/5/1453–1454.
37 LoB, MS3219/4/18, MB to JW, 24 Sep 1795.
38 LoB, MS3147/8/1.
39 LoB, MS3147/3/90, JWJ to WW, 26 Oct 1795.
40 LoB, MS3147/3/90, JWJ to WW, 28 Oct 1795.
41 LoB, MS3147/8/; MS3219/6/7, JWJ to Peter Ewart, 21 Jan 1797.
42 LoB, MS3147/32/23, JWJ to WW, 31 Oct 1795.
43 LoB, MS3147/3/90, JWJ to WW, 14 Nov 1795.
44 LoB, MS3147/3/90, JWJ to Peter Ewart., 14 Nov 1795; MS3147/3/249/59, Peter Ewart to JWJ, 17 Nov 1795.
45 LoB, MS3147/32/23, WW to JWJ, 16 Nov 1795.
46 Patent, AD 1794 June 2, No. 1993.
47 LoB, MS3147/3/90, JWJ to WW, 18 Nov 1795.
48 LoB, MS4282, JWJ to JS, 20 Dec 1795.
49 LoB, MS3147/3/34/6, MB to JWJ, 21 Jan 1796.
50 Dickinson 1937, 168–9.
51 LoB, MS3147/3/46/6, MB to JWJ, 21 Jan 1796; MS3147/3/34/8, MRB to JWJ, 24 Jan 1796.
52 LoB, MS3147/3/90, B&W to Gilbert Hamilton, 5 Feb 1796.
53 LoB, MS3147/3/34/11, MRB to JWJ, 7 Feb 1796; LoB, MS3147/3/90, JWJ to James Lawson, 17 Mar 1796.
54 Dickinson and Jenkins 1927, 268, 277.
55 LoB, MS3147/3/34/10, MRB to JWJ, 6 Feb 1796.
56 LoB, MS3147/4/; MS3147/5/1449, Feb 1796 identified with letters: COS, COT, COU, COV, COY.
57 LoB, MS3147/4/145; MS3147/5/1448.
58 LoB, MS3147/4/145; MS3147/5/1455.
59 LoB, MS3147/3/90, MRB to Snedshill Iron Furnace, 16 Mar 1796, MRB to W Reynolds and Co, 17 Mar 1796.
60 LoB, MS3147/3/90, JWJ to James Lawson, 17 Mar 1796.
61 LoB, MS3147/3/90, JWJ to Barnes, 25 Mar 1796.
62 LoB, MS3147/3/19/5, MB to MRB, 25 May 1796; MS3147/3/59/14, JWJ to JS, 26 May 1796; MS3147/3/328/1, JS to JW, 27 May 1796.
63 LoB, MS3147/3/19/9, MB to MRB, 20 Jun 1796; MS3147, JS to MRB, 20 Jun 1796.
64 LoB, MS3147/5/1453.
65 Ibid.
66 LoB, MS3147/3/281/71, JWJ to James Lawson, 12 Jul 1796.
67 LoB, MS3219/4/14/15, JWJ to JW, 14 Jul 1796.
68 LoB, MS3147/3/249/63, Peter Ewart to JWJ, 15 Sep 1796.
69 LoB, MS3147/9/1.
70 LoB, MS3147/5/1454.
71 LoB, MS3147/3/19/12, MB to JWJ, 1 and 2 Dec 1796.
72 LoB, MS31475/1448.
73 LoB, MS31475/1450.
74 LoB, MS3147/9/15.
75 LoB, MS3219/6/7, JWJ to Peter Ewart, 21 Jan 1797.
76 LoB, MS3147/3/329/1, JS to B&W, 2 Feb 1797.
77 LoB, MS3147/3/9, JWJ to Peter Ewart, 24 Feb 1797.
78 LoB, MS3147/3/249/65, Peter Ewart to JWJ, 24 Mar 1797.
79 LoB, MS3219/6/7, JWJ to Peter Ewart, 29 Mar 1797; MS3147/5/1448.
80 LoB, MS3147/6/2/E/21, Peter Ewart to JWJ, 12 Apr 1797.
81 LoB, MS3147/9/15.
82 LoB, MS3219/6/7, JWJ to WW, 3 Jun 1797.
83 LoB, MS3147/3/282/49, JWJ to James Lawson, 26 Aug 1797.
84 LoB, MS3147/3/91, JWJ to MRB, 10 Jun 1797.
85 LoB, MS4282, MB to JS, 8 Jul 1797.
86 LoB, MS3147/9/1; MS3219/6/141A; MS3147/32/23, JWJ to MRB, 10 Aug 1797; MS3147/3/35/8a, MRB to JWJ, 20 Sep 1797; MS3147/3/35/10, MRB to JWJ, 13 Oct 1797.
87 LoB, MS3147/9/1; MS3219/6/141A.
88 LoB, MS3147/9/1.
89 LoB, MS3147/3/35/10, MRB to JWJ, 13 Oct 1797.
90 LoB, MS3147/9; MS3147/35/10, MRB to JWJ, 13 Oct 1797.
91 LoB, MS3219/6/141A.
92 LoB, MS3147/3/35/11, MRB to JWJ, 9 Nov 1797.
93 LoB, MS3147/4/203, f 66; MS3147/9/1.
94 LoB, MS3147/6/2e, Peter Ewart to JWJ, 17 Feb 1798.

95 LoB, MS3219/6/7, JWJ to Peter Ewart, 7 Mar 1798.
96 LoB, MS3782/13/39/150, JWJ to MRB, 1 Sep 1798.
97 LoB, MS3782/13/39/152, JWJ to MRB, 16 Sep 1798.
98 LoB, MS3147/5/1454.
99 LoB, MS3147/3/47/32, JWJ to MRB, 9 Nov 1798.
100 LoB, MS3147/3/479/1, Memorandum. Dates of Mr Murdock's Experiments upon the light obtained from coal gas ... Apr 1805.
101 LoB, MS3147/9/1.
102 Ibid.
103 Ibid, see contemporary index.
104 LoB, MS3147/9/16; MS3147/9/17.
105 LoB, MS3147/3/287.
106 LoB, MS3782/13/98/7, ff 1–62.
107 Clegg 1866, 5.
108 LoB, MS3147/3/95, JWJ to Ashworth Clegg, 11 Mar 1800; MS3147/3/41/12, MRB to JWJ, 20 Jul 1803.
109 LoB, MS3147/9/16; MS3147/9/17.
110 LoB, MS3147/3/76/12, GW to JWJ, 11 Dec 1798.
111 LoB, MS3147 (MRB to JWJ, 15 Dec, B&W Box 38/4).
112 LoB, MS3147/3/36/20a, MRB to JWJ, 27 Dec 1798; LoB, MS3147/5/1448.
113 Dickinson and Jenkins, 170–2.
114 LoB, MS3147/3/48/4, JWJ to MRB, 9 Jan 1799.
115 LoB, MS3147/3/37/2, MRB to JWJ, 11 Jan 1799.
116 LoB, MS3147/3/379, MRB to JWJ, 1 Feb 1799.
117 LoB, MS3147/3/37/3, MRB to JWJ, 17 Jan 1799.
118 LoB, MS3147/3/48/7, JWJ to MRB, 20 Jan 1799.
119 LoB, MS3147/37/4, MRB to JWJ, 21 Jan 1799.
120 LoB, MS3147/4/145.
121 LoB, MS3147/5/1448, dated 10 Apr 1799.
122 LoB, MS3147/4/321, List of engines made at Soho, *c* 1775–*c* 1833; MS3147/9/30.
123 LoB, MS3147/3/76/16, GW to MRB, 26 Feb 1799.
124 LoB, MS3147/3/48/24, JWJ to MRB, 18 Mar 1799.
125 LoB, MS3147/3/48/30, JWJ to MRB, 16 Apr 1799.
126 LoB, MS3147/3/48/43, JWJ to GW, 1 May 1799.
127 LoB, MS3147/3/76/28, GW to MRB, 20 May 1799.
128 LoB, MS3147/3/29/4, JW to MRB, 24 May 1799.
129 LoB, MS3147/3/48/50, JWR to MRB, 10 Jun 1799.
130 LoB, MS3147/3/37/47, MRB to JWJ, 16 Jun 1799.
131 LoB, MS3147/3/48/54, JWJ to MRB, 29 Jun 1799.
132 LoB, MS3147/3/48/68, JWJ to MRB, 15 Aug 1799.
133 LoB, MS3147/3/76/31, GW to MRB, 14 Sep 1799.
134 LoB, MS3147/3/76/32, GW to JWJ, 17 Sep 1799.
135 LoB, MS3147/4/172.
136 LoB, MS3147/4/321.
137 LoB, MS3147/3/94, JWJ to William Murdoch, 28 Feb 1800.
138 LoB, MS3147/3/49/17a, JWJ to MRB, 1 Oct 1800.
139 LoB, 3147/3/49/14, JWJ to MRB, 2 Oct 1800.
140 LoB, MS3147/4/84.
141 LoB, MS3147/3/9/1; MS3147/9/26.
142 LoB, MS3147/9/26.
143 LoB, MS3147/12/8; MS3147/9/26.
144 LoB, MS3147/5/145; MS3147/9/26.
145 LoB, MS3147/9/1.
146 LoB, MS3782/13/98/7.
147 LoB, MS3147/3/479/1.
148 Clegg, 6.
149 LoB, MS3782/13/98/7, ff 51–62.
150 LoB, MS3147/5/1488; *The Engineer*, 27 Sept 1895.
151 LoB, MS3147/4/321; LoB, MS3147/9.
152 LoB, MS3147/3/48/50, JWJ to MRB, 10 Jun 1799.
153 LoB, MS3147/3/52/8, JWJ to MRB, 6 Jun 1803.
154 LoB, MS3147/3/52/9, JWJ to GW, 8 Jun 1803.
155 LoB, MS3147/5/1453; MS3147/9/1.
156 LoB, MS3147/9/1.
157 LoB, MS3147/4/2839; MS3147/4/321.
158 LoB, MS3147/9/1.
159 LoB, MS3147/4/233; former reference B&W Box 50/3, Agreement 22 Jan 1800; current reference not found.
160 LoB, MS3147/9/1.
161 LoB, MS3147/5/1453; MS3147/9/1.
162 LoB, MS3147/3/47/32, JWJ to MRB, 9 Nov 17; MS3219/2/17, JWJ to GW, 31 May 1804.
163 LoB, MS3147/5/1454; MS3147/9/1; MS3219/6/39.
164 LoB, MS3147/5/706c.
165 LoB, MS3147/3/60/8, JWJ to JS, 10 Aug 1804.
166 LoB, MS3147/9/1.
167 LoB, MS3147/5/804.
168 LoB, MS3147/5/1453.
169 LoB, MS3147/9/16.
170 LoB, MS3147/9/1.
171 Clegg, 13.
172 Griffiths 1992, 257–8.
173 LoB, MS3147/9/1.
174 LoB, MS3219/6/141/A; MS3147/4/321.
175 LoB, MS3147/9/1; MS3219/6/141/A.
176 LoB, MS3147/9/1.
177 Ibid.
178 LoB, MS3147/5/1454.
179 LoB, MS3147/9/1; MS3147/9/23 and 9/27.
180 LoB, MS3147/3/1455.
181 LoB, MS3147/5/821 (McConnel & Kennedy portfolio).
182 LoB, MS3147/9/1; MS3219/6/141A; MS3147/9/28.
183 LoB, MS3147/3/288/5, John Murdock to JWJ, 12 Feb 1812.
184 LoB, MS3147/5/1454.
185 LoB, MS3147/32/23, William Murdoch to JWJ, 23 Sep 1816.
186 See Ince, Fig 17.
187 LoB, MS3147/5/1454.
188 LoB, MS3147/9/1.
189 LoB, MS3147/4/28; MS3147/4/321; Ince, 58; MS3147/5/1346.
190 Ince, Figs 19 and 20.
191 LoB, MS3147/5/1454.
192 LoB, MS3147/9/1.
193 Henderson 1966, 133–4.
194 Hall 1925, 10–11.
195 LoB, MS3147/9/1.
196 Ince, 33, 58, 67–8.
197 LoB, MS3147/9/1.
198 Jacob's Map of Smethwick, *c* 1828, LoB, MS275a; MS3147/9/1.
199 LoB, MS3147/9/1.
200 LoB, MS3147/12/28/60, William Murdoch Jr to James Brown, 22 May 1823.
201 LoB, MS3147/3/12/28/93, JWJ to James Brown, 24 Oct 1823.
202 LoB, MS3147/5/1454.
203 LoB, MS3147/4/286; MS3147/5/95.
204 LoB, MS3147/5/1452; MS3147/9/1.
205 LoB, MS3147/9/1.
206 Ibid.
207 Ince, 33.
208 LoB, MS3147/9/1.
209 LoB, MS3147/4/119; MS3147/4/84.
210 LoB, MS3147/4/84; MS3147/4/120.
211 LoB, MS3147/9/1.
212 LoB, MS3147/4/284; MS3219/6/141A; MS3147/4/95.
213 LoB, MS3147/5/1452; MS3147/4/84.
214 LoB, MS3147/9/1.
215 Ince, 33; Gale 1961, 83.
216 LoB, MS3147/10/75–77.
217 LoB, MS3147/9/1.
218 LoB, MS3147, B&W to H Smith, 13 Oct 1847, B&W vol 121.
219 LoB, MS3147, B&W to H Smith, 14 Aug 1847, B&W vol 121.
220 LoB, MS 3147/31/3; photographs taken on the closure of the Soho Foundry in 1895.
221 LoB, MS3147/9/1.
222 Ibid.
223 LoB, MS3147/5/1346.
224 LoB, MS3147/4/98; MS3147/9/2.
225 LoB, MS3147/9/2.
226 Ibid.
227 Avery Deeds at Soho Foundry Office.

228 LoB, MS3147/5/1454.
229 LoB, MS3147/9/18.
230 LoB, MS3147/5/1445.
231 LoB, MS3147/9/2.
232 Cooke *c* 1997, 33.
233 Ince, 36.
234 LoB, MS3147/3/134, Gilbert Hamilton to H W Blake, 19 Jun 1850.
235 *Midland Counties Herald*, Apr 1851.
236 Ince, 39, 62.
237 Demidowicz 1998 for Sandwell Metropolitan Borough Council.
238 *The Engineer*, 17 Sep, 8 Oct 1869.
239 Ibid.
240 Ince, 43; LoB, MS3147/3/161, W H Darlington to James Watt & Co, 12 Dec 1892.
241 LoB, MS3147/4/75.
242 Avery Deeds at Soho Foundry Office.
243 Smith 1967, 549; Ince, 44.
244 *Birmingham Daily Post*, 20, 23 May 1895.
245 www.gracesguide.co.uk/W._and_T._Avery; LoB, MS1588.
246 LoB, MS3147/10/75–77.
247 LoB, MS3147/9/18.
248 LoB, MS3147/10/76–77.
249 *Birmingham Daily Post*, 5 Apr, 7 Nov 1895.
250 *The Engineer*, 27 Sep, 4 Oct, 18 Oct, 1 Nov 1895, 28 Feb 1896.
251 *The Engineer*, 24 May 1895.
252 *The Engineer*, 27 Sep 1895.
253 *The Engineer*, 24 May 1895; LoB, MS3147/31/3; MS1149/3–48.
254 *The Engineer*, 10 Sep, 17 Dec 1909; 14 Nov 1919.
255 *The Engineer*, 17 Dec 1909.
256 Bailey 1985; Lines 1990; the latter included the Soho Manufactory but not the Foundry.
257 Falconer 1980.
258 Crossley 1992 for English Heritage.
259 These were all listed in 1987; the gates date from 1837, 18 years after James Watt died.
260 Royal Commission on the Historical Monuments of England 1996.
261 Demidowicz 1998; this had been preceded by a short report by the Royal Commission on the Historical Monuments of England 1996; mint could be considered to be listed by reason of curtilage.
262 LoB, MS3147/7/36a and 36b.
263 Finn 2000.
264 Demidowicz 2002 for Sandwell Borough Council and English Heritage.
265 Material from this report has been extensively used in the writing of this chapter. The report included a history of the development of the site during the Avery period from 1895 to the present day, Demidowicz 2002, 72–8.
266 Joyce and Haywood 2002 for Sandwell Metropolitan Borough Council and the Heritage Lottery Fund.
267 Belford, Demidowicz and Hislop 2003 for Sandwell Council and English Heritage.
268 Demidowicz 2002, Fig 85.
269 Belford, Demidowicz and Hislop, 12 and Fig 8.
270 Demidowicz 2002, 72–8 and Fig 81.
271 Belford, Demidowicz and Hislop, 1.
272 Upson 2003, Parts A, B & C in two vols, for Sandwell Metropolitan Borough Council.
273 The Avery buildings included the former weighbridge shop, platform weighing machine shops and the power house.
274 Sandwell Metropolitan Borough Council, DC/06/46537, 21 Sep 2006.

Chapter 8

1 Cannadine 1984, 131–72; Beaudoin 2000, 7–13; Stearns 2015; Williamson 1987, 269–92.
2 Berg 1985, 40; Szostak 1991, 223; Huberman 1996, 152.
3 Berg 1994, 1–33.
4 Wrigley and Schofield 1981; Crafts 1985; Wrigley 1989.
5 Harris 1998, 349–64; typescript of talk, dated Jan 1995.
6 VCH, Birmingham vol 8, 8–14; Hopkins 1989, 31, 118–19.
7 Ure [1935] 1970, 140–3.
8 Mantoux 1928, 36–42.
9 Tann 1970, 3.
10 400 quoted in LoB, MS3782/1/16, 158, MB to John Lewis, 13 Jul 1765; 600 quoted in Shaw 1801, 117; 700 quoted in LoB, MS3782/12/2, 34, MB to Thomas Gilbert, 2 Feb 1771; 1,000 quoted in *Swinney's Directory of Birmingham* 1775.
11 LoB, MS3782/13/126, endorsed 'Measurment [*sic*] of Shops in the Soho Manufactory Xmas 1777', dated Nov 1776 at top of document.
12 Quoted by Briggs 1987, 186.
13 Hopkins, 56–7.
14 Berg 1985, 231.
15 LoB, MS3782/12/1, 66, MB to J H Ebinghaus, 2 Mar 1768; BMT, photocopy notes of a Frenchman's journey around England before 1782 (source unknown).
16 Tann 1970, 3.
17 LoB, MS3782/12/102/6.
18 Fitzmaurice 1875, 400.
19 Mare and Quarrell 1938, 97.
20 LoB, MS3782/12/102/6.
21 Mantoux, 36.
22 LoB, MS3782/12/72/19, John Scale to MB, 3 Jul 1778.
23 Hall 1925, 9.
24 Roll 1930, Chapter 3.
25 Bedfordshire Record Office, L31/114/2/18, Lord Grantham's Diary, 2 Jul 1799.
26 Fitzmaurice, 400.
27 LoB, MS3782/13/126.
28 Morgan 1992, 253, 255.
29 Cule 1935.
30 Morgan, 255.
31 Goodison 1974, 11–12; Goodison 2002, 21 quoting Wedgwood; Delieb and Roberts 1971, 57.
32 Dickinson and Jenkins 1927.
33 Dickinson 1937, 203, quoting from memoir of Boulton by Watt.
34 Dickinson 1937, 205.
35 LoB, MS3147/31/3.
36 Shaw, 117.
37 Morgan, 253.
38 Tann 1970, 151–7; Jones 1985, 20–4, 35–6.
39 Lob, MS3782/13/126.
40 Guildhall Library London, MS7253/5.
41 Dickinson 1963, A E Musson's introduction to 2nd edition, no pagination; Tann 1970, 75.
42 Dickinson and Jenkins, 148–56.
43 Hopkins, 34–5, 55–8.
44 Morgan, 255.
45 Henderson 1966, 131.
46 Comparing the size of the largest industrial sites in the country at this time is fraught with difficulty. Size could be measured physically, but should this be exclusively floor area or include curtilage also? The number of workers employed is an alternative measure and in the case of the Manufactory its size has been discussed on p 209, both in terms of curtilage and workforce. The latter could vary greatly, however, with economic conditions. There is no doubt that the Manufactory would figure in any league of the largest industrial complexes at the beginning of the 19th century, but the full membership and order of this league may never satisfactorily be established. Other candidates for the top league would include New Lanark Mill, Scotland; Cromford Mill, Derbyshire; Coalbrookdale, Shropshire; naval dockyards at Portsmouth, Deptford, Chatham and Woolwich; the Carron Ironworks, Scotland; the Etruria pottery works, Staffordshire; and Murray's cotton mill, Manchester.
47 Morgan, 253.
48 West Yorkshire Archaeology Service 1996, 1. There are two foundry buildings at the Round Foundry, neither of them round, as this was the name given to the fitting shop, the so-called Rotundo. The rectangular buildings were both in existence by 1802, one earlier that the other, but the 1796 date suggested for the former is not certain. They both measured approximately 27.5m × 12.5m, which compares with the 30m × 22m of the original Soho Foundry, extended another 15m × 22m, by 1801–2.

49 Historic England 2013, 8–9.
50 List description for The Old Foundry, Lowndes Road, Dudley: https://historicengland.org.uk/listing/the-list/list-entry/1262873, also quoting Earl 1996.

Appendix 1

1 Jones 1994.
2 LoB, MS3782/1/16, f 1A, MB to Samuel Wyatt, 26 Apr 1765; MS3782/1/16, ff 149–50, MB to Wm Rigg, 2 Jul 1765 (*see* p 12).
3 LoB, MS3147/5/717e.
4 Ibid.
5 Lob, MS3147/5/707a–d (Calcutta); MS3147/5/708a–c (Bombay).
6 LoB, MS3782/13/120, Particular of the Builders Work, Aug 1825; Details of the Mechanists Work, Aug 1825.
7 LoB, MS3147/5/714e.
8 Electronic Distance Meter.
9 LoB, MS3147/5/714c.
10 The full analysis of the results is available in a comprehensive report, Barker, Reynolds and Dinn 1996.

Appendix 2

1 Cule 1935, 5.
2 LoB, MS3782/1/1; MS3782/1/4.
3 Cule, 212, 214.
4 LoB, MS3782/2/4, ff 204, 256–9; MS3782/12/44/73, William Nelson to MB, 2 Mar 1799.
5 LoB, MS3782/13/82, Agreement with J Bownas, 31 Dec 1809; MS3782/13/126, Memorandum of Agreement.
6 LoB, MS3782/13/126 [previously 294/29, 74, 95].
7 LoB, MS3782/13/126 [previously 294/116B–118, 121–2].
8 LoB, MS3782/2/1, ff 2, 33, 41, 44.
9 LoB, MS3782/13/91 [previously 284/131, 133, 165].
10 LoB, MS3782/6/182 [previously 282/122]; *Post Office Directory Birmingham, Warwickshire, Worcestershire, Staffordshire* (1854).
11 Staffordshire Record Office, D564/16.
12 Demidowicz 1998.
13 LoB, MS3782/2/1, ff 170, 152, 159.
14 LoB, MS3782/11/31, Memorandum of Agreement, 24 Jan 1853; Staffordshire Record Office, D564/16.
15 LoB, MS3782/5/1.
16 Dickinson 1937, 167, 171; Dickinson and Jenkins 1927, 346–7.
17 An important study of the Soho Foundry business from the point of view of production is to be found in Ince 2000.
18 Gale 1961, 83–4.
19 Demidowicz 1998.
20 LoB, MS3147/5.

Bibliography

Bibliography

Primary sources

The principal source consulted has been the vast Soho Collection, lodged in the Archives and Collections in the Library of Birmingham.

It is divided into three main parts:
MS3782 formerly the Matthew Boulton Papers
MS3147 formerly the Boulton and Watt Papers
MS3219 formerly the Muirhead Papers, united later with the acquisition of the James Watt Papers by Birmingham City Council in 1994

This constitutes the most important single collection of business records of the late 18th and 19th century. Its breadth and depth is astonishing, and without the 800 or more references to items in the collection, this book could not have been written. Consulting this material, however, has excavated only a small quarry in a very large mountain. It would be impossible, therefore, to summarise its extent and contents, and I draw attention to the detailed guides that are available on open shelves in the Archives Department, following its comprehensive re-cataloguing between 1998 and 2003.

All of MS3219 and parts of the two other collections are available in the Archives online catalogue (Library of Birmingham website).

For the Soho Foundry, in addition, there is also an extensive archive in the Avery Museum at the Foundry, but it is now closed and not available for public consultation. A detailed guide to its contents for the history of the Foundry can be found in Demidowicz (1998).

Unpublished reports

Barker, P B, Reynolds, J and Dinn, J 1996 *A Report for Time Team on a Ground Probing Radar Survey carried out at the Soho Manufactory*. Handsworth, Birmingham. 6 vols

Belford, P, Demidowicz, G and Hislop, M 2003 *An Historical Environment Assessment (with Ecological Statement) of the Soho Foundry, Foundry Lane, Smethwick, West Midlands*. For Sandwell Council and English Heritage

Crossley, D 1992 *Monuments Protection Programme: The Iron and Steel Industries Step 1 Report*. For English Heritage

Demidowicz, G 1998 *The Soho Foundry Mint, Smethwick: A Documentary and Archaeological Study*. For Sandwell Metropolitan Borough Council

Demidowicz, G 2002 *The Soho Foundry, Smethwick, West Midlands: A Documentary and Archaeological Study*. For Sandwell Borough Council and English Heritage

Demidowicz, G and Molyneux, N 1996 *Research Design for the Time Team Archaeological Investigation of the Soho Manufactory and Mint, Birmingham*

Finn, N 2000 *The Mint Building, Soho Foundry, Smethwick: Archaeological Evaluation and Photographic Survey*. University of Leicester Archaeological Service, Report no 2000/142 for Sandwell Metropolitan Borough Council

Historic England 2013 *Designation Scheduling Selection Guide: Industrial Sites*

Jones, L R 1994 *An Archaeological Evaluation at South Road, Soho, Handsworth, Birmingham*, BUFAU Report no 326

Joyce, N and Haywood, F 2002 *Health and Safety Structural Condition Survey, Soho Foundry, Foundry Lane, Smethwick*. For Sandwell Metropolitan Borough Council and the Heritage Lottery Fund

Royal Commission on the Historical Monuments of England 1996 *Soho Foundry, Foundry Lane, Smethwick, West Midlands: Historic Buildings Report*

Royal Commission on Historical Monuments of England 1997 *Supplementary Report [on Erecting Shop Soho Foundry]*

Upson, A 2003 *Soho Foundry, Smethwick, West Midlands: Conservation Plan*, Parts A, B & C in two vols. For Sandwell Metropolitan Borough Council

West Yorkshire Archaeology Service 1996 *The Round Foundry, Water Lane, Leeds. Preliminary Archaeological Assessment*. West Yorkshire Archaeology Service

Theses and dissertations

Cule, J E 1935 'The financial history of Matthew Boulton, 1759–1800', unpublished MComm thesis (University of Birmingham)

Earl, J 1996 'The Stourbridge Ironworks – evolution of an industrial site', MA thesis (University of Birmingham)

Loggie, V A 2011 'Soho depicted: prints, drawings and watercolours of Matthew Boulton, his manufactory and estate, 1760–1809' unpublished PhD thesis (University of Birmingham)

Powell, J S 1977 'The Birmingham coiners 1780–1816', MA thesis (Sussex)

Smith, B M D 1967 'A history of the firm of W & T Avery Ltd 1730–1939' unpublished Faculty of Commerce thesis (University of Birmingham

Secondary sources

Building News
Birmingham Daily Post
Midland Counties Herald
Post Office Directory Birmingham, Warwickshire, Worcestershire, Staffordshire
Swinney's Directory of Birmingham
Whites Directory of Birmingham
The Engineer
Articles in *The Engineer*
'Sale of Soho Foundry' May 24 1895, 449
'The Soho Foundry No I', Sep 27 1895, 305–8
'The Soho Foundry No II', Oct 4 1895, 340–1
'The Soho Foundry No III', Oct 18 1895, 392–3
'The Soho Foundry No IV', Nov 1 1895, 425–6
'A Curious Old Steam Engine', 28 Feb 1896, 208–9
'Boulton & the Soho Works', Sep 10 1909, 259–61
'Some Recollections of Soho Foundry, its Men and Methods', by Charles H Wall, Dec 17 1909, 624–7
'The Boulton and Watt Relics', by Edgar C Smith, Nov 14 1919, 637–40

This group of articles published in *The Engineer* on the closure of the Soho Foundry (1895), the centenary of Matthew Boulton's death (1909) and the centenary of James Watt's death (1919) constitute an important secondary source providing descriptions and illustrations as either engravings or photographs of steam engines and machinery. There is detailed technical analysis and the 17 Dec 1909 article is extremely useful on the layout of the Soho Foundry and working methods based on information provided by Courtney Darlington, who assisted his father, a manager at the works.

Published articles and chapters

Apling, H 1968 'Matthew Boulton: His coins and tokens & medals'. *Seaby Coin and Medal Bulletin*, Sep, 308–16

Beaudoin, S M 2000 'Current debates in the study of the Industrial Revolution'. *OAH Magazine of History* **15**(1), Fall, 7–13

Cannadine, D 1984 'The past and present in the English Industrial Revolution, 1880–1980'. *Past and Present* **103**, 131–72

Demidowicz, G 2009a 'Power at the Soho Manufactory and Mint', *in* Dick, M (ed) *Matthew Boulton: A Revolutionary Player*. Studley: Brewin Books, 116–31

Demidowicz, G 2009b 'A walking tour of the Three Sohos', *in* Mason, S (ed) *Matthew Boulton: Selling What All the World Desires*. New Haven, CT: Yale University Press, 101–5

Demidowicz, George 2013 'The origins of the Soho Manufactory and its layout', *in* Quickenden, Kenneth, Baggott, Sally and Dick, Malcolm (eds) *Matthew Boulton: Enterprising Industrialist of the Enlightenment*. Farnham: Ashgate, 67–83

Gale, W K V 1961 'Soho Foundry: Some facts and fallacies'. *Transactions of the Newcomen Society* **34**, 72–87

Gould, B M 1969 'Monsieur Duret, craftsman at Soho'. *Numismatic Circular* **57**, 270–7

Harris, J E 1986 'Michael Alcock and the transfer of Birmingham technology to France before the Revolution'. *Journal of European Economic History*, 7–57. Reprinted in Harris, J 1992 *Essays in Industry and Technology in the Eighteenth Century; England and France*. Hampshire: Variorum

Harris, J E 1998 'Matthew Boulton: A slight adjustment of the halo', *in* Merger, M and Barjot, D *Les entreprises et leurs réseaux: Hommes, capitaux, techniques et pouvoirs, XIXe–XXe siècles: mélanges en l'honneur de François Caron*. Paris: La Sorbonne, 349–64

Hawker, C R 'Eighteenth-century token notes from Matthew Boulton's letters; the Glasgow Halfpenny', *Seaby Co in and Medal Bulletin*, 833 (Sep 1988), 199–204; 834 (Oct 1988), 227–30; 843 (Sep 1989), 200–2; 844 (Oct 1989), 227–30

Ince, Laurence 2000 'The Soho Engine Works 1796–1895'. *Stationary Power: The Journal of the International Stationary Steam Engine Society*, **16**

Hall, J W 1925 'Joshua Field's diary of tour in 1821 through the Midlands with an Introduction and Notes'. *Transactions of the Newcomen Society* **6**, 1–41

Margolis, R 1988 'Matthew Boulton's French ventures of 1791 and 1792; Tokens for the Monneron Frères of Paris and Isle de France'. *British Numismatic Journal* **58**, 102–9

Margolis, R 1990 'The Soho Mint's token coinage of 1791 for Barbados'. *Spink Numismatic Circular* **98**, Jul and Aug, 200

Pelham, R A 1963 'The water-power crisis in Birmingham in the eighteenth century'. *University of Birmingham Historical Journal* **11**(1), 79–82

Pelham, R A 1964 'Some new light on Matthew Boulton'. *The Engineer*, 20 March, 503–4

Pollard, J G 1968 'Matthew Boulton and J.-P. Droz'. *The Numismatic Chronicle*, 7 ser, **8**, 241–52

Pollard, J G 1971 'Matthew Boulton and the reducing machine in England'. *The Numismatic Chronicle*, 7 ser, **11**, 311–17

Skempton, A W 1971 'Samuel Wyatt and the Albion Mill'. *Architectural History* **14**, 53–73

Symons, D 2009a '"Bringing to Perfection the Art of Coining': What did they make at the Soho Mint," *in* Mason, S (ed) *Mathew Boulton: Selling What All the World Desires*. New Haven, CT: Yale University Press, 89–98

Symons, D 2009b 'Matthew Boulton and the Royal Mint', *in* Dick, M (ed) *Matthew Boulton: A Revolutionary Player*. Studley: Brewin Books, 170–84

Tann, J 1998 'Two knights at Pandemonium: A worms-eye view of Boulton Watt & Co., c. 1800–1820'. *History of Technology* **20**, 47–72

Tann, J and MacLeod, C 2016 'Empiricism afloat – Testing steamboat efficacy'. *International Journal of Engineering and Technology* **86**(2), 228–43

Tungate, S 2009a 'Matthew Boulton's mints; copper to customer', *in* Mason, S (ed) *Matthew Boulton: Selling What All the World Desires*. New Haven, CT: Yale University Press, 80–8

Tungate, S 2009b 'Technology, art and design in the work of Matthew Boulton; Coins, medals and tokens produced at the Soho Mint', *in* Dick, M (ed) *Matthew Boulton: A Revolutionary Player*, 185–200

Tungate, S 2013 'Workers at the Soho Mint (1788–1809)', *in* Quickenden, Kenneth, Baggott, Sally and Dick, Malcolm (eds) *Matthew Boulton: Enterprising Industrialist of the Enlightenment*', Farnham: Ashgate, 179–98

Williamson, J G 1987 'Debating the British industrial revolution'. *Explorations in Economic History* **24**(3), 269–92

Books

Anon 1885 *John Wyatt, Master Carpenter and Inventor, Compiled from Original Manuscripts*. London: Hamilton, Adams

Aston, M and Taylor, T 1998 *The Atlas of Archaeology*. London: Dorling Kindersley

Bailey, B 1985 *A Guide to Britain's Industrial Past*. London: Whittet Books

Ballard, P, Loggie, V and Mason, S 2009 *A Lost Landscape: Matthew Boulton's Gardens at Soho*. Chichester: Phillimore

Bennett, William 1937, 1939 *John Baskerville, the Birmingham Printer: His Press, Relations, and Friends*, 2 vols. Birmingham: City of Birmingham School of Printing

Berg, M 1985 *The Age of Manufactures. Industry, Innovation and Work in Britain, 1700–1820*. Oxford: Blackwell

Berg, M 1994 *The Age of Manufactures, 1700–1820*. London and New York: Routledge

Briggs, A 1987 *Victorian Cities*. Harmondsworth: Penguin

Boucher, C T G 1963 *John Rennie, 1761–1821: The Life and Work of a Great Engineer*. Manchester: Manchester University Press

Clay, R and Tungate, S 2009 *Matthew Boulton and the Art of Making Money*. Studley: Brewin Books

Clegg, S 1866 *A Practical Treatise on the Manufacture and Distribution of Coal-gas*. London: John Weale

Connor, P 1984 *Michael Angelo Rooker*. London: Batsford

Cooke, I G H [c 1997] *The Nineteenth-century Diaries of a Birmingham Engineer: William Garland*. London: Metro

Cooper, D R 1988 *The Art and Craft of Coinmaking: A History of Minting Technology*. London: Spink & Son

Colvin, H 1995 *A Bibliographic Dictionary of British Architects* 3rd ed New Haven and London: Yale

Crafts, N R F 1985 *British Economic Growth during the Industrial Revolution*. Oxford: Clarendon Press

Crook, J M and Port, M H 1973 *The History of the King's Works, 1782–1851*, 6. London: HMSO

Delieb, E and Roberts, M 1971 *The Great Silver Manufactory: Matthew Boulton and the Birmingham Silversmiths 1760–1790*. London: Studio Vista

Dent, R K 1894 *The Making of Birmingham*. Birmingham

Dick, M (ed.) 2009 *Matthew Boulton A Revolutionary Player*. Studley: Brewin Books

Dick, M and Croft, K 2019 *The Power to Change the World: James Watt (1736–1819): A Life in 50 Objects*. Alcester: West Midlands History

Dickinson, H W 1935 *James Watt: Craftsman and Engineer*. Cambridge: Cambridge University Press

Dickinson, H W 1937 *Matthew Boulton*. Cambridge: Cambridge University Press

Dickinson, H W 1963 *A Short History of the Steam Engine*. London: Frank Cass

Dickinson, H W and Jenkins, R 1927 *James Watt and the Steam Engine*. Oxford: Clarendon Press

Dilworth, D 1976 *The Tame Mills of Staffordshire*. London and Chichester: Phillimore

Doty, R 1998 *The Soho Mint and the Industrialization of Money*. London: British Numismatic Society

Falconer, K 1980 *Guide to England's Industrial Heritage*. New York: Holmes & Meier

Fitzmaurice, Lord E 1875 *Life of William, Earl of Shelburne*. London: MacMillan

Gale, W K V 1948 *Soho Foundry*. Smethwick: W & T Avery

Gale, W K V and Seaby, W A 1982 *Boulton, Watt and the Soho Undertakings*. Birmingham: Birmingham Science Museum

Goodison, Nicholas 1974 *Ormolu: The Work of Matthew Boulton*. London: Phaidon

Goodison, Nicholas 2002 *Ormolu*. London: Christie's

Griffiths, John 1992 *The Third Man: The Life and Times of William Murdoch, 1754–1839*. London: A. Deutsch

Harris, J 1992 *Essays in Industry and Technology in the Eighteenth Century; England and France*. Hampshire: Variorum

Henderson, W O 1966 *J C Fisher and his Diary of Industrial England: 1814–51*. London: Frank Cass

Hills, R L 2005 *James Watt, Volume 2: The Years of Toil, 1775–1785*. Ashbourne: Landmark

Hopkins, E 1989 *Birmingham: The First Manufacturing Town in the World 1760–1840*. London: Weidenfeld & Nicolson

Huberman, M 1996 *Escape from the Market: Negotiating Work in Lancashire*. Cambridge: Cambridge University Press

Jones, Edgar 1985 *Industrial Architecture in Britain 1750–1939*. London: Batsford

Jones, J M 1984 *Manors of North Birmingham*. Birmingham: City of Birmingham Education Dept

Jones, P M 2008 *Industrial Enlightenment, Science, Technology and Culture in Birmingham and the West Midlands 1760–1820*. Manchester: Manchester University Press

Keir, J [1809] 1947 *Memoir of Matthew Boulton*. Birmingham

Lines, C 1990 *Companion to the Industrial Revolution*. New York: Facts on File

Mantoux, P 1928 *The Industrial Revolution of the Eighteenth Century*. London: Cape

Mare, M L and Quarrell, W H 1938 *Lichtenberg's Visits to England*. Oxford: Clarendon Press

Mason, S (ed) 2009 *Matthew Boulton: Selling What All the World Desires*. New Haven, CT: Yale University Press

Michaelis-Jena, R and Merson, W (eds) 1988 *A Lady Travels: Journeys in England and Scotland from the Diaries of Johanna Schopenhauer*. London: Routledge

Morgan, K (ed) 1992 *An American Quaker in the British Isles: The Travel Journals of Jabez Maud Fisher, 1775–1779*. Oxford: Oxford University Press

Muirhead, J P 1854 *The Origin and Progress of the Mechanical Inventions of James Watt: Illustrated by his Correspondence with his Friends and the Specifications of his Patents*, 3 vols. London: J. Murray

Pardoe, F E 1975 *John Baskerville of Birmingham, Letter-Founder & Printer*. London: F Muller

Quickenden, Kenneth, Baggott, Sally and Dick, Malcolm (eds.) 2013 *Matthew Boulton: Enterprising Industrialist of the Enlightenment*. Farnham: Ashgate

Rickman, T M 1901 *Notes on the Life and in the Several Imprints of the Works of Thomas Rickman, F.S.A., Architect*. London: G J W Pitman

Robinson, E and Musson, A E 1969 *James Watt and the Steam Revolution*. New York: Kelley

Roll, E 1930 *An Early Experiment in Industrial Organisation: Being a History of the Firm of Boulton and Watt, 1775–1800*. London: Longmans

Rolt, L T C [1965] 1986 *Tools for the Job*. London: HMSO

Russell, B 2014 *James Watt: Making the World Anew*. London: Reaktion Books

Selgin, G 2011 *Good Money: Birmingham Button Makers, The Royal Mint, and The Beginnings of Modern Coinage, 1775–1821*. Ann Arbor: University of Michigan Press

Shaw, S 1801 *The History and Antiquities of Staffordshire*, vol. ii. London

Smiles, Samuel 1904 *Lives of the Engineers: Boulton and Watt*. London: Murray

Stearns, P N 2015 *Debating the Industrial Revolution*. London: Bloomsbury

Stephens, W B 1969 (ed) *A History of the County of Warwick*. Vol VII London: Oxford University Press

Sweeney, J O 1981 *A Numismatic History of the Birmingham Mint*. Birmingham: Birmingham Mint

Szostak, R 1991 *The Role of Transportation in the Industrial Revolution: A Comparison of England and France*. Buffalo, NY: McGill-Queen's University Press

Tann, J 1970 *The Development of the Factory*. London: Cornmarket Press

Tann, J (ed.) 1981 *The Selected Papers of Boulton and Watt, Volume I: The Engine Partnership 1775–1825*. Cambridge, MA: MIT Press

Thomson, J 2003 *The Scot Who Lit the World: The Story of William Murdoch Inventor of Gas Lighting*. Glasgow: Janet Thomson

Tomory, L 2012 *Progressive Enlightenment: The Origins of the Gaslight Industry 1780–1820*. Cambridge, MA: MIT Press

Uglow, J 2002 *The Lunar Men: The Friends who Made the Future*. London: Faber

Ure, A [1835] 1970 *The Philosophy of Manufactures*. London: Charles Knight

Ward, J T 1970 *The Factory System Vol 1: Birth and Growth*. Newton Abbot: David and Charles, 140–3

Williams, T L 1981 *A History of the British Gas Industry*. Oxford: Oxford University Press

Wrigley, E A 1989 *Continuity, Chance and Change: The Character of the Industrial Revolution in England*. Cambridge: Cambridge University Press

Wrigley, E A and Schofield, R S 1981 *The Population History of England, 1541–1871*. Cambridge: Cambridge University Press

Index

Page numbers in **bold** refer to figures, page numbers in *italic* refer to tables.